GW00585722

Mining for Wisdom within Delusion

The Tsadra Foundation Series

published by Snow Lion, an imprint of Shambhala Publications

Tsadra Foundation is a U.S.-based nonprofit organization that contributes to the ongoing development of wisdom and compassion in Western minds by advancing the combined study and practice of Tibetan Buddhism. Taking its inspiration from the nineteenth-century nonsectarian Tibetan scholar and meditation master Jamgön Kongtrül Lodrö Tayé, Tsadra Foundation is named after his hermitage in eastern Tibet, Tsadra Rinchen Drak. The Foundation's various program areas reflect his values of excellence in both scholarship and contemplative practice, and the recognition of their mutual complementarity.

Tsadra Foundation envisions a flourishing community of Western contemplatives and scholar-practitioners who are fully trained in the traditions of Tibetan Buddhism. It is our conviction that, grounded in wisdom and compassion, these individuals will actively enrich the world through their openness and excellence.

This publication is part of the Tsadra Foundation's Translation Program, which aims to make authentic and authoritative texts from the Tibetan traditions available in English. The Foundation is honored to present the work of its fellows and grantees, individuals of confirmed contemplative and intellectual integrity; however, their views do not necessarily reflect those of the Foundation.

Tsadra Foundation is delighted to collaborate with Shambhala Publications in making these important texts available in the English language.

MINING FOR WISDOM WITHIN DELUSION

Maitreya's

Distinction between Phenomena and the Nature of Phenomena

and Its Indian and Tibetan Commentaries

Translated and introduced by
Karl Brunnhölzl

Snow Lion
Boston & London
2012

Snow Lion
An imprint of Shambhala Publications, Inc.
Horticultural Hall
300 Massachusetts Avenue
Boston, Massachusetts 02115
www.shambhala.com

© 2012 by Tsadra Foundation
All rights reserved. No part of this book may be reproduced in any form or by any means, electronic or mechanical, including photocopying, recording, or by any information storage and retrieval system, without permission in writing from the publisher.

9 8 7 6 5 4 3 2 1

First Edition
Printed in the United States of America

♾This edition is printed on acid-free paper that meets the American National Standards Institute Z39.48 Standard.
♻Shambhala makes every attempt to print on recycled paper.
For more information please visit www.shambhala.com.

Distributed in the United States by Random House, Inc., and in Canada by Random House of Canada Ltd

Library of Congress Cataloging-in-Publication Data

Maitreyanātha.
[Dharmadharmatāvibhaṅga. English]
Mining for wisdom within delusion: Maitreya's Distinction between phenomena and the nature of phenomena and its Indian and Tibetan commentaries / translated and introduced by Karl Brunnhölzl.
pages cm.—(The Tsadra Foundation series)
Includes bibliographical references and index.
ISBN-13: 978-1-55939-395-9 (alk. paper)
1. Maitreyanātha. Dharmadharmatāvibhaṅga. 2. Yogācāra (Buddhism)—Early works to 1800. I. Brunnhölzl, Karl. II. Vasubandhu. Dharmadharmatāvibhaṅgavṛtti. III. Raṅ-byuṅ-rdo-rje, Karma-pa III, 1284–1339. Chos daṅ chos ñid rnam par 'byed pa'i bstan bcos kyi rnam par bśad pa'i rgyan. English. IV. 'Gos Lo-tsa-ba Gźon-nu-dpal, 1392–1481. Theg pa chen po rgyud bla ma'i bstan bcos kyi 'grel bśad de kho na ñid rab tu gsal ba'i me loṅ. English.
V. Title.
BQ3080.D5322E53 2012
294.3'85—dc23
2011053331

Contents

Abbreviations:

AS	*Asiatische Studien*
C	Cone *Tengyur*
D	Derge Tibetan Tripiṭaka
DDV	*Dharmadharmatāvibhāga*
DDV (K)	Versified version of the *Dharmadharmatāvibhāga* (D4023)
DDV (P)	Prose version of the *Dharmadharmatāvibhāga* (D4022)
DDVV	Vasubandhu's *Dharmadharmatāvibhāgavṛtti*
DDVV (S)	Sanskrit fragment of the *Dharmadharmatāvibhāgavṛtti*
DLC	Dagtsang Lotsāwa's commentary on DDV (Stag tshang lo tsā ba shes rab rin chen 2007)
G	Ganden *Tengyur*
GC	Gö Lotsāwa's commentary on DDV ('Gos lo tsā ba gzhon nu dpal 2003b, pp. 453–70)
J	Johnston's Sanskrit edition of the *Ratnagotravibhāgavyākhyā*
JAOS	*Journal of the American Oriental Society*
JIABS	*Journal of the International Association for Buddhist Studies*
JIBS	*Journal of Indian and Buddhist Studies* (Indogaku Bukkyōgakku Kenkyū)
JIP	*Journal of Indian Philosophy*
KCA	Kamalaśīla's *Avikalpapraveśadhāraṇīṭīkā*
LBC	Lobsang Balden Dendzin Nyentra's commentary on DDV (Blo bzang dpal ldan bstan 'dzin snyan grags n.d.)
LDC	Lobsang Dayang's commentary on DDV (Blo bzang rta dbyangs 1975–76)

LZC	Khenpo Lodho Zangpo's commentary on DDV (Lodho Zangpo 1982)
MC	Mipham's commentary on DDV (c. 1990c)
N	Narthang *Tengyur*
OED	Rangjung Dorje's commentary on DDV (Rang byung rdo rje 2006b)
P	Peking Tibetan Tripiṭaka
RC	Rongtön's commentary on DDV (Rong ston shes bya kun gzigs 1998)
RGVV	*Ratnagotravibhāgavyākhyā*
SC	Śākya Chogden's commentary on DDV (Śākya mchog ldan 1988c, pp. 149–55)
SGC	Khenpo Shenga's commentary on DDV (Gzhan phan chos kyi snang ba 1987)
Taishō	Taishō Shinshū Daizōkyō (The Chinese Buddhist Canon). Ed. J. Takakusu and K. Watanabe. Tokyo: Taishō Shinshū Daizōkyō Kanko kai, 1970.
TBRC	Tibetan Buddhist Resource Center (www.tbrc.org)
TOK	Jamgön Kongtrul Lodrö Tayé's *Treasury of Knowledge* (Kong sprul blo gros mtha' yas 1982)
VV	Vairocanarakṣita's *Dharmadharmatāvibhāgakatipayapadavivṛtti*

Preface

This translation and study of Maitreya's *Distinction between Phenomena and the Nature of Phenomena* and several of its commentaries is foremost a journey through the vast landscape of Indian and Tibetan Yogācāra teachings, discussing the origin and permutations of ordinary deluded consciousness in its many forms as well as the process of its transition to the nonconceptual and nondual wisdom of a buddha. It is also intended as a small contribution to the body of English renderings of essential works by the Karmapas and other major lineage figures of the Tibetan Karma Kagyü School and to the growing collection of materials for English speakers who wish to pursue the course of studies at Western institutions of higher Buddhist learning that follow the curricula of Tibetan monastic colleges. Last but not least, all the materials contained in this book are not only scholarly documents, but bear great significance for practicing the Buddhist path and making what is described in them a living experience.

The introduction discusses "the five dharmas of Maitreya," their transmission from India to Tibet, and a number of assertions about the views contained in these texts. In particular, the structure and the central topics of the *Dharmadharmatāvibhāga*—the notions of "fundamental change" and nonconceptual wisdom—are explored in greater detail. The translation section contains English renderings of the *Dharmadharmatāvibhāga* in its prose and versified versions as well as the full commentaries by Vasubandhu (fourth century), the Third Karmapa, Rangjung Dorje[1] (1284–1339), and Gö Lotsāwa Shönnu Bal[2] (1392–1481). These are supplemented by excerpts from other Indian and Tibetan commentaries from all four schools of Tibetan Buddhism. Also included is a translation of the *Dhāraṇī of Entering Nonconceptuality* (*Avikalpapraveśadhāraṇī*), with excerpts from Kamalaśīla's commentary, because this text is an important source for the *Dharmadharmatāvibhāga* and is also quoted frequently in its commentaries by the Third Karmapa and Gö Lotsāwa.

My deep gratitude and respect go to Khenchen Tsültrim Gyamtso Rinpoche for his profound and detailed teachings on Maitreya's *Dharmadharmatāvibhāga* and Mipham Rinpoche's commentary in the late 1980s and early 1990s.

I am ever appreciative and thankful for the generous support by the Tsadra Foundation, which has changed my life in a profound way and has made the translation and research in this and other volumes possible. Many thanks also go to Jeff Cox and Sidney Piburn from Snow Lion Publications for their readiness and efforts to publish this book, and to Steve Rhodes for his skilled and meticulous editing. I am also very grateful to Stephanie Johnston for preparing the layout and the index.

If there is anything in this book that sounds good, makes sense, and serves as an antidote to confusion and suffering, may it be relished as originating from realized masters and scholars truly vast in learning. Everything else, including all mistakes, can safely be said to be mine.

It is my hope that this work may be a contributing cause for the buddha heart of H.H. the Seventeenth Gyalwang Karmapa, Ogyen Trinley Dorje, swiftly embracing all sentient beings in whatever ways suitable. May it in particular be of assistance in transplanting and sustaining both the great scholarly and meditative traditions of the Karma Kagyü lineage in the English-speaking world since they were initiated and fostered by all the Karmapas as a means to liberate beings from their experiencing delusive afflictive phenomena that obscure their minds' true nature of being peaceful and at ease.

Seattle, March 13, 2011

INTRODUCTION

"The five dharmas of Maitreya" and their transmission from India to Tibet

Among modern scholars, Maitreya's authorship of the five texts that the Tibetan tradition considers as being authored by Maitreya—the *Abhisamayālaṃkāra*, *Mahāyānasūtrālaṃkāra*, *Madhyāntavibhāga*, *Dharmadharmatāvibhāga*, and *Ratnagotravibhāga* (*Uttaratantra*)—continues to be disputed. Positions include a total denial of a historic person named Maitreya, the author of these texts not being the bodhisattva called Maitreya, but some human master with this name, and these works being composed by Asaṅga and/or other persons (such as *Sāramati). All five texts have been compared in terms of form, terminology, and contents, with some of them (*Mahāyānasūtrālaṃkāra*, *Madhyāntavibhāga*, and *Dharmadharmatāvibhāga*) showing greater similarities than others (*Abhisamayālaṃkāra* and *Uttaratantra*), but it is naturally problematic to decide questions of authorship solely on the grounds of such criteria.

The Chinese Buddhist tradition also speaks of "the five works of Maitreya," but considers them as consisting of the *Yogācārabhūmi*, a **Yogavibhāga*,[3] the *Mahāyānasūtrālaṃkāra*, the *Madhyāntavibhāga*, and the *Vajracchedikāvyākhyā*.[4] The *Uttaratantra* is ascribed to a certain *Sāramati (whom modern scholars either consider as a person different from Maitreya or as just one of his epithets). The *Abhisamayālaṃkāra* was never translated into Chinese and seems to be completely unknown in the Chinese Buddhist tradition. As for the *Dharmadharmatāvibhāga*, there is only a single very late Chinese translation by Fa-tsun (1902–1980) in 1936.

The designation "the five dharmas of Maitreya"[5] in the Tibetan tradition for the above five texts is not of Indian origin and is also unknown in the earliest catalogues of Tibetan translations from Sanskrit[6] (both compiled in the ninth century). It is hard to say when this expression was used first. However, by the eleventh century, at least some Indian texts considered all the above five texts to be authored by Maitreya.[7] As for their being translated into Tibetan, only two of them were translated during the early translation period—the *Mahāyānasūtrālaṃkāra* by Gawa Baldse[8] and the *Madhyāntavibhāga* by Yeshé Dé[9] (both eighth century). The remaining three were translated during the eleventh century. The

Abhisamayālaṃkāra was translated by Ngog Lotsāwa Loden Sherab[10] (1059–1109) (present version in the *Tengyur*). The *Dharmadharmatāvibhāga* was translated by Sengé Gyaltsen[11] and Tsültrim Gyalwa,[12] with the latter being revised by Su Gawé Dorje[13] (all preserved in the *Tengyur*). The *Uttaratantra* was first translated by Atiśa (980–1054) and Nagtso Lotsāwa Tsültrim Gyalwa, then by Ngog Lotsāwa (present version in the Tengyur), Patsab Lotsāwa Nyima Trag[14] (born 1055), and later by Jonang Lotsāwa Lodrö Bal[15] (1299/1300–1353/1355) and Yarlung Lotsāwa Tragpa Gyaltsen[16] (1242–1346). The *Blue Annals* adds that Marpa Topa Chökyi Wangchug[17] (1042–1136) is also reported to have translated all five Maitreya works.[18]

There are a number of Kagyü, Jonang, Sakya, and Nyingma sources[19] that speak about the transmission of the Maitreya texts and the lineage of the *Shentong* teachings. According to Kongtrul Lodrö Tayé[20] (1813–1899), who is known to rely greatly on Tāranātha, the intention of the sūtras of the third dharmacakra was elucidated by the four works of Maitreya except the *Abhisamayālaṃkāra* and by Nāgārjuna's collection of praises. In India, the meaning of these texts was explained and spread widely by Asaṅga, Vasubandhu (both fourth century), Candragomī (sixth/seventh century), their followers, Ratnākaraśānti, and others. It is also well known, Kongtrul says, that Dharmapāla (530–561) composed a treatise called *Bright Appearance*[21] that commented on Nāgārjuna's sixfold collection of reasoning and the *Mūlamadhyamakakārikā* in particular as bearing the intention of the third dharmacakra.[22] However, while the general philosophical system of Maitreya's texts—the contents of the *Abhisamayālaṃkāra*, *Mahāyānasūtrālaṃkāra*, and *Madhyāntavibhāga*—was explained in detail through many excellent teaching traditions, such as those of Dignāga and Sthiramati, the uncommon philosophical system of these texts was sustained in such a way that only the supreme disciples transmitted it orally, with the texts of the *Dharmadharmatāvibhāga* and *Uttaratantra* being hidden away as treasure texts.

According to the historical records of the tradition of Dsen Kawoché, the *Dharmadharmatāvibhāga* and the *Uttaratantra* were not known to other paṇḍitas[23] in India until the eleventh century, when the mahāsiddha Maitrīpa (1012–1097) rediscovered these texts inside an old stūpa and then received direct instructions on them from Maitreya.[24] Gö Lotsāwa's *Blue Annals* agrees with this and adds that it seems to be true because the great Indian treatises (such as the *Abhisamayālaṃkārālokā*) quote the *Madhyāntavibhāga* and the *Mahāyānasūtrālaṃkāra* but never mention the *Dharmadharmatāvibhāga* and *Uttaratantra*.[25] Maitrīpa then taught the *Dharmadharmatāvibhāga* and *Uttaratantra* to paṇḍita *Ānandakīrti who, disguised as a beggar, traveled to Kashmir. There he transmitted these texts to the Kashmiri paṇḍita Sajjana, who gave copies to paṇḍita Jñānaśrī and others.[26]

Sajjana was the elder son of paṇḍita Sugata and the grandson of the siddha and paṇḍita Ratnavajra,[27] who was the central one among the six gatekeeper paṇḍitas of Vikramaśīla and also a teacher of the translator Rinchen Sangpo[28] (958–1055). At Vikramaśīla, Ratnavajra mainly taught the five texts of Maitreya, Dignāga's and Dharmakīrti's works on *pramāṇa*, and the Buddhist tantras for many years. Upon his return to Kashmir, he established a number of centers for the study of the sūtra and tantra traditions.[29] He also wrote a still extant, but unfortunately unavailable, commentary on the *Uttaratantra*,[30] which should shed considerable light on the interpretation of this text in this particular lineage that was subsequently transmitted into Tibet by Dsen Kawoché. As a possible glimpse into this commentary by Ratnavajra, the Eighth Karmapa[31] says that there are three ways of distinguishing what is of expedient and what is of definitive meaning in the three dharmacakras as presented by the *Saṃdhinirmocanasūtra*, the *Uttaratantra*, and Nāgārjuna and his followers. The Kashmiri paṇḍita Ratnavajra, the Karmapa says, explains the distinction in the *Uttaratantra* as follows:

> The wheel that introduces to the path of peace is of expedient meaning. The wheel of maturation is the wheel that is predominantly of definitive meaning, but also contains some parts of expedient meaning. The wheel of prophecy is the wheel of nothing but the definitive meaning.[32]

Sajjana's son, Mahājana, also received the transmission of the Maitreya texts from his father and grandfather. Like Su Gawé Dorje (eleventh century; see below), he was also active in western Tibet, translated the *Dharmadharmatāvibhāgavṛtti*, and helped in compiling the versified version of the *Dharmadharmatāvibhāga*.[33]

As for the transmission of the five works of Maitreya from India to Tibet, there are the two principal lineages through Ngog Lotsāwa and Dsen Kawoché (a.k.a. Trimé Sherab), who both traveled to Kashmir and studied the Maitreya works with the great paṇḍita Sajjana at the same time. The former lineage is often called "the exegetical tradition of the dharma works of Maitreya" (*byams chos bshad lugs*), while the latter represents "the meditative tradition of the dharma works of Maitreya" (*byams chos sgom lugs*).[34]

As for Dsen Kawoché, he was a student of Trapa Ngönshé[35] (1012–1090) and traveled to Kashmir at age fifty-five (1076). When he met Sajjana he said, "Since I am old now, I won't study many teachings. However, I wish to make the dharmas of the Bhagavān Maitreya my 'death dharma.'[36] Therefore, please instruct me properly in them." Upon this request, Sajjana taught him the Maitreya works by relying on the translator Su Gawé Dorje.[37] The latter is also said to have written a (now lost) commentary on the *Uttaratantra* that contained his notes of Sajjana's teachings.[38] In Tholing in western Tibet, Su Gawé Dorje also revised an earlier translation of the prose version of the *Dharmadharmatāvibhāga* (by Śāntibhadra and Tsültrim Gyalwa). Another translator present at the time in Kashmir, called Padma Sengé,[39] also received explanations from Sajjana similar to those given to Dsen, and it appears that Padma Sengé composed an (equally lost) extensive commentary on the *Mahāyānasūtrālaṃkāra* that contained his notes of Sajjana's explanations.

Dsen Kawoché and Su Gawé Dorje returned to Tibet before Ngog Lotsāwa (who stayed in Kashmir for seventeen years). In their homeland, they taught the Maitreya works (in particular, the *Dharmadharmatāvibhāga* and *Uttaratantra*) to many masters in Central Tibet, such as a certain Changrawa.[40] The latter taught them to Tarma Dsöndrü (1117–1192) of Chö Dodé Boog,[41] who was a holder of the Shijé[42] lineage and composed an extensive commentary on the *Mahāyānasūtrālaṃkāra* in several volumes (now lost). The *Blue Annals* mentions the existence at that time of an anonymous Tibetan commentary on the *Uttaratantra* that was referred to as "a ṭīkā on the *Uttaratantra* in the tradition of Dsen" and supplemented its explanations on the text with pith instructions on meditation practice. According to the *Blue Annals*, there were also a number of short texts, such as the *Repository of Wisdom* (*Ye shes kyi bzhag sa*), that contained pith instructions of the Dsen tradition.[43] In addition, Gö Lotsāwa says, the great Kashmiri paṇḍita Śākyaśrībhadra (1140s–1225) is reported to have given pith instructions on the five works of Maitreya on Mount Sinpori[44] near Gyantsé,[45] but they do not exist at present (that is, at the end of the fifteenth century). Likewise, Gö Lotsāwa says, he has not heard of the instructions of the Dsen tradition nowadays resting with any kalyāṇamitra.[46]

Tāranātha, Kongtrul, and other sources who obviously follow them also refer to the eleventh-century siddha Yumowa Mikyö Dorje[47] as being another major figure in the transmission of the *Shentong* view.[48] There is little information about Yumowa, but the Jonang School considers him as its founder. Jonang histories of the Kālacakratantra say that he was a student of a certain Candranātha and a paṇḍita from Kashmir. Yumowa was a master of the Kālacakratantra and his teachings were initially passed on through his family line and several other masters, with Dölpopa Sherab Gyaltsen[49] (1292–1361) already being about the tenth lineage holder.[50] Yumowa's only preserved works consist of the *Fourfold Cycle of Luminous Lamps*.[51] These texts deal with the correct practice of the six-branch yoga of the Kālacakratantra and treat some of the topics on which Dölpopa elaborated later (without, however, using his specific terminologies, such as *rangtong*, *shentong*, and ālaya-wisdom).[52] Thus, Tāranātha says that Yumowa is "the founder of the philosophical system of mantric *Shentong*."[53]

According to the *Blue Annals*, in the tradition of Ngog Lotsāwa, who composed two commentaries on the *Uttaratantra* (the shorter one being still available; see below), there were many who wrote commentaries on this text, such as the third abbot of Sangpu Nëutog,[54] Shang Tsépong Chökyi Lama[55] (born eleventh century; one of the four main students of Ngog), Chaba Chökyi Sengé[56] (1109–1169), and his two students Tenpagpa Mawé Sengé[57] and Dsangnagpa Dsöndrü Sengé[58] (both born twelfth century).[59]

Various assertions about the nature and the view of the five Maitreya texts in the Tibetan tradition

In the different schools of Tibetan Buddhism, there is just about every possible interpretation as to what Maitreya's texts comment on and which of them belong to Yogācāra (what Tibetans call "Mere Mentalism" (*sems tsam*)), Yogācāra-Madhyamaka, *Svātantrika-Madhyamaka, *Prāsaṅgika-Madhyamaka, *Shentong* Madhyamaka, or "Great Madhyamaka." However, despite these differences, what is clear for most commentators is that, in terms of their contents, these five texts cover the entire range of the mahāyāna teachings.

Ngog Lotsāwa

The early Kadampa master Ngog Lotsāwa's synopsis of the *Uttaratantra*[60] starts by saying that when Maitreya elucidated the intention of the words of the Buddha in an unmistaken manner, he composed the *Uttaratantra*, which explains the precious sūtra collection of definitive meaning (the dharma wheel of irreversibility)[61] that teaches the single principle of the dharmadhātu and thus the meaning of all dharma specifications that are utterly pure and beyond doubt. Therefore, it presents the ultimate true reality of the mahāyāna. Through explaining the meanings of the sūtra collections of expedient meaning, the remaining four texts turn their audiences into vessels for the exposition of the perfect supreme dharma because they present seeming reality and the ultimate in dependence on the thinking of others.

Jomdendé Rigpé Raltri

Another famous Kadampa master, Jomdendé Rigpé Raltri[62] (1227–1305), gives a synopsis of the essential gist of each one of the works of Maitreya. The *Abhisamayālaṃkāra*, which starts with the homage, says that, on the path of accumulation, bodhisattvas practice by focusing on the three knowledges as the objects. Through the four trainings as the nature of clear realization, one practices the path in the form of the six pāramitās. Their motivation consists of the armorlike practice—threefold generosity preceded by taking refuge, ethics (relinquishing the mental engagements of śrāvakas and pratyekabuddhas), patience (not retaliating), vigor (striving for the retinue of the mahāyāna), dhyāna (not being blended with other yānas), and prajñā (dedicating everything to enlightenment). All these should be embraced by not conceptualizing the three spheres. The equipment of the bhūmis consists of the ten pāramitās and the main purifications of the bhūmis. The *Mahāyānasūtrālaṃkāra* speaks about making the conduct of bodhisattvas a living experience, which consists of the engagement through aspiration on the impure bhūmis and the superior intention on the pure bhūmis. During the preparatory stage, their motivation that arises from knowing the benefit is to aspire for the mahāyāna dharma. Then, within the state of unmistakenly striving to search the dharma for their own welfare, bodhisattvas apply that motivation through teaching the dharma for the welfare of others. As the main part of practice, they practice the dharma for their own welfare and give instructions and directions for the welfare of others. As the conclusion, their conduct for both their own welfare and that of others should be embraced by skill in means. Their conduct on the pure bhūmis consists of both vast and profound ways of conduct. The benefit of all that is that, through having made the mahāyāna dharma a living experience, the disease of the afflictions is pacified. When practicing the dharma, mastery is gained. When the dharma is held in one's mind, all benefits in this and future lives will arise. Thus, it is like a wish-fulfilling gem. The *Dharmadharmatāvibhāga* gives the pointing-out instruction that, without recognizing the nature of phenomena, one's own mind appears as the conceptions of the eight consciousnesses, but none of them really exist. What is real is the appearing of the nature of phenomena, while these eight do not appear. The afflictions arise through clinging to the mistaken conceptions that appear as the inner mind and the outer world and its inhabitants. Since the cognition in which conceptions and dualistic appearances have ceased abides as the nature of phenomena, it is the nonconceptual wisdom of meditative equipoise. During subsequent attainment, everything appears like an illusion, without any clinging to it. The *Madhyāntavibhāga* says that, through mentally relinquishing the world, one dedicates everything to enlightenment for the sake of all sentient beings. One begins with this during the paths of accumulation and preparation, engages in it in an illusionlike manner on the first bhūmi, practices it in an approximately concordant way on the eighth bhūmi, and accomplishes its perfection on the tenth bhūmi and the buddhabhūmi. The means to do so is to aspire for the equality of oneself and others. The other pāramitās are the aids in order to manifest nonconceptual wisdom through mastering samādhi, which consist of practicing the ten dharma activities, undistracted calm abiding, and unmistaken superior insight. The *Uttaratantra*, which ends with the dedication, explains in detail the essence of the other four Maitreya texts—natural luminosity—through the seven vajra points and the nine examples. This luminosity is the self-aware self-lucidity that is free from clinging, through the stains of the dualistic appearances of apprehender and apprehended, to genuine primordial wisdom as being such wisdom. Having decided on this, the extreme of extinction is eliminated through this wisdom being awareness, while the narrow view of permanence is brought to an end as follows. Since the nature of the mind is unchanging, just like space, it is recognized to be the expanse that is untainted by the afflictions that arise from false imagination. This is what the Maitreya texts describe for the fortunate ones through guiding them with pointing fingers.

The Gelugpa School as exemplified by Lobsang Dayang

The Gelugpa School unanimously holds that the *Abhisamayālaṃkāra* teaches on the middle turning of the wheel of dharma (prajñāpāramitā) and represents the view of *Yogācāra-Svātantrika-Madhyamaka. The *Uttaratantra* is also regarded as a commentary on the intention of the middle turning, but represents the *Prāsaṅgika-Madhyamaka view. Both texts are said to explain that all phenomena (including buddha nature) are empty of any nature of their own (in fact, the notion of buddha nature is considered as just another term for the emptiness of all phenomena, which is a nonimplicative negation). The *Mahāyānasūtrālaṃkāra*, *Madhyāntavibhāga*, and *Dharmadharmatāvibhāga* are said to teach on the third turning and consist of nothing but Mere Mentalism (understood as asserting the ultimate existence of dependent mind and thus being inferior to Madhyamaka).

The introduction in the commentary on the *Dharmadharmatāvibhāga* by the Mongolian Gelugpa master Lobsang Dayang[63] (1867–1937) agrees with this Gelugpa position on the five texts of Maitreya, saying that they were composed as commentaries on the intentions of the entire teachings of the mahāyāna in terms of view, conduct, and fruition. For the *Abhisamayālaṃkāra* and the *Uttaratantra* comment on the intention of the Buddha's teachings in terms of the Niḥsvabhāvavādins, while the other three Maitreya texts comment on the intention of his teachings in terms of Mere Mentalism. In particular, the *Mahāyānasūtrālaṃkāra*, *Madhyāntavibhāga*, and *Dharmadharmatāvibhāga* distinguish the expedient and definitive meanings in the Buddha's teachings according to the *Saṃdhinirmocanasūtra*. Following this sūtra, the

Madhyāntavibhāga, through dividing phenomena into the three natures, primarily teaches the middle way free from the extremes of permanence and extinction. The *Dharmadharmatāvibhāga* is based on the three natures taught in the *Madhyāntavibhāga* and describes phenomena as the dependent nature that is the basis for the arising of the mistakenness of the imaginary nature (the appearances of the duality of apprehender and apprehended), thus being the basis for the establishment of saṃsāra. The nature of phenomena is the perfect nature—the dependent nature empty of the imaginary nature (its being empty of the duality of apprehender and apprehended)—that is the support for attaining nirvāṇa. The *Mahāyānasūtrālaṃkāra* is a text that, based on such presentations, determines in detail how to proceed on the mahāyāna path.

As for the *Dharmadharmatāvibhāga*, against the explicit words of the text and all its commentaries, Lobsang Dayang criticizes Rongtön's comments that phenomena and the nature of phenomena are to be understood as synonyms of saṃsāra and nirvāṇa, respectively. For he says that all knowable objects are included in phenomena and the nature of phenomena, while saṃsāra and nirvāṇa do not include all knowable objects. For this he gives the following two reasons. That phenomena and the nature of phenomena include all knowable objects is stated by both the words of the *Dharmadharmatāvibhāga* and Vasubandhu's commentary (which is correct). However, he says, there are no sūtras or treatises on them that explain all imaginary and dependent phenomena as making up saṃsāra while everything that is the perfect nature is nirvāṇa, nor is such asserted by any scholars (which is incorrect, since precisely this is explained in, for example, the *Madhyāntavibhāga*, the *Mahāyānasaṃgraha*, OED, and SC).[64] Therefore, in general, Lobsang Dayang says, phenomena and the nature of phenomena are here synonyms for seeming reality and ultimate reality, respectively. As for the main explicit teaching of the *Dharmadharmatāvibhāga*, the text's intention is that the basis of saṃsāra is the impure dependent nature, while the support of nirvāṇa is the perfect nature that consists of phenomenal identitylessness. Here Lobsang Dayang refers to Gyaltsab Darma Rinchen's[65] (1364–1432) commentary on the *Abhisamayālaṃkāra* as supporting his explanation:

> In the *Dharmadharmatāvibhāga*, [what is taught as] phenomena is the basis for the establishment of saṃsāra—the really established dependent [nature] that appears as the duality of apprehender and apprehended. What is taught as the nature of phenomena empty of any substantially different apprehender and apprehended is the support for attaining liberation by virtue of having become familiar with it after having focused on it.

As for the defining characteristic of phenomena, Lobsang Dayang says that it consists of the dependent nature, which is the sphere of false imagination (consisting of the six consciousnesses). Then he claims that this passage in the *Dharmadharmatāvibhāga* teaches that the imaginary appearances of the mistaken cognition that is false imagination do not exist ultimately, while the mistaken cognition that is false imagination itself does exists ultimately. As "reasons" for this claim, Lobsang Dayang adduces a passage from DDVV ("It is without referents because a nature of appearances is not established. It is mere conception because appearances exist merely as mistakenness.") and *Madhyāntavibhāga* I.1ab ("False imagination exists. Duality is not present in it."). However, obviously, none of these two quotes speaks about any *ultimate* existence of false imagination or the dependent nature. Nevertheless, Lobsang Dayang also declares here that Rongtön was unable to elucidate what he himself claims because Rongtön apparently took the dependent nature to be ultimately nonexistent (which is, of course, perfectly in line with standard Yogācāra explanations).

Thus, Lobsang Dayang tries to read the Gelugpa claim of an ultimately real dependent nature in the system called "Mere Mentalism" into the *Dharmadharmatāvibhāga*, which is not only not warranted by the text or Vasubandhu's commentary, but also contradicts Lobsang Dayang's own above equation of phenomena (the dependent nature) with seeming reality. Moreover, if the dependent nature existed ultimately, it would have to be the nature of phenomena, which (according to Lobsang Dayang) is "the perfect nature that consists of phenomenal identitylessness." But if the ultimately existent dependent nature were the nature of phenomena that is phenomenal identitylessness, how could it at the same time be, as he says, "the mistaken cognition that is false imagination"? Also, if both false imagination and the nature of phenomena existed ultimately, there would be two ultimate realities, but no seeming reality or saṃsāra. Moreover, Lobsang Dayang later (in the section on the defining characteristics of nonconceptual wisdom) surprisingly follows RC in saying that both the imaginary and the dependent natures do not appear for nonconceptual wisdom. However, if, as he claims, the dependent nature were ultimately real, it should be perceived as such by the ultimately valid cognition of nonconceptual wisdom. By following RC here, Lobsang Dayang also invalidates his above critique of Rongtön taking the dependent nature to be ultimately nonexistent.

Dölpopa and Sabsang Mati Paṇchen

By contrast, Dölpopa says in his *Mountain Dharma* and elsewhere that all five Maitreya texts teach nothing but *Shentong* Madhyamaka, and that even the *Abhisamayālaṃkāra* does not contain what is known as *rangtong*. Tāranātha (1575–1635), in his *Essence of Other-Emptiness* and other works, agrees with this.[66]

The introduction to a commentary on the *Uttaratantra*[67] by Sabsang Mati Paṇchen (1294–1376), a student of Dölpopa who also had strong Sakya ties, explains that the Abhisamayālaṃkāra elucidates the second turning of the wheel of dharma. The *Mahāyānasūtrālaṃkāra* discusses the view and the conduct of the third turning, and the remaining three texts of Maitreya explain the view of the third turning by way of analyzing the dharmadhātu. Mati Paṇchen further emphasizes that the teachings of the third turning (including the *Saṃdhinirmocanasūtra*) go beyond Mere Mentalism. If it is argued that the notion of mind's natural luminosity in the works of Maitreya does not withstand Madhyamaka reasoning, one should treat the Buddhist tantras in the same manner (which nobody in the Tibetan tradition does) since they discuss the very same luminosity.

Butön Rinchen Drub

Butön Rinchen Drub's (1290–1364) *History of Buddhism*[68] rejects the position of some that the *Mahāyānasūtrālaṃkāra* and *Madhyāntavibhāga* pertain to the abhidharma; the *Dharmadharmatāvibhāga* and the *Uttaratantra*, to the sūtras; and the *Abhisamayālaṃkāra*, to the vinaya. Butön classifies the *Abhisamayālaṃkāra* as a commentary on the second turning, with its primary subject being the hidden meaning of the prajñāpāramitā sūtras—the knowledge of the path to buddhahood. The other four works of Maitreya elucidate the third turning, with the *Mahāyānasūtrālaṃkāra* containing a summary of the entire mahāyāna dharma. The *Madhyāntavibhāga* distinguishes extremes (existence, nonexistence, permanence, and extinction) from the middle way of avoiding them. It contains seven topics—the three natures, the obscurations, true reality, the remedies for the obscurations (profound meditation and its sphere), and the supreme yāna (the mahāyāna). The *Dharmadharmatāvibhāga* distinguishes between the afflicted phenomena of saṃsāra and the nature of these phenomena—nirvāṇa. The *Uttaratantra* bears its name because it is the highest one (*uttara*) within the continuum (*tantra*) of the mahāyāna teachings. The word *uttara* can also be understood as referring to the last or latest teachings of the mahāyāna. The text discusses the three jewels, buddha nature (the dhātu), the result that is enlightenment, the sixty-four qualities of a buddha, and enlightened activity.[69]

Gorampa Sönam Senge

In the later Sakya School, it is the works of Gorampa Sönam Sengé[70] (1429–1489) that are usually taken to be authoritative. One of his commentaries on the *Abhisamayālaṃkāra*[71] discusses the twenty Indian texts associated with Maitreya[72] in general and how the five works of Maitreya in particular explain the sūtras. Gorampa starts by reporting the positions of some earlier scholars. Some assert that the Maitreya works are definitely five in terms of determining the meanings of the three piṭakas. Among them, the *Mahāyānasūtrālaṃkāra* and *Uttaratantra* determine the meaning of the sūtras because the former does so in a general way without distinguishing between expedient and definitive meanings, while the latter determines the meaning of the sūtras of definitive meaning in particular. The *Abhisamayālaṃkāra* determines the vinaya because the uncommon vinaya of the mahāyāna consists of taming the afflictions and this text teaches their remedies. The *Madhyāntavibhāga* and *Dharmadharmatāvibhāga* determine the abhidharma because they ascertain the general and specific characteristics of phenomena.

According to others, the Maitreya works are definitely five in terms of determining the meanings of individual sūtras and determining them in common, respectively. The *Mahāyānasūtrālaṃkāra*, *Abhisamayālaṃkāra*, and *Uttaratantra* respectively determine the meanings of the *Buddhabhūmisūtra*, *Śatasāhasrikāprajñāpāramitāsūtra*, and *Dhāraṇīśvararājaparipṛcchāsūtra*. The *Madhyāntavibhāga* and *Dharmadharmatāvibhāga* determine the meanings of the sūtras in common because the former teaches the progressive stages of the path of a single person becoming a completely perfect buddha, while the latter demonstrates those among these progressive stages that pertain to the path which is specific to the mahāyāna.

Yet others hold that the Maitreya works are definitely five in terms of being primary (bodylike) and secondary (limblike) texts. The *Abhisamayālaṃkāra*, *Mahāyānasūtrālaṃkāra*, and *Madhyāntavibhāga* belong to the first category because they respectively determine the meanings of the vinaya, sūtra, and abhidharma scriptures. The *Uttaratantra* and *Dharmadharmatāvibhāga* make up the second category because the former shows that the *Mahāyānasūtrālaṃkāra*'s teaching about the existence of sentient beings whose disposition is cut off is of expedient meaning and then establishes all sentient beings as being endowed with the tathāgata heart. The *Dharmadharmatāvibhāga* teaches the progressive stages of the path that are special to the mahāyāna, which are not taught in the *Madhyāntavibhāga* though the latter teaches the stages of the path of all yānas in common.

Finally, Gorampa presents the Sakya School's own position. The sūtras to be explained by the five Maitreya works are those that are specific to the mahāyāna. Among them, those that are of expedient meaning are sūtras like the *Saṃdhinirmocanasūtra*. Those that are of definitive meaning are the prajñāpāramitā sūtras, the *Dhāraṇīśvararājaparipṛcchāsūtra*, *Tathāgatagarbhasūtra*, *Ratnadārikāparipṛcchāsūtra*, *Sthirādhyāśayaparivartasūtra*, *Anūnatvāpūrṇatvanirdeśasūtra*,[73] *Śrīmālādevīsūtra*, *Sarvabuddhaviṣayāvatārajñānālokālaṃkārasūtra*, and so on. Among the sūtras of definitive meaning, the *Abhisamayālaṃkāra* ascertains the meaning of those that determine a single disposition because it explains solely the prajñāpāramitā sūtras. The *Uttaratantra* comments on the meaning of those sūtras that determine several dispositions because it explains the above-mentioned sūtras of definitive meaning. As for the sūtras of expedient meaning, they are clarified by the *Madhyāntavibhāga* and *Dharmadharmatāvibhāga* because both ascertain the meanings of the *Saṃdhinirmocanasūtra* and so on. The *Mahāyānasūtrālaṃkāra* comments on various sūtras of expedient and definitive meanings for the following reasons. It comments on the sūtras of expedient meaning by way of explaining that, in the context of the ground, there are sentient beings whose disposition is cut off. Also, in the context of the path, the sūtras that ascertain all phenomena as being without arising are taught to be of expedient meaning. Likewise, through demonstrating, in the context of the fruition, that the certainty about there being only a single yāna ultimately is of expedient meaning, the text teaches that, ultimately, there are three yānas. It also comments on the sūtras of definitive meaning by way of teaching that, in the context of the ground, all sentient beings are endowed with the tathāgata heart; in the context of the path, teaching the six pāramitās and the four means to attract those to be guided; and, in the context of the fruition, giving the presentation of the three kāyas and the four wisdoms.

As for Maitreya's purpose in connecting his five texts with the sūtras, since he is actually a perfect buddha who is only displaying the way of being of a bodhisattva on the tenth bhūmi, one may wonder why he does not simply compose texts on his own without commenting on the words of Buddha Śākyamuni. The reason why he links his works to the sūtras is to make those to be guided understand that those teachings which follow the words of a teacher who demonstrates the twelve deeds of a fully enlightened buddha are pure, whereas those that do not follow these words are not pure. As *Uttaratantra* V.16 and V.20 says:

Thus, based on trustworthy scriptures and reasoning,
I expounded this [treatise] in order to purify just myself
And also for the sake of supporting those who are endowed
With intelligence, confidence, and consummate virtue.

In this world, there is no one wiser than the Victor,
No other one anywhere who is omniscient and properly knows supreme true reality in its entirety.
Therefore, one should not deviate from the sūtras that are taught to be definitive by the seer himself.
Otherwise, this will harm the genuine dharma through destroying the guidance of the sage.

As for the manner in which the five works of Maitreya explain the meanings of these sūtras, the *Abhisamayālaṃkāra* teaches the meaning of the prajñāpāramitā sūtras by way of summarizing it in the eight clear realizations. The *Uttaratantra* teaches the meaning of the sūtras of definitive meaning mentioned above by way of summarizing it into the seven vajra points (the three jewels, buddha nature, enlightenment, its qualities, and its enlightened activity). The *Madhyāntavibhāga* teaches both the progressive stages of the path of the common yāna and those that are specific to the mahāyāna. The *Dharmadharmatāvibhāga* teaches by way of distinguishing the bearers of the nature of phenomena (saṃsāra) and the nature of phenomena (nirvāṇa). The *Mahāyānasūtrālaṃkāra* explains the meanings of many sūtras of expedient and definitive meanings by way of summarizing them into five points, which are illustrated through five examples (such as hand-beaten gold).[74]

Śākya Chogden

Śākya Chogden (1428–1507), Gorampa's contemporary and rival in the Sakya School, wrote two texts that deal exclusively with the view and the practice of the five Maitreya texts. His *Illumination of the Definitive Meaning of the Five Maitreya Dharmas*[75] generally classifies the Maitreya texts as commentaries on the second and third turnings of the wheel of dharma. In brief, the *Abhisamayālaṃkāra*, *Mahāyānasūtrālaṃkāra*, and *Madhyāntavibhāga* are mahāyāna treatises in general and, since their contents are related to the sūtra collection that teaches the vast aspect of the Buddha's teachings, they teach the paths of all three yānas in detail. The *Uttaratantra* and the *Dharmadharmatāvibhāga* accord in teaching only the definitive meaning and only the path of the mahāyāna.

However, these five texts cannot be divided according to the distinctive features of the usual Tibetan mahāyāna doxographical categories of "Mere Mentalism" and "Madhyamaka" because the intention of all five consists of the particular kind of Madhyamaka (*Shentong*) that is found in Maitreya's own texts and the commentaries on their intention by Asaṅga, Vasubandhu, and so on. Neither Asaṅga nor Vasubandhu explained any of Maitreya's texts as Mere Mentalism and, though they commented on the intentions of the *Abhisamayālaṃkāra* (in the *Bṛhaṭṭīkā*)[76] and the *Uttaratantra* (in the *Ratnagotravibhāgavyākhyā*) as being Madhyamaka, they did not do so in accord with *Rangtong* Madhyamaka (the *Ratnagotravibhāgavyākhyā* comments solely according to the *Shentong* Madhyamaka system, while not containing even a speck of *Rangtong* explanations). Thus, even the *Abhisamayālaṃkāra* and the *Uttaratantra* do not match the kind of Madhyamaka that consists of *Svātantrika and *Prāsaṅgika. If, as other Tibetans claim, all Madhyamaka texts had to accord with Nāgārjuna's *Mūlamadhyamakakārikā* and Candrakīrti's *Madhyamakāvatāra*, all *Svātantrika-Madhyamaka works as well as Nāgārjuna's *Bodhicittavivaraṇa*, *Dharmadhātustava*, and other texts would not be Madhyamaka either. For these Tibetans assert that the *Madhyamakāvatāra* refutes the *Svātantrika view, while the *Bodhicittavivaraṇa* and so on explain that nondual wisdom is ultimate reality. Also, once they accept the *Uttaratantra* as a Madhyamaka text, the *Mahāyānasūtrālaṃkāra*, *Madhyāntavibhāga*, and *Dharmadharmatāvibhāga* must also be Madhyamaka works because there is no difference between these four in that they all explain the duality of apprehender and apprehended as the imaginary nature and nondual wisdom as ultimate reality. Furthermore, it is very clear that the latter three texts do not represent Mere Mentalism because *Mahāyānasūtrālaṃkāra* VI.8b says:

> Then, it is realized that mind does not exist either.

Also, *Madhyāntavibhāga* I.6cd states:

> Based on nonobservation,
> Nonobservation arises.

Vasubandhu's *Bhāṣya* comments on this:

> Based on the nonobservation of referents, the nonobservation of mere cognizance[77] too arises.[78]

Likewise, the *Dharmadharmatāvibhāga* says, "By virtue of not observing any referents, they engage in not observing mere cognizance [either]." In addition, these three texts and all their Indian commentaries contain solely explanations on the dependent nature being illusionlike, whereas there is not a single passage in them about the dependent nature being really existent.

As for the order of the five Maitreya texts, Śākya Chogden holds it to be different from the usual one mentioned above. He says that the *Abhisamayālaṃkāra*, the *Mahāyānasūtrālaṃkāra*, and the *Uttaratantra* are the first three treatises because they are connected with specific mahāyāna sūtras and thus were composed for the sake of easily understanding the meanings of these respective sūtras. The *Madhyāntavibhāga* and the *Dharmadharmatāvibhāga* come last because they teach the progressive stages of making the respective paths taught in the first three texts a living experience. In detail, the *Abhisamayālaṃkāra* is the first text that Maitreya composed because it is a commentary on the intention of the sūtras of the middle turning and those that determine emptiness. His second text is the *Mahāyānasūtrālaṃkāra* because its parts on the view come from the abhidharma teachings in the third turning and its parts on conduct are comments on the intentions of various kinds of sūtras. Also, it establishes the middle turning as the Buddha's words and then identifies the ultimate definitive meaning in this second turning through the manner in which it is commented on in the third turning. The *Uttaratantra* was composed third because, through presenting the ultimate definitive meaning found in the first two texts as the basis of the intention behind the teachings on buddha nature, it explains that this nature pervades all sentient beings and that there is only a single yāna. Therefore, it is the commentary on the intention of the final parts within the final turning. For until Maitreya had finished teaching on prajñāpāramitā and emptiness in detail, he did not teach on buddha nature and the single yāna. Fourth comes the *Madhyāntavibhāga* because it was composed for the sake of explaining that the ultimate definitive meaning of the *Abhisamayālaṃkāra*, which is identified by the *Mahāyānasūtrālaṃkāra*, represents the middle way, linking it with the conduct found in the sūtras, and then teaching the manner of the progressive stages of familiarizing with it. The final text is the *Dharmadharmatāvibhāga* because it was composed for the purpose of teaching the manner of the progressive stages of familiarizing with the definitive meaning of the *Uttaratantra*. The *Madhyāntavibhāga* does not teach these progressive stages because it does not speak about the ground of the latent tendencies of ignorance,[79] the practices to purify it, and uncontaminated karma, nor does it go beyond the principle of the three yānas. Just like the *Uttaratantra*, the *Dharmadharmatāvibhāga* speaks of only a single yāna because it explains that the final fundamental change[80] pertains solely to the mahāyāna. Thus, it says that, by virtue of the existence of the ground of the latent tendencies of ignorance in the inferior nirvāṇas without remainder, śrāvaka and pratyekabuddha arhats must eventually take birth again and enter the path of the mahāyāna. It is through the power of familiarizing with the nature of phenomena that they are then able to relinquish this ground of latent tendencies too.

As for identifying the definitive meaning of these five texts, what is explicitly taught by the *Abhisamayālaṃkāra* is the same as the explicit teaching in the sūtras of the second turning of the wheel of dharma—the nonimplicative negation of being empty of the duality of apprehender and apprehended. However, this alone is not suitable as the definitive meaning since it does not go beyond being a conceptual isolate (an "elimination-of-other").[81] Therefore, it is definitely nothing but a direct object of conception, but not suitable as the sphere of personally experienced wisdom. Therefore, the ultimate definitive meaning of the *Abhisamayālaṃkāra* is primarily identified in the *Madhyāntavibhāga* (which Maitreya himself declared to be a Madhyamaka text) and also in the *Mahāyānasūtrālaṃkāra* because the definitive meaning of the middle turning depends on what is identified as this meaning in the final turning, which is the wisdom without the duality of apprehender and apprehended. This wisdom can be considered in terms of being something that bears the nature of phenomena or being the nature of phenomena itself, but what is meant here is solely the latter. For *Mahāyānasūtrālaṃkāra* XIII.19cd says:

> Apart from the mind that is the nature of phenomena no other
> mind
> Is proclaimed to be luminous in nature.

Also, *Madhyāntavibhāga* I.13ab says that "the defining characteristic of emptiness consists of the nonbeing of duality and the being of this nonbeing." Thus, there is no difference whatsoever in the way in which the ultimate view taught by these three texts is identified. However, they differ in their ways of teaching how to make this view a living experience through engaging in it since the *Abhisamayālaṃkāra* explains it by combining the progression of the implicit teaching of the prajñāpāramitā sūtras (the clear realizations) with the progression of their explicit teaching (emptiness). On the other hand, the *Madhyāntavibhāga* and the *Mahāyānasūtrālaṃkāra* explain the view through combining the definitive meaning of the middle turning as identified by the final turning with the ways of conduct that are found in many sūtras of the final turning. Also, the nature of the definitive meaning of the *Uttaratantra* and the manner in which this nature is identified in it do not differ from the nature of the definitive meaning of the *Abhisamayālaṃkāra*, *Mahāyānasūtrālaṃkāra*, and *Madhyāntavibhāga*. For the definitive meaning that is determined in the latter two texts by way of the three natures is nothing other than what the *Uttaratantra* explains. Also, Maitreya does not identify the buddha heart that is found in the *Uttaratantra* without this being preceded by the reasonings in his *Mahāyānasūtrālaṃkāra* that teach the dependent nature to be illusionlike. However, this does not mean that the *Uttaratantra* just repeats what the *Mahāyānasūtrālaṃkāra* and the *Madhyāntavibhāga* say because their ways of explanation differ. The *Mahāyānasūtrālaṃkāra* and the *Madhyāntavibhāga* just teach the final definitive meaning, but they do not explain it from the point of view of its qualities. This aspect is explained in the *Uttaratantra* through the seven vajra points and through taking the nondual wisdom at the time of the ground as the basis of purification, which, by virtue of the purification of the adventitious stains to be purified during the time of the path, undergoes the fundamental change as being buddha wisdom at the time of the fruition.

As for the identification of the definitive meaning of the *Dharmadharmatāvibhāga* (here called "the nature of phenomena"), it is exactly the same as in the *Mahāyānasūtrālaṃkāra* and the *Madhyāntavibhāga* because it is explained as the entity that is empty of what is to be put to an end (the imaginary nature that consists of apprehender and apprehended) within the basis of purification that is the dependent nature. However, the *Mahāyānasūtrālaṃkāra* and the *Madhyāntavibhāga* differ in determining the view and then teaching the manner of familiarizing with it through one's engagement in the six pāramitās, bodhicitta, and so on for countless eons, whereas the *Dharmadharmatāvibhāga* teaches the progressive familiarization with the view from the perspective of mentally engaging in the nature of phenomena alone. In brief, when determining the view in the works of Maitreya, that which is existent must be the dharmadhātu and emptiness, which must be what is called "the wisdom empty of the duality of apprehender and apprehended" and also bears the name "perfect nature."

In particular, the False Aspectarians are established as Mādhyamikas because they refute the philosophical system of Mere Mentalism and put forth their own system, which is superior to Mere Mentalism. There are no scriptures that explain the False Aspectarians as Mere Mentalists, whereas there is the *Madhyāntavibhāga* that teaches the False Aspectarians to be Mādhyamikas. Also, if someone were established as a Mere Mentalist merely by virtue of being explained to be a Yogācāra, it would absurdly follow that all Yogācāra-Mādhyamika masters such as Śāntarakṣita are Mere Mentalists. In Indian doxographical classifications, the twofold division of Mere Mentalists into Real and False Aspectarians and of Mādhyamikas into *Svātantrikas and *Prāsaṅgikas did not exist because there are no scriptural sources for such divisions. These divisions are not justified through reasoning either because doxographical classifications are made from the perspective of the view, but there is no difference in terms of the view between *Svātantrikas and *Prāsaṅgikas. On the other hand, the twofold classification of Madhyamaka into *Rangtong* and *Shentong* is clearly evident in the texts of the two great mahāyāna traditions of Nāgārjuna and Maitreya/Asaṅga.

As for the ultimate compatibility of the traditions of Nāgārjuna and Asaṅga, Śākya Chogden says that the unsurpassable tradition of Nāgārjuna is to practice meditation according to the manner of *Shentong* after having sealed it with the *Rangtong* view. The unsurpassable tradition of Asaṅga is to assert *Shentong* when presenting one's philosophical system during subsequent attainment, but to rest evenly in the state of sheer lucid awareness during meditative equipoise, without mentally engaging in any reference points or characteristics whatsoever.

In his *Illuminating the Stages of the Path of the Five Maitreya Dharmas*,[82] Śākya Chogden repeats the main points above and adds that, at the time of studying and reflecting, all five Maitreya works ascertain the entirety of seeming reality as being self-empty. What they teach with regard to the time of meditating is to rest in meditative equipoise in ultimate reality alone. Thus, even the *Abhisamayālaṃkāra* teaches both *rangtong* and *shentong*. In the context of studying and reflecting, the temporary definitive meaning in the *Abhisamayālaṃkāra* must be explained in accordance with how the Niḥsvabhāvavādins comment on it because what is to be experienced (later) through direct yogic valid perception first needs to be identified correctly in the context of study and reflection. However, the manner in which emptiness is determined in the *Abhisamayālaṃkāra* during the time of studying and reflecting, which accords with the explicit teaching of the prajñāpāramitā sūtras, is geared toward negating all conceptions of clinging to any characteristics of knowable objects from the perspective of ordinary consciousness, but not geared toward resting in meditative equipoise in the spacelike lack of characteristics from the perspective of nonconceptual wisdom. For the former emptiness is only a conceptual isolate and therefore not suitable from the perspective of wisdom. In the context of identifying what is to be experienced through having become familiar with emptiness through meditation, this emptiness must be explained according to Asaṅga's and Vasubandhu's way of commenting because what is to be experienced through yogic valid perception needs to be identified in the specific context of meditation (versus study and reflection).[83] In general, the *Abhisamayālaṃkāra*'s philosophical system is nothing other than what Asaṅga explains.

The same author's *Explanation of the Origin of Madhyamaka*[84] says that the main subject of both the *Abhisamayālaṃkāra* and the *Uttaratantra* is the Madhyamaka that represents the intention of the prajñāpāramitā sūtras as commented on through the third turning of the wheel of dharma. In the

Abhisamayālaṃkāra, the hidden meaning of these sūtras—the clear realizations—is identified from the perspective of the wisdom that is free from apprehender and apprehended, and the text's seventy points ascertain all phenomena as *rangtong* in accordance with the explicit teachings of these sūtras. Similarly, in the *Uttaratantra*, when emptiness and the tathāgata heart are identified, both the way of negating the object of negation and the identification of the object that is to be made a living experience are clearly explained in the manner of *shentong*. Moreover, if the view of the three other Maitreya texts belonged to Mere Mentalism, all presentations of the five paths, the ten bhūmis, and the fruitional buddhabhūmi in them would have to be deprecated as not being in accord with how things actually are. Thus, all mahāyāna texts composed by Asaṅga and Vasubandhu, as well as all those by Dignāga and his spiritual heirs, represent nothing but the Madhyamaka of the definitive meaning, which is nothing other than the intention of the prajñāpāramitā sūtras as commented on in the sūtras of the third turning.

Other Sakyapas

The anonymous contemporary editor of the commentaries on the *Madhyāntavibhāga* and *Dharmadharmatāvibhāga*[85] by the Sakya master Rongtön Shéja Künsi[86] (1367–1449) explains that the *Abhisamayālaṃkāra* is the text that teaches the meanings of the precious prajñāpāramitā sūtras through matching them with the pith instructions on the progressive stages of the path to enlightenment. The *Mahāyānasūtrālaṃkāra* teaches the essential points of practice of the *Abhisamayālaṃkāra* through compiling them from many different sūtras. The *Madhyāntavibhāga*'s five chapters on the defining characteristics, the obscurations, true reality, cultivating the remedies, and the unsurpassable yāna teach on the practices of calm abiding and superior insight in particular. Their topic is the distinction between the middle and the extremes of all phenomena that consist of the three natures—the imaginary nature of the duality of apprehender and apprehended, the dependent nature that is falsely imagined as the imaginary nature, and the perfect nature that is empty of all extremes, such as existence and nonexistence. The *Dharmadharmatāvibhāga* finely distinguishes between phenomena (saṃsāra) and the nature of phenomena (nirvāṇa). Phenomena consist of apprehender and apprehended—the imaginary and dependent natures that are the seeds for wandering in the three realms of saṃsāric existence. The nature of phenomena is the perfect nature—the fundamental mode of being of being empty of apprehender and apprehended. The *Uttaratantra* establishes a single yāna in accordance with the final view of Madhyamaka.

The concluding verses of the contemporary Khenpo Lodho Zangpo's[87] commentary on the *Dharmadharmatāvibhāga* say that Maitreya's texts represent the true Madhyamaka of being free from all reference points, which is beyond "other-empty" and "self-empty" and represents the fundamental change that is the inseparability of appearances (phenomena) and the dharmadhātu (the nature of phenomena):

> [There are] the explanation that Madhyamaka is a permanent
> entity,
> Which is empty of what is other (conditioned phenomena),
> And the clinging to the emptiness of being self-empty—
> The view that represents the extreme of extinction.
> In order to be liberated from both of these,
> The utter freedom from all extremes of reference points
> Is explained through the excellent intention of the protector
> Maitreya.
>
> Through the virtue of having made these efforts here,
> May the fundamental change of the inseparability
> Of appearing phenomena and the dhātu of dharmatā manifest
> And may the welfare of sentient beings be promoted
> Through the three kāyas—the maṇḍala of the victors—
> For as long as [saṃsāric] existence lasts.[88]

Mipham Rinpoche

As for the Nyingma School, Mipham Rinpoche's (1846–1912) introduction in his commentary on the *Dharmadharmatāvibhāga*[89] says that the five Maitreya works comment on the intentions of the entire teachings of the Buddha. Some scholars hold that all five represent a unity, while others reject this notion because these texts disagree in what they teach ultimately, such as explaining three yānas or a single yāna as being the definitive meaning. In our own system, they are held to be commentaries on the intentions of distinct sets of teachings by the Buddha. Some assert that the first one and the last one are commentaries on the intention of Madhyamaka, while the middle three are commentaries on the intention of Mere Mentalism. Others hold that only the *Mahāyānasūtrālaṃkāra* is a Mere Mentalist text, while the other four are Madhyamaka. Yet others think that the *Abhisamayālaṃkāra* is Madhyamaka, while the other four represent Mere Mentalism. Some assert that the intention of all five is Mere Mentalism, while others think that all five are Madhyamaka.

Ultimately, however, the *Abhisamayālaṃkāra* comments on the intention of the middle turning of the wheel of dharma (prajñāpāramitā) and the *Uttaratantra* comments on the definitive meaning of the final turning (the intention of the sūtras that teach the sugata heart). Both assert a final single disposition and a final single yāna, thus according in their intention in those regards with the meaning of Madhyamaka. The *Mahāyānasūtrālaṃkāra* is a synopsis that comments on the intentions of the majority of the remaining sūtras. Most of what is said in it, such as a single disposition and a single yāna not being definite, is mainly a commentary on the intention of the sūtras of Mere Mentalism.[90] The *Madhyāntavibhāga* and the *Dharmadharmatāvibhāga* teach the vast and the profound sides, respectively, of the general yāna.

Though the latter two texts extensively teach on the three natures and the nonexistence of outer objects, it is in no way definite for them to be exclusive Mere Mentalist texts merely by virtue of these features. It is also not contradictory to present the intention of Madhyamaka through these terminologies since the *Laṅkāvatārasūtra* teaches the five dharmas, the three natures, the eight consciousnesses, and the two kinds of identitylessness as the general dharma terminologies of the entire mahāyāna and since the three natures also appear in the Maitreya Chapter of the prajñāpāramitā sūtras. However, there is no word or reasoning in any of those two texts by Maitreya that suggests a really established consciousness empty of duality as asserted by the Mere Mentalists. Thus, there is not only no flaw whatsoever in explaining them to be unbiased commentaries on the intention of the general yāna, but this is precisely the true nature of these texts.

In particular, the *Madhyāntavibhāga* gives a detailed explanation of the vast paths of the three yānas, while the *Dharmadharmatāvibhāga* determines nonconceptual wisdom—the heart essence of the topics of all profound sūtras—in accordance with the Yogācāra-Madhyamaka principle of the two realities in union. Since this is the profound meaning of the definitive secret of the view, all followers of the mahāyāna must realize the view in this way and therefore there is no problem in commenting on it according to either Madhyamaka or Mere Mentalism. For example, though various Mādhyamika and Mere Mentalist masters comment on the prajñāpāramitā sūtras in their texts according to their own distinct positions, the ultimate intention of these texts is Madhyamaka. Likewise, there is no contradiction when those who assert the *Dharmadharmatāvibhāga* as being a treatise according to Mere Mentalism explain it in that way through applying their own mental dexterity. However, ultimately, this text clearly teaches the ultimate profound point of the mahāyāna—nonconceptual wisdom, just as it is. Therefore, it is a general commentary on the entire collection of the profound sūtras. In this text the manner of asserting the seeming (the bearers of the nature of phenomena) accords with Mere Mentalism, while the manner of asserting the ultimate (the nature of phenomena) accords with Madhyamaka. Thus, its final intention consists of Madhyamaka and can be understood as the manner of teaching the essential point of the mahāyāna view by way of the union of Mere Mentalism and Madhyamaka.

Khenpo Shenga

The great Nyingma scholar Khenpo Shenga[91] (1871–1921) says in the prologue to his annotational commentary on Haribhadra's *Abhisamayālaṃkāravivṛti*[92] that the five works of Maitreya were taught as commentaries on the intentions of the entire mahāyāna. Among them, the *Abhisamayālaṃkāra* explains the intention of the sūtras that teach profound emptiness. It is based and draws on all prajñāpāramitā sūtras (such as the large, medium, and brief ones). From among the three turnings of the wheel of dharma, it comments on the intention of the sūtras of definitive meaning from the middle turning on the lack of characteristics and belongs to the category of pith instructions on profound emptiness. It was composed for the purpose of guiding those who are ignorant about how the stages of clear realization—the hidden meaning of the prajñāpāramitā sūtras—are to be made a living experience. The *Mahāyānasūtrālaṃkāra*, the *Madhyāntavibhāga*, and the *Dharmadharmatāvibhāga* explain the intention of the sūtras that teach vast activity, and the *Uttaratantra* clarifies the intention of the sūtras that teach the inconceivable nature of phenomena. These texts were given for the sake of guiding three types of persons—the three middle treatises were composed for those to be guided through the philosophical system of Mere Mentalism; the *Abhisamayālaṃkāra*, for those to be guided through the teachings of the *Svātantrika system; and the *Uttaratantra*, for those to be guided through the teachings of the *Prāsaṅgika system. Also, these five texts are taught as the remedies for six kinds of wrong ideas. As the remedies for (1) the clinging to entities and (2) the clinging to the lack of entities, respectively, the *Abhisamayālaṃkāra* teaches the lack of any nature and all the stages of the paths. The *Mahāyānasūtrālaṃkāra*, the *Madhyāntavibhāga*, and the *Dharmadharmatāvibhāga* were taught for those who are temporarily unable to understand the meaning of the freedom from extremes. Thus, these texts teach the intentions, the indirect intentions, the three natures, and so on as the remedies for (3) taking this meaning literally. They also teach the infinite varieties of the aspect of skillful means as the remedy for (4) lacking interest in the vast aspect of the teachings and the narrow-minded wish to merely meditate on identitylessness. The *Uttaratantra* teaches that all sentient beings possess the buddha heart as the remedy for (5) the five faults, such as faintheartedness.[93] As the remedy for (6) the idea that, if all beings have buddha nature, there can be neither any decrease of flaws nor any increase in qualities, the text differentiates this in terms of various presentations, examples, utterly pure buddhahood, and so on.

Düjom Rinpoche

The Nyingma School of Tibetan Buddhism by the late head of this school, Düjom Rinpoche (1904–1988), states that there are two Madhyamaka systems—the outer coarse one and the inner subtle one. The latter is referred to as Great Madhyamaka, the highest among the philosophical systems of the sūtrayāna. Its meaning is revealed in the texts of Maitreya and in Nāgārjuna's collection of praises, which subsume the essence of the definitive meaning of both the second and third turnings of the wheel of dharma. In particular, concerning this Great Madhyamaka,

> . . . the regent Ajita has extensively analysed the meaningful intention of the topics of vast significance which revealed all things in terms of the three essential natures. This he did by means of discourses connected with the irreversible intention of the final turning of the doctrinal wheel and with the utter purity of the three spheres [of subject, object, and their interaction].[94]

The Third Karmapa

In the Kagyü School, the introduction to OED by the Third Karmapa says that the five treatises of Maitreya represent a single continuous effort on his behalf. Thus, homage is only paid at the beginning of the *Abhisamayālaṃkāra*, while the end of the *Uttaratantra* contains the dedication. According to this order, the *Abhisamayālaṃkāra* was composed first because prajñāpāramitā is like the mother of all texts that teach the paths and fruitions of all yānas which give birth to all four noble ones.[95] Thus, this text was composed in order to clearly teach prajñāpāramitā, the middle turning of the wheel of dharma. By saying that the diverse other sūtras of the three yānas accord with this point, the *Mahāyānasūtrālaṃkāra* ascertains that they belong to the scope of what is to be understood and clearly realized. Thus it illuminates the meanings of all teachings in all three turnings. As a summary of this, the *Madhyāntavibhāga* explains merely how to engage in the defining characteristics of the factors to be relinquished and their remedies, the obscurations of these, true reality, abiding in the manner of cultivating the remedies plus their results, and the unsurpassable yāna.[96] The *Dharmadharmatāvibhāga* summarizes all of what is taught in this way further, saying that everything is contained in phenomena (saṃsāra) and the nature of phenomena (nirvāṇa). It illuminates the path, including its fruition, which consists of the manner of engaging in the five dharmas and the three natures (both of which elucidate the principle of the two realities) as well as in the true reality of the eight consciousnesses—the nonconceptual wisdom that bears the names "fundamental change," "buddha heart," and "dharmakāya." The text thus primarily teaches the manner of practically engaging in *tathāgatagarbha*, which is equated with the stainless nature of phenomena, nonconceptual wisdom, the dharmakāya, the perfect nature, and prajñāpāramitā. Implicitly, it also teaches the liberations of all śrāvakas and pratyekabuddhas. Therefore, it resembles a gate to enter all the words of the Buddha and the treatises on them. The *Uttaratantra* summarizes the meanings of the sūtras of the last turning and of those that teach the buddhayāna. It teaches the actuality of the nature of phenomena (the basic nature of buddhahood that is the final definitive meaning), which lies not within the sphere of any ordinary beings, śrāvakas, or pratyekabuddhas. This nature is taught as its being associated with adventitious stains, stainless enlightenment, its qualities, its enlightened activity, and the manner of engaging in it.[97] Thus, one should know that all the words of the Buddha's teaching and the treatises on it are summarized in these five texts.[98]

Gö Lotsāwa

Gö Lotsāwa's *Blue Annals*[99] explains the following on the assertions of different early Tibetan commentators on the *Uttaratantra*. Both Ngog and Dsangnagpa hold *tathāgatagarbha* to be ultimate reality, but they state that ultimate reality is not even a mere referent object (*zhen yul*), let alone being an object of terms and conceptions. On the other hand, Chaba Chökyi Sengé asserts that ultimate reality consists of the nonimplicative negation of all entities being empty of real existence and that this negation does serve as a referent object of terms and conceptions. Those who follow the tradition of Dsen Kawoché hold that, since the naturally luminous nature of the mind is *tathāgatagarbha*, it is the powerful vital cause of buddhahood.[100] Rendawa Shönnu Lodrö[101] (1348–1412) first took the *Uttaratantra* to be a treatise of the Mere Mentalist system and composed a commentary in accordance with that system. However, when he stayed in solitary retreat later, he sang a spontaneous dohā:

> Therefore, seeing our own mind, this inseparability of being aware and empty,
> To exist in all sentient beings in a pervasive manner,
> Through examples such as a treasure below the earth and the womb of a pregnant woman,
> [Maitreya] declared that all beings are endowed with *tathāgatagarbha.*

The *Blue Annals* concludes by saying that there are people who claim that Dölpopa is wrong in asserting *tathāgatagarbha* to be really existent and permanent, but it appears that it is due to his kindness that there are many in Central Tibet who take the *Uttaratantra* as their yidam.[102]

Gö Lotsāwa's commentary on the *Uttaratantra* says that, in general, this text teaches the meaning of all yānas and that all words of the Buddha are authentic. However, the primary meaning of this text concerns the last or unsurpassable turning of the wheel of dharma and it also shows the difference between the expedient and the definitive meanings of the Buddha's words.[103] The *Uttaratantra* explains enlightenment as stainless suchness, while the *Dharmadharmatāvibhāga* calls it "the nature of phenomena," which means the same as suchness. Also, both texts say that the fundamental change has the same meaning as suchness.[104] The *Uttaratantra* identifies nonconceptual wisdom as the cause of enlightenment and the *Dharmadharmatāvibhāga* explains it as the cause of the fundamental change. In sum, the *Dharmadharmatāvibhāga* appears to be something like a commentary on the second chapter (on enlightenment) of the *Uttaratantra.*[105] Uniquely among all commentators on the *Uttaratantra*, Gö Lotsāwa explicitly links not only this text to the Mahāmudrā in the tradition of Maitrīpa, Sahajavajra, Gampopa, and other Kagyü masters,[106] but does the same with three of the other four treatises by Maitreya.

In this regard, Gö Lotsāwa's *Blue Annals*[107] quotes Gampopa's (1079–1153) statement that "the text for this Mahāmudrā of ours is this *Mahāyānottaratantraśāstra* composed by the Bhagavān Maitreya." The text continues on Maitrīpa's specific prajñāpāramitā-based approach to Mahāmudrā by saying that it

> is clearly explained in Sahajavajra's *Tattvadaśakaṭīkā* as the wisdom of suchness that has the three characteristics of its nature being pāramitā, being in accordance with the secret mantra, and its name being "Mahāmudrā." Therefore, the Mahāmudrā of prajñāpāramitā of lord Gampopa was described by lord Götsangpa as being a doctrine of Maitrīpa.[108]

In particular, Gö Lotsāwa's *Uttaratantra* commentary links the contents of this text to the four yogas of Mahāmudrā. He does so both directly and through his comments on the *Dharmadharmatāvibhāga* within his commentary on the *Uttaratantra*[109] (as mentioned above, he takes the former to be a commentary on the second chapter of the latter). The specific way in which Gö Lotsāwa links the *Dharmadharmatāvibhāga* to the four yogas of Mahāmudrā is through the four yogic practices (*prayoga*)[110] as the third point in the explanation of nonconceptual wisdom. Since he also quotes the *Laṇkāvatārasūtra*, the *Mahāyānasūtrālaṃkāra*, and the *Madhyāntavibhāga* in this context, he establishes their connection with Mahāmudrā too.[111] In Yogācāra texts, these four yogic practices are typically said to correlate to the four factors conducive to penetration of the path of preparation, which are also discussed in detail in the *Abhisamayālaṃkāra*. Thus, implicitly, this text can also be regarded as a basis for Mahāmudrā practice.[112]

The Seventh Karmapa

The Ocean of Texts on Reasoning by the Seventh Karmapa, Chötra Gyatso (1454–1506), explains:

> . . . the final intention of the *[Pramāṇa]samuccaya* and the seven treatises [by Dharmakīrti] is represented by the Madhyamaka that was transmitted from Maitreya via Asaṅga and his brother, which is also in accord with the Madhyamaka texts of Nāgārjuna and his spiritual heirs.[113]

The very same is said in the introduction to the contemporary edition of the Seventh Karmapa's text by the tutor of the Seventeenth Karmapa, Khenchen Thrangu Rinpoche (born 1933),[114] and also by the First Karma Trinlépa, Choglé Namgyal (1456–1539).[115] The latter also states:

> The meaning that is taught in the tantras, the bodhisattva
> commentaries,[116]
> Many sūtras, and by those who follow the [five] dharmas of Maitreya
> Represents the *shentong* held by Rangjung Dorje . . .[117]

The Eighth Karmapa

The Eighth Karmapa, Mikyö Dorje's[118] (1507–1554), colophon to his new edition of the Seventh Karmapa's *Ocean of Texts on Reasoning* says:

> It is appropriate to also refute this philosophical system of
> Vijñapti[vādins].
>
> Nevertheless, the statement that lucid and aware mere mind,
> Which is taught as being really established ultimately
> In the sevenfold collection and the sūtra of Dignāga and
> [Dharma]kīrti,
> Abides as Madhyamaka was made by the victor Maitreya
>
> To the great noble master Asaṅga
> In order to guide Vasubandhu,
> Proclaiming that the three latter dharmas of Maitreya[119] and the
> system
> That extensively teaches the dharma principles of Vijñapti[vāda]
> are Madhyamaka.[120]

The same author's commentary on the *Abhisamayālaṃkāra* explicitly and repeatedly says that both Maitreya's and Nāgārjuna's systems are Madhyamaka[121] and that, in commenting on the texts by Maitreya, one must follow Asaṅga and Vasubandhu,[122] who are also (Great) Mādhyamikas and definitely not so-called Mere Mentalists.[123]

In his commentary on the *Madhyamakāvatāra*, the Eighth Karmapa reports the position of his main teacher, the First Sangyé Nyenpa, Dashi Baljor (1457–1519)[124] on the texts of Maitreya:

> All these five dharma works by Maitreya are established as commentaries on the intentions of the entirety of the words of the Buddha in the causal and fruitional mahāyāna for the following reasons. As for the middle three treatises [*Mahāyānasūtrālaṃkāra, Madhyāntavibhāga,* and *Dharmadharmatāvibhāga]*, it is not the case that they do not teach the principle of the Madhyamaka dharma in an ancillary way, but their explicit teaching is the distinct system of Yogācāra.[125] The first dharma work of Maitreya [*Abhisamayālaṃkāra]* is a treatise common to Madhyamaka and Yogācāra. The last dharma work of Maitreya *[Uttaratantra]* is a treatise common to sūtra and tantra.[126]

Jamgön Kongtrul Lodrö Tayé

Jamgön Kongtrul Lodrö Tayé's introduction to his commentary on the *Uttaratantra* states:

> First [Maitreya] composed the *Abhisamayālaṃkāra,* which teaches the coarse dharma terminology of the Great Madhyamaka of definitive meaning in merely an abbreviated manner. Then, in the *Mahāyānasūtrālaṃkāra, Madhyāntavibhāga,* and *Dharmadharmatāvibhāga,* he explained it clearly and extensively. Finally, in the *Uttaratantra,* he ascertained the fine details of the philosophical system of the uncommon meaning of the sūtras [that teach] on the [tathāgata] heart.[127]

Furthermore, his introduction also states that the *Dharmadharmatāvibhāga* is like a commentary on the second chapter of the *Uttaratantra* and that the former's term "nature of phenomena" and the latter's term "stainless suchness" have the same meaning.[128]

The same author's TOK[129] classifies the *Abhisamayālaṃkāra* as a commentary on the second turning of the wheel of dharma, with its view being *Rangtong* Madhyamaka, while the other four texts are commentaries on the third turning and belong to *Shentong* Madhyamaka. In addition, TOK[130] refers to Śākya Chogden as dividing *Shentong* Madhyamaka into the two subschools of Yogācāra-Mādhyamikas, who follow the explanatory principles of the first three works of Maitreya (*Abhisamayālaṃkāra, Mahāyānasūtrālaṃkāra,* and *Madhyāntavibhāga*), while the "Mādhyamikas of Certainty about the Ultimate" follow the explanatory principles of the *Uttaratantra.* In terms of the nature of the view, TOK says, these two systems show no great differences. However, the system of the first three Maitreya texts explains that, ultimately, there are three yānas and so on. Also, these texts do not use certain explanatory principles found in the *Uttaratantra,* such as there being only a single yāna ultimately and the notions of "the ground of the latent tendencies of ignorance" and "rebirth through uncontaminated karma." One should understand that these two systems, for the two types of beings to be trained (common and uncommon), respectively represent cutting through reference points through study and reflection and the manner of explaining certainty about the ultimate through meditation.

Most Tibetans say that the first three Maitreya works are not Madhyamaka texts because they explain that, ultimately, there are three yānas. However, according to the masters who follow *Shentong,* one cannot claim that these texts are not Madhyamaka merely on account of the first three Maitreya texts explaining that śrāvakas and pratyekabuddhas, after they have entered the nirvāṇa without remainder, do not enter the path of the mahāyāna. For the presentation that something is Madhyamaka is made from the perspective of the view, and what the mighty scholar Kamalaśīla and others explained as the distinctive features of Madhyamaka—(1) as emptiness, all knowable objects are of the same taste, (2) the basic element (the *sugatagarbha*) pervades all sentient beings, and (3) they are all capable of becoming enlightened—apply to these three texts as well.

Dölpopa said that there is no difference in the view of the five works of Maitreya. Also, what the *Abhisamayālaṃkāra* explains is not the view of *rangtong*, and none of those five texts contain any explanations about the cut-off disposition or the ultimate existence of three yānas. Thus, Dölpopa does not make the above twofold distinction of a higher and a lower system within *Shentong* Madhyamaka.

The Tibetans explain that this Madhyamaka system of the first three texts of Maitreya is "the system of the False Aspectarian Mere Mentalists." However, generally speaking, the conventional terms "real [aspect]" and "false aspect," which are based on the system of the Mere Mentalists, are just applied by Tibetans as they please. All that one finds in that regard in the original texts are the two types of passages that prove that the consciousness which appears as a referent is a real or a false aspect of consciousness appearing as a referent. In particular, Śākya Chogden says:

> If one asserts that the view of the *Uttaratantra* is the view of Mere Mentalism, there are no scriptures or reasonings that would prove that this is the case. The reasons for this are as follows. In this system [of the *Uttaratantra* itself], no scriptures or reasonings appear that could serve as valid cognitions [for such a position]. [But] if one applies proofs and invalidations [that accord with such a position] to some scriptures and reasonings that one has taken from other systems, one will never find a Mādhyamika who asserts the Madhyamaka view without flaw. [Also,] venerable Maitreya and Asaṅga explained that [the *Uttaratantra*] is a Madhyamaka [text]. If it is not established as such [a text] even through [their testimony], one will not find any other referees who could serve as the authorities for this teaching. Through the argument that [Nāgārjuna] is a noble one and was prophesied by the Sugata, Bhāviveka[131] and Kamalaśīla have proved that the scriptural system of Nāgārjuna is Madhyamaka. That [very same argument] applies in this case [to Asaṅga] as well.

> If something were not Madhyamaka because it explains the perfect [nature] as ultimate reality, how could the many earlier and later Tibetans be Mādhyamikas who assert that the factor of emptiness [in the sense] of a nonimplicative negation is ultimate reality?
>
> Therefore, in Maitreya's and Asaṅga's own system, there are no explanations that there are [any] other discourses [of the Buddha] or treatises [that comment on them] which teach a Madhyamaka view outside of this very Madhyamaka that is taught in the last dharma of Maitreya. One will understand [that this is the case] by merely reading not only just the root texts of Maitreya, but also the four synopses[132] and the two summaries[133] [by Asaṅga]. For it is clear in this very system that it lucidly explains that the sūtras which teach all phenomena as lacking a nature are not to be taken literally. If one accepts them as something to be taken literally, one becomes a proclaimer of [the extreme of] extinction.

Thrangu Rinpoche

According to Thrangu Rinpoche's contemporary commentary on the *Dharmadharmatāvibhāga*,[134] the different positions on the Maitreya texts include the claims that all five belong to the "Mind-only School"; that the *Abhisamayālaṃkāra* and the *Uttaratantra* represent Madhyamaka, while the other three belong to "Mind-only"; and that only the *Abhisamayālaṃkāra* represents Madhyamaka, with the other four being "Mind-only." However, in terms of practice, it is necessary to settle that appearances are nothing but mind (even in the Madhyamaka view), to resolve that mind is empty, and to realize this emptiness in meditation. The view of the "Mind-only School" is to claim that this mind is truly existent, but such is not said anywhere in the texts of Maitreya. Thus, from that point of view, it can be said that all five belong to Madhyamaka. In particular, the *Dharmadharmatāvibhāga* and the *Uttaratantra* present the view of the *Shentong* Madhyamaka School in that they both teach *sugatagarbha*.

The Dharmadharmatāvibhāga *and its major topics*

The different versions of the text

In his essay "Search for Sanskrit Manuscripts in Tibet" (Sāṃkṛtyāyana 1935), Sāṃkṛtyāyana reported the existence of a five-folio manuscript in Māgadhī script authored by Maitreya called *Dharmadharmatāpravibhāgasūtra*. Unfortunately Sāṃkṛtyāyana only presented the opening stanza, the first three and the last two sentences, and the colophon (the entire text is not available at present). A comparison with the Tibetan of DDV shows that the text is obviously a Sanskrit prose version of DDV.

In the Tibetan *Tengyur*, the *Dharmadharmatāvibhāga* is preserved in three different versions. There are two prose versions (D4022 and the one embedded in Vasubandhu's DDVV) as well as a versified version (D4023). As Mathes and others[135] have already shown in detail, there are clear terminological correspondences between the versified version (translated by Sengé Gyaltsen) and the prose version contained in DDVV (translated by Ngog Lotsāwa), while the independent prose version D4022 (translated by Tsültrim Gyalwa and further edited by Su Gawé Dorje) often diverges from standard Tibetan translation terminology as it is used by Ngog and followed by Sengé Gyaltsen (however, when compared to the prose version of DDV as contained in the available Sanskrit fragment of DDVV, D4022 often reflects the Sanskrit better than the other two versions). Somewhat peculiarly, the versified version often uses both variants of the Tibetan found in D4022 versus the prose version in DDVV that are used to translate a given Sanskrit term. Though the colophon of the versified version says that it was "translated" by Mahājana and Sengé Gyaltsen, the above facts suggest that it was most probably compiled in Tibetan on the basis of the two already existing Tibetan translations of the prose version and that there was no original Sanskrit versified form of DDV. This is further supported by the fact that both Vasubandhu's commentary and the earliest available Tibetan commentary—the Third Karmapa's OED—comment on the prose version (all later Tibetan commentaries use the versified version).

A summary of the Dharmadharmatāvibhāga

Introduction

To give a brief overview of the contents of DDV, its introductory section (lines 1–35 in the versified version) first provides the distinction and the defining characteristics of phenomena and the nature of phenomena (1–23), that is "what appears as duality and how it is designated" and "suchness, which lacks any distinction between apprehender and apprehended, or [between] objects of designation and what designates them." Phenomena make up all appearances in saṃsāra, which are nothing but manifestations or projections of false imagination (what is to be relinquished), while the nature of phenomena is suchness, nonconceptual wisdom, and nirvāṇa (what is to be directly perceived). Just like illusions, phenomena do not really exist but appear, thus causing afflictions and suffering. On the other hand, the nature of phenomena does exist ultimately, but does not appear for ordinary beings as long as it is obscured by the appearances of false imagination. Second (24–31), "the rationale" for both the ultimate nonexistence of phenomena and their seeming appearance is that both these elements are necessary in order to account for mistakenness and unmistakenness as well as affliction and purification. Third (32–35), when investigated, phenomena and their nature are neither the same nor different.

Detailed explanation of phenomena

The section that explains phenomena in detail (36–87) contains six points, with (1)–(3) (36–45) corresponding to the three main points in the introduction (defining characteristic, rationale, and phenomena and their nature being neither one nor different). Points (4) and (5) (46–79) consist of the twofold "matrix of phenomena" or the twofold manner in which phenomena manifest—the world as the environment and the sentient beings that live in it. The world as the surroundings of sentient beings is experienced as something in common among them. As for sentient beings, certain elements (such as behaviors, qualities, and faults) are also experienced in common, while others (such as happiness, suffering, karma, bondage, and liberation) are strictly individual "private" experiences. In general, however, both the world and the beings in it consist of nothing but a multitude of individual mind streams. That certain groups of beings (such as humans) experience a seemingly common external world is only due to the fact of the mind streams of these beings containing similar imprints that appear to each one of them individually as their own projections of a world, but are mistaken by all of them for constituting an actual shared environment outside of their individual mind streams. The text also makes it clear that the minds of others can never be a direct object of another mind, be it in ordinary states of mind or in meditation. Thus, the text (and the Yogācāra system in general) maintains that whatever is perceived is nothing but appearances in individual mind streams, without thereby falling into the extreme of solipsism. Point (6) (80–87) discusses "the nonexistence of the appearance of apprehender and apprehended." What appear as objects do not exist externally apart from mind as the perceiver, in which they appear. Consequently, what appear as the apprehenders of such objects do not exist either. Nevertheless, by virtue of beginningless latent tendencies, the seeming duality of apprehender and apprehended keeps appearing to ordinary beings.

Detailed explanation of the nature of phenomena

The bulk of DDV (70%) contains the detailed presentation of the nature of phenomena (88–300). Though DDV first defines the nature of phenomena in a more negative way by excluding what it is not ("suchness, which lacks any distinction between apprehender and apprehended, or [between] objects of designation and what designates them"), the text also speaks of suchness in a positive way as being existent and illustrates its natural and unchanging purity and qualities through the examples of space, gold, and water remaining unchanged throughout all kinds of obscurations. Thus, the goal of the mahāyāna path is to see through the illusory nature of the obscuring appearances of false imagination and to directly perceive the primordially existent true nature of all phenomena instead. This is the fundamental change in which all adventitious stains are eliminated and everything appears as nothing but suchness.

DDV presents the nature of phenomena in six points. Point (1) (88–94)—the defining characteristic—was already covered in the introduction above. (2) "The matrix of the nature of phenomena" (95–96), or where the nature of phenomena is found, consists of all phenomena as well as the Buddha's teachings that explain this nature. (3) "Penetration" (97–100) refers to the path of preparation of properly engaging in the mahāyāna scriptures through conceptual study, reflection, and meditation. (4) "Contact" (101–4) represents the path of seeing, on which the nature of phenomena is realized directly in a nonconceptual manner for the first time. (5) "Recollection" (105–8) is the path of familiarizing with what was seen on the path of seeing, thus gradually eliminating all afflictive and cognitive obscurations.

(6) "The arrival at the true nature of the nature of phenomena" (109–300) is the main subject of the entire text (60% of DDV). It is explained as "the

fundamental change" in ten points, which represents the most detailed discussion of this topic in Buddhist literature. (a) "The nature" of the fundamental change (121–25) refers to the direct appearance of suchness without any adventitious stains whatsoever.[136] (b) The threefold "substance" or "entity" of the fundamental change (126–33), that is, what changes into suchness, consists of mind appearing as the outer world, mind appearing as sentient beings, and the dharmadhātu as found in the sūtras all having changed into suchness, which respectively result in the manifestation of pure buddha realms and the realization of qualities, the ability to teach the profound and vast dharma, and the direct perception of everything that is to be known. (c) "The persons" who undergo this fundamental change (134–39) are twofold—the foundation that is the suchness of the mind streams of buddhas and bodhisattvas changes completely so that it is free from all obscurations, while the fundamental changes of śrāvakas and pratyekabuddhas are only partial. (d) "The distinctive features" of the fundamental change (140–46) are the attainment of the dharmakāya, sāmbhogikakāya, and nairmāṇikakāya with their respective qualities and activities. (e) "The prerequisites" for the fundamental change (147–51) consist of previous aspiration prayers, the mahāyāna teachings as the focal object, and the training on the ten bhūmis.

(f) The sixth point—nonconceptual wisdom as "the foundation" of the fundamental change (152–239)—is the main topic (25% of DDV) in the discussion of the fundamental change and may be considered the heart of DDV.[137] The explanation of nonconceptual wisdom in six points starts with (1) its "focal objects" (159–64)—the mahāyāna teachings, aspiring for them, gaining certainty about them, and completing the accumulations of merit and wisdom. (2) "The relinquishment of characteristics" (165–72) consists of abandoning the characteristics of the four progressively more subtle conceptions about antagonistic factors, their remedies, suchness, and realization (as explained in detail in the *Avikalpapraveśadhāraṇī*). (3) The fourfold "correct yogic practice" to approach nonconceptual wisdom (173–78) consists of the four well-known mahāyāna *prayogas* of observing all phenomena as being nothing other than mind, not observing them as external objects, not observing the observer or apprehender of such objects either, and observing that the duality of apprehender and apprehended is actually unobservable. (4) "The defining characteristics" of nonconceptual wisdom (179–97) are threefold. The first characteristic (abiding) means that nonconceptual wisdom rests in the nondual and inexpressible nature of phenomena. The second characteristic (nonappearance) means that duality, designations, sense faculties, objects, cognizance, and the outer world do not appear for nonconceptual wisdom. The third characteristic (appearance) means that all phenomena appear equal to space during meditative equipoise and appear like illusions during subsequent attainment. Thus, nonconceptual wisdom is "ungraspable, indemonstrable, ungrounded, without appearance, without cognizance, and without base" (as also explained in the *Avikalpapraveśadhāraṇī* and the *Kāśyapaparivarta*).[138] (5) "The benefit of nonconceptual wisdom" (198–202) is the attainment of the dharmakāya, supreme bliss, mastery over seeing the suchness and the variety of all knowable objects, and mastery over the manifold ways of teaching as is appropriate for different beings.

(6) "The thorough knowledge of nonconceptual wisdom"[139] (203–39) is fourfold. (a) "The knowledge about its being a remedy" (209–15) means that nonconceptual wisdom remedies the fivefold clinging to what is nonexistent—clinging to phenomena, persons, change (the arising and ceasing of phenomena), any difference between phenomena and the nature of phenomena, and denial (even denying the imputed existence of phenomena and persons). (b) "The thorough knowledge of the defining characteristic" (216–20) of nonconceptual wisdom refers to the exclusion of five misconceptions about what nonconceptual wisdom is. These five consist of mistaking it for the total absence of any mental engagement, mundane meditative states such as the second dhyāna and above, the complete subsiding of conceptions (such as when sleeping, being drunk, or fainting), matter, or just thinking of nonconceptuality. (c) "The knowledge of its distinctive features" (221–26) refers to the five features of being nonconceptual, not being limited in its scope of realizing all specific and general characteristics of all knowable objects, not abiding in saṃsāra or nirvāṇa, remaining even in the nirvāṇa without any remainder of the skandhas, and being unsurpassable. (d) "The knowledge of its functions" (227–39) refers to the five functions of its distancing itself from the movement of conceptions, granting unsurpassable bliss, freeing from the afflictive and cognitive obscurations, engaging in all aspects of knowable objects through the wisdom that is attained subsequent to the nonconceptual wisdom of meditative equipoise, and, finally, purifying buddha realms, maturing sentient beings, and granting omniscience.

(g) The seventh among the ten points of the fundamental change—"the mental engagement" (240–68)—means to realize that, by virtue of being ignorant about suchness, the delusive appearance of actually nonexistent false imagination and duality out of the ālaya-consciousness prevents the appearance of the nature of phenomena, and that the latter appears once the former two cease to appear. The manner of approaching such realization consists again of the fourfold correct yogic practice as explained above.

(h) "The trainings" to accomplish the fundamental change (269–85) consist of the level of engagement through aspiration (the path of preparation), the direct realization on the first bhūmi (the path of seeing), the remaining six impure and three pure bhūmis (the path of familiarization), and the effortless and uninterrupted enlightened activity of a buddha (the path of nonlearning). In due order, these four stages are said to correspond to the above four stages of "penetration," "contact," "recollection," and "the arrival at the true nature of the nature of phenomena" (points three to six of the nature of phenomena).

(i)–(j) The last two points of the fundamental change—"the shortcomings of there being no fundamental change" and "the benefits of there being this fundamental change" (286–96)— are fourfold each, with the benefits being the reverse of the shortcomings. As for the shortcomings, if there were no fundamental change, there would be no support for the afflictions not operating, no support for engaging in the path, no basis for designating those persons who have passed into nirvāṇa, and no basis for designating the differences between the realizations of śrāvakas, pratyekabuddhas, and buddhas.

Finally, DDV concludes by providing examples (297–300) for both the fleeting nature of the adventitious stains (just like illusions, dreams, and so on) and the immutability of the nature of phenomena—suchness or mind's natural luminosity—as the ever-unchanging foundation of the fundamental change that is only revealed once the stains have been eliminated (just like space, gold, and water).

The fundamental change

As mentioned above, the two main—and closely related—topics of the *Dharmadharmatāvibhāga* are the fundamental change and nonconceptual wisdom. The discussion of the fundamental change covers 60% of the entire text (being the most detailed treatment of this topic in any treatise) and the explanation of nonconceptual wisdom makes up 70% of that discussion. Thus, it seems appropriate to explore these two topics further and provide some more context for them.

Meaning of the term "fundamental change"

In the Sanskrit term *āśrayaparivṛtti* or *āśrayaparāvṛtti*, *āśraya* means "basis," "matrix," "foundation," "source," or "origin." It generally refers to something to which something else is annexed or with which something is closely connected or on which something depends or rests. This can also be a person or a thing in which some quality is inherent or retained. *Āśraya* can also mean "body," "seat" or "place of refuge." More specifically, it refers to the five sense faculties and the mental sense faculty as being the recipients of their respective objects. The primary meaning of the verbal noun *parivṛtti* is "turning about," "rolling," and "revolution." It can also mean "change," "transmutation," "removal," "end(ing)," "termination," "moving to and fro," "dwelling in a place," "returning (into this world)," "exchange," and "surrounding" (*parāvṛtti* also has all of these meanings plus "turning back or round or away from" and "rebounding"). The compound *āśrayaparivṛtti* is a *tatpuruṣa* compound, which can be taken to mean "change *of* the foundation," "change *within* the foundation," and "change *by means* of the foundation." Though the first one is the most common meaning, all three have been suggested as glosses by different Indian commentators.

According to Schmithausen, there seems to be a tendency of *parivṛtti* positively emphasizing replacement through something new (and implying removal of something old), while *parāvṛtti* negatively emphasizes removal of the old (implying replacement with something new). Thus, when these terms are used in the sense of "termination" or "removal" of something (such as impurity), both naturally imply replacement by something else (such as purity). Generally, however, it is clear that these two terms are used interchangeably, which is further evidenced by both consistently having been translated as *chüan-i* into Chinese and mostly as *gnas (yongs su) gyur (pa)* into Tibetan, though one also finds *(gnas) gzhan du gyur pa* and *gnas 'phos pa* for *parāvṛtti*.[140]

In its use in Buddhist texts, both the origin and the context of the term *āśrayaparivṛtti* are usually soteriological in nature, indicating (in one way or the other) a change from saṃsāric confusion and suffering to nirvāṇic wisdom and freedom. Thus, the term generally emphasizes the result of the process rather than the process itself or its origin. However, there is a great variety of different explanations as to what exactly changes into what. Also, often no real change of anything into anything is implied, but the result of the fundamental change is simply the revelation of the underlying true reality of all phenomena. This result can be the new state of that foundation (such as the state of the purity of suchness or buddha nature) or the foundation itself in this new state (such as suchness or buddha nature itself, once it has been purified).

There are a great number of Buddhist scriptures in which the term *āśrayaparivṛtti* (or *āśrayaparāvṛtti*) is used with reference to a variety of different states or processes. It is beyond the scope of this book to provide an exhaustive overview of all the ways in which this term is employed and understood in different texts, but some characteristic examples (primarily from Yogācāra works, in which the term appears most frequently) shall highlight its main meanings and contexts.[141]

Āśrayaparivṛtti in the sūtras

The *Śrāvakabhūmi* extensively quotes a no longer existent **Revatasūtra*.[142] Though this sūtra does not contain the word *āśrayaparivṛtti*, it uses the term *āśrayapariśuddhi* ("the purity of the foundation") in a very similar sense (see below).

In the *Saṃdhinirmocanasūtra*, the single passage that treats the notion of fundamental change is X.1–2.[143] There, the fundamental change is described as the dharmakāya of buddhas, which differs from the vimuktikāya as representing the fundamental changes of śrāvakas and pratyekabuddhas.

> "Mañjuśrī, the defining characteristic of the dharmakāya of the tathāgatas is the perfect accomplishment of the fundamental change that is the outcome of having intensely cultivated the bhūmis and pāramitās. This [fundamental change] is to be understood as having the characteristic of inconceivability for two reasons—because it is without reference points and free from anything to be formed (*mngon par 'du bya ba med pa)* and because sentient beings cling to reference points and what is to be formed."
>
> "Bhagavan, how is it, are the fundamental changes of śrāvakas and pratyekabuddhas also to be called dharmakāya?" "Mañjuśrī, they are not to be called [dharmakāya]." "Bhagavan, what should they be called then?" "Mañjuśrī, they are the vimuktikāya. Mañjuśrī, in terms of the vimuktikāya, tathāgatas, śrāvakas, and pratyekabuddhas are the same and equal. In terms of the dharmakāya, [the tathāgatas] are superior. As for being superior in terms of the dharmakāya, it is superior by virtue of its immeasurable distinct qualities, which are not easy to illustrate."[144]

The *Laṅkāvatārasūtra* occasionally uses the term *āśrayaparāvṛtti* (sometimes just *parāvṛtti* and *vyāvṛtti*). However, there are no actual explanations of the term itself and the sūtra's notoriously heterogeneous nature makes it difficult to reveal a precise and consistent meaning of its uses of "fundamental change." The only passage that comes close to a gloss of the term is found in X.151:

> Once the dependent has become pure
> And is thus free from conception,
> What [it] has changed [into] is suchness
> And [its] abode is one in which conception is eliminated.[145]

In other words, the fundamental change is described here as the dependent nature's having become purified from all conception, that is, mind's false imagination or delusive construction of the duality of apprehender and apprehended (the imaginary nature). The result of the fundamental change is suchness (the perfect nature) and the state in which that suchness abides is that it is absolutely free from such conception.[146]

Usually, the sūtra says that the ālaya-consciousness, which is consistently identified with *tathāgatagarbha*, is to be thoroughly purified[147] and several passages speak about the removal of the impregnations of negative tendencies from the ālaya-consciousness.[148] As in the following passage, the fundamental change is said to apply to the ālaya-consciousness—the *tathāgatagarbha*—and to happen throughout the ten bhūmis.

> If the ālaya-consciousness, which is known as "tathāgata heart," has not changed, the seven operating consciousnesses do not cease . . . Through seeing the five dharmas, the three natures, and the identitylessness of phenomena, the tathāgata heart becomes still when the evolution of the progression of the bhūmis has changed. Thus, it cannot be agitated by the views of the path of the tīrthikas.[149]

On the other hand, some passages refer to buddhahood and nonconceptual wisdom as the complete fundamental change or even the removal of all eight consciousnesses.[150] Similarly, the sūtra says:

> In those endowed with yoga, in whom mind, mentation, and the mental consciousness have undergone the fundamental change, who have relinquished the conceptions of apprehender and apprehended that are appearances of their own minds, and who have attained the bhūmi of a tathāgata and the personally experienced wisdom of the noble ones, discriminating notions about entities and nonentities do not arise.[151]

Furthermore, verse X.832[152] declares that the ālaya is the pure foundation of all beings, which exists without stains, just like mercury. In sum, it is not clear whether the ālaya-consciousness remains after the fundamental change and if so, in what form.

In particular, the sūtra describes the result of the fundamental change as liberation and seeing suchness, which are based on realizing all appearances to be nothing but expressions of one's own mind:

> The cessation of the causes that are the latent tendencies of consciousness—beginningless reference points and impregnations of negative tendencies—and their fundamental change through understanding that external referents are the appearances of one's own mind are liberation, Mahāmati, not destruction.[153]

> Immediately upon the fundamental change and having comprehended and realized [everything] as being the appearances of one's own mind, the mind that rests within the movement of conceptions, is spurred on by former virtue, and is learned in all scriptures sees suchness just as it is.[154]

The text also relates the fundamental change to nonarising and the freedom from the extremes of existence and nonexistence.

> Entities not arising from causes
> Are free from conceiving and what is conceived.
> Being liberated from the sides of existence and nonexistence
> Is nonarising, I declare.
>
> The mind liberated from appearance
> Is free from the two natures.[155]
> The fundamental change
> Is nonarising, I declare.[156]

Suzuki summarizes the meaning of "fundamental change" in the *Laṅkāvatārasūtra* as follows:

> . . . when we are removed from the influence of false discrimination, the whole Vijñāna system woven around the Ālaya as centre experiences a revulsion toward true perception (*parāvṛtti).* This is the gist of the teaching of the *Laṅkāvatāra.*
>
> This revulsion marks the culmination of the practical psychology of the *Laṅkāvatāra,* for it is through this fact that the realisation of *Pratyātmāryajñānagocara*[157] is possible, and this realisation is the central theme of the discourse. As this event takes place in the Ālaya, or what is the same thing, in the Tathāgata-garbha, which is the basis of all things, it is known as *āśraya-parāvṛtti,* a revulsion at the basis. Āśraya means that on which anything is dependent, and in this case the Ālaya is the Āśraya on which hangs the working of the Vijñānas and consequently the birth of the whole universe.

The new orientation takes place when the ego-centric and evil-creating discrimination based upon the dualism of subject and object ceases by the realisation that there is no external world besides what is perceived within the self; and this realisation is effected by the cultivation of the intellect known as non-discriminative and transcendental (*nirvikalpa-lokottara-jñāna*) . . . We must now look in the opposite direction, towards the quarter where no Vikalpa takes place, and where no evolution (*pravṛtti*) of the Vijñānas has set in. An opening must be made to the non-discriminative and transcendental intellect. This opening is called revulsion. The eye that used to open to the external world . . . now turns within to see what lies here. It is in this inner world that so many things we have been looking after are accessible now: the Inner Perception,[158] Nirvana, Tathatā, Emancipation, Prajñāpāramitā, the cessation of the seven Vijñānas, etc.

This sudden turning is in a sense re-turning, the Ālaya or Tathāgata-garbha returns by this to its original purity (*śuddha*), happiness (*sukha*), and eternal nature which is above *pravṛtti* and *nirvṛtti* (arise and disappearance). The Ālaya has been contaminated by external impurities (*āgantukleśa*) amassed by all kinds of philosophising (*vitarkadarśana*) based on the discrimination of subject and object.[159]

Āśrayaparivṛtti in the abhidharma and vinaya

The term *āśrayaparivṛtti* does not appear in Pāli. However, in the abhidharma tradition preserved in the Chinese canon, the term occurs in the *Mahāvibhāṣa* in the context of imperceptible form (*avijñaptirūpa*) as the basis for the transformation of the elements[160] and in Dharmatrāta's *Saṃyuktābhidharmahṛdayaśāstra* as the third point in a list of five factors that bring about the elimination of afflictions through the supramundane path.[161]

As for the *Abhidharmakośa*, Vasubandhu's *Bhāṣya*[162] on II.36c has the Sautrāntikas use the notion of *āśrayaparāvṛtti* in the sense of the *āśraya* no longer containing any seeds that are capable of giving rise to afflictions, just as burned seeds cannot sprout. Yaśomitra's *Vyākhyā* says that *āśraya* here stands for the entire psychophysical continuum (*ātmabhāva*) of the five skandhas. On IV.56, Vasubandhu[163] comments that the mind streams of those on the path of seeing and of arhats become stainless through their old foundations having changed (*parivṛtti*) into their respective new foundations (*pratyagrāśraya*). Thus, the fundamental change in this sense is said to apply only to stream-enterers and arhats (as the two most significant changes of one's whole being on the path), but not to once-returners and nonreturners. Generally, the *Abhidharmakośa* explains *āśraya* as the body and thus, according to Yaśomitra, *pratyagrāśraya* refers to a new fresh body (*abhinavaśarīra*) in the sense of having attained a certain path only recently. In his comments on VII.34,[164] however, Yaśomitra—quite unusual for a Sautrāntika author—equates *āśrayaparivṛtti* with the dharmakāya.

There are a few cases of *āśrayaparivṛtti* being used as referring to sex changes from female to male or male to female. For example, this meaning of the term is found in the *Mahāyānasūtrālaṃkārabhāṣya* on XI.4, which gives an eightfold definition of the vinaya, and in the *Viniścayasaṃgrahaṇī*'s presentation of five possibilities of becoming free from having broken certain monastic vows that apply only to monks or only to nuns.[165] In general, the notion of sex change is sometimes discussed (without, however, using the word *āśrayaparivṛtti*) in its relevance to monastics in the vinaya scriptures and elsewhere.[166]

Āśrayaparivṛtti in the *Yogācārabhūmi*

Given the heterogeneous nature of different parts of the *Yogācārabhūmi*,[167] like many other terms, the notion of *āśrayaparivṛtti* is described in various ways. In the historically older parts of the text, which still rely strongly on the traditional abhidharma system, the foundation (*āśraya*) usually indicates the entire psychophysical continuum (*ātmabhāva*) or the six inner āyatanas, which are freed from all physical and mental impregnations of negative tendencies (*dauṣṭhulya*), and then are sometimes said to be replaced by another *āśraya*. For example, the *Śrāvakabhūmi* (the oldest part of the *Yogācārabhūmi*) says several times that, through the path of cultivating calm abiding and superior insight, the *āśraya* that is affected by the impregnations of physical and mental negative tendencies gradually disappears and is replaced by an *āśraya* that is characterized by a sense of joyful ease of body and mind (*praśrabdhi*).[168]

In line with the notion of exchanging or replacing one *āśraya* with another one and this replacement including both physical and mental elements, the *Vastusaṃgrahaṇī* states that the fundamental change of the six inner āyatanas associated with ignorance (*avidyā*) means that they cease and are replaced by the six āyatanas associated with awareness (*vidyā*). However, unlike the above explanation in the *Śrāvakabhūmi*, this does not refer to the path of cultivating meditation but to its soteriological result:

> When [yogins], based on studying the genuine dharma as the power that is the external factor and by virtue of internal proper mental engagement, give rise to the correct view, they thereby relinquish

> ignorance and give rise to awareness. Since thus their foundation has changed and the impregnations of negative tendencies within it have been completely purified, [already] in this life their six āyatanas that are associated with the element of ignorance cease, while [the six āyatanas that are] associated with the element of awareness arise.[169]

In this vein, that text[170] also says that liberation is the fundamental change that consists of the foundation (one's psychophysical existence) having become something in which the afflictions can absolutely not arise again. This comes about through the arising of the fully-relinquishing remedy, which completely purifies all impregnations of negative tendencies that belong to the afflictions.

The *Bodhisattvabhūmi*[171] contains a similar explanation about the impregnations of negative tendencies related to rebirth in the lower realms being removed from the *āśraya* of bodhisattvas on the level of engagement through aspiration, which results in these bodhisattvas on the path of seeing—"the level of pure superior intention (*śuddhāśrayabhūmi*)"—no longer committing any actions leading to rebirth in the lower realms and thus never again falling into these realms.

In the context of the above-mentioned fundamental change through cultivating calm abiding and superior insight, the *Śrāvakabhūmi* also discusses the four results of yoga and their relationship—(1) the cessation of the foundation (*āśrayanirodha*), (2) the replacement or exchange of the foundation (*āśrayaparivarta*), (3) the cognition of the focal object (*ālambanaparijñāna*), and (4) the delight in that object (*ālambanābhirati*):

> Here (1) the cessation of the foundation is the gradual ceasing of the [old psychophysical] foundation that is associated with the impregnations of the negative tendencies in those who are involved in cultivating the mental engagement of [meditative] practice, thus being (2) replaced by the [new psychophysical] foundation that is associated with joyful ease (*praśrabdhi*). This cessation of the foundation and this replacement of the foundation constitute the goal of [practicing] yoga.
>
> As for (3) the cognition of the focal object and (4) the delight in the focal object, there are the cognition of the focal object and the delight in the focal object that precede the cessation of the foundation and the replacement of the foundation. [That is,] when the cognition of the focal object and the delight in the focal object function as the dominant [conditions], the [old] foundation ceases and

> is replaced [by the new one]. There are [also] the cognition of the focal object and the delight in the focal object that are preceded by the purity of the foundation *(āśrayapariśuddhi)*. [That is,] when this purity of the foundation functions as the dominant [condition], the pure cognition as well as the enjoyment of the focal object operate at the time of having accomplished what is to be done.[172]

Similarly, in the context of how the afflictions are relinquished, the *Viniścayasaṃgrahaṇī*[173] says that they are to be relinquished through the cognition of the focal object and the delight in the focal object (these two factors thus being the causes or means for relinquishing the afflictions). The afflictions can be said to have been relinquished completely by virtue of the cessation of the old foundation and its replacement by the new foundation (these two thus being the result of the relinquishment of the afflictions).

As mentioned above, the *Śrāvakabhūmi* extensively quotes a **Revatasūtra* as the scriptural source for *āśrayaparivṛtti*. Though the citations from this sūtra only use the term *āśrayapariśuddhi* ("the purity of the foundation"), its discussions of this term show a clear correspondence to how the *Śrāvakabhūmi* describes *āśrayaparivṛtti*. For example, the text says[174] that yogins who meditate diligently come in contact with, attain, and directly perceive four types of purity. Among these, (1) the purity of the foundation comes about by virtue of the purification of all impregnations of negative tendencies (meaning such tendencies both physical and mental); (2) the purity of focal objects, by virtue of discriminating the entities to be known; (3) the purity of mind, by virtue of being free from desire; and (4) the purity of wisdom, by virtue of being free from ignorance.

Later, the *Bodhisattvabhūmi*[175] elaborates on these four kinds of purity as they pertain to buddhahood. Among them, (1) the purity of the foundation consists of (a) its total lack of all impregnations of negative tendencies (plus their latencies) that accord with the afflictions as well as (b) the power over assuming, remaining in, and leaving one's body as one pleases. Thus, unlike in certain other parts of the *Yogācārabhūmi* (in particuar the *Śrāvakabhūmi*), this purity consists not just of the negative aspect of the elimination of the impregnations of negative tendencies but also of the positive aspect of the complete power over appearing in different physical manifestations as one pleases. Several passages in the *Viniścayasaṃgrahaṇī* also attribute the power over all phenomena to the final fundamental change of buddhahood.[176] (2) The purity of focal objects is explained as in the *Śrāvakabhūmi* above. (3) The purity of mind means to be free from all impregnations of negative tendencies in the mind due to having accumulated all virtues in the mind. (4) The purity of wisdom refers to being free from all impregnations of negative tendencies that accord with ignorance, thus mastering wisdom due to lacking any obscurations of wisdom with regard to any knowable objects.

Sāgaramegha's *Bodhisattvabhūmivyākhyā*[177] comments on these four purities by identifying them with the fundamental change of a buddha. In "the purity of the foundation," "foundation" refers to "name and form," that is, the five skandhas. Its "purity" is the fundamental change of the inconceivable dhātu. Among the two kinds of latent tendencies, śrāvakas and pratyekabuddhas relinquish only the latent tendencies of the afflictions, but buddhas are superior in relinquishing the entirety of both these and the latent tendencies that are the impregnations of the negative tendencies of maturation. This is due to their having cultivated the accumulations of merit and wisdom for three incalculable eons. The purity of the foundation is the kāya of a tathāgata—natural luminosity—abiding in a stainless manner because it is free from all adventitious stains, just like water, gold, and space.[178] This is called "the dharmakāya," which includes the other two buddhakāyas and their functions. "One's own body" refers to the svābhāvikakāya or dharmakāya, which, through the power of effortless aspiration prayers, can be manifested as one pleases. "Assuming" refers to nairmāṇikakāyas residing in Tuṣita and so on. "Remaining" means to remain for the sake of sentient beings as long as saṃsāra lasts, or to have the mastery over remaining through blessing one's lifespan. "Leaving" refers to displaying the great nirvāṇa of a buddha, or to having the mastery over ending one's life. This fundamental change is said to be free from reference points since it is inconceivable due to being endowed with distinguished features in terms of its nature and its conditions. As for the purity of wisdom, śrāvakas and pratyekabuddhas are liberated through prajñā, while buddhas possess the pure wisdom that is completely perfect in all respects. In brief, through understanding that the four kinds of purity will arise, if there is the fundamental change, one should therefore understand that it is their primary cause. Consequently, this fundamental change is expressed as being inconceivable because it serves as the foundation of many inconceivable buddhadharmas.

In the newer sections of the *Yogācārabhūmi* that are more in accord with the mahāyāna approach (primarily the *Viniścayasaṃgrahaṇī* and the *Bodhisattvabhūmi*), the notion of fundamental change is usually explained in the sense of relinquishing the entire ālaya-consciousness and revealing pure suchness or the dharmadhātu, all of which (in line with the Yogācāra denial of matter) pertains solely to the mental realm. For example, a passage at the beginning of the *Viniścayasaṃgrahaṇī* discusses the relationship between the ālaya-consciousness and the fundamental change and that the latter is in fact the relinquishment of the former:

> Since the ālaya-consciousness contains the elements of everything that consists of the reference points of formations, [yogins] concentrate, collect, and gather them in this ālaya-consciousness. Having gathered them [in that way], [yogins] cause the fundamental change by virtue of the cause that consists of their having relied on and cultivated suchness through the cognition of focusing on it. Immediately upon having undergone that fundamental change, the ālaya-consciousness is to be declared as having been relinquished. Since it has been relinquished, all afflictiveness is also to be declared as having been relinquished. The fundamental change of the ālaya-consciousness is to be understood as its remedy and what is inimical [toward it].
>
> The ālaya-consciousness is impermanent and entails appropriating [the five skandhas], whereas the fundamental change is permanent and lacks appropriating because of the change through the path of focusing on suchness. The ālaya-consciousness is endowed with the impregnations of negative tendencies, whereas the fundamental change is absolutely free from all impregnations of negative tendencies. The ālaya-consciousness is the cause for the afflictions operating and is not the cause for the path operating, whereas the fundamental change is not the cause for the afflictions operating and is the cause for the path operating because it is the cause for [the path] continuing but not the cause of its production. The ālaya-consciousness has no power over virtuous and neutral phenomena, whereas the fundamental change has power over all virtuous and neutral phenomena.[179]

Later, the *Viniścayasaṃgrahaṇī* makes it explicitly clear that the result of the fundamental change does not consist of, or is not caused by, the ālaya-consciousness, but of that which is its remedy—the uncontaminated dharmadhātu:

> It is to be understood that the continuation of the supramundane dharmas that have arisen is due to the generation of the power of the fundamental change. This [fundamental change] is called "the remedy of the ālaya-consciousness," "what is not the ālaya,"[180] "the uncontaminated dhātu," and "what is free from reference points."[181]

The *Nirupadikā Bhūmi* of the *Yogācārabhūmi* (discussing the nirvāṇa without remainder) also describes the fundamental state as being the uncontaminated dhātu, which is said to be nothing but the pure suchness that cannot be determined or reified in any way:

> What is the final freedom (*nirvṛti)* that is unassailable? It is the uncontaminated dhātu that is not associated with any bases [of saṃsāric existence], is antagonistic to the operation of any afflictions and sufferings, and is characterized by being the fundamental change . . . With this in mind, the Bhagavān said that this final freedom cannot be determined in the profound, vast, and immeasurable [dhātu] . . . because it cannot be demonstrated as existent or nonexistent and because it cannot be demonstrated as form or anything different from form, nor as feeling, discrimination, formation, or consciousness, nor as anything different from [feeling, discrimination, formation, or] consciousness. For what reason? Because it is characterized by pure suchness and is absolutely stainless. Thus, it is called "the final freedom that is unassailable."[182]

In that vein, the section on the nirvāṇas with and without remainder of the skandhas in the *Viniścayasaṃgrahaṇī* (*Sopadikā Bhūmi* and *Nirupadikā Bhūmi*) describes even the final fundamental change of an arhat in a mahāyāna sense in terms of unchanging suchness and the uncontaminated dharmadhātu. This fundamental change is unchangingly existent, permanent, and blissful. It is disconnected from the six āyatanas and arises from the cultivation of the path of focusing on suchness as its object. It has the characteristics of being free from reference points and is the utter purity of the dharmadhātu. Just as in the above passage, the *Viniścayasaṃgrahaṇī* refers here again to the fundamental change being the cause or foundation for the afflictions not operating and the path operating. If the fundamental change did not exist, there would be no such foundation (this is elaborated in the *Dharmadharmatāvibhāga*'s section on the four flaws if there were no fundamental change):

> "If the six āyatanas of an arhat [remain] exactly as they arose and occurred [before having become an arhat and thus] have not ceased and not changed into something other, with the six āyatanas lacking any change what is their fundamental change that [must be] other than those [āyatanas]? If the fundamental change that [must be] other than those [āyatanas] did not exist, with that foundation being equal before and after why would it be that the afflictions cease and the path operates in that [foundation]?" Answer: The fundamental change of an arhat exists, but it should not be expressed as being other or not other than the six āyatanas. "Why is that?" Because such a fundamental change is constituted by pure suchness, has the disposition of suchness, has the seed of suchness, and is accomplished by virtue of suchness,[183] but suchness should not

be expressed as being other or not other than the six āyatanas. How it should not be expressed in this way was already taught above. Therefore, to ask whether the fundamental change is other or not other than the six āyatanas is inappropriate.

If the fundamental change did not exist, such a flaw [as voiced above] would definitely follow because it would follow that the afflictions occur in an arhat, while the path does not occur. Therefore, one should understand that the fundamental change definitely exists. Also the Bhagavān had this very fundamental change in mind when he said:

> Afflictiveness consists of the latent tendencies of clinging
> To the imaginary nature.
> What is purified consists of
> The lack of those latent tendencies of clinging.
>
> Here these two are the contaminated dhātu
> And the fundamental change—
> The uncontaminated dhātu—
> Which is unsurpassable purity.

. . . It should also be understood that the apprehending of characteristics by arhats who have undergone the fundamental change is more eminent than their former apprehending of characteristics. However, just like suchness, since [their apprehending] is in accord with [having to be] personally experienced, it cannot be expressed adequately to others [by saying], "I perceive such and such characteristics." . . .

The fundamental change of those who dwell in [the nirvāṇa] with the remainder of the skandhas is [still] connected with the six āyatanas, whereas the fundamental change of those who dwell in the [nirvāṇa] without the remainder of the skandhas is not connected with the six āyatanas. "If the fundamental change of those who have fully passed into the dhātu of the nirvāṇa without the remainder of the skandhas is not connected with the six āyatanas, how could it be present without the foundation of the six āyatanas?" Answer: The fundamental change of an arhat did not arise from the causes that are the six āyatanas, but it arose from the cause that is the cultivation of the path of focusing on suchness. Therefore, no matter whether the six āyatanas exist or do not exist, there is no change into anything other in the fundamental change, let alone it showing any deterioration. This dhātu is neither what is to be understood nor what is to be relinquished.[184] Therefore, it is not what is to be ceased either.

"Is the fundamental change of those who have fully passed into the dhātu of the nirvāṇa without the remainder of the skandhas to be described as existent or to be described as nonexistent?" Answer: It is to be described as existent.

"Through which characteristics is [this fundamental change] to be described?" Answer: It has the characteristic of being free from reference points and the characteristic of the utter purity of the dharmadhātu.

"Why is [this fundamental change of the nirvāṇa without remainder] to be described as existent?" Answer: Because the true nature of this fundamental change within the dhātu of the nirvāṇas with the remainder of the skandhas and without the remainder of the skandhas is undisturbable. For, based on this true nature being undisturbable, it is not reasonable for it to exist before [during the nirvāṇa with remainder] and then not to exist later [during the nirvāṇa without remainder]. This dharma [that is the fundamental change] neither originated, nor arose, nor was it accomplished, but it has become clear like water, has become immaculate like gold, and has become free from clouds and fog like space. Therefore, it is to be described as existent.

"Is it to be described as permanent or is it to be described as impermanent?" Answer: It is to be described as permanent. "Why is that?" Answer: Because it is constituted by the purity of suchness, because it is unoriginated, because it is unarisen, and because it is unceasing.

"Is it to be described as blissful or is it to be described as not blissful?" Answer: It is to be described as blissful in terms of ultimate bliss, but not in terms of the bliss that is a feeling. "Why is that?" Answer: Because it is completely beyond all afflictions and all sufferings arising from them.[185]

Later, the *Viniścayasaṃgrahaṇī*[186] confirms that, through the fundamental change in arhats, all afflictions, including their seeds that could mature in the future, have been destroyed completely. The *Manobhūmi*[187] just says generally that, at the time of the parinirvāṇa of yogins who have undergone the fundamental change, all their seeds of afflicted phenomena have undergone this change. In another passage, the *Viniścayasaṃgrahaṇī*[188] differentiates between the nirvāṇas of śrāvakas, pratyekabuddhas, and buddhas. Though the nirvāṇas without remainder of all three are equal in terms of being free from obscurations, the difference is that śrāvaka (or pratyekabuddha) arhats, due to having the disposition of śrāvakas (or pratyekabuddhas) and lacking the previous aspiration prayers of buddhas, do not act for the welfare of others in their nirvāṇas without remainder.[189]

As for the nature of the great enlightenment of buddhas (the first point of five that describe this enlightenment in the *Śrutamayī Bhūmi*), the *Viniścayasaṃgrahaṇī* says that great enlightenment is the fundamental change that is superior to those of śrāvakas and pratyekabuddhas. Its nature is to be understood through the following four aspects. (1) It is the foundation for the supramundane path operating in the mind stream of a buddha. Otherwise, without relying on this fundamental change, that supramundane path would not arise and not continue to operate. Also, if the path could operate despite there being no fundamental change, it would have to operate even in ordinary beings right from the start. (2) This fundamental change is also the foundation for the afflictions, including their latent tendencies, not operating. Otherwise, without relying on this fundamental change, the fact that the afflictions, including their latent tendencies, do not operate in a buddha's mind would not be observable. (3) The fundamental change is also the result of having examined well all knowable objects, that is, the result of having scrutinized the suchness or true reality of all knowable objects. Otherwise, even the very nature of the buddhadharmas would have to be understood, relinquished, and brought to cessation. (4) The fundamental change has the characteristic of being the pure dharmadhātu because of having overpowered all characteristics. Otherwise, if the fundamental change were not the pure dharmadhātu, it would be something impermanent and conceivable, but it is in fact permanent and inconceivable.[190]

Similarly, the *Bodhisattvabhūmi* uses the term "fundamental change" for the buddhabhūmi, which is attained immediately after the vajralike samādhi and is the supreme fundamental change of bodhisattvas:

> After having fulfilled their heart's desire, [bodhisattvas] go beyond the conduct of bodhisattvas and the bhūmis of bodhisattvas and dwell in the conduct of a tathāgata and the bhūmi of a tathāgata. Their fundamental change [comes about] by virtue of having relinquished without exception even the most deep-seated impregnations of negative tendencies that are a part of the cognitive obscurations. The fundamental change of these [tathāgatas] is unsurpassable. All other fundamental changes of bodhisattvas up through the most supreme state [of bodhisattvas] are to be understood as being surpassable.[191]

This means that the fundamental change on the buddhabhūmi represents the final culmination in a series of lower levels of fundamental changes along the path of bodhisattvas. Thus, as shown in some other texts too, the notion of "fundamental change" can obviously also be used for certain temporary achievements on the path and not only for a final resultant state.

Sāgaramegha's *Bodhisattvabhūmivyākhyā*[192] comments here that the relinquishment of all obscurations, including even the most deep-seated impregnations of negative tendencies, is the attainment of the supreme and unsurpassable fundamental change because it is completely perfect in all respects, without any stains, and consists of the dharmakāya.

The *Viniścayasaṃgrahaṇī*[193] provides a further example of describing this final fundamental change not only as being a state free from all stains but as being endowed with positive qualities, using the well known three examples of water, gold, and space that are also found in the *Dharmadharmatāvibhāga* and elsewhere. The *Viniścayasaṃgrahaṇī* equates the fundamental change with the unconditioned nirvāṇa that is the pure dharmadhātu. This nirvāṇa is a state of extinction in the sense of afflictions and suffering having utterly subsided but not in the sense of total nonexistence. In this, it resembles the clarity of water, which is nothing but the purification of its turbidity, but the purification of its turbidity does not lead to its clarity not existing anymore. Likewise, the purity of gold is nothing but its being freed from stains but this being freed from stains does not make its purity nonexistent. Also, the purity of space is nothing but its being freed from clouds, mist, and so on but this being freed does not cause its purity to be nonexistent. Likewise, the purity of the dharmadhātu is still present after what obscures it has been eliminated. This purity of the dharmadhātu is suchness, which clearly manifests by virtue of the elimination of all characteristics through having cultivated correct cognition. This elimination of characteristics resembles someone dreaming of being carried away by the waters of a river, making great efforts to exit this river, and then awakening through these very efforts, upon which the waters of that dream river are no longer perceptible. In its final state, the foundation (suchness or the dharmadhātu) is said to be "perfected" because it is absolutely unassailable by any affliction or harm. The sphere of the buddhas—those who fully realize this suchness—is completely pure true reality, everything is directly perceptible for them, and they have power over everything.

Finally, the *Viniścayasaṃgrahaṇī* also presents the notion of fundamental change in the context of the four remedies:

> The path that arises from study and reflection is the invalidating remedy. The supramundane path is the relinquishing remedy. Its

> result—the fundamental change—is the sustaining remedy. The mundane path of familiarization is the distancing remedy.[194]

This means that the final fundamental change is understood as the resultant state of the foundation—unconditioned suchness—being irreversibly freed from all obscurations.

Āśrayaparāvṛtti in the *Mahāyānasūtrālaṃkāra*

The *Mahāyānasūtrālaṃkāra* uses the term "fundamental change" frequently (in its ninth, eleventh, and fourteenth chapters) and primarily explains it in terms of three different, yet interrelated sytems—the five skandhas, the eight consciousnesses, and the three natures.

According to the commentaries by Vasubandhu and Sthiramati, the six verses IX.12–17 are explicitly devoted to the notion of fundamental change. In the introduction to his comments on IX.12, Sthiramati explains the term in two ways based on the five skandhas. First, once everything in the five skandhas up through the afflicted mind has become pure, the dharmadhātu has become pure, and when the ālaya-consciousness has become pure, it functions as nonconceptual wisdom. Second, once the emptiness within the five skandhas in general has become pure, the dharmadhātu has become pure. In particular, when the eight consciousnesses have become pure, they operate as the four wisdoms:

> Here "foundation" refers to the five skandhas from the skandha of form up through the skandha of consciousness. After the afflictive and cognitive obscurations that exist in these skandhas have been relinquished, the dharmadhātu has become pure and has become nonconceptual wisdom. This is called "fundamental change." In this regard, when the four skandhas of form, feeling, discrimination, and formation as well as [everything] in the skandha of consciousness from the eye consciousness up through the afflicted mind have become pure, the dharmadhātu becomes pure. When the ālaya-consciousness has become pure, it becomes nonconceptual wisdom.
>
> Or when the emptiness that exists in form, feeling, discrimination, formation, and the eight consciousnesses has become pure, the dharmadhātu becomes pure. From among the eight consciousnesses, when the ālaya-consciousness has become pure, it becomes mirrorlike wisdom. When the afflicted mind has become pure, it becomes the wisdom of equality. When the mental consciousness

> has become pure, it becomes discriminating wisdom. When the five [sense] consciousnesses, from the eye [consciousness] up through the body [consciousness] have become pure, they become all-accomplishing wisdom. The attainment of these five—the four wisdoms and the pure dharmadhātu—is called "the five fundamental changes into something else."[195]

In detail, verse IX.12 identifies buddhahood as the fundamental change that is endowed with all pure buddha qualities:

> Wherever the seeds of the afflictive and cognitive obscurations,
> ever present since primordial time,
> Are destroyed through all kinds of very extensive relinquishments,
> Buddhahood is attained as the fundamental change[196] endowed
> with the supreme qualities of the pure dharmas,
> Which is obtained through the path of utterly pure wisdom that is
> nonconceptual and very vast in scope.

In his comments, Sthiramati[197] takes this verse to be in accordance with the second understanding of "fundamental change" that he presented above—once all afflictive and cognitive obscurations are relinquished, the fundamental change consists of the four wisdoms and the pure dharmadhātu as well as all special buddha qualities. In detail, Sthiramati says, this verse describes the removal of the antagonistic factors of buddhahood and the remedies through which it is attained. The relinquishment of the latent tendencies of the two obscurations being "very extensive" refers to the path of supramundane wisdom from the first to the tenth bhūmis. "All kinds" means that the wisdoms on each one of these bhūmis have nine degrees in terms of lesser, medium, and great. "Wherever" refers to someone's mind in which the two obscurations have been purified through applying these remedial wisdoms, which is the meaning of "attaining the fundamental change." Once the two obscurations are relinquished in this way, this fundamental change consists of the attainment of the five dharmas (the four wisdoms and the pure dharmadhātu) as well as the unique qualities of a buddha (such as the ten powers and four fearlessnesses), all of which are supreme since śrāvakas and pratyekabuddhas do not possess them. The path of supramundane wisdom is twofold—utterly pure nonconceptual wisdom and the pure mundane wisdom of subsequent attainment, whose scope consists of all knowable objects. Utterly pure nonconceptual wisdom sees all phenomena to be empty, just like space. The pure mundane wisdom of subsequent attainment sees all entities of worldly realms in the three times as illusions and mirages.

Verse IX.13 explains the superiority of the fundamental change that is buddhahood when compared to the fundamental changes of śrāvakas and pratyekabuddhas. Sthiramati[198] says that tathāgatas (that is, those who realize the dharmadhātu just as it is) rest firmly in the realization of the uncontaminated dhātu that is the fundamental change. Just as if standing on top of Mount Meru, they behold all sentient beings, be they near, far, good, or bad, and look upon them with great compassion. They even have compassion for śrāvakas and pratyekabuddhas, who delight in the dharma but end up just dwelling in their own solitary nirvāṇas without promoting the welfare of the beings in saṃsāra, and lacking omniscient wisdom due to not having relinquished the cognitive obscurations. Needless to say then that the buddhas have even greater compassion for worldly beings, who have not gained liberation from saṃsāra but are always tormented by many sufferings.

Verse IX.14 plays on the word "fundamental change" by adding ten different prefixes or modifiers to the Sanskrit word *vṛtti* in *āśrayaparāvṛtti*, most of which highlight the dynamic and positive character of the most fundamental change that is called "buddhahood." According to Sthiramati,[199] this verse teaches the ten distinct qualities of that fundamental change. It is said to be a "pro-change" (*pravṛtti*) because it is always engaged in the welfare of others—all sentient beings. It is a "super-change" (*udvṛtti*) since it is the best of all phenomena, superior to any mundane phenomena, and even superior to the fundamental change of supramundane śrāvakas. As for the term "nonchange (of the foundation)" (*avṛtti*), "foundation" refers to the state that is the result of change, which is a state of nonchange in the sense of the inactivity of the three causes of afflictions (that is, the presence of objects, improper mental engagement, and not having relinquished the latencies of both). It is a "counter-change" (*nivṛtti*) since it does not engage in afflictions or nonvirtue, and counteracts selfish actions. It is an "ongoing change" (*āvṛtti*) since it functions all the time (once this fundamental change has occurred, its operation will never decline until the end of saṃsāra) and engages in all the remedies for afflicted phenomena. It is a "change that is dual" (*dvayā vṛtti*) because it first engages in demonstrating becoming fully enlightened and finally engages in demonstrating nirvāṇa. It is a "change that is nondual" (*advayā vṛtti*) because, ultimately, it neither engages in saṃsāra nor in nirvāṇa. For, by virtue of being endowed with prajñā, what is conditioned is relinquished, and by virtue of possessing compassion, what is unconditioned is relinquished. It is a "change that is equal" (*samā vṛtti*) because as far as being liberated from all afflictions goes, it is equal in śrāvakas, pratyekabuddhas, and buddhas. It is a "change that is distinct" (*viśiṣṭā vṛtti*) because it is superior to the fundamental change of the śrāvakas by virtue of the relinquishment of the cognitive obscurations and the qualities of the powers, the fearlessnesses, and so on. It is a "change that is omnipresent" (*sarvagā vṛtti*) because the three yānas engage all sentient beings in an omnipresent way. This fundamental change of the tathāgatas is endowed with all those supreme qualities, which are the uncontaminated dharmas, or the remedies for all afflictions. Therefore, it operates in a very vast manner. To these ten variations of *vṛtti* in the context of *āśrayaparāvṛtti*, one may as well add *vyāvṛtti* in IX.11, which refers to the elimination of all vices and sufferings.

Verses IX.15–17 further describe the omnipresence of the fundamental change that is buddhahood. Sthiramati[200] explains that, just as space is omnipresent in all entities in the three times, the uncontaminated dharmadhātu exists and is omnipresent in the mind streams of all sentient beings. This is to be understood here in terms of buddhas experiencing and accepting all beings as not being different from themselves in a perfect manner. Buddhahood has the nature of the dharmadhātu, and once the characteristic of the omnipresence of the dharmadhātu is realized on the first bhūmi, a state of mind of perceiving oneself and all beings as equal is attained. Through further cultivating this throughout the remaining bhūmis, at the time of buddhahood this all-encompassing experience is perfected. This is what is called "being omnipresent in the hosts of beings."[201]

As for why sentient beings do not realize the dharmadhātu and do not see buddhas, though the dharmadhātu always exists and is omnipresent in them, verse IX.16 says that, just as the moon is not seen in a vessel that is without water or is broken, the mind streams of beings are either like an empty vessel through not being filled with the accumulations of merit and wisdom, or their mind streams are impaired through being full of afflictions and evil deeds. Despite such beings having the nature of a buddha, they do not see it. Of course, the reverse applies for beings whose mind streams are endowed with merit and wisdom.

Verse IX.17 teaches that if there are suitable beings to be guided in whose mind streams a certain accumulation of merit and wisdom exists, buddhas are born, are seen by them, and demonstrate the manner of attaining nirvāṇa. Once the buddhas have guided those beings to their respective goals, they pass into nirvāṇa and are not seen anymore. This is compared to fire blazing in a place with fuel, but becoming extinct when that fuel has been burned.

Later in the same chapter, verses IX.41–47 describe the various fundamental changes of the skandhas (primarily that of consciousness) in somewhat different terms.[202] Here Sthiramati repeatedly glosses "fundamental change" as "having become pure." In other words, the ordinary skandhas cease and are replaced by their pure equivalents—many different kinds of mastery over phenomena, wisdom, and so on. Verse IX.41 says:

In the fundamental change of the five sense faculties,
Supreme mastery is attained
Over the perception of all their objects
And the arising of twelve hundred qualities in all of them.

This represents the fundamental change of the skandha of form as represented by the five sense faculties, which occurs on the first bhūmi and results in two kinds of mastery. First, each one of the sense faculties is able to perform the perceptive functions of all five. Second, bodhisattvas on the first bhūmi attain twelve sets of one hundred qualities, such as seeing, in a single moment, one hundred buddhas, resting in one hundred samādhis, and so on. Here Sthiramati has someone object, "If (according to Yogācāra) external objects do not exist and thus are like horns of a rabbit, how can the sense faculties undergo a fundamental change?" He answers that the treatises that teach "mere consciousness" (*vijñānamātra*) explain the six inner āyatanas as the arising of the five sense consciousnesses and the mental consciousness by virtue of the latent tendencies of apprehender and apprehended existing in the ālaya-consciousness. The six outer āyatanas refer to the fact that what appear as visible form, sound, and so on arise from those six consciousnesses. Therefore, the Vijñaptimātravādins also possess the distinction between inner and outer āyatanas. Through gradually having studied, reflected, and meditated on all three realms of saṃsāra being merely mind and so on, bodhisattvas eliminate any discriminating notions about form and so on. When they thus have relinquished their mistakenness about form and so on, it is the resultant relinquishment of their former mistakenness of internally clinging to each one of the inner āyatanas that is called "fundamental change." Since they attain twofold mastery by virtue of that, it is reasonable to speak of a fundamental change even without any external objects.

The next four verses explain the fundamental change of the skandha of consciousness, which consists of the fundamental changes of the afflicted mind (mentation), the sense consciousnesses, the conceptual consciousness, and the ālaya-consciousness. The first three of these fundamental changes occur on the eighth bhūmi, while the fundamental change of the ālaya-consciousness happens at the very end of the tenth bhūmi (during the vajralike samādhi). Verse IX.42 says:

In the fundamental change of mentation,
Supreme mastery is attained
Over utterly stainless nonconceptual
Wisdom ensuing from mastery.

Sthiramati explains that nonconceptual wisdom is associated with and springs from the mental consciousness because the support of the mental consciousness is the afflicted mind (being the mental sense faculty), just as the support of the eye consciousness is the eye sense faculty. During the time of ordinary beings, for as long as the afflicted mind has not undergone the fundamental change, it is associated with four afflictions—views about a self, self-conceit, attachment to that self, and ignorance about it. The afflicted mind also mistakenly engages the ālaya-consciousness as being a self and what is "mine." In accordance with this mistaken engagement of the afflicted mind, the mental consciousness that depends on it also engages objects such as form in mistaken ways. Though such objects do not exist, the mental consciousness is attached to them by thinking that they do exist. Once the afflicted mind has undergone the fundamental change by virtue of the relinquishment of the views about a self and "mine," it becomes the wisdom of equality, and thus bodhisattvas attain supreme mastery over stainless nonconceptual wisdom ("ensuing from mastery" in IX.42d refers to the preceding twofold mastery due to the fundamental change of the five sense faculties). When the afflicted mind has undergone the fundamental change, it becomes nonconceptual wisdom. It is nonconceptual because it does not conceive of apprehender and apprehended. It is stainless because afflictive and cognitive obscurations have been relinquished (or because it is free from the above four afflictions). While the afflicted mind is impure, it focuses on the ālaya-consciousness as a self and what is "mine." But when it has become pure and is the wisdom of equality, it focuses on nonconceptual wisdom as equality, without any notion of a self or what is "mine." Therefore, when the afflicted mind has undergone the fundamental change, bodhisattvas attain the mastery over focusing on nonconceptual wisdom. The wisdom of equality that focuses on nonconceptual wisdom always operates for the welfare of all sentient beings and does so together with all the kinds of wisdoms of mastery, which include nonconceptual wisdom and the pure mundane wisdom that is attained subsequent to it as well as the above-mentioned two masteries over the sense faculties engaging all objects and over the twelve hundred qualities. Note that the *Mahāyānasūtrālaṃkāra* here describes wisdom as the result of the fundamental change and not as its foundation or cause (as the *Dharmadharmatāvibhāga* and *Uttaratantra* do).

As for the fundamental change of the five sense consciousnesses and their objects, verse IX.43 says:

> In the fundamental change of the apprehender and its referents,
> Supreme mastery is attained
> Over pure realms in order to display
> Enjoyments just as one pleases.

Once the five sense consciousnesses ("apprehender") and their referents (including the objects of the sixth consciousness) have undergone the fundamental change, there is the twofold mastery over pure realms and the display of enjoyments within them. As long as external objects have not undergone the fundamental change, there appears to be impurity in the environment (such as thorns, shards, and ravines), but when they have become pure, these objects appear as buddha realms with a ground having the colors of beryl, crystal, gold, and so on. As long as the five sense consciousnesses are impure, they are only able to focus on and experience their respective limited objects. Once they have undergone the fundamental change, it is ponds of nectar, wish-fulfilling trees, and so on in those buddha realms that are displayed to the sense consciousnesses.

The fundamental change of the conceptual consciousness is explained in verse IX.44:

> In the fundamental change of conception,
> Supreme mastery is attained
> Over wisdom and activities
> Unimpeded at all times.

As long as the conceptual consciousness is impure, it conceives of all kinds of phenomena (such as forms and sounds), but when it has undergone the fundamental change, bodhisattvas attain the twofold mastery over permanent and unimpeded wisdom and activity. Here "wisdom" refers to mirrorlike wisdom, the wisdom of equality, discriminating wisdom, and all-accomplishing wisdom. "Unimpeded at all times" means that these wisdoms know all phenomena at all times, not just some at some times. "Activities" refers to the enlightening activities of emanations—from Akaniṣṭha all kinds of emanations that demonstrate becoming enlightened and so on are always displayed in an uninterrupted manner.

Finally, the fundamental change of the ālaya-consciousness is described in verse IX.45:

> In the fundamental change of the foundation,
> Supreme mastery is attained
> Over the nonabiding nirvāṇa
> In the stainless state of the buddhas.

The focal object of the ālaya-consciousness is the entire great ground of the world as the container or abode for the world of sentient beings. This is also the abode of all kinds of plants and trees. In addition, the ālaya-consciousness is the foundation of all virtuous and nonvirtuous latent tendencies, and all bodies, possessions, and places are also nothing but this ālaya-consciousness appearing as these bodies and so on. For all these reasons it is called "foundation." Once the ālaya-consciousness and its object have undergone the fundamental change, the tathāgatas reside in the uncontaminated dhātu and thus attain the mastery over the nirvāṇa of not abiding in either saṃsāra or nirvāṇa.[203]

The following two verses IX.46–47 describe the fundamental changes of the skandhas of feeling and discrimination, respectively:

> In the fundamental change of sexual union,
> Supreme mastery is attained
> Over the blissful state of a buddha
> And being unafflicted upon seeing spouses.

Once the state of sexual union has undergone the fundamental change, that is, once one is free from sexual desire, one attains the twofold mastery over the blissful samādhi of buddhas that is free from all reference points and over afflictions not arising even when seeing beautiful females.

> Turning away from the discrimination of space,
> Supreme mastery is attained
> Over a wealth of desired objects
> And the evolutions of movement and form.

"The discrimination of space" refers to thinking that what is unobstructive is like space, while what is obstructive is form. Through relinquishing this discrimination, one attains threefold mastery. Accomplishing "a wealth of desired objects" means that, through attaining "the samādhi of the sky treasure," all necessities flow from space as one wishes. "The evolutions of movement and form" refers to moving in an unobstructed manner (such as passing through walls) and dissolving forms (when thinking of making everything into space, all phenomena become like space).

Thus, the text explicitly explains eleven kinds of fundamental change (in terms of the five sense faculties, the four kinds of consciousness, feelings, and discrimination).[204] Finally, verse IX.48 speaks of an infinite number of fundamental changes:

> Thus, infinite masteries are asserted
> In infinite fundamental changes

By virtue of the inconceivable all-accomplishment
Within the stainless foundation of the buddhas.

In conclusion, all the detailed facets of all the fundamental changes of the five skandhas are in fact innumerable and can be looked up in the different sūtras in which they are described. Likewise, the masteries that are attained through these fundamental changes are innumerable, as are the enlightened activities for the welfare of sentient beings that arise from these masteries (such as different nirmāṇakāyas). As for when and where these masteries and enlightened activities are attained, they are all attained when abiding within the stainless foundation of the buddhas—the changeless and ever-pure dharmadhātu.

Verse IX.56 defines the nature of the uncontaminated dharmadhātu in terms of being free from all obscurations and possessing inexhaustible mastery over twofold wisdom:

It has the characteristic of the suchness of all phenomena
Being pure of the two obscurations.
It [also] has the characteristic of the inexhaustible mastery
Over the wisdom of the real and [the wisdom] whose object that is.

Though this verse does not mention the term "fundamental change," all its Indian commentaries (except for the *Bhāṣya*) explain it through the threefold fundamental change of suchness, the impregnations of negative tendencies, and the path that is also found in the *Abhidharmasamuccaya* (see below). According to Sthiramati,[205] the suchness of all conditioned, unconditioned, contaminated, and uncontaminated phenomena refers to emptiness. The suchness that is the emptiness of the buddhabhūmi has the characteristic and nature of being free from the afflictive and cognitive obscurations. This is the fundamental change of suchness. "The wisdom of the real" (*vastujñāna*) refers to the pure mundane wisdom that is attained subsequent to this fundamental change, while "the real" (*vastu*) refers to the nonconceptual wisdom that is the characteristic of the fundamental change of the ālaya-consciousness, which is the dependent nature. This nonconceptual wisdom (of meditative equipoise) is known in an unmistaken manner through the pure mundane wisdom of subsequent attainment, but not through any other kind of wisdom. This describes the fundamental change of the ālaya-consciousness, which is the support for the impregnations of negative tendencies. The word "that" in IX.56d refers to the dharmadhātu, which means that nonconceptual wisdom focuses on the dharmadhātu. This describes the fundamental change of the path.[206] Through the pure mundane wisdom of subsequent attainment focusing on nonconceptual wisdom, inexhaustible mastery is attained because this pure mundane wisdom realizes the nature of nonconceptual wisdom in an unmistaken manner. Also, nonconceptual wisdom attains inexhaustible mastery over suchness—the dharmadhātu—because nonconceptual wisdom settles one-pointedly on the dharmadhātu. This describes the nature of the dharmadhātu.[207]

Asvabhāva's *Ṭīkā*[208] agrees that IX.56 represents this threefold fundamental change. He likewise identifies "the wisdom of the real" as the wisdom of subsequent attainment, and "that" in IX.56d as the dharmadhātu. However, he says that "the real" refers to the ālaya-consciousness—the dependent nature. Still, this describes the fundamental change of the impregnations of negative tendencies—when the dependent nature has undergone the fundamental change, it becomes the sphere of the wisdom that is attained subsequent to nonconceptual wisdom, but not the sphere of other wisdoms. Nonconceptual wisdom attains mastery over suchness because it rests in meditative equipoise at will, while the wisdom that is attained subsequent to this meditative equipoise attains mastery over the dependent nature in the sense of being unmistaken about it.

The *Buddhabhūmisūtra*, which says that buddhahood consists of five dharmas—the pure dharmadhātu, mirrorlike wisdom, the wisdom of equality, discriminating wisdom, and all-accomplishing wisdom,[209] concludes with four verses that are identical to *Mahāyānasūtrālaṃkāra* IX.56–59.[210] Just like Sthiramati and Asvabhāva, Śīlabhadra's (529–645) commentary on this sūtra, the *Buddhabhūmivyākhyāna*[211] as well as the *Buddhabhūmyupadeśa*[212] also explain the verse that corresponds to IX.56 as the threefold fundamental change of suchness and so on.

In particular, Śīlabhadra explains this threefold fundamental change in relation to the purity of the dharmadhātu and the four wisdoms. The dharmadhātu is completely pure once it is free from the seeds of the two obscurations by virtue of having attained the utterly pure path of supramundane wisdom. This is called "the fundamental change of suchness," which occurs right after the vajralike samādhi. "The real" refers to the dependent nature, which is the object of mirrorlike wisdom—"the wisdom of the real." "That" does not refer to the wisdom of the real, but to the dharmadhātu, which is also the object of mirrorlike wisdom, because the latter is present as the personally experienced wisdom that observes the dharmadhātu for as long as saṃsāra exists. Thus, mirrorlike wisdom is the wisdom that is the common locus of perceiving both the dependent nature and the dharmadhātu. In that way, all phenomena are the objects of mirrorlike wisdom because it observes all generally and specifically characterized phenomena.

From another perspective, the wisdom of the real and the wisdom that has the dharmadhātu as its object represent a division in terms of counterparts.

What is called "mirrorlike wisdom" is the fundamental change by virtue of the foundation of all impregnations of negative tendencies—the ālaya-consciousness—having become free from all these impregnations without exception. What is labeled with the conventional term "pure dependent nature" is the nature of mind without any conceptions. It is through imputing the general statement "This is the sheer real" onto this nature that it is expressed by the term "the real." Once the foundation of the impregnations of negative tendencies has undergone the fundamental change, mirrorlike wisdom has the cognitive aspect of what observes and what is observed being equal. In this sense, it is the wisdom of equality.

The pure mundane wisdom that is attained subsequent to mirrorlike wisdom has the cognitive aspect of differentiating its own conceptions. Its object is the dependent nature that has undergone the fundamental change. This subsequently attained wisdom is nothing but the discriminating wisdom because when it discriminates its own conceptions, its object is the twofold wisdom of the real and the dharmadhātu. This is the characteristic of the inexhaustible mastery over these two, which teaches the fundamental change in terms of the path.

Once the afflicted mind has undergone the fundamental change, through its observation of the mirrorlike wisdom observing the dharmadhātu it becomes the wisdom of equality—once suchness is completely pure, inexhaustible mastery over that is attained too. Since mirrorlike wisdom is present for as long as saṃsāra lasts by virtue of its being permanent in terms of being a continuity, the attainment of inexhaustible mastery is reasonable, and the same applies to the wisdom of equality. This inexhaustible mastery refers to effortless perception by virtue of merely wishing such. That the wisdom of subsequent attainment likewise possesses inexhaustible mastery over the sheer real—the pure dependent nature—is by virtue of its unmistakenness. The wisdom of subsequent attainment matches this pure dependent nature, which is the nature of lacking all mistakenness. Since that wisdom is what observes this umistaken dependent nature, it is established as being unmistaken too. Still, it is referred to as being mundane because it has the cognitive aspect of being conceptual (in a subtle way). Nevertheless, it observes its own conceptions in a manner that concords with self-awareness. Therefore, its cognitive aspect of differentiating its own conceptions appears in an unmistaken manner.

On *Mahāyānasūtrālaṃkāra* IX.60 on the three kāyas, the *Bhāṣya* says that the dharmakāya has the nature of the fundamental change. Sthiramati[213] matches the fundamental changes of the eight consciousnesses into the four wisdoms with the three kāyas, explaining that the dharmadhātu is called "dharmakāya" once it has become mirrorlike wisdom through the relinquishment of the stains of apprehender and apprehended in the ālaya-consciousness. As for the sāmbhogikakāya, once the afflicted mind has undergone the fundamental change, it becomes the wisdom of equality, and once the mental consciousness has undergone the fundamental change, it becomes the discriminating wisdom. Once the sense consciousnesses have undergone the fundamental change, the activities of maturing sentient beings through the twelve deeds of a buddha are called "the nairmāṇikakāya."

In *Mahāyānasūtrālaṃkāra* XI.15–18, the fundamental change is related to the three natures. They are illustrated by the example of a magical illusion, such as the appearances of elephants and so on (the imaginary nature) being created based on a piece of wood (the dependent nature). Just as the audience perceives the piece of wood that is the cause of the illusory appearances of elephants and so on once these illusory appearances vanish, when the fundamental change occurs, false imagination is perceived as it truly is. Thus, just as people who are no longer under the magician's spell act as they please with regard to that piece of wood that was taken as the foundation of the illusion, once the fundamental change occurs, yogins can act as they please. Sthiramati[214] comments that when the duality of apprehender and apprehended is realized to be nonexistent, that is, once the fundamental change of the ālaya-consciousness (the dependent nature) occurs, the perfect nature is observed as the aspect of the freedom from duality, just like seeing a rope when one no longer sees it as a snake. Once the fundamental change of the ālaya-consciousness occurs, the dependent nature comes to lack the twofold error of apprehender and apprehended. Through the pure mundane wisdom that is attained subsequent to that, false imagination—the dependent nature—is realized in an unerring manner, that is, as the characteristic of being free from the duality of apprehender and apprehended. Once the fundamental change of the dependent nature, that is, the relinquishment of apprehender and apprehended, occurs, the yogins who perceive this dependent nature unerringly also act unerringly because they do not see the mistakenness of duality anymore. Consequently, they act as they please because they are without attachment to and fear of dualistic appearances.

Verses XI.44–46 take up the themes of IX.41–45, saying that the fundamental change of the ālaya-consciousness in all its manifestations results in the uncontaminated dharmadhātu, while the fundamental change of the remaining seven consciousnesses results in the four kinds of mastery on the three pure bhūmis:

> By virtue of the change of the seeds,
> The change of what appear as places, referents,
> And bodies is the uncontaminated dhātu,
> Which is the omnipresent foundation.

By virtue of the change of mentation, perception,
And conception, there is fourfold mastery
Over nonconceptuality, [pure] realms,
Wisdom, and activity.

It is held that there is fourfold mastery
On the three bhūmis, such as the Immovable—
Two masteries on one [bhūmi]
And one on each of the others.

Sthiramati[215] comments that "seeds" refers to the ālaya-consciousness with all its latent tendencies of afflictive and cognitive obscurations (or apprehender and apprehended). Once it has undergone the fundamental change through becoming free from the stains of apprehender and apprehended, what appear as ordinary places (the outer environment), referents (the objects of the six consciousnesses), and bodies (the six sense faculties) respectively turn into buddha realms with grounds of gold and so on, wish-fulfilling trees and so on, and buddha bodies (including the qualities described in IX.41 above). The uncontaminated dhātu that is the fundamental change of these three elements is called "liberation." This foundation of liberation is omnipresent because all śrāvakas, pratyekabuddhas, and bodhisattvas engage in it (this verse corresponds to IX.45).

"Mentation" refers to the afflicted mind that always regards the ālaya-consciousness as one's self. "Perception" consists of the five sense consciousnesses, and "conception" is the mental consciousness. Once these seven consciousnesses have undergone the fundamental change by virtue of coming to an end, the four kinds of mastery are attained. Once the afflicted mind has undergone the fundamental change, on the eighth bhūmi bodhisattvas attain the mastery over nonconceptual wisdom because the afflicted mind in its impure state focuses on the ālaya-consciousness, while its fundamental change means to focus solely on nonconceptual wisdom (corresponding to IX.42). Once the five sense consciousnesses have undergone the fundamental change, also on the eighth bhūmi bodhisattvas attain the mastery over pure buddha realms (corresponding to IX.43). Once the mental consciousness has undergone the fundamental change, on the ninth bhūmi they attain the mastery over wisdom through being endowed with the four kinds of discriminating awareness[216] and on the tenth bhūmi, the mastery over enlightened activity by virtue of the five supernatural knowledges (corresponding to IX.44).

Verses XIV.28–29 say that the first bhūmi represents the first actual fundamental change, which consists of supramundane nonconceptual wisdom free from duality and without stains. Sthiramati[217] comments that, upon the arising of the mahāyāna path of seeing, bodhisattvas relinquish apprehender and apprehended and also the afflictions that can be relinquished through seeing. This is called "the fundamental change of the ālaya-consciousness of bodhisattvas" and it is by virtue of this fundamental change that one speaks of the first bhūmi. This initial level of the fundamental change of the ālaya-consciousness happens after one incalculable eon on the mahāyāna path, but its fundamental change continues for two more such eons up to buddhahood.

Verses XIV.45–46 further describe this ultimate fundamental change at the time of buddhahood as follows:

> The attainment of the vajralike samādhi
> That cannot be destroyed by thoughts
> Is the final fundamental change,
> Unstained by all obscurations.
>
> Omniscience is attained—
> The unsurpassable state,
> Abiding in which one's activity
> Is for the benefit of all sentient beings.

Sthiramati[218] explains that, though there is a fundamental change on the first bhūmi too, it is not the final fundamental change because it is only the fundamental change that is attained through being free from the obscurations that can be relinquished through the path of seeing. The ultimate fundamental change consists of the relinquishment of even the most subtle latent tendencies through the vajralike samādhi, which has the immediate result of the ālaya-consciousness being free from all afflictive and cognitive obscurations on the buddhabhūmi. This is the state of unsurpassable omniscient wisdom, which is one's own consummate welfare. Through dwelling in this nonconceptual wisdom and in order to benefit all sentient beings and make them happy, buddhas also possess the realization of pure supramundane wisdom, thus teaching the dharma and so on, which is the consummate welfare of others.[219]

Finally, similar to what DDV says about the arrival at the nature of phenomena (nothing but stainless suchness appearing, while adventitious stains do not appear any more), verses XIX.53–54 explain that the fundamental change means that true reality appears while unreal dualistic delusion no longer appears:

> For childish beings, with true reality being obscured,
> What is not true reality appears everywhere.

Having eliminated it, for bodhisattvas
True reality appears everywhere.

It should be understood that what does not appear and what does appear
Are what is unreal and what is real, respectively.
This fundamental change
Is liberation because [one then can] act as one wishes.

According to Sthiramati,[220] though saṃsāra has the nature of nirvāṇa, in ordinary beings true reality is obscured by their tendencies of clinging to a self and really existing phenomena. Thus, they do not see emptiness, which actually exists, but they naturally perceive the actually nonexistent phenomena of apprehender and apprehended, just as when mistakenly not seeing an existent rope, but seeing it as a nonexistent snake. Bodhisattvas lack the clinging to a self and phenomena and thus they naturally see true reality—emptiness—while not seeing any duality, just as correctly seeing an existent rope, while not seeing it as a nonexistent snake. When existent emptiness—true reality—is seen and the nonexistent characteristics of apprehender and apprehended are not seen anymore, the ālaya-consciousness—the dependent nature—has undergone the fundamental change. This fundamental change is liberation and nirvāṇa. Just as people liberated from bondage can do what they please, once this fundamental change occurs, bodhisattvas are liberated because they have gained mastery over their minds, which abide like space without any appearance of characteristics. Thus, no matter what they encounter, they are able to act as they please without being bound by any attachment or aversion.

Note that this description in terms of the appearance and nonappearance of true reality and duality in ordinary beings and bodhisattvas, respectively, as well as the adventitious nature of the stains of dualistic appearances corresponds exactly to what the *Dharmadharmatāvibhāga* states repeatedly, such as when it identifies the nature of the fundamental change as the appearance of suchness and the nonappearance of adventitious stains (see below).[221]

Āśrayaparivṛtti in the *Dharmadharmatāvibhāga*

As mentioned above, the description of the fundamental change in this text represents the most detailed discussion of this topic in Buddhist literature. However, interestingly (and somewhat ironically), despite that fact, the explanations in the *Dharmadharmatāvibhāga* are usually not referred to in other works that discuss the notion of fundamental change.

In the *Dharmadharmatāvibhāga*, the notion of fundamental change is explained through the ten points of (1) its nature, (2) its substance or entity, (3) the persons who undergo this change (śrāvakas, pratyekabuddhas, and bodhisattvas), (4) its distinctive features (the three buddhakāyas with their respective qualities and activities), (5) its prerequisites (previous aspiration prayers, the mahāyāna teachings as the focal object, and the training on the ten bhūmis), (6) its foundation (nonconceptual wisdom), (7) the mental engagement that leads to it (the four yogic practices), (8) the trainings to accomplish it (the five paths), (9) the shortcomings of there being no fundamental change, and (10) the benefits of there being this change.

The most important ones among these ten are points (1), (2), and (6). The nature of the fundamental change is that pure suchness directly appears in a complete manner, while its adventitious stains no longer appear. The entity of the fundamental change is that mind appearing as the outer world, mind appearing as the beings in it, and the dharmadhātu in the scriptures all are revealed as nothing but pure suchness. The foundation or support (*āśraya*) of the fundamental change is the nonconceptual wisdom that is free from the duality of apprehender and apprehended. Vasubandhu's DDVV comments on these three points as follows:

> That [everything] is an object as nothing but this [suchness] is called "the arrival at its nature," which is the perfection of the fundamental change because [suchness] has the nature of this [fundamental change]. Since there are [already certain degrees of] change during the phases of the path of seeing and so on too, here the perfection [of this fundamental change] is taught because the stains have been relinquished without exception . . . The nature of the fundamental change refers to suchness having become stainless in terms of adventitious stains not appearing and in terms of nothing but suchness appearing . . . The entity of the fundamental change consists of the threefold change of the suchness by virtue of the difference in terms of [what] this [suchness] is connected [to] and the difference in terms of the results [of this threefold fundamental change] . . . the foundation of the fundamental change is nonconceptual wisdom because it is attained through this foundation.[222]

Thus, in DDV and DDVV, both the temporary and the final fundamental changes refer to suchness having been purified—to certain degrees and completely so, respectively. Thus, the manifestation of pure suchness is strictly speaking only the result of the fundamental change, not the actual process of the fundamental change. As for the flaws, if there were no such fundamental change, Vasubandhu says:

> Without a support due to there being no fundamental change, how could abiding in the nature of phenomena, in which henceforth afflictions do not arise, operate? Therefore, just as with the support for the afflictions operating, there must be a support for their [not operating]. [Otherwise, this] constitutes the flaw of there being no support for the afflictions not operating.
>
> Likewise, just as contaminated consciousness operates with a support, its remedy must also do so with a support. Therefore, [without such a support] there is the flaw of there being no support for engaging in the path.
>
> Furthermore, for example, in the case of a person in saṃsāra, the skandhas are designated as "[being in] saṃsāra." Likewise, there must be a basis for designating the persons who have passed into parinirvāṇa. First, it is not tenable that mind is this [basis] because the ceasing of the antagonistic factors and the arising of their remedies is simultaneous and also because two contrary [phenomena] within the same support are untenable, just as a cold and a warm sensation are untenable within the same support. In addition, [there must be the basis for designating persons who have passed into nirvāṇa] because there would be no basis for [such a] designation once [a saṃsāric person] has passed into the nirvāṇa without any remainder of the skandhas. Therefore, there must be a basis for designating the persons who have passed into nirvāṇa that corresponds to the skandhas [as the basis for designating persons in saṃsāra]. [Otherwise, there is] the flaw of there being no basis for designating the persons who have passed into nirvāṇa.
>
> The fourth [flaw] is the flaw of there being no basis for designating the differences between the three [types of] enlightenment.
>
> Therefore, the fundamental change that functions as the entity that is [such] a basis exists.[223]

As for the fundamental change referring to the revelation of unchanging suchness upon its merely being freed from adventitious stains, without any transformation of anything into anything else, Vasubandhu says:

> "When something has undergone this fundamental change, it has changed into something else. Consequently, how is what has undergone the fundamental change not something that is altered?" Therefore, [Maitreya] says that the manner in which there is a fundamental change without it referring to something that is altered is established through examples. Examples for the fundamental

change are space, gold, water, and so on. For example, space is [always] nothing but pure by nature. It is only by virtue of its being associated with adventitious fog and so on that this [purity] is not realized, but it is [seen to be] pure by virtue of [eventually] becoming free from such [adventitious obscurations]. Since it is not the case that impure [space] becomes pure, it is not that its being pure arises [newly]. Rather, it is just that [its purity] is observed by virtue of its being free from causes for not observing it. It is also not that one should claim space to be something that is altered through its being observed as being utterly pure.

In the same way, gold too solely remains in [its state of] being immaculate. It is just not observed [as being immaculate] by virtue of its being covered over by adventitious stains, but it is observed [as being immaculate] by virtue of [eventually] becoming free from such [stains]. It is also not that [its being immaculate] has arisen by virtue of this observing.

Likewise, water [always] remains totally clear. It is just not observed [as being clear] by virtue of this water being associated with earth substances, but it is observed [as being clear] by virtue of being free from those earth substances. It is also not that, by virtue of observing [its clarity], [this clarity] has arisen in such a way that it has not been present [before] in this substance of water that represents a continuous stream [of individual moments]. Nor is it that one should claim the substance of water to be something that is altered through its being observed as being clear.

In the same way, in the fundamental change too, natural luminosity is not something that did not exist before, but it does just not appear by virtue of adventitious stains appearing. This is just as with [space, gold, and water, respectively, appearing] to be impure, not immaculate, and turbid. By virtue of being free from these [adventitious stains], [natural luminosity] appears. However, it is not that it arises, in such a way that it has not been present [before], by virtue of the appearance of an alteration due to the nature of phenomena entailing [such an] alteration. Since there is no such [alteration], the nature of phenomena and the fundamental change that is constituted by it are permanent.

Here, [the fundamental change of the nature of phenomena] is taught through the examples of gold and water as being congruent with their properties only in terms of their qualities, without considering their [respective material] substances. Through the example of space, however, it is taught in its entirety. Through the

> phrase "and so on," other similar such kinds [of examples] are to be understood [as being appropriate] too, such as a cloth and so on remaining in its [state of] being clean through having become free from stains.[224]

Āśrayaparivṛtti in the *Uttaratantra* and *RGVV*

In the *Uttaratantra* itself, the term appears only once, in verse V.7, which summarizes *tathāgatagarbha* as the object of buddhas alone in four points. In this verse, "the foundation" (*āśraya*) refers to obscured *tathāgatagarbha* (the fourth vajra point) and "its change" (*tatparāvṛtti*) means enlightenment (the fifth vajra point), which is nothing but *tathāgatagarbha* having become unobscured.

Uttaratantra I.23ab explains the fourth through seventh vajra points (buddha nature enshrouded in obscurations, buddha enlightenment, its qualities, and its activity) through equating *tathāgatagarbha* with "suchness with stains" (*samalā tathatā*) and buddhahood (the purified *tathāgatagarbha*), with "stainless suchness" (*nirmalā tathatā*). RGVV further explains those four vajra points by way of equating this stainless suchness with the final fundamental change of buddhahood, that is, the dharmakāya:

> Suchness with stains is the dhātu that is not liberated from the cocoon of the afflictions, which is called "the tathāgata heart." Stainless suchness is the very same [dhātu] that is characterized by the fundamental change on the buddhabhūmi, which is called "the dharmakāya of a tathāgata." The stainless buddha qualities are the supramundane buddhadharmas (such as the ten powers) within that very dharmakāya of a tathāgata that is characterized by the fundamental change. The activity of the victors consists of the distinct unsurpassable actions of these very buddhadharmas (such as the ten powers) . . .[225]

On *Uttaratantra* I.44, RGVV[226] comments that *tathāgatagarbha* is endowed with the fruitional qualities of nonlearning that are inseparable from it and consist of uncontaminated supernatural knowledges, wisdom, and relinquishment. The five supernatural knowledges resemble the light of the flame of an oil lamp because they have the characteristic of overcoming the darkness of the antagonistic factors of the wisdom of experiencing true reality. The wisdom of the termination of contaminations (*āsravakṣaya*) resembles the heat of that flame because it has the characteristic of burning the entire fuel of karma and afflictions. The termination of contaminations that is the fundamental change resembles the color of the flame because it has the characteristic of the completely stainless and pure luminosity of this fundamental change. It is stainless by virtue of the relinquishment of the afflictive obscurations; pure, by virtue of the relinquishment of the cognitive obscurations; and luminous, by virtue of not having the nature of these two adventitious stains.

At the begining of the *Uttaratantra*'s second chapter (on buddha enlightenment), RGVV comments that the nature of that fundamental change is the purity of *tathāgatagarbha*, while its cause consists of twofold wisdom:

> Suchness with stains has been discussed [in the first chapter]. Now stainless suchness shall be treated. Here what is stainless suchness? Since [this suchness] is free from all kinds of stains in the uncontaminated dhātu of the buddha bhagavāns, it is presented as the fundamental change. In brief, this is to be understood in terms of eight points. What are these eight points? . . . They are the point of [its] nature, the point of [its] cause, the point of [its] result, the point of [its] function, the point of [its] endowment [with qualities], the point of [its] manifestation, the point of [its] permanence, and the point of [its] inconceivability.
>
> Here the Bhagavān called the dhātu that is not liberated from the cocoon of the afflictions "the tathāgata heart." Its purity is to be understood as being the nature of the fundamental change.
>
> Wisdom is twofold—supramundane nonconceptual [wisdom] and the mundane [wisdom] that is attained subsequent to it. This mundane and supramundane wisdom—the cause of the fundamental change—is indicated through the term "attainment" [in *Uttaratantra* II.1]. [Here] "attainment" refers to that through which [the fundamental change] is attained.[227]

Later RGVV confirms that the manner of attaining the enlightenment of tathāgatas consists of the fundamental change.[228]

Furthermore, the purity of the nature of the fundamental change that is buddhahood consists of both the natural primordial purity of *tathāgatagarbha* and its having become free from all adventitious stains at the end of the path:

> As for it being said that "purity is the nature of the fundamental change," here, in brief, purity is twofold—natural purity and the purity of being without stains. Here natural purity is [in itself] liberation, but it is not [yet] freed because the luminous nature of mind has not become freed from adventitious stains. The purity of being without stains is [both] liberation and freed because the luminous

> nature of mind has become freed from all adventitious stains without exception, just like water and so on [having become freed from] silt and so on.[229]

As for the twofold wisdom that is the cause of the fundamental change, RGVV adds that this wisdom has the function of accomplishing the welfare of oneself and others and that the fundamental change is called "a result of freedom" (from all adventitious stains).[230]

In sum, the way in which RGVV understands "fundamental change" is in terms of a fundamental change of buddha nature—ever unchanging yet temporarily obscured suchness—having become free from all adventitious stains. However, unlike in other texts, suchness is not just the pure object to be focused on in order to attain liberation, but, as *tathāgatagarbha*, it is understood as the innermost nature of every being's mind, which is the very subject that eventually realizes its own pure nature.

It should also be noted that the first point in the explanation of enlightenment in the *Uttaratantra* and RGVV corresponds to the first point in the presentation of the fundamental change in DDV (both these points refer to the fundamental change as stainless suchness and both are called "its nature"). The following four points of DDV on the fundamental change also describe this fundamental change in the sense of being a fundamental change in terms of suchness (*tathatāparivṛtti*). DDV's sixth point—"the foundation" (nonconceptual wisdom)—corresponds to the second point of the *Uttaratantra*'s explanation of *bodhi* (twofold wisdom as the cause of enlightenment).[231] Directly or indirectly, the remaining six points of the *Uttaratantra* on enlightenment are also discussed in DDV's section on the nature of phenomena. In both DDV and the *Uttaratantra*, the notion "fundamental change" clearly refers to the result (stainless suchness, buddhahood, or dharmakāya) and not to the process.

Āśrayaparivṛtti in the *Abhidharmasamuccaya*

Asaṅga's *Abhidharmasamuccaya* speaks about the fundamental change at the end of its discussion of the reality of the path and seems to present a brief synopsis of the principal ways and contexts in which the notion of fundamental change was employed in the different layers of the *Yogācārabhūmi*:

> What is the final path? It is the vajralike samādhi—by virtue of cutting through all impregnations of negative tendencies, by virtue of relinquishing everything that is connected [with these tendencies], and by virtue of attaining everything that is free [from these

> tendencies]. Immediately after that [samādhi], there is the total[232] fundamental change, [which consists of] the knowledge of the termination [of all contaminations], the knowledge of [their] non-arising [in the future], and the ten dharmas of nonlearning[233] . . .
>
> What is the total fundamental change? It is (1) the fundamental change of mind [upon] the attainment of the path of nonlearning, (2) the fundamental change of the path, and (3) the fundamental change of the impregnations of negative tendencies.[234]

Sthiramati's *Abhidharmasamuccayavyākhyā*[235] explains this threefold fundamental change as follows. (1) "The fundamental change of mind upon the attainment of the path of nonlearning" refers to the naturally luminous mind that is the nature of phenomena having become free from all adventitious afflictions without exception. This is also called "the fundamental change of suchness." (2) "The fundamental change of the path" means that, once clear realization occurs on the mundane path, it has changed into the supramundane path. The latter is also called "the path of learning" because there still remain tasks to be accomplished. Once all antagonistic factors are eliminated through being free from attachment to the three realms, this is presented as the perfectly complete fundamental change that is the nature of this path. (3) "The fundamental change of the impregnations of negative tendencies" refers to the ālaya-consciousness being free from even the most subtle latent tendencies of all afflictions.

Āśrayaparivṛtti in the *Mahāyānasaṃgraha*

The various occurrences of the notion of fundamental change in the *Mahāyānasaṃgraha* generally rely and elaborate on the templates of explaining the fundamental change that are found in the *Mahāyānasūtrālaṃkāra* (that is, the skandhas, the three natures, and the eight consciousnesses). A unique feature of the *Mahāyānasaṃgraha*'s presentation is that it also defines the fundamental change by way of the impure or afflicted form of the dependent nature turning into its pure form.

The first chapter of the *Mahāyānasaṃgraha*, on the ālaya-consciousness, describes the cause of the fundamental change as "the latent tendencies for listening," which are the natural outflow of the pure dharmadhātu, giving rise to "the supramundane mind" as the remedy of the ālaya-consciousness, and thus are the seeds of the dharmakāya:

> "How could the maturational consciousness[236] with all the seeds, which is the cause of afflicted phenomena, be the seed of its remedy,

that is, supramundane mind? Since supramundane mind is not contained in [the minds of ordinary beings], the latent tendencies of this [supramundane mind] do not exist [in them]. But if these latent tendencies do not exist [in them], it must be stated from which seeds they arise." [Supramundane mind] originates from the natural outflow of the pure dharmadhātu, that is, the seeds which are the latent tendencies for listening. You may wonder, "What are these latent tendencies for listening, anyway? Are they of the nature of the ālaya-consciousness or are they not? If they were of the nature of the ālaya-consciousness, how could they be suitable as the seeds of its remedy? And if they are not of its nature, then look at what the matrix of these seeds of latent tendencies for listening is." What these latent tendencies for listening in dependence on the enlightenment of a buddha are, which matrix they enter, and that they enter the maturational consciousness in a manner of coexisting with it—all this is like [a mixture of] milk and water. They are not the ālaya-consciousness because they are the very seeds of its remedy.[237]

Small latent tendencies turn into medium latent tendencies, and these medium latent tendencies then turn into great latent tendencies, all this by virtue of being associated with listening, reflection, and meditation that are performed many times. The small, medium, and great latent tendencies for listening are to be regarded as the seeds of the dharmakāya. Since they are the remedy for the ālaya-consciousness, they are not of the nature of the ālaya-consciousness. [In the sense of being a remedy,] they are something mundane, but since they are the natural outflow of the supramundane—the utterly pure dharmadhātu—they are the seeds of supramundane mind. Although this supramundane mind has not originated yet, they are the remedy for being entangled [in saṃsāra] through the afflictions, the remedy for migrating in the lower realms, and the remedy that makes all wrongdoing vanish. They are what is in complete concordance with meeting buddhas and bodhisattvas.

Though beginner bodhisattvas are mundane, [these latent tendencies] should be regarded as being included in the dharmakāya and [those of] śrāvakas and pratyekabuddhas as being included in the vimuktikāya. They are not the ālaya-consciousness, but included in the dharmakāya and vimuktikāya, respectively.[238] To the extent that they gradually shine forth in a small, medium, and great way, to that same extent the consciousness of complete maturation wanes and undergoes the fundamental change too.[239] If it has undergone the fundamental change in all aspects, that consciousness becomes devoid of seeds and is also relinquished in all aspects.

> You may wonder, "How is it that the ālaya-consciousness, which abides together with what is not the ālaya-consciousness like water and milk, can wane in all aspects?" It is like geese drinking [by separating] milk from water.[240] It is also similar to the fundamental change when, being free from mundane desire, the latent tendencies of the state of not being in meditative equipoise wane, while the latent tendencies of the state of being in meditative equipoise increase."[241]

Later in that chapter,[242] the text justifies the existence of the ālaya-consciousness by explaining why the fundamental change can only happen on the basis of the ālaya-consciousness and not based on the sense consciousnesses or the mental consciousness alone.

In its third chapter, on how to engage in the three natures, the *Mahāyānasaṃgraha* explains the fundamental change as making contact with the dharmakāya through having cultivated the latent tendencies for listening and thus achieving nonconceptual omniscient wisdom and all buddha qualities:

> Why do [bodhisattvas] engage in that "mere cognizance"? The cognitions of [nonconceptual and unmistaken] supramundane calm abiding and superior insight focus on [all] the miscellaneous dharmas [of the mahāyāna, whose general characteristic is suchness], and the subsequently attained [nonconceptual] cognition in terms of various kinds of cognizance [realizes all phenomena to be nothing but imaginations of apprehender and apprehended]. Through these [cognitions], they relinquish all seeds in the ālaya-consciousness, together with their causes, and thus increase the seeds of making contact with the dharmakāya [that is, cultivating the mahāyāna latent tendencies for listening. Finally,] having undergone the fundamental change,[243] they perfectly accomplish all the buddhadharmas and thus attain omniscient wisdom.[244]

The *Mahāyānasaṃgraha*'s ninth chapter, on perfect fruitional relinquishment, says that the nonabiding nirvāṇa of bodhisattvas is the fundamental change in which all afflictions have been relinquished, but, for the welfare of sentient beings, saṃsāra is not abandoned. Uniquely among all presentations of the fundamental change in Yogācāra texts (maybe following the *Laṅkāvatārasūtra*), the *Mahāyānasaṃgraha* here (and also in Chapter Ten below) says that "foundation" refers to the dependent nature, while its "change" means that the afflicted aspect of this dependent nature ceases and changes into its purified aspect. In general, the text presents six kinds of fundamental change:

> The relinquishment of bodhisattvas is the nonabiding nirvāṇa. Its defining characteristic is the fundamental change of having abandoned the afflictions while not having abandoned saṃsāra. Here saṃsāra is the aspect of the dependent nature that belongs to what is afflicted. Nirvāṇa is the aspect of this very [dependent nature] that belongs to what is purified. "The foundation" is what belongs to both these aspects—the dependent nature. [Its] "change" [means that], after the remedy of the dependent nature has arisen, [its] afflicted aspect ceases and it turns into [its] purified aspect.[245]
>
> In brief, this [fundamental] change is sixfold. (1) [There is] the change that consists of weakening and expanding, because only small afflictions occur or do not occur [at all] in those in whom, through the power of aspiration, the latent tendencies for listening are present [in a stable manner] and who are endowed with refraining [from afflictions].
>
> (2) The change through realization is the one of bodhisattvas having entered the bhūmis. For up through the sixth bhūmi, [both] the appearances of true reality [during meditative equipoise] and what is not true reality [during subsequent attainment] are present.
>
> (3) The change through familiarization is the one of those [bodhisattvas] who [still] possess [some cognitive] obscurations. For [from the seventh] up through the tenth bhūmis, all characteristics disappear, while true reality appears.
>
> (4) The change in terms of the completely perfect fruition is the one of those who are without [any] obscurations. For, [for them,] all characteristics disappear, utterly pure true reality appears, and they have attained the mastery over all characteristics.
>
> (5) The inferior change is the one of the śrāvakas [and pratyekabuddhas] because they realize [only] personal identitylessness and completely abandon saṃsāra through having turned their backs on saṃsāra.
>
> (6) The vast change is the one of bodhisattvas because they realize phenomenal identitylessness and, through seeing this very [saṃsāra] as being peaceful,[246] relinquish the afflictions and yet do not abandon [saṃsāra].
>
> Which flaw would accrue if the inferior change were the one of bodhisattvas? Through not considering the welfare of sentient beings, they would go beyond the true nature of bodhisattvas, and

thus there would be the shortcoming of their [liberation] being equal to the liberation of the followers of the hīnayāna.

What is the benefit of the vast [fundamental] change of bodhisattvas? The benefit is that, by virtue of [having] the foundation of their own fundamental change, they attain mastery over all saṃsāric phenomena. Therefore, through displaying [themselves] in all realms [by assuming] the bodies of all sentient beings and through their various skills in the means to guide [beings], they guide them to and establish them in the higher realms and all three yānas.

Here are [some] verses:

For childish beings, with true reality being obscured,
What is not true reality appears everywhere.
Having eliminated it, for bodhisattvas
True reality appears everywhere.

It should be understood that what does not appear and what
 does appear
Are what is unreal and what is real, respectively.
This fundamental change
Is liberation because [one then can] act as one wishes.[247]

When the knowledge of the sameness
Of saṃsāra and nirvāṇa has arisen,
Consequently, at that time,
That very saṃsāra becomes nirvāṇa.

Therefore, saṃsāra
Is neither abandonded nor not abandoned.
Consequently, nirvāṇa is also
Neither attained nor not attained.[248]

The tenth chapter, on perfect fruitional wisdom (the three kāyas), equates the final fundamental change with the dharmakāya, which is described through ten points. Among these, (1) its characteristics, (2) its attainment, (3) its mastery, and (5) its constitution are particularly relevant in terms of discussing the fundamental change. (1) As for the characteristics of the dharmakāya, the text says:

In brief, the characteristics should be known as five. (a) [The dharmakāya] has the characteristic of the fundamental change because when the aspect of the dependent nature that belongs to what is afflicted (all obscurations) has come to an end, it has changed into the aspect of the dependent nature that is liberated from all obscurations, belongs to what is purified, and abides as the mastery over all dharmas.[249]

(b) [The dharmakāya] has the characteristic of having the nature of pure dharmas because the ten masteries are attained through having perfected the six pāramitās. For the mastery over lifespan, the mastery over mind, and the mastery over necessities represent the perfection of the pāramitā of generosity. The mastery over karma and the mastery over birth represent the perfection of the pāramitā of ethics. The mastery over creative willpower is the perfection of the pāramitā of patience. The mastery over aspiration prayers is the perfection of the pāramitā of vigor. The mastery over the miraculous powers that consists of the five supernatural knowledges is the perfection of the pāramitā of dhyāna. The mastery over wisdom and the mastery over dharma represent the perfection of the pāramitā of prajñā.[250]

(c) [The dharmakāya] has the characteristic of nonduality because all phenomena are nonentities by virtue of having the characteristic of existence and nonexistence being nondual, while [the dharmakāya] is the entity that has the characteristic of emptiness. [The dharmakāya also] has the characteristic of the nonduality of conditioned and unconditioned phenomena because it is not formed by karma and afflictions, but masters the display of unconditioned appearances. [The dharmakāya also] has the characteristic of the nonduality of being one or different because the matrix of all buddhas is not different in it, while innumerable mind streams [of bodhisattvas attain] fully perfect enlightenment . . .

(d) [The dharmakāya] has the characteristic of permanence because it has the characteristic of being pure suchness, [is attained through] the force of previous aspiration prayers, and its activity is never completed.

(e) [The dharmakāya] has the characteristic of inconceivability because pure suchness is to be personally experienced, is without compare in the world, and is not the sphere of dialecticians.[251]

As for (2) the attainment of the dharmakāya, the text presents the principal means or causes for achieving the fundamental change that is the dharmakāya:

> How is the dharmakāya attained for the first time through contact? Through the wisdoms of nonconceptuality and subsequent attainment that focus on [all] mahāyāna dharmas in combination having excellently cultivated the five aspects [of practice],[252] the accumulations are gathered well in all respects. Through the vajra-like samādhi, [which has this name] because it destroys the subtle obscurations that are difficult to destroy, [the dharmakāya] is free from all obscurations right at the end of that [samādhi]. Therefore, [the dharmakāya] is attained through these [factors] by virtue of the fundamental change.[253]

(3) The mastery of the dharmakāya is said to be attained through the fundamental changes of the five skandhas:

> Through how many kinds of masteries is the mastery of the dharmakāya attained? In brief, mastery is attained through five kinds. (1) Through the fundamental change of the skandha of form, the mastery over [pure buddha] realms, kāyas, the excellent major and minor marks, infinite voices, and the invisible mark on the crown of the head [is attained]. (2) Through the fundamental change of the skandha of feeling, the mastery over infinite and vast blissful states without wrongdoing [is attained]. (3) Through the fundamental change of the skandha of discrimination, the mastery over teaching [is attained] through all groups of words, groups of phrases, and groups of letters. (4) Through the fundamental change of the skandha of formation, the mastery over creation, transformation, gathering retinues, and gathering the immaculate dharmas [is attained]. (5) Through the fundamental change of the skandha of consciousness, the mastery over mirrorlike [wisdom], [the wisdom of] equality, discriminating [wisdom], and all-accomplishing [wisdom is attained]. Through [those], mastery is attained.[254]

(5) "What constitutes the dharmakāya" is also explained through the notion of fundamental change, which here has six aspects:

> Through how many buddhadharmas is the constitution of the dharmakāya to be understood? In brief, it is constituted by six aspects. (1) [It is constituted] by the buddhadharma that is [its] purity because the dharmakāya is attained through the [fundamental] change of the ālaya-consciousness.[255] (2) [It is constituted] by maturation because matured wisdom is attained through the

> change of the physical sense faculties. (3) [It is constituted] by dwelling because [its] dwelling by virtue of immeasurable wisdom is attained through the change of dwelling in sense pleasures and so on. (4) [It is constituted] by mastery because [its] mastery over the wisdom of supernatural knowledges unimpeded in all worldly realms is attained through the change of various purposeful activities. (5) [It is constituted] by conventional [expressions] because [its] mastery over knowing [all] the teachings that satisfy the minds of all sentient beings is attained through the change of the conventional expressions about what is seen, heard, perceived [by the remaining three sense consciousnesses], and known [by the conceptual consciousness]. (6) [It is constituted] by removal because the knowledge of removing all harm to all sentient beings is attained through the change that is the removal of all harms and flaws.[256]

Finally, the text[257] says that one of the reasons why the sāmbhogikakāya is not the svābhāvikakāya is that the former is the result of the fundamental change of the sense consciousnesses and the mental consciousness, while the latter is the result of the fundamental change of the ālaya-consciousness.

Āśrayaparāvṛtti in the *Triṃśikākārikā*

Verse 29 of Vasubandhu's *Triṃśikā* says:

> Then, it is no-mind and nonperception—
> It is supramundane wisdom.
> This is the fundamental change
> By virtue of having relinquished the twofold impregnations of
> negative tendencies.

Sthiramati's *Triṃśikābhāṣya* comments on this by saying that the fundamental change of buddhas refers to the ālaya-consciousness ceasing and changing into the dharmakāya, while the fundamental changes of śrāvakas (and pratyekabuddhas) result in the vimuktikāya:

> . . . based on the path of seeing, yogins who engage in mere cognizance give rise to the consummate fruition through progressively going higher and higher. Since there is no mind there that is an apprehender and no perception of apprehended referents, [line 29a says] "no-mind and nonperception." Since it is not familiar and

does not arise in the world and is nonconceptual, it is said to be beyond the world, which is said to be supramundane wisdom.

After wisdom, in order to teach that there is a fundamental change, [line 29b] says, "This is the fundamental change." Here, "foundation" refers to the ālaya-consciousness with all the seeds. As for its change, once the entity that consists of the impregnations of negative tendencies, [karmic] maturation, and the latent tendencies of duality has come to an end, it changes into the entity that consists of what is truly workable, the dharmakāya, and nondual wisdom. "Through relinquishing what is this fundamental change attained?" Therefore, [line 29b] says "by virtue of having relinquished the twofold impregnations of negative tendencies." "Twofold" refers to the impregnations of the negative tendencies of the afflictive obscurations and the impregnations of the negative tendencies of the cognitive obscurations. "Impregnations of negative tendencies" are the unworkable ālaya, that is, the seeds of the afflictive and cognitive obscurations. As for the fundamental change, the one that is attained through having relinquished the impregnations of the negative tendencies that exist in śrāvakas is said to be "the vimuktikāya." The one that is attained through having relinquished the impregnations of the negative tendencies that exist in bodhisattvas is said to be "what is called the dharma[kāya] of the great sage." It is taught that, by virtue of the difference between the two kinds [of obscurations], [there is] a surpassable and an unsurpassable fundamental change.[258]

Āśrayaparāvṛtti in the *Madhyāntavibhāgaṭīkā*

Though the *Madhyāntavibhāga* itself does not mention the term "fundamental change," Sthiramati's *Madhyāntavibhāgaṭīkā* uses it, such as when glossing pure suchness as having the nature of the fundamental change.[259] Sthiramati also equates the fundamental change (of the ālaya-consciousness) with the dharmakāya, the perfect nature, and the nirvāṇa without remainder.[260] In particular, Sthiramati elaborates on Vasubandhu's *Madhyāntavibhāgabhāṣya* on I.16 as follows.[261] The divisions of emptiness are being afflicted and pure as well as being with and without stains. Being afflicted refers to false imagination, while its relinquishment means being pure. However, at the times of being afflicted and pure, there is nothing but emptiness that is afflicted or pure. That emptiness is presented as afflicted and pure, respectively, is based on its not having or having undergone the fundamental change. By virtue of the flaws of noncognition and wrong cognition, those who are not learned cling to apprehender and apprehended and their mind streams become stained by afflictions such as desire. Thus, it is due to emptiness not appearing for them that it is considered as "stained." By virtue of the noble ones realizing true reality, they lack mistaken states of mind. Thus, in them, emptiness is spotless like space and appears in an uninterrupted manner, due to which it is referred to as "having relinquished the stains." It is in this way that emptiness is to be regarded as depending on being afflicted and being pure, but one should not think that its nature is stained because it is luminous by nature.

Some may object that different phases are not seen in what is unchanging, whereas change is connected to arising and ceasing. Therefore, since emptiness is a phenomenon that entails change in that it is first with and later without stains, why would it not be impermanent? In answer, Sthiramati says that there is no change of emptiness from its phase of being afflicted to its phase of being pure, but it always remains as true reality and thus does not change into anything else. Here "change" refers to emptiness becoming free from adventitious stains, but not to its nature changing into anything else. Therefore, its nature is completely pure, similar to space, gold, and water. Since these do not have the nature of their stains, they never change into being of the nature of these stains. Therefore, both when they are stained by adventitious stains and when they have become pure of them, their natures do not change into anything else.[262] On the other hand, those who claim that the very same entity first has the defining characteristic of being afflicted and later has the nature of being pure will never be able to deny that such an entity is a phenomenon that is altered due to its having changed into being of another nature. Nor will those who think that both being afflicted and being pure are adventitious be able to explain the fundamental change as the irreversible attainment of nirvāṇa. Therefore, emptiness is not impermanent.

Āśrayaparāvṛtti in Ratnākaraśānti's *Prajñāpāramitopadeśa* and *Khasamanāmaṭīkā*

Ratnākaraśānti's *Prajñāpāramitopadeśa* describes the result of the fundamental change as the remainder of the pure elements of the mind, which are revealed after its afflicted elements have been eliminated. This is buddhahood and the irreversible fundamental change of liberation from saṃsāra, in which the ālaya-consciousness ceases to exist, while the pure elements of mind continue to operate forever. Though the liberated minds of śrāvaka and pratyekabuddha arhats and buddhas are said to be equally pure, the qualities of buddhas as the full expression of mind's natural luminosity are far greater than those of śrāvakas and pratyekabuddhas:

> In these three [types of] arhats[263] the ālaya-consciousness will come to an end. How does it come to an end? It is the fundamental change—after the part that is the locus of the afflicted characteristics of the continuum of mind has come to an end, the purified part [of this continuum] operates for as long as there is space. Through the latent tendencies that represent the seeds of all afflicted phenomena having been completely severed, the ālaya-consciousness, which is the locus of those [afflicted] entities, is relinquished. That is, by virtue of the seeds having been terminated, no afflicted phenomena will arise [again]. At that point, the foundation [of mind's continuum] is called "uncontaminated dhātu" because it is of one taste, just like space. By virtue of the seeds having been terminated, the consciousnesses that appear as bodies, places, and possessions will not arise [again], which is also called "the vimuktikāya." Therefore, the vimuktikāya of buddha bhagavāns is not distinct from [those of] śrāvakas and pratyekabuddhas because the vimuktikāyas of all of them are without difference, just like pure crystals.
>
> [However,] the dharmakāya is more eminent than those [vimuktikāyas] because [in] buddhas the termination of afflicted phenomena means the fundamental change of the vimuktikāya in all respects. This is [nothing other than] the dharmakāya because it is the foundation of the dharmas of completely perfect buddhas. For the dharmakāya functions as the foundation of the buddhadharmas. Why is it their foundation? Because it is produced by the power of the immeasurable accumulations of merit and wisdom as well as by aspiration prayers. By virtue of [buddhas] being distinguished by the dharmakāya, the buddhadharmas that consist of the sāmbhogikakāya and nairmāṇikakāya are immeasurable. Therefore, [the dharmakāya's] being more eminent than the [vimuktikāyas of śrāvakas and pratyekabuddhas] is as in the example of the sun, moon crystals *(candrakānta),* and sun crystals *(sūryakānta)* not being different from other gems in terms of merely their purity, but being much more eminent in terms of their radiance.[264]

The three kinds of fundamental change listed at the beginning of Ratnākaraśānti's *Khasamanāmaṭīkā* (his commentary on the *Khasamatantra*) resemble the three types of fundamental change in the *Abhidharmasamuccaya* above, but Ratnākaraśānti explains them in somewhat different ways. He presents three kinds of foundation or support (*āśraya*) that change—the ālaya-consciousness as the support of the impregnations of negative tendencies, the support that is the path, and the support that is suchness. Accordingly, the ways in which each one of these supports undergoes the fundamental change are different—becoming exhausted, changing from being mundane to being supramundane, and changing in the sense of becoming completely free from adventitious stains, respectively. The entirety of this threefold fundamental change of buddhas consists of the three kāyas, each one being explained as "spacelike" (*khasama*) in its own way:

> Here the vajradhara, the Bhagavān, represents the enlightenment of all buddhas that has the characteristic of the fundamental change. "Foundation" [means] support,[265] which is threefold. (1) As for the support that has the characteristic of being the mind stream, for as long as it is the support of the latent tendencies that are the seeds of afflicted phenomena (called "the impregnations of negative tendencies"), it is called "the ālaya[-consciousness]." Later, through having cultivated for a long time the path of the noble ones that is free from reference points, what is called "ālaya[-consciousness]"—the consciousnesses that appear as if being places, bodies, and possessions—becomes exhausted and those afflicted phenomena which have [already] arisen vanish, while those which have not [yet] arisen do not arise at all. Therefore, by virtue of having that character, it is certain that [the ālaya-consciousness] ceases. [Its fundamental] change is the certainty that [mind keeps] operating as [its] infinite character of luminosity free from reference points, which is like the pure sky. This is the fundamental change of the buddhas in terms of the impregnations of negative tendencies. It is also described as "the uncontaminated dhātu" of the [buddhas] because it bears the seeds of the uncontaminated buddhadharmas.
>
> (2) It is also the support that is the path of the [buddhas]. Its change [means] that it completely ceases in its form of having a mundane nature, while operating in its completely supramundane form.
>
> (3) Also the suchness of all phenomena is the support of the [buddhas]. Its change refers to [its] total purity of all adventitious obscurations.
>
> [Thus,] what is the change of the support of the impregnations of negative tendencies, the support that is the path, and the support that is suchness represents the enlightenment of the [buddhas]. This is referred to as the support that is the dharmakāya and the kāya of the buddhadharmas, which is called "svābhāvikakāya" because it abides forever as the self-nature of both suchness and luminosity. This is the vajradhara, the Bhagavān, having the characteristic of buddha enlightenment and being like space by nature.

[Thus,] its nature is the kāya that is [its] essence (*svābhāvikaḥ kāyaḥ*). Therefore, it is like space because it has the nature of the suchness of nonappearance, infinite purity, and luminosity *(nirābhāsānantasuviśuddhaprakāśa).*

Since [buddhahood] as the sāmbhogakāya has various aspects, it is not like space in terms of the manner of [its] aspects. However, it is like space in terms of the manner of [its] appearance *(pratibhāsa).* The dharmakāya experiences phenomena as spacelike suchness in an unobscured manner and the sāmbhogakāya determines them accordingly because it is the natural outflow of this experience. How does it determine [phenomena]? Because it determines them as not existing as the appearances of apprehender and apprehended. [In the case] of childish beings, the natural outflow of experiencing a jar is [their] certainty about [its] existence. It is with regard to the clear experience of the [appearing] aspect of a jar, which is existent yet free from expression, that childish beings determine [that jar] as existent, which is due to the power of their habitual tendencies of being close to previous [instances of such] certainty [about existence]. Likewise, though the buddhas are free from expression, the sāmbhogakāya determines its own aspects to be nonexistent. This determination is indicated here by the term "appearance." This appearance is twofold—perception *(saṃvedana)* and designation *(upalakṣaṇa).* Therefore, the sāmbhogakāya is also like space in terms of the manner of the appearance of the buddhas.

The nirmāṇakāya is also very much like space because illusionists [always] determine the nonexistence of the persons and so on that they themselves have created. [Likewise,] the vajradhara is the one who gives rise to all buddhas. These too are like space because they are his natural outflow.[266]

Āśrayaparivṛtti in the two *Bṛhaṭṭīkās* on the prajñāpāramitā sūtras

There are two closely related commentaries on the prajñāpāramitā sūtras from a Yogācāra perspective that speak about *āśrayaparivṛtti.* According to Vasubandhu's commentary on the three longest prajñāpāramitā sūtras, the *Śatasāhasrikāpañcaviṃśatisāhasrikāṣṭādaśasāhasrikāprajñāpāramitābṛhaṭṭīkā*, at the time of the final fundamental change of the dharmadhātu the perfect nature on the one side and the imaginary and dependent natures on the other side (which appear to be indifferentiable for ordinary mistaken beings) finally become separated:

> [The sūtra] says, "Bhagavan, how are all phenomena unmixed?" When the two of the imaginary [nature] and the perfect [nature] are one (that is, abide in a manner of not being distinct) at the time of saṃsāra, the two abide without difference. This is called "being mixed." When the fundamental change has taken place progressively through the power of the natural outflow of the utterly pure dharmadhātu (study, reflection, meditation, and so on), [the dharmadhātu] abides as the utterly pure and stainless nature in which the two of the perfect [nature] and the imaginary [nature] have become distinct. At that point this is called "being unmixed."[267]

Note that the *Bṛhaṭṭīkā* usually speaks of all three natures, but sometimes summarizes all phenomena into two of them—the imaginary nature and the perfect nature—which are then used in contradistinction. It is clear from the contexts and also from an explicit statement in the *Bṛhaṭṭīkā* that in such cases the dependent nature is included in the imaginary nature.[268] In addition, when passages of the *Bṛhaṭṭīkā* that use only the imaginary and perfect natures reappear in Jagaddalanivāsin's *Āmnāyānusāriṇī* (a commentary on the *Prajñāpāramitāsūtra in Eight Thousand Lines*), the *Āmnāyānusāriṇī* usually explicitly adds the dependent nature on the side of the imaginary nature, thus making it very clear that the former is included in the latter. Accordingly, the slightly paraphrased version of the above passage in the *Bṛhaṭṭīkā* in the *Āmnāyānusāriṇī*[269] says that "at the time of saṃsāra, the imaginary [nature], the dependent [nature], and the perfect [nature] are one" and that, after the fundamental change, "the perfect [nature] has become distinct from the imaginary [nature] and the dependent [nature]."

Obviously, this is just another way of phrasing (through using the framework of the three natures) the above stance of the *Uttaratantra*, the DDV, and so on that, at the time of buddhahood, mind's natural luminosity (or buddha nature) is finally completely freed from its adventitious stains through realizing that these stains never really existed in the first place, but were only imaginary (later this became one of the most fundamental *Shentong* positions).

The *Bṛhaṭṭīkā* also relates the fundamental change to the notion of *tathāgatagarbha*:

> The perfect nature of inner and outer phenomena is called "the suchness of all phenomena," that is, it is exemplified by "the suchness of form," "the suchness of sound," "the suchness of smell," and so on. The fundamental change of the *tathāgatagarbha* of all buddhas—the dharmakāya—is the second one, called "the suchness of the dharmadhātu," because it is the foundation of all buddhadharmas.[270]

> During the state of ordinary beings, since *tathāgatagarbha* is naturally completely pure, it lacks being afflicted. When it has undergone the fundamental change, just like space, it also lacks any being purified that has not occurred before. Therefore, [the sūtras] say that it is "neither afflicted nor purified."[271]

> That which has undergone the fundamental change through a fourfold change[272] and is completely pure is called "the characteristic of lacking being afflicted and lacking being purified."[273]

> As for "the nirvāṇa of bodhisattvas," it refers to the utterly pure fundamental change. This fundamental change thus has the nature of all afflictive and cognitive obscurations having passed into parinirvāṇa and the nature of [all] karmic maturations having passed into parinirvāṇa. Therefore, it is nirvāṇa. Thus, it is unlike [the nirvāṇas of] both śrāvakas and pratyekabuddhas, but performs the welfare of sentient beings for as long as saṃsāra exists. Therefore, it is not nirvāṇa.[274]

The *Āmnāyānusāriṇī* explains that the perfect nature is the remainder that represents the final fundamental change of all ultimately nonexistent imaginary and dependent phenomena:

> The intention [here] is this: Since the imaginary and the dependent are nonexistent, the elder *(sthavira)* too lacks the nature of the imaginary and dependent. Therefore, the perfect nature is what serves as the remainder . . . Those in whom all imaginary and conceived phenomena have undergone the fundamental change realize the phenomenon that is devoid of the characteristics of those [phenomena] and is inexpressible. They abide [in it] at all times, but worldly beings and dialecticians do not realize it. Therefore, it is profound.[275]

Āśrayaparivṛtti in the *Kāyatrayāvatāramukha* and its *Vṛtti*

Nāgamitra's *Kāyatrayāvatāramukha*[276] discusses the characteristics of nonconceptual wisdom and the fundamental change as well as their close relationship. Verses 66–68 say:

> Since nonconceptual wisdom
> Understands, relinquishes,

And directly perceives the three natures,
Its fruition—the three kāyas—is attained.

Apart from nonconceptual wisdom
There is no other genuine wisdom.
Apart from the knowable object that is the dharmadhātu
There is no other genuine knowable object.

By virtue of the particulars of [that] knowable object and wisdom,
Duality becomes nonduality
And conceptuality, nonconceptuality—
Such is the fundamental change.

Jñānacandra's *Kāyatrayavṛtti*[277] explains this fundamental change in terms of the three natures, nonconceptual wisdom, and the dharmadhātu. The three kāyas are said to be the fruition of supramundane nonconceptual wisdom simultaneously understanding the imaginary nature, relinquishing the dependent nature, and directly perceiving the perfect nature. The three kāyas are not the fruition of anything else because there is no true reality other than nonconceptual wisdom (the ultimate subject) and the dharmadhātu (the ultimate object). For other cognitions dwell on superimposed entities and other objects manifest as mistaken aspects. As for the dharmakāya being constituted by the fundamental change, duality—the false imaginary nature that has the characteristics of apprehender and apprehended—becomes nonduality because it does not appear as its own nature anymore. The dependent nature is the nature of conceptions, and once it does not appear under the aspect of duality, this is "the fundamental change." If this fundamental change is analyzed, it is conceived of by virtue of the particulars of the ultimate object (the dharmadhātu) and the ultimate subject (wisdom). Verses 80–85 say:

The fundamental change
Is asserted as the foundation of that [wisdom].
Since there would be two flaws,
Mind is not the foundation of that [wisdom].

Since it does not obstruct movement
And therefore provides room,
Space is asserted as the foundation
Of everything that appears as form.

Likewise, upon the fundamental change,
That [wisdom] operates,

> [But] it does not in the foundation with flaws.
> Therefore, it is the foundation of that [wisdom].
>
> Wisdom and the fundamental change,
> These two are mutually asserted
> As the entity that is the foundation,
> Just like conceptions [arising] from the root mind.
>
> Just as conceptions arise
> From the root mind,
> It is held that when they arise,
> They likewise make it flourish.
>
> Similarly, based on the fundamental change,
> Genuine and pure
> Nonconceptual wisdom arises,
> Which is what accomplishes that [change].

Jñānacandra comments that suchness—and not mind—is the foundation of nonconceptual wisdom, which can only operate freely once this foundation is unobscured. At the same time, suchness and nonconceptual wisdom depend on and mutually enhance each other:

> It may be said, "What is the foundation of nonconceptual wisdom? Is it mind or is it something other? If it were mind, something else would exist where [mind] exists, [meaning that] that wisdom would [likewise] be referential discursiveness (*spros pa).* But if [the foundation] is something other, it must be shown [what it is]." Therefore, [the text] says:
>
> > The fundamental change
> > Is asserted as the foundation of that [wisdom].
>
> The fundamental change refers to suchness—it is the foundation of wisdom. "Why does [this foundation] not refer to mind?" Therefore, [the text] says:
>
> > Since there would be two flaws,
> > Mind is not the foundation of that [wisdom].

If mind were the foundation [of wisdom], two flaws would occur. Why? Because it is asserted that "mind" *(citta)* applies to the aspect of what is accumulated (*cita*) and variegated *(citra)*.[278] If [mind] were [the foundation of wisdom in] the first [sense], it would not be suitable [as that foundation] because it brings forth all the seeds of those in saṃsāra without exception. Nor is it [suitable as the foundation in] the second [sense] because, [unlike mind, wisdom] lacks the operating consciousnesses. Also, mind is what determines the entities that have the aspect of generalities, whereas supramundane wisdom is the opposite of that. Therefore, [the Buddha] said, "Rely on wisdom, but do not rely on consciousness." This means that, since the [latter] does not operate according to the way things actually are, one should not rely on it. Since wisdom is what determines things as they actually are, one should rely on it. "But without an example, how could one understand this?" Therefore, [the text] says:

Since it does not obstruct movement
And therefore provides room,
Space is asserted as the foundation
Of everything that appears as form.

Likewise, upon the fundamental change,
That [wisdom] operates,
[But] it does not in the foundation with flaws.

This teaches that, for example, space provides room since it does not obstruct the continual flow of the movement of phenomena that have form. Therefore, space is called "foundation." Likewise, upon the fundamental change, nonconceptual wisdom arises, but it does not arise in any way for as long as the foundation is associated with flaws. The conclusion is:

Therefore, it is the foundation of that [wisdom].

"In that case, suchness is the foundation (*gnas)* since [wisdom] arises based on it. [However, that wisdom is then] something else called 'that which is based [on that foundation]' *(gnas pa)* [for] these two are clearly postulated [here]." Therefore, [the text] says:

Wisdom and the fundamental change,
These two are mutually asserted
As the entity that is the foundation

This teaches the following. Both of these come about through their mutual powers. Therefore, it is not that categorically just one serves as the foundation, but [the fact of being] the entities that are the foundation and what is based [on it] exist in both. Without the fundamental change, nonconceptual wisdom does not arise, and without wisdom, there is no fundamental change. Therefore, what is described in this context applies to both together, just as in the case of the root [mind] and conceptions. "How is that?" Therefore, [the text] says:

> Just like conceptions [arising] from the root mind.

> Just as conceptions arise
> From the root mind,
> It is held that when they arise,
> They likewise make it flourish.
>
> Similarly, based on the fundamental change,
> Genuine and pure
> Nonconceptual wisdom arises

For example, when the various seeds that are present in the ālaya-consciousness mature, conceptions arise in the manner of a mutual cause-and-result [relationship with the ālaya-consciousness]. [For,] at that time, they [in turn] produce seeds in that very ālaya-consciousness and make it flourish. Later, the result of this flourishing is the arising of [further] conceptions [from it]. Similarly, it is taught that, when nondual wisdom arises based on the fundamental change, it is held that [this wisdom] is the very agent that accomplishes the fundamental change. Therefore, [the text] says:

> Which is what accomplishes that [change].[279]

Āśrayaparivṛtti in the *Dharmadhātustava*

Verse 88 of the *Dharmadhātustava* says:

> The abode of buddhadharmas
> Fully bears the fruit of practice.
> This fundamental change
> Is called the "dharmakāya."

The Third Karmapa's commentary explains this verse under the heading of the fundamental change being the dharmakāya's very own essence, which consists of the perfect nature free from all afflictive and cognitive obscurations of the ālaya-consciousness:

> Once all ten bhūmis have been completed, the vajralike samādhi destroys the ālaya-consciousness, which is the ground of the latent tendencies of ignorance. At that point, [bodhisattvas] receive the empowerment of great light rays bestowed [by all buddhas] and become buddhas [themselves]. As for this stage, the abode of all dharmas' ultimate own essence, once the miragelike afflictive obscurations and cognitive obscurations are purified through the infinite practices of the activities [of bodhisattvas] on many bhūmis, it fully bears the naturally luminous perfect nature. This is taught to be "the fundamental change," which is called the "dharmakāya."[280]

Āśryaparivṛtti in the *Munimatālaṃkāra*

Abhayākaragupta's *Munimatālaṃkāra* explains the fundamental change as the fundamental change of the eight consciousnesses into the pure dharmadhātu and the four wisdoms (together presented as five wisdoms):[281]

> When the nature of the suchness of all phenomena (the unmistaken nature, true reality, emptiness) has become utterly free from the seeds of the two obscurations by virtue of having attained the path of utterly pure supramundane wisdom, this is called "the fundamental change of the completely pure dharmadhātu, suchness." This is also the uncontaminated dharmadhātu. It is wisdom—the wisdom of the utterly pure dharmadhātu. For it abides for endless time by virtue of observing [the dharmadhātu] as what is to be personally experienced. [Both] the dharmadhātu and all phenomena are observed by mirrorlike wisdom because it observes [both] the general and specific characteristics [of phenomena].
>
> What has solely the character of conception and is the support of all impregnations of negative tendencies is the ālaya-consciousness. It is nothing but [its] fundamental change by virtue of having become free from all impregnations of negative tendencies without exception through the power of the remedies that is called "mirrorlike wisdom." . . .

The other three wisdoms also are fundamental changes. Master Candragomī says:

> The fundamental change of the afflicted mind
> Is to be called mirrorlike wisdom.
> The discriminating wisdom
> Is the one of the mental consciousness.
>
> These two represent the sāmbhogikakāya
> Because they teach enjoyment of the dharma
> And because the great
> Bodhisattvas enjoy the dharma.
> . . .
> The consciousnesses of the five sense faculties
> Apprehend all referents—
> For the welfare of all sentient beings
> Sheer all-accomplishment is attained.
>
> This is always and everywhere,
> In accordance with time and in accordance with the thinking [of beings],
> The nairmāṇikakāya of the buddhas
> Because it is the cause of all emanations.
> . . .

In this way these five wisdoms arise as the completely pure supramundane seeming [reality] from the supremely uncontaminated dharmadhātu—they have its nature.[282]

Āśrayaparivṛtti in Madhyamaka texts

Occasionally the term "fundamental change" is also found in Madhyamaka texts, such as Avalokitavrata's *Prajñāpradīpaṭīkā* saying:

> It is said that when it is seen that objects such as form are neither being, nor nonbeing, nor [both] being and nonbeing, there are no conceptions that apprehend in mistaken ways. Therefore, the ālaya-consciousness has undergone the fundamental change and true reality—called "phenomenal identitylessness"—is realized. Consequently, it is the mere negation of being and nonbeing

> that is called "the middle path," but there is nothing whatsoever in between these two.[283]

And:

> The essence of mind is natural luminosity. Having put an end to this [mind being ensnared by itself] means the liberation from adventitious obscurations and the fundamental change . . . This teaches [the manner of] bondage by virtue of adventitious obscurations and the manner of liberation and the fundamental change by virtue of seeing phenomenal identitylessness.[284]

And:

> Consummate wisdom is constituted by the fundamental change—mirrorlike wisdom, the wisdom of equality, discriminating wisdom, and all-accomplishing wisdom.[285]

Jayānanda's *Madhyamakāvatāraṭīkā* declares:

> After the afflictions to be relinquished [through seeing] have been relinquished by virtue of seeing [the reality of] suffering through the [dharma] readiness [with regard to suffering], the foundation has undergone the fundamental change. The wisdom through which that fundamental change is realized is called "the dharma cognition of suffering."[286]

Furthermore, in typical Yogācāra fashion, the text also describes the pure dharmadhātu and the four wisdoms (mirrorlike wisdom and so on) as resulting from the fundamental changes of the eight consciousnesses.[287]

Āśrayaparivṛtti in the Tibetan commentaries on the *Dharmadharmatāvibhāga*

The Third Karmapa's OED generally quotes extensively from the ninth and tenth chapters of the *Mahāyānasaṃgraha* on the fundamental change. In particular, OED matches DDV's main distinction between phenomena and the nature of phenomena with the three natures and equates the perfect nature with the fundamental change:

> Here, in terms of the defining characteristics [of knowable objects], the two that are the imaginary and dependent [natures] are explained as representing the obscurations and phenomena. The perfect [nature]—the fundamental change—is said to be the nature of phenomena.[288]

Similar to the *Mahāyānasaṃgraha* and its commentaries, OED explicitly relates the notion of fundamental change to the three natures. However, while the *Mahāyānasaṃgraha* describes the fundamental change as the change of the dependent nature from its impure form into its pure form, OED says that it is characterized by the disappearance of both the imaginary and dependent natures, while the nature of phenomena—the perfect nature—alone is perceived:

> Once it is liberated from afflicted phenomena, the dependent—as mere cognizance—comes to be without the imaginary. Therefore, once cognizance embraced by purified phenomena has undergone the fundamental change, it becomes the perfect [nature]. Consequently, the nonobservation of both the imaginary and the dependent [natures] as well as the observation of the nature of phenomena occur together.[289]

The final fundamental change in terms of the three natures at the end of the bodhisattva path of familiarization, with nothing but the perfect nature—suchness—remaining, is also explained as the fundamental change of the eight consciousnesses into the five wisdoms:

> "As for the arrival at its nature" means "having reached the end [of the path]." This [nature] is suchness—the nature of the two [aspects of] the perfect [nature] (unchanging suchness and unmistaken suchness, which is nothing other). Once this [suchness] has become without the stains of the imaginary and the dependent [natures], since all knowable objects are without duality they are naked wisdom, that is, they appear as nothing but suchness. After mind, mentation, and consciousness have undergone their fundamental change, this is their perfection as the natures of the five wisdoms. Here "change" refers to the path of familiarization having reached its end.[290]

OED supplements its more detailed explanation of what changes into what by quoting *Mahāyānasaṃgraha* X.4 and *Mahāyānasūtrālaṃkāra* XIV.44–46 (see above) and then says:

> That which undergoes the fundamental change is the ālaya-consciousness. That through which it undergoes the fundamental change is the dharmakāya that is the natural outflow [of the stainless dharmadhātu]. That into which there is a fundamental change is the stainless dharmakāya. The way in which the fundamental change happens is that the two nonexistent phenomena [—the imaginary and dependent natures—] become pure and the existent nature of phenomena appears. The time during which the fundamental change occurs is fourfold—aspiration, contact, recollection, and instantaneously becoming its nature. As for the fundamental change with its distinctive features that will be explained [below in DDV] through ten points, through the [first] six points (including the progression) it is taught as buddhahood [by Maitreya].[291]

As for the nature of this fundamental change being the revelation of the unchanging luminous nature of the mind and its seeming obscuration in ordinary confused beings, OED says:

> Adventitious stains are one's own stainless and naturally luminous mind as such, but by virtue of this very [mind] being ignorant of itself, cognizance appears in a dualistic way as if it were [a separate] apprehender and apprehended. Miragelike mental conceptions arise, and these false imaginations obscure luminous suchness. If these obscurations do not appear, suchness will appear, just as in the example of water appearing to be clear and transparent once it has become pure of silt. This is the nature of the fundamental change. The *Mahāyānasūtrālaṃkāra* says:
>
> > When murky water becomes clear,
> > [Its] transparency does not arise from elsewhere,
> > But is just its becoming free from pollution.
> > The same goes for the purity of your own mind.
> >
> > It is held that mind, which is always naturally luminous,
> > Is [only] blemished by adventitious flaws.
> > Apart from the mind that is the nature of phenomena, no other mind
> > Is proclaimed to be luminous in nature.[292]
>
> Luminosity and natural emptiness are not tainted by the nature of conceptions since conceptions are [nothing but] nonexistents that appear. This is stated many times, such as in the *Dharmadhātustava:*

About water at the time of spring,
What we say is that it's "warm."
Of the very same [thing], when it's chilly,
We just say that it is "cold."

Covered by the web of the afflictions,
It is called a "sentient being."
Once it's free from the afflictions,
It should be expressed as "buddha."[293]

Also the *[Hevajra]tantra* says:

Sentient beings are buddhas indeed.
However, they are obscured by adventitious stains.
If these are removed, they are buddhas.[294,295]

As for the entity of the fundamental change (or what changes), OED[296] elaborates by matching the threefold fundamental change of suchness with the eight consciousnesses. (1) The fundamental change of the cognizance that appears as the external world refers to the fundamental change of the five sense faculties and their objects. (2) The fundamental change of the dharmadhātu of the sūtra collection refers to the purity of the clinging to the characteristics of the dharma (such as words, phrases, and letters) as well as the mastery over them. This is the fundamental change of the sixth consciousness in its conceptual and nonconceptual aspects. (3) The fundamental change of the dhātu of sentient beings which is not in common refers to the fundamental change of the ālaya-consciousness and the afflicted mind.

On the four flaws that would follow if there were no fundamental change, OED comments as follows:

First, the flaw of there being no support for the afflictions not operating. If there were not the nature of the fundamental change (the permanent dharmakāya), afflictions could not but operate again in their support that is the ālaya-consciousness because it is the result of having accumulated the entirety of false imagination and the [other] consciousnesses are produced by it. [However,] if there is the arising of the uncontaminated wisdom that is supported by the support which is the dharmakāya, the afflictions do not operate [again] because their remedy is blazing, [just as,] for example, darkness does not occur in the sun.

Second, the flaw of there being no support for engaging in the path. If one needs to definitely generate the five uncontaminated paths in due order, one relies on the support that is nonconceptual wisdom (the unchanging perfect [nature]) in order to manifest attainment through relying on ultimate practice. The natural outflow of this [wisdom]—unmistaken study, reflection, and meditation—produces fruitions that are increasingly pure. However, it is not feasible for purity to arise from an impure support because it is not tenable for something uncontaminated to arise from something contaminated—[these two] are mutually exclusive, just like light and darkness.

Third, the flaw of there being no basis for designating the persons who have passed into nirvāṇa. As for saṃsāra with its three contaminated realms, it is through the causal karmas that are produced by ignorance and formations that the three [realms of saṃsāric] existence, which are based on craving and grasping, are established. Likewise, it is based on the uncontaminated pure karmas of nirvāṇa that the vimuktikāya exists as being designated as arhats, pratyekabuddhas, or bodhisattvas, and also the final great perfect enlightenment must exist. If both saṃsāra and nirvāṇa had the same support, there would be great flaws. It is contradictory for antagonistic factors to be relinquished and their remedies to have the same support. Also, when the mind ceases, mistakenness ceases, and therefore the perfect [nature] that is wisdom would cease too. If the perfect [nature] were to cease too in this manner, it would be conditioned. Consequently, the nature of phenomena and the dharmakāya, which are unconditioned, would absolutely not exist either, and if such is accepted, it would represent the view of Kaṇāda.[297] Since the pure dharmas would be meaningless, it is not in order to regard the four noble ones as being nonexistent. Therefore, [with the fundamental change existing,] it is tenable to designate the persons who have passed into nirvāṇa.

Fourth, the flaw of there being no basis for designating the differences between the three [types of] enlightenment. As for the three [types of] enlightenment, the differences in terms of liberation based on the support that is the dharmadhātu are as follows. Śrāvakas are liberated through relinquishing the afflictive obscurations (including their support) of clinging to a personal self. In addition to that, pratyekabuddhas are only endowed with the liberation of having relinquished the conceptions about the apprehended with regard to phenomena because they gain slight mastery over

> samādhis such as The Sky Treasure, which are based on unconditioned uncontaminated phenomena. As for bodhisattvas, from the path of seeing onward they realize that any identities of persons and phenomena do not exist. Thus, through relying on the familiarization [with this twofold identitylessness] in order to eradicate the stains of these [identities], they are liberated from the ground of the latent tendencies of ignorance and thereby become buddhas. Therefore, based on the support that is the dharmakāya, it is feasible to designate these three differences in terms of liberation. Thus, it is feasible to designate the three [types of enlightenment]—the enlightenment of having relinquished the afflictions, the enlightenment of having relinquished the apprehended, and complete enlightenment. However, if there were no such [fundamental] changes, since there would also be no differences with regard to the sheer ālaya-consciousnesses that are not in common coming to an end, the three [types of enlightenment] would not be feasible. If the very [ālaya-consciousness] were the support of enlightenment, the fundamental change of what is supported would not be tenable in any respect because causes and results as well as factors to be relinquished and remedies would be mistaken.[298]

Finally, the three concluding examples of space, gold, and water for the fundamental change in DDV are explained by OED similar to DDVV, but OED equates the nature of phenomena with the perfect nature and also adduces the *Uttaratantra*'s nine examples of buddha nature being obscured by various adventitious stains as pertaining to this context of the ultimate fundamental change:

> For example, space is nothing but pure by nature. Therefore, by virtue of certain conditions (such as fog or mist) in the world, one can observe the statements, "The sky is not pure," and "It is pure" [when] it is clear and free [from these conditions]. However, it is not suitable to claim such because of a change of the nature of space. With its own nature being pure, empty, and unconditioned, it is indeed not in order for it to either become pure by virtue of itself or become pure by virtue of something else. Nevertheless, mistaken minds that connect mere conventional terms to it cling to space as being pure and impure, [but] this is nothing but an error. Likewise, though it may appear as if the naturally pure nature of phenomena—the perfect [nature]—has become free from the fog and mist of conceptions, it is not asserted that this perfect [nature] changes

[in any way]—it is absolutely without any arising or ceasing in terms of itself, others, both, or neither.

In the same way, the fact of gold remaining in its state of being immaculate is not changed by any stains, and the fact of water remaining clear and moist is not changed in its nature even if it becomes associated with sullying factors, [such as] silt. Likewise, all that happens to the unmistaken path and the pure dharmas is that they just become associated with stains and sullying factors through the conceptions of ignorance, but it is not asserted that these uncontaminated dharmas [—the path and the pure dharmas entailed by cessation—] change. Consequently, naturally luminous stainlessness is unconditioned and changeless. Therefore, though the nature of phenomena is referred to by the conventional term "fundamental change," it is also called "permanent."

The words "and so on" refer to its being like a buddha [statue] existing in the shroud of a [decaying] lotus, honey existing amidst bees, a grain in its husks, gold in filth, a treasure in the earth, a tree [sprouting] from a fruit, a precious statue in tattered rags, a cakravartin in the belly of a destitute woman, and a golden statue in clay. [In due order, the respective obscuring factors in these nine examples correspond to the following mental obscurations.] The four that consist of the three latencies of desire, hatred, and ignorance, as well as the intense arising of all [three], are the factors to be relinquished through cultivating the mundane paths.
The ground of the latent tendencies of ignorance is the factor to be relinquished through the cognition of realizing the foundation of knowable objects. The [afflictive] factors to be relinquished through seeing are relinquished through the path of seeing. The [afflictive] factors to be relinquished through familiarization are relinquished through [the path of] familiarization. The cognitive obscurations of the impure bhūmis are relinquished through the two wisdoms of meditative equipoise and subsequent attainment. The cognitive obscurations of the pure [bhūmis] are relinquished through the vajralike [samādhi]. Thus, [the corresponding obscured factors in the nine examples correspond to] the buddha heart, the [single] taste of the [profound] dharma, the essence of its meaning, natural luminosity, changelessness, the unfolding of wisdom, the dharmakāya, the sāmbhogikakāya, and the nairmāṇikakāya, [all of which] represent the pure unchanging and spontaneously present nature . . . [The *Uttaratantra also says]:*

> There is nothing to be removed from it
> And not the slightest to be added.
> Actual reality is to be seen as it really is—
> Whoever sees actual reality is liberated.
>
> The basic element is empty of what is adventitious,
> Which has the characteristic of being separable.
> It is not empty of the unsurpassable dharmas,
> Which have the characteristic of being inseparable.[299]

This teaches the defining characteristics of the emptiness endowed with the supreme of all aspects, free from the extremes of superimposition and denial.[300]

Rongtön's RC[301] comments on these examples by saying that space and so on are examples for the matrix of the fundamental change—the natural nirvāṇa. For, though space may be associated with clouds, space does not have the nature of clouds nor vice versa, and therefore they coexist in a manner of being separable. Since space is pure of the nature of clouds and clouds are pure of the nature of space, one also speaks of "purity by nature." The same applies for gold being covered by a film and water being murky. Or these examples for the fundamental change can be understood as follows. Though the natural nirvāṇa is naturally pure before, it is associated with adventitious stains and therefore is impure. Later this very natural purity has become pure of adventitious stains and therefore one speaks of "the attainment of the fundamental change." This corresponds to the manner in which space is naturally pure before and later has become pure of clouds as well as the manner in which gold and water become free from a film and silt, respectively.

Gö Lotsāwa's GC starts by quoting RGVV on the fundamental change and then explains the meaning of this term:

[The *Ratnagotravibhāgavyākhyā]* says:

> Here you may wonder, "What is stainless suchness?" It is that which is presented as the fundamental change because of being free from all kinds of stains in the uncontaminated dhātu of the buddha bhagavāns. In brief, this should be understood in terms of eight points.[302]

As for accepting the expression "stainless suchness," first it is asked [here], "What is the nature of stainless suchness?" Stainless suchness is that which is presented as the fundamental change of the sovereigns who are the buddha bhagavāns. You may wonder, "In this, what does 'foundation' and what does 'change' refer to?" The "foundation" is the uncontaminated dhātu and the meaning of "change" is "coming to an end"[303] because all stains or obscurations (with afflictive and cognitive obscurations as the divisions of their aspects) in this dhātu have become separated [from it] and come to an end. [The *Abhidharmasūtra] says:*

> The dhātu of beginningless time
> Is the foundation of all phenomena.

Thus, because suchness has functioned as the foundation or support of afflicted phenomena since beginningless time, it is also to be described as "host" (gnas po). [Nāgamitra's] *Kāyatrayāvatāra* says:

> The host having changed into something else . . .[304]

Accordingly, it is called "fundamental change" because, through having changed into another nature later, it functions as the support for the purified qualities.[305]

Thus, different from DDVV, OED, and other commentaries, GC obviously takes suchness as being the single foundation of both afflicted and purified phenomena, which is repeated several times in GC. The text even says that suchness "changes into another nature," thus being the support for pure qualities. Compare also Gö Lotsāwa's comments on RGVV on II.1:

> . . . what is expressed by the name "tathāgata heart" is the basic element or cause which is not liberated from the cocoon of the afflictions, that is, which serves as the foundation *(gnas)* for the production of afflictions. It is a foundation because it functions as the support for afflictiveness. Once it has become pure of its stains, including their latent tendencies, and this has become irreversible, it does not function as the foundation for afflictions [anymore] and has therefore reversed from [what it was] before. Since it [now] functions as the support for purified phenomena alone, it should be understood as the nature of the fundamental change. The two that [are called] "basic element" *(khams)* and "fundamental change" are only differentiated by virtue of there being or not being stains—their nature is this very suchness.[306]

Though this explanation accords with what was said above, it also relativizes what GC means by "support" and "changing its nature" since suchness itself remains unchanged, whether it is stained or unstained. The manner in which it serves as a support for afflicted phenomena is thus rather nominal, that is, in the sense of the *Uttaratantra*'s explanation that conditioned phenomena depend on space. Thus, this is a different way of suchness being a support than its being a support for the pure buddha qualities, which are intrinsic to its nature. This is also made clear earlier in GC:

> Here, as for comprehending the nature [of the fundamental change], it is suchness that has become stainless, which is in terms of adventitious stains not appearing at all and suchness appearing in all respects. Through having reversed its functioning as the support for adventitious stains, [suchness] functions as the support that is the [very] nature of the appearance of suchness, but it does not function as the support for producing [the appearance of suchness]. Therefore, it is said to "have become its [own] nature." This fundamental change also needs to be expressed by the term "buddhahood" (*sangs rgyas)*. For, by virtue of all stains not arising again, it is pure *(sangs),* and by virtue of all knowable objects appearing as nothing but suchness, it has unfolded *(rgyas).* This corresponds to what the *Kāyatrayāvatāra* says:
>
> > Apart from stainless suchness
> > And nonconceptual wisdom,
> > There are no other dharmas
> > Of the buddhas whatsoever.[307]
>
> Here, on the buddhabhūmi, both the relinquishment of being without stains and the wisdom of realizing suchness have the nature of the single luminous wisdom. Therefore, both are suchness, the nature of phenomena, and the foundation of phenomena.[308]

GC also explains that the threefold fundamental change in terms of the suchness of the world, sentient beings, and the scriptures refers to the fundamental change by virtue of what comes to an end, whereas the division of the fundamental change in terms of śrāvakas, pratyekabuddhas, and bodhisattvas (including the latter's qualities of the three kāyas) refers to that which arises instead or that into which there is change. Furthermore, the direct cause of the fundamental change is nonconceptual wisdom, which is in turn caused by proper mental engagement (point seven of the explanation of the fundamental change in DDV).[309]

As for the four flaws of there being no fundamental change, GC comments as follows:

> First, [without this fundamental change,] it follows that there is no obstacle [for the afflictions] that constitutes the support for the afflictions henceforth not operating and not arising in the mind stream. Since beginningless time the afflictions have been operating again and again by way of being an uninterrupted series [of moments], but if they do not arise [during some] later [period], one should be certain that there is an obstacle to this [arising]. It is said that this obstacle is nothing but the fundamental change. This is comparable to [the fact that] guests who had [regularly] entered a hotel before are not able to enter it [anymore] due to the host rebelling against it . . .
>
> As for the second flaw, the path of liberation consists of the [ten] powers and so on of the buddhabhūmi. When these remain by way of being an uninterrupted series, it is certain that there exists a stable support for them, just as it is certain that, when water remains [somewhere] in a steady manner, there exists some stable ground beneath it. Since the support of these qualities is nothing but the fundamental change, if one has the view of there being no such [support], it is the ignorance and the doubts in terms of lacking trust in the fruition that constitute the [second] flaw.
>
> [Third,] if there were no stable continuum called "fundamental change" in the states of śrāvakas and pratyekabuddhas having passed into the nirvāṇa without remainder, there would also be no basis in these states for designating the persons who are called "arhats." Also, if there were no stable continuum of wisdom after having become a buddha, there would be no basis for designating the persons who are called "buddhas." For example, in the state of saṃsāra too, [people] accept a mental continuum that is the basis for being designated as Devadatta and so on . . . Therefore, the [third] flaw consists of the doubts about [the Buddha and the saṃgha as objects of] refuge due to lacking trust in the three [kinds of] persons who have passed into nirvāṇa.
>
> As for the fourth flaw, [without a fundamental change] there would be no differences between the three [types of] enlightenment—being enlightened about the four realities through the enlightenment of śrāvakas, pratyekabuddhas being enlightened about dependent origination, and buddhas being enlightened about all knowable objects without exception. In this way, there would

> be no mental continuum called "fundamental change" whatsoever once śrāvakas and pratyekabuddhas have passed into [their respective] nirvāṇas without remainder. Therefore, there is the flaw of it then following that these two would not enter the mahāyāna. If one views it in that way, there is the flaw of having doubts about the path of the single yāna.[310]

GC's manner of explaining DDV's concluding examples of space, water, and gold is quite unique. He even holds that Vasubandhu's DDVV represents Madhyamaka:

> As for the explanation of the fundamental change, which is characterized by being the nature of phenomena, the fundamental change is not something arisen newly, but exists from the start. Its examples are that it is like space merely being seen newly by virtue of having become free from obscurations, while its nature existed before. Also, though gold exists before, it is merely seen later by virtue of having become free from tarnish. Water is clear by its very nature right from the start, but what is new is [just] the seeing [of its clarity] by virtue of [its] turbidities having settled. Thus, [Vasubandhu's] commentary [says]:
>
>> [The fundamental change of the nature of phenomena] is taught through the examples of gold and water as being congruent with their properties only in terms of their qualities, without considering their [respective material] substances. Through the example of space, however, it is taught in its entirety.[311]
>
> [Accordingly,] that space is taught to be congruent with the properties of the fundamental change is by virtue of both [of its following] qualities—being a substance that operates by way of being an uninterrupted series and [eventually] becoming observed as opposed to not having been observed [before]. Through this, it is clear that this commentary by master [Vasubandhu] represents the Madhyamaka system. For, in the great Yogācāra texts, it is not explained that there exists a naturally pure continuum within the continuum of afflicted phenomena such as ignorance, while such is explained in this [commentary]. Also the root [text] itself clearly speaks of the difference in terms of nonexistence and existence, respectively, with regard to phenomena and the nature of phenomena. Therefore, this matches well with the explanation in the *Uttaratantra*[312] here that

> [the tathāgata heart] is empty of adventitious stains, but not empty of qualities.

The way in which Gö Lotsāwa interprets the three examples of space and so on is quite uncommon in that he takes all three to illustrate the natural luminosity of mind as being a "substance that operates by way of being an uninterrupted series [of moments] (*rgyun gyis 'jug pa'i rdzas*)." In the context of the *Uttaratantra*'s discussion of buddha nature being all-pervading in all three of its states (being impure, partly pure, and completely pure), Gö Lotsāwa[313] explicitly confirms this by saying that Vasubandhu's explanation of all three examples entails the existence of a continuum. Thus, Gö Lotsāwa seems to understand the permanence of the nature of phenomena as an endless and uninterrupted continuation of moments, of which only the continuum of space is a fully congruent example, whereas gold and water also represent continua, but are not everlasting. That Gö Lotsāwa indeed takes the nature of phenomena, the fundamental change, and nonconceptual wisdom to be continua of moments is confirmed by him shortly after:

> Therefore, it is not the case that space—which is the mere existence of providing room, has a momentary nature, and possesses a continuum—is nonexistent. Here, in terms of time, the space at the beginning of an eon is not the space at the time of [its] destruction [and thus also momentary in a sense]. In terms of location, the very substance that is the mere existence of providing room within a golden container is not the mere existence of providing room in an earthen container. Likewise, the moments of the basic element of sentient beings, which has the property of awareness and operates by way of being an uninterrupted series, do not turn into the moments of buddha wisdom. However, the two mere existences of providing room in a golden and an earthen container, respectively, are not different in type. Likewise, the nonconceptuality of buddhas and the nonconceptuality of sentient beings are very much similar in kind, and there also are conventional expressions for their being one . . .[314]

In this sense, the nature of phenomena, the fundamental change, and nonconceptual wisdom all can be taken as the momentary continuity of the stainless true nature of the mind. This is also made clear in GC's comments on the defining characteristic of the nature of phenomena, saying that "the commentary [by Vasubandhu] explains [the nature of phenomena] to be nothing but the continuum of stainless mind,"[315] which is supported by referring to *Mahāyānasūtrālaṃkāra* XIII.19 and DDVV, both saying that the nature of phenomena is the pure luminous mind. Interestingly, what shows for Gö Lotsāwa that DDVV belongs to the Madhyamaka tradition is both this momentary nature of the nature of phenomena as the continuum of luminosity and the fact that this luminosity is observed after not having been observed before. For, he says, the great Yogācāra treatises do not explain that there is a naturally pure continuum of luminosity within the continuum of the afflictions. However, it is unclear what exactly Gö Lotsāwa means by "great Yogācāra treatises." Maybe he refers to passages like *Mahāyānasaṃgraha* I.45–49, in which a clear line is drawn between an impure ālaya-consciousness and a pure supramundane mind, which does not exist in the mind streams of ordinary beings but arises from the latent tendencies for listening that are the natural outflow of the pure dharmadhātu (however, it is also stated there that these latent tendencies abide together with the ālaya-consciousness as a continuum until the latter dissolves).[316]

According to Śākya Chogden's SC,[317] DDV's detailed explanation of the fundamental change dispels any ignorance about the fundamental state and the final fruition of all three yānas. In the term "fundamental change," "foundation" refers to the true nature of the mind in all three yānas and "change" means that, through the power of becoming familiar with this nature, afflicted phenomena do not manifest by virtue of purified phenomena manifesting. The ultimate foundation of both kinds of phenomena indeed exists as nothing other than dharmadhātu wisdom. However, through the explanation by way of dividing the sheer fundamental change in terms of isolates into the ālaya-consciousness and ālaya-wisdom, it is easy to identify, respectively, what is to be relinquished and what is to be made a living experience. It may be argued that if the fruition is explained to be the fundamental change, ground and fruition are presented as being the same. However, there is no problem because it is explained that, at the time of meditative equipoise, there is nothing to be removed or added. Therefore, there is no need to depend on any efforts in terms of the fundamental change.

Mipham Rinpoche's MC[318] explains that once suchness has become without adventitious stains, all phenomena appear as nothing but suchness since their mode of appearance and their actual mode of being are the same in all respects. Though the sheer fundamental change exists already on the first bhūmi, its full completion occurs only at buddhahood. When not having undergone the fundamental change yet, what consists of forms and the sounds of speech is suitable to appear as being in common with others, while the mind is not so in common. At the time of the fundamental change, all phenomena just appear as suchness, and there are no differences or impurities. Therefore, everything appears in the special manner of being nothing but pure self-appearance. Nevertheless, from the perspective of the appearances of those who have not undergone such a fundamental change, this very suchness appears in different ways as buddhas, their teachings, and so on.

Mipham Rinpoche provides a lengthy explanation of the four flaws of there being no fundamental change[319] because, he says, they were not discussed in detail in previous Indian and Tibetan commentaries. If there were no fundamental change of the factors to be relinquished having been relinquished and the realizations having been attained through the path, first, there would be no support for already relinquished afflictions not operating again in the mind stream. For example, in the case of the factors to be relinquished through seeing not arising again in the mind stream of a bodhisattva in which they have been relinquished, it is by virtue of that bodhisattva having attained a fundamental change in which the mind stream has changed that there is no chance for these factors to be relinquished to operate again in that mind stream. Otherwise, if the mind stream had not undergone the fundamental change, even if the obscurations have already been relinquished one time, they would arise again just as before. The same applies up through the buddhabhūmi—when a mind stream has not undergone the fundamental change, it serves as a support for the operating of the respective factors to be relinquished, but when it has undergone the fundamental change, it serves as the support for those factors to be relinquished not operating. It may be said, "Once the seeds to be relinquished are destroyed, just like seeds burned by fire, they simply do not arise again. So, even if there is no 'fundamental change,' how is that contradictory to their not rearising?" Though the seeds to be relinquished are destroyed, this relinquishment needs to be presented by indicating the distinctive features of the mind stream in which it happened, but it is not feasible in terms of a mind stream that shows no such distinctive features. For, without demonstrating this relinquishment through specifying that certain distinctive features of a mind stream in which remedial wisdom has been generated represent "the termination of contaminations," one does not know the manner in which the seeds have been destroyed either. Thus, it is by virtue of these distinctive features of a fundamental change, when compared to before, that the seeds to be relinquished do not rearise in a mind stream in which they have been terminated, but this is unlike the case of the support having become nonexistent after the continuum of the mind stream has become extinct. Therefore, that contaminations arise in mind streams with certain distinctive features and do not arise in mind streams with certain others is by virtue of not having or having attained a fundamental change, respectively, just as there is no chance for appearances of falling hairs in an eye without blurred vision.

Second, there would be no support for the operating of the path that is the remedy for the factors to be relinquished. For the supports for respectively higher paths operating in the distinctive mind streams that are referred to as "a person on the path of seeing," "a person on the second bhūmi," and so on are the respectively preceding fundamental changes, and without the respectively preceding ones, the arising of the respectively following ones is not possible. This is comparable to there being no chance for the stem and so on of a plant growing if there is no fundamental change of its seed into its sprout. For the respective fundamental changes along the path, both the conventional terms for these fundamental changes and their actualities apply, just as the actuality of the buddhabhūmi is called "the path of nonlearning."

Third, what is taken as the basis for being designated as "a saṃsāric person" is a continuum of the contaminated skandhas. Likewise, what is taken as the basis for being designated as "a nirvāṇic person" is the fundamental change of this continuum into being uncontaminated. Without that fundamental change there would be no basis for designating the sheer continuum of the skandhas (such as the mind) as a nirvāṇic person, just as there is no such basis during the phase of the skandhas not having undergone that fundamental change before. Furthermore, there would be no basis for designating the persons who have passed into nirvāṇa within the dhātu without any remainder of the skandhas (as asserted by the śrāvakas and pratyekabuddhas) as "those who have passed into nirvāṇa." For if there were no fundamental change, such a designation would be a name without any basis, just like the term "horns of a rabbit." You may think, "Even if there is no fundamental change here, what is wrong with that? To designate the mere cessation of the previous skandhas as 'nirvāṇa' is just like referring to the termination of an illness as 'being without illness.'" If there is the certainty that the continuum of the previous skandhas has become extinct and does not arise again, it is exactly this that represents the existence of the fundamental change of that continuum. For this fundamental change consists of both the support for the certainty that "this person has passed into nirvāṇa and does not fall into saṃsāra again" and the basis for such a designation. Therefore, one cannot claim that such a fundamental change does not exist. However, if one claims its nonexistence, the extinction and the lack of rearising of the continuum of the previous skandhas do not exist either because both the support and the basis of designation of this extinction and lack of rearising do not exist. Though bodhisattvas, through the path of the mahāyāna, also pass into nirvāṇa within the dhātu without any remainder of the contaminated skandhas, they pass into the particular nirvāṇa in which the stream of uncontaminated kāyas and wisdoms is uninterrupted. In that case, there is obviously no need to mention that this represents the nature of their fundamental change.

Fourth, the flaw of there being no basis for designating the differences between the three types of enlightenment is by virtue of these types of enlightenment actually being classified due to the differences of their respective fundamental changes. That is, the three types of enlightenment must be presented by virtue of the differences in terms of their being pure of certain parts of the obscurations or of all of them. However, without the fundamental change there would be no basis for designating such differences. At the time of passing into nirvāṇa within the dhātu without any remainders of the skandhas, there would be no basis with regard to which one could designate these differences between the three types of enlightenment. Therefore, all explanations on their qualities of relinquishment and realization being greater or lesser and so on would be pointless, just like explanations on whether the son of a barren woman is handsome or not.

As for the examples of space, gold, and water, MC[320] says that, in terms of their actual mode of being, all phenomena are primordially without any stains (such as apprehender and apprehended). However, this actual mode of being is obscured under the sway of mistakenness and thus, in terms of their mode of appearance, phenomena appear as if being impure. During that time one says that they "did not undergo a fundamental change." Once the actual mode of being and the mode of appearance concord in all respects through the power of these stains having been eliminated by the path, the final fundamental change is attained. You may wonder, "Isn't it the case that the nature of phenomena is not feasible as having the nature of primordial purity, but actually entails a change because it entails two different phases—not having and having undergone the fundamental change?" This is not the case. Primordially pure space is associated with adventitious fog and so on; gold, with dirt; water, with silt; and the sun, with obscurations such as clouds, but their respective natures are not impaired by these obscurations. Also, when their natures free from these obscurations have become manifest, it is not that these natures arise newly. Likewise, it is through the power of having become free from adventitious stains that the fundamental change is attained. This fundamental change is to be understood as merely the fact that the actuality of natural luminosity, which did not appear before by virtue of having been obscured by adventitious stains, appears later by virtue of the power of the path.

Khenpo Lodho Zangpo's LZC[321] glosses the fundamental change as "the fundamental change of emptiness and dependent origination" in the sense of realizing that "the nature [of phenomena] is emptiness and appearances are dependent origination." The three examples for the fundamental change at the end of DDV refer to a dispute about what is unconditioned. In itself, the fundamental change is not something that entails change. For, though the phenomena that appear as the conditioned bearers of the nature of phenomena undergo a fundamental change, in the nature of phenomena—emptiness free from reference points—any nature is not established, and therefore change is not established either. LZC follows DDVV in saying that the fundamental change is taught through the examples of gold and water as being congruent with their properties only in terms of their qualities, without considering their respective (material) substances. However, contrary to DDVV ("Through the example of space, however, it is taught in its entirety"), LZC explains that, though the example of space concords with the fundamental change in terms of its (immaterial) substance, it is only an example that concords with a fraction of the qualities of the fundamental change, but not in its entirety. For *Uttaratantra* IV.96cd says:

> It is similar to space and yet dissimilar
> In that [the latter] is not the basis of virtue.[322]

Conclusion

As the variety of the above descriptions of the notion of "fundamental change" show, there is a development of this concept in Buddhist texts, ranging from a simple replacement of a defiled psychophysical structure with a purified psychophysical structure through entirely mental forms of fundamental change to the mere revelation of the primordially existing ultimate nature of the mind through the change that consists of recognizing the adventitious nature of the stains that seem to have obscured it, without any change or replacement of anything by anything.

As illustrated by the texts presented above, the "foundation" in the term "fundamental change" may refer to the body, the entirety of one's psychophysical existence (*ātmabhāva*), the five skandhas, the physical and/or mental impregnations of negative tendencies, the six inner āyatanas, the impure or afflicted dependent nature, the ālaya-consciousness, all eight consciousnesses, adventitious stains, the impure elements of the mind stream, suchness, emptiness, the nature of phenomena, the dharmadhātu, nonconceptual wisdom, the nature of the mind, or *tathāgatagarbha*. "Change" may refer to the removal of something (either the removal of something in something or the removal of this very something) and its being explicitly or implicitly replaced by something else, the purification of something, the change of something into something else, the revealing of something without any change within this something through merely eliminating what obscured it, (or the very foundation within which any of the above "changes" take place, but which remains changeless itself). Thus, the outcome of this process may be something entirely new, a new form of something preexisting, or the unobscured manifestation of what existed primordially. Though some texts do not explicitly specify the result of the fundamental change, others identify it in many different ways, such as the purified dependent nature, the pure elements of the mind stream, stainless suchness, purified emptiness, the uncontaminated dharmadhātu, the dharmakāya, all kinds of masteries (over phenomena, wisdom, and so on), or the *tathāgatagarbha* endowed with twofold purity (naturally pure and pure of adventitious stains). According to Paramārtha's translations and works (preserved only in Chinese), the fundamental change refers to the change of the ālaya-consciousness into "the pure consciousness" (*amalavijñāna*).

In sum, when the *āśraya* in *āśrayaparivṛtti* is the psychophysical continuum of an ordinary being or the ālaya-consciousness, it is to be removed and replaced by something else, but when it refers to the nature of phenomena or buddha nature, it is to be revealed. However, with Schmithausen, one could also say that the purification of suchness and so on as *āśraya* is only a special case of *āśrayaparivṛtti*'s general principle of eliminating afflictions or impurities, that is, one in which the nature of what changes (suchness and so on) is not affected, while what seems to be "removed" are only adventitious stains that never really existed in the first place. Thus, while some Yogācāra texts still refer to a process of nonconceptual wisdom and/or the qualities of the dharmakāya being developed or gradually increasing along the path, others speak clearly about merely revealing what has always been present as ultimate reality.

Despite their great variety, all these descriptions of the fundamental change entail both a negative aspect (relinquishment) and a positive aspect (attainment or purity), thus usually designating both a process and its outcome. By keeping in mind that the term "fundamental change" is used in Yogācāra texts sometimes to refer more to the first and sometimes more to the second aspect, many seeming contradictions in their differing ways of describing or applying this term can be resolved.

All of this also shows that the most common translation of *āśrayaparivṛtti* as "transformation of the basis" may be appropriate in certain cases, but as far as unchanging suchness, the dharmadhātu, natural purity, buddha nature, or the luminous nature of the mind are concerned, the whole point of the notion of "fundamental change" is that there is absolutely no transformation of anything into anything else. Rather, the revelation of mind's primordially pure state, which from the perspective of the path appears as fruitional enlightenment, only manifests as a change from the perspective of deluded mind—mind seeming to be obscured before and then unobscured later. This is definitely the meaning of "fundamental change" in the *Dharmadharmatāvibhāga*, the *Uttaratantra*, and others of the above works. As explained there, this kind of fundamental change does not refer to any change in nature, just as the sun first being covered by clouds and then being free from clouds would not be called a transformation of the clouds into the sun, or even any transformation of the sun itself. It is solely from the perspective of those who watch the sun that its state seems to have changed in terms of first being with and then without clouds. It is clear that the presence or absence of clouds does not affect the nature of the sun itself in any way, but just our perception of it. In fact, for the sun itself, there is not even a question of whether it has transformed or changed, let alone how. In this vein, *Mahāyānasūtrālaṃkāra* IX.22 says:

> Though without difference between before and after,
> It is immaculate in terms of all obscurations.
> Being neither pure nor impure,
> Suchness is held to be buddhahood.

Sthiramati's commentary explains the unchanging nature of suchness as the emptiness that is always empty and naturally luminous, be it at the time of being an ordinary person or a buddha. The removal of adventitious stains is as adventitious as these stains themselves:

> "Purity" is said to mean having the nature of being afflicted before and then the stains having become nonexistent later through having cultivated the path, with "before" referring to the time of an ordinary being, and "later" to the time of full buddhahood. But the dharmakāya of a buddha is held to be of the nature of suchness, emptiness. Emptiness has the nature of being empty and naturally luminous even at the time of ordinary beings. Also later, at the time of full buddhahood, it has the nature of being empty and naturally luminous. Therefore, in its nature of purity, there is no difference. Since there is nothing to be purified in that [nature], it is not pure. Nevertheless, at the time of fully perfect buddhahood, through the power of having cultivated the path, the adventitious stains—afflictive obscurations and cognitive obscurations—become nonexistent. Thus, since [suchness] becomes pure later, this is the meaning of [its] "not being impure either."[323]

Mahāyānasūtrālaṃkāra XIII.18–19 declares:

> When murky water becomes clear,
> [Its] transparency does not arise from elsewhere,
> But is just its becoming free from pollution.
> The same goes for the purity of your own mind.

It is held that mind, which is always naturally luminous,
Is [only] blemished by adventitious flaws.
It is stated that there is no other mind apart from
The naturally luminous mind of dharmatā.

Sthiramati[324] comments that what is referred to as "murky water having become pure" means nothing but that its primordially existing natural transparency appears upon having become separated from adventitious pollution. In other words, water never has the nature of pollution, but is naturally clear and transparent. Likewise, naturally pure mind is said to have become pure upon being freed from adventitious stains. Naturally pure luminous mind covered by adventitious stains is like a pure crystal—when covered by mud, its purity is not seen. "Naturally pure mind" refers to the nondual dharmatā of the mind, that is, the perfect nature, whereas any other kinds of mind—the minds that represent the dependent nature—are not explained to be pure mind. For dependent minds are always stained by the afflictions and other mental factors, and they also arise and cease momentarily. Therefore, they are not suitable as naturally luminous mind. On the other hand, the perfect nature is said to be naturally luminous because it is not stained by saṃsāric contaminations and does not arise and cease momentarily. Thus, naturally pure luminous mind refers to the suchness of mind.

Furthermore, when Yogācāra texts speak about "change" in terms of the eight consciousnesses or adventitious stains, they usually do not refer to a real change since all these consciousnesses or stains are typically explained to be delusive and illusionlike, and thus actually nonexistent in the first place. The only "change" is the realization of exactly this fact. Thus, there is actually no change in terms of the object, but only in terms of the realizing subject, which again happens only from the perspective of the (seemingly) evolving wisdom of the path, but not in terms of the fundamentally unchanging nature of nonconceptual wisdom. Therefore, at any given time on the path, there is never any change in substance or nature (both on the side of what is to be relinquished and the side of what is to be attained)—all that happens is a cognitive change, or a change in one's outlook on oneself and the world. Thus, there is only a revelation of the way things actually have always been once the delusion of what is projected onto it is seen through. In addition, nonconceptual wisdom as both the underlying foundation and the result of this fundamental change is clearly described in terms of the dynamics of an enlightened mind, and not as sheer emptiness or an inert state. Consequently, as far as the notion of "fundamental change" refers to this process of uncovering mind's fundamental nature, even when it is sometimes described in Buddhist texts as if there were a transformation of one "entity" into another "entity," or of something impure (such as the skandhas or mental afflictions) into something pure (such as the pure skandhas or wisdoms), this is just a conventional or expedient way of teaching. As the Eighth Karmapa's commentary on the *Abhisamayālaṃkāra* says:

> Those present-day followers of [Mahā]mudrā whose confusion is even a hundred thousand times bigger than this exclaim, "Through refining the ālaya-consciousness into something pure, it turns into the result of mirrorlike wisdom." This is not justified for the following reasons. Something like this does not appear in any of the traditions of the mahāyāna, and what does not appear [there also] does not appear in the sense of something that is obtained through reasoning. A presentation of the ālaya-consciousness as the cause and mirrorlike wisdom as its result is not something that is obtained through reasoning. Rather, with respect to the mode of being of causes and results in terms of [such] causes and results in the abhidharma that actually fulfill these functions[325] (that is, what produces and what is produced), the ālaya-consciousness and mirrorlike wisdom are not adequate as a cause and a result that fully qualify as such. Also, since the very nature of the ālaya-consciousness is [nothing but] the adventitious stains, it is presented as impure. No matter how it may be refined by something else, it will not turn into something pure. It is not possible within the sphere of knowable objects that something impure turns into something pure, or that something pure turns into something impure.[326]

This also highlights the two reasons why, from the perspective of the path, any fundamental change is possible at all. First, what seems to "change" (the adventitious stains) can appear to change precisely because it is merely an unreal and deceiving mental construct in the first place. Secondly, these fictitious mental projections are only superimposed onto, and occur nowhere else than within, the undeceiving ground of true reality, which is their actual nature, just to be revealed. In other words, though sentient beings' delusional seeming reality has no beginning, for individual beings it can end. On the other hand, ultimate reality has neither beginning nor end.

Thus, realizing buddhahood means nothing but to recognize the true nature of the mind, which can never be altered through its opposites, such as mistakenness and afflictions. Once the latter are fully seen through and recognized as adventitious illusory phenomena, mind will not revert to them. In other words, unlike water being reheatable over and again, once the nature of the mind is known directly for what it is, it is impossible to unknow it. As Dharmakīrti says in his *Pramāṇavārttika*:

> The nature without adversity
> That is actual reality is not harmed
> Through what is contrary, even with effort,
> Since mind [naturally] settles in its [own] sphere.[327]

As for when the fundamental change takes place, as seen above, it is mostly explained as happening on the buddhabhūmi. However, *Mahāyānasūtrālaṃkāra* XIV.28–29 and the *Bodhisattvabhūmi* say that the first occurrence of the fundamental change is on the first bhūmi, while the *Mahāyānasūtrālaṃkārabhāṣya* on VI.9 and XI.34 also relates the fundamental change to the path of familiarization.[328] Thus, in a more general sense, as also the *Mahāyānasūtrālaṃkāra*'s above verses on the fundamental change of the eight consciousnesses on different bhūmis show, the notion of fundamental change can be understood as a continuous process throughout the ten bhūmis that culminates in the attainment of buddhahood as the final fundamental change. What is common to every level of this process is that the respective changes are irreversible, though they are further enhanced and expanded up to the buddhabhūmi.

Nonconceptual wisdom

The above discussions of the fundamental change in a variety of texts already included a number of explanations on nonconceptual wisdom, but the primary Indian Buddhist texts that systematically discuss this topic are the *Dharmadharmatāvibhāga* and the *Mahāyānasaṃgraha*. Thus, the following presentation of nonconceptual wisdom is not an exhaustive documentation of this topic in Buddhist literature (which is far beyond the scope of this study), but is limited to those two texts and excerpts from their commentaries as well as some additional materials from the *Mahāyānasūtrālaṃkāra*, the *Kāyatrayāvatāramukha*, and the latter's commentary.

Nonconceptual wisdom in the *Dharmadharmatāvibhāga*[329]

In general, DDV says that nonconceptual wisdom is the foundation or support (*āśraya*) of the fundamental change (the sixth point in the text's explanation of *āśrayaparivṛtti*). However, it is not taken as the foundation that changes or the result of the fundamental change (which is suchness or the nature of phenomena). Rather, DDVV explains nonconceptual wisdom as being the cause of the fundamental change because the latter is attained through the former. Likewise, GC says that the direct cause of the fundamental change is nonconceptual wisdom, which is in turn caused by proper mental engagement (point seven of the explanation of the fundamental change in DDV). In detail, nonconceptual wisdom is explained through the following six points.

(1) The four focal objects of nonconceptual wisdom consist of the mahāyāna teachings, aspiring for them, gaining certainty about them, and completing the accumulations of merit and wisdom. This means to first rely on spiritual friends who teach the vast and profound mahāyāna. Based on that, aspiration for the dharma taught by them arises, followed by gaining doubt-free certainty about it through reasonings that are inspired by one's aspiration, and completing the accumulations by way of mentally engaging in a proper manner in the meaning about which one has gained certainty. However, if one of these four factors is missing, the result of nonconceptual wisdom will not arise.

(2) The relinquishment of characteristics through nonconceptual wisdom refers to the four kinds of conceptions about antagonistic factors, their remedies, suchness, and realization. (a) The antagonistic factors consist of the afflictions and the fourfold clinging to impermanent sentient beings as being permanent; to what is empty and conditioned as being real entities; to saṃsāra (which has the nature of the three sufferings) as being really existent; and to identityless phenomena as having an identity. These are characteristics of mistakenness because they cause bondage in saṃsāra. (b) The remedies consist of the antidotes for the afflictions (such as the meditation on repulsiveness as an antidote for desire) and understanding what is conditioned as being impermanent, everything imaginary as being empty, all beings in saṃsāra as not being beyond the three sufferings, and nirvāṇa as being peace because all phenomena are identityless and free from being "mine." These are the remedies of saṃsāra because they liberate from nonvirtue. (c) However, if one clings to those factors to be relinquished and their remedies as characteristics, one will not be liberated. Since they are without arising and ceasing, they are unconditioned by nature. This is the suchness of all phenomena, which is the ultimate remedy of both antagonistic factors and remedies. It is the focal object of nonconceptual wisdom, but in order for nonconceptual wisdom to arise, any conceptions about this suchness are to be relinquished too. (d) The characteristic of realization refers to conceptions about the cognizing subject of suchness, that is, all realizations on the path, training in and perfecting the qualities, and the fruition of buddhahood with its enlightened activity. The first two characteristics of the factors to be relinquished and their remedies are gradually eliminated on the paths of accumulation and preparation; the

characteristic of suchness, on the seven impure bhūmis; and the characteristic of realization, on the three pure bhūmis.

(3) The fourfold correct yogic practice to attain nonconceptual wisdom consists of the four *prayoga*s of observing all phenomena as being nothing other than mere mind, thus not observing any phenomena as external objects, consequently not observing any observer of external objects either, and finally observing the suchness that is the unobservability of the duality of apprehender and apprehended. These four make up the levels of heat, peak, poised readiness, and the supreme dharma of the path of preparation. This is the progressive way in which nonconceptual wisdom is generated in the mind stream because it is easy to realize that external referents lack a nature of their own, while it is more difficult to realize that the apprehender is unobservable too.

(4) Nonconceptual wisdom is defined through three characteristics—resting in the very essence of the nature of phenomena, resting in it without appearances, and resting in it with appearances. (a) Nonconceptual wisdom abides or rests in the nondual and inexpressible nature of phenomena as its focal object. (b) What does not appear for this wisdom are duality, designations, sense faculties, objects, cognizance, and an external world since all phenomena that appear in these ways are obscurations of nonconceptual wisdom. Thus, if these phenomena do not appear, the nature of phenomena will appear. This nonconceptual wisdom cannot be grasped as the duality of apprehender and apprehended because nonduality is its very nature. It cannot be demonstrated through any designations to express it. It is not grounded on the sense faculties. It lacks any appearance of objects, such as form. It is not cognizance because it is without anything to be aware of and anything that is aware. It is without base because it is not an entity that is a base. (c) The manner in which all phenomena appear for nonconceptual wisdom is that during meditative equipoise they appear equal to space since nonconceptual wisdom lacks all characteristics of a cognizing subject and all clinging to any characteristics. During subsequent attainment phenomena appear as the union of appearance and emptiness, just like illusions, dreams, and so on, because they are realized to be unreal.

(5) The fourfold benefit of nonconceptual wisdom is the attainment of the dharmakāya, including its enlightened activity, by virtue of the ultimate fundamental change of being free from the two obscurations, supreme uncontaminated bliss beyond all forms of contaminated bliss due to having attained all buddha qualities, mastery over the pure, spontaneous, and unmistaken seeing of the suchness and the variety of all knowable objects, and mastery over the many ways of teaching as they are appropriate for different beings. The first two benefits represent one's own welfare, while the latter two are the welfare of others.

(6) Among the fourfold thorough knowledge of nonconceptual wisdom, (a) the knowledge about its being a remedy refers to nonconceptual wisdom remedying the fivefold clinging to what is nonexistent: (1)–(2) clinging to nonexistent phenomena and persons as being referents and having an identity, (3) clinging to nonexistent change (clinging to the arising and ceasing of nonexistent phenomena), (4) clinging to a difference between phenomena and the nature of phenomena, while there is no difference, and (5) clinging to the denial of taking phenomena and persons to be utterly nonexistent because of denying their nominal imputed existence. The first four clingings are superimpositions because of clinging to what is ultimately nonexistent as being existent, while the fifth one represents the denial of the conventional existence of mere appearances.

(b) The thorough knowledge of the defining characteristic of nonconceptual wisdom refers to the exclusion of five misconceptions about what nonconceptual wisdom is. (1) Nonconceptual wisdom is not the total absence of mental engagement. Though the cognitions of small children or someone just being spaced out do not engage in the reference points of worldly conventions, these beings are not liberated through that. In nonconceptual wisdom's direct seeing of the nature of phenomena, all reference points have vanished. Without any reference point on the object side to engage in anymore, on the subject side any mental engagement in such reference points naturally subsides. However, this does not mean that this wisdom lacks wakefulness and one-pointed sharp mindfulness. It is also not without any cognitive capacity and clarity since it directly realizes the nature of phenomena without any dualistic split into apprehender and apprehended. (2) Nor is nonconceptual wisdom the transcendence of conceptions in the sense of lacking any coarse or subtle conceptual analysis. Therefore, though all mundane meditative states from the second dhyāna of the form realm onward are without such analysis, they lack the qualities of nonconceptual wisdom. (3) Nonconceptual wisdom is not the complete subsiding of conceptions either. Otherwise, being asleep, intoxicated, having fainted, and the meditative absorption of cessation[330] would also qualify as nonconceptual wisdom. (4) Nor is nonconceptual wisdom something like inert and unconscious matter, which simply lacks conceptions by its very nature. (5) Nonconceptual wisdom is also not the picturing of nonconceptuality. This means that the actual defining characteristic of nonconceptual wisdom is that which observes true reality. Unlike in a visual consciousness and so on, the nature of that realization does not involve any variety or multiplicity. Thus, nonconceptuality means completely letting go of all discursiveness and reference points, in particular with regard to true reality, such as trying to pinpoint a certain meditative experience, thinking, "This is nonconceptuality." Naturally, nonconceptual wisdom does not just mean a state of trying not to think or imagine anything either, or just trying to think, "I shall not think." For all such cases are simply subtle thoughts or grasping.

In sum, nonconceptual wisdom means not seeing anything to be observed, nor apprehending anything as anything whatsoever. However, this perceptual mode is actually the seeing of the suchness of all phenomena. From the perspective of ordinary beings, nonconceptual wisdom cannot be demonstrated at once in an affirmative manner. Therefore, though its nature is to not conceive of anything, through unerringly realizing that the nature of phenomena is unobservable as anything whatsoever, nonconceptual wisdom does not apprehend it as anything. However, this wisdom is not taught to be nonconceptual by virtue of not cognizing anything at all or by virtue of a total cessation of cognition. Therefore, though nonconceptual wisdom does not conceive of any reference points at all, within the sphere of the basic nature being unobservable the appearances of personally experienced wisdom dawn from within.

(c) The knowledge of the distinctive features of the nonconceptual wisdom of buddhas and bodhisattvas refers to its being superior to the wisdoms of śrāvakas and pratyekabuddhas through five points. Śrāvakas and pratyekabuddhas conceive of saṃsāra as a flaw and of nirvāṇa as a quality. Their wisdoms are limited because they focus merely on the general characteristics of the four realities of the noble ones. They also abide somewhere because they abide in nirvāṇa. Their wisdoms are not lasting either because they become extinct in the nirvāṇa without remainder. Also, they are surpassed by buddha wisdom. On the other hand, the wisdom of buddhas and bodhisattvas is (1) nonconceptual because it does not conceive of flaws or qualities in terms of saṃsāra and nirvāṇa. (2) It is unlimited because it takes as its objects the specific and general characteristics of all knowable objects, precisely as they are. Or it is not limited in terms of relinquishment and realization, but completely perfect. (3) It is nonabiding. For through prajñā and compassion, respectively, it does not abide in either saṃsāra or nirvāṇic peace and therefore neither adopts nirvāṇa nor rejects saṃsāra. (4) It is lasting because, by virtue of the dharmakāya as its foundation being permanent, its continuum does not even become extinct in the nirvāṇa without remainder and therefore always operates for the welfare of beings as long as saṃsāra lasts. (5) It is unsurpassable because there is nothing more supreme than it. In brief, the wisdom of buddhas and bodhisattvas is taught to be nonconceptual because of the purity of saṃsāra and nirvāṇa, knowing all that is to be known by wisdom, and being the unity of emptiness and compassion (that is, having attained the unconditioned dharmakāya).

(d) The knowledge of the fivefold function of nonconceptual wisdom refers to (1) its distancing itself from the movement of conceptions because it has overcome the arising of the latent tendencies of ignorance about suchness. (2) It accomplishes unsurpassable, unmistaken, and lasting bliss because of realizing the suchness and variety of all knowable objects. (3) It makes one attain the freedom from all afflictive and cognitive obscurations because it overcomes all contaminations, including their latent tendencies. (4) The wisdom that is attained subsequent to the nonconceptual wisdom during meditative equipoise engages unimpededly in all aspects of knowable objects. (5) By virtue of the great fundamental change of all eight consciousnesses, nonconceptual wisdom purifies buddha realms, matures sentient beings, and grants omniscience. These five functions accomplish the fruition that consists of the three kāyas.

As mentioned above, in terms of their contents, points seven and eight (mental engagement and training) of DDV's presentation of the fundamental change also pertain to nonconceptual wisdom. DDVV explicitly includes these two points under its discussion of nonconceptual wisdom, saying that point seven belongs to the defining characteristics of nonconceptual wisdom, while point eight elucidates the training in order to attain this wisdom.

In more detail, DDVV explains the mental engagement in nonconceptual wisdom as follows. For ordinary beings, false imagination (the ālaya-consciousness, from which the other seven consciousnesses arise) appears, while actually not existing. Due to its seeming appearance, the actually existing nature of phenomena does not appear. However, once false imagination does not appear anymore due to having been recognized as what it is (unreal), the nature of phenomena appears naturally. The manner in which bodhisattvas mentally engage in nonconceptual wisdom is through the four yogic practices. By virtue of observing that false imagination appears, but does not exist, they engage in observing everything as mere cognizance, because cognizance is the appearing of duality. By virtue of observing everything as mere cognizance, they engage in not observing any referents because it is nothing but cognizance that appears as referents, and therefore external referents do not exist. By virtue of not observing any referents, they engage in not observing mere cognizance either because it is not established as this very cognizance. For if there are no referents to be cognized, cognizance is not reasonable. By virtue of not observing this cognizance (that is, by virtue of not observing apprehender and apprehended), they engage in observing the lack of difference between those two. For apprehender and apprehended are not different since they do not exist as two in the first place. Thus, the very nonobservation of apprehender and apprehended is the observation of the lack of difference between these two because a difference can only be cognized if there are two distinct phenomena. This is the manner of mental engagement on the path of preparation resulting in the path of seeing. Thus, the eventual nonobservation of apprehender and apprehended—that is, the observation of nondual suchness—represents nonconceptual wisdom. This nonconceptual wisdom lacks any external or internal objects, as in the case of the eyes and so on. It is also free from being a subject that observes any objects because it is characterized by not observing any characteristics whatsoever.

Finally, the entire progression of the training in order to attain nonconceptual wisdom consists of the five paths.

Nonconceptual wisdom in the *Mahāyānasaṃgraha*

Besides this explanation of nonconceptual wisdom in DDV and its commentaries, the most extensive discussion of this topic in Indian Buddhist literature is found in the eighth chapter of the *Mahāyānasaṃgraha* and its commentaries by Vasubandhu and Asvabhāva.[331] The text presents nonconceptual wisdom—superior prajñā—primarily through the seventeen points of (1) its nature, (2) its matrix, (3) its basis, (4) what is observed, (5) its cognitive aspect, (6) answer to objections, (7) its being a support, (8) its aids, (9) its maturation, (10) its natural outflow, (11) its outcome, (12) its culmination, (13) its benefits, (14) its classification, (15) its examples, (16) its effortless accomplishment of activity, and (17) its profundity.

(1) Similar to what is said in point (6b) in DDV above, the nature of nonconceptual wisdom refers to the exclusion of five aspects—(a) the complete lack of mental engagement, (b) mental states beyond the levels that entail examination and analysis, (c) the cessation of discriminations and feelings, (d) the nature of form, and (e) picturing true reality.

(2) As for the matrix of nonconceptual wisdom, it does not arise from mind in the sense that it does not function like ordinary consciousness (thinking or focusing on referents). On the other hand, without any mind at all, nonconceptual wisdom cannot manifest either. For otherwise it would just be like matter.

(3) The basis or cause of nonconceptual wisdom is the proper mental engagement in the latent tendencies for listening, which results in the correct familiarization with the Buddha's teachings.

(4) What is observed by nonconceptual wisdom is the inexpressibility of phenomena—the suchness of identitylessness.

(5) The cognitive aspect of nonconceptual wisdom is signlessness with regard to its observed object, which means to refrain from mentally engaging in any characteristics. Thus, it is the very lack of any cognitive aspects that is nonconceptual wisdom's unique cognitive aspect.

(6) It may be objected, "If all phenomena are inexpressible, what do we conceive of?" Meaning only derives from correctly pronouncing (verbally or mentally) a sequence of syllables, thus conceptually connecting them. As for

the reason why all phenomena are inexpressible, though the object of expression and what expresses it are mutually dependent, their nature is entirely different. The object one wishes to express is a specifically characterized phenomenon that can be perceived directly, while the means to express that object is a term or image in the conceptual mind. Since a conceptual image can never really capture the uniqueness of a concrete object, nothing is ever expressed.

(7) Nonconceptual wisdom is the support of all activities of bodhisattvas during subsequent attainment because they flourish through it.

(8) The aids of nonconceptual wisdom are the other five pāramitās.

(9) The maturation of nonconceptual wisdom is twofold. Through making efforts in cultivating nonconceptual wisdom, one is born into the maṇḍala of a nairmāṇikakāya. Through attaining the actuality of nonconceptual wisdom, one is born into the maṇḍala of a sāmbhogikakāya. This twofold maturation is the very remedy for the ordinary maturation of karmic actions.

(10) The natural outflow of nonconceptual wisdom consists of its specific ways of manifesting and flourishing in all subsequent lives by way of being continuously reborn into the above two buddha maṇḍalas.

(11) The outcome of nonconceptual wisdom consists of the ten bhūmis. The first bhūmi is the primary outcome of nonconceptual wisdom because the very essence of all bhūmis is attained on it. During the remaining nine bhūmis, nonconceptual wisdom is progressively perfected in all its aspects.

(12) The culmination of nonconceptual wisdom happens due to attaining the three pure kāyas and the ten masteries over lifespan and so on.

(13) The benefit of wisdom is to be like space in three ways. Just like space, the wisdom due to preparatory application is untainted by coarse evil actions. This is caused by one's confidence and devoted interest in actual nonconceptual wisdom, which serves as the remedy for falling into the lower realms. Just like space, the actual nonconceptual wisdom is untainted by any obscurations and is endowed with attainment and perfection. When bodhisattvas demonstrate rebirths in all kinds of worldly realms, their wisdom of subsequent attainment is untainted by worldly phenomena, just like space.

(14) The classification of nonconceptual wisdom is that the wisdom due to preparatory application is like a mute wishing to experience an object, but not experiencing it and also not being able to speak about it. The actual nonconceptual wisdom is like a mute experiencing that object, but still not being able to express it. Subsequently attained wisdom is like a person who experiences that object and is also able to speak about it. Or these three wisdoms are respectively like the five sense consciousnesses wishing to experience an object, but not experiencing it and also not being able to conceptualize it; those five consciousnesses experiencing that object; and the mental consciousness both experiencing and conceptualizing that object. Or they are like someone

not knowing a treatise and wishing to know it, experiencing the dharma, and experiencing its meaning, respectively.

(15) The examples for nonconceptual wisdom and subsequently attained wisdom are a person with closed eyes and open eyes, respectively. Or nonconceptual wisdom is like space—it is all-pervasive since all phenomena are pervaded by the single taste of emptiness; it is untainted since all those phenomena do not affect it; and it neither has any conceptions nor can it be conceived by others. Subsequently attained wisdom is like forms appearing in that space since it can be conceived.

(16) The nonconceptual and effortless activity of nonconceptual wisdom is like wish-fulfilling jewels and celestial cymbals performing their specific activities without any thoughts or efforts.

(17) The profundity of nonconceptual wisdom is that it never bears on one thing or any other thing, is neither knowledge nor nonknowledge, and is not different from what it knows. Since there is nothing to be conceived, all phenomena are naturally nonconceptual. For all these reasons this wisdom is nonconceptuality.

Furthermore, for the nonconceptual flux of wisdom, there is no appearance of any referents. Hence, it is to be realized that referents do not exist, and without them there is no cognizance either.

Nonconceptual wisdom is in fact nothing other than prajñāpāramitā, which fully completes all pāramitās by way of abandoning five kinds of abiding—(1) the tīrthikas' abiding in the clinging to a self, (2) abiding in the conceptions of bodhisattvas who do not yet see true reality, (3) abiding in the two extremes of saṃsāra and nirvāṇa, (4) abiding in the clinging of being content with just the relinquishment of the afflictive obscurations, and (5) abiding in the dhātu of the nirvāṇa without any remainder of the skandhas and thus disregarding the welfare of sentient beings.

The five points of difference between the wisdoms of śrāvakas and bodhisattvas are the same as in point (6c) in DDV above, but they are explained a little bit differently. Unlike the wisdom of śrāvakas, the one of bodhisattvas is (1) nonconceptual since it does not conceive of any phenomena; (2) unlimited in terms of realizing true reality in an exhaustive manner, engaging in all aspects of all knowable objects, and serving the welfare of all sentient beings; (3) nonabiding since it is the nonabiding nirvāṇa; (4) everlasting since it never becomes exhausted in the dhātu of nirvāṇa; and (5) unsurpassed since there is no yāna more superior to it.

Nonconceptual wisdom in the *Mahāyānasūtrālaṃkāra*

Apart from the statements about nonconceptual wisdom in the *Mahāyānasūtrālaṃkāra* found above in the context of the fundamental change, verses VI.6–10 describe the bodhisattva's approach to nonconceptual wisdom throughout the five paths:[332]

> Having gathered the utterly infinite accumulations
> Of merit and wisdom, bodhisattvas
> Gain certainty in their reflection about phenomena,
> Thus realizing that the way of being of referents derives from
> [mental] discourse.[333]
>
> Once they understand that referents are mere discourse,
> They dwell in the mere mind that appears as those [referents].
> Then they directly realize the dharmadhātu
> Free from the characteristics of duality.
>
> The mind is aware that nothing other than mind exists.
> Then it is realized that mind does not exist either.
> The intelligent ones are aware that both do not exist
> And abide in the dharmadhātu, in which these are absent.
>
> The power of the nonconceptual wisdom of the intelligent,
> Which is always and in all respects accompanied by equality,
> Clears the dense thicket of the collection of flaws on that foundation,
> Just as a great antidote does with poison.
>
> Being well established in the excellent dharma spoken by the sage
> And having placed their insight in the dharmadhātu of the root,
> The wise realize that the flow of mindfulness is mere conception
> And travel swiftly to the far shore of the ocean of qualities.

Vasubandhu's, Sthiramati's and Asvabhāva's commentaries agree that VI.6–9 refer to the paths of accumulation, preparation, seeing, and familiarization, though they present slightly different boundary lines for the first three paths. According to Vasubandhu and Sthiramati, VI.10 teaches the greatness of ultimate nonconceptual wisdom, and Sthiramati and Asvabhāva say that VI.10 corresponds to the final path of nonlearning.

Sthiramati explains that, among the two kinds of the ultimate, verses VI.1–5 have taught the ultimate that is true reality. Verses VI.6–10 teach the ultimate that has the characteristic of nonconceptual wisdom in order to show how bodhisattvas realize phenomenal identitylessness through that nonconceptual wisdom and thus attain buddhahood. In particular, verses VI.6–9 teach the extraordinary means of bodhisattvas to attain nirvāṇa, that is, engaging in ultimate wisdom as the remedy for being oppressed by mistakenness.

In detail, in the first among these five verses, the accumulation of merit consists of paying homage and service to buddhas, while the accumulation of wisdom consists of listening to, reflecting, and meditating on the dharma taught by those buddhas. Or merit consists of practicing generosity, ethics, and patience for one incalculable eon, while wisdom refers to the cultivation of dhyāna and prajñā (vigor belongs to both accumulations). Or merit refers to the practice of the first five pāramitās, while wisdom is the cultivation of the pāramitā of prajñā. "Certainty in the reflection about phenomena" means that these bodhisattvas, based on their samādhi of familiarizing with all their accumulations of merit and wisdom as being impermanent, suffering, empty, and identityless, determine without any doubt that all phenomena, including the Buddha's teachings, are impermanent, suffering, empty, and identityless. Upon having gathered the two accumulations and gained certainty about phenomena in that way, bodhisattvas understand that all seemingly external referents arise from no other cause than mind's ongoing conceiving activity. At this point, they dwell in the samādhi of attaining the illumination of the prajñā of realizing that. Thus, the first three lines of VI.6 correspond to the path of accumulation, while the last line refers to the level of heat of the path of preparation.

The first line of the second verse means that bodhisattvas do not only understand but now see clearly and directly how apprehended phenomena arise from the mind, which is the samādhi of the increase of that illumination of prajñā (the level of peak). The second line says that they then rest in these phenomena as being mere mind free from anything apprehended, which is the samādhi of penetrating a part of true reality, that is, the lack of something apprehended (corresponding to the level of poised readiness). The third and fourth lines refer to the path of seeing on which, immediately after the last part of the path of preparation, nonconceptual wisdom directly perceives the dharmadhātu without apprehender and apprehended.

The third verse teaches the causes and means of how the dharmadhātu becomes manifest on the path of seeing (last line), thus referring to the level of the supreme dharma of the path of preparation (first three lines). At the time of poised readiness, the obscurations in terms of the apprehended are relinquished. At the time of the supreme dharma, bodhisattvas realize that, without anything apprehended, there is no apprehender either. They understand that there is no phenomenon outside of the mind and thus no mind that would apprehend such external phenomena. Thus, at the end of the level of the supreme dharma, the obscurations in terms of both apprehender and apprehended are relinquished and the path of seeing arises immediately after that, perceiving the dharmadhātu without any duality. Therefore, the last level of the path of preparation is referred to as the samādhi that immediately precedes the path of seeing. The direct realization of the dharmadhātu also means that all afflictions to be relinquished through seeing have been eliminated.[334]

The fourth verse teaches the path of familiarization. Through the power of the nonconceptual wisdom of bodhisattvas, the poison of the obscurations is continuously eliminated from the second through the tenth bhūmis. "In all respects accompanied by equality" refers to the entirety of both internal and external entities being seen as empty. This wisdom is called "nonconceptual" because of conceiving neither apprehender nor apprehended. "That foundation" refers to the ālaya-consciousness, that is, the dependent nature.[335] Thus, "the collection of flaws" consists of the latent tendencies of the afflictive obscurations and of apprehender and apprehended that exist in, and are based on, the ālaya-consciousness. These latent tendencies, which have been accumulated and clung to since beginningless time, are like a dense thicket because they are subtle and thus difficult to know and to relinquish. Just as a few drops of a powerful antidote can turn all the poison in a jar into medicine and are also able to eliminate poison when ingested, the nonconceptual wisdom of the path of familiarization eliminates the poisonlike subtle afflictions and so on that are to be relinquished through familiarization and they become something else—their fundamental change is the attainment of the nonconceptual wisdom of the buddhabhūmi.

As for the fifth verse, at the end of the path the insight of bodhisattvas is well established in the ultimate of the dharmas taught by the Buddha. As for "having placed their insight in the dharmadhātu of the root," the mind of bodhisattvas who engage in the ultimate wisdom and focus on the meanings of all the mahāyāna sūtras by combining them into one is called "root mind." Or this term refers to the mind of focusing on all the meanings of the dharmas of the mahāyāna as a whole without focusing on the distinct names, words, and letters of the mahāyāna sūtras. Through the insight or prajñā connected with this root mind, these bodhisattvas focus on the dharmadhātu, familiarize with it, and keep it in mind.[336] At that point, they even relinquish their understanding that the dharmas concordant with enlightenment and so on, about which they are mindful, arise from the mind stream and are mere mind. Such bodhisattvas who do not even conceive of mere mind are called "wise."[337] That they "travel swiftly to the far shore of the ocean of qualities" means that they quickly attain buddhahood with all its qualities, such as the ten powers and the four fearlessnesses.[338]

Furthermore, verse XIV.43 says that nonconceptual wisdom is what purifies all buddha qualities, while verses XVI.8–13 state that all six pāramitās are associated with nonconceptual wisdom. Vasubandhu[339] explains that this is so because they are connected with the realization of phenomenal identitylessness. Sthiramati[340] also says that nonconceptual wisdom is the means to completely perfect all the pāramitās.

Nonconceptual wisdom in the *Kāyatrayāvatāramukha* and its commentary

In addition to nonconceptual wisdom being discussed in Nāgamitra's *Kāyatrayāvatāramukha* in the context of the fundamental change as presented above, a number of its other verses provide further details on the characteristics of this wisdom. Verse 6 says:

> Apart from stainless suchness
> And nonconceptual wisdom,
> There are no other dharmas
> Of the buddhas whatsoever.

Jñānacandra's commentary[341] glosses "stainless" as "free from adventitious stains." Nonconceptual wisdom is what observes suchness, which means that is the wisdom in which what observes and what is observed are equal. All knowable objects have the nature of stainless suchness and nonconceptual wisdom because any other natures are delusive due to being objects that are reference points and because buddhas lack any reference points.

Verses 70–73 say:

> Just as it is asserted that the dharmadhātu
> Is constituted by nonduality,
> Nonconceptual wisdom too
> Is constituted by not seeing any duality.
>
> Since it is unconditioned, since it is nondual,
> And since it is the existence of nonduality,
> It is empty of being something previously nonexistent and so on.
> Nonduality is asserted to be other.
>
> What represent the clarity and unclarity
> Of nonconceptual wisdom
> Do not exist in all minds
> That are clear and unclear.

> The realization of what is nondual
> Is called "clarity."
> The realization of what is dual
> Should be understood as being unclarity.

Jñānacandra[342] explains that, just as the dharmadhātu is constituted by the lack of the false imaginary nature, wisdom is also characterized by seeing the lack of apprehender and apprehended.[343] However, it is not that, by virtue of nonconceptual wisdom not seeing any duality, it is one of the four kinds of nonexistents. Nonconceptual wisdom is neither something that did not exist before nor something that has become nonexistent after having been destroyed, because arising and ceasing appear only in conditioned phenomena. Nor is wisdom a case of something not existing in something else, such as a horse not existing in a cow or a cow not existing in a horse, since it is the lack of both apprehender and apprehended. However, being the lack of that duality does not mean that wisdom is something absolutely nonexistent since it exists as that very nonduality. If it were a nonentity, it would be nonexistent too, but since it is constituted by being nonduality, there is no flaw. Thus, nondual wisdom is the opposite of imaginary entities.

"The clarity and unclarity of nonconceptual wisdom" are its features that are not found in other kinds of mind. This does not mean that clarity and unclarity exist simultaneously in this wisdom, but they refer to different phases. Thus, "the realization of what is dual" refers to the perception of the pure mundane wisdom that is attained subsequent to supramundane wisdom ("the realization of what is nondual"). This pure mundane wisdom refers to the time of applying conventional terms because of realizing the two referents that are called "apprehender and apprehended."

Verse 77 and its commentary[344] say that, just as an arrow keeps flying by virtue of previously having been shot through the efforts of one's hands and so on, nonconceptual wisdom keeps operating through the force of previous aspiration prayers.

Verses 102–104 connect nonconceptual wisdom to the middle path and mere cognizance, with the latter being understood as dependent origination. The manner to give rise to nonconceptual wisdom is through cultivating the four yogic practices of observing everything as mere cognizance and so on as described above:

> The nonconceptual wisdom
> That arises from the middle path
> Cannot be attained
> Through the views of permanence or extinction.

What is called "the middle path"
Is not tenable here in any respect
As anything other, if examined by reasoning,
Than the very being of mere cognizance.

Those who wish for perfect enlightenment,
In order to give rise to nonconceptual wisdom,
Should always apply themselves
To familiarizing with mere cognizance.

According to the commentary,[345] if the middle path is analyzed, it is mere cognizance, which primarily refers to dependently arising entities. Since the dependent nature is sheer mistakenness and therefore appears as apprehender and apprehended, if it existed in the way it appears, it would represent the extreme of permanence or existence. But if it were nothing whatsoever, it would represent the extreme of extinction or nonexistence because the basis of imputation must be accepted as being existent. Therefore, those who wish for buddhahood should always familiarize with everything being mere cognizance. If they thus see the appearing of cognizance, while not seeing everything as having the nature of real entities, they eventually do not perceive mere cognizance either since there is no apprehender without anything apprehended. Therefore, through being free from any conceptions in terms of apprehender and apprehended, nonconceptual wisdom will arise effortlessly.

Verses 110–114 and their commentary[346] say that the cause for the arising of nonconceptual wisdom is the elimination of dualistic conceptions, but not the total lack of any mental engagement in conceptions. True mental disengagement comes about through relinquishing all clinging and all conceptions about characteristics. Without engaging in characteristics, bodhisattvas then enter the dharmadhātu without characteristics. To the degree that they disengage from duality and engage in nonduality, their afflictive and cognitive obscurations are relinquished and thus suchness and nonconceptual wisdom become pure.

Verse 150 and its commentary[347] explain that nonconceptual wisdom is nonconceptual because all bases for conceptions are relinquished. It is effortless because it operates through the power of previous aspiration prayers. It is free from attachment because it is unobstructed with regard to all knowable objects. It is the self-awareness of buddhas because it cannot be explained to others.

In sum, the progressive purification of suchness, or the nature of phenomena, is both accomplished and realized through nonconceptual wisdom. In other words, starting with the first direct realization of suchness on the path of seeing, the false imagination of dualistic appearances that obscures the true nature of phenomena is gradually dissolved by nonconceptual wisdom. To speak of this dissolution of obscuring false imagination is the same as speaking of entering the wisdom that is completely free from such imagination or conception. With the nature of buddhahood being stainless suchness, nonconceptual wisdom is both the entrance into that nature and inseparable from it. That is, at buddhahood there is no nonconceptual wisdom apart from stainless suchness, nor is there any stainless suchness apart from nonconceptual wisdom. As the above texts explain, buddhahood as the final result of the fundamental change means that adventitious stains, which obscured suchness, no longer appear, while all that appears at this point is nothing but stainless suchness. Nonconceptual wisdom is the fundamental awareness to which this suchness appears in a completely unobscured manner. This wisdom is the only state of mind for which the nature of phenomena, which is entirely free from reference points, can appear because nonconceptual nondual wisdom is the sole cognition that does not entertain or grasp on to any reference points. Therefore, the ultimate subject and object are absolutely identical in their lack of any stains or reference points. Consequently, unlike in any other kind of cognition, they are completely indistinguishable as a separate subject and object, though they are explained as the ultimate subject and object from the perspective of beings with dualistic minds. In other words, stainless suchness refers to unobscured true reality, just as it is, while nonconceptual wisdom is the realization of this reality in an unobscured manner. Though these two terms emphasize the ultimate cognitive object and subject, respectively, as amply illustrated by Yogācāra texts, each one of them on their own point to and represent the nondual experience of mind's nature realizing itself, which cannot be expressed adequately by our ordinary epistemological terms rooted within a subject-object frame of reference.

The commentaries on the Dharmadharmatāvibhāga

The Indian commentaries

Vasubandhu's *Dharmadharmatāvibhāgavṛtti* (DDVV; 24 pages) is the only available actual Indian commentary on DDV and is the one on which all Tibetan commentaries rely greatly. Though the entire Sanskrit text of DDVV was found recently, it is not available yet. There is, however, a Sanskrit fragment of the text (DDVV (S)) that was published as an appendix in Lévi's edition of the *Mahāyānasūtrālaṃkāra* (Lévi 1907).[348] DDVV closely follows the words of the prose version of DDV and provides mostly quite brief comments on them, without giving any general explanations. In line with DDV, DDVV does not mention the three natures, while almost all Tibetan commentaries interpret DDV as being based on and teaching this typical exegetical template of Yogācāra.[349]

Vairocanarakṣita's (eleventh/twelfth century) *Dharmadharmatāvibhāgakatipayapadavivṛtti* (VV) is a one-folio Sanskrit manuscript which was first mentioned in Gokhale 1977. It is not an actual commentary, but only provides brief glosses of certain terms in DDV (thus, it cannot be assessed whether VV is based on the prose version or the versified version). VV does not mention the three natures either.

The Tibetan commentaries

As for the Tibetan commentaries perused in the present study, Jomdendé Rigpé Raltri wrote a very brief summary of the main points of DDV (Bcom ldan rig pa'i ral gri 2006; 4 pages) without providing any further explanations.

The earliest available actual Tibetan commentary on DDV (composed in 1320), which is also by far the longest one, is the Third Karmapa's *Ornament That Explains* The Treatise on The Distinction between Phenomena and the Nature of Phenomena (OED; 126 pages). This text is the only Tibetan commentary that comments on the prose version of DDV. Rangjung Dorje declares all five Maitreya texts to form a unity and clearly uses them in that way in OED. He states that OED is generally based on the intentions of both Asaṅga and Nāgārjuna. As for OED's contents in general and its additional explanations in particular, it greatly and primarily relies on the other four Maitreya texts, the *Mahāyānasaṃgraha* (quoted twenty-five times), and Vasubandhu's *Triṃśikā* (seven verses). OED extensively quotes the *Mahāyānasūtrālaṃkāra* (eighty-one verses), the *Uttaratantra* (eighteen verses; referring to another six), the *Abhisamayālaṃkāra* (twelve verses), and the *Madhyāntavibhāga* (eleven verses). The text also cites Nāgārjuna's *Yuktiṣaṣṭikā* (six verses), *Mūlamadhyamakakārikā* (two verses), and *Dharmadhātustava* (two verses). In its comments on DDV's sections on "the relinquishment of the four kinds of characteristics" and "the thorough knowledge of nonconceptual wisdom," OED explicitly refers to and bases its explanations on the *Avikalpapraveśadhāraṇī*.

Though OED greatly relies on DDVV, it goes far beyond it in that it offers more or less detailed general discussions of the nonexistence of external objects (supported by Dignāga's *Ālambanaparīkṣā* and its autocommentary), the five paths and the ten bhūmis (mainly based on the *Mahāyānasaṃgraha*, *Mahāyānasūtrālaṃkāra*, *Abhisamayālaṃkāra*, and *Madhyāntavibhāga*), the nature of the afflictive and cognitive obscurations, the eight consciousnesses, the five wisdoms, and the three kāyas. OED also describes the perfect nature as the "ālaya," while the imaginary and dependent natures are equated with the "ālaya-consciousness," which resembles the later distinction into "ālaya-wisdom" and "ālaya-consciousness" by Dölpopa and others. The eight consciousnesses are said to be the obscurations, while the first four of the five wisdoms (mirrorlike wisdom, the wisdom of equality, discriminating wisdom, and all-accomplishing wisdom) represent the intrinsic stainlessness of these consciousnesses, which is nothing but the perfect nature. The fifth wisdom (dharmadhātu wisdom) is the matrix within which the other four display.

Following DDV, OED explains the four "yogic practices" (*prayoga*) found in many mahāyāna texts twice. However, OED's first presentation respectively relates these four to the path of preparation, the path of seeing, the second through seventh bhūmis, and the eighth through tenth bhūmis, while its second explanation follows the standard matching of those four practices with the four levels of the path of preparation (following *Mahāyānasūtrālaṃkāra* XIV.23–27).

Among all of Rangjung Dorje's works, OED gives the most detailed presentations of nonconceptual wisdom, the notion of "fundamental change," and the three natures. It also connects the latter with the threefold lack of nature and repeatedly states that both the imaginary and the dependent natures are the obscurations and are not established ultimately, while the perfect nature (consisting of suchness and nonconceptual wisdom) is empty of both the imaginary and the dependent natures. Though the latter is a typical *Shentong* position, OED clearly warns against any kind of reification of the perfect nature, saying that it is the sheer lack of phenomena and is absolutely without any arising or ceasing in terms of itself, others, both, or neither. Of particular interest is that OED is the only commentary on DDV that repeatedly equates the nature of phenomena, nonconceptual wisdom, the fundamental change, and the perfect nature with the notion of *tathāgatagarbha*.

Rongtön's *Excellent Instruction That Explains* The Distinction between Phenomena and the Nature of Phenomena, *Called The Great Drum of the Gods* (RC; 28 pages) closely follows DDVV, but also interprets DDV through the exegetical template of the three natures. RC is often formulated in a syllogistic style and usually does not provide much additional explanation.

The Sakya master Dagtsang Lotsāwa Sherab Rinchen[350] (born 1405) wrote his *Exposition of* The Distinction between Phenomena and the Nature of Phenomena in 1469 (DLC; 15 pages). Though it often follows DDVV, it also presents a number of its own original explanations.

Gö Lotsāwa's untitled commentary (GC; 41 pages) is embedded in his commentary on the *Uttaratantra* (composed in 1473). It introduces the second chapter of the *Uttaratantra* by explaining the section of DDV that discusses the nature of phenomena. With this section covering about two thirds of DDV and GC also addressing DDV's main topic of the section on phenomena or dualistic appearances, GC represents an almost complete commentary on DDV of a highly original nature. GC starts by saying that DDV can be considered as a commentary on the second chapter of the *Uttaratantra*.[351] The reasons for this are that "stainless suchness" in the *Uttaratantra* corresponds to "the nature of phenomena" in DDV, with both texts explaining that stainless suchness consists of the fundamental change, whose cause is nonconceptual wisdom. The end of GC states that the distinction between the existent nature of phenomena (suchness or mind's luminosity) and nonexistent phenomena in DDV matches the explanation in the *Uttaratantra* that the ultimately existent *tathāgatagarbha* is empty of adventitious stains, but not empty of buddha qualities. In both texts, the fundamental change indicates a primordial ultimate that is described in positive terms and is revealed by eliminating ultimately nonexistent adventitious stains, as illustrated by the examples of primordially pure space, gold, and water, which only need to be discovered by removing adventitious stains, but do not need to be newly created.

Just like DDVV, but unlike almost all other Tibetan commentaries, GC does not mention the three natures. GC frequently quotes the *Avikalpapraveśadhāraṇī*, in particular in its long section on the relinquishment of the four kinds of conceptions, which presents the two different exegetical approaches on this text's central notion of "mental nonengagement." First, as for Kamalaśīla's analytical approach of mental nonengagement (which he explains as being "the prajñā of discriminating true reality," whose outcome is the state of mental nonengagement), GC offers a digest of Kamalaśīla's *Avikalpapraveśadhāraṇīṭīkā* on the four types of conceptions. According to GC, this is the approach for people of inferior faculties. The second approach, for those of higher faculties, is found in Maitrīpa's *Tattvadaśaka* and his student Sahajavajra's *Tattvadaśakaṭīkā*, with the latter being cited at length by GC. In this nonanalytical approach based on pith instructions, mental nonengagement means that even beginners take the approach of directly resting in the natural luminosity of whatever conceptions that appear in the mind, which is nothing other than Mahāmudrā. In this vein, GC's section on the four steps of the correct yogic practice even matches these four with the four yogas of Mahāmudrā.

Śākya Chogden's short untitled commentary (SC; 7 pages), which is found at the end of his *Opening the Jewel Casket, A Treatise That Elucidates the Stages of the Path of the Five Maitreya Dharmas* (Śākya mchog ldan 1988c), is not a word-by-word commentary on DDV, but only discusses a few of its essential points, some of them in a quite general manner.

Mipham Rinpoche's *Commentary on the Verses of* The Distinction between Phenomena and the Nature of Phenomena, *The Distinction between Wisdom and Appearance*[352] (MC; 52 pages) was composed in 1894. It usually follows DDVV and RC, but is more detailed and also adds new material. In particular, MC elaborates on the nonexistence of external objects, the minds of others never being a direct object of someone else's mind (be it in meditative equipoise or outside of it), the nonexistence of the apprehender in dependence on the nonexistence of the apprehended, the five defining characteristics of nonconceptual wisdom (such as its being ungraspable), the five factors that are to be excluded as being nonconceptual wisdom (such as being the mere absence of any mental engagement), and the four flaws if there were no fundamental change.

Khenpo Shenga's interlinear commentary (SGC; 22 pages), in his typical style, consists almost entirely of a literal copy of DDVV, without any additional explanations.

The Gelugpa Tragar Tulku, Lobsang Balden Dendzin Nyentra[353] (1866–1928), wrote *A Commentary on* The Distinction between Phenomena and the Nature of Phenomena, *The Essence of the Path* (LBC; 34 pages). It closely follows both DDVV and RC (for the most part actually being a literal copy of the latter), without offering further explanations.

Lobsang Dayang composed his *Excellent Explanation That Comments on* The Distinction between Phenomena and the Nature of Phenomena, *Opening the Jewel Casket* (LDC; 41 pages) in 1926.[354] The colophon of the text says that it is based on the explanations of Tsongkhapa and his spiritual heirs as well as "the good parts of Rongtön's *Ṭīkā*." This is quite an understatement, since, just like LBC, LDC is largely a literal copy of RC. However, at times LDC criticizes RC's comments and differs significantly from it when discussing the standard Gelug positions on the five texts of Maitreya and Mere Mentalism, as illustrated above. Lobsang Dayang's concluding verses state that he has not seen any commentaries on DDV in his own Gelugpa tradition.[355]

The contemporary commentary by the late Sakya Khenpo Lodho Zangpo (LZC; 39 pages) was published in 1982 and, with a few exceptions, closely follows DDVV.

Akhu Sherab Gyatso's list of rare texts mentions two commentaries on DDV by Ngog Lotsāwa and Chaba Chökyi Sengé,[356] while Khenpo Appey's bibliography of Sakya literature[357] lists a commentary by Sönam Gyaltsen[358] (1312–1375). However, none of these texts is preserved at present.

Thus, not counting Jomdendé Rigpé Raltri's brief summary, the currently available Tibetan commentaries on DDV consist of four from the Sakya tradition and two each from the Kagyü, Nyingma, and Gelug schools. The translation section below contains English renderings of the prose and versified versions of DDV, as well as DDVV, OED, and GC. In addition, relevant excerpts from VV are found in the notes to the translation of DDVV, while excerpts from all other Tibetan commentaries are provided in the notes to OED.

English commentaries

The contemporary senior abbot of the Karma Kagyü School, Khenchen Thrangu Rinpoche, gave a brief and rather general oral commentary on DDV, which was translated into English by Jules Levinson and published in 2004 as *Distinguishing Dharma and Dharmata by Maitreya.*

There is also a contemporary commentary on DDV by master Tam Shek-wing (born 1935) that is primarily based on DDVV and MC, while also occasionally bringing in a Dzogchen perspective (published in Chinese in 1999).[359] A richly annotated English translation by Henry Shiu, which also includes excerpts from Tam Shek-wing's public lectures on his text in Toronto in 2000, is found in Robertson 2008 (vol. 2, pp. 439–512).

TRANSLATIONS

The Prose Version of The Distinction between Phenomena and the Nature of Phenomena

In Indian language: Dharmadharmatāvibhāga[360]
In Tibetan language: Chö dang chönyi nampar jépa
[In English: The Distinction between Phenomena and the Nature of Phenomena][361]

I pay homage to Youthful Mañjuśrī.

Since something is to be relinquished after being understood
And something else is to be made fully perceptible,
Therefore, this treatise was composed out of the wish
To distinguish these two through their defining characteristics.

All this is summarized into two, that is, into phenomena and the nature of phenomena.[362] What is characterized by phenomena is saṃsāra. What is characterized by the nature of phenomena is the nirvāṇa of the three yānas.

What appears as duality and how it is designated is false imagination, which is the defining characteristic of phenomena. The appearance of what does not exist is false. Being without referents in all [respects], imagination is mere conception.

The defining characteristic of the nature of phenomena is suchness, which lacks any distinction between apprehender and apprehended, or [between] objects of designation and what designates them.

The mistakenness due to what does not exist appearing is the cause of afflictiveness, just like seeing illusory elephants and so on, and also because what exists is not seen either.

If any one of these two—nonexistence and appearance—did not exist, mistakenness, unmistakenness, afflicted phenomena, and purified phenomena would not follow.

These two are neither one nor different because there is a difference as well as no difference in terms of existence and nonexistence.

The realization of phenomena through six points is unsurpassable—comprehending the defining characteristic, the rationale, their being neither one nor different, their matrix,[363] what is in common and not in common, and the nonexistence of the appearance of apprehender and apprehended.

The defining characteristic, the rationale, and not being one or different are as in the brief introduction [above].

Their matrix consists of what cycles in what—the world of sentient beings and the container. The world of the container consists of the cognizances that seem to be in common. The world of sentient beings consists of what is in common and what is not in common.

Birth, behavior, care, defeat, qualities, and faults cause each other and therefore are in common by virtue of mutual domination. The abode, cognizance, karma, happiness, suffering, death and transition, birth, bondage, and liberation are not in common by virtue of not being in common.

What appears as something apprehended that is in common and external is the cognizance that is the apprehender, but there is no referent that is apart from cognition because such is common.

The apprehended [objects] (the referents that are consciousness) that are not in common and are the minds and so on of others do not mutually serve as objects for the [two types of] cognizances that are the apprehenders [while] being or not being in meditative equipoise, respectively. Because for those who are not in meditative equipoise, their own conceptions appear and because [for] those who are in meditative equipoise, it is a reflection of the [mind of another] that appears in [the form of] the experiential object of samādhi.

If what appears as the apprehended does not exist, it is established that what appears as the apprehender does not exist either. Therefore, the realization of the nonexistence of the appearance of apprehender and apprehended is established. For arising without beginning is established. For while the two are not established at all, they are commonly known.

The realization of the nature of phenomena through six aspects is unsurpassable—the realization of the defining characteristic, the matrix, penetration, contact, recollection, and the arrival at its nature.

The defining characteristic is as in the brief introduction.

The matrix consists of all phenomena and the collection of the words of all sūtra collections that represent the twelve branches of the Buddha's speech.

Penetration is the entire path of preparation that consists of the proper mental engagement which relies on the sūtra collection of the mahāyāna.

Contact is the realization and experience of suchness through the path of seeing because the correct view is attained, which is by virtue of direct training.

Recollection is the entire path of familiarization that eliminates the stains of what consists of the factors concordant with enlightenment just as one has made contact with it.

As for the arrival at its nature, by virtue of suchness having become without stains, in all respects, nothing but suchness appears, which is the perfection of the fundamental change.

The realization of the fundamental change through ten points is unsurpassable—realizing the nature, the entity, the persons, the distinctions, the prerequisites, the foundation, the mental engagement, the trainings, the shortcomings, and the benefits.

As for realizing the nature, in stainless suchness adventitious afflictions and suchness do not appear and appear, respectively.

The realization of the entity refers to the change of the cognizance that is the common container into suchness, the change of the dharmadhātu of the sūtra collection into suchness, and the change of the cognizance that is the dhātu of sentient beings which is not in common into suchness.

As for realizing the persons, the first two are the changes into suchness that are those of buddhas and bodhisattvas. The latter one refers also to those of śrāvakas and pratyekabuddhas.

The realization of the distinctive features refers to the distinctive feature of the pure realms of buddhas and bodhisattvas and the distinctive feature of having attained the dharmakāya, the sāmbhogika[kāya], and the nairmāṇikakāya, which is due to the distinction of having obtained seeing, instruction, and mastery, respectively.

The realization of the prerequisites is by virtue of the distinctive feature of previous aspiration prayers, the distinctive feature of the focal object that is the mahāyāna teaching, and the distinctive feature of training on the ten bhūmis.

The realization of the focal objects through four points is by virtue of the mahāyāna teaching, aspiring for it, being certain [about it], and the completion of the accumulations.

The realization of the relinquishment of characteristics through four points is by virtue of relinquishing the characteristics of antagonistic factors, remedial factors, suchness, and the dharmas of realization. Through this, corresponding to this enumeration, it is taught as the relinquishment of the characteristics that are coarse, middling, subtle, and associated for a long time.

The realization of the correct yogic practice, also in four points, is by virtue of the yogic practice of observation, the yogic practice of nonobservation, the yogic practice of the nonobservation of observation, and the yogic practice of the observation of nonobservation.

The realization of the defining characteristics in three points is by virtue of abiding in the nature of phenomena due to abiding in the nature of phenomena that is nondual and inexpressible. It is [also] by virtue of nonappearance because what appear as duality, how it is designated, sense faculties, objects, cognizance, or the world as the container do not exist. Through these, the defining characteristic is clearly taught as it is described in the sūtras: "Nonconceptual wisdom is ungraspable, indemonstrable, ungrounded, without appearance, without cognizance, and without base." It is [also] by virtue of appearance because all phenomena are seen like the center of space and because all conditioned phenomena are seen like illusions and so on.

The realization of the benefit in four points is by virtue of attaining the dharmakāya in a complete manner, by virtue of attaining the supreme state of bliss, by virtue of attaining mastery over seeing, and by virtue of attaining mastery over instruction.

The realization by virtue of thorough knowledge in four points consists of the thorough knowledge of [being a] remedy, the thorough knowledge of the defining characteristic, the thorough knowledge of the distinctive features, and the thorough knowledge of the functions.

Here the thorough knowledge of [being a] remedy refers to nonconceptual wisdom, that is, [its being] a remedy for clinging to these five—phenomena, persons, change, difference, and denial—in terms of their having a real nature. The thorough knowledge of the defining characteristic refers to its specific characteristic that is the exclusion of these five—lacking mental engagement, transcendence, complete subsiding, what is naturally [nonconceptual], and picturing. The thorough knowledge of the distinctive features is by virtue of the distinctive features of the five factors of being nonconceptual, not being partial, nonabiding, lasting, and being unsurpassable. The thorough knowledge of the functions refers to the distinctive features of function that are fivefold—distancing conceptions, granting unsurpassable bliss, uniting with the freedom from afflictive and cognitive obscurations, engaging in all aspects of knowable objects through the wisdom that is attained subsequent to it, and purifying buddha realms, maturing sentient beings, and bestowing the knowledge of all aspects.

As for the realization of mental engagement, as it is said, bodhisattvas who wish to realize nonconceptual wisdom engage mentally as follows: due to being ignorant about suchness since beginningless time, false imagination consists of what contains all seeds (the cause for what is not real appearing as duality) and also what is based on it yet different. Here what entails cause and result appears, but it is not real. By virtue of appearing in such a way, the nature of that does not appear. By virtue of that not appearing, the nature of phenomena does appear. When bodhisattvas mentally engage in this in a proper manner, they realize nonconceptual wisdom.

By virtue of such observing, they realize focusing on mere cognizance. By virtue of focusing on mere cognizance, they realize that all referents are nonobservable. By virtue of all referents being nonobservable, they realize that mere cognizance is not observed either. By virtue of not observing that [cognizance], they realize that a difference between those two is not observable. Those two not being observable as such is nonconceptual wisdom—it lacks an object and lacks observation because it is characterized by not observing any characteristics.

The realization of the training is fourfold by virtue of the training through aspiration on the level of engagement through aspiration (this is the phase of discernment), by virtue of the training in discriminating awareness on the first bhūmi (this is the phase of contact), by virtue of the training in familiarization on the six impure bhūmis and also on the three pure ones (this is the phase of recollection), and by virtue of the training in completion on the buddhabhūmi because the deeds of a buddha are effortless and uninterrupted (this is the phase of the arrival at the nature of the [nature of phenomena]).

As for realizing the shortcomings, [they occur] if there is no fundamental change. The shortcomings are fourfold—the shortcoming of there being no support for the afflictions not operating, the shortcoming of there being no support for engaging in the path, the shortcoming of there being no support for presenting conventional terms for persons having passed into nirvāṇa, and the shortcoming of there being no support for presenting conventional terms for the differences between the three types of enlightenment.

Based on the opposites of those, the existence of the fundamental change should be known as [entailing] a fourfold benefit.

One should understand that these are the ten points of how to realize the fundamental change.

That nonexistent phenomena appear corresponds to, for example, illusions, dreams, and so on. Examples for the fundamental change are that it corresponds to space, gold, water, and so on.

This concludes The Distinction between Phenomena and the Nature of Phenomena *composed by noble Maitreya. It was translated, edited, and finalized by the Indian abbot paṇḍita Śāntibhadra and the great editor-translator and fully ordained monk Tsültrim Gyalwa. It was corrected and finalized by the Kashmirian junior abbot paṇḍita Parahita and the great editor-translator and fully ordained monk Gador at the practice place that is the temple of Toling.*[364]

Maṅgalaṃ

The Versified Version of The Distinction between Phenomena and the Nature of Phenomena

In Indian language: Dharmadharmatāvibhāgakārikā
In Tibetan language: Chö dang chönyi nampar jépe tsig le'ur jepa
[In English: The Stanzas on The Distinction between Phenomena and the Nature of Phenomena]

I pay homage to the protector Maitreya.

Something is to be relinquished after being understood
And something else is to be made fully perceptible.
Therefore, this treatise was composed out of the wish
To distinguish the defining characteristics of these two.

If one summarizes all these,
They should be known as twofold
Because everything is included
In phenomena and likewise the nature of phenomena.

Here what constitutes phenomena
Is saṃsāra. What constitutes
The nature of phenomena is the three yānas'
Nirvāṇa.

Here the defining characteristic of phenomena
Is what appears as duality and how it is designated.
It is false imagination
Because what does not exist appears.
Therefore, it is false.
Since it is without referents [in] all [respects]
And is mere conception, it is imagination.

Furthermore, the defining characteristic of the nature of phenomena
Is suchness, which lacks any distinction
Between apprehender and apprehended,
Or [between] objects of designation and what designates them.

Because of the appearance of what does not exist, mistakenness
Is the cause of afflictiveness,
Just like the appearance of illusory elephants and so on,
And because what exists does not appear either.

If any one of these two—nonexistence and appearance—
Did not exist, mistakenness and unmistakenness,
And likewise afflicted phenomena
And purified phenomena, would not be tenable.

These two are neither one
Nor are they distinct
Because there is a difference as well as no difference
In terms of existence and nonexistence.

Through six points, the comprehension
Of phenomena is unsurpassable—
Through comprehending the defining characteristic, the rationale,
Their being neither one nor different,
Their matrix in common and not in common,
And the nonexistence of the appearance
Of apprehender and apprehended.

Here the defining characteristic, the rationale,
And being neither one nor different
Are as in the brief introduction.

When something cycles in something,
That makes up their matrix—
The realm of sentient beings and the realm of the container.
The realm of the container is in common—
The cognizances that seem to be in common.
The realm of sentient beings is what is in common
Or what is not in common.

Birth, behavior,
Care, defeat,
Benefit, harm,[365]
Qualities, and faults are causes
For each other by virtue of mutual domination.
Therefore, they are in common.

Since the abode, cognizance,
Happiness, suffering, karma, death and transition,
Birth, bondage,
And liberation are not in common,
They are the matrix that is not in common.

What appears as something apprehended that is external
And in common is the cognizance that is the apprehender.
External to consciousness,
There is no referent
Because such is in common.

The other, the apprehended [objects] not in common—
The referents that are cognizance—
Are the minds and so on of others.
For the cognizances that are the apprehenders
[While] being or not being in meditative equipoise,
They do not mutually serve as objects.
Because for those who are not in meditative equipoise,
Their own conceptions appear and
Because for those who are in meditative equipoise,
What appears is a reflection
That is the experiential object of samādhi.

If it is established that what appears as the apprehended does not exist,
It is established that what appears as the apprehender does not exist [either].
By virtue of that, the comprehension
Of the nonexistence of what appears as apprehender
And apprehended is established because beginningless
Arising is established.
For while the two are not established at all,
They are commonly known.

The comprehension of the nature of phenomena
Through six points is unsurpassable—
Through comprehending the defining characteristic, the matrix,
Penetration, contact,
Recollection, and the arrival
At its nature.

The defining characteristic is as in the introduction.
The matrix consists of all phenomena
And all the sūtra collections of the Buddha's speech.

Here penetration
Is the entire path of preparation that consists of
The proper mental engagement which relies
On the sūtra collection of the mahāyāna.

Because the correct view is attained, contact
Is the experience

And attainment of suchness in a direct
Manner through the path of seeing.

What consists of the factors concordant with enlightenment
Of the path of familiarizing with the actuality that was seen
Through contact is recollection
Because it eliminates the stains of that.

As for the arrival
At its nature, once suchness
Has become without stains,
All appears as nothing but suchness,
Which is the perfection
Of the fundamental change. Through ten points

The comprehension of the fundamental change
Is unsurpassable
Through comprehending the nature, the substance, the persons,
The distinctions, the prerequisites, the foundation,
The mental engagement, the trainings,
The shortcomings, and the benefits.

Here, as for comprehending the nature,
It is stainless
Suchness in terms of
Adventitious stains and suchness
Not appearing and appearing, respectively.

The comprehension of the substantial entity
Refers to the cognizance that is the common container
Having changed into suchness,
The dharmadhātu of the sūtra collection
Having changed into suchness,
And the cognizance that is the dhātu
Of sentient beings which is not in common
Having changed into suchness.

As for comprehending the persons,
The first two are the changes
Of suchness that are those of buddhas
And bodhisattvas.
The latter one refers to those of śrāvakas
And pratyekabuddhas too.
The comprehension of the distinctive features
Is by virtue of the distinctive feature of the pure realms

Of buddhas and bodhisattvas
And the distinctive feature of having attained
Seeing, instruction, and mastery
Through the attainment of the dharmakāya,
The sāmbhogika[kāya], and the nairmāṇikakāya, respectively.

The comprehension of realizing the prerequisites
Refers to the distinctive feature of previous aspiration prayers,
The distinctive feature of the focal object
That is the mahāyāna teaching, and the distinctive feature
Of training on the ten bhūmis.

The comprehension of the foundation or support
Is by virtue of nonconceptual wisdom
Being comprehended through six points—
Through comprehending the focal objects, the relinquishment of characteristics,
The correct yogic practice,
The defining characteristics, the benefit,
And the thorough knowledge.

Here, first, the comprehension
Of the focal objects should be understood as four points
By virtue of the mahāyāna teaching,
Aspiring for it, being certain [about it],
And the completion of the accumulations.

Second, the comprehension of the relinquishment
Of characteristics in four points
Is by virtue of relinquishing the characteristics
Of what is antagonistic, remedies,
Suchness, and realization.

Through this, in due order,
This is the relinquishment of the characteristics
That are coarse, middling, subtle,
And associated for a long time.

The comprehension of the correct
Yogic practice in four points
Is the yogic practice of observation,
The yogic practice of nonobservation,
The yogic practice of the nonobservation of observation,
And the yogic practice of the observation of nonobservation.

Here the comprehension of the defining characteristics
Should be understood through three points—
By virtue of abiding in the nature of phenomena
Due to abiding in the nature of phenomena
That is nondual and inexpressible.

It is [also] by virtue of nonappearance because there is nothing
That appears as duality, how it is designated,
Sense faculties, objects, cognizance,
Or the world as the container.

Therefore, nonconceptual wisdom's
Defining characteristic is described through this
As in the sūtras: "Ungraspable,
Indemonstrable, ungrounded,
Without appearance, without cognizance,
And without base."

It is [also] by virtue of appearance because
All phenomena appear equal to the center of space
And because all conditioned phenomena
Are appearances like illusions and so on.

The comprehension of the benefit in four points
Is the attainment of the dharmakāya in a complete manner,
The attainment of supreme bliss,
The attainment of mastery over seeing,
And the attainment of mastery over teaching.

The comprehension of the thorough knowledge
Should be understood through four points—
The thorough knowledge of [being a] remedy,
The thorough knowledge of the defining characteristic,
The thorough knowledge of the distinctive features,
And the thorough knowledge of the five functions.

Here the knowledge of [being a] remedy
Refers to nonconceptual wisdom
Because it is taught to be the remedy
For the fivefold clinging to nonexistents—
Clinging to phenomena and persons,
Change, difference,
And denial.
The thorough knowledge of the defining characteristic
Refers to its own defining characteristic that is the exclusion

Of the fivefold clinging to
Mental nonengagement, transcendence,
Complete subsiding, what is naturally [nonconceptual], and picturing.

The thorough knowledge of the distinctive features
Refers to the fivefold distinctive features
That are the factors of being nonconceptual,
Not being limited,
Nonabiding, lasting,
And being unsurpassable.

Finally, the thorough knowledge of the functions
Refers to the distinctive features of five kinds of function—
Distancing conceptions,
Granting unsurpassable bliss,
Freeing from the afflictive
And cognitive obscurations,
Engaging in all aspects
Of knowable objects through the wisdom

That is attained subsequent to it,
And purifying buddha realms,
Maturing sentient beings,
And granting and bestowing
The knowledge of all aspects.

As for the comprehension of mental engagement,
Bodhisattvas, who are
The persons who wish to comprehend
Nonconceptual wisdom,
Engage mentally as follows:

Through being ignorant about suchness,
The imagination of what is unreal
Is "what contains all seeds"
(The cause for what does not exist appearing as duality)

And the continuum[366] that is based on it yet different.
Therefore, what entails cause and result
Appears, but it does not exist.

It appears and the nature of these phenomena does not appear.
By virtue of its not appearing, the nature of phenomena does appear.
If they mentally engage in this in a proper manner,
Bodhisattvas engage in
Nonconceptual wisdom.

By virtue of such observing, they observe
Mere cognizance. By virtue of observing [them]
As mere cognizance, they do not observe referents.
By virtue of not observing referents,
They do not observe mere cognizance [either].
By virtue of not observing that [cognizance], they engage in
Observing the lack of difference between those two.

To not observe these two as being different
Is nonconceptual
Wisdom—it lacks an object and lacks observation
Because it is characterized
By not observing any characteristics.

To enter the bhūmis through the training
Should be understood as being fourfold—
By virtue of the training through aspiration
On the level of engagement through aspiration
(This is the phase of penetration),
By virtue of the training in discriminating direct
Realization [on] the first bhūmi
(This is the phase of contact),
By virtue of the training through familiarization
[On] the six impure bhūmis
And the three pure bhūmis
(This is the phase of recollection),
And by virtue of the training in completion
Because the deeds of a buddha are effortless
And uninterrupted
(This is the phase of the arrival
At its nature).

As for comprehending the shortcomings,
These are the four shortcomings of
There being no fundamental change—
The flaw of there being no support for the afflictions not operating,
The flaw of there being no support for engaging in the path,
The flaw of there being no basis for designating
The persons who have passed into nirvāṇa,
And the flaw of there being no basis for designating
The differences between the three [types of] enlightenment.
The comprehension of the benefit (the opposite)
Should be known as being fourfold.

Examples for nonexistent phenomena appearing
Are being like illusions, dreams, and so on.
If examples for the fundamental change are given,
It is like space, gold, water, and so on.

This concludes The Verses on the Distinction between Phenomena and the Nature of Phenomena *composed by the protector Maitreya. They were translated, edited, and finalized by the Kashmirian paṇḍita Mahājana and the translator and fully ordained monk Sengé Gyaltsen.*

Maṅgalaṃ

Vasubandhu's Commentary on *The Distinction between Phenomena and the Nature of Phenomena*

{27b}[367] In Indian language: Dharmadharmatāvibhāgavṛtti
In Tibetan language: Chö dang chönyi nampar jépe drelpa
[In English: A Commentary on The Distinction between Phenomena and the Nature of Phenomena]

I pay homage to the Bhagavān Ajita.[368]

To Ajita, who realized that the world had gone astray from the path
Through its mistakenness of clinging to the literal meaning
And who thus proclaimed this [treatise] by summarizing the teachings,
To this guru I bow with my palms folded together.

Having studied it with [my] gurus,[369]
I make an effort in order to discriminate a bit,
Word by word and to [the best of] my abilities,
The profound meaning of this condensed treatise granted by him.[370]

> **Since something is to be relinquished after being understood**
> **And something else is to be made manifest,**
> **Therefore, this treatise was composed out of the wish**
> **To distinguish these two due to their defining characteristics.**

As for [the lines] "**Since something is to be relinquished after being understood and something else is to be made manifest,**" in due order, they are given in terms of phenomena, which have the defining characteristic of afflictiveness, and the nature of phenomena, which is characterized by the fundamental change that has the defining characteristic of being purified. As for "**to distinguish these two due to their defining characteristics,**" this means that they are not [distinguished] due to being different objects. The meaning of the remaining [parts of this verse] is understood by itself.

It may be said, "What [is the meaning of] 'to distinguish these two due to their defining characteristics'? Is it that just phenomena and the nature of phenomena are distinguished, while others are not. Or is it that [everything] comes down to only these two?" To answer, this is not a distinction through singling them out as two from among a [larger] multitude. "How is it then?" [Everything] that the Bhagavān presented (such as skandhas, dhātus, and āyatanas) is included [in these two]. Therefore, [Maitreya says,]

> **All this is twofold.**

If you wonder why, [this is,]

> **because it is included in phenomena and the nature of phenomena.**

If skandhas, dhātus, āyatanas, {28a} and so on are summarized, they are of **two** kinds, that is, **phenomena and the nature of phenomena**. Here [Maitreya] speaks of "**this**" for the sake of identifying what is explained in this teaching [of the Buddha]. Saying "**all**" is for the sake of indicating that [everything in] the [Buddha's teaching] is [included in] just this [distinction of phenomena and the nature of phenomena] **because** anything that is other than these [two] **is** either **included in** them or does not exist.

It may be said, "If [these two] are discussed without difference in this way, one does not understand the distinction by way of saṃsāra and nirvāṇa such that [one knows] what consists of what." Therefore, [Maitreya] says:

> **What constitutes phenomena is saṃsāra.**

Here, since phenomena are what have the defining characteristic of afflictiveness, **saṃsāra**—which has the nature of this [afflictiveness]—**is** described as being "**what constitutes phenomena.**" As for the other one, [Maitreya says]:

> **What constitutes the nature of phenomena is the nirvāṇa of the three yānas.**

Since nirvāṇa is what is to be attained through the three yānas, it is described as "the nirvāṇa through the three yānas." Or, since it is both the three yānas and nirvāṇa, it **is** called "**the nirvāṇa of the three yānas.**"[371] Here, since the nature of phenomena is what has the defining characteristic of being the fundamental change, the nirvāṇa that consists of this [fundamental change] is described as "**what constitutes the nature of phenomena.**"

It may be said, "Saṃsāra and nirvāṇa are indeed characterized in this way by phenomena and the nature of phenomena, respectively. However, since their defining characteristics have not been described, one does not understand these very phenomena as to what their defining characteristic is like." Therefore, for the sake of teaching their defining characteristic [Maitreya] says:

> **What appears as duality and according designations is false imagination, which is the defining characteristic of phenomena.**

What appears as duality and according designations refers to what appears as duality and {28b} what appears as according designations. Here [this includes] (a) the entities of apprehender and apprehended (such as the eyes and form) that appear as duality and (b) what appear as the according designations that are based on the [former]. Respectively, these have the natures of being the supports for designating a nature and distinctive features. [Both] constitute **false imagination.** Through saying that this "**is the defining characteristic of phenomena,**" the defining characteristic of phenomena is described in an unmistaken and complete manner.

Here, as for the hermeneutical etymology of "false," [Maitreya says:]

> **Since what does not exist appears, it is false.**

Why? These phenomena are **not existent.** As for the hermeneutical etymology of the word *pari* and the word *kalpa* [in *parikalpa* ("imagination")], [Maitreya continues:]

> **In all [respects], it is without referents**[372] **and is mere conception. Therefore, it is imagination.**

It is without referents because a nature of appearances is not established. It **is mere conception** because appearances exist merely as mistakenness. This completes the explanation of the defining characteristic of phenomena.

As for the defining characteristic of the nature of phenomena, [Maitreya says:]

> **The defining characteristic of the nature of phenomena is suchness, which lacks any distinction between apprehender and apprehended, or [between] objects of designation and what designates them.**

What **lacks any distinction between apprehender and apprehended** and what lacks any distinction between **objects of designation and what designates them is suchness.** This is **the defining characteristic of the nature**

of phenomena. According to this order, [it consists of this twofold] lack of distinction because it is without duality and because it is inexpressible, respectively. For that in which there is no distinction is called "lacking distinction." If there were duality or an object of designation and what designates it ([such as saying,] "This is what is apprehended" and "This is the apprehender" or "This is the object of designation" and "This is what designates it"), there would be a distinction. However, since there is none, it is the suchness that lacks any distinction. Through saying that this is "the defining characteristic of the nature of phenomena," the defining characteristic of the nature of phenomena is taught in an unmistaken and complete manner.

As for what is the defining characteristic of phenomena that was taught above, [Maitreya elaborates:]

> **The mistakenness by virtue of what does not exist appearing is the cause of afflictiveness.**

Since what is not existent appears, it is the **appearing** of **what does not exist**. Therefore, one should realize that it is mere **mistakenness**. {29a} Because of that, it **is** also **the cause of afflictiveness**. For, through clinging to it, the threefold afflictiveness[373] arises thereafter. You may wonder, "What is this appearing of what does not exist like?" [Maitreya] says:

> **It is like the appearing of illusory elephants and so on.**

For example, **elephants and so on** as well as riches, grain, and so on that are produced as [magical] **illusions** do not exist in the ways they appear, but still **appear. Like**wise, false imagination also appears while not existing.

> **And furthermore, because what exists does not appear either.**

"Mistakenness" is carried over [as the subject of this phrase]. Here, as for "**because what exists does not appear either**," it is also because of what exists—twofold identitylessness—not appearing that this is mistakenness. For, in the world, one sees it in such a way that, [in the case of mistaking a cairn for a human,] the nonappearing of a cairn (which exists) and the appearing of the shape of a human [instead] (which does not exist) are the defining characteristics of mistakenness.

It may be said, "By virtue of what point is it then not held that one of the two—nonexistence and appearance—does not exist?" [Maitreya] says:

> **If any one of these two—nonexistence and appearance—did not exist, mistakenness, unmistakenness, afflicted phenomena, and purified phenomena would not be tenable.**

If there were only nonexistence but no **appearance**, there would be no **mistakenness** because the [latter] is absent. For one [cannot] be mistaken about what is nonexistent being nonexistent. If there were no mistakenness, there would be no **unmistakenness** either because unmistakenness entails being preceded by the [former]. Therefore, **afflicted phenomena would not** exist either because they entail the cause that is mistakenness. If these [afflicted phenomena] did not exist, there would be no **purified phenomena** either because purified phenomena entail being preceded by afflicted phenomena. Therefore, **if** the [appearance] **did not exist**, since one would be liberated without effort, this would contradict direct perception.

But if there were only appearance and no **nonexistence**, in that case, because nonexistence is absent, there would be no mistakenness. For if appearances were established as their nature [in the way they appear], they would not be mistaken. {29b} If there were no mistakenness, just as above, the remaining would not exist either. Therefore, the actions of persons would be pointless, thus contradicting what is reasonable. For, in the world too, [to perceive] a cairn and a person that are established as [two] separately [existent entities as being separate] is not[374] labeled as mistakenness.

This concludes the explanation of the defining characteristic of phenomena (what appears as duality and according designations) and the defining characteristic of the nature of phenomena[375] (lacking those distinctions).

You may wonder, "In that case, should phenomena and the nature of phenomena be accepted as being one or as being different?" [Maitreya] says:

> **These two are neither one nor are they distinct because there is [a difference as well as][376] no difference in terms of existence and nonexistence.**

"**These two**" refers to the two of phenomena and the nature of phenomena, which **are not** held to be the same **or** to be different. Why is that? **Because there is a difference as well as no difference in terms of existence and nonexistence.** First,[377] it is not tenable that phenomena and the nature of phenomena are the same. Why? Because there is a difference in terms of [their] being existent and nonexistent, respectively. The nature of phenomena is existent, while phenomena are nonexistent. Therefore, how could these two that entail this difference in terms of [the one] being existent and [the other] being nonexistent be one? Nor are they different. Why? Because there is no difference in terms of [their] being existent and nonexistent, respectively. You may wonder, "How are they not different?" Because the [existent] nature of phenomena is constituted by the mere nonexistence of phenomena. For it lacks any distinctions in terms of something apprehended and so on. This completes the explanation that phenomena and the nature of phenomena are neither one nor distinct.

It may be said, "Still, among these two that are thus not different, how does one comprehend phenomena, or how does one comprehend them well?" [Maitreya] says:

> **The comprehension of phenomena through six points is unsurpassable—**

That is, [one comprehends phenomena] **through** the **six** [points] that will be explained. They are as follows:

> **Through comprehending the defining characteristic, the rationale, their being neither one nor distinct, their matrix in common and not in common, and the nonexistence of the appearance of apprehender and apprehended.**

Here

> **the defining characteristic,** {30a} **the rationale, and their being neither one nor distinct are as in the introduction.**

It should be understood that these three [points] **are as in the introduction**, that is, they are **the defining characteristic, the rationale, and their being neither one nor distinct.**[378] As for the defining characteristic, what appears as duality and according designations is false imagination. This is the defining characteristic of phenomena. As for the rationale, if any one of these two—nonexistence and appearance—did not exist, there would be the flaw of mistakenness, unmistakenness, afflicted phenomena, and purified phenomena not being tenable. Therefore, through accepting both [nonexistence and appearance], they are established as having [their respective] results. As for their being neither one nor being distinct, this is "because there is a difference as well as no difference in terms of existence and nonexistence." Thus, [these three] are as in the introduction.

As for the matrix [of phenomena, Maitreya says]:

> **Their matrix consists of what cycles[379] in what—the realm of sentient beings and the realm of the world.**

Here **what cycles** and **in what** it cycles refer to **the matrix** of phenomena. In due order, it consists of the entities that are the supported and the support—**the realm of sentient beings and the realm of the world.** Here

> **the realm of the world consists of the cognizances that seem to be in common.**

[This is] because consciousnesses that appear as the [world] arise in all sentient beings in their individual mind streams. As for the other one, [Maitreya continues]:

> **The realm of sentient beings consists of what is in common and what is not in common. Birth, behavior, benefit, harm, qualities, and faults are in common because they are causes for each other by virtue of mutual domination.**

The **births, behaviors** (such as looking [at each other]), **benefits, harms, qualities, and faults** that exist in individual mind streams are described as **the realm of sentient beings that is in common because they are causes for each other by virtue of mutually dominating** the arising of consciousnesses [in other beings] that appear as those [phenomena of birth and so on]. That [Maitreya] speaks of "[mutual] domination," while [the basic meaning] is [already] established through [the phrase] "because they are causes for each other," {30b} is for the sake of excluding causes that are objects [as opposed to dominating causes].

You may wonder, "How is it that this [realm of sentient beings] **is not in common?**" [Maitreya] says:

> **The abode, cognizance, karma, happiness, suffering, death and transition, birth, bondage, and liberation are not in common.**

The abode is the ālaya-consciousness because the latent tendencies of the cognizances that appear as certain ones [among the remaining phenomena of sentient beings that are not in common] abide in it. **Cognizance** refers to the operating consciousnesses. **Karma** is virtuous, nonvirtuous, or neutral. The remaining ones are to be understood according to the sūtras. Since the abode and so on are without form[380] and since they are to be experienced individually, they do not represent any causes for the arising of cognizances that mutually appear to individual mind streams as these [phenomena that are not in common]. Therefore, they are described as "the realm of sentient beings that **is not in common.**"

It may be said, "Why is it that the cognizances that are [appearing as] physical and verbal karmic actions are not included under [the category of] 'behavior' [above] despite their being causes for the arising of cognizances that mutually appear as such [physical and verbal actions]?" To answer, the cognizances that are [appearing as] body and speech are indeed included under "behavior," but they are not the cognizances that are [appearing as] karmic actions. These [latter cognizances that are referred to as physical and verbal karmic actions] are taught in terms of their being virtuous or nonvirtuous, through which they are understood as constituting the [corresponding] karmas of the [cognizances that appear as physical and verbal behaviors].[381] The cognizances that appear as such [karmas] are not causes for those cognizances that appear as such [karmas] to arise mutually [to different mind streams]. Therefore, the cognizances that are [appearing as] physical and verbal karmas are not in common.

As for comprehending the nonexistence of the appearance of apprehender and apprehended, [it first means] to comprehend that what appears as the apprehended does not exist. Therefore, [Maitreya] says the following in terms of comprehending that what appears as the apprehended does not exist:

> **In the cognizance that is the apprehender and appears as something apprehended[382] that is in common and external, there is no referent that is external to consciousness because such is universal.**[383]

[This is] because **the** very **cognizance that is the apprehender and appears as** a cognizance that is [appearing as] the container arises in each individual mind stream. **In** this cognizance that is the apprehender, **there is no** other cognizance that is the apprehender and **is external** to that consciousness that appears as the [container]. {31a} [As such then,] this very cognizance does not serve as an object of others. Since cognizances that are [appearing as] the container **are universal** [to all beings], cognizances that appear as the [container] arise in [all] individual mind streams, [though they do so in individually distinct ways]. Therefore, the cognizance of one [being] does not serve as an object of others. Consequently, there are no **referents**. This also excludes [the existence of any] cognizances that are something apprehended which is in common in terms of the realm of sentient beings.

As for the other one [(the realm of sentient beings that is not in common), Maitreya says:]

> **The apprehended [objects]—the referents that are cognizance—that are not in common and are called "the minds and[384] mental**

> **factors of others" do not mutually serve as objects for either of the two [types of] cognizances that are the apprehenders [while] being or not being in meditative equipoise, respectively.**

If you wonder why, [this is]

> **because for those who are not in meditative equipoise,[385] their own conceptions appear**

Because for those who are not in meditative equipoise, what serves as the object is their very own **cognizance**[386] that is **the apprehended** which **appears** for **their own conceptions**. Therefore, **the minds** and so on **of others** are **not** the **objects** of those [who are not in meditative equipoise]. As for the others, [Maitreya says:]

> **and because even for those who are in meditative equipoise,[387] it is a reflection of the [mind of another][388] that appears in [the form of] the experiential object of samādhi.**

"The minds of others and so on are not [their] objects" is carried over [as the subject]. **Because even for** the cognizance of **those who are in meditative equipoise**, what serves as the object is the very cognizance that is **the experiential object of samādhi** and **appears** as **a reflection of the** [mind of another]. Therefore, the minds of others and so on are not the objects of those [in meditative equipoise] either. In this way, since nothing but one's own cognizance is the object, there are no referents that are external to consciousness. Since such [referents] do not exist, what appears as the apprehended does not exist.

> **If it is established that what appears as the apprehended does not exist, it is also established that what appears as the apprehender does not exist.**

For **if the apprehended does not exist, the apprehender does not exist** [either]. It is to be understood that,

> **by virtue of that, the comprehension of the nonexistence of the appearance of apprehender and apprehended is established** in due order.

You may wonder why that is.

> **For arising without beginning is established.**

What is arising without beginning is the ignorance about suchness, which is the appearing of a duality that does not exist—{31b} the cause of mistakenness. Therefore, **arising without beginning is established**, that is, completely established. Consequently, what appears as apprehender and apprehended does not exist because this twofold[389] mistakenness is not real. **By virtue of that**, what **appears** as **apprehender and apprehended does not exist**. If you wonder why, [the answer is:]

> **For while the two are not established at all, they are commonly known.**[390]

This is to be understood by virtue of the following reason. Though **the two are not established at all**, one sees the arising of consciousnesses that are in contradiction [to this][391] and so on. That through which one thoroughly understands this is described as the unsurpassable comprehension of phenomena. This completes the explanation of the comprehension of phenomena.

Now the comprehension of the nature of phenomena is to be discussed. Therefore, in that regard, [Maitreya] says:

> **The comprehension of the nature of phenomena through six points is unsurpassable.**

That is, **through** the following **six** [points] that will be explained:

> **For it is comprehension of the defining characteristic, the matrix, discernment, contact, recollection, and the arrival at its nature.**

Here

> **The defining characteristic is as in the introduction.**

[As] it was said, "The defining characteristic of the nature of phenomena is suchness, which lacks any distinction between apprehender and apprehended, or [between] objects of designation and what designates them." Here

> **The matrix consists of all phenomena and all sūtra collections included in the twelve branches of the Buddha's speech.**

"**All phenomena**" refers to form and so on. **The twelve branches** consist of sūtras, proclamations in song, and so on. That [Maitreya] mentions these two is in terms of their making up afflicted phenomena and purified phenomena, respectively. Here

> **Discernment is the entire path of preparation that consists of the proper mental engagement which relies on the sūtra collection of the mahāyāna.**

"**The entire** [path of preparation]" refers to its being constituted by study, reflection, and meditation because the [nature of phenomena] is **discerned** through those [three]. Here

> **Contact is** {32a} **the attainment and experience of suchness in a direct manner through the path of seeing because the correct view is attained.**

"**Contact**" refers to the discriminating awareness **of suchness through the path of seeing.** This is described as "**attainment and experience.**" For "attainment and experience" refers to the very attainment *being* experience. You may wonder, "How is this experience to be presented?" [Maitreya] says that [it occurs] "**in a direct manner.**" He taught this in the sense of experience being nothing but what makes [suchness] fully perceptible.

Since recollection follows immediately after the point of contact, it is taught [next]:

> **Recollection is the entirety of what consists of the factors concordant with enlightenment—the path of familiarizing with [the nature of phenomena] as it was seen for the sake of eradicating the stains of this [level].**

Here **the path of familiarization** immediately after the path of **seeing** is called "**recollection.**" Through recollecting the determination of the [nature of phenomena] on the already attained path [of seeing], one orients [one's mind toward it again and again]. You may wonder, "For what sake is this?" [Maitreya] says, "**for the sake of eradicating the stains of this** [level]." The gist of this is that it is for the sake of relinquishing the remaining stains that have the characteristic of being factors to be relinquished through familiarizing with suchness.

Since the arrival at its nature follows immediately after recollection, it is taught [next]:

As for the arrival at its nature, once suchness has become without stains, all appears as nothing but suchness

Here **once suchness has become without stains**, because the remaining stains have been relinquished through the path of familiarization, it is through the path of completion that anything **appears as nothing but suchness** in **all** respects. For through being free from all stains, [everything] has become nothing but suchness. That [everything] is an object in being nothing but that [suchness] is[392] called "**the arrival at its nature**,"[393]

which is the perfection of the fundamental change

because [suchness] has the nature of this [fundamental change]. Since there are [already certain degrees of] change during the phases of the path of seeing and so on too, here **the perfection** [of this fundamental change] is taught because the stains have been relinquished without exception.

You may wonder, "How should one comprehend this fundamental change {32b} and how does its comprehension become unsurpassable?" [Maitreya] says:

The comprehension of the fundamental change through ten points is unsurpassable—

that is, [it is comprehended] **through** the following **ten points** that will be explained:

through comprehending the nature, the entity,[394] the persons, the distinctions, the prerequisites, the foundation, the mental engagement, the trainings, the shortcomings, and the benefits.

As for the first one here,

As for comprehending its nature, it is stainless suchness in terms of adventitious stains and suchness not appearing and appearing, respectively.

The nature of the fundamental change refers to suchness having become stainless **in terms of adventitious stains not appearing and** in terms of nothing but **suchness appearing.** That through which one thoroughly understands this is described as the unsurpassable **comprehension of the nature** [of the fundamental change]. Here

The comprehension of the entity refers to the change of the suchness of the cognizance that is the common container,[395] the change of the suchness of the dharmadhātu of the sūtra collection, and the change of the suchness of the cognizance that is the dhātu of sentient beings which is not in common.

The entity of the fundamental change consists of the threefold **change of suchness**[396] by virtue of the difference in terms of [what] this [suchness] is connected [to][397] and the difference in terms of the results [of this threefold fundamental change]. For the distinct[398] results in terms of appearance, instruction, and seeing are different.[399] Here

As for comprehending the persons, the first two are the fundamental changes of suchness of buddhas and bodhisattvas.

[These two] are not [the fundamental changes] of others because they are not in common [with others].

The latter one refers also to those of śrāvakas and pratyekabuddhas.

It is also the one of buddhas and bodhisattvas because it is in common.

The comprehension of the distinctive features is by virtue of the distinctive feature of the purity of the realms of buddhas and bodhisattvas

The distinctive feature of the purity of realms is [a distinctive feature] of the [fundamental change] **of buddhas and bodhisattvas**, but not of the [fundamental change] of śrāvakas and so on {33a} because those [realms] appear [to the latter] as having highs and lows.[400]

And the distinctive feature of having attained seeing,[401] instruction, and mastery—the attainment[402] of the dharmakāya, the sāmbhogika[kāya], and the nairmāṇikakāya, respectively.

Here it is to be understood that **the distinctive feature of having attained seeing** is by virtue of fully perceiving all aspects of knowable objects. The distinctive feature of having attained [the ability of] **instruction** is by virtue of [buddhas and bodhisattvas] teaching the profound, vast, amazing,[403] and immeasurable[404] in many different ways. The distinctive feature of having attained **mastery** is by virtue of having attained the immeasurable and unimpeded qualities (such as the supernatural knowledges) that constitute the support for accomplishing [beneficial] activities for [all] sentient beings.[405] One should understand that these, in due order, refer to **the attainment[406] of the dharmakāya, the sāmbhogika**[kāya], **and the nairmāṇikakāya.**

> **The comprehension of the prerequisites is by virtue of the distinctive feature of previous aspiration prayers, by virtue of the distinctive feature of the focal object that is the mahāyāna teaching, and by virtue of the distinctive feature of training on the ten bhūmis.**

Here, by virtue of the three distinctive features that are the **prerequisites,** the fundamental change of buddhas and bodhisattvas is more eminent than [those of] śrāvakas and pratyekabuddhas. Among these three kinds of distinctive features, the distinctive feature of aspiration prayers **is by virtue of the distinctive feature of previous aspiration prayers,** that is, because of the aspirations for great[407] enlightenment. The distinctive feature of focusing is **by virtue of the distinctive feature of the focal object that is the mahāyāna teaching,** that is, because of the focal object of all dharmas in combination and without combining them[408] and because of the focal object of their suchness. The distinctive feature of training is **by virtue of the distinctive feature of training on the ten bhūmis,** that is, because of the distinctive[409] training in cultivating the remedies for the obscurations for the sake of relinquishing all of them. Here

> **the foundation**

of the fundamental change is **nonconceptual wisdom** because it is attained through this foundation. You may wonder, "How is this [foundation] **comprehended?**" [Maitreya] says that it

> **refers to comprehending nonconceptual wisdom through six points. This comprehension in six points** {33b} **is by virtue of the focal objects, the relinquishment of characteristics, the correct yogic practice, the defining characteristics, the benefit, and the thorough knowledge.**

Here

> **The comprehension of the focal objects through four points is**

through [the four][410] that will be explained right below. They are as follows:

> **by virtue of the mahāyāna teaching, aspiring for it, being certain [about it], and the completion of the accumulations.**

The focal objects for the arising[411] of nonconceptual wisdom consist of **the mahāyāna teaching, aspiring for it, being certain** about it, **and the completion of the accumulations.** For if anyone [of these] is lacking, it does not arise. Through this, the complete comprehension of the focal objects should be clear.[412] Here it is to be understood that

> **the comprehension of the relinquishment of characteristics through four points is by virtue of relinquishing the characteristics of antagonistic factors, remedies, suchness, and the dharmas of[413] realization.**

Here **the relinquishment of the characteristic of antagonistic factors is by virtue of relinquishing the characteristics of** desire and so on. The relinquishment of the characteristic of [their] **remedies** is by virtue of relinquishing the characteristics of [meditating on] repulsiveness and so on. The relinquishment of the characteristic of **suchness** is by virtue of relinquishing even the characteristics[414] of any efforts in terms of [thinking,] "This is suchness." The relinquishment of the characteristic of **the dharmas of realization** is by virtue of relinquishing the characteristics of the attained realizations through familiarization[415] on the bhūmis.

> **Through this, in due order, they are described as the relinquishment of the characteristics[416] that are coarse, middling, subtle, and associated for a long time.**

This should be understood as follows. **The characteristic** of the antagonistic factors is **coarse** because they are the causes of the impregnations of negative tendencies and because they are easy to identify.[417] The characteristic of [their] remedies is **middling** because it is the remedy for the [former]. The characteristic of suchness is **subtle** because it is the remedy for everything that is other than it. The characteristic of realization is **that** with which one **is associated for a long time** because it is the result of familiarization. {34a} Here

> **The comprehension of the correct yogic practice through four points is**

as follows:

> **through the yogic practice of observation**

because of the **observation** of [everything as] mere cognizance;

> **through the yogic practice of nonobservation**

because of the **nonobservation** of [external] referents;

> **through the yogic practice of the nonobservation of observation**

because of **the nonobservation** of mere cognizance, if there are no referents, because cognizance is not tenable without any referents of cognizance;[418]

> **and through the yogic practice of the observation of nonobservation**[419]

because of **the observation of** nonduality through the **nonobservation** of duality. Here

> **The comprehension of the defining characteristics through three points**

is as follows. It

> **is by virtue of abiding in the nature of phenomena due to abiding in [its] defining characteristic**[420] **of being nondual and inexpressible,**

that is, because of the [nature of phenomena] being the focal object [of nonconceptual wisdom].

> **It is [also] by virtue of nonappearance because duality, according designations, sense faculties, objects, cognizance, and the world as the container do not appear.**

Where **duality, according designations, sense faculties, objects, cognizance, and the world as the container do not appear**, that is nonconceptual wisdom.

You may wonder, "In that case, what is taught [as this defining characteristic of nonconceptual wisdom]?" [Maitreya] says:

> **Through this, the defining characteristic of nonconceptual wisdom is described according to the sūtras as "ungraspable, indemonstrable, ungrounded, without appearance, without cognizance, and without base."**[421]

Here, because it cannot be grasped as the duality that consists of the entities of apprehender and apprehended,[422] it is **ungraspable**. It is **indemonstrable** because it cannot be demonstrated through designations. It is **ungrounded** because it is not grounded on the sense faculties (such as the eyes). It is **without appearance** because it is not [something with] an object. For it lacks any appearance of objects, such as form. It is **without cognizance** because it is not cognizance. It is **without base** because it is not an entity that is a base.[423]

> **It is [also] by virtue of appearance because all phenomena appear equal to the center of space,** {34b}

that is, **because all** its characteristics of [being] a [cognizing] subject[424] have been relinquished,

> **and because all conditioned phenomena appear like illusions and so on,**

that is, **because** they are realized to be false **appearances**. The phrase "**and so on**" [means that] they should [also] be regarded as [being like] mirages, dreams, and so on. Here

> **the comprehension of the benefit through four points is by virtue of attaining the dharmakāya in a complete manner,**

that is, **by virtue of** the fundamental change;

> **by virtue of attaining the supreme state of bliss,**

that is, because of having relinquished contaminated **bliss** and always having the nature of the [uncontaminated bliss];

> **by virtue of [attaining] mastery over seeing,**[425]

that is, because of realizing the suchness and the variety of knowable objects;

> **and by virtue of attaining mastery over instruction,**

that is, because of engaging in the manifold ways of teaching as it is appropriate. Since it is the cause of attaining these four kinds of benefit, **the benefit** of this wisdom is described in **four points.**

> **The comprehension of the thorough knowledge in four points consists of the thorough knowledge of [being a] remedy, the thorough knowledge of the defining characteristic, the thorough knowledge of the distinctive features, and the thorough knowledge of the functions. Here the thorough knowledge of [being a] remedy is due to nonconceptual wisdom being the remedy for the fivefold clinging to nonexistents, that is, phenomena, persons, change, difference, and denial.**

As for "**nonconceptual wisdom being the remedy for the fivefold clinging to nonexistents,**" the understanding that this is the case is called "**the thorough knowledge of** [its being a] **remedy.**" The fivefold clinging to nonexistents consists of clinging to nonexistent **phenomena** and clinging to nonexistent **persons** (that is, clinging to nonexistent referents),[426] clinging to nonexistent **change** (that is, clinging to the arising and ceasing of phenomena), clinging to nonexistent **difference** because of clinging to phenomena and the nature of phenomena as being distinct, **and** clinging to the **denial** of [taking phenomena and persons to be] nonexistent {35a} because of even denying the imputed existence of phenomena and persons.

> **The thorough knowledge of the defining characteristic is by virtue of its specific defining characteristic of excluding the five factors of lacking mental engagement, transcendence, complete subsiding, what is naturally [nonconceptual], and picturing.**

First, it is not reasonable that nonconceptual wisdom has the nature of nonconceptuality by virtue of **lacking mental engagement** in [any] conception. If it were nonconceptual by virtue of lacking mental engagement in conception, the cognitions of small children, fools, and so on would also be nonconceptual [wisdom]. Nor is it reasonable for it to have the nature of the **transcendence** of conceptions. If it had the nature of this transcendence, to rest evenly in the meditative absorptions of the second dhyāna and so on would therefore also constitute this [nonconceptual wisdom] because [mental states] without examination and analysis are without conceptions. It is also not reasonable for it to have the nature of conceptions having **completely subsided**. If it were nonconceptual by virtue of conceptions having completely subsided, consequently [the minds of] those who are asleep, intoxicated, or have fainted would also constitute such [nonconceptual wisdom] because they do not entertain conceptions during these states. If it were nonconceptual merely by virtue of being so **naturally**, objects such as [material] forms would also be nonconceptual [wisdom] because they do not entertain conceptions due to being immovable. Nor is it reasonable that it is the **picturing** of the very aspect of nonconceptuality. If one is in the process of mentally engaging [by thinking], "Nonconceptuality is like that" or "This is nonconceptuality," this wisdom[427] does not arise because the mental engagement of conceiving and designating [something] as nonconceptuality is also nothing but an aspect of conceptuality. Therefore, one should understand that this wisdom {35b} is free from **the specific characteristics of these five factors**. Here

> **The thorough knowledge of the distinctive features is by virtue of the five distinctive features of being nonconceptual, unlimited, nonabiding, lasting, and unsurpassable.**

This is because this wisdom is more eminent than [those] of śrāvakas and pratyekabuddhas **by virtue of five distinctive features**. For their wisdoms entail conceptions because śrāvakas and pratyekabuddhas conceive of the qualities of nirvāṇa and the flaws of saṃsāra. [Their wisdoms] are limited because they focus merely on the general characteristics of the four realities of the noble ones. They also abide [somewhere because they abide in nirvāṇa. [Their wisdoms] are not lasting either because they become extinct in the nirvāṇa without any remainder of the skandhas, just as it is explained in the sūtra [passages] on [the path] being like a raft.[428] They are also surpassable because buddha wisdom surpasses them.

The wisdom of buddhas and bodhisattvas is more eminent by virtue of **the** five **distinctive features** that are the opposites of these. [It is eminent] by virtue of being **nonconceptual** because it does not conceive of flaws or qualities in terms of saṃsāra and nirvāṇa. It is **unlimited** because what it takes as its objects are the specific and general characteristics of all knowable objects, precisely as they are. It is **nonabiding** because it neither adopts nirvāṇa nor rejects saṃsāra. It is **lasting** because, by virtue of the dharmakāya ([its] foundation) being permanent, its continuum does not even become extinct in the nirvāṇa without any remainder of the skandhas. It is **unsurpassable** because there is nothing more supremely eminent than it. Here

> **The thorough knowledge of the functions is by virtue of the fivefold distinctive features of function—distancing conceptions, accomplishing unsurpassable bliss, freeing from the afflictive and cognitive obscurations, {36a} engaging in all aspects of knowable**

> **objects through the wisdom that is attained subsequent to it, and purifying buddha realms, maturing sentient beings, and granting the knowledge of all aspects.**

This wisdom performs **the** following **five functions.** It **distances** [itself] from the movement of **conceptions** because it has overcome the arising [of the latent tendencies of ignorance about suchness]. It **accomplishes unsurpassable bliss** because, through realizing the suchness and variety of [all] knowable objects, it accomplishes all eminent, unmistaken, and lasting bliss. It makes one attain the **freedom from the afflictive and cognitive obscurations** because it overcomes the contaminations, including their latent tendencies. **The wisdom that is** the [cognizing] subject with the specific characteristic of being **attained subsequent to** the nonconceptuality [during meditative equipoise] also **engages in all aspects of knowable objects.** In addition, it is **purifying buddha realms, maturing sentient beings, and granting the knowledge of all aspects.**

> **As for the comprehension of mental engagement, bodhisattvas who wish to engage in nonconceptual [wisdom] by all means engage mentally by thinking the following:**

As for teaching the progression [of this, Maitreya says]:

> **False imagination consists of what contains all seeds,**

that is, it **consists of** the ālaya-consciousness. [It is]

> **the cause for what does not exist appearing as duality**

because it is seized by the latent tendencies of clinging to **duality,**

> **and the other continuum that is based on that,**

which is understood as the operating consciousnesses. As for [false imagination occurring] "**due to being ignorant about suchness,**" [it means that it occurs] due to the latent tendencies of ignorance that [exist] **since beginningless time.**[429]

> **Therefore,**

that is, because of ignorance being the cause of mistakenness,

> **what entails cause and result appears,[430] but does not exist.**

False imagination {36b} always **appears** to cognition, **but does** definitely **not exist**. Furthermore,

> **by virtue of its appearing, the nature of phenomena does not appear,**

that is, suchness **does not appear.**

> **By virtue of its not appearing, the nature of phenomena does appear**

because the [nature of phenomena] is characterized by the lack of that [false imagination].

Through their **mentally engaging** through aspiration,

> **bodhisattvas who mentally engage in this way engage in nonconceptual wisdom.**

[This phase] consists of the path of preparation.

> **By virtue of such observing,**

that is, **observing** that false imagination appears, but does not exist, and so on,

> **they engage in observing [everything] as mere cognizance**

because **cognizance** is the appearing of duality.

> **By virtue of observing [everything] as mere cognizance, they engage in not observing any referents**

because it is nothing but **cognizance** that appears as referents, and therefore external **referents** do not exist.

> **By virtue of not observing any referents, they engage in not observing mere cognizance [either]**

because cognizance is **not** established as this very **cognizance** [either]. For if there are **no referents** to be cognized, cognizance is not reasonable [either].

By virtue of not observing that [cognizance],

that is, **by virtue of not observing** apprehender and apprehended,

they engage in observing the lack of difference between those two

because there is no difference between those two by virtue of their not existing as two. It should be understood that the very nonobservation of those two as the natures of apprehender and apprehended is the **observation** of **the lack of difference between those two** because a difference is [only] cognized if there are two [distinct phenomena].

Here the nonobservation of these two,

that is, **the nonobservation of** apprehender and apprehended,

is nonconceptual wisdom,

which teaches the subject matter. Thus, bodhisattvas who wish to comprehend **nonconceptual wisdom** in this way mentally engage in it in such a way. In this manner, {37a} [Maitreya] teaches what he taught before—that the mental engagement in this way is the comprehension of nonconceptual wisdom. That

it lacks an object

[is said] for the sake of excluding that it is something that has **an object** as in the case of the eyes and so on. For even though [nonconceptual wisdom] lacks [any] observing, [one may think that the fact of its] having an object exists.[431] [That it]

lacks observing

teaches that it is not **observing** objects such as form

because it is characterized by not observing any characteristics.

This conclude the explanation of the defining characteristics of wisdom and their comprehension.

Now, if you wonder how bodhisattvas train, [Maitreya] teaches the training in attaining this wisdom.

> **The comprehension of the training is also fourfold by virtue of the training through aspiration on the level of engagement through aspiration (this is the very phase of discernment taught above).**

[One also trains]

> **by virtue of the training in direct realization on the first bhūmi**

because this is the **direct realization** of the dharmadhātu through the path of seeing.

> **(This is the very phase of contact taught above).**

[One further trains]

> **by virtue of the training in familiarization on the six impure bhūmis,**

that is, the second **bhūmi** and so on. They are **impure** because one [still] entertains characteristics. [Then one trains]

> **on the three pure bhūmis,**

that is, on the eighth one and so on. They are **pure** because one does not entertain characteristics. For [their] remedy—the path—operates all by its own.

> **(This is the phase of recollection taught above).**

[Finally one trains]

> **by virtue of the training in completion on the buddhabhūmi because the deeds of a buddha are effortless and uninterrupted.**

That by virtue of which one immediately attains **the uninterrupted deeds of a buddha** is called "**the training in completion.**"

> **(This is the very phase of the arrival at the nature of the [nature of phenomena] taught above).**

This is **the very arrival at the nature of the** [nature of phenomena] because of having become the nature of this wisdom and therefore {37b} being of one taste with the wisdom of the fundamental change. Here

> **As for comprehending the shortcomings, these are the four shortcomings of there being no fundamental change,**

that is,

> **the shortcoming of there being no support for the afflictions not operating.**

If there were no fundamental change, without a support due to **there being no fundamental change**, how could abiding in the nature of phenomena, in which henceforth afflictions do not arise, operate? Therefore, just as with the support for the afflictions operating, there must be a support for their [not operating]. [Otherwise, this] constitutes **the flaw of there being no support for the afflictions not operating.**

Likewise, just as contaminated consciousness operates with a support, its remedy must also do so with a **support**. Therefore, [without such a support,] there is

> **the flaw of there being no support for engaging in the path.**

Furthermore, for example, in the case of a person in saṃsāra, the skandhas are designated as "[being in] saṃsāra." Likewise, there must be a basis for designating the persons who have passed into parinirvāṇa. First, it is not tenable that mind is this [basis] because the ceasing of the antagonistic factors and the arising of their remedies is simultaneous and also because two contrary [phenomena] within the same support are untenable, just as a cold and a warm sensation are untenable within the same support. In addition, [there must be that basis for designating persons who have passed into nirvāṇa] because there would be no basis for [such a] designation once [a saṃsāric person] has passed into the nirvāṇa without any remainder of the skandhas. Therefore, there must be a **basis for designating the persons who have passed into nirvāṇa** that corresponds to the skandhas [as the basis for designating persons in saṃsāra]. [Otherwise, there is]

> **the flaw of there being no basis for designating the persons who have passed into nirvāṇa.**

The fourth [flaw] is

> **the flaw of there being no basis for designating the differences between the three [types of] enlightenment.**

Therefore, the fundamental change that functions[432] as the entity that is [such] a basis exists.

> **One should know that, when there is the fundamental change, the opposites of those are the four kinds of benefit. Thus, {38a} one should understand that these are the ten points of comprehending the fundamental change.**

It has already been explained how false imagination appears, but does not exist.[433] Nevertheless, [some] examples that give rise to confidence in this shall be described here. Therefore, [Maitreya] says:

> **Examples for nonexistents appearing are illusions, dreams, and so on.**

For **example**, though **illusions, dreams, and so on** are observed, they are not existent. Likewise, phenomena **appear**, but are definitely **nonexistent**. The phrase "and so on" means that one should also understand "antelope thirst,"[434] the city of gandharvas, and so on as well as mirages, echoes, [reflections of] the moon [in] water, and so on [to be suitable examples].

As for it having been explained how comprehending the fundamental change is unsurpassable through those ten points, it may be asked, "When something has undergone this fundamental change, it has changed into something else. Consequently, how is what has undergone the fundamental change not something that is altered?" Therefore, [Maitreya] says that the manner in which there is a fundamental change without it referring to something that is altered is established through examples.

> **Examples for the fundamental change are space, gold, water, and so on.**

For **example, space** is [always] nothing but pure by nature. It is only by virtue of its being associated with adventitious fog and so on that this [purity] is not realized,[435] but it is [seen to be] pure by virtue of [eventually] becoming free from such [adventitious obscurations]. Since it is not the case that impure [space] becomes pure, it is not that its being pure arises [newly]. Rather, it is just that [its purity] is observed by virtue of its being free from causes for not observing it. It is also not that one should claim space to be something that is altered through its being observed as being utterly pure.

In the same way, **gold** too solely remains in [its state of] being immaculate. It is just not observed [as being immaculate] by virtue of its being covered over by adventitious stains, but it is observed [as being immaculate] by virtue of [eventually] becoming free from such [stains]. It is also not that [its being immaculate] has arisen by virtue of this observing. {38b}

Likewise, **water** [always] remains totally clear. It is just not observed [as being clear] by virtue of this water being associated with earth substances, but it is observed [as being clear] by virtue of being free from those earth substances. It is also not that, by virtue of observing [its clarity], [this clarity] has arisen in such a way that it has not been present [before] in this substance of water that represents a continuous stream [of individual moments]. Nor is it that one should claim the substance of water to be something that is altered through its being observed as being clear.

In the same way, in **the fundamental change** too, natural luminosity is not something that did not exist before, but it does just not appear by virtue of adventitious stains appearing. This is just as with [space, gold, and water, respectively, appearing] to be impure, not immaculate, and turbid. By virtue of being free from these [adventitious stains], [natural luminosity] appears. However, it is not that it arises—in such a way that it has not been present [before]—by virtue of the appearance of an alteration due to the nature of phenomena entailing [such an] alteration. Since there is no such [alteration], the nature of phenomena and the fundamental change that is constituted by it are permanent. Here [the fundamental change of the nature of phenomena] is taught through the examples of gold and water as being congruent with their properties only in terms of their qualities, without considering their [respective material] substances. Through the example of space, however, it is taught in its entirety. Through the phrase "**and so on**," other similar such kinds [of examples] are to be understood [as being appropriate] too, such as a cloth and so on abiding in its [state of] being clean through having become free from stains.

This concludes A Commentary on The Distinction between Phenomena and the Nature of Phenomena *composed by master Vasubandhu. It was translated by the Kashmirian paṇḍita Mahājana and the translator Loden Sherab.*

Sarva maṅgalam

The Third Karmapa's Ornament That Explains *The Treatise on The Distinction between Phenomena and the Nature of Phenomena*

{489} I pay homage to all buddhas and bodhisattvas.

You were empowered so that your body of the qualities of a victor is complete.
Through the wheel of your ocean of wisdom, you were victorious over the māras.
You display an ocean of enlightened activity for beings who possess the disposition—
To the son of the victors, Ajita, I pay homage.

Through your powerful aspiration prayers to see the actuality of the nature of phenomena,
You illuminated the teachings—to the lineage of gurus
Such as noble Asaṅga and Vasubandhu
I always pay homage with respect and venerate it as much as I can.

So that the profound that is beyond being an object of [ordinary] persons—
This manner of distinguishing between phenomena and the nature of phenomena—
May appear in my own mind
And may be realized by those who possess the dharma, I make an effort [here].

The completely perfect {490} Buddha, by virtue of being endowed with compassion beyond measure, taught the eighty-four thousand collections of dharma, and the children of the victor collected his words again and again. Nevertheless, seeing that the light of the mahāyāna is slightly obscured for those with inferior aspirations, the great bodhisattva Maitreya composed these five dharmas of Maitreya.[436] He composed the *Abhisamayālaṃkāra* to clearly teach prajñāpāramitā, the middle [cycle of the] Buddha's words, which is the dharma wheel of the lack of characteristics. The *Mahāyānasūtrālaṃkāra* illuminates the meanings of all teachings of the sūtra collections in all [dharma wheels], the first one, the middle one, and so on. {491} The *Madhyāntavibhāga* teaches the meanings of the defining characteristics [of afflicted and purified phenomena] up through the unsurpassable yāna. The *Dharmadharmatāvibhāga* elucidates the meanings of saṃsāra and nirvāṇa. The *Uttaratantra* summarizes the meanings of the sūtras of the last [cycle of the] Buddha's words and of those that teach the buddhayāna.

As for the arrival of these [texts] in this human realm, at the time when eight hundred years had elapsed after the Tathāgata had passed into nirvāṇa, through the power of former aspiration prayers, noble Asaṅga and Vasubandhu were born as the sons of the Brahman woman *Prakāśaśīlā.[437] When noble Asaṅga had practiced for twelve years on Mount Kukkuṭapāda, [Maitreya] showed his face to him and they went to Tuṣita. Having listened [there] to the yogācārabhūmis in one hundred thousand [lines][438] and so on for fifty human years,[439] he returned to the human realm and elucidated the teachings. He composed [many] treatises that provide a synopsis of all the teachings [of the Buddha], such as the fivefold bhūmi collection and the twofold collection of synopses.[440] He is also prophesied in the *Mañjuśrīmūlatantra*:

> The fully ordained monk called Asaṅga,
> Who is learned in the meanings of the treatises,
> In many ways distinguishes
> The expedient meaning and the definitive meaning of the sūtra collections.
> In order for the teachings to remain for a long time,
> He summarizes the meaning of the true reality of the sūtras.

The supreme one among the learned, Vasubandhu, also composed [many texts] such as the eightfold *prakaraṇa* collection and commentaries on the dharmas of Maitreya and so on.[441] {492}

Though [there are all these] vast [teachings], in particular, this *Distinction between Phenomena and the Nature of Phenomena* illuminates the path, including its fruition, which consist of the manner of engaging in the five dharmas and the three natures ([both of] which elucidate the principle of the two realities) as well as in the true reality of the eight consciousnesses—the nonconceptual wisdom that bears the name "fundamental change," that is, the buddha heart, the dharmakāya. Implicitly, it also teaches the liberations of all śrāvakas and pratyekabuddhas. Therefore, it resembles a gate to enter all the words of the Buddha and the treatises [on them].

Thus, to teach this [text] in a clear manner, this [commentary] has two parts:

1) The title and the homage spoken by the translators
2) The actual treatise

1. The title and the homage spoken by the translators

In Indian language: **Dharmadharmatāvibhāga**
In Tibetan language: **Chö dang chönyi nampar jépa**
[In English: **The Distinction between Phenomena and the Nature of Phenomena**]

I pay homage to the Bhagavān Ajita.

[The title and the homage] being adduced by the translators at the beginning of the treatise [has the following] three purposes. Through providing [the title] in Indian language at the beginning, trust in [the authentic origin of] the dharma [that the text contains] arises. Since Sanskrit is the supreme of languages, [the mentioning of the title in Sanskrit] plants [some] tendencies [for this language in the mind] and is of great blessing. Through translating it into Tibetan, one understands the connection between the title and its meaning. The purpose is that, through the title, one understands the meaning, and through the meaning, one remembers the title. To match both [the Sanskrit and the Tibetan titles] has the purposes of understanding whether the terms [in the Tibetan] are justified or wrong, understanding that they accord in meaning, {493} and remembering the great kindness [of the translators]. Though such is stated, the royal decree [for translating Buddhist texts into Tibetan simply] provides the following rule: "Follow this order of stating the title of the dharma that is translated at the beginning and paying homage." Therefore, I refrain from saying much [more] here.

When [the title] is translated, **dharma** [means] "phenomena" (*chö*). As for **dharmatā**, the syllable *tā*[442] [indicates] the nondual dharma, that is, "the nature of phenomena" (*chönyi*). **Vibhāga** [means] "distinction" (*nampar jépa*). Thus, [this refers to] the distinction between the factors to be relinquished and their remedy, describing [how] the title accords with the meaning. The detailed explanation of this is found below. As for the homage, here the translators and paṇḍitas pay homage to the author of the treatise, noble Maitreya, with body, speech, and mind so as to [be able to] complete the translation and be in accord with the style of genuine [beings]. As for [Maitreya] being called "Ajita," it is [one of his] epithets. Since the Victor prophesied, "You will become a buddha after me," those in the pure abodes proclaim, "You are the invincible one."

2. The actual treatise

This has three parts:

1) Presentation of the body [of the text][443]
2) The actual topics
3) Conclusion [through] examples [and their] meanings

2.1. Presentation of the body [of the text]

> **Since something is to be relinquished after being understood**
> **And something else is to be made fully perceptible,**[444]
> **Therefore, this treatise was composed out of the wish**
> **To distinguish these two through their defining characteristics.**[445]

Here some may think that this just states the [author's] commitment to explain [the distinction between phenomena and the nature of phenomena] without paying homage. {494} [However,] these five treatises represent a single continuous effort [by Maitreya]. In order for these five to ascertain the meaning of the entire teachings, it is evident that homage is paid at the beginning [of the five texts] in the *Abhisamayālaṃkāra*, while the completion part in the *Uttaratantra* teaches the dedication. [Through this,] one also realizes the order of these [five texts] as follows. [The *Abhisamayālaṃkāra*] was composed first because prajñāpāramitā is like the mother of all texts that teach the paths and fruitions of all wonderful yānas which give birth to all four noble ones. [By saying] that the diverse [other] sūtras of the three yānas accord with this point just mentioned, the *Mahāyānasūtrālaṃkāra* ascertains that they belong to the scope of what is to be understood and clearly realized. As a summary of this, the *Madhyāntavibhāga* explains merely how to engage in the defining characteristics of the factors to be relinquished and their remedies, the obscurations of these, true reality, abiding in the manner of cultivating the remedies plus their results, and the unsurpassable yāna.[446] If all of what is taught in this way is summarized further, everything is contained in this comprehension of phenomena and the nature of phenomena [that is taught here in the *Dharmadharmatāvibhāga*]. The *Uttaratantra* teaches the actuality of the nature of phenomena—the basic nature of buddhahood, the final definitive meaning—which lies not within the sphere of any ordinary beings, śrāvakas, or pratyekabuddhas. {495} [This nature is taught as] its being associated with [adventitious] stains, stainless enlightenment, its qualities, [its] enlightened activity, and the manner of engaging [in it].[447] Thus, one should know that all the words of the Buddha's teaching and the treatises [on it] are summarized [in these five texts].

This single verse [above] teaches the [set of] "purpose and connection" at the beginning of the treatise, which is fourfold—the two kinds of purpose, the connection in order to realize what is to be adopted and to be relinquished, and the characteristics of the subject matter as well as the distinction in terms of the means of expression.[448] You may wonder, "What is the point in teaching the purpose at the beginning?" Those who rely on the meaning [rather than the words] engage [in a text] through first seeing the purpose [for doing so]. Therefore, the purpose [here] consists of understanding, based on this discussion of phenomena and the nature of phenomena, that phenomena consist of afflicted phenomena (saṃsāra) and understanding that the nature of phenomena has the defining characteristic of being what is purified. The essential purpose is to engage, based on this [understanding], in what is to be adopted and to be relinquished. In this way, there manifests the connection of realizing, "The subject matter and the means of expression of the treatise are such and such." Therefore, the statement about purpose and connection is given at the beginning.

The basis for the manifestation [of the fourfold set] of purpose and connection through the actual body of the treatise consists of the meaning of phenomena and the nature of phenomena (the subject matter) being taught by this treatise (the statements that are the means of expressing [this subject matter]). Through this, based on the mere connection of [such] statements and [the meanings] that entail these statements being interdependent, the knowledge of realizing what is to be adopted and to be relinquished {496} arises and, through this condition, [one understands] the purpose of engaging in the path. The essential purpose is that, through having engaged in the path, the wisdom of the fundamental change will be realized.

Having explained the enumeration and the order of this pair of purpose and connection in this way in general, [in the above phrase] "**something is to be relinquished after being understood**," what is to be relinquished is the false imagination that gives rise to all contaminated afflicted phenomena and suffering and makes one wander in the cycle of saṃsāra forever. "**Something else is to be made fully perceptible**" refers to the stainless nature of phenomena, the buddha heart, nonconceptual wisdom, prajñāpāramitā, the dharmakāya. Through the realization that is connected to the correct view based on the pure buddhadharma that is its natural outflow, one comprehends this [nature], ascertains it, [makes it] appear, and completes it through familiarizing with it.[449] For this reason, having realized the connection between phenomena and the nature of phenomena in terms of what is to be adopted and to be relinquished, respectively, the subject matter (the defining characteristics of phenomena and the nature of phenomena) is taught as having the defining characteristics that are explained below. Therefore, the distinction in terms of the means of expression [is found in the phrase] "**out of the wish to distinguish these two through their defining characteristics.**" Since all knowable objects are contained in phenomena and the nature of phenomena, [Vasubandhu's] commentary[450] says that this refers to the distinction of their defining characteristics, but it is neither a distinction in terms of different objects nor a distinction in terms of singling out these two [—phenomena and their nature—] from among a [larger] multitude.[451] {497}

The nature [of phenomena and their nature] consists of the three natures, with saṃsāra [consisting] of the imaginary and the dependent [natures], while the perfect [nature]—suchness and perfect wisdom—represents nirvāṇa.[452] Therefore, this is a division by way of defining characteristics, but not [in terms of] different objects. For example, just as when a rope is mistaken for being a snake, the imaginary [nature] is [like the snake for which the rope is mistaken, that is,] a nonexistent that [seems to] appear. The dependent [nature] is [like] the rope—it appears, but it does not really exist[453] in the way [it appears], that is, it is a collection of threads that appears as merely a [certain] color and shape [to the eyes]. The perfect [nature] is (a) the snake's and the rope's very own nature of lacking real existence and (b) unmistaken self-awareness, since [such awareness] is without mistakenness about what appears [to it].[454] Therefore, [phenomena and their nature] do not exist as different objects. This very point is also expressed by noble Nāgārjuna:

> Between saṃsāra and nirvāṇa
> There is not the slightest difference.
> Between nirvāṇa and saṃsāra
> There is not the slightest difference.[455]

Furthermore, the domain of everything [in] saṃsāra and nirvāṇa is the dharmadhātu, which is their general characteristic. The *Madhyāntavibhāga* says:

> Except for the dharmadhātu
> There is thus no phenomenon.
> Therefore, it is the general characteristic,
> And this is the unmistakenness about it.[456]

As for [this distinction] not referring to singling out two [—phenomena and their nature—] from among a [larger] multitude, [Vasubandhu's] commentary[457] says that the entirety of the Bhagavān's presentations of skandhas, dhātus, āyatanas, and so on, when summarized, {498} is twofold, that is, [it consists of] phenomena and their nature.

As for [the above phrase] "**this treatise was composed**," it is the Bhagavān Maitreya who authored this principle of comprehending all [the Buddha's presentations through the distinction of phenomena and the nature of phenomena].[458]

This concludes the explanation of the presentation of the body of the treatise. Since conceptual refutations and affirmations and so on are of little meaning, I let them be [here].

2.2. The actual topics

This has two parts:

1) Brief introduction
2) Detailed explanation

2.2.1. Brief introduction

This has seven parts:

1) General instruction
2) The distinction of both [phenomena and the nature of phenomena]
3) The defining characteristic of phenomena
4) The defining characteristic of the nature of phenomena
5) The reason for mistakenness
6) If one does not exist, they do not appear as two
7) Not asserting them as being one or different

2.2.1.1. General instruction

> **All this is twofold because it is included in phenomena and the nature of phenomena.**

"**All this**" refers to the entire multitude that makes up saṃsāra and nirvāṇa. It **is twofold**—the factors to be relinquished (the **phenomena** of saṃsāra) **and** the liberation from them (**the nature of phenomena**—the nirvāṇa that is to be made fully perceptible through the three yānas).[459] In this general instruction, one does not know [yet] what consists of what. Therefore, [the text continues with:]

2.2.1.2. The distinction of both [phenomena and the nature of phenomena]

> **What constitutes phenomena is saṃsāra. What constitutes the nature of phenomena is the nirvāṇa of the three yānas.**

Here **saṃsāra** {499} is explained to consist of false imagination—the mind with stains, the ālaya-consciousness. This refers to all contaminated virtuous, nonvirtuous, and neutral **phenomena** that make up the three realms. The *Madhyāntavibhāga* says:

> False imagination [consists of]
> The minds and mental factors of the three realms.[460]

The nature of phenomena consists of the unchanging and unmistaken perfect [nature]. Its own nature **is the nirvāṇa of the three yānas** of śrāvakas, pratyekabuddhas, and bodhisattvas.[461] It is also explained that this refers to the phenomena that make up what is free from attachment (the reality of cessation) and what frees from attachment (the reality of the path). It is called "the stainless dharmadhātu and the very profound dharmakāya that is its natural outflow."[462] Respectively, [these two] are taught by the names "buddha" and "dharma." The *Uttaratantra* [says]:

> By virtue of its being inconceivable, free from the dual,
> nonconceptual,
> Pure, manifesting, and remedial,
> It is what is and what makes free from attachment, respectively—
> The dharma that is characterized by the two realities.
>
> Freedom from attachment consists of
> The two realities of cessation and the path.[463]

And

> The dharmakāya is to be known as twofold—
> The utterly stainless dharmadhātu
> And its natural outflow, teaching
> The principles of profundity and diversity.[464]

This is also explained as the following synonyms—{500} "buddha," "dharma," "the inseparable actuality," "the disposition," "suchness," "attaining the fruition," "the true undeceiving ultimate," "primordial peace." [In the *Uttaratantra*] we find:

> [They] are the inseparability of the buddha qualities,
> The disposition for that being obtained just as it is,
> Its true nature being without falsity and deception,
> And its being natural primordial peace.[465]

One speaks of a "yāna" by virtue of its proceeding somewhere or proceeding through it. For this reason, since those who engage in the mahāyāna must manifest the seeing of all knowable objects, the eminent sūtras speak of the ālaya-consciousness as the foundation of knowable objects; the three natures, as the defining characteristics of knowable objects; mere cognizance, as the engagement in them; the six pāramitās, as the causes and results of engaging in them; the ten bhūmis, as the means of familiarization; the three trainings (the vajra of bodhisattvas, as the training in ethics; [the samādhis of] the heroic stride, the sky treasure, and so on, as [the training in] samādhi; and nonconceptual wisdom, as the training in prajñā); the nonabiding nirvāṇa, as the fruition in terms of relinquishment; and the three kāyas, as the fruition in terms of attainment. The *Mahāyānasaṃgraha* says:

> The foundation of knowable objects, [their] defining
> characteristics, the engagement in them,
> The causes and results of this, its divisions,
> The three trainings, {501} and their fruitional
> Relinquishment and wisdom constitute the eminence of the
> supreme yāna.[466]

Here, in terms of the defining characteristics [of knowable objects], the two that are the imaginary and dependent [natures] are explained as representing the obscurations and phenomena. The perfect [nature]—the fundamental change—is said to be the nature of phenomena. Therefore, this includes all ten topics [of the *Mahāyānasaṃgraha*]. Another enumeration of these is stated in the *Laṅkāvatārasūtra*:

> In the five dharmas, the [three] natures,
> The eight consciousnesses,
> And the two kinds of identitylessness
> The entire mahāyāna is included.[467]

Thus, it refers to the five dharmas and the three natures. [Elsewhere in this text] we find:

> Names, causal features, and imagination
> Are the defining characteristics of the [first] two natures.
> Perfect wisdom and suchness
> Are the defining characteristics of the perfect [nature].[468]

Thus, names and causal features represent the imaginary [nature] and imagination is the dependent [nature]. These two [natures] make up phenomena. Perfect wisdom refers to the uncontaminated phenomena that consist of [the realities of] cessation and the path. Suchness is the nature of the two realities that is present in all knowable objects, that is, the lack of nature of all phenomena. Among these [latter] two, the former is the unmistaken perfect [nature] and the latter is the unchanging perfect [nature].[469] Among these three [natures], the latter one[470] is called "ālaya," while the former two [natures] are called "ālaya-consciousness." Since the other consciousnesses—the afflicted mind and the six collections—are in {502} a mutual [relationship of] dependent origination with [the ālaya-consciousness], the eight consciousnesses are explained to be the obscurations. It is taught that the four wisdoms are the stainlessness of these consciousnesses and therefore the perfect nature, with the dharmadhātu wisdom being like the matrix of all of these [wisdoms]. Therefore, [these consciousnesses and wisdoms] represent the factors to be relinquished and their remedies, [respectively].

For this reason, the assertion by some people who present the unfolding disposition based on the ālaya-consciousness and thus [claim] that the dharmas during subsequent attainment that accomplish the two kāyas arise from the ālaya-consciousness is wrong.[471] Also, since the sūtras and tantras explain that this [unfolding disposition] relinquishes the ālaya-consciousness by way of overcoming it through the vajralike [samādhi], a philosophical system with the assertion that buddhas do not possess wisdom came about, [but] such is wrong [too]. This is also [stated] in the *Mahāyānasaṃgraha*:

> "Why is it called 'ālaya-consciousness'?" All afflicted phenomena that entail arising adhere to it as [its] resultant entities, or it adheres to them as [their] causal entity. Therefore, it is the ālaya-consciousness.[472]

Thus, [the ālaya-consciousness] is identified in terms of afflicted phenomena, but purified phenomena are not included in it. Furthermore, in the context of explaining the dominant condition, [the *Mahāyānasaṃgraha*] says:

> Just as the ālaya-consciousness is the cause of afflicted phenomena, these afflicted phenomena are presented in turn as the causal condition for the ālaya-consciousness since no other causal condition is observable.[473]

This [relationship between the ālaya-consciousness and all afflicted phenomena] {503} is the basis of saṃsāric dependent origination, the "dependent origination of differentiating the nature." Based on it, the twelve [links] of "the dependent origination of differentiating what is desired and undesired" come about.[474] The dependent origination of nirvāṇa consists of the two [aspects of the perfect nature]—the unchanging and the unmistaken. [Respectively, these two] should be understood as twofold—the two realities in terms of the nature of knowable objects and the two realities in terms of the convention of the pure mind that is the knower [of this nature]. These are respectively explained as the two dharmakāyas. They represent the remedy for the ālaya-consciousness. The *Mahāyānasaṃgraha* states:

> "How could the maturational consciousness with all the seeds, which is the cause of afflicted phenomena, be the seed of its remedy, that is, supramundane mind? Since supramundane mind is not contained in [the minds of ordinary beings], the latent tendencies of this [supramundane mind] do not exist [in them]. But if these latent tendencies do not exist [in them], it must be stated from which seeds they arise." [Supramundane mind] originates from the natural outflow of the pure dharmadhātu, that is, the seeds which are the latent tendencies for listening.[475]

Because these [latent tendencies of the supramundane mind] and the stains exist as a mixture right now, [the text continues]:

> What these latent tendencies for listening in dependence on the enlightenment of a buddha are, which matrix they enter, and that they enter the maturational consciousness in a manner of coexisting with it—all this is like [a mixture of] milk and water. They are not the ālaya-consciousness because they are the very seeds of its remedy.[476]

{504} Therefore, as taught below, the dharmakāya originates from uncontaminated dharmas, but since the basic element of the stainless dharmakāya exists right now, the dharmas that are its natural outflow arise. Look at this in detail in the *Mahāyānasaṃgraha* and the *Yogācārabhūmi*. [I summarize] what is emphatically taught here in [some] intermediate verses:

> In the sky of the great dharmadhātu,
> The characteristics of saṃsāra and nirvāṇa are like illusions.
> The perfect [nature as] the dependent origination of the nature of phenomena
> [Consists] of the dharmakāya and the dharmas that are its natural outflow.

What appears while not existing is the dependent origination
Of the causes and results of nonrealization,[477] conception,
imagination,
And the ālaya-consciousness that is based on them.

When you understand these two in an unmistaken way,
This is the prajñā of distinguishing saṃsāra and nirvāṇa,
Which is praised by the victors.

Nowadays, most scholars and siddhas
Resemble blind people speaking about grabbing an elephant.
Therefore, take seriously what is elucidated here
In this [treatise on] phenomena and the nature of phenomena.

Having taught the distinction [between phenomena and the nature of phenomena] in this way, [the text continues with]

2.2.1.3. The explanation of the defining characteristic of phenomena

This is taught through three parts:

1) The actual defining characteristic
2) Hermeneutical etymology [of false imagination]
3) The meaning of imagination

2.2.1.3.1. The actual defining characteristic

What appears as duality and the according designations is false imagination, which is the defining characteristic of phenomena.

What appears as duality consists of the six apprehended objects (which appear as forms, sounds, smells, tastes, tangible objects, and phenomena) and {505} the six apprehenders (the consciousnesses of the eyes, ears, nose, tongue, body, and mind). As for **the according designations**, based on conceptions, [names are imputed, such as,] "This is form." Based on the distinct features of color and shape that derive from such [form], for example, something white and round in the sky is labeled with the name "moon." Based on such imputations, one apprehends characteristics and so on of this white and round referent. [So,] what appears to be designated in these ways is [also] false imagination. Thus, **phenomena** consist of what, based on the twelve āyatanas, [appear as] duality and the according designations. This is the instruction on the complete and unmistaken **defining characteristic** [of phenomena].[478]

2.2.1.3.2. Hermeneutical etymology of this [false imagination]

> **Since what does not exist appears, it is false.**

Since these phenomena are **not existent**, yet are **appearing, they are false.** You may wonder how it is that they do not exist. Though childish beings think that something like a [visible] form is really existent, it [actually] lacks real existence. The śrāvakas cling to something like a vase not being really existent as something singular in the way [it appears], but being composed of many minute particles, with these particles being really existent. However, if these particles are divided into ten or six sides by virtue of their parts, it is established that they are not really existent. Thus, if the object is not really existent, how could it be reasonable that the cognition which apprehends the [apprehended] aspect that [appears as] a vase is unmistaken? {506} This is [obvious] from the words of the great being [Maitreya]:

> If there is nothing apprehended, there is no apprehender of it.
> Without this, consciousness does not exist either.[479]

Therefore, it is established that [external] referents do not really exist. [At the same time,] they still appear, that is, by virtue of the dependent origination of object, sense faculty, and cognition, they appear as mere cognizance in the form of the aspects of color and shape, [such as] the aspect that is a vase. Master Dignāga says [in his *Ālambanaparīkṣāvṛtti*]:

> The nature of internal knowable objects is that which appears as if it were external—this is [what appears as] a referent. While there are no external referents, that which appears as if it were external definitely exists internally—this is the object condition.[480]

Internal knowable objects are nothing but mere cognizance. Since nothing but this appears as the aspects of object, sense faculty, and cognition, these function as if they were object condition, dominant condition, and immediate condition, [respectively,] for each other. Therefore, this cognizance is called "dependent."[481] The *Mahāyānasūtrālaṃkāra* says:

> What appear as three aspects each
> Are the characteristics of apprehender and apprehended,
> Which are false imagination,
> The characteristic of the dependent.[482]

What appear as [the three aspects of] places, referents, and bodies are not at all established as having the natures of such [places and so on]. They are nothing but mere conceptions that exist as mere mistaken appearances. For these reasons, one speaks of "false imagination" and "the imaginary." This is twofold—the nominal imaginary and the imaginary without any characteristics.[483] In brief, [the imaginary] consists of names {507} and causal features. The [above] three [aspects of] what is apprehended as well as the three [aspects of] the apprehender—the afflicted mind, the apprehenders that are the five [sense] doors, and the sixth [consciousness] (the mental [consciousness], including conception)—appear in these ways, but are not really existent. Therefore, they constitute false imagination.

2.2.1.3.3. Teaching yet another meaning of imagination

> **In all [respects], it is without referents and is mere conception.**
> **Therefore, it is imagination.**

[Appearances] do not really exist as referents, but they appear. Thus,[484] it is by virtue of beginningless latent tendencies (such as those of forms and feelings) that the causal features of referents appear at present, that they appear as if they were referents, and that they are discriminated [as such. All this] makes up the nominal imaginary [nature]. [The *Mahāyānasūtrālaṃkāra*] says:

> The causal features of referents
> As designated, their latent tendencies,
> And the appearance of referents through them
> Constitute the imaginary characteristic.[485]

By virtue of having labeled something white and round in the sky as "moon," when its name is pronounced, even if this referent is not [visible], a white and round aspect comes to mind. [Likewise,] with regard to the aspect that has the shape of a round belly and so on, one thinks, "This is a vase."[486] These are [instances of] the imaginary [nature]. [The *Mahāyānasūtrālaṃkāra*] says:

> That referents appear like [their] names {508}
> And names [like their] referents
> Is the cause of false conception,
> Which is the defining characteristic of the imaginary.[487]

Both kinds of the imaginary **are mere conception** and expressions that are based on conception, and thus **are without referents. Therefore, they are** called "**imagination.**" Since those who cling to them, just as deers chasing after a mirage, create nothing but suffering, this is pointless.[488] This completes the explanation of the characteristic of phenomena.

2.2.1.4. The defining characteristic of the nature of phenomena

> **The defining characteristic of the nature of phenomena is suchness, which lacks any distinction between apprehender and apprehended, or [between] objects of designation and what designates them.**

The appearance of the duality of **apprehender and apprehended** is not really existent. Therefore, the fact that this duality actually does not exist is the basic nature that is the nature of phenomena. As for [this nature] **lacking any** difference **between objects of designation and what designates them**, nonduality cannot be expressed, just as when Mañjuśrī rejoiced in Vimalakīrti not saying anything.[489] This is the basic nature that is the perfect [nature]. The imaginary is absolutely nonexistent, and if that nonexistent is realized to be nonexistent, this is unmistakenness, which is consequently existent. However, on the level of seeming reality, both existents and nonexistents are equal in being nothing but mere cognizance. Ultimately, within nonconceptual wisdom, both saṃsāra (the lack of peace) and nirvāṇa (peace) {509} cannot be discriminated as different. Therefore, this is the perfect [nature]. As the *Mahāyānasūtrālaṃkāra* states:

> Being nonexistent, existent,
> And the equality of existence and nonexistence;
> The lack of peace and peace; and nonconceptuality
> Are the defining characteristics of the perfect.[490]

You may wonder, "How is the perfect [nature] to be understood as twofold here?" The unchanging [perfect nature] is expressed through the name "emptiness" because it is empty of the characteristics of both the imaginary and the dependent [natures].[491] Since this is never other, it is called "suchness." Because it is the unmistaken actuality to be realized, it is "the true end." Because it is the cessation of the [above] two characteristics [(the imaginary and the dependent)], it is "signlessness." Because it is the sphere of the noble ones, it is "the ultimate." Because it is the cause of the dharmas of the noble ones, it is the "dharmadhātu." These are its synonyms. As the *Madhyāntavibhāga* says:

> If emptiness is summarized,
> Suchness, the true end,

Singlessness, the ultimate,
And dharmadhātu are its synonyms.

By virtue of not being other, not being mistaken,
Putting an end to [signs], being the sphere of noble ones,
And being the cause of the dharmas of the noble ones,
The meanings of these synonyms match the [above] order.[492]

Here, the unmistaken perfect nature is the nature of the wisdom of the noble ones that is produced by perfect prajñā. Its enumerations are said to be the ten [kinds of] unmistakenness, {510} that is, being unmistaken about letters, their meaning, mental engagement, not straying away, the specific characteristic, the general characteristic, impurity and purity, what is adventitious, nonaversion, and lack of arrogance. This is taught in detail [in the *Madhyāntavibhāga*]:

Letters, meaning, mental engagement,
Not straying away, the two characteristics,
Impurity and purity, what is adventitious,
Nonaversion, and lack of arrogance.[493]

In brief, [these two aspects of the perfect nature] are to be understood as the following division. The former is the dharmakāya that is the stainless dharmadhātu, and the latter is the very profound dharmakāya, which is the natural outflow [of this stainless dharmadhātu]. Through these, **the defining characteristic of the nature of phenomena** is taught in a complete and unmistaken manner.[494]

You may wonder, "If there is no mistakenness in the nature of phenomena, while mistakenness itself does not really exist, how [can there be] mistakenness?" [The answer is given in the following section.]

2.2.1.5. The manner of being mistaken

This is discussed through three points:

1) The appearing of what does not exist
2) The example [for false imagination]
3) The manner of what exists not appearing

2.2.1.5.1. The appearing of what does not exist

The mistakenness by virtue of what does not exist appearing is the cause of afflictiveness.

While **not existing**, based on the dependent [nature] the threefold **afflictiveness** [of afflictions, karma, and birth][495] arises, which is **mistakenness.** How does it arise? In dependence on the seeds that are the latent tendencies of expression,[496] cognizance arises [in the form] of (1) the body, (2) the body-possessor, (3) the experiencer, (4) the objects to be experienced by the [preceding three], (5) the experiencers [of those objects], (6) time, (7) numbers, (8) places, and (9) conventional expressions. {511} From the seeds that are the latent tendencies of views [about a real identity], cognizance arises [in the form] of (10) the distinctions between a self and others. From the seeds of the branches of [saṃsāric] existence, cognizance arises [in the form] of (11) the deaths and transitions of the happy realms and the miserable realms. In these [eleven kinds of] cognizance, all realms, beings, and birthplaces are included. They constitute the false imagination that is the dependent characteristic. The fact that, based on this, nothing but this mere cognizance **appears** as referents, though there are no referents, is the imaginary [nature].[497] Then, the threefold afflictiveness of afflictions, karma, and life makes one suffer. Since these are nothing but mere conception, it is taught that "there are no referents."[498] One should understand that glorious Dharmakīrti too had this in mind, when he said:

> What is connected with conception
> Does not entail the clear appearance of referents.[499]

Thus, one should not entertain views that assert external referents. Also the *Yuktiṣaṣṭikā* says:

> Since the buddhas said
> That the world entails the condition of ignorance,
> Why should it not be justified
> That this world is conception?
>
> Once ignorance has ceased,
> Why should it not be clear
> That that which will cease
> Was imagined by ignorance?[500]

2.2.1.5.2. The example [for false imagination]

> **It is like the appearing of illusory elephants and so on.**

Elephants, horses, riches, **and so on** that are produced by a [magical] **illusion appear**, {512} but they do not exist in the way [they appear]. **Like**wise, false imagination does not exist, yet still appears.[501] Noble Nāgārjuna's *Mahāyānaviṃśikā* states:

> How sentient beings experience objects
> Is exactly like in the case of illusions.
> Beings have the nature of illusions—
> Just like them, they originate dependently.[502]

2.2.1.5.3. The nonappearance of what exists

> **And furthermore, because what exists does not appear either.**

Thus, [false imagination] is also mistakenness **because what exists**—the twofold identitylessness that is to be realized through the three yānas—**does not appear**. As the *Mahāyānasūtrālaṃkāra* says:

> Therefore, what is this particular kind of darkness
> Of not seeing what exists and seeing what does not exist?[503]

Since the two [kinds of] the perfect [nature] exist, but are not seen, this is mistakenness. Also the *Yuktiṣaṣṭikā* states:

> The victors have declared
> That nirvāṇa alone is real,
> So which wise one would think
> That the rest is not delusive?[504]

Since that [ultimate] reality is not realized, this is mistakenness. In a mundane context, it resembles the thought of mistaking an [existent] cairn for a [nonexistent] human being. In these ways, the reasons for being mistaken are understood.

2.2.1.6. If one does not exist, [phenomena and the nature of phenomena] are not tenable as two

> **If any one of these two—nonexistence and appearance—did not exist, mistakenness, unmistakenness, afflicted phenomena, and purified phenomena would not be tenable.**

Through [mistakenly using] the reasons of **nonexistence and appearance,** [respectively], {513} one either conceives of appearances as existent (such as being real, an agent, or a self), or one thinks that these appearances—despite being established [as mere appearances]—are [utterly] nonexistent. This is called "mistakenness" for two reasons. If something is just utterly nonexistent, it is not possible to be mistaken about its very nonexistence. Or if there indeed existed the slightest real [entity], its existence would be without mistakenness. Furthermore, **if mistaken** cognition **did not exist**, the existence of **unmistaken** cognition would not be reasonable either because it depends on the [former]. If both did not exist, being **afflicted** in mistaken saṃsāra **and** also the nirvāṇa that is its **purified** state **would not be tenable.** If one accepts that these are not tenable, everything would simply be meaningless. Therefore, what would be the point of presenting saṃsāra and nirvāṇa? Or if [one thinks that] either an everlasting saṃsāra or effortless liberation are reasonable, [both of these notions] contradict direct perception. Through realizing the reasons for being mistaken by virtue of nonexistence and appearance, one also sees dependent origination. Through realizing that appearances are empty of reality, just like illusions, the correct cognition of directly realizing that they are free from arising and ceasing [appears]. Based on this [cognition], yogic valid perception occurs, through which liberation takes place. This point accords with what noble Nāgārjuna says [in his *Yuktiṣaṣṭikā*]:

> You are not liberated from this [saṃsāric] existence
> Through being or through nonbeing.
> Great beings are liberated
> Through fully understanding being and nonbeing.[505] {514}

2.2.1.7. Not asserting [phenomena and the nature of phenomena] as being one or different

You may wonder, "In this case, should phenomena and the nature of phenomena be accepted as being the same or should they be taken as being different?"

> **These two are neither one nor are they distinct because there is a difference as well as no difference in terms of existence and nonexistence.**

It is not suitable if phenomena and the nature of phenomena are accepted to be one. If the nature of phenomena—the perfect [nature]—is definitely **existent**, whereas phenomena, just like mirages, do **not** really **exist** at all, how could they be accepted as one? Furthermore, the nature of phenomena would be seen through merely seeing the bearers of this nature, and any efforts [on the path] would [thus] be pointless. Therefore, [because] **there is a difference** in these ways, they **are not** accepted as **one**. You may wonder, "How is it then not suitable to accept them as being different?" This is [not tenable] for the following reasons. The direct appearance of the nature of phenomena is nothing but this mere cognizance, which [mistakenly appears as] the imaginary and the dependent [natures], appearing without the characteristics of such cognizance, and the nature of phenomena consists of the sheer lack of phenomena. For example, though a rope may [mistakenly] appear as a snake, its [sheer] abiding as nothing but a rope lacks any difference in terms of the existence or nonexistence of a snake [in it]. Likewise, in terms of appearing and being empty abiding in an inseparable manner, phenomena and the nature of phenomena are not established as different. Thus, it is not reasonable that they are two. {515} "So, how are they then?" They are free from being the same or other.[506] The *Mahāyānasūtrālaṃkāra* says:

> Mind is what appears as twofold:
> It appears as desire and such, and likewise,
> It appears as confidence and so on.
> There is no other phenomenon that is affliction and virtue.[507]

Through seeing in this way that phenomena and their nature are taught as the three natures and are not suitable to be the same or different, the unmistaken characteristics of all knowable objects will be realized.[508] This point is also expressed in the *Triṃśikā*:

> Whichever entity is imagined
> By whichever imagination
> Is the imaginary nature,
> Which is unfindable.[509]

Thus, the imaginary is the appearance of what does absolutely not exist. [The *Triṃśikā* continues:]

> The dependent nature, on the other hand,
> Is conception that arises from conditions.[510]

Through the potentials of object, sense faculty, and cognition, [the dependent nature] arises as if it were the cognizance that entails apprehender and apprehended. [The *Triṃśikā* continues:]

The perfect [nature] is its
Always being free from the former.

Therefore, it is said to be neither other
Nor not other than the dependent,
Just like impermanence and such.
When the one is not seen, the [other] one is not seen [either].[511]

The perfect [nature] is said to be the lack of the characteristics of the former two [(the imaginary and the dependent natures)].[512] Therefore, the cognizance that appears [dualistically] but does not exist [in that way] is called "dependent." If it is free from those characteristics, it is the perfect [nature]. However, by virtue of cognizance being mistaken, there arises the imaginary [nature] of thinking that [dualistic cognition]—despite not existing [that way]—is really existent. Therefore, cognizance [as such] {516} and the dependent [nature] are not accepted to be one or different.

Thus, the imaginary lacks real existence, while the dependent—mere cognizance—exists. However, through seeing that [this mere cognizance] lacks the duality of apprehender and apprehended, the perfect [nature] will be seen. This is taught in detail below. Also noble Nāgārjuna says in his *Bodhicittavivaraṇa*:

As for the imaginary, the dependent,
And the perfect [natures],
Their nature is the single character of emptiness.
They are imputations onto mind.[513]

The *Mahāyānasaṃgraha* discusses this in very great detail.[514] [This concludes] the brief introduction of the treatise.

2.2.2. Detailed explanation

This has two parts:
1) [The explanation of] comprehending phenomena
2) The explanation of comprehending the nature of phenomena

2.2.2.1. [The explanation of] comprehending phenomena

This has two parts:
1) Brief introduction
2) Detailed explanation

2.2.2.1.1. Brief introduction

> **The comprehension of phenomena through six points is unsurpassable—**

The six that are taught [here] are the following:

> **Through comprehending the defining characteristic, the rationale, their being neither one nor distinct, their matrix in common and not in common, and the nonexistence of the appearance of apprehender and apprehended.**

Through these **six** one excellently **comprehends phenomena**. They are taught because all means to realize the manner in which [phenomena] are the factors to be relinquished are included in them.[515]

2.2.2.1.2. Detailed explanation

This has three parts:

1) The first three [points] being as in the brief introduction [above]
2) [The explanation of comprehending] the matrix [of phenomena] {517}
3) The explanation of comprehending the nonexistence of the appearance of apprehender and apprehended

2.2.2.1.2.1. The first three [points] being as in the brief introduction [above]

> **The defining characteristic, the rationale, and their being neither one nor distinct are as in the introduction.**

[These points] **are** exactly **as** what was taught **in the** brief **introduction** above.[516] [The passage] "What appears as duality and according designations is false imagination, which is the defining characteristic of phenomena" represents the summary of **the defining characteristics** of the imaginary and the dependent [natures]. As for **the rationale**, if any one of these two—nonexistence and appearance[517]—did not exist, there would be the flaw of mistakenness, unmistakenness, afflicted phenomena, and purified phenomena not being tenable. Therefore, through temporarily accepting both [nonexistence and appearance], their entailing [their respective] results is established.[518] As for **not** accepting them to **be one or** different, [this is taught through the passage] "because there is a difference as well as no difference in terms of existence and nonexistence." Thus, whether phenomena and the nature of phenomena exist or do not exist as different is exactly as was already explained above in the brief introduction.

2.2.2.1.2.2. The matrix of phenomena

This has two parts:
1) Brief introduction
2) Detailed explanation

2.2.2.1.2.2.1. Brief introduction

> **Their matrix consists of what cycles in what—the realm of the world and the realm of sentient beings.**

What cycles are **sentient beings** (the supported) and **in what** they cycle is **the realm of the world** [(the support)]. In both [cases], it is the ālaya-consciousness that is taught by [the term] "**realm.**" In the sense of being that which possesses all seeds, {518} it consists of those two realms that are the support and the supported, respectively. The *Vajraśikhara[mahāguhyayogatantra]* says:

> The ālaya, from which all seeds arise,
> Is held to be the nature of [everything] internal and external.[519]

2.2.2.1.2.2.2. Detailed explanation

This has two parts:
1) [Their matrix that is] in common
2) [Their matrix that is] not in common

2.2.2.1.2.2.2.1. [Their matrix that is] in common

> **The realm of the world consists of the cognizances that seem to be in common.**

[First, as for the realm of the world,] there is nothing whatsoever that exists externally, such as the real external referents that are asserted by some tīrthikas and the Vaibhāṣikas. However, since the consciousnesses that appear as such [external phenomena] arise in all sentient beings in their respective mind streams, [Maitreya] speaks of "**cognizances that seem to be in common.**" For certain [phenomena] such as colors and shapes appear as if common [to everybody], but none of them is [really] in common. A single entity such as a tree appears as good to some and as unpleasant and different to some [others]. Likewise, hungry ghosts, hell beings, humans, and gods engage in seeing [what humans perceive as] water in different ways—as pus and blood, [molten] lead, water, and nectar, respectively. Furthermore, if there were really existing referents in an external **realm of the world**, they would not appear to cognition because they are not feasible as having either a connection of identity or a causal one[520] with cognition. [In general,] what appears to cognition has necessarily the [same] identity as this [cognition] or is something that is caused by it, but if it is not connected [to cognition in either way], it does necessarily not appear [to it] either, just like [the appearances in] dreams and unseen entities.[521] {519}

Second, as for the explanation of the realm of sentient beings, the brief description [says]:

> **The realm of sentient beings consists of what is in common and what is not in common.**

In detail:

> **Birth, behavior, benefit, harm, qualities, and faults are in common because they are causes for each other by virtue of mutual domination.**

As for "**birth**," both being born from a womb and being born from dominant conditions[522] are causes that are mutually [perceptible and thus] in common. [Likewise,] **behavior** (such as looking [at each other]), creating **benefit**, **harm**, and giving rise to **qualities** such as ethics **and** the **faults** of nonvirtue **are** [all] referred to as "seemingly **in common**." That [Maitreya] speaks of "[mutual] **domination**," while [the meaning] is [already] established through[523] [the phrase] "**because they are causes for each other**," is for the sake of excluding causes that are objects. For if causes that are objects are not excluded, [the set of what is in common in the realm of sentient beings] overextends into [the set of the common] realm of the world.[524]

2.2.2.1.2.2.2.2. Explanation of [their matrix that is] not in common

> **The abode, cognizance, karma, happiness, suffering, death and transition, birth, bondage, and liberation are not in common.**

The abode is the ālaya-consciousness because the latent tendencies of the cognizances that appear as the [remaining phenomena of sentient beings] abide in it. This corresponds to the example of the ocean being the abode of water, with all rainwater and rivers gathering [in it] and rainwater arising from it [as clouds and so on]. **Cognizance** {520} refers to the six operating consciousnesses because they cognize objects. **Karma** is threefold—virtuous, nonvirtuous, and neutral karmas. Likewise, the individual experiences of **happiness** and **suffering; death and transition; birth**[525] in the three [realms of saṃsāric] existence; as well as the mind stream being in **bondage** through the afflictions **and** [its] **liberation** from that [bondage] **are not in common.** Since the abode and so on are without form and are to be experienced personally, they do not represent any causes for the arising of cognizances that mutually appear in individual mind streams. Therefore, they are described as "the realm of sentient beings that is not in common."[526]

It may be said, "Why is it that the cognizances that are [appearing as] body and speech are not included here under [the category of] 'behavior' [above] despite their being causes for the arising of cognizances that mutually appear as the [body and speech]?" To explain, the cognizances that are [appearing as] body and speech are indeed included under "behavior," but they are not the cognizances that are [appearing as] karma. Here [these latter cognizances that are referred to as physical and verbal karmas] are taught in terms of their being virtuous or nonvirtuous through which they are understood as constituting the [corresponding] karmas [of the cognizances that appear as physical and verbal behaviors]. The cognizances that are taught as being virtuous and nonvirtuous are not causes for the arising of the cognizances that [mutually] appear as such [virtue and nonvirtue]. Therefore, the cognizances that are [appearing as] physical and verbal karmas are also not in common.[527]

2.2.2.1.2.3. The manner of comprehending the nonexistence of the appearance [of apprehender and apprehended]

This has two parts:

2.2.2.1.2.3.1. Comprehending the nonexistence of the appearance of the apprehended

> {521} **In the cognizance that is the apprehender**[528] **and appears as something apprehended that is in common and external, there is no referent that is external to consciousness because such is common to all.**

Though there are six **external apprehended** [objects], they are explained here [to be] the cognizances that [appear as the world which] is the container. Therefore, the other [part of this passage] is understood implicitly. Consequently, what **appears as** the cognizances that [appear as] the container (a semblance of a realm that is the world) is **the** very **cognizance that is the apprehender**, which is what arises in each individual mind stream. Therefore, **there is no** other **referent that is external** to, and other than, this very cognizance, but this cognizance does not serve as an object of others. If you wonder why, what arises in an individual cognizance is not in common [with others], just like the appearing of objects in a dream. You may wonder, "So why do we speak of 'seemingly in **common**' then?" Two persons may equally dream about a golden vase in their dreams when asleep, and when they wake up, the color and shape [of this vase seems] to match [for them] and [their sense of] referring to "I" and "me" seems to match [too]. This **is** called "seemingly **in common**," but there are no real matching objects that are external referents. All thoughts that external referents exist, that hidden referents exist, and so on originate from latent tendencies of mistakenness dwelling in the mind stream, but there are no [external] referents. Āryadeva also says [in his *Jñānasārasamuccaya*]:

> "Something that has parts" does not exist,
> And minute particles do not exist [either].
> What [seems to] appear distinctly is [actually] unobservable—
> Experiences are like a dream.[529]

In a rope there is no snake and the rope itself, when split up in its many threads and minute particles, does not really exist either, {522} nor is it established as a referent that is other than a mere appearance. Therefore, all experiences are explained to be like a dream. Dignāga states [in his *Ālambanaparīkṣāvṛtti*]:

> Even if minute[530] particles were
> The causes of cognizance [based on] the sense faculties,
> Since [cognizance] does not appear as such [particles], its objects
> Are not minute particles, just as the sense faculties [are not]. [1]

> What is called "an object" refers to its own nature being apprehended by a cognition because [this cognition] arises as [bearing] the aspect of that [object]. Though minute particles may be taken to be the causes of such [cognitions], they are not like [those objects that are nothing but cognizance appearing as those aspects], just as the [material] sense faculties [are not objects of cognition]. Thus, first, minute particles [in themselves] are not the focal objects [of cognition].
>
> [Secondly,] as for a conglomerate [of many such particles], though it may be taken to be what appears as the [aspect that is the object of cognizance],
>
> > The [cognition] does not [arise] from that as which it appears. [2a]
>
> It is reasonable that something which produces a cognizance that appears as this very [something] is the focal object [of this cognizance] because it is explained that it is, in this way, a condition for

the arising of this [cognizance]. [However,] a conglomerate is not like that,

> For it does not exist substantially, just like two moons. [2b]

By virtue of the [eye] sense faculties being deficient, two moons may be seen [because of cataracts]. Though this may be taken to be [the cognition] that appears as such [two moons], [two moons] are not its object. Likewise, due to its not existing substantially, a conglomerate is not the cause [of a cognition]. Therefore, it is not [its] focal object.

> Thus, in both cases, something external
> Is not suitable as an object of the mind. [2cd][531]

This teaches the entire reasoning [why external referents cannot be objects of cognition]. If this is realized in such a manner, it represents the comprehension of the meaning of the nonexistence of the apprehended.[532] {523}

You may wonder, "Though there are no apprehended [objects] that are in common, are there real apprehended referents that are not in common?" [Maitreya] says:

> **The apprehended [objects]—the referents that are cognizance—that are not in common and are the minds and mental factors of others do not mutually serve as objects for either of the two [types of] cognizances that are the apprehenders [while] being or not being in meditative equipoise, respectively.**

This is taught in order to dispel the mistakenness of thinking that, [in the case of] two different **cognizances that are not in common**, the one could **serve as the object** of the [other] one. If you wonder why, [Maitreya] continues:

> **Because for those who are not in meditative equipoise, their own conceptions appear and because even for those who are in meditative equipoise, it is a reflection of the [mind of another] that appears in [the form of] the experiential object of samādhi. The minds of others and so on are not their objects.**[533]

The minds of others and so on are not the objects of those [who are not in meditative equipoise] **because for those who are not in meditative equipoise,** it is their own cognizance—the apprehended which **appears** to **their own conceptions**—that serves as the object. The minds of others and so on are not the objects of those [in meditative equipoise] either **because even for** the cognizances of **those who are in** mundane **meditative equipoise**, what serves as the object is [again] this very cognizance which is the apprehended—[in this case] **the experiential object of samādhi that appears** as **a reflection of the** [mind of another]. You may wonder, "If there are no objects that are other [(such as the minds of others)] in both cases, what is it that appears [for cognizance]?" Since it is nothing but one's own cognizance that is the object, {524} there are no external referents that are other than consciousness, and since such [referents] do not exist, what appears as the apprehended does not really exist. [This is] what is found in [Vasubandhu's] commentary.[534]

2.2.2.1.2.3.2. Comprehending the nonexistence of the appearance of the apprehender

> **If it is established that what appears as the apprehended does not exist, it is also established that what appears as the apprehender does not exist. By virtue of that, the comprehension of the nonexistence of the appearance of apprehender and apprehended [is established].**

If apprehended referents are **not** real, the cognition that apprehends them is mistakenness. Therefore, **it is established that the apprehender does not** really **exist** [either]. Consequently, through understanding that there are no different real referents that are apprehender and apprehended, **the comprehension of the nonexistence of the appearance of apprehender and apprehended** [is established]—since nonduality is not tainted by any conventional characteristics, it is inexpressible. The *Abhisamayālaṃkāra* says:

> If apprehended referents do not exist like that,
> Can these two[535] be asserted as the apprehenders of anything?
> Thus, their characteristic is the emptiness
> Of a nature of an apprehender.[536]

Glorious Dharmakīrti also says [in his *Pramāṇavārttika*]:

> Given the lack of anything that has the nature of a referent,
> How could what bears its appearance apprehend referents?
> True—such I do not know either.[537]

It may be said, "[But] an appearance without an external referent is not tenable as the apprehension of a referent." This is true—it is taught that ordinary beings are not able to understand that referents appear, while there is no apprehender and apprehended. "In that case, while there are no real referents that constitute the duality of apprehender and apprehended, what is this appearance [of duality]?" {525} [Maitreya] says:

> **For arising without beginning is established.**[538]

As for "**without beginning,**" it is twofold—no beginning in terms of an earliest point in the continuum of time and there being no real substance to begin with, with this [case] here referring to both.[539] The continuum of mistaken latent tendencies has no end because there is no beginning or end of saṃsāra. As for the appearing of duality while it does not exist, just as with magical illusions and optical illusions, it is impossible to establish these as real referents merely through conceptions. If there existed real referents in the mistakenness of saṃsāra, there would be a great flaw. The *Mahāyānasūtrālaṃkāra* says:

> Being habituated to it since beginningless time,
> The view about an identity needs not be produced.
> If there were a person, everybody would be
> Either liberated without effort or not liberated [at all].[540]

If the person and the self really existed, liberation would never be attained and if the [self] itself were liberation, one would be liberated without effort. Therefore, it is wrong [to assume the real existence of referents, be they a self or anything else].

If one comprehends phenomena in such a way, this is the meaning of phenomena. [Maitreya] continues:

> **For while the two are not established at all, they are commonly known.**

Thus, by virtue of understanding that **the two**—the imaginary and the dependent [natures]—**are not at all established** as real, it is said that "the dependent origination of the nature of phenomena is seen in dependence on phenomena." This is also stated in the *Madhyāntavibhāga*:

> If it were not defiled,
> All beings would be liberated.
> If it did not become pure,
> Efforts would be fruitless. {526}

It is neither defiled nor undefiled,
Neither pure nor impure.[541]

Noble Nāgārjuna states [in his *Yuktiṣaṣṭikā*]:

In dependent origination,
What could beginning and end be?

How could what has arisen earlier
Be put to an end later?
Devoid of any end in terms of earlier and later,
The world appears like an illusion.[542]

In detail, this is discussed in the *Saṃdhinirmocana[sūtra]* and the *Yogācārabhūmi*.[543] This completes the explanation of the unsurpassable comprehension of phenomena.

2.2.2.2. The explanation of comprehending the nature of phenomena

This has two parts:
1) Brief introduction
2) Detailed explanation

2.2.2.2.1. Brief introduction

The comprehension of the nature of phenomena through six points is unsurpassable.

These are the following **six** [points] that will be explained [below]:

For it is comprehension of the defining characteristic, the matrix, discernment, contact, recollection, and the arrival at its nature.[544]

This is the summarized teaching on these [points].

2.2.2.2.2. Detailed explanation

This has seven parts:
1) Defining characteristic
2) The matrix of the nature of phenomena
3) The path of preparation
4) The path of seeing
5) The path of familiarization (recollection)

6) The path of completion (arrival)
7) Explanation of the fundamental change of those

2.2.2.2.2.1. Defining characteristic

The defining characteristic is as in the introduction.

This **is** what was stated above: "**The defining characteristic** of the nature of phenomena is suchness, which lacks any distinction between apprehender and apprehended, or [between] objects of designation and what designates them." {527} This is the perfect nature, for which numerous synonyms are given in all the sūtras and tantras. Glorious Nāropa says:

This very being empty is awareness, mind.
Also bodhicitta is just this.
The tathāgata heart is nothing but this.
Great bliss is precisely this.

What is called "secret mantra" is just this.
The reality of valid cognition is exactly this.
The fourth empowerment is this.
Connate joy is nothing but this.

The pāramitās are precisely this.
Unity is simply this.
Great Madhyamaka is solely this.
Vairocana is this.

Vajrasattva is simply this.
The sixth family is only this.
The buddha disposition is just this.
Many enumerations, such as these,
Which are stated in the sūtras and tantras,
Are for the most part based on this.

As for the meaning of noble Nāgārjuna's statement that all phenomena lack a nature, the nature of all phenomena is that they neither arise by nature nor cease by nature. For this reason, since they are not real as being permanent or extinct, coming or going, or one or different, they are free from reference points. Therefore, they are both "all phenomena" and "the lack of a nature." The enumerations [of this lack of nature] are "the lack of nature in terms of characteristics," "the lack of nature in terms of arising," and "the ultimate lack of nature," which are taught in relation to the imaginary, {528} the dependent, and the perfect [natures], respectively. One should understand that all [kinds of] emptiness are also divisions [that are derived] from this.[545]

2.2.2.2.2.2. The matrix of the nature of phenomena

> **The matrix consists of all phenomena and all sūtra collections included in the twelve branches of the Buddha's speech.**

As for "**all phenomena**," all the phenomena taught above are **the matrix** of the nature of phenomena because the nature of phenomena is these very phenomena being empty of any specific and general characteristics. The *Mahāyānasaṃgraha* says:

> In the dependent, the imaginary does not exist.
> The perfect exists in it.
> Therefore, with regard to these two, in the [dependent]
> Nonobservation and observation occur together.[546]

Once it is liberated from afflicted phenomena, the dependent—as mere cognizance—comes to be without the imaginary. Therefore, once cognizance embraced by purified phenomena has undergone the fundamental change, it becomes the perfect [nature]. Consequently, the nonobservation of both the imaginary and the dependent [natures] as well as the observation of the nature of phenomena occur together.[547] Therefore, all saṃsāric phenomena are the matrix of the nature of phenomena.

As for purified phenomena, they are **the twelve branches of the Buddha's speech**—(1) the **sūtra collection**, (2) proclamations in song, (3) prophecies, (4) narratives, (5) reports on [the Buddha's] former lives, (6) counsels, (7) [discourses on] marvelous qualities, {529} (8) proclamations in verses, (9) joyful aphorisms, (10) legends, (11) ascertaining [discourses], and (12) very extensive discourses.[548] These constitute the pure dharma of a buddha—the uncontaminated dharma. They are the natural outflow of the dharmakāya and thus [also] the matrix of the nature of phenomena. This explanation that both [phenomena and the dharma] are the matrix of the nature of phenomena in these ways is given in terms of what is to be personally experienced [through nonconceptual wisdom].[549]

It is the words of childish beings to say, "Through attaining the final samādhi, which is a particular instance of the nonassociated formations that are words, phrases, and letters in terms of factors to be relinquished and their remedies, one manifests miraculous powers in a chiliocosm. Pratyekabuddhas attain all samādhis through shaking a trichiliocosm."[550] This is just like saying that a cakravartin who wields power over [all] four continents does not wield power over Jambudvīpa, but that a powerful cakravartin wields power over Jambudvīpa. That much elaboration shall suffice [here].

As for the cognitive obscurations, the ten bhūmis are described in terms of the factors to be relinquished and their remedies that perfect nonconceptual wisdom—prajñāpāramitā. The *Madhyāntavibhāga* says:

> The actuality of omnipresence, the actuality that is supreme,
> The natural outflow that is the supreme purpose,
> The actuality of nonclinging,
> The actuality of the mind streams not being different,
>
> The actuality of neither affliction nor purity,
> The actuality of no difference,
> The actuality of neither decrease nor increase,
> And the matrix of fourfold mastery.
>
> Ignorance about the dharmadhātu— {530}
> The ten nonafflictive obscurations—
> Are the antagonistic factors of the ten bhūmis.
> Their remedies are the bhūmis.[551]

[Vasubandhu's] commentary on this says:

> It is the nonafflictive ignorance about the ten aspects of the dharmadhātu—such as the actuality of omnipresence—that obscures the ten bodhisattvabhūmis in due order because it represents their antagonistic factor. This is as follows. On the first bhūmi [bodhisattvas] realize the actuality of the omnipresence of the dharmadhātu as this actuality of omnipresence, through which they attain [the realization of] the equality of themselves and others. On the second one they realize [the dharmadhātu] as the actuality that is supreme, through which they think, "Therefore, we shall make efforts in universal practice, that is, the practice to purify it in all aspects." On the third one they realize its natural outflow that is the supreme purpose. Through this, they recognize study—the natural outflow of the dharmadhātu—to be supreme and therefore, for this purpose, [are willing to] even plunge themselves into a fire pit that has the size of the greatest chiliocosm in a trichiliocosm. On the

fourth one they realize it as the actuality of nonclinging. Thus, they even reverse craving for the dharma. On the fifth one they realize the actuality of the mind streams not being different—they realize the equality of pure mind and intention in ten aspects. On the sixth one {531} they realize the actuality of neither affliction nor purity because they realize that, in the actuality of dependent origination, there is no phenomenon that is either afflicted or pure. On the seventh one they realize the actuality of no difference. For, by virtue of the lack of characteristics, different characteristics of phenomena (such as the sūtras) do not transpire. On the eighth one they realize the actuality of neither decrease nor increase. For, by virtue of having attained the poised readiness for the dharma of nonarising, they do not see any decrease or increase with regard to afflicted or purified phenomena.[552]

Fourfold mastery refers to what is conducive to manifesting [full] mastery over nonconceptuality, mastery over pure realms, mastery over wisdom, [and mastery over enlightened activity]. [The *Abhisamayālaṃkāra* says]:

Being skilled in the full accomplishment
Of signlessness, generosity, and so on,
Within this complete realization of all aspects,
Are asserted as the factors conducive to liberation.

They are fivefold—the confidence of focusing on the Buddha and so on,
The vigor whose sphere consists of generosity and so on,
The mindfulness of the consummate intention,
Nonconceptual samādhi,

And the prajñā of knowing
Phenomena in all aspects.[553]

Thus, by virtue of [bodhisattvas] being endowed with the marvelous possession of the five dharmas such as confidence, they attain buddhahood, while those with inferior aspiration fall into the inferior yānas. Maitreya says:

It is held that perfect enlightenment is easy to realize
By those who are sharp, and hard to realize by the dull.[554]

[2.2.2.2.2.3. **The path of preparation**

> **Discernment is the entire path of preparation that consists of the proper mental engagement which relies on the sūtra collection of the mahāyāna.]**

Here, since the **discerning** path of preparation {532} is accomplished through **the proper mental engagement which relies** solely **on the sūtra collection of the mahāyāna** (the very vast sūtras and the prajñāpāramitā [sūtras]), it **consists of** all four branches of penetration.[555] Therefore, [the text] speaks of "**the entire path of preparation.**"[556] You may wonder, "How is that [to be understood]?" It is to be understood [through] the following five—the pure defining characteristic of knowable objects,[557] [the persons] who engage in it, where they engage, how they engage, and the progression of such engagement. As for the first one, the *Mahāyānasaṃgraha* says:

> The state of being impregnated with lots of study is not included in the ālaya-consciousness. Similar to the ālaya-consciousness, it represents seeds, [but these here] consist of the proper mental engagement that has the form of arising as the aspects of the dharma and [its] meanings ([which thus] resemble phenomena that are apprehendable entities)—the mental discourses that are endowed with the view.[558]

This is called "the disposition." Its nature is the stainless dharmadhātu and its natural outflow is the distinctive feature of the uncontaminated dharmas. Since it [abides] together with the six āyatanas, we also find in the *Bodhisattvabhūmi*[559] that the [naturally abiding] disposition is [referred to as] the distinctive feature of the six āyatanas. Therefore, the *Abhisamayālaṃkāra* [states]:

> Because the dharmadhātu is indivisible,
> Divisions of the disposition are not tenable.
> But by virtue of the divisions of the phenomena founded on it,
> Its divisions are expressed.[560]

"What is founded on it" {533} refers to the arising of supreme, middling, and minor aspirations, respectively, for the awakening of the latent tendencies for listening, which depends on the enlightenment of a buddha. The *Uttaratantra* [states]:

The disposition is to be known as twofold,
Being like a treasure and a fruit tree—
The naturally abiding one without beginning
And the supreme accomplished one.

It is held that the three kāyas are attained
By virtue of these two dispositions—
The first kāya, by virtue of the first one,
And the latter two, by virtue of the second one.[561]

Since the light of the dharma and its meaning—the natural outflow that is based on the dharmakāya—appears as if it increases and unfolds [on the path], one speaks of the "unfolding [disposition]." Therefore, [the *Mahāyānasūtrālaṃkāra* says]:

Aspiration for the dharma is the seed,
Which is born from the supreme pāramitā[562]

As for such unfolding arising from the manner in which one aspires, since "pāramitā," "nonconceptuality," and "the basic element that is the [tathāgata] heart" are equivalents, it is said that "it arises from that." As for that through which [the disposition] unfolds, [the *Mahāyānasūtrālaṃkāra* continues]:

In the womb of the bliss arisen from dhyāna,
And compassion is its nourishing nanny.[563]

Dhyāna and samādhi produce bliss in oneself and others, and compassion makes one not fall into [the nirvāṇa of personal] peace. Therefore, [the *Uttaratantra*] declares that those

Are the children who take after the sages.[564]

This is [the explanation of] the pure defining characteristic of knowable objects.

As for who engages [in this characteristic], the *Mahāyānasaṃgraha* [says]:

> Because they have impregnated their mind streams with having studied the mahāyāna dharma a lot, have already pleased the limitless buddhas who appeared, are endowed with one-pointed aspiration [for the mahāyāna dharma], and have excellently gathered the roots

> of virtue, {534} it is the bodhisattvas who have excellently gathered the accumulations of merit and wisdom.[565]

As for where they engage, the same [text] states:

> In this [process of] mental discourse that is endowed with the view, appears as the dharma and its meanings, and arises from the cause that is the mahāyāna dharma, [bodhisattvas] engage on the level of engagement through aspiration, the path of seeing, the path of familiarization, and the path of completion. For, respectively, they aspire for the proclamation that all phenomena are mere cognizance, realize this exactly as it is, familiarize with the remedies for all obscurations, and are [finally] without obscurations.[566]

You may wonder, "In what manner do they engage?" [The text] continues:

> They engage through generating the power of the roots of virtue, training the mind in three ways, relinquishing four things, and cultivating the calm abiding and superior insight of focusing on the dharma and its meaning through constant and devoted application and heedfulness.[567]

The threefold training of the mind consists of the three mindsets of not being fainthearted, ([thinking,] "If limitless humans have attained enlightenment, why should I not attain it?"), thinking, "[With this mindset] I shall perfect the pāramitās," and [thinking, "I shall] effortlessly obtain a succession of [births in the] pleasant realms."[568] The relinquishment of four [things] consists of the following four—relinquishing the mental engagements of śrāvakas and pratyekabuddhas, engaging in the mahā[yāna] through relinquishing concerns and doubts, relinquishing clinging and attachment to phenomena as "me" and what is "mine," and {535} relinquishing all characteristics that may be present or be placed before one's conception.[569] The others will be taught below.

As for the progression of such engagement, the *Mahāyānasaṃgraha* states that [bodhisattvas] observe [letters and referents as well as their natures and distinctive features] as being mere mental discourse and rely on the four investigations of names, referents, and the imputations of a nature and distinctive features, with both being unobservable.[570] Through relying on this,

> At the time of the lesser poised readiness for the nonexistence of referents,[571] the samādhi of attaining the illumination [of the prajñā

> about the nonexistence of something apprehended that is different from mind] serves as the basis [of the branch] of what is conducive to penetration that is heat. At the time of greater such poised readiness, the samādhi of the increase of this illumination serves as the basis of peak. During the fourfold understanding of things as they really are, one engages in mere cognizance and ascertains that there are no referents, which is the samādhi of penetrating a part of the actuality of true reality. It serves as the basis of [the branch of what is conducive to penetration that is] poised readiness, which is approximately concordant with reality. Thereafter, the dismantling of the notion of mere cognizance represents the samādhi immediately before [the path of seeing], which is regarded as the basis of the supreme mundane dharma. One should understand that these samādhis are close to clear realization.[572]

This is also discussed in detail in the *Mahāyānasūtrālaṃkāra*'s [fourteenth] chapter on the instructions and directions.[573]

As for the path of preparation of the common yāna, the four foundations of mindfulness, the four correct efforts, and the four limbs of miraculous powers {536} [make up] the path of accumulation, while one progresses on the path of preparation through the five faculties and five powers. These are discussed in the *Madhyāntavibhāga* and the *Mahāyānasūtrālaṃkāra*, so I do not explain them here out of fear of being too wordy.

Here "discernment" refers to the concordant cause of nonconceptual [wisdom]—the samādhi that entails the discernment through study, reflection, and meditation in order to enter the path of seeing (the cause of buddha enlightenment).

2.2.2.2.2.4. The path of seeing

> **Contact is the attainment and experience of suchness in a direct manner through the path of seeing because the correct view is attained.**

In the common yāna the *Śrāvakabhūmi* says that, in terms of relying on the four realities, suffering is what is to be understood; its cause (the origin [of suffering]), what is to be relinquished; cessation, what is to be manifested; and the path (the factors concordant with enlightenment), what is to be familiarized with. Through relying on that, one attains the path of preparation that causes one to go beyond the desire realm. Then one relies on the cognitions, subsequent cognitions, poised readinesses, and subsequent readinesses with regard to these four realities and attains the path of seeing of the fifteen or sixteen moments [of the prajñā of realizing the four realities] being associated with [resting in] the first dhyāna or any dhyāna among the six levels [of dhyāna].[574]

What [bodhisattvas] comprehend and make fully perceptible here is the dharma that is even more marvelous than these—the light of nonconceptual wisdom. {537} This means to comprehend the principles of the three natures. The *Mahāyānasaṃgraha* says:

> Thus, through comprehending the characteristics of referents, which are [nothing but] appearances of mental discourse, bodhisattvas comprehend the imaginary nature. Through comprehending mere cognizance, they comprehend the dependent nature. You may wonder, "How do they comprehend the perfect nature?" They comprehend it by putting an end to the notion of mere cognizance too. At that point, for bodhisattvas who have dissolved the notion of referents, there is no chance that the mental discourse that arises from the causes which are the latent tendencies of the dharma they have listened to could arise as any appearance of referents. Therefore, not even an appearance as mere cognizance arises. When such bodhisattvas rest, with regard to all referents, in names without conceptions[575] and dwell in the dharmadhātu in a direct manner, there arises their nonconceptual wisdom, in which what is observed and what observes are equal. In this way, such bodhisattvas comprehend the perfect nature . . . In this way, these bodhisattvas comprehend the characteristics of knowable objects through comprehending their being mere cognizance. Through having comprehended this, they enter the bhūmi Supreme Joy, excellently realize the dharmadhātu, are born in the lineage of the tathāgatas, and attain an equal mind toward all sentient beings, an equal mind toward all bodhisattvas, and an equal mind toward all buddhas. {538} This is the path of seeing.[576]

Also the *Mahāyānasūtrālaṃkāra* teaches this:

> The mind is aware that nothing other than mind exists.
> Then it is realized that mind does not exist either.
> The intelligent ones are aware that both do not exist
> And abide in the dharmadhātu, in which these are absent.[577]

Here, as for the branches of enlightenment, [this text says]:

It is held that the branches of enlightenment
Are presented for those who have entered the bhūmis,[578]

The reason for this is

Because they are the ones who realize the equality
Of all phenomena and sentient beings.[579]

Since the wisdoms of suchness and variety engage in [all] knowable objects and unfold them, correct mindfulness resembles the [precious] wheel. [The *Mahāyānasūtrālaṃkāra* continues]:

Mindfulness operates everywhere
So as to conquer unconquered knowable objects.[580]

Since the prajñā of fully discriminating phenomena overcomes all wrong characteristics, it resembles the [precious] elephant:

Their discrimination overcomes
All characteristics of conceptions.[581]

Since the vigor that is uninterrupted until having reached the end is swift, it resembles the [precious] horse:

Vigor progresses toward
Enlightenment without exception.[582]

Since the joy[583] about the increase of the brilliance of the ocean of the mahāyāna dharma expands the light of wisdom, it resembles the [precious wish-fulfilling] jewel:

Since the brilliance of the dharma increases,
They are always filled with joy.[584]

Since the suppleness of the mind stream liberates from the two obscurations, including their latent tendencies, {539} it resembles the [precious] queen due to the attainment of lasting bliss:

Since it liberates from all obscurations,
They are blissful through suppleness.[585]

Since the intended aim—riches [through samādhis such as] The Sky Treasure—arises from the samādhis, including their foundations that are based on the fourth dhyāna, [samādhi] resembles the [precious] householder:

> From samādhi there comes
> The fulfillment of the intended aim.[586]

Since the equanimity of engaging in the equality of meditative equipoise and subsequent attainment means to abide as one wishes without straying into [saṃsāric] existence or [nirvāṇic] peace, it resembles the [precious] general:

> Through equanimity, they abide
> In all [situations] just as they wish,[587]

For the reason of having attained all seven in this way, [bodhisattvas are]

> Always at their best by virtue of abiding
> Through subsequent attainment and nonconceptuality.[588]

These are the [seven] branches of enlightenment, and these seven arise in ways that resemble the seven precious items [of a cakravartin].

With the nature of the path of seeing—the discrimination of phenomena—resting upon mindfulness, final deliverance occurs through vigor, and samādhi expands the qualities. The three of suppleness, joy, and equanimity represent the branch of the lack of afflictions.[589] [The *Madhyāntavibhāga* says]:

> The branch of the nature, the branch of the matrix,
> The third being the branch of final deliverance,
>
> The fourth being the branch of benefit,
> And three aspects being the branch of the lack of afflictions.[590]

This explains what the branches are like. Likewise, {540} the chapter on the instructions [in the *Mahāyānasūtrālaṃkāra*] discusses this in detail:

> Furthermore, they attain the wisdom
> That is free from apprehending duality,
> Supramundane, unsurpassable,
> Nonconceptual, and stainless.

> This—their fundamental change—
> Is asserted as the first bhūmi.[591]

In brief, once the afflictions that are factors to be relinquished through seeing are relinquished, the two kinds of identitylessness are seen **in a direct manner**, one makes **contact** with the [doors to] liberation that consist of the triad of emptiness, signlessness, and wishlessness, and **attains** the samādhi of the light of nonconceptual wisdom. This is **the path of seeing** of bodhisattvas—the first bhūmi—which is more eminent than [the one in] the common presentation [of the path of seeing].[592]

2.2.2.2.2.5. Explanation of the path of familiarization

> **Recollection is the entirety of what consists of the factors concordant with enlightenment—the path of familiarizing with [the nature of phenomena] as it was seen for the sake of eradicating the stains of this [level].**

Immediately after the path of seeing, through **familiarizing** [with the nature of phenomena] **as it was seen** [on the path of seeing], one familiarizes with it in order to arrive at its very own nature. Therefore, this is the path of familiarization. Through the **recollection** of nonconceptual wisdom[593] one familiarizes [with what was seen] **for the sake of eradicating** the remainder of the afflictions that are to be relinquished through familiarization and the tenfold nonafflictive cognitive obscurations that obscure the ten bhūmis. Since [that recollection] brings this [eradication of both obscurations] to its completion, {541} it is a **path**. As for **the** dharmas that are **concordant with enlightenment**, one cultivates the thirty-seven dharmas of the common yāna that are concordant with enlightenment, the thirty-four [aspects] of bodhisattvas, the thirty-nine [aspects] of buddhas, and so on,[594] that is, everything that consists of the focal objects, [cognitive] aspects, and phenomena to be observed [that bodhisattvas have to realize]. As for how one trains in this, the *Mahāyānasaṃgraha* [says]:

> "In this way bodhisattvas who have entered the bhūmis and thus have attained the path of seeing engaged in mere cognizance. How do they train on the path of familiarization?" On the ten bhūmis as they are described, which embody all sūtra collections, [bodhisattvas] familiarize [with the nature of phenomena] through the supramundane and subsequently attained wisdoms of calm abiding and superior insight that focus on [all mahāyāna dharmas] in

> combination[595] for many billions of eons. Because of that, they undergo the fundamental change and thus train in order to attain the three kāyas of a buddha.[596]

Likewise, the *Mahāyānasūtrālaṃkāra* [states]:

> Then, on the remaining bhūmis
> On the path of familiarization,
> They train in cultivating
> The two kinds of wisdom.[597]

You may wonder, "How do they train in the two wisdoms?" [The text continues]:

> That nonconceptual wisdom
> Purifies the buddha qualities.[598]

[This is] because the nature of meditative equipoise is nothing but nonconceptual wisdom and therefore {542} masters the perfection of the qualities of the dharmakāya.

> The other one matures sentient beings
> In accordance with their respective situations.[599]

The wisdom of subsequent attainment matures buddha realms and sentient beings in an illusionlike manner because it represents the function of nonconceptual wisdom.[600]

> After the completion of two incalculable [eons]
> Familiarization is fully accomplished.[601]

[The first] six bhūmis [of the path of familiarization last] one incalculable [eon] and the [next] three [also last] one [such eon] because the three trainings are completed in this [amount of time]. You may wonder, "How is that?"

> Having realized the nature of phenomena here,
> They further train in superior ethics,
> Superior mind, and superior prajñā.[602]

Having realized the actuality of the nature of phenomena on the first bhūmi, [bodhisattvas] perfect the pāramitā of generosity. On the second [bhūmi] ethics become pure. On the third one they are endowed with patience and on the fourth one, with vigor. Therefore, since the mind is pure, they engage in [the training in] superior mind, through which the pāramitās of dhyāna and prajñā become pure on the fifth and sixth [bhūmis], respectively. As for the reason, {543} [the *Mahāyānasūtrālaṃkāra* says]:

> But prajñā has two spheres.
>
> The true reality of phenomena
> And the activities of not knowing it, knowing it, and so on
> Constitute the spheres of prajñā.
> Therefore, it is presented on two bhūmis.[603]

Thus, the result of having trained on these six bhūmis is taught to be fourfold:

> There are four other kinds of result
> Of the trainings and familiarization.[604]

As for the first one of these, on the seventh bhūmi skill in means becomes pure. Therefore, one attains the signlessness with effort:

> The first result is the state
> Of signlessness with effort.[605]

As for the second [result], effort subsides too and thus [mind] turns into the very dharmakāya. Through touching the dhātu of nonconceptuality, and through mentation, perception, and conception becoming nonexistent,[606] [bodhisattvas] touch the secret of the buddhas. Then, at that moment, all buddhas rouse them from their [meditative equipoise that] lacks appearances and they obtain the limitless appearances of wisdom, through which they obtain a pure realm. For this reason,

> The same without effort
> And the purity of the realm
> Are asserted as the second result.[607]

This is the pāramitā of aspiration prayers because an ocean of realms becomes pure merely through aspiring so.

As for the third [result], since [bodhisattvas] mature an inexpressible ocean of realms of sentient beings in a single instant, this is the pāramitā of power.

For they have manifested the four [kinds of] discriminating awareness {544} [and thus] are the powerful sovereigns of all phenomena.

The accomplishment of maturing sentient beings[608]

Immediately after that, through the liberations of an ocean of samādhis and the completion of all dhāraṇīs, [bodhisattvas] gain mastery over engaging in all worldly realms with an ocean of emanations and gathering an ocean of disciples to guide on a single hair in a [single] pore. Through this, the tenth bhūmi of the pāramitā of wisdom represents the culmination of excellent familiarization. On that [bhūmi], what accords with phenomena that [appear as] duality and according designations is not present as anything that has a connection of identity or causality with the nature of phenomena. Also the *Uttaratantra* says:

> [Like within a lotus, . . .
>
> Like a buddha, . . .]
>
> The beginningless natural stainlessness
> Of the mind within the beginningless cocoons
> Of afflictions that are not connected to
> The dhātu of sentient beings is declared to be.[609]

Therefore, here the matrix is inseparable purity and, in the sense of [being its] natural outflow, [its realization] depends on one's personal experience. Thus, as for the nonexistence and existence of phenomena and the nature of phenomena, respectively, it has been taught above that [phenomena] do not exist, but still appear. On the other hand, it is not contradictory that what exists [—the nature of phenomena—] is without stains and yet must become pure. As the *Mahāyānasūtrālaṃkāra* says:

> Phenomena do not exist and yet are observed.
> There is no affliction and yet there is purity.
> These are to be understood like an illusion and such
> And like space, respectively.[610]

This is to be understood in the detailed teachings in this [text].[611] {545}

When relying on this foundation [(the nature of phenomena)], the third [point] that comes up [in this discussion of the nature of phenomena here] is the path of preparation. Therefore, to explain it [Maitreya] said, "Discernment is the entire path of preparation that consists of the proper mental engagement which relies on the sūtra collection of the mahāyāna."

Here, among the five paths, the path of accumulation serves as the cause of that discernment. When just [starting to] engage in the distinction between phenomena and the nature of phenomena, one relies on mere aspiration [for the nature of phenomena] and engages in many factors that are conducive to merit[612] over a long time. Through this, one causes the dispositions of the three yānas to arise as the [respective] unfolding [dispositions] from the naturally abiding [disposition]. As we find in the *Mahāyānasūtrālaṃkāra*:

> [Bodhisattvas,] who set out for incalculable eons,
> Increase their aspiration,
> Thus being as full of virtuous dharmas
> As the ocean is of water.[613]

Here the foundation of final deliverance that is based on the delicate aspirations for the twofold hīnayāna [of śrāvakas and pratyekabuddhas] is said to be like the past causes of noble *Mārgadhṛti.[614] However, here, in the unsurpassable yāna, since [bodhisattvas] must understand the above-explained foundation of knowable objects and their characteristics[615] and then engage in them, [the foundation of final deliverance here] consists of the triad of studying, reflecting on, and familiarizing with [that foundation and its characteristics]. Therefore, [bodhisattvas] engage in inconceivable causes. Consequently, as for the factors conducive to liberation, in one's buddha nature (the basic element with stains) enlightenment, the qualities, and enlightened activity exist in oneself, but they are fettered by the two obscurations. Seeing this, {546} [bodhisattvas] see the principles of a buddha endowed with twofold purity (someone like [Śākya]muni), the dharma, and the saṃgha.[616] Through this, they understand confidence and the six pāramitās (such as generosity) as being the causes and results [of engaging in the characteristics of knowable objects]. Then [they understand] the vigor of aspiring for the training [in these pāramitās] as well as the consummate motivation—the mindfulness which entails the aspiration prayers that are connected to the welfare of others and not only one's own welfare. As for understanding that the foundation [of all this] is nonconceptual wisdom, they understand the samādhi of contemplation and the prajñā of realizing [all] phenomena just as discussed above. [All of this is] for the sake of the great liberation of a buddha.

Furthermore, we find in the *Sāgaramatiparipṛcchasūtra*:

> "You may wonder, 'What are their afflictions that are the causes for saṃsāra and are congruently associated with roots of virtue?' They

are as follows—never being content with [their efforts in] seeking out the accumulation of merit, taking rebirths in [saṃsāric] existence as they wish, striving to meet buddhas, never being weary of maturing sentient beings, making efforts in grasping the genuine dharma, exerting themselves in whatever activities of [benefit for] sentient beings there are, not being separated from the thinking of being attached to the nature of phenomena, and not rejecting their connections to the pāramitās. Sāgaramati, no matter through what bodhisattvas train, they are not tainted by the flaws of the afflictions. {547} These are the afflictions that are congruently associated with roots of virtue." Again, [Sāgaramati] spoke, "Bhagavan, if these are roots of virtue, for what reason are they called 'afflictions'?" [The Buddha] said, "Sāgaramati, here these afflictions that have such a nature connect bodhisattvas with the three realms—the three realms originate from the afflictions. Since bodhisattvas are skilled in means and have given rise to the power of the roots of virtue, they connect with the three realms as they please. Therefore, [these afflictions] are called 'the roots of virtue that are congruently associated with afflictions.' They are referred to [as afflictions] because they connect [bodhisattvas] with the three realms for as long as these exist, but not because they afflict the mind."

Furthermore, [this sūtra] discusses this in ten verses starting with the following:

After the children of the victors have realized this unchanging
Nature of phenomena, their seeing of those
Who are born and so on by virtue of
The blindness of ignorance is marvelous.

In detail, two [verses] discuss the first bhūmi; the third and fourth, the [following] six bhūmis; the fifth one, the eighth [bhūmi]; three others, the qualities of the tenth bhūmi; and the following two, the manner in which [these qualities] are not and are different, respectively, from [those of] a buddha. The same is also discussed in the *Śrīmāla[devī]sūtra* and the *Mahāparinirvāṇa[sūtra]*.

As for the rationale too being taught by the scriptures, {548} [the following statement] is [internally] contradictory: "The bodhisattvas who have attained all four dhyānas on the path of preparation and then go, through their miraculous powers, to other worlds in order to venerate buddhas and listen to the dharma engage in the path of seeing (the first bhūmi) without having attained the fourth dhyāna." [In the *Abhisamayālaṃkāra*] we find the following [that speaks] directly on the signs [of irreversibility of bodhisattvas on the path of seeing]:

Turning away from discriminating notions of form and so on,
Firmness of mind, turning away
From both the inferior yānas,
Dissolution of the branches of the dhyānas and so on . . .[617]

Furthermore, if [bodhisattvas] on the path of seeing wish, in a single moment of mind they [are able to] cultivate one hundred samādhis and thus shake one hundred realms and so on. By virtue of such attainments, [it is clear that] they have attained the fourth dhyāna and overcome the enemies [of the afflictions. The *Mahāyānasūtrālaṃkāra* says]:

And the accomplishment of samādhi and dhāraṇīs
Are the supreme results.
These four kinds of result
Are based on the four bhūmis.[618]

In this way, the six and the [following] four pāramitās [among the ten pāramitās] are taught as the causes and the results, respectively, of engaging in the characteristics of knowable objects on the path of familiarization, and the division of familiarizing with that [engagement] is taught as the ten bhūmis. In detail, [this is explained in] the chapters on the pāramitās in the *Mahāyānasaṃgraha* and the *Mahāyānasūtrālaṃkāra*.[619] The purifications [of the ten bhūmis] are discussed in [the section on] the purifications of the bhūmis in the *Abhisamayālaṃkāra*,[620] the *Bodhisattvabhūmi*, and the *Daśabhūmikasūtra*. {549}

Here, as for the difference between the paths of familiarization of bodhisattvas and śrāvakas, during the four dhyānas and the four formless [absorptions] of the śrāvakas the seeds of the latencies of the afflictions (such as desire and anger) are relinquished through those levels [of samādhi] and the prajñā of [realizing] the four realities. [The śrāvakas] cultivate [the path of familiarization] because they strive solely for the peace that is beyond the three realms. It is therefore that the path of familiarization of the śrāvakas is labeled with the name "uncontaminated." As for bodhisattvas, though they attain that lack of afflictions of being beyond the three realms immediately upon attaining the path of seeing, out of great compassion they deliberately seize saṃsāra again and, knowing the afflictions of all sentient beings as far as space extends, they dispel them. By virtue of having attained skill in means, they see that all conceptions in terms of factors to be relinquished and remedies are necessary and therefore manifest and take them up willingly. It is therefore that the path of familiarization of bodhisattvas is labeled as "being contaminated." However, one should understand that, in terms of the definitive [meaning], the path of familiarization of bodhisattvas is without afflictions.

To explain the reason for this, there are both scriptures and reasonings. As for the first one, the *Uttaratantra* says:

> The root of the sufferings of death, sickness,
> And aging is removed by the noble ones.
> [Suffering] is born from the power of karma and afflictions,
> [But] they lack it because they lack these.[621]

As for the substantial [causes] (which are like firewood) of sickness, aging, and death (which are like fire) during the phase of impure [sentient beings], {550} [sickness and so on] arise by being preceded by improper mental engagement, karma, and afflictions. Bodhisattvas realize that, in those who have attained a body of mental nature, the ones [that are like firewood] do not appear at all and therefore the others [that are like fire] absolutely never blaze.

> Due to their character of compassion,
> They display birth, death, aging, and sickness,
> [But] they are beyond birth and so on,
> Because they see [the dhātu] as it really is.[622]

Bodhisattvas are connected to the roots of virtue and thus, based on their mastery over being reborn as they wish, perfectly connect with the three realms out of compassion. Though they display birth, aging, sickness, and death, these phenomena do not exist [for them]. Their mastery over karma is to see true reality as it is—this basic element being without arising and without ceasing. [Thus, bodhisattvas] attain the first two [masteries] on the eighth [bhūmi].[623] The ninth [bhūmi] represents their attainment of mastery over wisdom because they attain [the four kinds of] discriminating awareness. Through the tenth [bhūmi] they realize the mastery over [enlightened] activity because they promote the welfare of sentient beings through emanations just as they please.

[There follow some] intermediate verses:

> The path of familiarization is profound,
> Such as profound emptiness.
> This profundity is the liberation from the extremes
> Of superimposition and denial with regard to this.[624] {551}

It means liberation from the obscurations in terms of
Being pervasive, limited, excessive,
Equal, adopting, and relinquishing.[625]
Through nonconceptual wisdom,
Just as a great medicine for poison eliminates poison,
They are purified as equality.[626]

In nonconceptuality everything appears.
Through nonconceptuality everything is done.
Just as the two obscurations are eliminated
Through the wisdom with the power of nonconceptuality,
All power is accomplished
Through the samādhi of engaging in crossing in one leap.[627]

Moment by moment of mind,
[Bodhisattvas] venerate the buddhas, grasp all dharmas,
Purify realms, liberate sentient beings,
And train perfectly in the pāramitās.
Since [all] this is performed in an inconceivable manner,
It is the sphere of buddhas alone.

The children of the victors who attain the first bhūmi
Equal one hundred pratyekabuddhas.
Those who explain this in accordance with the path of
familiarization of śrāvakas
Compare the children of the victors to childish beings.

The cessation of realizing [everything] to be illusionlike
And the cessation of freedom and termination are different[628]—
They have the two natures of remedy and what is to be
relinquished, respectively.
It is mistaken to conceive as one
The conditioned and contaminated three realms
And the wisdom activity of uncontaminated karma—
This is similar to matching a miserable firefly
With the functions of the orb of the sun.

If the present-day learned and accomplished ones
Examine this principle well, it will be of great significance.

[This concludes] the explanation of the path of recollection.

2.2.2.2.2.6. The path of completion (arrival)[629]

> {552} **As for the arrival at its nature, once suchness has become without stains, all appears as nothing but suchness, which is the perfection of the fundamental change.**

This says that the nature of the two dharmakāyas of a buddha is nonconceptual wisdom. "**As for the arrival at its nature**" means "having reached the end [of the path]." This [nature] is **suchness**—the nature of the two [aspects of] the perfect [nature] (unchanging suchness and unmistaken suchness, which is [ultimately] nothing other [than unchanging suchness]). **Once** this [suchness] **has become without** the **stains** of the imaginary and the dependent [natures], since **all** knowable objects are without duality, they are naked wisdom, that is, they **appear as nothing but suchness.**[630] After mind, mentation, and consciousness have undergone their **fundamental change**, this **is their perfection** as the natures of the five wisdoms. Here "change" refers to the path of familiarization having reached its end.[631]

In [the seventh chapter of] the *Abhisamayālaṃkāra* this [fundamental change] is said to be instantaneous. It refers to the realization by virtue of all [uncontaminated] phenomena being contained in the nature of a single uncontaminated phenomenon, just as a water wheel moves in its entirety through a single spot to step on. At that point, the instant in terms of maturation is the nature of prajñāpāramitā, and all pure phenomena have become their own nature, being inseparable [from prajñāpāramitā]. Therefore, this is called "instantaneous wisdom."[632] {553} For this is the final realization that the imaginary and the dependent characteristics appear, but do not really exist and are dreamlike. Through this [realization], the consummate pure conduct of the pāramitās and the actuality of the nonreferentiality of all phenomena have become free from all obscurations, just like a person having awoken from being asleep. Therefore, at this point the knowledge of termination and nonarising is [due to the final] knowledge that all obscurations are terminated and due to the final perception that all phenomena do not arise. The *Mahāyānasaṃgraha* says:

> How is the dharmakāya attained for the first time through contact? Through the wisdoms of nonconceptuality and its subsequent attainment that focus on [all] mahāyāna dharmas in combination having excellently cultivated the five aspects [of practice],[633] the accumulations are gathered well in all respects. Through the vajralike samādhi, [which has this name] because it destroys the subtle obscurations that are difficult to destroy, [the dharmakāya] is free

> from all obscurations right at the end of that [samādhi]. Therefore, [the dharmakāya] is attained through these [factors] by virtue of the fundamental change.[634]

That which undergoes the fundamental change is the ālaya-consciousness. That through which it undergoes the fundamental change is the dharmakāya that is the natural outflow [of the stainless dharmadhātu]. That into which there is a fundamental change is the stainless dharmakāya. The way in which the fundamental change happens is that the two nonexistent phenomena [—the imaginary and dependent natures—] become pure and the existent nature of phenomena appears. The time during which the fundamental change occurs is fourfold—aspiration, contact, recollection, and instantaneously becoming its nature. {554} As for the fundamental change with its distinctive features that will be explained [below] through ten points, through the [first] six points, including the progression,[635] it is taught as buddhahood [by Maitreya]. The *Mahāyānasūtrālaṃkāra* says:

> Having attained the final familiarization,
> Bodhisattvas receive the empowerment.
>
> Having attained the vajralike samādhi
> That is unbreakable by conceptions,
> They undergo the final fundamental change,
> Being without the stains of all obscurations.
>
> They attain the unsurpassable state
> Of the knowledge of all aspects,
> Due to which [the activities] for the benefit
> Of sentient beings are accomplished.[636]

In detail, this is taught below.

2.2.2.2.2.7 Explanation of the fundamental change

This has three parts:

1) Connecting [passage]
2) [Brief] introduction
3) [Detailed] explanation

2.2.2.2.2.7.1. Connecting [passage]

> **The comprehension of the fundamental change through ten points is unsurpassable—**

The completely perfect **fundamental change** in terms of these [points] that are taught below teaches the **unsurpassable** fundamental change of buddhahood.[637] So what are these points?

2.2.2.2.2.7.2. Brief introduction

> **[through comprehending the nature, the entity, the persons, the distinctive features, the prerequisites, the foundation, the mental engagement, the trainings, the shortcomings, and the benefits.]**

The fundamental change is to be understood through these following ten points—teaching (1) what **the nature** of the fundamental change is, (2) which **entities** undergo the fundamental change, (3) which **persons** undergo the fundamental change, (4) **the distinctive features** of the fundamental changes of śrāvakas and pratyekabuddhas versus [the one of] the mahāyāna, (5) on which **prerequisites** it depends, (6) based on which **foundation** of the fundamental change this change takes place, (7) **the mental engagement** that is the cause of the fundamental change, (8) how to **train** on the path [that leads to] it, {555} (9) the existence of four **shortcomings** if there is no fundamental change, **and** (10) **the benefits** of its existence.[638]

2.2.2.2.2.7.3. Detailed explanation

This has ten parts:

2.2.2.2.2.7.3.1. Explanation of the nature of the fundamental change

> **As for comprehending the nature, it is stainless suchness in terms of adventitious stains and suchness not appearing and appearing, respectively.**

Adventitious stains are one's own **stainless** and naturally luminous mind as such, but by virtue of this very [mind] being ignorant of itself, cognizance appears in a dualistic way as if it were [a separate] apprehender and apprehended. Miragelike mental conceptions arise, and these false imaginations obscure luminous **suchness**. If these obscurations do **not appear, suchness** will **appear**, just as in the example of water appearing to be clear and transparent once it has become pure of silt. This is **the nature** of the fundamental change. The *Mahāyānasūtrālaṃkāra* says:

> When murky water becomes clear,
> [Its] transparency does not arise from elsewhere,

But is just its becoming free from pollution.
The same goes for the purity of your own mind.

It is held that mind, which is always naturally luminous,
Is [only] blemished by adventitious flaws.
Apart from the mind that is the nature of phenomena, no other mind
Is proclaimed to be luminous in nature.[639]

Luminosity and natural emptiness are not tainted by the nature of conceptions, {556} since conceptions are [nothing but] nonexistents that appear. This is stated many times, such as in the *Dharmadhātustava*:

About water at the time of spring,
What we say is that it's "warm."
Of the very same [thing], when it's chilly,
We just say that it is "cold."

Covered by the web of the afflictions,
It is called a "sentient being."
Once it's free from the afflictions,
It should be expressed as "buddha."[640]

Also the *[Hevajra]tantra* says:

Sentient beings are buddhas indeed.
However, they are obscured by adventitious stains.
If these are removed, they are buddhas.[641]

This is the nature of the fundamental change. Since it is understood in this way, it is explained that it is "**comprehended.**"[642]

2.2.2.2.2.7.3.2. Which entities undergo the fundamental change

The connecting [passage is]

The comprehension of the entity.[643]

There are three [such] **entities**. What are they? [This]

refers to the change of the suchness of the cognizance that is the common container, the change of the suchness of the dharmadhātu

of the sūtra collection, and the change of the suchness of the cognizance that is the dhātu of sentient beings which is not in common.

(1) Thus, as for **the cognizance that is the container**, at the time of being impure it appears as the world that is an impure realm, but when it has become pure, it therefore **changes** into a pure buddha realm. This refers to the factors that consist of the [five sense] objects and the five sense faculties. Maitreya says [in his *Abhisamayālaṃkāra*]:

The world of sentient beings is impure,
And so is the world that is the environment.
By virtue of accomplishing the purity of those, {557}
The purity of a buddha realm [appears].[644]

The *Mahāyānasūtrālaṃkāra* says:

In the fundamental change of perception and its referents,
Supreme mastery is attained
Over pure realms in order to display
Enjoyments just as one pleases.[645]

(2) **The dharmadhātu of the sūtra collection** refers to the purity of the clinging to the characteristics of the piṭakas of the dharma that make up the teaching[646] (such as words, phrases, and letters) as well as the mastery over them. This is the fundamental **change of** the sixth [consciousness]—mentation, including conceptions.[647] [In the *Mahāyānasūtrālaṃkāra*] we find:

In the fundamental change of conception,
Supreme mastery is attained
Over wisdom and activities
Unimpeded at all times.[648]

(3) **The dhātu of sentient beings which is not in common** is the ālaya-consciousness. It is called "not in common" because it is the result that is produced by the karmic formations—the seven consciousnesses—of each individual mind stream. Its fundamental change has two elements. The dharmakāya [is what manifests] through the element of the foundation—the ālaya—having become pure. Equality [is what manifests] through the fundamental **change of** the element that is the active agent—the afflicted mind. [The *Mahāyānasūtrālaṃkāra*] says:

In the fundamental change of mentation,
Supreme mastery is attained
Over utterly stainless nonconceptual
Wisdom ensuing from mastery.[649]

And

In the fundamental change of the foundation,
Supreme mastery is attained
Over the nonabiding nirvāṇa
In the stainless state of the buddhas.[650]

In brief, {558} [these entities that undergo the fundamental change] are referred to as three because they are [three] different results in terms of appearance, instruction, and beholding.[651]

2.2.2.2.2.7.3.3. The persons who undergo the fundamental change

This has two parts:
1) [The fundamental changes that are] not in common
2) The fundamental change that is in common

2.2.2.2.2.7.3.3.1. [The fundamental changes that are] not in common

As for comprehending the persons, the first two are the fundamental changes of suchness of buddhas and bodhisattvas.

Śrāvakas and pratyekabuddhas do not need the [first] **two** [kinds of fundamental change explained above] because they strive for [personal] peace without purifying the container and [all] phenomena [in general]. However, **buddhas and bodhisattvas** need them because they display kāyas, wisdoms, and enlightened activities by virtue of their mastery over all realms and phenomena. Therefore, [these two fundamental changes] are called "not in common with śrāvakas and pratyekabuddhas."

2.2.2.2.2.7.3.3.2. [The fundamental change that is] in common

The latter one refers also to those of śrāvakas and pratyekabuddhas.

What is taught [above] by "the dhātu of sentient beings which is not in common" is the factor of the ālaya-consciousness, which functions as the foundation of all afflictions of the three realms. This must be relinquished by all noble ones because the afflictive obscurations, including their foundation, are the [common] factors to be overcome. Since all [noble ones] are equal in being liberated from these [factors to be relinquished], [such relinquishment] is also taught as "the vimuktikāya. The following [lines] in the *Saṃdhinirmocanasūtra* also teach just this:

> This uncontaminated dhātu of those who are liberated
> Is not anything that can be designated as two or one.[652] {559}

2.2.2.2.2.7.3.4. Instruction on the distinctive features of the fundamental change

This has two parts:
1) The distinctive feature in terms of realms
2) The distinctive feature in terms of attainment

2.2.2.2.2.7.3.4.1. The distinctive feature in terms of realms

> **The comprehension of the distinctive features is by virtue of the distinctive feature of the purity of the realms of buddhas and bodhisattvas**

After the factors that consist of the consciousnesses—the characteristics that exist in the ālaya and appear as objects—have been purified, all **buddhas and bodhisattvas** possess **the purity of** [their] **realms**, and their display is also unimpeded. This is because they have gained mastery over the profound dependent origination with regard to apprehending specifically characterized phenomena without there being a creator of realms. Since the śrāvakas do not purify the aspect of the container in this way, it appears [to them] in common with other sentient beings. [The container] of the pratyekabuddhas is purified a little bit, but since they leave it behind and enter the uncontaminated [dhātu], [their purification of the container] is pointless.

2.2.2.2.2.7.3.4.2. The distinctive feature in terms of attainment

> **And by virtue of the distinctive feature of having attained seeing, instruction, and mastery through the attainment of the dharmakāya, the sāmbhogika[kāya], and the nairmāṇikakāya, respectively.**

The dharmakāya is the mastery over **seeing** the entirety of the suchness and variety of knowable objects. **The sāmbhogika**[kāya] refers to the **instruction**

in, and the mastery over, the profound and vast dharma—it teaches many amazing doors [of dharma]. **The nairmāṇikakāya** is the **attainment** and display of inconceivable qualities that are the foundation for accomplishing [all kinds of beneficial] activities for sentient beings. {560} Śrāvakas and pratyekabuddhas do not have these [kāyas].[653]

2.2.2.2.2.7.3.5. Explanation of comprehending the distinctive features of the prerequisites

> **The comprehension of the prerequisites is by virtue of the distinctive feature of previous aspiration prayers, by virtue of the distinctive feature of the focal object that is the mahāyāna teaching, and by virtue of the distinctive feature of training on the ten bhūmis.**

The comprehension of the prerequisites—the causes for attaining the fruition of the three kāyas—**is** through three points. (1) **Previous aspiration prayers** start on [the level of] engagement through aspiration, [continue through] accomplishing the ten great aspiration prayers[654] on the bhūmis of pure superior intention,[655] and [culminate in] the perfect accomplishment of aspiration prayers on the eighth [bhūmi], that is, engaging [as] in the immeasurable exemplary life story of Samantabhadra. This is the prerequisite of pure speech.

(2) As for **the distinctive feature of the focal object**, [bodhisattvas] focus on prajñāpāramitā, in which the entirety of the mahāyāna is combined into one in a nonconceptual manner. Through focusing on all [mahāyāna] dharmas individually without combining them, they engage in [their] being illusion-like. Through focusing on the suchness of all these [dharmas], the power for **teaching the mahāyāna** dharmas arises because they engage in it through limitless dhāraṇīs and discriminating awarenesses.

(3) **The distinctive feature of training on the ten bhūmis** is due to relinquishing the two obscurations, including their latent tendencies, and attaining supreme wisdom and thereby making the activity of accomplishing the qualities of the ten pāramitās unimpeded for as long as saṃsāra lasts.[656] {561}

In this way, the prerequisites for wisdom and enlightened activity becoming pure by virtue of aspiration prayers, focal object, and training are taught. This point is also [explained] in the chapter on the generation of bodhicitta [in the *Mahāyānasūtrālaṃkāra*]:

> Because of accomplishing the ten great aspiration prayers,
> It should be understood as magnanimous.

> Because of not becoming weary by hardships over a long time,
> It should be realized to be enthusiasm.
>
> Because of realizing the closeness to enlightenment
> And acquiring the means and prajñā for that,
> It should be understood as pure intention,
> While skill [in means] comes on another level.
>
> Through mentally engaging in how things are,
> Through realizing the conceptuality of that,
> And through not conceptualizing this [realization],
> It should be understood as final deliverance.[657]

Thus, [the above] accords with what the *Mahāyānasūtrālaṃkāra* says about buddhahood being accomplished through training in magnanimity, enthusiasm, pure intention, and final deliverance. For śrāvakas and pratyekabuddhas, these [trainings] are pointless because they aspire to exit saṃsāra all by themselves, seize the dharma [only] temporarily like a raft, and possess the limited trainings that make them go beyond the three realms through their own respective levels.

In this way, these five [points] of nature, entity, persons, distinctions, and prerequisites (which have the nature of being what is founded on [the foundation that is nonconceptual wisdom]) are taught based on the factors to be relinquished and their remedies.

2.2.2.2.2.7.3.6. Instruction on the foundation of all this, based on which the fundamental change takes place

{562} This has two parts:

1) Brief introduction
2) Detailed explanation

2.2.2.2.2.7.3.6.1. Brief introduction

The connecting [passage]:

> **The comprehension of the foundation refers to comprehending nonconceptual wisdom through six points.**

The brief introduction to these **six**:

> **[This comprehension in six points]**[658] **is by virtue of the focal objects, the relinquishment of characteristics, the correct yogic**

> **practice, the defining characteristics, the benefit, and the thorough knowledge.**

When **comprehending** the **nonconceptual wisdom** of the buddha bhagavāns, such **comprehension is by virtue of** examining (1) **the focal objects** through which one engages in [this wisdom], (2) which conceptions about **characteristics** are **relinquished**, (3) how one **practices** this [wisdom], (4) of which kind its **defining characteristics** are, (5) what its **benefit** is, **and** (6) that nonconceptual wisdom is known through **the knowledge** of certain [points].[659]

2.2.2.2.2.7.3.6.2. Detailed explanation

This has six parts—from among the six above,

2.2.2.2.2.7.3.6.2.1. Explanation of the fourfold comprehension of the focal objects

The brief introduction:

> **The comprehension of the focal objects through four points**

What are those four?

> **is by virtue of the mahāyāna teaching, aspiring for it, being certain [about it], and the completion of the accumulations.**

In the *Uttaratantra* this [wisdom] is taught through the term "basic element." Here it is discussed under the term "nonconceptual wisdom." In the prajñāpāramitā [texts] it is treated under the name "prajñāpāramitā." In the *Mahāyānasaṃgraha* we find:

> There is no difference between prajñāpāramitā and nonconceptual wisdom.[660] {563}

Therefore, [the *Uttaratantra* says]:

> As for what is to be awakened, awakening,
> Its branches, and what causes awakening, in due order,
> One point is the cause and three
> Are the conditions for its purity.[661]

[The *Ratnagotravibhāgavyākhyā*] says that since all knowable objects are included in these four topics, the first one is the point of what is to be realized.

The second one is its realization, that is, enlightenment. Its branches are the [buddha] qualities. Since these qualities function as the conditions for realization, they [also] represent the enlightened activity. As for the explanation of the basic element and the [three] jewels, the basic element is to be understood as the cause and the three jewels, as the conditions. From both this cause and these conditions, the result—enlightenment, qualities, and enlightened activity—arises.[662] Therefore, the basic element, which bears the conventional term "cause," is the nature of nonconceptual wisdom. When the thirty-two-fold enlightened activity[663] of a buddha (the condition [for the realization of other beings]) operates, the three jewels (which are based on [this enlightened activity being labeled as buddha, dharma, and saṃgha through] the terms of these other [beings]) arise. It is therefore that [Maitreya] speaks here of "**the mahāyāna** dharma." Thus, [a buddha's] **teaching** the dharma refers to [those to be guided] attaining those conditions [of enlightened activity manifesting to them in the form of the three jewels], which appear as if being external. Based on that, **aspiration** [for the three jewels] arises [in them]. If they aspire [for these jewels], they engage [in them] through **being certain** [about them], which leads to the arising of vigor. If that is present, through engaging in [gathering] the two accumulations they will **complete the accumulations**. However, if one of these four [factors] is lacking, nonconceptual wisdom does not arise in the form of the result. This is why these **four focal objects** are taught. Consequently, the *Uttaratantra* says the following about them, including their progression:

> They make the confident resolve, {564}
> "This inconceivable object exists,
> It can be attained by someone like me,
> And its attainment possesses such qualities."
>
> Thereby, bodhicitta—the receptacle
> Of qualities such as confidence, vigor,
> Mindfulness, dhyāna, and prajñā—
> Is present in them at all times.
>
> Since that [mind] is always present,
> The children of the victors are irreversible
> And reach the completion
> And purity of the pāramitā of merit.[664]

You may wonder, "It is said that, based on such focal objects, the characteristics of conceptions about the existence of that on which one focuses are blazing. Therefore, how could this be nonconceptual wisdom?"

2.2.2.2.2.7.3.6.2.2. Instruction on the comprehension of the relinquishment of characteristics

> **The comprehension of the relinquishment of characteristics through four points is to be understood[665] by virtue of relinquishing the characteristics of antagonistic factors, remedies, suchness, and the dharmas of realization.**

What is to be taught here are (1) the nature of these four **characteristics**, (2) their order, and (3) what is eliminated based on what. (1a) The **antagonistic factors** are the [four kinds of] clinging to impermanent sentient beings as being permanent, clinging to what is empty and conditioned as being [real] entities, clinging to [saṃsāric] existence (which has the nature of the three sufferings) as being really existent, and clinging to identityless phenomena as having an identity. These are characteristics of mistakenness {565} because they cause bondage in saṃsāra. They are not in accordance with correct cognition. (1b) The **remedies** consist of understanding that what is conditioned is impermanent, understanding that everything imaginary is empty, understanding that all who wander in [saṃsāric] existence are not beyond the three sufferings, and understanding that nirvāṇa is peace because all phenomena lack an identity and what is "mine." These are the remedies of saṃsāra—those characteristics that are remedies cause liberation from nonvirtue. Therefore, they are common to [all] three yānas. (1c) As for **suchness**, both the factors to be relinquished and their remedies are mere cognizance. If one clings to them as characteristics, one will not be liberated from the imaginary and the dependent [natures]. Since the cognizances of the [factors to be relinquished and their remedies], which are produced through the conceptions of factors to be relinquished and their remedies, are without arising and ceasing, they are unconditioned by nature. This is the nature of phenomena that is the perfect [nature]. Those who see the buddha heart as [consisting of the pāramitās of supreme] purity, self,[666] bliss, and permanence[667] are the children of the victors. (1d) The characteristic of **realization** refers to training and perfecting the qualities (such as the fourfold mastery) as well as the enlightened activity.

(2) As for the order [of these four characteristics, Maitreya says]:

> **Through this, in due order, they are described as coarse, middling, subtle, and what is associated for a long time.**

The characteristic of the antagonistic factors is **coarse** because they are the causes of the impregnations of negative tendencies and are easy to understand. {566} The characteristic of their remedies is **middling**. The characteristic of suchness is **subtle** because it is the mere focusing on the appearance of nonconceptual wisdom and is the remedy for everything that is other than it. Since the characteristic of realization is the result of familiarization, it is **that** with which [a bodhisattva] **is associated for a long time** because it remains up to the end of the continuum [of the ten bhūmis].[668]

(3) As for what is eliminated based on what, in the *Avikalpapraveśadhāraṇī*[669] the afflictions are relinquished through the remedies eliminating the conceptions to be relinquished, that is, [through] clinging to [saṃsāric] existence as the factor to be relinquished and clinging to suchness as the remedy.[670] Among these [four characteristics], since it is necessary to accomplish the fruition that consists of the two kāyas, through making them unequalled the two [characteristics] of factors to be relinquished and remedies are eliminated on [the paths of] accumulation and preparation; [the characteristic of] suchness, on the seven impure bhūmis; [the characteristic of] realization (the fruition), on the three pure bhūmis; and the last of all characteristics, through the vajralike samādhi. These are discussed through the example of a gem that exists beneath the earth—in due order, [things] like earth, stones, silver, gold, and various precious gems are removed and then a precious gem (a beryl) comes forth.[671]

[2.2.2.2.2.7.3.6.2.3. The correct yogic practice]

To explain the mind that trains in focusing on the elimination of those characteristics in such a way, [Maitreya gives] the general instruction:

> **The comprehension of the correct yogic practice through four points**

What are these **four**?

> **is through the yogic practice of observation,** {567} **through the yogic practice of nonobservation, through the yogic practice of the nonobservation of observation, and through the yogic practice of the observation of nonobservation.**

First, on the path of preparation, **the yogic practice of** the **observation** of all dharmas and their meanings as being mere cognizance relinquishes the entirety of the imaginary and makes [bodhisattvas] see that their own awareness does not exist as the duality of apprehender and apprehended. The *Triṃśikā* says:

For as long as consciousness
Does not dwell in mere cognizance,
The aftereffects of twofold grasping
Will not come to a halt.[672]

Then, on the path of seeing, [bodhisattvas] cultivate **the yogic practice of** the **nonobservation** of mind—this mere cognizance—too because this very cognizance has the nature of the dependent. For, since [this cognizance] has the nature of the apprehender, if they do not go beyond it, they do not see the perfect [nature]. [The *Triṃśikā* continues]:

But "all this is mere cognizance"
Refers to this observing too—
Anything that is propped up before [the mind]
Means not dwelling in "merely that [cognizance]."[673]

If there are no referents, cognizance is not tenable. Therefore, this is called "the yogic practice of nonobservation." It is what relinquishes [both] apprehender and apprehended. The *Triṃśikā* says:

When consciousness itself
Does not observe any focal object,
It rests in the very being of mere consciousness
Since there is no apprehender without something apprehended.[674]

Based on **the yogic practice of the nonobservation**[675] of cognition in this way, what is **observed** is nonconceptual wisdom. {568} This is the beginning of the fundamental change. [The *Triṃśikā* states]:

Then, it is no-mind and nonperception—
It is supramundane wisdom.
This is the fundamental change
By virtue of having relinquished the twofold impregnations of
negative tendencies.[676]

Thus, through the nonobservation of the mind with the duality of apprehender and apprehended, which is impaired by the afflictions, supramundane wisdom will be observed. Based on this nonconceptual wisdom, the two impregnations of negative tendencies that are to be relinquished through seeing and familiarization, respectively, will be relinquished. Also the *Mahāyānasūtrālaṃkāra* teaches the above order [of this]:

The mind is aware that nothing other than mind exists.
Then, it is realized that mind does not exist either.
The intelligent ones are aware that both do not exist
And abide in the dharmadhātu, in which these are absent.[677]

Then [this text continues]:

The power of the nonconceptual wisdom of the intelligent,
Which is always and everywhere accompanied by equality,
Clears the dense thicket of the collection of flaws on that foundation,
Just as a great antidote does with poison.[678]

Thus, based on that, the two obscurations are eliminated. In this way, up through the seventh bhūmi, [bodhisattvas] proceed through the training in the equality of [saṃsāric] existence and peace [as it is still] based on the characteristic of suchness.[679]

Immediately upon seeing the eighth bhūmi, when conception, mentation, and perception have become pure, fourth, **the training in the observation of nonobservation** arises. For example, even while knowing one's swimming in a great river in a dream {569} to be a dream, one still makes intense efforts to reach the other shore. However, immediately upon waking up, nothing whatsoever [of all this] appears and one is free from [any] effort. Likewise, while nonconceptual wisdom appears on the [first] seven bhūmis, [bodhisattvas] still make intense efforts to train in the wisdoms of meditative equipoise and subsequent attainment. Immediately upon attaining buddhahood, being free from such efforts, there will be no [such] appearances. [Also,] immediately upon that,[680] as many tathāgatas as there are sand grains in the River Gaṅgā show their faces and rouse [these bodhisattvas] who rest in the dhātu of nonconceptuality. They rouse them [by saying], "O children of good family, this dhātu of the lack of appearance is in common with śrāvakas and pratyekabuddhas. However, without resting in it, look at our inconceivable kāyas, wisdoms, realms, dharmas, and enlightened activities!" Based on this cause, [those bodhisattvas] engage in training in aspiration prayers, dhāraṇīs, discriminating awarenesses, [pure] realms, and the ornament of the heart of enlightenment[681] through giving rise to limitless appearances of wisdom while not conceptualizing [anything]. Therefore, this is called "the training in the observation of nonobservation" and also "the characteristic of the fruition."[682]

Such is the synopsis of what the *Daśabhūmikasūtra* and also the *Laṅkāvatārasūtra* say. The summary of this is found in an old translation [of the latter]:

By relying on mere mind
Those of good fortune relinquish it too.
By relying on mere mind
They must even go beyond nonappearance. {570}
If a yogin rests in nonappearance,
He does not see the mahāyāna.

[Kamalaśīla's] Madhyamaka-*Bhāvanākrama* [says]:

The yogin who rests in nonappearance
Sees the mahāyāna.

Thus, his reference to [just] the last part of the [newer] translation does not consider the detailed explanation preceding it and thus takes it to be a quote on meditative equipoise being without appearances, which I see as an error.[683]

2.2.2.2.2.7.3.6.2.4. The defining characteristics of nonconceptual [wisdom]

This has three parts:
1) The characteristic of how it abides
2) The characteristic of nonappearance
3) The characteristic of appearance

2.2.2.2.2.7.3.6.2.4.1. The characteristic of how it abides

The connecting [passage]:

The comprehension of the defining characteristics through three points

You may wonder, "How does nonconceptual wisdom abide as the unchanging perfect [nature]?" [This]

is by virtue of abiding in the nature of phenomena due to abiding in the nature of phenomena that is nondual and inexpressible.

This corresponds to what was taught above as the defining characteristic of **the nature of phenomena**. With this in mind, the [sūtras] say:

No matter whether buddhas have arrived or not arrived in the world, [this] is the very abiding of the true nature of phenomena.[684]

2.2.2.2.2.7.3.6.2.4.2. The characteristic of nonappearance

> **It is [also] by virtue of nonappearance because duality, according designations, sense faculties, objects, cognizance, and the world as the container do not appear.**

What appears as the **duality** of apprehender and apprehended; {571} what is conceived as names and referents that are **designated** by virtue of latent tendencies; the triad of **sense faculties, objects**, and **cognizance** that appears as the triad of what is internal, external, and in between, respectively; and **the world as the container** that appears to the mind as if it were a referent that is other [than mind]—all these are enumerations of what appear as the aspects of the imaginary and the dependent [natures]. Since [all phenomena] that appear in these ways are obscurations of nonconceptual wisdom, [anything] that **appears** as these does **not** exist [in it]. Therefore, to match this with the sūtras, [Maitreya] says:

> **Thus, through this, the defining characteristic of nonconceptual wisdom is described according to the sūtras as "ungraspable, indemonstrable, ungrounded, without appearance, without cognizance, and without base."**

Therefore, since [nonconceptual wisdom] cannot be grasped as the duality of apprehender and apprehended, it is **ungraspable**[685] because the actuality of nonduality is its nature. It is **indemonstrable** because it cannot be demonstrated through names and words to express it. Since it is not grounded on the sense faculties (such as the eyes), it is **ungrounded** because it is the emptiness of the internal.[686] Since external objects (such as form) do not exist outside, it is **without appearance**—the emptiness of the external. Cognizance is the dependent, and since its referents do not exist, [nonconceptual wisdom] is [also] **without cognizance** because it is without anything to be aware of and anything that is aware. Since it is not an entity that is a base, it is **without base** because it is the emptiness of the great.[687] If [the above six phenomena] do not appear as [explained here], {572} the [true] actuality will appear.[688] Therefore, the meaning of being without obscurations is that there is no appearance of names, characteristics, and imagination.[689]

2.2.2.2.2.7.3.6.2.4.3. The characteristic of appearance

> **It is [also] by virtue of appearance because all phenomena appear equal to the center of space and because all conditioned phenomena appear like illusions and so on.**

By virtue of meditative equipoise [bodhisattvas] are free from all clinging to [any] characteristics of [any among] **all phenomena**. Therefore, [all phenomena] are **equal to the center of space** because the unchanging perfect [nature] is seen. Through the cognition that is attained subsequent to that, **all conditioned phenomena appear like illusions**, mirages, echoes, and dreams, and therefore are mere appearances because the nature of [all kinds of] saṃsāra is seen. In detail, according to what is said in the sūtra collection, the inner body consists of the illusionlike appearances of the six sense faculties. Objects do not exist and yet appear, just like dreams. They are also like reflections and optical illusions. Sounds are like echoes. The appearances of samādhi are like [the reflection of] the moon in water. All that appears as [saṃsāric] existence is like a magical creation.[690] As for seeing all factors to be relinquished and remedies like illusions, [the *Mahāyānasūtrālaṃkāra* says]:

> Just like an illusory king being defeated
> By another illusory king—
> The dispassionate children of the victors
> Regard all dharmas [in this way].[691]

The *Mahāyānasaṃgraha* discusses this in detail:

> The aspect of the nonconceptual {573}
> Wisdom of all bodhisattvas
> Is the signlessness
> In the observed object to be known.[692]
>
> Having the nature of connection,
> What is conceived [as meaning] is nothing other than that.
> Through connecting letters with each other,
> Meaning comes from connecting them.
>
> Without an expression, wisdom
> Does not engage in an object of expression.
> [But] since [the two] are contradictory, nothing is expressed.
> Therefore, everything is inexpressible.[693]
>
> Nonconceptual wisdom
> Is the support of the activities of bodhisattvas
> During subsequent attainment
> Since they flourish [through it].

The aids of the nonconceptual
Wisdom of all bodhisattvas
Are said to be the two paths,
Which have the nature of the five pāramitās.[694]

The maturation of the nonconceptual
Wisdom of all bodhisattvas
Are the two buddha maṇḍalas
By virtue of application and attainment.[695]

The natural outflow of the nonconceptual
Wisdom of all bodhisattvas
Is asserted as its specific manifestations
In all subsequent lives.[696]

The outcome of the nonconceptual
Wisdom of all bodhisattvas
Is to be known as the ten bhūmis
Since it is attained and then perfected.[697]

The culmination of the nonconceptual
Wisdom of all bodhisattvas happens
Due to attaining the three pure kāyas
And due to attaining the supreme masteries.[698]

Nonconceptual wisdom
Is like space, untainted {574}
By all kinds of grave evil deeds
And because of mere confidence and devoted interest.[699]

In brief, because the imaginary and the dependent natures do not appear, suchness and the unmistaken [perfect nature] that engages it appear. This is called "nonconceptual wisdom," which does not mean not cognizing anything at all.[700]

2.2.2.2.2.7.3.6.2.5. Explanation of the fourfold comprehension of the benefit

Therefore, the connecting [passage says]:

The comprehension of the benefit through four points

What are these?

is by virtue of attaining the dharmakāya in a complete manner, by virtue of attaining the supreme state of bliss, by virtue of [attaining] mastery over seeing, and by virtue of attaining mastery over instruction.

This is **the benefit** of nonconceptual wisdom. Though **the dharmakāya** is its very nature, "**in a complete manner**" refers to [its] entailing enlightened activity. The *Abhisamayālaṃkāra* says:

The factors concordant with enlightenment, the immeasurables,
The liberations, the ninefold
Progressive meditative absorptions,
The ten totalities,

The āyatanas of overpowering,
Divided into eight kinds,
Dispassion, knowledge through aspiration,
The supernatural knowledges, the discriminating awarenesses,

The four purities in all respects,
The ten masteries, the ten powers,
The four fearlessnesses,
The three ways of nothing to hide,

The threefold foundation of mindfulness,
The true nature of being without forgetfulness, {575}
The latent tendencies being overcome,
Great compassion for beings,

The eighteen qualities that are said
To be unique to a sage,
And the knowledge of all aspects—
The dharmakāya is described as these.[701]

Thus, the 144 particular instances [of the qualities of the dharmakāya] are explained in twenty-one sets. By virtue of having completed these, [buddhas] are endowed with lasting uncontaminated **bliss**. As for the meaning of "**seeing**," [buddhas have mastery over seeing] because they see all knowable objects in their suchness and variety. On **the mastery over instruction**, the *Mahāyānasūtrālaṃkāra* says:

But the speech of the sugatas is infinite
And has sixty inconceivable branches.

This speech with frequent repetitions
Through well formulated phrases,
Which expound, discriminate, and remove doubts,
Is for those who understand through concise statements and elaboration.

Being pure of the three spheres,
The teaching of the buddhas is beneficial.
It should also be understood
As being free from the eight flaws.

Laziness, lack of understanding,
Inopportunity, uncertainty,
Not removing doubts,
Inconclusiveness,

Weariness, and stinginess—
These are asserted as the flaws of speech.
Since the teaching of the buddhas
Lacks these, it is unsurpassable.[702]

Thus, this refers to mastery over the speech that teaches through sixty branches,[703] [well] formulated [phrases], all detailed and brief [forms of teaching], {576} the arising of all qualities, and being free from these eight faults of speech.[704]

Having explained the fourfold benefit [of nonconceptual wisdom] in this way, [there follows]

2.2.2.2.2.7.3.6.2.6. The comprehension of the thorough knowledge

This has five parts:

1) [Brief] introduction
2) [Explanation of nonconceptual wisdom being] the remedy of five [factors]
3) [Explanation of its] specific characteristic of excluding five [factors]
4) [Explanation of its] five distinctive features
5) Explanation of its being endowed with five functions

2.2.2.2.2.7.3.6.2.6.1. [Brief] introduction

> **The comprehension of the thorough knowledge in four points consists of the thorough knowledge of [being a] remedy, the thorough knowledge of the defining characteristic, the thorough knowledge of the distinctive features, and the thorough knowledge of the functions.**

You may wonder, "How is nonconceptual wisdom to be **known**?" It is to be **known** through **four points**.

[2.2.2.2.2.7.3.6.2.6.2. Explanation of nonconceptual wisdom being the remedy of five factors]

[First] you may wonder, "For what is this [nonconceptual wisdom] a remedy?"

> **Here the thorough knowledge of [being a] remedy is due to nonconceptual wisdom being the remedy for the fivefold clinging to nonexistents, that is, phenomena, persons, change, difference, and denial.**

Therefore, [the factors] that are to be overcome by **nonconceptual wisdom** are the following five—despite their nonexistence, (1) clinging to **phenomena** as having an identity, (2) clinging to **persons** as having an identity, (3) clinging to phenomena as arising and ceasing (their **changes** despite their nonexistence), (4) clinging to **difference** (clinging to phenomena and the nature of phenomena as being different despite their not existing as being different), **and** (5) **denial** (denying even the existence of merely imputedly existent phenomena and persons). {577} One should understand that nonconceptual wisdom **is the remedy for** these **five**. This teaches the meaning of comprehending the relinquishment of the two extremes ([such as] the two identitylessnesses, lacking arising, lacking ceasing, and being free from being one and different) that is discussed in the *Madhyāntavibhāga*.[705]

2.2.2.2.2.7.3.6.2.6.3. Explanation of the defining characteristic

> **The thorough knowledge of the defining characteristic is by virtue of its specific characteristic of excluding the five factors of lacking mental engagement, transcendence, complete subsiding, what is naturally [nonconceptual], and picturing.**

Through the teachings on "nonconceptual wisdom" one should understand **its specific characteristic of excluding** these [above five] errors. (1) Some assert that nonconceptual wisdom is the mere **lack of mental engagement**. This is not the case—a lack of conceptions about aspects exists even in small children, but one is not liberated through that. (2) The vanishing of examination and analysis is called "**transcendence.**" This is not nonconceptual wisdom either because the second dhyāna and so on are [states] without examination and analysis,[706] but [also] lack the qualities [of nonconceptual wisdom]. (3) Nor is it reasonable for [this wisdom] to have the nature of conceptions having **subsided completely**—[the states of] being asleep, being intoxicated, and having fainted would also be this [wisdom] because these states are without conceptions. (4) Nor is it reasonable for **what** does **naturally** not entertain conceptions to be this [nonconceptual wisdom]. {578} If such were the case, objects such as form would also be this [wisdom] because it is by their very nature that they do not have conceptions. (5) "Nonconceptual" [also indicates] that it is not reasonable for **picturing** to be this [wisdom]. For if one mentally engages [by thinking], "Nonconceptuality is like that," such a thought about [nonconceptuality] is nothing but a conception.

Thus, nonconceptual wisdom is what is free from these **five factors**. In brief, fools who have not learned designations, the mere vanishing of examination and analysis, the temporary [states of] conceptions being at peace in the dhyānas and unconsciousness, being something like matter, and the apprehension of mental characteristics are taught to be the [five] factors that do not accord with nonconceptual wisdom.[707] Therefore, [the *Mahāyānasaṃgraha* describes] its nature as follows:

> It neither bears on that nor on something else.
> It is neither knowledge nor nonknowledge.
> Not being different from what is known,
> This knowledge is nonconceptuality.
>
> Since there is nothing to be conceived,
> All phenomena are explained
> To be naturally nonconceptual.
> Therefore, this wisdom is nonconceptuality.[708]

The manner of this teaching on the nature of the nonconceptual prajñā of buddhas and bodhisattvas in the *Mahāyānasaṃgraha* is discussed in this text here in the manner of eliminating its antagonistic factors.

2.2.2.2.2.7.3.6.2.6.4. Explanation of the five kinds of distinctive features

> {579} **The thorough knowledge of the distinctive features is by virtue of the five distinctive features of being nonconceptual, unlimited, nonabiding, lasting, and unsurpassable.**

This wisdom[709] is more eminent than [those of] śrāvakas and pratyekabuddhas **by virtue of five distinctive features.** How is it eminent? [The wisdoms of] śrāvakas and pratyekabuddhas entail conceptions because they understand saṃsāra as a flaw and nirvāṇa as a quality. [These wisdoms] are limited because they focus merely on the general characteristics of the four realities of the noble ones. They also abide [somewhere] because they abide in nirvāṇa. [Their wisdoms] are not lasting either because they become extinct in the nirvāṇa without any remainder of the skandhas. For this is explained in the sūtra [passages] on [the path] being like a raft. They are also surpassable because buddha wisdom surpasses them.

[The wisdoms of] buddhas and bodhisattvas are [characterized] by the five distinctive features that are the opposites of the [above]. (1) They are **nonconceptual** because they do not conceive of flaws or qualities of [saṃsāric] existence and peace. (2) They are **unlimited** because what they take as their objects are the specific and general characteristics of all knowable objects, precisely as they are. (3) They are **nonabiding** because, [without abiding in saṃsāric] existence through prajñā and without abiding in [nirvāṇic] peace through compassion, they train in there being nothing to be adopted or to be rejected. (4) They are **lasting** because, by virtue of the dharmakāya as their foundation being permanent, their continuum does not become extinct even in the nirvāṇa without any remainder of the skandhas. {580} (5) They are **unsurpassable** because there is nothing more eminent above them. In brief, [the wisdoms of buddhas and bodhisattvas] are taught to be nonconceptual because of the purity of [saṃsāric] existence and peace, knowing [all] that is to be known by wisdom, and being the unity of emptiness and compassion, that is, having attained the unconditioned dharmakāya and the consummate state.[710]

2.2.2.2.2.7.3.6.2.6.5. Explanation of the five functions of wisdom

> **The thorough knowledge of the functions is by virtue of the five-fold distinctive features of function—distancing conceptions, accomplishing unsurpassable bliss, freeing from the afflictive and cognitive obscurations, engaging in all aspects of knowable objects through the wisdom that is attained subsequent to it, and purifying buddha realms, maturing sentient beings, and granting the knowledge of all aspects.**

This wisdom performs the following **five functions**. (1) As for **distancing conceptions**, the root of mistakenness consists of conceptions and the [beginningless] arising [of the latent tendencies of ignorance about suchness].[711] The nature in which such does not exist arises as a matter of course in seeing that all aspects are without arising. (2) As for **unsurpassable bliss**, by virtue of not lacking the knowledge of all knowable objects, [this wisdom] is **accomplishing** skill in means. Such occurs due to having accomplished the nature of uncontaminated bliss by virtue of being free from the three [kinds of] suffering. {581} (3) As for **the afflictive** obscurations, through realizing that the intense arising of desire, anger, pride, ignorance, doubt, the five kinds of views, and the twenty secondary afflictions comes from the conceptions that depend on subject and object, [nonconceptual wisdom] liberates [from them]. Through looking inward at the ālaya-consciousness, [the afflicted mind] functions as the support for the arising of the afflictions, and this mentation that dwells in the ālaya exists in all three realms as a latency that is to be relinquished through familiarization. Through not conceiving both imputed and innate [afflictive obscurations] and realizing that they are illusionlike, [nonconceptual wisdom] is **freeing from** [these obscurations]. Through this, the contaminations,[712] including their latent tendencies, are overcome.[713] (4) Once being liberated from ignorance through this, without characteristics and conceptions, all focal objects appear in an illusionlike manner and there arises [the wisdom of subsequent attainment that is] **engaging in all aspects of** [these illusionlike] **knowable objects**. (5) As taught above, through the great fundamental change of mentation, perception, and conception, [nonconceptual wisdom] is **purifying buddha realms, maturing sentient beings, and granting** (that is, causing the attainment of) **the knowledge of all aspects**. [These three] are also a **function** of nonconceptual wisdom. This principle is found[714] [in the *Uttaratantra*] in the following manner:

> Their mind [set] on accomplishing [beneficial] activity
> Is perpetually blazing like fire,
> While always being immersed in
> The absorption of the dhyāna of peace.[715]

As for the last three [above] being taken as a single function [by Maitreya], {582} they represent a single function because three distinct [functions] are perfected through the single [factor of] nonconceptuality. Among those five functions, [the first and third] depend on conceptions and the two obscurations as the factors to be relinquished. The others are based on what is to be attained.[716]

If [the above five points] are understood in this way, this is called "the comprehension of the thorough knowledge." This comprehension of the thorough knowledge should be understood according to the *Avikalpapraveśadhāraṇī*. One should understand that, after the setting of this sūtra, what is taught consists of the manner of the correct training, entering the dhātu of nonconceptuality, its characteristics, the signs of having entered it, its activity, an example, and, through the other remaining [passages], the means [to enter that dhātu].[717] [However,] I do not write down the words of the sūtra [here] out of fear of being too wordy.

2.2.2.2.2.7.3.7. Explanation of the mental engagement

This has two parts:

1) Through what [bodhisattvas] engage mentally
2) The manner in which they engage mentally and the progression [of that]

2.2.2.2.2.7.3.7.1. Through what [bodhisattvas] engage mentally

> **As for the comprehension of mental engagement, bodhisattvas who wish to engage in nonconceptual [wisdom] by all means engage mentally by thinking the following:**

Because they definitely need **to engage in nonconceptual** [wisdom] (the foundation [of the fundamental change]), those who have the mindset for engaging in the supreme yāna, have the ***courageous*** mindset for great ***enlightenment***, and have the welfare of sentient beings in ***mind*** should **engage mentally** in the following manner.[718]

2.2.2.2.2.7.3.7.2. The manner in which they engage mentally and the progression [of that]

This has three parts:

1) Examination of the manner of being mistaken by virtue of the ālaya, conditions, and ignorance appearing, but not really existing {583}
2) The manner of mental engagement
3) The progression of realization

2.2.2.2.2.7.3.7.2.1. Examination of the manner of being mistaken by virtue of the ālaya, conditions, and ignorance appearing, but not really existing

> **False imagination—what contains all seeds (the cause for what does not exist appearing as duality) and the other continuum that is based on that—[occurs] due to being ignorant about suchness.[719] Therefore, what entails cause and result appears, but it does not exist.**

As taught above, [one part of false imagination] is the ālaya-consciousness **that contains all seeds**. Based on the **imagination** that, while not existing in actual reality, forms karmas through the seven collections [of consciousness], [the ālaya-consciousness] arises subsequently through being produced and accumulated by that [false imagination]. For **the cause for** the **duality** of apprehender and apprehended **appearing** from it while **not existing** is [its] being seized by the latent tendencies of clinging to duality. **The other continuum that is based on that** consists of the six operating consciousnesses that appear as if arising from object conditions. The seventh [consciousness] abides in the ālaya and provides the power for the arising and ceasing [of the other six consciousnesses], which is explained as "the mentation [that is the mind] immediately after these six have ceased." It is also referred to as "the dhātu or āyatana of mentation." Through the condition of [mentation] being afflicted by virtue of being associated with the four afflictions that look inward,[720] **suchness** is not recognized. **Due to** that, [mind] is mistaken, and [this mistakenness] arises from the latent tendencies of ignorance that [exist since] beginningless time.[721] **Therefore**, this represents **being ignorant** [about suchness], which is the cause of mistakenness. Consequently, **what entails** mutual **causes and results appears**, {584} **but it does not** really **exist**.[722] For example, through mistaking a rope for a snake one is afraid, and being afraid produces further mistakenness. Thus, in all respects, suffering resembles a snake not existing in a rope and yet appearing. Glorious Rāhulabhadra says:

> Just as [when mistaking] a rope [for] a black poisonous snake,
> One becomes afraid merely through seeing [it].
> O friends, people with clinging
> Are fettered by the flaw of two objects.[723]

Having understood this, [there follows]

2.2.2.2.2.7.3.7.2.2. The manner of mental engagement

> **By virtue of its appearing, the nature of phenomena does not appear. By virtue of its not appearing, the nature of phenomena does appear. Bodhisattvas who mentally engage in this way engage in nonconceptual wisdom.**

This is the manner of mental engagement on the path of preparation. Through the imaginary, which consists of apprehender and apprehended, **appearing** while not existing, what **does not appear** is the focusing on **the nature of phenomena**, which is established primordially, on the unmistaken path of engaging in that [nature], and on the fruition of that [path]. Therefore, one is mistaken. **By virtue of** that [nature] appearing and apprehender and apprehended **not appearing**, true reality and the path with its fruition **do appear. Bodhisattvas who mentally engage in this way engage in nonconceptual wisdom.**[724] This is also [stated] in the *Mahāyānasūtrālaṃkāra* and the *Mahāyānasaṃgraha*:

> [There is] the investigation of names
> And referents being mutually adventitious {585}
> And the investigation of the two kinds
> Of imputation as being mere such [imputations].
>
> Through understanding how things really are,
> With referents not existing, [there is only] threefold conception,
> And since that does not exist [either], one engages in
> The threefold seeing that it does not exist.[725]

Thus, this says that when the cognizances that [appear as] names, causal features, and imagination do not exist, the triad of the nature, [its] stainlessness, and the path [toward that stainlessness] is observed.

2.2.2.2.2.7.3.7.2.3. Explanation of the progression of that [realization]

This has five parts:
1) Observing as cognizance
2) Not observing any referents
3) Not observing cognizance
4) Observing no difference
5) Explanation of the nature

2.2.2.2.2.7.3.7.2.3.1. Observing as cognizance

> **By virtue of such observing, they engage in observing [everything] as mere cognizance.**

At the time of the lesser illumination [of the prajñā about the nonexistence of something apprehended that is different from mind] on the path of preparation, through realizing the principle explained above, [bodhisattvas] **observe** both mistaken and unmistaken cognizances **as** not really existing as anything other than **mere cognizance**. Through this, [the level of] heat arises. Bodhisattvas who have excellently gathered the accumulations attain the causes for calm abiding and superior insight through the nine methods of settling the mind[726] and the eleven mental engagements.[727] Through being endowed with the dhyānas, they focus on the three doors of superior insight[728] and the six discriminations of entities[729] and thus engage in [mere] cognizance. [The *Mahāyānasūtrālaṃkāra* says]:

> Then, having become such,
> Bodhisattvas in meditative equipoise,
> Except for mental discourse, {586}
> Do not see any referents.[730]

Thus, they **engage in** [mere] cognizance.

2.2.2.2.2.7.3.7.2.3.2. Not observing any referents

> **By virtue of observing [everything] as mere cognizance, they engage in not observing any referents.**

At the time of this illumination [of prajñā] having become middling, when [everything] appears **as mere cognizance, any** external **referents** are **not observed**. This is [the level of] peak because the illumination of phenomena is stable. [The *Mahāyānasūtrālaṃkāra*] continues:

> In order to increase the illumination of phenomena,
> They make stable efforts.
> Through the increase of the illumination of phenomena,
> They abide in mere mind.[731]

2.2.2.2.2.7.3.7.2.3.3. Explanation of engaging in not observing cognizance

> **By virtue of not observing any referents, they engage in not observing mere cognizance [either].**

If **any referents** do **not** exist, **mere cognizance** is **not** established [either] because cognizance depends on referents. This is [the level of] approximately concordant poised readiness. [The *Mahāyānasūtrālaṃkāra* says]:

> Through this, they see all appearances
> Of referents as being mind.
> At this point, they relinquish
> The distraction of the apprehended.[732]

Since cognizance does not appear as the duality [of apprehender and apprehended], [the next point is]

2.2.2.2.2.7.3.7.2.3.4. Observing no difference

> **By virtue of not observing that [cognizance], they observe the lack of difference between those two.**

Those who do **not observe** cognizance do not **observe the two** of apprehender and apprehended. Both of them are alike in appearing as mere cognizance and {587} they are also alike in that there is no really existing apprehender if there is no really existing apprehended. Therefore, they **lack** [any] **difference**. This is the contact with [the level of] the supreme dharma. [The *Mahāyānasūtrālaṃkāra* says]:

> Then, solely the distraction
> Of the apprehender remains.
> At that point, they swiftly
> Touch upon the uninterrupted samādhi.
>
> Thus, immediately upon that,
> The distraction of the apprehender is relinquished.[733]

Thus, to familiarize with this progression [of realization] constitutes the more eminent path of preparation of the mahāyāna. [The *Mahāyānasūtrālaṃkāra*] states:

> In due order, these [phases]
> Should be known as being heat and so on.[734]

2.2.2.2.2.7.3.7.2.3.5. Explanation of the nature

> **The nonobservation of these two in this way is nonconceptual wisdom—it lacks an object and lacks observation because it is characterized by not observing any characteristics.**

The lack of appearance **of these two** (apprehender and apprehended), all phenomena [appearing] like the center of space, and all knowable objects appearing like illusions and so on constitute the path of seeing. Through cultivating it, all stains are eliminated and this is perfected through **lacking** any **observation** of the six **objects** on the inside or outside **and not observing any**

characteristics of factors to be relinquished and remedies as well as the characteristics of suchness and the fruition. This is just as taught above.[735]

Such characteristics are clearly discussed in detail in the prajñāpāramitā [texts]:

> Nonentities, entities,
> Superimposition, denial, {588}
> Oneness, difference, nature,
> Distinctive features, and names and referents exactly as they are.[736]

As for these ten, the *Mahāyānasaṃgraha* says:

> (1) [The Buddha] stated the following as the meaning of the remedy for the conception of nonentities: "While existing as bodhisattvas, . . ." (2) He stated the following as the meaning of the remedy for the conception of entities: ". . . they do not really see bodhisattvas." (3) He stated the following as the meaning of the remedy for the conception of superimposition: "They do not really see the name 'bodhisattva.' They do not really see prajñāpāramitā. They do not really see 'engagement' [in it]. They do not really see forms. Nor do they see feelings, discriminations, formations, and consciousness. Why is that? Because names are empty of any nature of their own . . ." (4) He stated the following as the meaning of the remedy for the conception of denial: "It is not by virtue of emptiness [that form is empty] . . ." (5) He stated the following as the meaning of the remedy for the conception of oneness: "What is the emptiness of form is not form . . ." (6) He stated the following as the meaning of the remedy for the conception of difference: "Nor is it anything other than form. Form is emptiness. {589} Emptiness is form." (7) He stated the following as the meaning of the remedy for the conception of a nature: "Subhūti, it is as follows: 'Form' is just a name . . ." (8) He stated the following as the meaning of the remedy for the conception of distinctive features: "A nature does not arise, does not cease, is not afflicted, and is not purified." (9) He stated the following as the meaning of the remedy for the conception of referents being exactly as their names: "Based on fabricated names, phenomena are discriminated and conventional expressions are asserted in accordance with random names. Then [people] cling [to referents] in exactly the same way in which they labeled them with such conventional expressions." (10) He stated the following as the meaning of the remedy for the conception of names being

exactly as their referents: "Bodhisattvas do not really see all these names. Since they do not really see them, they have no clinging." What [the Buddha] had in mind [here] is that [bodhisattvas do not see names] exactly as their referents are. Just as with form, the same is to be applied to [all skandhas] up through consciousness. As the remedy for these ten distractions, nonconceptual wisdom is taught in all prajñāpāramitā [texts]. Thus, the entire meaning of the prajñāpāramitā [texts] should be understood as being [contained in] antagonistic factors and remedies.[737]

Furthermore, if one summarizes all purified phenomena, {590} they are of four kinds:

(1) Natural purity is suchness, emptiness, the true limit, signlessness, the ultimate, and also the dharmadhātu. (2) Stainless purity refers to this very [natural purity] not having any obscurations. (3) The complete purity of the path to attain this [unstained purity] consists of all the dharmas concordant with enlightenment, the pāramitās, and so on. (4) The pure focal object in order to generate this [path] is the teaching of the genuine dharma of the mahāyāna. In this way, since this [dharma] is the cause for purity, it is not the imaginary [nature]. Since it is the natural outflow of the pure dharmadhātu, it is not the dependent [nature either]. All purified phenomena are included in these four kinds [of purity].
[There follow two summarizing] verses:

The teachings about illusions and so on refer to what is present,
The teachings about nonexistence refer to the imaginary,
While the teachings about the perfect
Refer to the fourfold purity.

This purity consists of being natural,
Stainless, the path, and the focal object.
[All] pure phenomena
Are included in these four kinds.[738]

All focal objects of mental engagement are taught through being included in this. This concludes the explanation of comprehending the defining characteristics of wisdom.

2.2.2.2.2.7.3.8. Comprehending the training

This has two parts:

1) Brief introduction {591}
2) Detailed explanation

2.2.2.2.2.7.3.8.1. Brief introduction

> **The comprehension of the training is also fourfold**

This teaches that bodhisattvas attain this wisdom if they **train** in certain ways.

2.2.2.2.2.7.3.8.2. Detailed explanation

This has four parts:

1) [The paths of] accumulation and preparation
2) [The path of] seeing
3) [The path of] familiarization
4) The [path of] completion

2.2.2.2.2.7.3.8.2.1. [The paths of] accumulation and preparation

> **by virtue of the training through aspiration on the level of engagement through aspiration (this is the phase of discernment),**[739]

[The paths of] accumulation and preparation were [already] taught in the explanation of the [first] six [points of] comprehending the nature of phenomena. Accordingly, bodhisattvas who are endowed with the [mahāyāna] disposition, by virtue of the foundation of knowable objects, the knowable objects (the three natures), the engagement in these characteristics, the manner in which to engage in them, and the progression of the three trainings, study the principles of what is relinquished and what is attained—the mahāyāna piṭaka that is a natural outflow of the dharmadhātu. By virtue of that, they give rise to the factors conducive to liberation through the five dharmas such as confidence,[740] generate the earthlike bodhicitta, attain the goldlike one of the unchanging superior intention and the one that is like the waxing moon in which the qualities become special ([this bodhicitta's] further and further [increase]), and attain the firelike one that consumes apprehender and apprehended and arises from meditation.[741] This is **the training through aspiration**. Through the armor[like practice] of the six pāramitās and the practice of engagement,[742] [bodhisattvas] take the **aspiration** for the foundation that is the dharmakāya—the basic element of nonconceptual wisdom—as their object. It is through the cognitions that focus on that that they, based on the accumulation of the causes of calm abiding and superior insight, {592} engage in those focal objects. Through having engaged in them, they train in the path of [the factors conducive to] penetration [with its four levels of] heat, peak, poised readiness, and the supreme dharma. Therefore, [the paths of accumulation and preparation] are called "the training through aspiration."

When [bodhisattvas] train in this manner, they need to relinquish the five flaws and rely on the eight remedial applications. [The *Madhyāntavibhāga* says]:

> Laziness, forgetting the instructions,
> Dullness and agitation,
> Nonapplication, and application—
> These are asserted as the five flaws.[743]

As the remedies for laziness, they should make efforts in dispelling it through striving, effort, confidence, and suppleness. As the remedy for forgetting the instructions, they should give rise to mindfulness and not forget them. When dullness and agitation arise, they should dispel them through being embraced by alertness. If they, after thoughts have subsided, do not apply [the appropriate remedies to the arising of dullness and agitation], they should unfold [the appropriate] remedial thoughts through the intention [to apply those remedies]. When they are distracted by remedial thoughts and apply [these remedies] too forcefully, they should rest evenly through equanimity. Through training in this manner, all five faculties of mastery[744] arise, and, through not being suppressable by māras and the hīnayāna, these turn into the five powers. [The *Mahāyānasūtrālaṃkāra* says]:

> The path of calm abiding should be known
> As the synopsis of the names of the dharma.
> The path of superior insight should be known
> As the analysis of their meanings.
>
> The path of unity should be known
> To be their combination.
> A fainthearted mind should be made firm
> And agitation should be pacified.
>
> Then, once evenness with regard to the focal object
> Is attained, they should rest in equanimity.[745] {593}

Through relying on this, the illuminations taught above arise, which represent the training in **discernment**. Thus, the focal objects, the aspects, and the training are taught in general [here]. The signs [of this training], the differences between [this training in] the hīnayāna and mahāyāna, [its] qualities, and so on are as discussed in detail in the [texts on prajñā]pāramitā and the *Bodhisattvabhūmi*.[746]

2.2.2.2.2.7.3.8.2.2. Explanation of the path of seeing

> **by virtue of the training in direct realization on the first bhūmi (this is the phase of contact),**

Once the characteristics of cognizance are eliminated through focusing on the dhātu of nonconceptuality, as [the cognitive] aspect [of meditative equipoise], all phenomena appear like the center of space, but [bodhisattvas] engage in the power [of phenomena] during subsequent attainment and do so in an illusionlike manner. This is the path of seeing and **the first bhūmi.** The distinctions, the focal objects, and the aspects of its sixteen moments in terms of śrāvakas and pratyekabuddhas versus bodhisattvas are discussed in the *Abhisamayālaṃkāra*. I do not write them down [here] out of fear of being too wordy. This [first bhūmi] is called "the **contact** with the samādhi of the light of nonconceptual wisdom."

Here, through their pure superior intention, [bodhisattvas] generate the bodhicitta of the complete pāramitā of generosity that is like a treasure.[747] Their going for refuge is obtained through the nature of phenomena and they attain samādhis such as the illusionlike one and the one of heroic stride. Calm abiding and superior insight have become a unity and they attain inexhaustible total recall (dhāraṇī). {594} These and other things are discussed in all sūtras in infinite specifications.[748]

2.2.2.2.2.7.3.8.2.3. Explanation of the path of familiarization

> **by virtue of the training in familiarization on the six impure bhūmis and the three pure bhūmis (this is the phase of recollection)**[749]

The six bhūmis that consist of the second one and the following [still] entail conceptual characteristics and thus their conduct is [slightly] **impure. The three** that consist of the eighth one and the following operate naturally of their own accord without characteristics and without effort. Therefore, they are **pure.**[750] The *Mahāyānasaṃgraha* says the following in its section that teaches relinquishment:

> The change through realization is the one of bodhisattvas having entered the bhūmis. For up through the sixth bhūmi, [both] the appearances of true reality [during meditative equipoise] and what is not true reality [during subsequent attainment] are present. The change through familiarization is the one of those [bodhisattvas]

> who [still] possess [some cognitive] obscurations. For [from the seventh] up through the tenth bhūmis, all characteristics disappear, while true reality appears. The change in terms of the completely perfect fruition is the one of those who are without [any] obscurations. For [for them,] all characteristics disappear, utterly pure true reality appears, and they have attained the mastery over all characteristics.[751]

As taught above in detail, [all] afflictive and cognitive obscurations are relinquished. On the six impure bhūmis [of the path of familiarization], [bodhisattvas] attain the ultimate generation of bodhicitta as the aspects of ethics being [like] a jewel mine, {595} patience being [like] an unruffled ocean, vigor being [like] a vajra that crushes the obscurations, the mountain of dhyāna that is not moved by distractions, the medicine of prajñā that pacifies the disease of the latencies, and being like a friend who holds one through skill in means. Then, [the generations of ultimate bodhicitta] on the three pure bhūmis are the [wish-fulfilling] jewel of aspiration prayers that are fulfilled as aspired, the sun of the power to dispel the darkness of the minds of sentient beings and mature the qualities [of a buddha], and the wisdom that is the beautiful song of the dharma. As [the types of bodhicitta] that arise on these three bhūmis in common, [bodhisattvas also] manifest [the ones] that are like the king of unimpeded strength, the treasure-vault of the maturation of the two accumulations, the highway of enlightenment, the vehicle of progressing through compassion and emptiness being of equal taste, and the fountain of the inexhaustible ocean of dhāraṇīs and self-confidence. At the end of the continuum of the tenth bhūmi, the bhūmi of receiving empowerment arises, on which there occur [the generations of bodhicitta that resemble] the pleasant melody of the speech that is equal to all sounds, the river of the wisdom mind that endlessly flows in saṃsāra, and the cloud that spreads as physical emanations within an ocean of realms. These [last three] constitute the completion of uncontaminated karma.[752]

As for these ten bhūmis, as explained before, after the nature of phenomena has been realized on the first one, on the second one [bodhisattvas] engage in [the training in] superior ethics. On the third, fourth, and fifth they complete the training in [superior] mind. {596} On the sixth one they finish the training in prajñā. Through this, on the four [bhūmis] that consist of the seventh one and the following they attain the fourfold accomplishment of the results of these [trainings].

As for the hermeneutical etymologies of these bhūmis, [the name of the first bhūmi] is Supreme Joy because [the bodhisattvas on it] are endowed with special supramundane joy. The second bhūmi [is The Stainless One] because ethics is without any stains of being corrupted. The third bhūmi is The Illuminating One because it produces the great radiance of samādhi. The fourth bhūmi is The Radiating One because it burns the remainders of the two obscurations through the dharmas that are concordant with enlightenment. The fifth bhūmi is Difficult to Master because it equally masters [saṃsāric] existence and peace, which are difficult to master. The sixth bhūmi is The Facing One because prajñā trains in both saṃsāra and nirvāṇa. The seventh bhūmi is Gone Afar because it is joined with the path of the single progress of [all] buddhas that is without characteristics. The eighth bhūmi is The Immovable One because it is not moved by either characteristics or effort. The ninth bhūmi is The Excellent One[753] because the [four] discriminating awarenesses are completed. The tenth bhūmi is The Dharma Cloud because samādhis and dhāraṇīs pervade [all of] space. At the end of this [bhūmi] one has power over the complete enlightened activity of the three kāyas. Therefore, it is the bhūmi of receiving empowerment. Once these twelve bhūmis (including [the bhūmi of] engagement through aspiration) have been completed, this is final buddhahood, which is [the level of] the arrival at the nature of the [nature of phenomena]. {597} The scriptural passages about the etymology[754] of these [bhūmis] are stated in the *Mahāyānasūtrālaṃkāra* and the *Bodhisattvabhūmi*. [There follow some] summarizing verses:

> Nonconceptual wisdom,
> By its nature, is meditative equipoise
> And subsequent attainment is its function,
> Just like a fire and its consuming a thicket.
>
> Aspiring for the dharma and superior intention represent prajñā.
> Dhyāna and compassion are the means.
> Through means and prajñā being inseparable,
> All characteristics placed before one are dispelled.
>
> Thus, the ten obscurations are eliminated, the ten bhūmis are completed,
> The ten pāramitās become pure,
> And the qualities of entering the ocean
> Of dhāraṇīs, samādhis, aspiration prayers,
> Wisdoms, and powers are completed.
>
> Through this, the basic element of the buddha heart is attained—
> Perfect buddhahood without bondage and liberation,
> Which is called "omniscience."

2.2.2.2.2.7.3.8.2.4. Explanation of the path of completion

> **and by virtue of the training in completion on the buddhabhūmi because the deeds of a buddha are effortless and uninterrupted (this is the phase of the arrival at the nature of the [nature of phenomena]).**

That immediately upon which **the uninterrupted deeds of a buddha** are attained is called "**the training in completion**." Through it, the basic element of a buddha is attained immediately upon [bodhisattvas on the tenth bhūmi] having definitely obtained the empowerment [by all buddhas]. Thus, [the mind stream of bodhisattvas] becomes of **the nature of the** [basic element] because the wisdom of the **effortless** three kāyas, together with their enlightened deeds, arises.[755] {598} This is taught in detail through [the chapter on] enlightenment [in the *Uttaratantra*]:

> Through nature, cause, fruition,
> Function, endowment, manifestation,
> And its permanence and inconceivability,
> The buddhabhūmi is determined.[756]

The nature is the purity of the basic element. The cause of that purity [becoming manifest] is what is taught through the terms that are studied—the pure dharmas that are a natural outflow [of this basic element]. These [dharmas] are what free from the two obscurations. The fruition is twofold—the dharmakāya and the rūpakāyas. The function is the unimpeded function of the wisdom that overcomes the obscurations in a nonconceptual manner and is uncontaminated [by them]. The endowment is to be endowed with the enlightened activity for the marvelous welfare of oneself and others. The manifestation is the threefold permanence of the three kāyas engaging in saṃsāra for as long as it lasts. This permanence is explained as being threefold in terms of [being so by] nature, in terms of continuity, and in terms of an uninterrupted series, respectively.[757] As for the reasons for that, [the *Uttaratantra*] says:

> By virtue of the causes being infinite, by virtue of the realms of
> sentient beings being inexhaustible,
> By virtue of being endowed with compassion, miraculous powers,
> wisdom, and fulfillment,
> By virtue of mastering [all] dharmas, by virtue of having
> vanquished the māra of death,

And by virtue of lacking any nature, the protector of the world is
permanent.[758]

These [reasons] are explained in detail [in the following verses] in the *Uttaratantra*.[759] The *Mahāyānasaṃgraha* says:

How should one regard the distinctive features of wisdom? They consist of the three kāyas—the svābhāvika[kāya], the sāmbhogika[kāya], and the nairmāṇikakāya. Here the svābhāvikakāya is {599} the dharmakāya of the tathāgatas because it is the foundation of mastery over all dharmas. The sāmbhogikakāya is characterized by various maṇḍalas of retinues of the buddhas and is based on the dharmakāya because it makes one experience the enjoyments of pure buddha realms and the mahāyāna dharma. The nairmāṇikakāya is [also] based on the dharmakāya because it displays the deeds starting with dwelling in the abode of Tuṣita up through displaying nirvāṇa.

[Here is] a summarizing verse on the divisions of this:

Characteristics, attainment,
Mastery, foundation, constitution,
Difference, qualities, profundity,
Recollection, and enlightened activity.

(1) The characteristics are five. (a) [The dharmakāya has the characteristic of] the fundamental change because when the aspect of the dependent nature that belongs to what is afflicted (all obscurations) has come to an end, it has changed into the aspect of the dependent nature that belongs to what is purified, is liberated from all obscurations, and abides as the mastery over all dharmas. (b) [As for its characteristic of having the nature of pure dharmas,] through having perfected [all] pure dharmas, the ten masteries are attained by virtue of the six pāramitās. (c) As for the characteristic [of nonduality,] all phenomena are nondual in the sense of having the nature of nonentities and being empty. Since both conditioned and unconditioned phenomena do not exist, mastery over both is attained. Also, buddhas do not exist as being one or different. (d) [The characteristic of] permanence is threefold.[760] (e) [The characteristic of] inconceivability is that [the fundamental change] is beyond dialectics.

(2) As for attainment, since the two obscurations are destroyed by the wisdoms of meditative equipoise and subsequent attainment, {600} this is attainment.

(3) The masteries are five because of the following. (a) Through the fundamental change of the skandha of form, [the mastery over pure buddha] realms, kāyas, the excellent major and minor marks, infinite voices, and the invisible mark on the crown of the head [is attained]. (b) Through the fundamental change of the skandha of feeling, the mastery over infinite and vast blissful states without wrongdoing [is attained]. (c) Because of the fundamental change of the skandha of discrimination, the mastery over teaching through words, phrases, and letters [is attained]. (d) Because of the fundamental change of the skandha of formation, the mastery over creation, transformation, gathering retinues, and gathering pure dharmas [is attained]. (e) Through the fundamental change of the skandha of consciousness, the ālaya changes into mirror-like [wisdom]; mentation, into [the wisdom of] equality; the sixth [consciousness], into discriminating [wisdom]; and the five [sense consciousnesses], into all-accomplishing [wisdom].

(4) [The dharmakāya's] being a foundation is threefold. (a) It is the foundation of great bliss because power, all-accomplishment, the taste of dharma, the boundless and eternally inexhaustible consummations of [its] meanings and qualities, and the seeing [of that] are attained. (b) It is the foundation of the sāmbhogikakāya because [the latter] matures bodhisattvas. (c) It is the foundation of various nairmāṇikakāyas because [the latter] mainly matures śrāvakas.

(5) What constitutes [the dharmakāya] is sixfold. The dharmakāya is constituted by (a) the pure buddhadharmas having become pure [by virtue of the fundamental change of] the ālaya[-consciousness]. The dharmakāya is [further] constituted by (b) the wisdom of maturation [by virtue] of the [fundamental] change of the physical sense faculties, {601} (c) boundless wisdom [by virtue] of the fundamental change of sense pleasures, (d) the wisdom that is unimpeded with regard to everything [by virtue] of the [fundamental] change of various purposeful activities, (e) satisfaction of [all] sentient beings through all teachings by way of conventions, and (f) the removal of all flaws of sentient beings through the removal [of all misfortunes and flaws].

(6) As for difference, in terms of foundation, intention, and enlightened activity, [the dharmakāyas of] all buddhas are equal. [However,] since numberless sentient beings become enlightened

as such [dharmakāyas], they are different. The sāmbhogikakāyas are also not different in terms of intention and enlightened activity, [but] they are different in terms of their supports. The same goes for the nairmāṇika[kāyas].[761]

(7) The qualities are summarized as sixty-four—the thirty-two of the dharmakāya and the thirty-two of the rūpakāyas. [In more detail,] they consist of the four purities in all respects, the four immeasurables, the eight liberations, the eight [kinds of] over-powering, the ten totalities, dispassion, the knowledge through aspiration, the four discriminating awarenesses, the six supernatural knowledges, the thirty-two major marks, the eighty minor marks, the ten powers, the four fearlessnesses, the three ways of nothing to hide, the threefold foundation of mindfulness, the latent tendencies being overcome, the true nature of being without forgetfulness, great compassion, the eighteen unique qualities of a buddha, [the knowledge of all aspects], and being endowed with the perfection of the six pāramitās. In [even more] detail, they are also said to be 640 millions. {602}

(8) If the inconceivable profound nature of the dharmakāya of a buddha is summarized, it is twelvefold. First, the profundity in terms of nirvāṇa, enlightened activity, and abiding:

> Nonarising is the arising of buddhas.
> They abide in nonabiding.
> They do everything effortlessly.
> They partake of the four foods.[762]

Second, the profundity in terms of the way of being, number, and enlightened activity:

> They are not different and yet immeasurable.
> Their enlightened activity is immeasurable and yet single.
> They are endowed with unfixed enlightened activity.
> The buddhas possess the three kāyas.

Third, the profundity in terms of fully perfect enlightenment:

> There is no fully perfect enlightenment whatsoever,
> [But] it is not that all [buddhas] are not buddhas.
> In each instant, they are immeasurable,
> Consisting of entities and nonentities.

Fourth, the profundity in terms of being free from attachment:

> They are neither desirous nor nondesirous.
> Through desire, they were delivered.
> Knowing desire and nondesire,
> They enter the true nature of desire.

Fifth, the profundity in terms of having relinquished the skandhas:

> The buddhas are beyond the skandhas,
> [But] they dwell in the skandhas.
> They are neither other than them nor not other.
> Through not relinquishing them, they pass well beyond.

Sixth, the profundity in terms of maturing sentient beings: {603}

> They are endowed with the enlightened activity in which all [their activities] merge—
> The victors thus resemble the waters in the ocean.
> They do not ponder about the welfare of others
> [Thinking,] "I did [that]. I am doing [this]. I will do [that]."

Seventh, the profundity in terms of seeing [the buddhas]:

> It is because of the flaws of sentient beings [if buddhas] do not appear,
> Just as the moon [does not reflect] in a broken container.
> Just like the sun, they pervade
> The entire world with the light of dharma.

Eighth, the profundity in terms of displaying nirvāṇa:

> To some they display perfect enlightenment
> And to some, nirvāṇa, just as a fire [illuminates and is extinguished, respectively].
> They are never nonexistent—
> The kāyas of the tathāgatas are permanent.

Ninth, the profundity in terms of abiding:

With regard to the dharmas that are not noble,
The human and the lower realms,
And the dharmas that are not pure conduct,
The buddhas are of superior nature and abode.

Tenth, the profundity in terms of displaying [their true nature]:

They move about everywhere,
[But] they do not move about anywhere.
They are seen in all places,
But they are not the sphere of the six sense faculties.

Eleventh, the profundity in terms of having relinquished the afflictions:

They tamed the afflictions, but did not relinquish them,
Just like a poison rendered impotent by a mantra.
It is by virtue of the afflictions that the buddhas
Terminated the afflictions and attained omniscience.

Twelfth, the profundity in terms of inconceivability:

For those who are endowed with great means,
The afflictions become branches of enlightenment {604}
And saṃsāra has the nature of nirvāṇa.
Therefore, the tathāgatas are inconceivable.

One should understand that these [twelve] teach the inconceivable profundity of the buddhas.

(9) Bodhisattvas should cultivate the following [seven] recollections of the buddhas. They should recollect, "[Since the buddhas] have obtained the supernatural knowledges that are unimpeded in all worldly realms, they are endowed with the principle of mastery over all phenomena" and "Since they are liberated from all stains, their kāyas are permanent." At all times, they should meditate as follows: "They are without any evil, without effort, [endowed with] immeasurable enjoyments, and, by virtue of taintless enlightenment, mature those who are not matured and liberate those who are matured."[763]

According to what is said in the *Ocean of the Samādhi of Recollecting the Buddha*,[764] beginners adopt the cross-legged position, immerse themselves in mindfulness, place a statue in front of them, and while meditating on it in a one-pointed manner, contemplate the inconceivable qualities [of the Buddha]. Having manifested such calm abiding and superior insight, they will swiftly experience all the buddhadharmas. As for the qualities [of this meditation], it is said that if one cultivates this samādhi of the present Buddha actually dwelling [in front of oneself] without interruption by anything else for seven days, one will definitely go to Sukhāvatī and attain the path of seeing. {605}

This completes the explanation of the path of completion.

2.2.2.2.2.7.3.9. Knowing the shortcomings [if there were no fundamental change]

This has two parts:

1) Brief introduction
2) Detailed explanation

2.2.2.2.2.7.3.9.1. Brief introduction

> **As for comprehending the shortcomings, these are the four shortcomings of there being no fundamental change—**

There must be the **fundamental change** that results from support and what is supported being different (as discussed above). Therefore,

2.2.2.2.2.7.3.9.2. Detailed explanation

This has four parts:

First,

> **the flaw of there being no support for the afflictions not operating,**

If **there were not** the nature of the fundamental change (the permanent dharmakāya), afflictions could not but operate again in their support that is the ālaya-consciousness because it is the result of having accumulated the entirety of false imagination and the [other] consciousnesses are produced by it. [However,] if there is the arising of the uncontaminated wisdom that is supported by the **support** which is the dharmakāya, **the afflictions do not operate** [again] because their remedy is blazing, [just as,] for example, darkness does not occur in the sun.[765]

Second,

> **the flaw of there being no support for engaging in the path**

If one needs to definitely generate the five uncontaminated **paths** in due order, one relies on the **support** that is nonconceptual wisdom (the unchanging perfect [nature])[766] in order to manifest attainment through relying on ultimate practice. The natural outflow of this [wisdom]—unmistaken study, reflection, and meditation—{606} produces fruitions that are increasingly pure. However, it is not feasible for purity to arise from an impure support because it is not tenable for something uncontaminated to arise from something contaminated—[these two] are mutually exclusive, just like light and darkness.[767]

Third,

> **the flaw of there being no basis for designating the persons who have passed into nirvāṇa**

As for saṃsāra with its three contaminated realms, it is through the causal karmas that are produced by ignorance and formations that the three [realms of saṃsāric] existence, which are based on craving and grasping, are established. Likewise, it is based on the uncontaminated pure karmas of nirvāṇa that the vimuktikāya exists as being designated as arhats, pratyekabuddhas, or bodhisattvas, and also the final great perfect enlightenment must exist. If both saṃsāra and nirvāṇa had the same support, there would be great **flaws**. It is contradictory for antagonistic factors to be relinquished and their remedies to have the same support. Also, when the mind ceases, mistakenness ceases, and therefore the perfect [nature] that is wisdom would cease too. If the perfect [nature] were to cease too in this manner, it would be conditioned. Consequently, the nature of phenomena and the dharmakāya, which are unconditioned, would absolutely not exist either, and if such is accepted, it would represent the view of Kaṇāda.[768] Since the pure dharmas would be meaningless, it is not in order to regard the four noble ones as being nonexistent. {607} Therefore, [with the fundamental change existing,] it is tenable to **designate the persons who have passed into nirvāṇa.**[769]

Fourth,

> **and the flaw**[770] **of there being no basis for designating the differences between the three [types of] enlightenment.**

As for **the three** [types of] **enlightenment**, the differences in terms of liberation based on the support that is the dharmadhātu are as follows. Śrāvakas are liberated through relinquishing the afflictive obscurations (including their support) of clinging to a personal self. In addition to that, pratyekabuddhas are only endowed with the liberation of having relinquished the conceptions about the apprehended with regard to phenomena because they gain slight mastery over samādhis such as The Sky Treasure, which are based on unconditioned uncontaminated phenomena. As for bodhisattvas, from the path of seeing onward they realize that any identities of persons and phenomena do not exist. Thus, through relying on the familiarization [with this twofold identitylessness] in order to eradicate the stains of these [identities], they are liberated from the ground of the latent tendencies of ignorance and thereby become buddhas. Therefore, based on the support that is the dharmakāya, it is feasible to **designate these** three **differences** in terms of liberation. Thus, it is feasible to designate the three [types of enlightenment]—the enlightenment of having relinquished the afflictions, the enlightenment of having relinquished the apprehended, and complete enlightenment. However, if **there were no** such [fundamental] changes, since there would also be no differences with regard to the sheer ālaya-consciousnesses that are not in common coming to an end, those three [types of enlightenment] would not be feasible. {608} If the very [ālaya-consciousness] were the support of enlightenment, the fundamental change of what is supported would not be tenable in any respect because causes and results as well as factors to be relinquished and remedies would be mistaken. These differences between the fundamental changes in the hīnayāna and the mahāyāna are also found in the *Mahāyānasaṃgraha*:

> The inferior fundamental change is the one of the śrāvakas because they totally abandon saṃsāra through realizing personal identitylessness and completely turning their back on saṃsāra. The vast fundamental change is the one of bodhisattvas because they realize phenomenal identitylessness and see this very [saṃsāra] as peace, thus relinquishing the afflictions while not abandoning [saṃsāra].[771]

[This completes] the instruction on the flaws of there being no fundamental change.[772]

2.2.2.2.2.7.3.10. Explanation of comprehending the benefits [of there being the fundamental change]

As for comprehending the benefits,

> **one should know that, when there is the fundamental change, the opposites of those are the four kinds of benefit.**[773]

As for the four benefits, when the pure dharmas that are supported by the support which is the dharmakāya increase and unfold, [the first one is] the benefit of the afflictive obscurations not arising at all. [The second one is] the benefit of the uncontaminated phenomena that are the reality of the path being tenable as the causes of accomplishing the dharmakāya. [The third one is] the benefit of the liberations of the three [kinds of] persons being tenable temporarily, though the final nirvāṇa is one. For through seeing that the obscurations—false imagination—are adventitious and thus relinquishing their respective [amounts], there exist the accomplishments of the respective fruitions of such [relinquishments]. {609} [The fourth one is] the benefit that, consequently, the three [types of] enlightenment are also tenable, due to which the three yānas are not contradictory [either]. **These four kinds** [of benefit] **should be known to be the benefits** of **there being the fundamental change.**[774]

> **[One should understand that these are the ten points of comprehending the fundamental change.]**

If one summarizes the meaning of all these [aspects of the] **fundamental change**[775] [that are explained] through **the ten points** discussed in these ways, everything that the *Mahāyānasūtrālaṃkāra*, the *Uttaratantra*, and the *Mahāyānasaṃgraha* say is included in just these [following verses]:

> For childish beings, with true reality being obscured,
> What is not true reality appears everywhere.
> Having eliminated it, for bodhisattvas
> True reality appears everywhere.
>
> It should be understood that what does not appear and what does
> appear
> Are what is unreal and what is real, respectively.
> This fundamental change
> Is liberation because [they then can] act as they wish.[776]

This teaches the nature [of the fundamental change]. You may wonder, "What happens through having engaged in and having attained it?" [The *Mahāyānasaṃgraha*] continues:

> Once the understanding
> That saṃsāra and nirvāṇa are equal
> Arises in them, consequently
> Saṃsāra becomes nirvāṇa.
>
> Therefore, saṃsāra
> Is neither abandoned nor not abandoned.

Therefore, nirvāṇa
Is neither attained nor not attained.[777]

In this way, all [aspects of the] fundamental change are explained. Now, [there follows]

2.3. Explanation through examples and conclusion of the treatise

This has three parts:

1) Examples for nonexistents appearing
2) Examples for the nature of the fundamental change being unchanging {610}
3) Instruction on the completion [of the treatise]

2.3.1. Examples for nonexistents appearing

Examples for nonexistent phenomena appearing are illusions, dreams, and so on.

Just as the appearances of horses, oxen, and so on that are created through an **illusion** do not exist in just the way [they appear], but are **nonexistents** that [nevertheless] **appear**, the imaginary [nature] should be understood as appearing but not existing. Just like the conditions [that produce an illusion] (such as pieces of wood, bones, and mantras), the conditions that are the dependent [nature] appear, but do not really exist as what [they appear to be]—they are nothing but mere cognizance. This meaning is also stated in the *Mahāyānasūtrālaṃkāra*:

False imagination is explained
To be just like an illusion.
Just like the aspect in which an illusion [appears],
It is explained as the mistakenness of duality.[778]

Likewise, since objects in **dreams** are also nothing but one's own mere cognizance, though they appear to be real [entities] (such as humans), they do not exist as anything other [than that cognizance]. Just so, mirages, echoes, [reflections of] the moon in water, rainbows, [what appears due to] blurred vision, and magical creations appear, but are not real as what [they appear to be].[779]

2.3.2. [Examples for] the nature of the fundamental change being unchanging

Examples for the fundamental change are space, gold, water, and so on.[780]

For **example, space** is nothing but pure by nature. Therefore, by virtue of certain conditions (such as fog or mist), in the world one can observe the statements "The sky is not pure," and "It is pure" [when] it is clear and free [from these conditions]. However, {611} it is not suitable to claim such because of a change of the nature of space. With its own nature being pure, empty, and unconditioned, it is indeed not in order for it to either become pure by virtue of itself or become pure by virtue of something else. Nevertheless, mistaken minds that connect mere conventional terms to it cling to space as being pure and impure, [but] this is nothing but an error. Likewise, though it may appear as if the naturally pure nature of phenomena—the perfect [nature]—has become free from the fog and mist of conceptions, it is not asserted that this perfect [nature] changes [in any way]—it is absolutely without any arising or ceasing in terms of itself, others, both, or neither.

In the same way, the fact of **gold** remaining in its state of being immaculate is not changed by any stains, and the fact of **water** remaining clear and moist is not changed in its nature, even if it becomes associated with sullying factors, [such as] silt. Likewise, all that happens to the unmistaken path and the pure dharmas is that they just become associated with stains and sullying factors through the conceptions of ignorance, but it is not asserted that these uncontaminated dharmas [—the path and the pure dharmas entailed by cessation—] change. Consequently, naturally luminous stainlessness is unconditioned and changeless. Therefore, though the nature of phenomena is referred to by the conventional term "**fundamental change**," it is also called "permanent."[781]

The words "**and so on**" refer to its being like a buddha [statue] existing in the shroud of a [decaying] lotus), honey existing amidst bees, a grain in its husks, gold in filth, {612} a treasure in the earth, a tree [sprouting] from a fruit, a precious statue in tattered rags, a cakravartin in the belly of a destitute woman, and a golden statue in clay. [In due order, the respective obscuring factors in these nine examples correspond to the following mental obscurations.] The four that consist of the three latencies of desire, hatred, and ignorance, as well as the intense arising of all [three], are the factors to be relinquished through cultivating the mundane paths. The ground of the latent tendencies of ignorance is the factor to be relinquished through the cognition of realizing the foundation of knowable objects. The [afflictive] factors to be relinquished through seeing are relinquished through the path of seeing. The [afflictive] factors to be relinquished through familiarization are relinquished through [the path of] familiarization. The cognitive obscurations of the impure bhūmis are relinquished through the two wisdoms of meditative equipoise and subsequent attainment. The cognitive obscurations of the pure [bhūmis] are relinquished through the vajralike [samādhi]. Thus, [the corresponding obscured factors in the nine examples correspond to] the buddha heart, the [single] taste of the [profound] dharma, the essence of its meaning, natural luminosity, changelessness, the unfolding of wisdom, the dharmakāya, the sāmbhogikakāya, and the nairmāṇikakāya, [all of which] represent the pure unchanging and spontaneously present nature. These [examples and their meanings] are found in the *Uttaratantra* and the *Tathāgatagarbhasūtra*.[782] [The *Uttaratantra* also says]:

> There is nothing to be removed from it
> And not the slightest to be added.
> Actual reality is to be seen as it really is—
> Whoever sees actual reality is liberated.
>
> The basic element is empty of what is adventitious,
> Which has the characteristic of being separable.
> It is not empty of the unsurpassable dharmas,
> Which have the characteristic of being inseparable.[783]

{613} This teaches the defining characteristics of the emptiness endowed with the supreme of all aspects, free from the extremes of superimposition and denial.[784]

2.3.3. Instruction on the completion [of the treatise]

> **This concludes *The Distinction between Phenomena and the Nature of Phenomena* composed by the noble protector Maitreya.**

[This treatise] teaches **the distinction between phenomena** (what appears as duality and according designations) **and the nature of phenomena** (suchness).

> In order to elucidate the essence of the teachings out of compassion
> For the beings of the degenerate times, the victor Ajita
> Composed *The Distinction between Phenomena and the Nature of Phenomena*
> So that those with intelligence [can] engage in it.
>
> Though [this text] is not within the sphere of fools like me,
> I commented on the profound by relying
> On the gist of the intentions of Asaṅga and Nāgārjuna.
> Through this virtue, may [all] enter the actuality free from extremes.[785]

This "Ornament That Extensively Comments on and Explains *The Distinction between Phenomena and the Nature of Phenomena*" was composed in a lucid manner by Rangjung Dorje, who is taken care of by the buddhas and bodhisattvas, upon [his wish to] illuminate it by himself, being requested by many learned and accomplished spiritual friends, and, in particular, being requested by the spiritual friend Kunga Jampa.[786]

It was translated by paṇḍita Mahājana and Loden Sherab.[787]

[This commentary] was composed during the first month of the Monkey Year [1320][788] at [Upper] Dechen.[789]

Gö Lotsāwa's Commentary on The Distinction between Phenomena and the Nature of Phenomena

{453}[790] With [the *Uttaratantra*'s] explanation of suchness with stains being finished, now, stainless suchness, which is labeled with the name "enlightenment," shall be discussed.[791] The meaning to be explained here has two points:

1) Brief introduction
2) Detailed explanation

1) [The *Ratnagotravibhāgavyākhyā*] says:

> Here, what is stainless suchness? Since [this suchness] is free from all kinds of stains in the uncontaminated dhātu of the buddha bhagavāns, it is presented as the fundamental change. In brief, this should be understood in terms of eight points.[792]

As for accepting the expression "stainless suchness," first, it is asked [here], "What is the nature of stainless suchness?" Stainless suchness is that which is presented as the fundamental change of the sovereigns who are the buddha bhagavāns. You may wonder, "In this, what does 'foundation' and what does 'change' refer to?" The "foundation" is the uncontaminated dhātu and the meaning of "change" is "coming to an end"[793] because all stains or obscurations (with afflictive and cognitive obscurations as the divisions of their aspects) in this dhātu have become separated [from it] and come to an end. [The *Abhidharmasūtra*] says:

> The dhātu of beginningless time
> Is the foundation of all phenomena.

Thus, because suchness has functioned as the foundation or support of afflicted phenomena since beginningless time, it is also to be described as "host" (*gnas po*). [*Nāgamitra's*] *Kāyatrayāvatāra* says:

> The host having changed into something else . . .[794]

Accordingly, it is called "fundamental change" because, through having changed into another nature later, it functions as the support for the purified qualities.[795] The *Dharmadharmatāvibhāga* says [the following on suchness as the nature of phenomena]:[796] . . . {455}

. . . These [verses] are to be explained here. [In the *Uttaratantra*] enlightenment is explained as stainless suchness. In the *Dharmadharmatāvibhāga* it is called "the nature of phenomena," which has the same meaning as suchness. Also, in both the [former] and the [latter texts] it is said that the fundamental change has the same meaning as suchness. As for the statement [in *Uttaratantra* II.7] that nonconceptual wisdom is the cause of enlightenment, [the same] is said in the *Dharmadharmatāvibhāga* in terms of [wisdom being] the cause of the fundamental change. {456} Since [the *Uttaratantra*] excellently explains the three kāyas in terms of manifestation and so on, the *Dharmadharmatāvibhāga* appears to be something like a commentary on this [second] chapter [of the *Uttaratantra*].[797]

Here "**the comprehension of the nature of phenomena**"[798] are the [beginning] words of the passage [in the *Dharmadharmatāvibhāga*] that teaches the distinctive features of the nature of phenomena. The comprehension of the nature of phenomena refers to the cognition of realizing [its] six distinctive features in an unmistaken manner because this is established through the words of this passage, just as in the phrase "the comprehension of the two realities." One comprehends **the defining characteristic** of the nature of phenomena, **the** support that is [its] **matrix**, the prajñā of **penetration** that consists of the mundane [part of the path], the path of seeing that represents the **contact** with and the full perception of the nature of phenomena, the path of familiarization that represents the relinquishment of subtle stains through the **recollection** of that [contact], and finally the nature of the fruition that is **the arrival at** the **nature of** suchness and [its] remaining without stains. **The comprehension of the nature of phenomena through** those **six points** makes up the **unsurpassable** yāna. These six represent three [main] points—what is to be understood, what is to be familiarized with, and the fruition to be attained. Among the [six points], the first one is what is to be understood, the middling four refer to familiarization, and the last one is the fruition.[799]

As for the first one, what is to be understood is **the defining characteristic** of the nature of phenomena, which **is as in the** brief **introduction**:

> **Furthermore, the defining characteristic of the nature of phenomena**
> **Is suchness, which lacks any distinction**
> **Between apprehender and apprehended,**
> **Or [between] objects of designation and what designates them.**

The **apprehended** consists of the six objects such as form **and** the **apprehender** consists of the six sense faculties such as the eyes. These two also point to the six consciousnesses [produced by them]. Thus, [apprehender and apprehended] consist of the objects, the sense faculties, and those consciousnesses which lack the conceptions that entail terms and referents. **Objects of designation** are the reflections of objects that appear to conceptions. **What designates them** are the reflections of terms together with the conceptions themselves. **The nature of phenomena** is free from ordinary beings' cognitions (such as [those of] the eyes), including their supports and their objects. It is also free from the conceptions that entail terms and referents, including their aspects. Therefore, what is called "the nature of phenomena" is the continuum of the mind that is of one taste, just like the expanse of space, because all phenomena of saṃsāra do not go beyond this nature either. With regard to this, some [say] that [the nature of phenomena] is either [suitable as] a nonimplicative negation [in the sense] of being the nonexistence of apprehender and apprehended or that it is suitable as an implicative negation [in the sense] of existing as this very nonexistence of nonduality. Though there are assertions of such [negations] being the nature of phenomena, here it is not like that because the commentary [by Vasubandhu] explains it to be nothing but the continuum of stainless mind.[800] For the *Mahāyānasūtrālaṃkāra* also says that it is the pure luminous mind:

> Mind is held to be always luminous by nature,
> Contaminated [only] by adventitious flaws.
> Apart from the mind that is the nature of phenomena,
> Another mind's luminosity in nature is not taught.[801]

Also, in [Vasubandhu's] commentary on this [*Dharmadharmatāvibhāga*] too it is taught as being luminosity.[802]

As for the adventitious stains, they consist of the nonconceptual sense consciousnesses and the conceptions that entail terms and referents. For all afflicted phenomena consist of conceptions, while the skandhas that are the maturations of these [afflicted phenomena] consist of the sense faculties together with their objects. Therefore, it is said that "the nature of the mind is empty of apprehender, apprehended, and conceptions." However, it is [also] said that "it is the [very] phenomena within the nature of phenomena of which it is empty." Thus, it is not that [phenomena] are negated through reasoning. Also the *Dharmadhātustava* says:

> Once conception and its concepts are relinquished
> With regard to phenomena whose principal is mind,

It's the very lack of nature of phenomena
That you should cultivate as dharmadhātu. {457}

What you see and hear and smell,
What you taste and touch, phenomena as well—
Once yogins realize them in this way,
The characteristics are complete.

Eyes and ears and also nose,
Tongue and body and the mind as well—
The six āyatanas fully pure.
This is true reality's own mark.[803]

Thus, [here the nature of phenomena] is explained as being the [very] phenomena of which it is empty—the six āyatanas, together with their objects.

As for "**the matrix**," it is the focal object of the conceptual cognitions that familiarize with suchness. For one familiarizes with suchness through focusing on **all phenomena** as [its] support, and familiarizes with them through taking **the Buddha's speech** (the means of expressing [all phenomena]) as the support [for such focusing]. However, the support for [this focusing] is the entire speech of the Buddha (such as the sūtra collection and the proclamations in song).

The **penetration** or discernment by prajñā through focusing on that focal object is primarily **the mental engagement** in accordance with the principle of suchness[804] through **relying** and focusing **on the sūtra collection of the mahāyāna**, and its nature is **the path of preparation**. The word "**entire**" refers to the cognitions in terms of study, reflection, and meditation that are the [mental] retinue of this preparation.

As for "**contact**," **through** the direct cognition of **the path of seeing** by virtue of having **attained the correct view** of the path of the noble ones, the object that is **suchness** is **experienced and attained in** accordance with **the direct manner** [of perception]. Through this the result of valid cognition is accomplished.

Recollection consists of the nature of **the factors concordant with enlightenment of the path of familiarizing with the actuality that was seen through** the path of seeing. [The *Abhisamayālaṃkāra*] says:

The path of familiarization consists of the repeated
Reflections, verifications, and absorptions
During the branches of penetration,
The path of seeing, and the path of familiarization itself.[805]

In this manner, [the path of familiarization] engages and rises again and again. Therefore, it is called "recollection" because it is mindfulness that links with many paths. **Because** the familiarization in this way **eliminates the** subtle **stains of that** suchness after the coarse ones have been overcome through the path of seeing, the ten bhūmis will be completed through the consummation of this familiarization.

"**The arrival at its nature**" refers to the cognitions of the path **arriving at** and abiding in the **nature of the** nature of phenomena. At the time of the path [bodhisattvas] have familiarized with all phenomena through focusing on them, but once a direct cognition has arisen, all phenomena of apprehender and apprehended do not appear [anymore], while only their suchness appears. When they rise from [that direct perception of suchness], [their perceptions during subsequent attainment] entail appearances that are not suchness. By virtue of [this process of alternating between meditative equipoise and subsequent attainment], the path of familiarization reaches its consummation. **Once suchness has become without stains, all appears as nothing but suchness.** The foundation of that—the very suchness that has functioned as the host of stains before—has changed into something else, **which is the perfection of the fundamental change**. In this way, what are called "the suchness that has become stainless" and "the fundamental change" have the very same meaning.

As for the phrase "**through comprehending**," it refers to comprehending the defining characteristic and is also to be applied to all other five [points of comprehending the nature of phenomena, such as] "comprehending the matrix." Though this is how the six dharmas through which one comprehends the nature of phenomena are, [in addition,] the fundamental change shall be explained in detail.

2) This **is** the **unsurpassable** yāna **through** the **ten points** of **comprehension** in order to realize and assimilate **the fundamental change**. It is to be understood in this way **through comprehending the nature**, comprehending **the substance** or the entity, comprehending **the persons**, comprehending **the distinctions**, comprehending **the prerequisites**, comprehending **the foundation**, comprehending **the mental engagement**, comprehending **the trainings**, comprehending **the shortcomings, and** {458} comprehending **the benefits**. Here these ten distinctive features represent two [topics]—the presentation of the fundamental change and the reasonings to establish it. Among these, the reasonings are taught by the last two comprehensions, while the first eight are summarized into (1) [its] nature, (2) [its] causes, and (3) the fruition. Among these, the five [points] up through the prerequisites are [its] nature. The foundation and the mental engagement are [its] causes. The trainings are the fruition.

(1) The nature consists of (a) the actual nature and (b) its division. (1a) Here, **as for comprehending the nature, it is suchness** that has become **stainless**, which is **in terms of adventitious stains not appearing** at all **and suchness appearing** in all respects. Through having reversed its functioning as the support for adventitious stains, [suchness] functions as the support that is the [very] nature of the appearance of suchness, but it does not function as the support for producing [the appearance of suchness]. Therefore, it is said to "have become its [own] nature." This fundamental change also needs to be expressed by the term "buddhahood" (*sangs rgyas*). For by virtue of all stains not arising again, it is pure (*sangs*), and by virtue of all knowable objects appearing as nothing but suchness, it has unfolded (*rgyas*). This corresponds to what the *Kāyatrayāvatāra* says:

> Apart from stainless suchness
> And nonconceptual wisdom,
> There are no other dharmas
> Of the buddhas whatsoever.[806]

Here, on the buddhabhūmi, both the relinquishment of being without stains and the wisdom of realizing suchness have the nature of the single luminous wisdom. Therefore, both are suchness, the nature of phenomena, and the matrix of phenomena.

(1b) From among the four ways of the division [of this nature of the fundamental change], (1ba) the division by way of connection consists of the division by way of the connection in terms of identity and the division by way of the connection in terms of causality. As for the division by way of the connection in terms of identity, since suchness is integral to everything, [this division] consists of the **change of the cognizance that is the common container into suchness, the change of the dhātu** of the **dharma** that is the meaning **of the sūtra collection**—the words of the Buddha, which are the natural outflow of this (dharmadhātu)—**into suchness, and the change of the cognizance that is the dhātu of sentient beings which is not in common into suchness.** [The nature of the fundamental change] is also to be understood as threefold through the division by way of the results caused by it, which is by virtue of the division of suchness in terms of the appearance of enlightened bodies, the instructions of enlightened speech, and the all-seeing of enlightened mind. Here as for "**entity**," just as in the case of calling an ox "substance" and the whiteness of that ox, "entity," it is nothing but a distinctive feature that is described as entity, whereas to say "**substance**" seems to be somewhat of an impurity in translation.

(1bb) "**As for** the division of **comprehending the persons,**" [among] the fundamental change of buddhas, the fundamental change from the path of seeing onward, and the fundamental change on the path of nonlearning, **the first two are the changes of suchness that are those of buddhas and bodhisattvas. The latter one refers to the** change of suchness **of śrāvakas and pratyekabuddhas too.** Since the former two do not exist in śrāvakas [and pratyekabuddhas], they are not in common, while the latter one exists in all noble ones and thus is in common. This is the division of the fundamental change into three by way of three [kinds of] persons.

(1bc) As for **the comprehension of** [this fundamental change] being more eminent than [those of] the yānas with inferior **distinctive features**, it is more eminent than [those of] śrāvakas and pratyekabuddhas by virtue of four distinctive features—**the distinctive feature of the pure realms of buddhas and bodhisattvas and** the teachers in those realms having the nature of the three kāyas. For the **seeing** of all knowable objects is **attained through the attainment of the dharmakāya**; the **instruction** on the profound and vast principles [of the dharma], through **the sāmbhogika**kāya; **and** the **mastery** over the causes for promoting the welfare of sentient beings (such as the supernatural knowledges), through the attainment of **the nairmāṇikakāya**. These also constitute the nature of the fundamental change.

(1bd) **The comprehension of** the distinctive feature of **realizing the purposes** or functions[807] {459} refers to the fundamental change of bodhisattvas being more eminent than [those of] śrāvakas and pratyekabuddhas by virtue of three distinctive features. It is more eminent by virtue of **aspiration prayers** ([its] cause), [its] **focal object** (the vast words of the Buddha), **and** the purification of **the ten bhūmis** ([its] nature). For the fundamental change of bodhisattvas performs those three functions, whereas the fundamental changes of śrāvakas and pratyekabuddhas do not. Here [the above-mentioned threefold division of the suchness of] the container, sentient beings, and the sūtra collections (assemblies of words) refers to the fundamental change by virtue of what comes to an end, whereas the latter [division here], which consists of the three that arise from the [former], refers to that into which there is change.

(2) As for the causes [of the fundamental change], (a) [its] direct cause is nonconceptual wisdom, while (b) the cause of the [latter] is proper mental engagement. (2a) First, **the comprehension of the foundation or support** of the fundamental change of buddhas **is nonconceptual wisdom**. Therefore, its comprehension consists of **comprehending the focal objects**, comprehending **the relinquishment of characteristics**, comprehending **the correct yogic practice**, comprehending **the defining characteristics**, comprehending **the benefit, and** comprehending **the thorough knowledge**. Thus, it **is**

comprehended through six points of comprehension. Here the first three are [its] causes; the defining characteristic, [its] nature; the benefit, [its] fruition; and the thorough knowledge, what makes one thoroughly know its antagonistic factors.

As for there being these six [points of] comprehending [nonconceptual wisdom] **here, first, the comprehension of the focal objects should be understood as four points.** What are these four? They are the words of the Buddha **teaching the mahāyāna, aspiring for these** words of the Buddha through studying them, **being certain** [about them] through the power of reasoning by virtue of reflecting [on them] (these three refer to searching for the focal objects), **and the completion of the accumulations** (from among the four wheels, having generated merit before).[808] If any of these four [focal objects] are lacking, the correct yogic practice will not arise.

[Second,] **the relinquishment of** the **characteristics** that arise and come up while being in the process of cultivating the training is the **second** one among these six comprehensions [of nonconceptual wisdom]. **The comprehension of** that [relinquishment of characteristics] has **four points,** which **is by virtue of relinquishing the characteristic of antagonistic** factors (afflicted phenomena), the characteristic of their **remedies** (meditating on repulsiveness and so on), the characteristic of **suchness** (the object), **and** the characteristic of **realization** (the attainment of the fruition). These should be understood from the very sūtra [(the *Avikalpapraveśadhāraṇī*)]:

> O sons of good family, here bodhisattva mahāsattvas hear the dharma related to nonconceptuality, place their intention on nonconceptuality, and then relinquish all characteristics of conceptuality. As the first of these [characteristics], they relinquish all characteristics of the conceptions about a nature, that is, about either apprehender or apprehended. These characteristics of the conceptions about a nature here consist of the characteristics with regard to contaminated entities. These contaminated entities are the five appropriating skandhas, that is, the appropriating skandha of form, the appropriating skandha of feeling, the appropriating skandha of discrimination, the appropriating skandha of formation, and the appropriating skandha of consciousness. How are those characteristics of the conceptions about a nature relinquished? What becomes perceptible by way of being an appearance [is relinquished] through not mentally engaging [in it].
>
> Once the [bodhisattvas] have gradually relinquished these characteristics of the conceptions about a nature, the characteristics of the conceptions that analyze the remedies, which are other than the

[former], occur and become perceptible by way of being appearances. They consist of the following—the characteristics of the conceptions that analyze generosity, {460} the characteristics of the conceptions that analyze ethics, the characteristics of the conceptions that analyze patience, the characteristics of the conceptions that analyze vigor, the characteristics of the conceptions that analyze dhyāna, and the characteristics of the conceptions that analyze prajñā, which [operate] either by way of analyzing a nature, by way of analyzing qualities, or by way of analyzing an essence. The [bodhisattvas] also relinquish these characteristics of the conceptions that analyze the remedies through not mentally engaging [in them].

Once the [bodhisattvas] have relinquished those [characteristics of the conceptions about the remedies], the characteristics of the conceptions that analyze true reality, which are other than the [former], occur and become perceptible by way of being appearances. They consist of the following—the characteristics of the conceptions that analyze emptiness, the characteristics of the conceptions that analyze suchness, the characteristics of the conceptions that analyze the true end, and the characteristics of the conceptions that analyze signlessness, the ultimate, and the dharmadhātu, which [operate] either by way of analyzing specific characteristics, by way of analyzing qualities, or by way of analyzing an essence. The [bodhisattvas] also relinquish these characteristics of the conceptions that analyze true reality through not mentally engaging [in them].

Once the [bodhisattvas] have relinquished those [characteristics], the characteristics of the conceptions that analyze attainment, which are other [than the former], occur and become perceptible by way of being appearances. They consist of the following—the characteristics of the conceptions that analyze the attainment of the first bhūmi up through the characteristics of the conceptions that analyze the attainment of the tenth bhūmi, the characteristics of the conceptions that analyze the attainment of the poised readiness for the dharma of nonarising, the characteristics of the conceptions that analyze the attainment of the prophecy, the characteristics of the conceptions that analyze the attainment of the purity of buddha realms, the characteristics of the conceptions that analyze the attainment of maturing sentient beings, the characteristics of the conceptions that analyze the attainment of the empowerment, up through the characteristics of the conceptions that analyze the attainment of the knowledge of all aspects, which [operate] either by way of analyzing specific characteristics, by way of analyzing

> qualities, or by way of analyzing an essence. The [bodhisattvas] also relinquish these characteristics of the conceptions that analyze attainment through not mentally engaging [in them].[809]

There are two approaches [of exegesis] here. Which are these two? The approach of the great master Kamalaśīla and the approach of venerable Maitrīpa and his spiritual heirs. As for the first one, I will write a little about its meaning by summarizing the *Nirvikalpapraveśadhāraṇīṭīkā* composed by that [master].

Here the four characteristics are the characteristic of analyzing a nature, the characteristic of analyzing the remedy, the characteristic of analyzing true reality, and the characteristic of analyzing attainment. From among them, "nature" refers to afflicted phenomena. Since they arise under the sway of ignorance without depending on effort, they are called "nature." "Remedy" refers to the six pāramitās such as generosity. "True reality" is emptiness, or the ultimate. "Attainment" consists of the eleven bhūmis such as Supreme Joy.[810] "Characteristics" refers to the discriminating notions of clinging to those four phenomena as being specifically characterized, which constitute the nature of what is to be relinquished. Here it is the [cognizing] subject of a characteristic that is expressed as "characteristic" because it is [the fact of] phenomena having specific characteristics that is called "characteristic," which is what is clung to. You may wonder, "Through what are these four characteristics relinquished?" They are relinquished through not becoming mentally engaged [in them]. "At which time [are they relinquished]?" Having first practiced calm abiding, [bodhisattvas] subsequently cultivate superior insight through the progression of the nine [ways of resting the] mind, such as "settling." {461} It is at this time [of cultivating superior insight] that [those characteristics] are relinquished. "When have they been relinquished?" One should speak of them as having been relinquished when the bhūmis are attained, [that is,] through the contact with suchness.

As for [the meaning of] "nonconceptual" here, [the *Avikalpapraveśadhāraṇīṭīkā*] says, "It is nonconceptual with regard to this . . . ," stating that [bodhisattvas] do not even conceptualize the object that is suchness. [The phrase] "because it does not conceptualize" refers to samādhi.[811] As for the antagonistic factor of "mental nonengagement," which is mental engagement, it refers to the conceptions that entail terms and referents or the conceptions of clinging to the distinctive features of these [terms and referents] as being [real] entities. Thus, the actual "mental nonengagement" is the nonconceptual samādhi of focusing on suchness. The cause of this [samādhi] is described as the inferential or discriminating prajñā of realizing that entities lack a nature of their own,[812] which is based on arguments such as dependent origination, lacking coming or going, or negating arising [in terms] of the four extremes.[813] When cultivating this discriminating [prajñā] in such a way, this discriminating [prajñā] subsides on its own and turns into resting in nonconceptuality, just as a fire arisen from rubbing two pieces of wood consumes these very pieces of wood [and then goes out].[814] Therefore, the cause that is discriminating prajñā is labeled by the name of [its] result—mental nonengagement.

You may wonder, "Of what kind is this result?" It is what is stated in this commentary [by Kamalaśīla]:

> In such a way, [through] the power of aspiration and through prajñā, yogins relinquished the entire web of characteristics of conceptions about existence and so on. Through a nonconceptual, nonanalyzing, and inexpressible mind of one taste, they should [then] cultivate, and dwell in, suchness in a very lucid manner without any effort through aspiring for this very [suchness].[815]

This refers to the stage of settling [the mind] at the beginning of the nine [ways of settling] mind. After having attained this [initial state], one cultivates [the stage of] settling [the mind] continuously and so on. In this [commentary] we find this is in detail:

> The mind stream that rests in this [state] should not be distracted. When one becomes distracted in between, one calms the [distraction] and again directs the mind toward this very [state] . . .[816]

Because it is said [in the *Avikalpapraveśadhāraṇī*] that, once the respectively former of the four characteristics has been relinquished, the respectively following arises, this represents a progressive [process of] familiarization [with nonconceptuality]. As for the [cognitive] aspects of how these characteristics arise, they constitute conceptions about a nature, qualities, an essence, and so on, which is said by relating these to the three [characteristics to be relinquished] that are the second one and so on.

The natures of the second [characteristic consist of the following. The nature of generosity] is the generosity [of providing material] possessions, fearlessness, and the dharma. The nature of ethics is to turn away from flawed conduct and to practice the dharma. The nature of patience is threefold—not to annoy, not to mind anything, and [the poised readiness] to understand [the dharma]. The nature of vigor is the delight in virtue. The nature of dhyāna is a one-pointed mind. The nature of prajñā is the correct discrimination of [all] entities. The qualities consist of being wealthy through generosity, [attaining] higher realms through ethics, [possessing] a handsome body through patience, [having] a united retinue of servants and uninterrupted wealth through vigor, being without sickness through dhyāna, and having sharp faculties, lots of [physical] pleasure and mental pleasure, as well as mastery over most groups of sentient beings through prajñā. Since "essence" is a synonym of "cause," it is what serves as the causes of great enlightenment through dedication.

As for the natures of [the third characteristic of] true reality, they are said to consist of emptiness by virtue of personal and phenomenal identitylessness, suchness by virtue of true reality never being anything other, the true end by virtue of being the unmistaken actuality, signlessness by virtue of being free from all characteristics, the ultimate by virtue of being the sphere of highest wisdom, and the dharmadhātu by virtue of being the cause of all buddhadharmas. As for the qualities, through familiarizing with these [natures] all buddhadharmas without exception {462} arise. "Essence" is also a synonym of "nature," thus referring to perfectly abiding by virtue of valid cognition.

As for the natures of the bhūmis [in terms of the fourth characteristic of attainment], they consist of Supreme Joy and so on, which are well known. The attainment of poised readiness for the dharma of nonarising, the prophecy, and the purity of [buddha] realms [all occur] on the eighth bhūmi. The maturation of sentient beings [by bodhisattvas happens] on the ninth bhūmi. The attainment of the empowerment [occurs] on the tenth bhūmi. As for the qualities, they consist of the number of qualities (such as seeing one hundred buddhas in a single moment) continuously increasing [on the bhūmis]. "Essence" is also a synomym of the term "crucial" because the buddhabhūmi is the unsurpassable one of all supramundane phenomena. Or [the buddhabhūmi] is also the essence by virtue being the basis of emanation since all welfare of oneself and others arises through it.

[The second approach of exegesis] is what we find in detail [in the *Tattvadaśaka*] by Maitrīpa and [the *Tattvadaśakaṭīkā* by his] spiritual heir [Sahajavajra]:

> Some may say, "However,[817] the Bhagavān taught that what you call 'the bodhicitta that is the suchness of the world being nondual' is the characteristic of the conceptions that analyze true reality; what you call 'the samādhi of reality as it is' is the characteristic of the conceptions that analyze remedial factors;[818] and what you call 'the true reality that, when realized, has the nature of enlightenment' is the characteristic of the conceptions that analyze fruition.[819] [He said that once the respective preceding characteristics have been relinquished through mental nonengagement, one by one,] the other characteristics become perceptible through the manner of appearing. Those others [too] are completely relinquished

through mental nonengagement. So how could this teaching in the *Avikalpapraveśa[dhāraṇī]* and [what you say] not be contradictory?" To that, some give the following temporary reply: "In terms of the [above-mentioned] accumulations [necessary] for meditation to arise,[820] first one [must] speak about [the triad of] what is to be proven, the means of proof, and true reality. For otherwise it would follow that the teachings are without any fruition. Later, when one has gained [sufficient] familiarity [in meditation], it is taught that the characteristics of what is to be proven and so on are relinquished since the operating of cognition in terms of characteristics too is to be relinquished. But the cognition that [still operates with the notions of what is to be proven and so on] is the very first one to be cultivated [on the path], so how should that contradict [what is said in the *Avikalpapraveśadhāraṇī*]?"

This is not the best answer, as it is insufficient. Therefore, [Maitrīpa's *Tattvadaśaka*] gives another answer:

> Even the vain presumptuousness about being free from duality,
> In like manner, is luminosity.[821]

The underlying intention of this is as follows. Those who fully penetrate this [see] true reality. In order to realize true reality,[822] it is taught that the three [types of] analysis[823] are to be relinquished, just like relinquishing the four extremes. [This is elucidated] through the following words [in Maitrīpa's *Sekanirdeśa*]:

> Those who do not dwell in remedial factors,
> Are not attached to true reality,
> And who do not wish for a fruition of anything,
> They understand Mahāmudrā.[824]

Here "Mahāmudrā" refers to the pith instructions on the true reality of Mahāmudrā that is fully penetrating the true reality of [all] entities. Also, as for those three analyses [above, Maitrīpa's *Mahāyānaviṃśikā]* says:

> The purity of the four extremes
> Is to rely on the four extremes.[825]

Thus, inasmuch as they are true reality, they are not to be relinquished. Therefore, this is not contradictory.

[In *Tattvadaśaka* 7cd,] being free from duality means being without duality. Vain presumptuousness about [being free from duality] refers to the conceptions that analyze true reality. Even that is [nothing but] luminosity since it lacks a nature and is naturally pure. Likewise, also the presumptuousness[826] in terms of something to be accomplished and the means of accomplishment is to be realized as the nature of luminosity.

However, as for [the phrase] "These characteristics are relinquished through not becoming mentally engaged [in them]" [in the *Avikalpapraveśadhāraṇī]*, here mental nonengagement does not refer to a complete absence of mental engagement, such as closing your eyes and then not seeing anything, like a vase or a blanket, at all. Rather, mental nonengagement refers to the very nonobservation of a nature of entities, be it through analysis or the guru's pith instructions. As it is said:

> Whether walking, standing, sitting,
> Or lying, rest in meditative equipoise.
> As for looking, hearing, smelling too,
> Touching, and tasting, {463}
>
> With the pure eye of prajñā,
> And through analysis and pith instructions,
> All phenomena are seen to be unborn,
> But that is nonseeing.[827]

Therefore, mental nonengagement with regard to characteristics means nothing but fully penetrating the very lack of characteristics. Also, those so-called "conceptions that analyze characteristics" are "analyses in terms of apprehending characteristics."[828] The Bhagavān has taught that those too are completely pure and unborn. As the Bhagavān says in the *Samādhirājasūtra*:

> A notion shows through that notion's
> Object and [its] grasping.
> And this notion is without grasping,
> Indicated through an object that is distinct.
>
> What is distinct is this notion,
> And such a distinct [notion] is taught.

A notion has not arisen by its nature,
And just so, a notion will not arise [ever].

We should laugh at this notion–
The one in whom a notion operates
Delights in the reference points of this notion,
And such a creator of notions is not liberated.

Whose notion has arisen,
And through whom did a notion arise?
Who engages in this notion,
And by whom is this notion stopped?

No phenomenon was found by the Buddha
For which a notion would occur.
Reflect on this meaning here,
And then no notion will occur [again].

When notions are unarisen,
Whose notion does then stop?[829]

Thus, to think, "This is unthinkable and nonconceptual" is just thinking and conception. However, it is not that [mental nonengagement] means that there is absolutely no cognition of the lack of nature. This is said in the Madhyamaka of union:[830]

In the yoga of nonconceptual mind,
The [mind] is without thinking, not conceptualizing,
The supreme of all aspects, yet without aspect,
With all faculties of mind,

The nature of entities and nonentities,
Yet devoid of entities and nonentities,
Liberated from the four extremes,
Yet equally endowed with the four extremes,

Not superimposed as various superimpositions,
And great bliss without attachment.[831]
The true reality of the antagonistic factors
Is the fruition—it cannot be analyzed through analysis.

Having arisen in dependence on such and such,
It is unarisen by nature.[832]
Since it is not matter, it is aware of itself,
Not a knower, and not something to be viewed.

Since it lacks a nature of its own, it is not enduring.
Since it lacks change, it is permanent.[833]

Guru [Maitrīpa] says [in his *Sekanirdeśa*]:

Related to being indistinct,
This thought is born dependent on conditions.
That alone is nirvāṇa—
So do not derange your mind![834]

and

Free from any fear of thoughts,
Just rest[835] at ease!

Likewise, the Bhagavān said [in the *Samādhirājasūtra]:*

When liberation is encountered,
All thinking [of it] is unthinkable.
When all thinking is unthinkable,
Then [liberation] just is unthinkable.

Just like sentient beings, so is thinking.
Just like thinking, so are the Victors.
The unthinkable Buddha
Explained just this as thinking.

In those who think that this is wonderful
No thought will ever arise [again].
Those who do not think of thinking
Will part with all their thinking.

Through thinking of it as unthinkable many times,
Having thought [like that] for a long time,
Thinking is not exhausted, but keeps arising,
Since such thinking is mistaken.

This thinking is great thinking,
The unsurpassable dharma-thinking.
Through this dharma-thinking
The thinking of true reality operates.[836]

Having these [stanzas] in mind, the Vajraguru [Maitrīpa] says [in his *Sekanirdeśa*]:

What is effortless wisdom
Is called "unthinkable."
What is made unthinkable by thinking,
That does not become unthinkable.[837]

[What is presented in the *Tattvadaśakaṭīkā*] here are the two passages on (1) a qualm [about the relinquishment of characteristics] and (2) the answers to that [qualm]. {464} (1) [The qualm is found in the first passage:] "Some may say, 'However, . . . not be contradictory?'" In this [passage] it is said that [according to the *Tattvadaśaka*] the characteristics of analyzing true reality, the remedy, and attainment are not relinquished. However, how is this not contradictory to the *Avikalpapraveśadhāraṇī*[838] stating that these three characteristics are relinquished? It is not asked here how to deal with the [first] characteristic of nature in [the context of] the dhāraṇī speaking of relinquishing four characteristics because this has already been taught through [line 3b in the *Tattvadaśaka*]:

Which is due to having the nature of nonattachment . . .[839]

(2) The answers are twofold—(a) an answer of others and (b) [Sahajavajra's] own answer. (2a) [The *Tattvadaśakaṭīkā* says,] "To that, some give the following temporary reply: '. . . how should that contradict [what is said in the *Avikalpapraveśadhāraṇī*]?'" As for the meaning [of this], it says the following. What is relinquished are the four characteristics related to the predicate to be proven with regard to the seeming bearers of the nature of phenomena, which is [their] lack of specific characteristics, and the means to prove [that], which are arguments such as dependent origination.[840] However, if an [inferential] valid cognition did not arise [in the first place], since there is no other means to relinquish those four characteristics, the teaching that says they are to be relinquished would be without fruition. Later on, through becoming familiar [with this] in meditation, the characteristics related to what is to be proven and so forth are relinquished too. Since inference is the remedy for characteristics, it is called "being without characteristics," which is by virtue

of its being a yoga of relinquishing [characteristics]. If this [inferential] cognition of being without characteristics is the first one to be cultivated, how could it contradict the *[Avikalpapraveśa]dhāraṇī*? It is through inference that characteristics are [deliberately] relinquished, while the relinquishment of characteristics that is not deliberate takes place at the time of (nonconceptual) meditation. Therefore, there is no contradiction.

(2b) Though this first answer here represents the position of Kamalaśīla, it is not the answer in terms of those with highest faculties. Therefore, our own approach [according to Maitrīpa and Sahajavajra] is as follows. [*Tattvadaśaka* 7cd says that] even the vain presumptuousness about the lack of duality—such as of a knower and what is known—is nothing other than luminosity. Hence, having understood that [such presumptuousness] has the nature of luminosity, one familiarizes [with it]. Since this is the familiarization with [the fact] that the conceptions about what is to be proven and the means of proof are luminosity too, this relinquishment of characteristics through knowing that, no matter how they may appear, their very own nature is luminosity, represents the approach for those with highest faculties, while the approach of Kamalaśīla is required for those with inferior faculties. The remaining explanations [in the *Tattvadaśakaṭīkā*] elucidate, through the sūtras and the guru's pith instructions, the way of meditation of the Madhyamaka of union, but I do not elaborate on this in detail.

Here master Kamalaśīla speaks [in his *Avikalpapraveśadhāraṇīṭīkā*] about the four characteristics as being the clinging to [real] entities, but does not describe [them as] anything else. However, the *[Avikalpapraveśa]dhāraṇī* itself says that "those [characteristics] become perceptible through the manner of appearing." Therefore, when the aspect of a vase appears for conception, through the power of that, clinging to an external vase arises. Therefore, it is the cause—this very aspect of a vase—that is called "characteristic." As for this kind [of characteristics], the coarse ones are relinquished on the first bhūmi. What appears for conceptions is put to an end on the seventh bhūmi, while [mind remains] associated with subtle nonconceptual appearances up through the tenth bhūmi. The [latter] are referred to as cognitive obscurations and are [only] put to an end without exception once the enlightenment of a buddha is attained. Therefore, by all means, also the appearances of nonconceptual saṃsāric cognitions must be relinquished. The meaning of this was explained many times before.

[The *Avikalpapraveśadhāraṇī*] says:

> "Very hard and solid rock mountain" means the kinds of formation that consist of afflictiveness and being engrossed in duality.[841]

Thus, after having referred to [characteristics as being] what is afflicted, [the text also] refers [to them] as duality. Also, above, [in the context of relinquishing the first among the four characteristics—the one of nature, the text glosses it as] "either apprehender or apprehended."[842] Since the distinctive feature of what appears as apprehender and apprehended is mentioned separately [here], this distinction [in the *Dharmadharmatāvibhāga*] into the two factors of "what appears as apprehender and apprehended" and "according designations" {465} is understood to also represent the meaning of this very *[Avikalpapraveśa]dhāraṇī* because this [distinction] is something like a commentary on the [latter].[843]

[It is taught] **through this**[844] set of four characteristics to be relinquished that, **in due order**, the first one is **coarse**; the second one, **middling**; the third one, **subtle**; **and** the fourth one, [the one with which bodhisattvas are] **associated for a long time**. That is, it is very subtle and must be relinquished even by those who have entered the bhūmis. **This is the relinquishment of characteristics** through nonconceptual wisdom.

As for the third [point of comprehending the foundation that is nonconceptual wisdom], **the comprehension of the correct yogic practice** (the cause [of nonconceptual wisdom]) is to be understood **in four points.** It **is the yogic practice of** the **observation** [of referents] as mere cognizance, then **the yogic practice of** the **nonobservation** of external referents, **the yogic practice of** realizing that, if there are no external referents, even the **observation** of mere cognizance is **nonobservable, and the yogic practice of the nonobservation** of both external [referents] and mere cognizance.[845] These are the four kinds [of yogic practice]. This sequence of the four yogas of this kind is also taught by [the following verses] in the *Laṅkāvatāra[sūtra]*:

> By relying on mere mind
> One does not imagine outer objects. . . .[846]

Also the *Mahāyānasūtrālaṃkāra* states:

> The mind is aware that nothing other than mind exists.
> Then it is realized that mind does not exist either.
> The intelligent ones are aware that both do not exist
> And abide in the dharmadhātu, in which these are absent.[847]

The same is also said in the *Madhyāntavibhāga*:

> Based on observation,
> Nonobservation arises.

> Based on nonobservation,
> Observation arises.
>
> Thus, observation is established
> As the nature of nonobservation.[848]

You may wonder, "Such is certainly the case, but if one holds that this text of the Bhagavān Maitreya is also a text of what is known as the yogas of Mahāmudrā, do the four yogas of this [Mahāmudrā][849] fit with those [four yogic practices in the *Dharmadharmatāvibhāga*]?" They do fit very well. The first [Mahāmudrā yoga] is to look inside and then to focus on [everything being] one's own mind. As for the explanation [in] the second [yogic practice] that there is nothing external, it is the [Mahāmudrā yoga of] freedom from reference points in which one realizes that all phenomena that are objects of the mind lack any basis or root. The realization that both what appears as [if] external and the inner mind free from reference points are of one taste is the yogic practice of the nonobservation of observation. To not meditate through deliberately focusing on even the nonduality of subject and object is called "nonmeditation," which is the fourth [Mahāmudrā] yoga.[850]

As for the fourth [point of comprehending nonconceptual wisdom] **here, the comprehension of the defining characteristics should be understood through three points**—the defining characteristic of abiding, the defining characteristic of nonappearance, and the defining characteristic of appearance. The defining characteristic of abiding is **by virtue of abiding in**, and focusing on, **the nature of phenomena due to abiding in**, and focusing on, **the nature of phenomena that is** the **nonduality** of apprehender and apprehended **and** without designation.

[The comprehension of the defining characteristics of nonconceptual wisdom] **is** [also] **by virtue of** the defining characteristic of **nonappearance because there is nothing** [in nonconceptual wisdom] **that appears as** the **duality** of apprehender and apprehended, **how it is designated**, the six **sense faculties**, the six **objects**, the six **cognizances** of those [objects], **or** even **the world as the container**. It is **for the** [reason] of those [six factors] not appearing that this nonconceptual wisdom is "**ungraspable, indemonstrable, ungrounded, without appearance, without cognizance, and without base**." Thus, **nonconceptual wisdom**'s six **defining characteristics are described as** they are found **in the** ***Avikalpapraveśasūtra***:

> What is nonconceptuality? Nonconceptuality is ungraspable, indemonstrable, unfounded, without appearance, noncognizance, and without base.[851]

[Nonconceptual wisdom] is unexaminable because it cannot be analyzed as the duality of apprehender and apprehended. The occurrence of "ungraspable" [corresponds to Sanskrit] "[a]rūpi" [in the *Dharmadharmatāvibhāga*], which applies to what can be grasped and what can be scrutinized. Therefore, [nonconceptual wisdom] is not an object of analysis and scrutiny.[852] This {466} teaches [its] defining characteristic of nonduality. [Also, nonconceptual wisdom] is indemonstrable because one is not able to describe it as it is through designations. This teaches [its] defining characteristic of lacking any designation. It is without support, or ungrounded, because it is not supported by, and grounded on, the sense faculties (such as the eyes). This teaches [its] defining characteristic of the sense faculties not appearing [in it]. It is without appearance because form and so on are not its objects. This teaches [its] defining characteristic of objects not appearing [in it]. It is not cognizance because it does not have the nature of the cognizances of the eyes and so on. This teaches [its] defining characteristic of consciousness not appearing [in it]. It is without base because it is not an entity that is a base for sentient beings. This teaches [its] defining characteristic of the world that is the container not appearing [in it].

[The comprehension of the defining characteristics of nonconceptual wisdom] **is** [also] **by virtue of** the defining characteristic of **appearance because** the characteristics of **all phenomena** do not appear and therefore [phenomena] are seen as being **equal** and identical **to the center of space, and because,** during the subsequent attainment that arises due to the power of that [seeing during meditative equipoise], **everything conditioned appears like** the eight examples of **illusions and so on**. This is also what the *[Avikalpapraveśa]-dhāraṇī* says:

> Through the nonconceptual wisdom that is not different from what is to be known, bodhisattva mahāsattvas who abide in the dhātu of nonconceptuality see all phenomena as being like the center of space. Through the wisdom that is attained subsequent to that [nonconceptual wisdom], they see all phenomena as being like illusions, mirages, dreams, optical illusions, echoes, reflections, [reflections of] the moon [in] water, and magical creations.[853]

As for the fifth [point of comprehending nonconceptual wisdom], **the comprehension of the benefit** should be understood **in four points**. It consists of the following four—**the attainment of the dharmakāya in a complete manner** (by virtue of the fundamental change), **the attainment of supreme bliss** (by virtue of having attained the highest abiding in bliss and thus having relinquished contaminated bliss and being the permanent [state] of lasting bliss),

the attainment of mastery over seeing [all] objects to be known (because of realizing the suchness and the variety of what is to be known), **and the attainment of mastery over teaching** the dharma (by virtue of teaching the dharma as it is individually appropriate). Here the attainment of the dharmakāya in a complete manner and the abiding in bliss are the dharmas of the enlightened body; seeing, the dharma of enlightened mind; and teaching, the dharma of enlightened speech.

As for the sixth [point], **the comprehension of the thorough knowledge should be understood through four points**. These four points are **the thorough knowledge of [being a] remedy, the thorough knowledge of the defining characteristic, the thorough knowledge of the distinctive features, and the thorough knowledge of the five functions.**

Here the first thorough knowledge, the knowledge [that nonconceptual wisdom is a] **remedy**, is fivefold **because nonconceptual wisdom is taught to be the remedy for the fivefold clinging** while [what is clung to] is **nonexistent—clinging to** the existence of an identity of **phenomena and** an identity of **persons** while they do not exist, clinging to what lacks arising by nature as arising and then **changing** (that is, perishing), clinging to [the two realities] as existing as something **different**, while ultimate reality does not exist apart from the seeming, **and** clinging to the **denial** of [taking phenomena and persons to be] nonexistent—clinging to phenomena and persons as being nonexistent despite their existing as mere imputations (this is the clinging to denial).

Second, **the thorough knowledge of the defining characteristic refers to its own defining characteristic that is the exclusion of the fivefold** antagonistic factors. These fivefold antagonistic factors are the **clinging to mental nonengagement, transcendence, complete subsiding, what is naturally** [nonconceptual], **and picturing**. Here, first, nonconceptual wisdom does not become nonconceptual wisdom merely by virtue of lacking mental engagement in [any] conception because, in the state of being a small child too, many [forms of] nonconceptual cognitions operate. Nor does the transcendence of conceptions {467} become nonconceptual wisdom merely by virtue of [its] being free from attachment to [conceptions] because the second dhyāna and so on that are free from attachment to those [conceptions] also exist in tīrthikas. [Nonconceptual wisdom] also does not become nonconceptual wisdom merely by virtue of the operation of conceptions having completely subsided temporarily because it would follow that deep sleep, having fainted, and so on also constitute nonconceptual wisdom since there is no operation of conceptions in these states. [Nonconceptual wisdom] does not become nonconceptual wisdom by virtue of having the very nature of lacking conception either because then it follows that form and so on also are nonconceptual wisdom. Nor is it reasonable for the picturing of nonconceptuality—a conception that apprehends [just] an aspect [of nonconceptuality], which appears to conception, as actually being nonconceptuality—to be nonconceptuality because this is [also nothing but] a conception.

Therefore, this negative "non-" in "nonconceptual" does not refer to the sheer nonexistence [of conceptions] because the sheer nonexistence of conceptions [also] exists in small children and [the state of] having fainted. [Nonconceptual wisdom] is not [nonconceptual] by virtue of being something other than conception either because then it follows that also form and so on are nonconceptual wisdom. Nor is it [nonconceptual] by virtue of applying this negative to something inferior because then it follows that the second dhyāna and a conception that dwells one-pointedly upon nonconceptual wisdom are also nonconceptual wisdom. Therefore, this negative [refers to] all conceptions that are designations and to the particular instances of what appears as the duality of apprehender and apprehended (what appear as the eighteen dhātus and the world that is the container). For they are called "conceptions" because, if examined correctly, they are [merely] something imagined, while not existing, whereas [nonconceptual wisdom] lacks any appearance of those [conceptions] and serves as the remedy for what appears as them. There does exist just a small amount of imagining [conceptions] during the phase of subsequent attainment, but these are [deliberately] retained by bodhisattvas for the sake of [being able to] venerate buddhas and benefit sentient beings.[854]

Third, **the thorough knowledge of the distinctive features** is more eminent than [those of] śrāvakas and pratyekabuddhas by virtue of **the** following **fivefold distinctive features** for the following reasons. [For] śrāvakas and pratyekabuddhas, it is the very conceptions about the flaws of saṃsāra and the qualities of nirvāṇa that represent [their] path, whereas the **nonconceptual** wisdom of buddhas and bodhisattvas does not conceive of saṃsāra and nirvāṇa as having flaws or qualities, respectively. [The wisdoms of] śrāvakas and pratyekabuddhas **are limited** by virtue of their making only the aspects of the four realities and dependent origination fully perceptible, whereas the nonconceptual [wisdom] of the mahāyāna is the [cognizing] subject of all knowable objects. Śrāvakas and pratyekabuddhas abide in nirvāṇa after having rejected saṃsāra, whereas buddhas and bodhisattvas are **not abiding** in saṃsāra or nirvāṇa through deliberately relinquishing or adopting [either of them]. The respective qualities of śrāvakas and pratyekabuddhas become extinct in the state of [the nirvāṇa] without remainder, whereas buddhas, despite having passed into [the state] without remainder, have **lasting** qualities for as long as space lasts. Though śrāvakas and pratyekabuddhas have attained their respectively final qualities, [through eventually having to enter the mahāyāna,] they still must search for other [qualities] that surpass [theirs], whereas there are **no** other [qualities] whatsoever to be searched for that **surpass** [those] of buddhas.[855]

The **final** thorough knowledge is **the thorough knowledge of the** five **functions** [of nonconceptual wisdom], which **refers to** nonconceptual [wisdom] performing **the** following **five functions** or activities. The **distinctive feature** of its nature is that it **distances** mere **conceptions.** [Its] **granting unsurpassable bliss** refers to buddhas abiding in bliss in an uninterrupted manner because this bliss is not interrupted by conceptions. Since it **frees from the afflictive and cognitive obscurations**, including their contaminations, consummate relinquishment is attained. [It also functions] because it causes the attainment of realizing and **engaging in all aspects of knowable objects through the wisdom that is attained subsequent to the** nonconceptual [wisdom in meditative equipoise]. Likewise, [it functions] because this subsequently attained [wisdom] **matures sentient beings,** {468} completely **purifies buddha realms, and grants and bestows the knowledge of all aspects** into [one's own] hands.

Here, through the thorough knowledge of [nonconceptual wisdom being a] remedy, [bodhisattvas] know what is to be relinquished. Through the thorough knowledge of [its] defining characteristic, they know through what [the former] is relinquished. Through the knowledge of [its] distinctive features, they know the differences in terms of in which [psychophysical] supports it exists and does not exist, respectively. [In particular,] through the knowledge of [its] being unsurpassable, they know that the motivation [of bodhisattvas—bodhicitta—] has been perfectly completed. Through the thorough knowledge of [its] function, they know [its] temporary activities.

As for the seventh [point of] comprehending the fundamental change, **the comprehension of mental engagement**, the above [point—the thorough knowledge—] represented the distinctive feature of the causes of comprehending the foundation [that is nonconceptual wisdom], in which nonconceptual wisdom referred to the wisdoms of noble buddhas and bodhisattvas. This [point] teaches that ordinary beings will [eventually] attain nonconceptual [wisdom] if they mentally engage in certain ways. This consists of two parts—how they should engage mentally and the manner in which they connect with nonconceptual [wisdom] through that [engagement].

First, as for **the persons who wish to comprehend nonconceptual wisdom,** [their psychophysical] support is [the one of] **bodhisattvas**. Therefore, at the beginning they should generate bodhicitta. They should mentally engage in [the fact] that the generation of bodhicitta is the striving for enlightenment, while the effective cause of enlightenment consists of nonconceptual wisdom. At the beginning of that they need to understand what conception is and that [wisdom] becomes nonconceptual by virtue of being free from that conception. [Thus,] they **mentally engage as follows** in what conception is as it will be explained [now]. **Through** the unawareness of being **ignorant about suchness**, one imagines **what appears as duality** while **not existing**, which is **the imagination of** [phenomena] as being real, while they are **unreal**. This is called "conception." The ālaya-consciousness **"that contains all seeds" is the cause for** this imagination. [From it,] **the continuum** or class [of false imagination] **that is based on it yet different**—the six operating consciousnesses—arises. Here this [continuum of the six consciousnesses] too is [understood as] conception. This false imagination **that entails** the ālaya-consciousness (the **cause**) **and** the operating consciousnesses ([its] results) arises from ignorance [as its] root. **Therefore**, those two [forms of] conception are what **appears** to cognition, **but does not exist** [as having any] nature ultimately. To cognitions in which **this** imagination manifestly **appears, the nature of phenomena** and suchness **do not appear. By virtue of this** imagination **not appearing, the nature of phenomena does appear.** For [in] the presentation of this nature of phenomena as emptiness, it is empty of imagination and therefore suchness is characterized by such being empty. **If bodhisattvas** examine imagination in this way and thus **mentally engage in this** nonexistence [of false imagination] **in a proper manner**, they **comprehend nonconceptual wisdom.**

Second, **such observing** is the observation that false imagination[856] lacks a nature, even though it appears. Such is called "**observing** [it] as **mere cognizance.**" **By virtue of** this **observing** [it] **as mere cognizance**, there arises the understanding that external **referents** are **not observed** because they lack a nature. **By virtue of** the understanding that **referents** are **not observed**, there arises the understanding that the apprehender, which is called "**mere cognizance**," does not have any nature either. **By virtue of** the understanding that the apprehender is **not observed** [either], [bodhisattvas] **engage in observing** suchness—**the lack of difference between those two** (apprehender and apprehended). Through this fourth yoga, they comprehend nonconceptual wisdom. Through mentally engaging in suchness, in which **these two** (apprehender and apprehended) are **not observed as being different, this nonconceptual wisdom is not observing any characteristics.** Therefore, it is described as "**lacking observation.**" Since it lacks observation, it is also described as "**lacking an object**" **because, by** such a lack of an object, this cognition **is characterized** [as being distinct] from other cognitions.[857]

(3)[858] Eighth, the comprehension of **the training** is **fourfold**—the training through aspiration, the training through discrimination, the training through familiarization, and the training in completion from the level of engagement through aspiration up through the buddha**bhūmi.** {469} Among these, **the training through aspiration** is the training **on the level of engagement through aspiration. By virtue of discriminating direct realization**, [bodhisattvas] train in **the first bhūmi (this is** called "**the phase of contact**" because they meet with suchness). **The training through familiarization** consists of **the six impure bhūmis** starting with the second bhūmi up through the seventh bhūmi **and the threefold bhūmis** that are **pure** of characteristics—the eighth one and so on (**these** nine **are the phase of recollection**). **Because** of training in **the deeds of a buddha** in an **effortless and uninterrupted** manner **by virtue of the training in completion**, it is also called a "training" (**this** training in completion **is the phase of the arrival at its nature**). Thus, it **should be understood** that the four trainings and their fruitions consist of the bhūmis from the engagement through aspiration up through the tenth bhūmi and the enlightened activity of the deeds [that are performed] after having become a buddha.

Ninth, **as for comprehending** the knowledge about **the shortcomings**, if one has the view **of there being no fundamental change, these are the four** kinds of **shortcomings** of this view. First, [without this fundamental change] it follows that **there is no** obstacle [for the afflictions] that constitutes the **support for the afflictions** henceforth **not operating** and not arising in the mind stream. Since beginningless time the afflictions have been operating again and again by way of being an uninterrupted series [of moments], but if they do not arise [during some] later [period], one should be certain that there is an obstacle to this [arising]. It is said that this obstacle is nothing but the fundamental change. This is comparable to [the fact that] guests, who had [regularly] entered a hotel before, are not able to enter it [anymore] due to the host rebelling against it. In the *Abhidharmasamuccaya* and other [texts] it is indeed explained that the path of liberation distances the afflictions,[859] but here it is to be understood that nothing but this very fundamental change is both the path of liberation and the reality of cessation because it ceases the afflictions.

As for the second flaw, **the path** of liberation consists of the [ten] powers and so on of the buddhabhūmi. When these remain by way of being an uninterrupted series, it is certain that there exists a stable support for them, just as it is certain that when water remains [somewhere] in a steady manner, there exists some stable ground beneath it. Since the **support** of these qualities is nothing but the fundamental change, if one has the view **of there being no** such [support], it is the ignorance and the doubts in terms of lacking trust in the fruition that constitute **the** [second] **flaw**.

[Third,] if there were no stable continuum called "fundamental change" in the states of śrāvakas and pratyekabuddhas **having passed into** the **nirvāṇa** without remainder, **there** would also **be no basis** in these states **for designating the persons who** are called "arhats." Also, if there were no stable continuum of wisdom after having become a buddha, there would be no basis for designating the persons who are called "buddhas." For example, in the state of saṃsāra too [people] accept a mental continuum that is the basis for being designated as Devadatta and so on. [As it is said]:

> It is based on a single continuum that
> A so-called "agent" and "experiencer" are taught.

Therefore, **the** [third] **flaw** consists of the doubts about [the Buddha and the saṃgha as objects of] refuge due to lacking trust in the three [kinds of] persons who have passed into nirvāṇa.

As for the fourth flaw, [without a fundamental change] **there** would **be no differences between the three** [types of] **enlightenment**—being enlightened about the four realities through the enlightenment of śrāvakas, pratyekabuddhas being enlightened about dependent origination, and buddhas being enlightened about all knowable objects without exception. In this way, there would be no mental continuum called "fundamental change" whatsoever once śrāvakas and pratyekabuddhas have passed into [their respective] nirvāṇas without remainder. Therefore, there is **the flaw of** it then following that these two would not enter the mahāyāna. If one views it in that way, there is the flaw of having doubts about the path of the single yāna.

Tenth, **the comprehension of the benefit should be known as being fourfold,** {470} that is, four qualities arising as **the opposites** of these four flaws. The opposite of the first flaw is trust in the relinquishment [of the afflictions]; the opposite of the second one, trust in the realization [of the nature of phenomena]; the opposite of the third one, trust in [the objects of] refuge; and the opposite of the fourth one, trust in the path of the single yāna. Here, since the continuum of wisdom is labeled as a person called "buddha," [one can also use the label] "of the buddhas," with buddhas representing the owners and the fundamental change being what is owned by them.

[Thus,] what is explained through these [ten points] is "the fundamental change," which is another name of suchness.

Now, in order to summarize the meaning of this treatise, [the lines] "**Examples for nonexistent phenomena** . . ." represent the synopsis of the meaning of the entire treatise without exception. Saṃsāra, which is characterized by being **phenomena**, is **appearing** while being **nonexistent**. As for its **examples**, it is referred to as "**being like illusions, dreams, and so on**." As for the explanation of **the fundamental change**, which is characterized by being the nature of phenomena, the fundamental change is not something arisen newly, but exists from the start. Its **examples** are that **it is like space** merely being seen newly by virtue of having become free from obscurations, while its nature existed before. Also, though **gold** exists before, it is merely seen later by virtue of having become free from tarnish. **Water** is clear by its very nature right from the start, but what is new is [just] the seeing [of its clarity] by virtue of [its] turbidities having settled. Thus, [Vasubandhu's] commentary [says]:

> [The fundamental change of the nature of phenomena] is taught through the examples of gold and water as being congruent with their properties only in terms of their qualities, without considering their [respective material] substances. Through the example of space, however, it is taught in its entirety.[860]

[Accordingly,] that space is taught to be congruent with the properties of the fundamental change is by virtue of both [of its following] qualities—being a substance that operates by way of being an uninterrupted series and [eventually] becoming observed as opposed to not having been observed [before]. Through this, it is clear that this commentary by master [Vasubandhu] represents the Madhyamaka system. For in the great Yogācāra texts it is not explained that there exists a naturally pure continuum within the continuum of afflicted phenomena such as ignorance, while such is explained in this [commentary]. Also the root [text] itself clearly speaks of the difference in terms of nonexistence and existence, respectively, with regard to phenomena and the nature of phenomena. Therefore, this matches well with the explanation in the *Uttaratantra* here that [the tathāgata heart] is empty of adventitious stains, but not empty of qualities.[861]

The three [texts] *Abhisamayālaṃkāra*, *Mahāyānasūtrālaṃkāra*, and *Madhyāntavibhāga* were well known to the scholars of the land of the noble ones from well before. Also, when master Haribhadra explained the *Abhisamayālaṃkāra*, he quoted passages from the [latter] two treatises too, whereas not even the names of the *Uttaratantra* and the *Dharmadharmatāvibhāga* appear [in his commentaries on the *Abhisamayālaṃkāra*]. The written texts of these two treatises—the *Uttaratantra* and the *Dharmadharmatāvibhāga*—were [only] found later by venerable Maitrīpa, and he studied them while having a direct vision of venerable Maitreya. [Later,] the paṇḍita called Ānandakīrti studied them with [Maitrīpa] and then explained them to Sajjana. This is what the followers of the system of Dsen [Kawoche] propagate.

In this way, "stainless suchness," "the fundamental change," and "enlightenment" are synonyms. Here the term "bodhi" refers to the flaws having become pure and cleansed and also refers to having realized and internalized the dharma. Therefore, it is [also] explained as "emptiness" because it is empty in terms of the tathāgata heart lacking [any] adventitious stains and has the nature of the qualities of wisdom.

Appendix 1: The Dhāraṇī of Entering Nonconceptuality

[1) The setting of the discourse][862]

{M1b} {D1b}[863] Thus have I heard at one time when the Bhagavān was residing in Rājagṛha[864] in the palace that is the heart of the nonconceptual dharmadhātu superior to all three realms,[865] together with a great gathering of bhikṣus and a great assembly of bodhisattvas. He was in the company of the bodhisattva mahāsattva Avikalpa, the bodhisattva mahāsattva Avikalpaprabhāsa, the bodhisattva mahāsattva Avikalpacandra, Nirvikalpavīra, Nirvikalpadharmanirdeśakuśala, Nirvikalpasvabhāva, Nirvikalpamati, Nirvikalpanāda, Nirvikalpaspharaṇa, Nirvikalpasvara, Nirvikalpamaheśvara,[866] Nirvikalpamahāmaitrīsvara, {D2a} and the bodhisattva Avalokiteśvara.[867]

[2) The opening of the discourse]

Then, surrounded by a retinue of many hundreds of thousands, the Bhagavān, looking forward, taught the dharma, beginning with the nonconceptuality of [all] phenomena[868] in the mahāyāna.

[3) The encouragement to retain]

Then the Bhagavān, having looked at the retinue of all the assembled bodhisattvas, said to the bodhisattvas, "Sons of good family, you must retain the dhāraṇī called 'Entering Nonconceptuality.' Those bodhisattva mahāsattvas who retain the dhāraṇī called 'Entering Nonconceptuality' accomplish the buddhadharmas very swiftly and always progress in a distinguished manner."

[4) The request]

Then the bodhisattva mahāsattva in the retinue whose name was Avikalpaprabhāsa rose from his seat, put his upper robe over one shoulder, placed his right knee cap on the ground, bowed in the direction of the Bhagavān with joined palms, and said to the Bhagavān, "Bhagavan, please teach the dhāraṇī of entering nonconceptuality, which bodhisattva mahāsattvas, upon having heard, will retain, read, mentally engage in a proper manner, and teach widely to others."

[5) Making the retinue into a proper vessel]

When he had spoken in that way, the Bhagavān answered, "Therefore, bodhisattva mahāsattvas, listen well and mentally engage properly, and I will explain the dhāraṇī of entering nonconceptuality." "Very well, Bhagavan," {D2b} said the bodhisattvas. They listened to the Bhagavān and the Bhagavān said the following to them.

[6) Taking one's stand]

O sons of good family, here bodhisattva mahāsattvas hear the dharma related to nonconceptuality, place their intention on nonconceptuality,[869]

[7) The correct practice to relinquish characteristics]

and then relinquish all characteristics of conceptuality. As the first of these [characteristics], they relinquish all characteristics of the conceptions about a nature, that is, about either apprehender or apprehended. These characteristics of the conceptions about a nature here consist of the characteristics with regard to contaminated entities. These contaminated entities are the five appropriating skandhas, that is, the appropriating skandha of form, the appropriating skandha of feeling, the appropriating skandha of discrimination, the appropriating skandha of formation, and the appropriating skandha of consciousness. How are those characteristics of the conceptions about a nature[870] relinquished? What becomes perceptible by way of being an appearance [is relinquished] through not mentally engaging [in it].[871]

Once the [bodhisattvas] have gradually relinquished these characteristics of the conceptions about a nature,[872] the characteristics of the conceptions that analyze the remedies, which are other than the [former], occur and become perceptible by way of being appearances. They consist of the following—the characteristics of the conceptions that analyze generosity, the characteristics of the conceptions that analyze ethics, {M2a} the characteristics of the conceptions that analyze patience, the characteristics of the conceptions that analyze vigor, the characteristics of the conceptions that analyze dhyāna, and the characteristics of the conceptions that analyze prajñā, which [operate] either by way of analyzing a nature, by way of analyzing qualities, or by way of analyzing an essence. The [bodhisattvas] also relinquish these characteristics of the conceptions that analyze the remedies through not mentally engaging [in them].[873]

Once the [bodhisattvas] have relinquished those [characteristics of the conceptions about the remedies], the characteristics of the conceptions that analyze true reality, which are other than the [former], occur and become perceptible by way of being appearances. {D3a} They consist of the following—the characteristics of the conceptions that analyze emptiness, the characteristics of the conceptions that analyze suchness, the characteristics of the conceptions that analyze the true end, and the characteristics of the conceptions that analyze signlessness, the ultimate, and the dharmadhātu, which [operate] either by way of analyzing specific characteristics, by way of analyzing qualities, or by way of analyzing an essence. The [bodhisattvas] also relinquish these characteristics of the conceptions that analyze true reality through not mentally engaging [in them].[874]

Once the [bodhisattvas] have relinquished those [characteristics], the characteristics of the conceptions that analyze attainment, which are other [than the former], occur and become perceptible by way of being appearances. They consist of the following—the characteristics of the conceptions that analyze the attainment of the first bhūmi up through the characteristics of the conceptions that analyze the attainment of the tenth bhūmi, the characteristics of the conceptions that analyze the attainment of the poised readiness for the dharma of nonarising, the characteristics of the conceptions that analyze the attainment of the prophecy, the characteristics of the conceptions that analyze the attainment of the purity of buddha realms, the characteristics of the conceptions that analyze the attainment of maturing sentient beings, the characteristics of the conceptions that analyze the attainment of the empowerment, up through the characteristics of the conceptions that analyze the attainment of the knowledge of all aspects, which [operate] either by way of analyzing specific characteristics, by way of analyzing qualities, or by way of analyzing an essence. The [bodhisattvas] also relinquish these characteristics of the conceptions that analyze attainment through not mentally engaging [in them].[875]

Once bodhisattva mahāsattvas have relinquished all aspects of the characteristics of conceptions through not mentally engaging [in them], they strive hard for the dhātu of nonconceptuality.[876] Though they have not yet made contact with the dhātu of nonconceptuality, there is the proper samādhi through which they will make contact with the dhātu of nonconceptuality.[877] {D3b}

[8) Entering the dhātu of nonconceptuality]

By virtue of pursuing that correct practice through reliance,[878] by virtue of pursuing it through familiarization, by virtue of pursuing it through enhancement, and by virtue of pursuing it through correct mental engagement, they make contact with the dhātu of nonconceptuality in a spontaneous and effortless manner and progressively purify it.[879]

[9) The characteristics of the dhātu of nonconceptuality]

Sons of good family, for what reason is the dhātu of nonconceptuality called "nonconceptual"? It is due to being beyond all conceptions that analyze, due to being beyond all conceptions in terms of demonstrating and illustrating,[880] due to being beyond all conceptions in terms of sense faculties, due to being beyond all conceptions in terms of objects, due to being beyond all conceptions in terms of cognizance, and due to not being the locus of any afflictive, secondary afflictive, and cognitive obscurations. Therefore, the dhātu of nonconceptuality is called "nonconceptual." What is nonconceptuality? Nonconceptuality is ungraspable, indemonstrable, unfounded, without appearance, noncognizance, and without base.[881]

[10) The signs of having entered it]

Through the nonconceptual wisdom that is not different from what is to be known, bodhisattva mahāsattvas who abide in the dhātu of nonconceptuality see all phenomena as being like the center of space. {M2b} Through the wisdom that is attained subsequent to that [nonconceptual wisdom], they see all phenomena as being like illusions, mirages, dreams, optical illusions, echoes, reflections, [reflections of] the moon [in] water, and magical creations.[882]

[11) Its benefits]

Therefore, they attain the vast mastery over dwelling in great bliss. They attain the vast great excellence of mind. They attain vast great prajñā and wisdom. They attain the vast mastery over great teaching.[883]

[12) Its activity]

At all times they will be able to promote all aspects of the welfare of all sentient beings. For effortless buddha activity is uninterrupted.[884] {D4a}

[13) Pointing out the dhātu of nonconceptuality through an example]

Sons of good family, it is thus. Assume that beneath very hard and solid rock mountain there is a great treasure full of all kinds of precious substances, that is, various great radiant precious substances that are wish-fulfilling jewels and consist of precious silver, precious gold, and various gems that are the cores of stone.[885] Then a person who wishes for a great treasure comes by. An [other] person who knows about that great treasure through supernatural knowledge says to the [first person], "O sir, beneath that very hard and solid rock mountain [there is] a great treasure full of radiant precious substances. Below that [treasure] [there is] a great treasure of the precious substance that is a wish-fulfilling jewel. So first you should dig up everything that has the nature of rock. Once you have dug up [all] that [rock], there will appear rock that appears to be silver. You should not think of this as being the great treasure, but fully know it [for what it is] and keep digging. Once you have dug out that [silver], there will appear rock that appears to be gold. You should not think of this as being the great treasure either, but fully know it [for what it is] too and keep digging. Once you have dug out that [gold], there will appear rock that appears to be various gems. You should not think of them as being the great treasure either, but fully know them [for what they are] and keep digging. Thus, O sir, having applied diligence, without [any further] exertion of digging you come to see the great treasure of the precious wish-fulfilling jewel without further effort. Through obtaining that great treasure of the precious wish-fulfilling jewel, you will be rich, having great wealth and great possessions, and be endowed with the power of [accomplishing] your own welfare and that of others."

Thus, O sons of good family, this example is given in order to make you understand the following meaning as best as possible. "Very hard and solid rock mountain" means the kinds of formation that consist of afflictiveness and being engrossed in duality. "A great treasure of the precious wish-fulfilling jewel below" refers to the dhātu of nonconceptuality. "The person who wishes for the great treasure of the precious wish-fulfilling jewel" {D4b} refers to a bodhisattva mahāsattva. "The person who knows about that great treasure through supernatural knowledge" refers to the arhat who is the Tathāgata, the completely perfect Buddha. "What has the nature of rock" refers to the characteristics of the conceptions about a nature. "Digging" means "not mentally engaging." "Rock that appears to be silver" stands for the characteristics of the conceptions that analyze the remedies. "Rock that appears to be gold" stands for the characteristics of the conceptions about emptiness and so on. "Rock that appears to be various gems" stands for the characteristics of the conceptions about attainment. "Obtaining the great treasure of the precious wish-fulfilling jewel" refers to making contact with the dhātu of nonconceptuality. Sons of good family, through adducing this example, the entering into nonconceptuality should be understood.[886]

[14) The means]

Sons of good family, how then do bodhisattva mahāsattvas who examine the characteristics of conceptions as taught [above] {M3a} enter the dhātu of nonconceptuality? Here, sons of good family, bodhisattva mahāsattvas who dwell in the dhātu of nonconceptuality, when the characteristics of the conceptions about a nature of form become perceptible [for them], examine them as follows. To entertain [the notion] "my form" is to entertain conceptions. To entertain [the notion] "the form of others" is to entertain conceptions. To entertain [the notion] "This is form" is to entertain conceptions. To entertain [the notions] "Form is arising, ceasing, afflicted, or purified" is to entertain conceptions. To entertain [the notion] "Form does not exist" is to entertain conceptions. To entertain [the notions] "[Form] neither exists by a nature of its own, nor does it exist as a cause, nor does it exist as a result, nor does it exist as karma, {D5a} nor does it exist as linkage, nor does it exist as a process" is to entertain conceptions. To entertain [the notion] "Form is mere cognizance" is to entertain conceptions. To entertain [the notion] "Just as form does not exist, so does the cognizance that appears as form not exist" is to entertain conceptions.

Therefore, sons of good family, bodhisattva mahāsattvas neither observe form nor do they observe the cognizance that appears as form. However, it is not that cognizance is utterly and completely nonexistent. Any other phenomenon apart from cognizance is not observable. This cognizance is not perceived as the lack of existence nor is the lack of existence perceived apart from cognizance. It is not that the lack of existence of the cognizance that appears as form and that cognizance are perceived as being one nor are they perceived as being different. It is not that the lack of existence of that cognizance is perceived as an existent nor is it perceived as a nonexistent. Sons of good family, what is not conceived by any aspects of all those conceptions—"the dhātu of nonconceptuality"—is not perceived either. Sons of good family, this is the way of entering the dhātu of nonconceptuality. In this way, bodhisattva mahāsattvas dwell in the dhātu of nonconceptuality. The same is to be applied to feeling, discrimination, formations, and consciousness; likewise, to the pāramitā of generosity, the pāramitā of ethics, the pāramitā of vigor, the pāramitā of dhyāna, and the pāramitā of prajñā; and likewise, to [everything] from emptiness and so on up through the knowledge of all aspects.

Sons of good family, bodhisattva {D5b} mahāsattvas, when the characteristics of the conceptions that analyze the knowledge of all aspects become perceptible [for them], examine them as follows. To entertain [the notion] "my knowledge of all aspects" is to entertain conceptions. To entertain [the notion] "the knowledge of all aspects of others" is to entertain conceptions. To entertain [the notion] "This is the knowledge of all aspects" is to entertain conceptions. To entertain [the notion] "The knowledge of all aspects is to be attained" is to entertain conceptions. To entertain [the notion] "The knowledge of all aspects relinquishes all afflictive and cognitive obscurations" is to entertain conceptions. To entertain [the notion] "The knowledge of all aspects is what is utterly purified"[887] is to entertain conceptions. To entertain [the notions] "The knowledge of all aspects is arising, ceasing, afflicted, or purified" is to entertain conceptions.[888] To entertain [the notion] "The knowledge of all aspects does not exist" is to entertain conceptions. To entertain [the notions] "The knowledge of all aspects neither exists by a nature of its own, nor does it exist as a cause, nor does it exist as a result, nor does it exist as karma, nor does it exist as linkage, nor does it exist as a process" is to entertain conceptions. To entertain [the notion] "The knowledge of all aspects is mere cognizance" is to entertain conceptions. {M3b} To entertain [the notion] "Just as the knowledge of all aspects does not exist, so does the cognizance that appears as the knowledge of all aspects not exist" is to entertain conceptions.

Therefore, just as bodhisattva mahāsattvas do not observe the knowledge of all aspects, so do they not observe the cognizance that appears as that [knowledge of all aspects]. However, it is not that the cognizance that is the [knowledge of all aspects] is utterly and completely nonexistent. Any other phenomenon apart from the cognizance that is the [knowledge of all aspects] is not observable. This cognizance is not perceived as the lack of existence nor is the lack of existence perceived apart from that cognizance. It is not that the lack of existence of the cognizance [that appears as the knowledge of all aspects] and that cognizance are perceived as being one {D6a} nor are they perceived as being different. It is not that the lack of existence of that cognizance is perceived as an existent nor is it perceived as a nonexistent. Sons of good family, what is not conceived by any aspects of all those conceptions[889]—"the dhātu of nonconceptuality"—is not perceived either. Sons of good family, this is the way of entering the dhātu of nonconceptuality. In this way, bodhisattva mahāsattvas dwell in the dhātu of nonconceptuality.[890]

Sons of good family, great is the merit of retaining, writing, preserving, and reading[891] this dharma specification. It is not equaled by giving away bodies as numerous as the sands of the River Gaṅgā. It is not equaled by giving away worldly realms as numerous as the sands of the River Gaṅgā that are full of gems.[892] It is not equaled by the amount of merit of giving away worldly realms as numerous as the sands of the River Gaṅgā that are full of buddha images. Then, at that point, the Bhagavān spoke the following two verses:

> The children of the Victor who reflected
> On nonconceptuality in this dharma,
> By transcending conceptions difficult to traverse,
> Gradually attain nonconceptuality.
>
> By virtue of that, bodhisattvas
> Discover the bliss of nonconceptuality,
> Which is peaceful, immovable, supreme,
> Powerful, and equal yet unequal.[893]

When the Bhagavān had spoken these words, the bodhisattva mahāsattva Avikalpaprabhāsa, the entire retinue, and the world with its gods, humans, asuras, and gandharvas rejoiced and praised the words of the Bhagavān.

Appendix 2: Topical outline of OED

1. The title and the homage spoken by the translators

2. The actual treatise

2.1. Presentation of the body [of the text]

2.2. The actual topics

2.2.1. Brief introduction

2.2.1.1. General instruction

2.2.1.2. The distinction of both [phenomena and the nature of phenomena]

2.2.1.3. The explanation of the defining characteristic of phenomena

2.2.1.3.1. The actual defining characteristic

2.2.1.3.2. Hermeneutical etymology of this [false imagination]

2.2.1.3.3. Teaching yet another meaning of imagination

2.2.1.4. The defining characteristic of the nature of phenomena

2.2.1.5. The manner of being mistaken

2.2.1.5.1. The appearing of what does not exist

2.2.1.5.2. The example [for false imagination]

2.2.1.5.3. The nonappearance of what exists

2.2.1.6. If one does not exist, [phenomena and the nature of phenomena] are not tenable as two

2.2.1.7. Not asserting [phenomena and the nature of phenomena] as being one or different

2.2.2. Detailed explanation

2.2.2.1. [The explanation of] comprehending phenomena

2.2.2.1.1. Brief introduction

2.2.2.1.2. Detailed explanation

2.2.2.1.2.1. The first three [points] being as in the brief introduction [above]

2.2.2.1.2.2. The matrix of phenomena

2.2.2.1.2.2.1. Brief introduction

2.2.2.1.2.2.2. Detailed explanation

2.2.2.1.2.2.2.1. [Their matrix that is] in common

2.2.2.1.2.2.2.2. Explanation of [their matrix that is] not in common

2.2.2.1.2.3. The manner of comprehending the nonexistence of the appearance [of apprehender and apprehended]

2.2.2.1.2.3.1. Comprehending the nonexistence of the appearance of the apprehended

2.2.2.1.2.3.2. Comprehending the nonexistence of the appearance of the apprehender

2.2.2.2. The explanation of comprehending the nature of phenomena

2.2.2.2.1. Brief introduction

2.2.2.2.2. Detailed explanation

2.2.2.2.2.1. Defining characteristic

2.2.2.2.2.2. The matrix of the nature of phenomena

2.2.2.2.2.3. The path of preparation

2.2.2.2.2.4. The path of seeing

2.2.2.2.2.5. Explanation of the path of familiarization

2.2.2.2.2.6. The path of completion (arrival)

2.2.2.2.2.7. Explanation of the fundamental change

2.2.2.2.2.7.1. Connecting [passage]

2.2.2.2.2.7.2. Brief introduction

2.2.2.2.2.7.3. Detailed explanation

2.2.2.2.2.7.3.1. Explanation of the nature of the fundamental change

2.2.2.2.2.7.3.2. Which entities undergo the fundamental change

2.2.2.2.2.7.3.3. The persons who undergo the fundamental change

2.2.2.2.2.7.3.3.1. [The fundamental changes that are] not in common

2.2.2.2.2.7.3.3.2. [The fundamental change that is] in common

2.2.2.2.2.7.3.4. Instruction on the distinctive features of the fundamental change

2.2.2.2.2.7.3.4.1. The distinctive feature in terms of realms

2.2.2.2.2.7.3.4.2. The distinctive feature in terms of attainment

2.2.2.2.2.7.3.5. Explanation of comprehending the distinctive features of the prerequisites

2.2.2.2.2.7.3.6. Instruction on the foundation of all this, based on which the fundamental change takes place

2.2.2.2.2.7.3.6.1. Brief introduction

2.2.2.2.2.7.3.6.2. Detailed explanation

2.2.2.2.2.7.3.6.2.1. Explanation of the fourfold comprehension of the focal objects

2.2.2.2.2.7.3.6.2.2. Instruction on the comprehension of the relinquishment of characteristics

2.2.2.2.2.7.3.6.2.3. The correct yogic practice

2.2.2.2.2.7.3.6.2.4. The defining characteristics of nonconceptual [wisdom]

2.2.2.2.2.7.3.6.2.4.1. The characteristic of how it abides

2.2.2.2.2.7.3.6.2.4.2. The characteristic of nonappearance

2.2.2.2.2.7.3.6.2.4.3. The characteristic of appearance

2.2.2.2.2.7.3.6.2.5. Explanation of the fourfold comprehension of the benefit

2.2.2.2.2.7.3.6.2.6. The comprehension of the thorough knowledge

2.2.2.2.2.7.3.6.2.6.1. [Brief] introduction

2.2.2.2.2.7.3.6.2.6.2. Explanation of nonconceptual wisdom being the remedy of five factors

2.2.2.2.2.7.3.6.2.6.3. Explanation of the defining characteristic

2.2.2.2.2.7.3.6.2.6.4. Explanation of the five kinds of distinctive features

2.2.2.2.2.7.3.6.2.6.5. Explanation of the five functions of wisdom

2.2.2.2.2.7.3.7. Explanation of the mental engagement

2.2.2.2.2.7.3.7.1. Through what [bodhisattvas] engage mentally

2.2.2.2.2.7.3.7.2. The manner in which they engage mentally and the progression [of that]

2.2.2.2.2.7.3.7.2.1. Examination of the manner of being mistaken by virtue of the ālaya, conditions, and ignorance appearing, but not really existing

2.2.2.2.2.7.3.7.2.2. The manner of mental engagement

Glossary: English–Sanskrit–Tibetan

English	Sanskrit	Tibetan
adventitious stains	āgantukamala	glo bur gyi dri ma
afflicted phenomena	saṃkleśa	kun nas nyon mongs pa
afflictive obscuration	kleśāvaraṇa	nyon mongs pa'i sgrib pa
ālaya-wisdom	—	kun gzhi'i ye shes
basic element	dhātu	khams
cognitive obscuration	jñeyāvaraṇa	shes bya'i sgrib pa
contaminated	sāsrava	zag bcas
correct imagination	bhūtaparikalpa	yang dag kun rtog
dependent (nature)	paratantra(svabhāva)	gzhan dbang (gi rang bzhin)
dharmas concordant with enlightenment	bodhipakṣadharma	byang chub phyogs chos
disposition	gotra	rigs
emptiness endowed with the supreme of all aspects	sarvākāravaropetā-śūnyatā	rnam kun mchog ldan gyi stong pa nyid
engagement through aspiration	adhimukticaryā	mos pas spyod pa
entity	bhāva/vastu	dngos po
factors conducive to liberation	mokṣabhāgīya	thar pa cha mthun
factors conducive to penetration	nirvedhabhāgīya	nges 'byed cha mthun
false imagination	abhūtaparikalpa	yang dag ma yin kun rtog

freedom from reference points	niṣprapañca	spros bral
fundamental change	āśrayaparivṛtti/ āśrayaparāvṛtti	gnas (yongs su) gyur pa
ground of the latent tendencies of ignorance	avidyāvāsanābhūmi	ma rig bag chags kyi sa
identitylessness	nairātmya	bdag med
imaginary (nature)	parikalpita(svabhāva)	kun brtags (kyi rang bzhin)
implicative negation	paryudāsapratiṣedha	ma yin dgag
impregnations of negative tendencies	dauṣṭhulya	gnas ngan len pa
imputedly existent	prajñaptisat	btags yod
innate	sahaja	lhan skyes
isolate	vyatireka	ldog pa
lack of nature	niḥsvabhāva	ngo bo nyid/rang bzhin med pa
latent tendencies for listening	śrutavāsanā	thos pa'i bag chags
latent tendency	vāsanā	bag chags
meditative absorption of cessation	nirodhasamāpatti	'gog pa'i snyoms 'jug
mental consciousness	manovijñāna	yid kyi rnam shes
mental nonengagement	amanasikāra	yid la mi byed pa
mentation	manas	yid
mere cognizance	vijñaptimātra	rnam rig tsam
Mere Mentalist	—	sems tsam pa
mere mind/Mere Mentalism	cittamātra	sems tsam
mind as such	cittatvam, cittam eva	sems nyid
natural outflow	niṣyanda	rgyu mthun pa
naturally abiding disposition	prakṛtisthagotra	rang bzhin gnas rigs

nature of phenomena	dharmatā	chos nyid
nonconceptual wisdom	nirvikalpajñāna	rnam par mi rtog pa'i ye shes
nondual wisdom	advayajñāna	gnyis med ye shes
nonentity	abhāva/avastu	dngos med
nonimplicative negation	prasajyapratiṣedha	med dgag
nonobservation	anupalabdhi, anupalambha	mi dmigs pa
nonreferential	anupalambha, anālambana	mi dmigs pa, dmigs med
path of accumulation	sambhāramārga	tshogs lam
path of familiarization	bhāvanāmārga	sgom lam
path of liberation	vimuktimārga	rnam grol lam
path of nonlearning	aśaikṣamārga	mi slob pa'i lam
path of preparation	prayogamārga	sbyor lam
path of seeing	darśanamārga	mthong lam
perfect (nature)	pariniṣpanna (svabhāva)	yongs grub (kyi rang bzhin)
personal identitylessness	pudgalanairātmya	gang zag gi bdag med
personally experienced (wisdom)	pratyātmavedanīya (jñāna) (svapratyātmāryajñāna)	so so rang rig (pa'i ye shes)
phenomenal identitylessness	dharmanairātmya	chos kyi bdag med
philosophical system	siddhānta	grub mtha'
purified phenomenon	vyavadāna	rnam par byang ba
reference point	prapañca	spros pa
referent	artha	don
result of freedom	visaṃyogaphala	bral ba'i 'bras bu
seeming (reality)	saṃvṛti(satya)	kun rdzob (bden pa)
self-aware(ness)	svasaṃvedana, svasaṃvitti	rang rig
subsequent attainment	pṛṣṭhalabdha	rjes thob

substantially existent	dravyasat	rdzas yod
superior intention	adhyāśaya	lhag pa'i bsam pa
three natures	trisvabhāva	ngo bo nyid/rang bzhin gsum
three spheres	trimaṇḍala	'khor gsum
true end	bhūtakoṭi	yang dag pa'i mtha'
true reality	tattva	de (kho na) nyid
ultimate (reality)	paramārtha(satya)	don dam (bden pa)
unconditioned (phenomenon)	asaṃskṛta	'dus ma byas
uncontaminated	anāsrava	zag med
unfolding disposition	paripuṣṭagotra	rgyas 'gyur gyi rigs
valid cognition	pramāṇa	tshad ma
views about a real personality	satkāyadṛṣṭi	'jig tshogs la lta ba
wisdom of knowing suchness	yathāvatjñāna	ji lta ba mkhyen pa'i ye shes
wisdom of knowing variety	yāvatjñāna	ji snyed mkhyen pa'i ye shes
yogic practice	prayoga	sbyor ba
yogic valid perception	yogipratyakṣapramāṇa	rnal 'byor mngon sum tshad ma

Glossary: Tibetan–Sanskrit–English

Tibetan	Sanskrit	English
kun brtags (kyi rang bzhin)	parikalpita(svabhāva)	imaginary (nature)
kun nas nyon mongs pa	saṃkleśa	afflicted phenomenon
kun rdzob (bden pa)	saṃvṛti(satya)	seeming (reality)
kun gzhi'i ye shes	—	ālaya-wisdom
khams	dhātu	basic element
'khor gsum	trimaṇḍala	three spheres
gang zag gi bdag med	pudgalanairātmya	personal identitylessness
glo bur gyi dri ma	āgantukamala	adventitious stains
'gog pa'i snyoms 'jug	nirodhasamāpatti	meditative absorption of cessation
rgyas 'gyur gyi rigs	paripuṣṭagotra	unfolding disposition
rgyu mthun	niṣyanda	natural outflow
sgom lam	bhāvanāmārga	path of familiarization
nges 'byed cha mthun	nirvedhabhāgīya	factors conducive to penetration
ngo bo nyid med pa	niḥsvabhāva	lack of nature
dngos po	bhāva/vastu	entity
dngos med	abhāva/avastu	nonentity
chos kyi bdag med	dharmanairātmya	phenomenal identitylessness
chos nyid	dharmatā	nature of phenomena
ji snyed mkhyen pa'i ye shes	yāvatjñāna	wisdom of knowing variety

ji lta ba mkhyen pa'i ye shes	yathāvatjñāna	wisdom of knowing suchness
'jig tshogs la lta ba	satkāyadṛṣṭi	views about a real personality
rjes thob	pṛṣṭhalabdha	subsequent attainment
nyon mongs pa'i sgrib pa	kleśāvaraṇa	afflictive obscuration
gnyis med ye shes	advayajñāna	nondual wisdom
btags yod	prajñaptisat	imputedly existent
thar pa cha mthun	mokṣabhāgīya	factors conducive to liberation
thos pa'i bag chags	śrutavāsanā	latent tendencies for listening
mthong lam	darśanamārga	path of seeing
de (kho na) nyid	tattva	true reality
don	artha	referent
don dam (bden pa)	paramārtha(satya)	ultimate (reality)
'dus byas	saṃskṛta	conditioned (phenomenon)
'dus ma byas	asaṃskṛta	unconditioned (phenomenon)
ldog pa	vyatireka	isolate
gnas ngan len pa	dauṣṭhulya	impregnations of negative tendencies
gnas (yongs su) gyur pa	āśrayaparivṛtti/ āśrayaparāvṛtti	fundamental change
rnam kun mchog ldan gyi stong pa nyid	sarvākāravaropetā-śūnyatā	emptiness endowed with the supreme of all aspects
rnam grol lam	vimuktimārga	path of liberation
rnam par byang ba	vyavadāna	purified phenomenon
rnam par mi rtog pa'i ye shes	nirvikalpajñāna	nonconceptual wisdom
rnam rig tsam	vijñaptimātra	mere cognizance
rnal 'byor mngon sum tshad ma	yogipratyakṣapramāṇa	yogic valid perception

spros pa	prapañca	reference point
spros bral	niṣprapañca	freedom from reference points
bag chags	vāsanā	latent tendency
bar chad med lam	ānantaryamārga	uninterrupted path
byang chub phyogs chos	bodhipakṣadharma	dharmas concordant with enlightenment
bral ba'i 'bras bu	visaṃyogaphala	result of freedom
sbyor ba	prayoga	yogic practice
sbyor lam	prayogamārga	path of preparation
ma yin dgag	paryudāsapratiṣedha	implicative negation
ma rig bag chags kyi sa	avidyāvāsanābhūmi	ground of the latent tendencies of ignorance
mi dmigs pa	anupalabdhi, anupalambha	nonobservation, nonreferential
mi slob lam	aśaikṣamārga	path of nonlearning
med dgag	prasajyapratiṣedha	nonimplicative negation
mos pas spyod pa	adhimukticaryā	engagement through aspiration
dmigs med	anupalambha, anupalabdhi	nonreferential, nonobservation
tshad ma	pramāṇa	valid cognition
tshogs lam	sambhāramārga	path of accumulation
rdzas yod	dravyasat	substantially existent
gzhan dbang (gi rang bzhin)	paratantra(svabhāva)	dependent (nature)
zag bcas	sāsrava	contaminated
zag med	anāsrava	uncontaminated
yang dag kun rtog	bhūtaparikalpa	correct imagination
yang dag pa'i mtha'	bhūtakoṭi	true end
yang dag ma yin kun rtog	abhūtaparikalpa	false imagination
yid	manas	mentation
yid la mi byed pa	amanasikāra	mental nonengagement

yongs grub (kyi rang bzhin)	pariniṣpanna (svabhāva)	perfect (nature)
rang bzhin gnas rigs	prakṛtisthagotra	naturally abiding disposition
rang bzhin med pa	niḥsvabhāva	lack of nature
rang bzhin gsum	trisvabhāva	three natures
rang rig	svasaṃvedana, svasaṃvitti	self-aware(ness)
rigs	gotra	disposition
shes bya'i sgrib pa	jñeyāvaraṇa	cognitive obscuration
sems nyid	cittatvam, cittam eva	mind as such
sems tsam	cittamātra	mere mind, Mere Mentalism
sems tsam pa	—	Mere Mentalist
so so rang rig (pa'i ye shes)	pratyātmavedanīya (jñāna) (svapratyātmāryajñāna)	personally experienced (wisdom)
lhag pa'i bsam pa	adhyāśaya	superior intention
lhan skyes	sahaja	innate

Notes

1 Tib. rang byung rdo rje.

2 Tib. 'gos lo tsā ba gzhon nu dpal.

3 This text is now lost, but is quoted in some other preserved Yogācāra works, such as in *Mahāyānasaṃgraha* III.17.

4 According to H. Shiu (Robertson 2008, p. 447), the earliest Chinese work to mention the term "the five texts of Maitreya" and to identify them with the above five works seems to be Dunlun's *Yujia lunji* (*Compendium of the Yogācāra Treatises*; Taishō vol. 42, p. 311b). As for the *Vajracchedikāvyākhyā*, the Chinese canon contains two commentaries on the *Vajracchedikāprajñāpāramitāsūtra* (Taishō 1510 and 1511). However, neither of them is ascribed to Maitreya, but they are attributed to Asaṅga and Vasubandhu, respectively.

5 Tib. byams chos sde lnga.

6 Tib. ldan dkar ma *and* 'phang thang ma.

7 As evidenced by the references to the *Dharmadharmatāvibhāga* and the *Uttaratantra* in Jñānaśrīmitra's and Ratnākaraśānti's works and Ngog Lotsāwa's synopsis of the *Uttaratantra* (see also Ruegg 1969, p. 35). Kong sprul blo gros mtha' yas 2005 (p. 7) claims that, according to Haribhadra, all five Maitreya texts were composed for the sake of Asaṅga. However, no such statement can be found in Haribhadra's works in the *Tengyur*.

8 Tib. ka ba dpal brtsegs.

9 Tib. ye shes sde.

10 Tib. rngog lo tsā ba blo ldan shes rab.

11 Tib. (zha ma) seng ge rgyal mtshan.

12 This is most probably Nagtso Lotsāwa Tsültrim Gyalwa (1011–1064; Tib. nag tsho lo tsā ba tshul khrims rgyal ba).

13 Tib. gzu dga' ba'i rdo rje.

14 Tib. spa tshab lo tsā ba nyi ma grags.

15 Tib. jo nang lo tsā ba blo gros dpal.

16 Tib. yar lung lo tsā ba grags pa rgyal mtshan.

17 Tib. mar pa do pa chos kyi dbang phyug. Though he also studied with Nāropa and his students as well as Maitrīpa, he is not to be confused with his older contemporay Marpa Chökyi Lodrö (1012–1097), the founder of the Kagyü School.

18 However, 'Ju mi pham rgya mtsho 1984 (fol. 25b.5–6) claims that, according to some historical records, all five dharma works of Maitreya had already been translated during the early translation period. Since great paṇḍitas such as Śāntarakṣita, Kamalaśīla, and so on dwelled in Tibet and the teachings were in full bloom in India at that time, MC says there is no doubt that there were translations of these texts. TOK (p. 460) says that an infinite number of sūtras of the third dharmacakra and commentaries on their intention were translated during the early translation period.

19 The ones used here include 'Gos lo tsā ba gzhon nu dpal 2003a (vol. 1, pp. 422–25), 'Gos lo tsā ba gzhon nu dpal 2003b (p. 4), Kong sprul blo gros mtha' yas 2005 (pp. 4–10), TOK (vol. 1, pp. 460–61 and vol. 2, pp. 543–44), Śākya mchog ldan 1975 (pp. 239–41), Kun dga' grol mchog 1981 (pp. 82–84), MC (pp. 5–6), RC (p. 142), Chos grags bstan 'phel 1990 (pp. 2–8), and Shes rab phun tshogs 2007 (pp. 2–9).

20 Tib. kong sprul blo gros mtha' yas.

21 Tib. dkar po rnam par 'char ba.

22 A similar statement about Dharmapāla is found in Śākya mchog ldan 1975 (p. 220). However, neither the *Tengyur* nor the Chinese canon contain such a text by Dharmapāla. In the Chinese canon, there is a commentary by him on Āryadeva's *Catuḥśataka* (Taishō 1571) which explains that text from a Yogācāra perspective.

23 This probably means paṇḍitas other than Asaṅga (to whom the Tibetan tradition attributes RGVV as a separate text, while others consider it to be a unit with the verses of the *Uttaratantra*) and Vasubandhu (who wrote the *Dharmadharmatāvibhāgavṛtti*). By extension, the unavailablity of the *Uttaratantra* and the *Dharmadharmatāvibhāga* in India for some time must have included RGVV and the *Dharmadharmatāvibhāgavṛtti*.

24 According to RC (p. 142), it was a disciple of Maitrīpa named *Aṇarakṣita who retrieved the Maitreya texts from a four-storied sandalwood stūpa and then passed them on to Sajjana and the latter's son, Mahājana.

25 Indeed, from the seventh to tenth centuries there seems to be no Indian text that quotes the *Uttaratantra* (though some of them discuss the topic of *tathāgatagarbha*), whereas the work is cited in a significant number of Indian Buddhist texts from the eleventh to thirteenth century. However, as Kano 2006 (p. 22) points out, there are two texts that indicate the possibility of the transmission of the *Uttaratantra* occurring at least throughout the eighth century. The *Sarvatathāgatatattvasaṃgraha* (late seventh to eighth century) uses terms such as *garbha*, *dhātu*, and *ratnagotra* in accordance with the *Uttaratantra* (see Matsunaga 1980, pp. 187ff. as well as Inui 1998 and 2000). Also, a Khotan-Saka hybrid Sanskrit fragment of the *Uttaratantra* (CH 0047 in the Stein collection at the India Office, edited in Bailey and Johnston 1935) from the end of the eighth century quotes *Uttaratantra* I.1, III.1–8, III.10, and V.3d, referring to the text as the *Ratnagotravibhāgaśāstra* by Maitreya. In any case, a Sanskrit manuscript of the *Uttaratantra* was brought to China by Ratnamati in 508 and was translated by him in ca. 511, so it must have still been available in India in the early sixth century. It is said that Bodhiruci's collaboration with Buddhasānta and Ratnamati (who both greatly emphasized the *tathāgatagarbha* teachings) in translating Vasubandhu's commentary on the *Daśabhūmikasūtra* came to an end over their disagreement as to whether *tathāgatagarbha* represents classical Yogācāra thought or not. In addition, Paramārtha (499–569) translated and widely taught a great number of Yogācāra and *tathāgatagarbha* materials in sixth-century China. Takasaki 1966 (pp. 45–54), 1989 (pp. 412–15), and 1999 discusses a number of texts from the sixth and seventh centuries that appear to have been influenced by the *Uttaratantra*. These are the **Buddhagotraśāstra* (Taishō 1610), the **Anuttarāśrayasūtra* (Taishō 669; both translated or even composed by Paramārtha), the **Dharmadhātvaviśeṣaśāstra* (Taishō 1627), and two Chinese translations of a *trikāya* chapter

in the *Suvarṇaprabhāsottamasūtra* (Taishō 664 and 665) which is absent in the Sanskrit and Tibetan versions of this sūtra. However, since these texts are only available in the Chinese canon and the **Buddhagotraśāstra* and the **Anuttarāśrayasūtra* are not unlikely to have been authored by Paramārtha, it is uncertain whether they are indeed translations of Indian texts. As for Maitrīpa having rediscovered the *Dharmadharmatāvibhāga* and the *Uttaratantra*, both texts are already quoted in two works by two teachers of Maitrīpa. Jñānaśrīmitra's (c. 980–1040) *Sākārasiddhiśāstra* mentions the *Dharmadharmatāvibhāga* by name and quotes what corresponds to lines 24 and 27 in DDV (K) (Jñānaśrīmitra 1987, p. 432.10–13) as well as a number of verses of the *Uttaratantra* (for details, see Kano 2006, pp. 33–38, 85, and 577–97). Likewise, Ratnākaraśānti's *Sūtrasamuccayabhāṣya* (D3935, fols. 297a.1–2 and 325a.6–7) quotes *Uttaratantra* I.28 and I.96–97. Though not entirely impossible, it seems somewhat unlikely that Maitrīpa's teachers only quoted the *Dharmadharmatāvibhāga* and *Uttaratantra* in their texts after their student Maitrīpa had rediscovered them.

26 LDC (fols. 18b.4–19a.5) also reports this account as being found in some commentaries (such as RC), but then quotes one of the Paṇchen Lamas as saying, "Though this account is surely fine in general, Atiśa and Nagtso Lotsāwa translated the root text of the treatise and its commentary (judging from the context and what LDC says below, this seems to refer not only to the *Uttaratantra* and RGVV, which were indeed translated by Atiśa and Nagtso, but also to DDV and DDVV, though there are no records that these two texts were also translated by them). Therefore, it is certain that Atiśa had studied the root text and its commentary from a teacher. However, since it is difficult to claim that this teacher could have been Maitrīpa, it needs to be examined whether this teaching was or was not obtainable from Maitrīpa alone." LDC then claims that, upon analysis according to this statement, it is clear that this teaching was not obtainable at the time from Maitrīpa alone. For Ngog Lotsāwa studied the DDV as progressively transmitted from Asaṅga and Vasubandhu up through the Kashmiri Jñānaśrī, but Maitrīpa does not appear in this lineage. Therefore, it is certain that this text existed before Maitrīpa in India until the Buddhist teachings became extinct there. Consequently, LDC says, the above account obviously only applies to the narrative of a particular place and time. Obviously both the *Blue Annals* and LDC refer to the Kashmiri paṇḍita Jñānaśrī (eleventh century) as having obtained the *Uttaratantra* and DDV. However, while the *Blue Annals* says that he received these texts from Sajjana via *Ānandakīrti and Maitrīpa, LDC claims a different lineage, starting with Asaṅga and Vasubandhu (without, however, providing any specifics or names). Jñānaśrī is known to have been active in western Tibet as a teacher-translator, playing an important role in spreading the teachings on valid cognition (*pramāṇa*) and the *Abhisamayālaṃkāra*. He also composed a number of texts preserved in the *Tengyur* (such as commentaries on the *Laṅkāvatārasūtra* and the *Heart Sūtra* as well as a *Pramāṇaviniścayaṭīkā*). However, to my knowledge, there are no accounts of his having received the *Uttaratantra*, DDV, and their commentaries from anybody but Sajjana, nor are there any records that he taught these texts to Ngog Lotsāwa. All available records agree that Ngog received teachings on these texts from Sajjana. Ngog also translated the *Uttaratantra* and RGVV together with Sajjana and collaborated with the latter's son, Mahājana, in translating DDV and DDVV. As for the above statement that it is difficult to claim Maitrīpa as the one who taught the *Uttaratantra*, DDV, and their commentaries to Atiśa, no reasons for this being "difficult" are given. Though it is indeed unlikely that Maitrīpa as the by far younger paṇḍita would have taught Atiśa, it is not entirely impossible, especially if he had indeed rediscovered these texts and received explanations on them from Maitreya in a vision. In any case, it is clear from the historical records that Atiśa became chief abbot of Vikramaśīla before Maitrīpa left it to meet his guru Śavari, and there are some accounts in the Tibetan tradition of how Atiśā and Maitrīpa met at Vikramaśīla. In sum, LDC's unsupported claims about a different lineage of the Maitreya texts having reached Ngog Lotsāwa sound very much like an attempt to establish an independent Kadampa—and thus Gelugpa—transmission of these texts that does not involve Maitrīpa as a forebear of the Kagyü School.

27 This is what is commonly accepted (see also Kong sprul blo gros mtha' yas 2005, p. 9), but Tāranātha 1980 (p. 302) refers to Mahājana as being the father of Sajjana and the son of Ratnavajra. However, the colophon of the *Putralekha* by Sajjana (D4187) says that it was translated by Mahājana and Marpa. Moreover, as a letter to a son, *Putralekha* IV.18c addresses and admonishes Mahājana by name.

28 Tib. rin chen bzang po.

29 Tāranātha 1980, pp. 295 and 301.

30 His *Rgyud bla ma'i 'grel pa* (172 fols.) is listed on p. 1403 of the *'Bras spungs dgon du bzhugs su gsol ba'i dpe rnying dkar chag*, Dpal brtsegs bod yig dpe rnying zhib 'jug khang, 2 vols. (Chengdu: Si khron mi rigs dpe skrun khang, 2005).

31 Mi bskyod rdo rje 2003, vol. 1, p. 35.

32 These three stages are based on *Uttaratantra* II.57–59, which speaks of making saṃsāric beings enter the path to the peace of śrāvakas and pratyekabuddhas, bringing śrāvakas and pratyekabuddhas to maturation in the mahāyāna, and then, on the eighth bodhisattvabhūmi, granting them the prophecy of their supreme enlightenment.

33 Given that Vasubandhu's *Dharmadharmatāvibhāgavṛtti* and early Tibetan commentaries comment on a prose version of the *Dharmadharmatāvibhāga* and due to textual correspondences between the *Dharmadharmatāvibhāgakārikā* (D4023) and the prose version of the *Dharmadharmatāvibhāga* contained in the *Dharmadharmatāvibhāgavṛtti* that are not found in the prose version on its own (D4022), it seems that there was no original kārikā version of the *Dharmadharmatāvibhāga*, but that it was abstracted from the prose version in the *Dharmadharmatāvibhāgavṛtti*.

34 The former is also referred to as "the tradition of studying and reflecting on the dharma works of Maitreya" (*byams chos thos bsam gyi lugs*). Ngog's interpretation of the *Uttaratantra* was later adopted in most points by the Sakya and Gelug schools. TOK (vol. 1, pp. 460–61) calls the two traditions *bshad pa'i bka' babs* and *sgrub pa'i bka' babs*, respectively, and says that they are asserted to hold the views of Madhyamaka versus Mere Mentalism. Shes rab phun tshogs 2007 (pp. 8–9) reports what the present tutor to the Seventeenth Karmapa, Khenchen Thrangu Rinpoche (born 1933), states about the main difference between the exegetical and the meditative traditions of the works of Maitreya. The former is said to explain the meaning of *tathāgatagarbha* mainly as the element that is the basic nature of phenomena in the sense of the empty dharmadhātu free from all reference points, which is the emptiness that is a nonimplicative negation and is explained in Nāgārjuna's collection of reasoning. The latter explains the meaning of *tathāgatagarbha* mainly as the element of luminosity that is wisdom and is characterized by being the emptiness that is a nonimplicative negation. That there in fact was (and still is) a meditative tradition of practicing the contents of the *Uttaratantra* is also highlighted by Rongtön saying in his *Stages of Meditation on the* Uttaratantra (Rong ston shes bya kun gzigs 1999, p. 529) that he presents the manner of making the *Uttaratantra* a living experience by summarizing the meaning that is explained in Nāropa's pith instructions.

35 Tib. grva pa mngon shes. He was instrumental in the transmission of the four medicine tantras in Tibet.

36 To make a teaching one's "death dharma" means that one takes it as the basis for one's practice when dying in order to attain buddhahood, become liberated from saṃsāra, or at least obtain another favorable rebirth.

37 Interestingly, the biography of Ra Lotsāwa Dorje Trag (Tib. rva lo tsā ba rdo rje grags; born 1016) states that Ngog Lotsāwa, together with Dsen Kawoché, Nyen Lotsāwa Tarma Trag (Tib. gnyan lo tsā ba dar ma grags), and others, had already studied the treatises of Maitreya

with paṇḍita Prajñāna, a teacher of Dsen, at the dharma council at Tholing organized by King Dsedé (Tib. rtse lde) in 1076 (Rva Ye shes seng ge, *Mthu stobs dbang phyug rje btsun rwa lo tsā ba'i rnam par thar pa kun khyab snyan pa'i rnga sgra*, Mtsho sngon mi rigs dpe skrun khang, 1989, p. 206.2–8). According to this, all Maitreya texts, including the *Uttaratantra* and the *Dharmadharmatāvibhāga*, would have been known at least in the Tholing area in western Tibet starting with that event.

38 See A khu Shes rab rgya mtsho's *Dpe rgyun dkon pa 'ga' zhig gi tho yig* (Lokesh Chandra 1963, vol. 3, no. 11338), which lists "an exposition of the *Uttaratantra* composed by the translator Su Gawé Dorje as his notes on what paṇḍita Sajjana taught" (*paṇḍita sajjana'i gsung la lo tsā ba gzu dga' rdor gyi zin bris byas pa'i rgyud bla ma'i rnam bshad*).

39 Tib. pad ma seng ge.

40 Tib. lcang ra ba.

41 Tib. 'phyos mdo sde sbug dar ma brtson 'grus.

42 Tib. zhi byed.

43 This text is by Kyodön Mönlam Tsültrim (Tib. skyo ston smon lam tshul khrims; 1219–1299), the eighth abbot of Nartang Monastery (from 1285 to 1299). It was recently published in *Bka' gdams gsung 'bum phyogs sgrig thengs gnyis pa*, Dpal brtsegs bod yig dpe rnying zhib 'jug khang nas bsgrigs, vol. 50 (Chengdu: Si khron mi rigs dpe skrun khang, 2007), pp. 293–304. There is also a *Theg chen rgyud bla ma'i gdams pa* by the same author (ibid., pp. 147–56). Both texts contain direct pointing-out instructions in accord with *Shentong* and Mahāmudrā based on the *Uttaratantra*. They are partly translated and analyzed in Mathes forthcoming and Brunnhölzl 2011a, pp. 190–94.

44 Tib. srin po ri.

45 Tib. rgyal rtse.

46 In effect, this means that, at least according to Gö Lotsāwa, "the meditative tradition of the Maitreya dharmas" had become extinct in Tibet at this time.

47 Tib. yu mo ba mi bskyod rdo rje.

48 See Kong sprul blo gros mtha' yas 2005 (p. 19), Chos grags bstan 'phel 1990 (p. 8), and Shes rab phun tshogs 2007 (p. 8).

49 Tib. dol po pa shes rab rgyal mtshan.

50 This tradition only became known as Jo nang after the founding of the monastery with that name by Künpang Tugjé Dsöndrü (Tib. kun spang thugs rje brtson 'grus; 1243–1313).

51 Tib. gsal sgron skor bzhi—*Zung 'jug gsal sgron*, *Phyag rgya chen po'i gsal sgron*, *'Od gsal gsal sgron*, and *Stong nyid gsal ba'i sgron me*.

52 Tib. kun gzhi ye shes. For more details, see Stearns 2010, pp. 43–45.

53 Tāranātha 1982–1987, vol. 2, p. 16: *sngags kyi gzhan stong grub mtha'i srol ka phye*. It is most probably due to Kongtrul's general great reliance on Tāranātha that he also mentions Yumowa in connection with *Shentong*.

54 Tib. gsang phu ne'u thog.

55 Tib. zhang tshe spong chos kyi bla ma.

56 Tib. phya pa chos kyi seng ge.

57 Tib. dan bag pa smra ba'i seng ge.

58 Tib. gtsang nag pa rigs pa'i seng ge. Interestingly, TOK (vol. 1, p. 461) includes a Gtsang nag pa in its list of upholders of the *Shentong* view. Chos grags bstan 'phel 1990 (p. 7) has an unidentifiable Gtsang nag pa Rigs pa'i seng ge. In both cases, most probably Dsangnagpa Dsöndrü Sengé is meant.

59 Kong sprul blo gros mtha' yas 2005 (p. 9) and Shes rab phun tshogs 2007 (p. 7) add a number of other early commentators on the *Uttaratantra* in this tradition, such as Ngog's main student, Trolungpa Lodrö Jungné (Tib. gro lung pa blo gros 'byung gnas), Nyangtrenpa Chökyi Yeshé (Tib. nyang bran pa chos kyi ye shes; both eleventh century), Sangpupa Lodrö Tsungmé (Tib. gsang phu pa blo gros mtshungs med; thirteenth/fourteenth century), Pagtru Gyaltsen Sangpo (tib. phag gru rgyal mtshan bzang po; 1350–1425), and Rongtön Shéja Künrig (Tib. rong ston shes bya kun rig; 1367–1449). Despite some of them using slightly different terminologies, all are said to agree with Ngog in explaining the meaning of *tathāgatagarbha* according to the exegetical tradition of the works of Maitreya. For extensive lists of Indian and Tibetan commentaries on the *Uttaratantra*, see Kano 2006 (pp. 611–18) and Burchardi 2006.

60 Rngog lo tsā ba blo ldan shes rab 1993, fol. 1b.2–2a.1.

61 This is the name of the third turning of the wheel of dharma in the *Dhāraṇīśvararājaparipṛcchāsūtra*.

62 Bcom ldan 'das rig pa'i ral gri 1981, pp. 167–69.

63 Blo bzang rta dbyangs 1975–1976, fols. 2a.1–3a.7 and 4b.5–5a.5.

64 For example, *Madhyāntavibhāga* I.3–4 explains in which ways false imagination manifests as saṃsāra (as referents, sentient beings, a self, and cognizance) and that liberation (nirvāṇa) comes about by virtue of the exhaustion of this false imagination. Also, lines III.10bd and Vasubandhu's *Bhāṣya* state that the imaginary nature (designation) and the dependent nature (cognizance) make up the coarse seeming reality, while the perfect nature alone is the subtle ultimate reality. *Mahāyānasaṃgraha* II.28–29 (D4048, fol. 19b.4–7) says, "'With what in mind did the Bhagavān teach in the *Brahmāparipṛccha[sūtra]* that the Tathāgata neither observes saṃsāra nor observes nirvāṇa?' He taught this by having in mind that there is no difference between saṃsāra and nirvāṇa because the dependent nature is [both] the imaginary and perfect natures. Thus, [in terms of] this very dependent nature being the phenomena of the imaginary, it is saṃsāra. [In terms of its] being the phenomena of the perfect [nature], it is nirvāṇa. . . . The existence of the imaginary nature in the dependent nature is that which is included in the set of what is afflicted. The existence of the perfect nature in the dependent nature is that which is included in the set of what is purified." OED (p. 497) states exactly what Lobsang Dayang denies: "The nature [of phenomena and their nature] consists of the three natures, with saṃsāra [consisting] of the imaginary and the dependent [natures], while the perfect [nature]—suchness and perfect wisdom—represents nirvāṇa." Likewise, SC (pp. 149–50) identifies phenomena as saṃsāra, consisting of the imaginary and the dependent natures, and the nature of phenomena as nirvāṇa, being the perfect nature. MC (fols. 4a.6–5a.2) also repeatedly equates phenomena and the nature of phenomena with saṃsāra and nirvāṇa, respectively. LZC (p. 3) says that all the Buddha's presentations of skandhas, dhātus, āyatanas, the four realities, the two realities, the three natures, and so on are included in seeming phenomena (nonexistents that appear) and the nature of phenomena (the dhātu that is the ultimate basic nature) because all of saṃsāra and nirvāṇa is included in these two.

65 Tib. rgyal tshab dar ma rin chen.

66 Tāranātha even wrote two commentaries on the *Heart Sūtra* from the perspective of *shentong* (Tāranātha n.d., vol. 17, pp. 571–759 and 759–83).

67 Sa bzang ma ti paṇ chen 'jam dbyangs blo gros rgyal mtshan 1999, pp. 16.1–17.2.

68 Bu ston rin chen grub 1931–32, vol. 1, pp. 50–54.

69 Together, these seven are known as "the seven vajra points." The sixty-four qualities consist of the thirty-two of the dharmakāya (the ten powers, the four fearlessnesses, and the eighteen unique qualities of a buddha) and the thirty-two major marks of the rūpakayas.

70 Tib. go rams pa bsod nams seng ge.

71 Go bo rab 'byams pa bsod nams seng ge 1979, fols. 3b.2–8a.3.

72 These are the five works of Maitreya, the five parts of the *Yogācārabhūmi* (*Bahubhūmivastu, Viniścayasaṃgrahaṇī, Vastusaṃgrahaṇī, Paryāyasaṃgrahaṇī,* and *Vivaraṇasaṃgrahaṇī*), the *Abhidharmasamuccaya* and the *Mahāyānasaṃgraha* by Asaṅga, and Vasubandhu's "eightfold *prakaraṇa* collection" (*prakaraṇa* means "treatise" or "mongraph"), which consists of his *Mahāyānasūtrālaṃkārabhāṣya, Madhyāntavibhāgabhāṣya, Dharmadharmatāvibhāgavṛtti, Vyākhyāyukti, Karmasiddhiprakaraṇa, Pañcaskandhaprakaraṇa, Viṃśatikākārikā,* and *Triṃśikākārikā.*

73 This sūtra is only preserved in Chinese translation (Taishō 668).

74 Verse 1 of the *Mahāyānasūtrālaṃkāra*'s prologue speaks of five points of explaining the mahāyāna and verse 2 provides the corresponding examples. According to Vasubandhu's *Bhāṣya* (D4026, fol. 130a.1–3), these five points are what is to be established, what is to be understood, what is to be conceived, what is inconceivable, and what is perfect (the latter is to be personally experienced and has the nature of the dharmas concordant with enlightenment). A rather extensive digest of Sthiramati's *Sūtrālaṃkāravṛttibhāṣya* (D4034, vol. mi, fols. 9a.1–14b.3) is provided here because it explains these five points and their corresponding examples in connection with (a) the five dharmas of the mahāyāna, (b) the three natures, and (c) three kinds of persons. Among these, (a) and (b) represent crucial Yogācāra concepts and also appear in OED and other commentaries below. (a) Among the five dharmas, (1) "names" are what worldly people use to label phenomena and through which they cling to these phenomena as existing by a nature of their own in exactly the ways in which they are labeled. Since it is difficult to convey to these people that the phenomena labeled with names do not exist by any nature of their own, their mistaken conceptions in this regard need to be refuted and the correct position needs to be established for them through logical arguments. Thus, the joy about what is to be established here resembles the joy of being beautifully ornamented by all kinds of jewelry crafted out of a lump of gold through the great efforts of an expert goldsmith. (2) Since external dependent entities (the apprehended) represent the bases for being labeled by names, they are called "causal features" (Skt. *nimitta* can mean both "cause" and "characteristic" and is to be understood in this double sense here). These entities are nothing but appearances that dependently originate from one's own mind. They are what is to be understood through teaching that they are external dependent origination, which is directly perceptible and thus undoubted by worldly persons, such as a sprout arising from a seed, leaves from a sprout, and so on. Thus, when one understands, upon being taught so without great efforts, that external entities are dependent origination, joy arises, which is comparable to the joy that arises upon seeing a fully bloomed lotus effortlessly opened by the sun. (3) "Conceptions" refers to the internal dependently originating entities of minds and mental factors that represent the apprehender. Through thinking properly by way of studying, reflecting, and meditating on the mahāyāna dharma, what is to be conceived is that external objects arise from the mind. In this way, one achieves an approximate relinquishment of afflicted phenomena and an approximate arising of purified phenomena. Just like the joy of someone close to starving feasting on delicious food, when those who are mentally starving due to not having studied, reflected, and meditated on the mahāyāna dharma feast on the nectar of this dharma through mentally engaging in it in a proper manner by way of studying it and so on, their hunger is pleasantly satisfied and they feel joy. (4) What is inconceivable is "suchness" because it is beyond the spheres of ordinary beings and

dialectics, is to be personally experienced by the noble ones, and lacks any comparable example in the world. Just as a learned person is filled with joy when receiving an excellently composed letter and realizing its consummate meaning in an unmistaken manner, buddhas and bodhisattvas are overjoyed when they, from the first bhūmi onward, directly see that suchness is personally experienced, beyond the sphere of dialectics, uncontaminated, and incomparable. (5) "Perfect wisdom" is not something to be explained, but refers to consummate direct realization. It has the nature of the dharmas concordant with enlightenment because it has the nature of minds and mental factors. However, it is not the nature of fools, but the uncontaminated nature to be personally experienced by the noble ones. It is referred to as "what is perfect" because it is the unmistaken perfect nature among the two aspects of the perfect nature (the other being suchness—the unchanging perfect nature). Just like the joy upon opening a casket richly filled with radiating jewels, buddhas and bodhisattvas feel supreme joy when afflictive and cognitive obscurations have been relinquished and thus the jewels of the dharmas concordant with enlightenment radiate in their mind streams. (b) As for relating these five points to the three natures, (1) what is to be established is that the imaginary nature is nonexistent because worldly people become afraid upon hearing words of nonexistence. However, this does not mean that the phenomena that are explained to be nonexistent are totally nonexistent in all respects. Rather, the intention behind explaining them to be nonexistent is that nonexistence refers to what is imagined by childish beings as apprehender and apprehended. The example of joy about being beautifully ornamented by all kinds of golden jewelry refers to the joy of the learned establishing that the imaginary nature is nonexistent and thus understanding it to be nonexistent in accordance with true reality. (2) The dependent nature consists of dependently originating minds and mental factors. Once the imaginary nature is established as lacking a nature of its own, the phenomena that consist of the dependent nature will be understood easily and joy will arise, just like the joy that arises upon seeing a fully bloomed lotus effortlessly opened by the sun. Therefore, the dependent nature is what is to be understood. (3) The dependent nature is also what is to be conceived. By virtue of being dependent, minds and mental factors lack a nature of their own. Therefore, one should properly conceive of the dependent nature in the manner of relinquishing nonvirtuous phenomena and cultivating virtuous phenomena, which will bring a joy that resembles the joy of someone starving feasting on delicious food. (4) As mentioned above, the perfect nature is twofold—suchness and nonconceptual wisdom. Suchness is inconceivable as explained before, and also because it is beyond all reference points and consciousness, thus being inconceivable for childish beings. Just as a learned person is filled with joy when unmistakenly realizing the consummate meaning of an excellent letter, bodhi-sattvas are overjoyed when they see suchness—the dharmadhātu—from the first bhūmi onward. (5) Nonconceptual wisdom (the unmistaken perfect nature) is to be personally experienced and realized by the noble ones. Just like the joy upon opening a casket richly filled with radiating jewels, bodhisattvas who see true reality feel supreme joy when the two obscurations have been relinquished and thus the precious nonconceptual dharmas concordant with enlightenment radiate in their mind streams. (c) As for relating the five points to three kinds of persons, ignorant persons are those who do not understand the words and meanings of the mahāyāna dharma. Doubtful persons are those who have doubts about whether the sūtra collection of the prajñāpāramitā sūtras and so on represents the mahāyāna or not. Those who cling to what is mistaken cling to the mahāyāna not being the mahāyāna and take the śrāvakayāna to be the mahāyāna. For the latter two kinds of persons, (1) the authentic mahāyāna is what is to be established, exemplified by the joy about gold jewelry as above. (2) To ignorant persons, the words, meanings, and defining characteristics of the mahāyāna are what is to be understood. Once they understand the mahāyāna after it has been taught to them, their joy about this resembles the joy that arises upon seeing a fully bloomed lotus effortlessly opened by the sun. (3)–(4) Since doubtful persons and those who cling to what is mistaken represent those who do not know how to establish the mahāyāna, they are also made to understand it through others teaching them. Thus, all three persons reflect on the mahāyāna's points to be conceived (such as skandhas, dhātus, and āyatanas). However, they should refrain from conceiving of four things that are inconceivable—the enlightened activity of buddhas, the karmas that establish all kinds of external entities, the karmas of practicing with gems, mantras, medicines, and secret teachings, and the spheres of the yogas of yogins. These are explained to be inconceivable because trying to conceive of them makes the mind agitated and crazed. If these persons reflect on what they should conceive and relinquish conceiving of what is inconceivable, joy will arise in them, which respectively resembles the joys of a starving person eating delicious food and a learned person eliminating errors when correctly understanding the meaning of an excellent letter. (5) When the three kinds of persons properly engage through conceiving what they should and avoiding grasping what is inconceivable, they will realize the dharmas concordant with enlightenment that are to be personally experienced. Just like the joy upon opening a jewel casket, when the afflictive and cognitive obscurations—the antagonistic factors of the mahāyāna and the pāramitās—are eliminated through the dharmas concordant with enlightenment functioning as their remedies, these dharmas radiate in the mind and there is great joy. In brief, the meanings of lacking a nature of their own are what are to be established. Minds and mental factors, which consist of the dependent nature, are what is to be understood. That very dependent nature should be conceived properly by way of relinquishing nonvirtuous phenomena and cultivating virtuous phenomena. The enlightened activity of buddhas and so on are explained to be inconceivable. Nonconceptual wisdom is the perfect nature to be personally experienced and realized, which has the nature of the dharmas concordant with enlightenment.

75 Śākya mchog ldan 1988b, pp. 5–18, 20–21, and 36.

76 As for the disputed authorship of this text (*Śatasāhasrikāpañcaviṃśatisāhasrikāṣṭādaśasāhasrikāprajñāpāramitābṛhaṭṭīkā*; D3808) and its frequent conflation with the *Śatasāhasrikāprajñāpāramitābṛhaṭṭīkā* (D3807; usually attributed to Daṃṣṭrāsena), see Sparham 2001 and Brunnhölzl 2010, endnote 98. The Eighth Karmapa's commentary on the *Abhisamayālaṃkāra* (Mi bskyod rdo rje 2003, vol. 1, pp. 8–9) explains that the claims by certain people that Vasubandhu did not comment on the intention of the prajñāpāramitā sūtras as being Madhyamaka just represent their being engaged in some partial and biased form of Madhyamaka. Furthermore, it is the Madhyamaka view held by Asaṅga that represents the final intention of the prajñāpāramitā sūtras and the *Abhisamayālaṃkāra*, with Haribhadra following this kind of Madhyamaka. Also, there is no way that Vasubandhu would comment on the intention of the prajñāpāramitā sūtras as being Mere Mentalism. Haribhadra's commentary does not say that Vasubandhu commented on the meaning of prajñāpāramitā as being *cittamātra*, but only says that he commented on it based on the fact that knowable objects are internal. However, merely this does not entail that Vasubandhu commented in such a way that this is the final intended meaning of the prajñāpāramitā sūtras. Moreover, even the Buddha himself taught many passages in the prajñāpāramitā sūtras that accord with *cittamātra*, but this can obviously not be explained as an inappropriate understanding on the side of the Buddha. Also, if someone commented on the intention of sūtras that teach Madhyamaka as being nothing but Mere Mentalism, they would waste the teachings. However, Vasubandhu cannot be said to ever waste the teachings, but is a unique ornament of the teachings.

77 Note that in Yogācāra "cognizance" (*vijñapti*) primarily indicates an appearance or an image within the mind. However, the term does not exclusively refer to what appears as an object, but also pertains to what appears as a cognizing subject—both the apprehending and the apprehended aspects are just dualistic appearances in the mind. Therefore, the frequent translation "representation" is not only problematic for this reason, but also because it can easily be misunderstood to mean that what appears in the mind as an object is a reflection of a real objective referent external to the mind, which contradicts the fundamental Yogācāra position that there are no such objects. There is also the common Yogācāra expression "cognizance that appears as such [referents]" (or "consciousness that appears as such"; *tadābhāsā vijñaptiḥ*/

tadābhāsaṃ vijñānaṃ), in which "cognizance" is clearly understood as mind and not just as something that appears in the mind (this expression is found in DDV, DDVV, Vasubandhu's *Viṃśatikā* 17a, Dignāga's Ālamabanaparīkṣā 5d, and other texts). In particular, the Yogācāra system holds that what appears in a being's mind as the world is not a representation of an external world, but it *is* the world of this being as projected by the mind of this being. In the minds of beings of the same type (such as humans), similar but still individual images of the world arise due to similar latent mental tendencies, which are then misconceived as being an actual common world out there.

78 D4027, fol. 3a.2–3.

79 This term, found in both the Śrīmālādevīsūtra and the *Uttaratantra* (I.138 and III.34), refers to the subtle remainders of the ālaya-consciousness that are present in the mind streams of śrāvaka and pratyekabuddha arhats and bodhisattvas on the ten bhūmis.

80 As will be seen in the introductory section on the "fundamental change" below, due to the many different ways in which the term *āśrayaparivṛtti* is used and understood in different texts, it is very difficult to translate it in a way that covers all of its many applications. Though more common renderings such as "transformation of the basis" or "revolution of the basis" may be appropriate in certain cases, in cases of a mere revelation of suchness and so on (which is the way in which the term is used in DDV), there is no transformation of anything into anything. The only way in which one can speak of a change here is that the state of suchness changes from its being obscured to its being unobscured, while there is no change whatsoever in suchness itself (similar to space being with and without clouds). Also, one cannot really say that, for example, "the ālaya-consciousness has transformed" because the texts usually explain either that the ālaya-consciousness is purified or that it ceases to exist altogether, but not that it is actually transformed into something else.

81 Tib. ldog pa gzhan sel gyi cha. An isolate, or an "elimination-of-other," refers to a concept of something that is arrived at through excluding everything that this something is not.

82 Śākya mchog ldan 1988c, pp. 40ff.

83 This accords with Śākya Chogden's repeated statements that the view of *rangtong* is the best one for cutting through all reference points, while the view of *shentong* is more helpful for describing and facilitating meditative experience and realization.

84 Śākya mchog ldan 1975, pp. 225–27.

85 RC, pp. 1–2.

86 Tib. rong ston shes bya kun gzigs.

87 Tib. blo gros bzang po.

88 LZC, p. 39.

89 MC, pp. 3–6.

90 In Tibet, there have been long-standing and complex debates about the questions of whether the *Mahāyānasūtrālaṃkāra*—as well as the *Madhyāntavibhāga* and *Dharmadharmatāvibhāga*—belongs to what Tibetans call "Mere Mentalism" (thus being inferior to Madhyamaka), whether it and the Yogācāra School teach that some beings have no disposition to attain enlightenment at all (and what exactly "disposition" means in this context), whether they assert three yānas ultimately, and so forth. For a discussion of these issues, see Brunnhölzl 2009, endnote 173.

91 Tib. gzhan dga'. His actual name is Shenpen Chökyi Nangwa (Tib. gzhan phan chos kyi snang ba) and he was the first main teacher at the famous monastic college of Dzongsar, founded by Dzongsar Khyentse Jamyang Chökyi Lodrö (Tib. rdzong gsar mkhyen brtse 'jam

dbyangs chos kyi blo gros; 1893–1959). Khenpo Shenga also greatly revived the Nyingma academic curriculum.

92 Gzhan phan chos kyi snang ba 1983b, pp. 71.6–74.6.

93 The other four are excessive self-cherishing, looking down on seemingly inferior beings, taking the adventitious stains to be real, and denying the existence of buddha nature as ultimate reality.

94 Bdud 'joms 'jigs bral ye shes rdo rje 1991, vol. 1, pp. 169–70.

95 These are buddhas and noble bodhisattvas, pratyekabuddhas, and śrāvakas.

96 These are the five chapter headings of the *Madhyāntavibhāga*.

97 These are the five chapter headings of the *Uttaratantra*.

98 Pp. 490–95.

99 'Gos lo tsā ba gzhon nu dpal 2003a, pp. 424–25.

100 Compare TOK (vol. 2, pp. 460–61), which says that, according to the Eighth Situpa, Chos kyi 'byung gnas (1699–1774), the texts in Dsen Kawoché's lineage accepted a really established self-aware self-luminous cognition empty of the duality of apprehender and apprehended to be the powerful vital cause of buddhahood.

101 Tib. red mda' ba gzhon nu blo gros.

102 That is, they take this text as the main basis of their practice.

103 'Gos lo tsā ba gzhon nu dpal 2003b, pp. 12.26–13.1.

104 Strictly speaking, this is not said in the *Uttaratantra* itself, but only in RGVV (J 79; D4025, fol. 85b.1–2): "Stainless suchness has the defining characteristic of the fundamental change on the buddhabhūmi and is that which is called 'the dharmakāya of a tathāgata.'"

105 'Gos lo tsā ba gzhon nu dpal 2003b, pp. 455.23–456.2 and 574.9–12.

106 Ibid., pp. 2.6–7, 5.10–21, and passim.

107 'Gos lo tsā ba gzhon nu dpal 2003a, vol. 2, pp. 847–48. The same quote is also found in TOK (vol. 3, pp. 375–76) and Mi bskyod rdo rje 1996 (p. 11), who says that the explicit teaching of Mahāmudrā is the sūtra tradition's Madhyamaka of emptiness free from reference points. Implicitly, the Mahāmudrā sytem also teaches the ultimate profound actuality of both sūtras and tantras—the ordinary and extraordinary *sugatagarbha*. With this in mind, Gampopa made his statement about the *Uttaratantra* (see right below) which is followed by many Kagyü masters such as Pamo Trupa Dorje Gyalpo (Tib. phag mo gru pa rdo rje rgyal po; 1110–1170) and Jigten Sumgön Rinchen Bal (Tib. 'jig rten gsum mgon rin chen dpal; 1143–1217).

108 Later, Jamgön Kongtrul's TOK (vol. 3, pp. 375–90) describes this particular type of Mahāmudrā as "Sūtra Mahāmudrā" as opposed to "Tantra Mahāmudrā" and "Essence Mahāmudrā." Both Gampopa's statement and the first sentence in the following citation are also found in this section of TOK (vol. 3, pp. 375–76 and 381). For more details, see also Brunnhölzl 2007a, pp. 131–37.

109 For details, see Mathes 2008, pp. 381–97.

110 These four are found in many mahāyāna sūtras and Yogācāra texts and are as follows. (1) Outer objects are observed to be nothing but mind (*upalambhaprayoga/dmigs pa'i sbyor ba*); (2) thus, outer objects are not observed (*anupalambhaprayoga/mi dmigs pa'i sbyor ba*); (3) with outer objects being unobservable, a mind cognizing them is not observed either (*upalambhānupalambhaprayoga/dmigs pa mi dmigs pa'i sbyor ba*); (4) not observing

both, nonduality is observed (*nopalambhopalambhaprayoga/mi dmigs dmigs pa'i sbyor ba*). As *Mahāyānasūtrālaṃkāra* XIV.28 and its *Bhāṣya* say, the full and direct realization of the nonduality of apprehender and apprehended (4) marks the beginning of the path of seeing. Besides Maitreya's *Mahāyānasūtrālaṃkāra* (VI.6–8, XI.47–48, and XIV.23–28), these four steps are also found in his *Dharmadharmatāvibhāga* (lines 173–78 and 257–63 in DDV (K)) and *Madhyāntavibhāga* I.6–7ab, Asaṅga's *Mahāyānasaṃgraha* III.13, Vasubandhu's *Triṃśikākārikā* 26–30 and *Trisvabhāvanirdeśa* 36–37ab, and *Laṅkāvatārasūtra* X.256–257. Ratnākaraśānti's explanations in his *Prajñāpāramitopadeśa* (D4079, fols. 156a.5–162.a.6), *Prajñāpāramitābhāvanopadeśa* (D4078, fols. 131b.5–133b.6), *Madhyamakālaṃkāravṛtti* (D4072, fols. 118a.7–119a.6), *Kusumāñjali* (D1851, vol. thi, fols. 41b.7–42a.7), and *Bhramahāra* (D1245, fols. 189b.7–190a.3) resemble these four steps more or less closely. In addition to the *Laṅkāvatārasūtra*, he also relates them to the *Avikalpapraveśadhāraṇī* (D142, fols. 4b.4–6a.3) and a verse from the *Guhyasāmajatantra*. Also some other Yogācāra-Madhyamaka texts quote the *Laṅkāvatārasūtra* and refer to these four stages, commenting on the last one from a Mādhyamika perspective, such as Śāntarakṣita's autocommentary on his *Madhyamakālaṃkāra* (D3885, fol. 79a–b) as well as Kamalaśīla's *Madhyamakālaṃkārapañjikā* (P5286, fols. 137a–138a) and first *Bhāvanākrama* (D3915, fol. 33a–b). For more details on the four yogic practices, see the Introduction below as well as the translation section.

111 GC, p. 465.4–16.

112 The Eighth Karmapa's commentary on the *Abhisamayālaṃkāra* also explains some of the contents of this text in relation to Mahāmudrā and frequently equates Mahāmudrā with prajñāpāramitā, suchness, the nature of phenomena, and so on (for details, see the Introduction in Brunnhölzl 2010).

113 Chos grags rgya mtsho 1985, vol. 2, p. 512.

114 Ibid., vol. 1, p. ca.

115 Ka rma 'phrin las pa 1975, vol. cha, p. 66.

116 These are Kalkin Puṇḍarīka's commentary on the *Kālacakratantra*, called *Vimalaprabhā* (Tib. 'grel chen dri med 'od); Vajragarbha's commentary on the *Hevajratantra*, called *Hevajrapiṇḍārthaṭīkā* (Tib. rdo rje'i snying 'grel); and Vajrapāṇi's commentary on the *Cakrasaṃvaratantra*, called *Lakṣābhidānāduddhṛtalaghutantrapiṇḍārthavivaraṇa* (Tib. phyag rdor stod 'grel).

117 Ka rma 'phrin las pa 1975, vol. cha, p. 91.

118 Tib. mi bskyod rdo rje.

119 These are the *Madhyāntavibhāga*, the *Dharmadharmatāvibhāga*, and the *Uttaratantra*.

120 Chos grags rgya mtsho 1985, vol. 4, p. 406.

121 Mi bskyod rdo rje 2003, vol. 1, pp. 103 and 182.

122 Ibid., vol. 1, p. 20 and vol. 2, p. 441.

123 Ibid., vol. 1, pp. 219 and 321ff.

124 Tib. sangs rgyas mnyan pa bkra shis dpal 'byor. The Sangyé Nyenpas are regarded as incarnations of the Indian paṇḍita Smṛtijñānakīrti (eleventh century), who stayed in Tibet for many years as a teacher and translator, being instrumental in initiating the later spread of the dharma there. According to Krang dbyi sun 1985 (pp. 3249 and 3255), the First Sangyé Nyenpa was born in 1457 and his next incarnation appeared in 1520. This fits with the biography of the Eighth Karmapa in Chos kyi 'byung gnas and 'Be lo tshe dbang kun khyab 1972 (vol. 2, p. 20.7), which says that Dashi Baljor passed away in 1519. However, the latter's biography in Dpa' bo

gtsug lag phreng ba 2003 (pp. 1200–1206) gives his year of birth as 1445 and says that he passed away at sixty-five. In the table of contents of Chos kyi 'byung gnas and 'Be lo tshe dbang kun khyab 1972, the editors Gyaltsan and Legshay say, "The work in hand gives the dates for this teacher as 1445–1509. These seem not to be in accordance with his relationship with the Seventh and Eighth Zhwanag Karma-pa." TBRC gives 1445/1457–1510/1525.

125 Literally, the Tibetan says *sems tsam* (Mere Mentalism), which is ever so often used in Tibetan texts to refer to the Yogācāra School in general or a specific part of it. What is meant in this context is clearly the classical Yogācāra system as presented by Maitreya, Asaṅga, and Vasubandhu, and not Mere Mentalism in its somewhat pejorative sense as what is refuted by, and subordinated to, Madhyamaka in the default Tibetan doxographical hierarchies.

126 Mi bskyod rdo rje 1996, p. 40.

127 Kong sprul blo gros mtha' yas 2005, pp. 6–7. For more details, see the beginning and the end of GC below.

128 Ibid., p. 24.

129 Vol. 1, pp. 449–50 and 460–62.

130 From here on, the remainder of this section is from vol. 2, pp. 544–46.

131 Modern scholars now agree that the spelling Bhāvaviveka is wrong. Correct is Bhāviveka or Bhavya.

132 These are the remaining parts of the *Yogācārabhūmi* besides the *Bahubhūmivastu*—the *Viniścayasaṃgrahaṇī*, *Vastusaṃgrahaṇī*, *Paryāyasaṃgrahaṇī*, and *Vivaraṇasaṃgrahaṇī*.

133 These are the *Abhidharmasamuccaya* and the *Mahāyānasaṃgraha*.

134 Thrangu Rinpoche 2004, pp. 73–74.

135 See Mathes 1996 (pp. 40–60) and Robertson 2008 (pp. 513–608).

136 Compare *Uttaratantra* I.23, which equates the *tathāgatagarbha* enshrouded in obscurations with "suchness with stains" (*samalā tathatā*) and equates the purified *tathāgatagarbha* with "stainless suchness" (*nirmalā tathatā*). RGVV on I.23 (J 23) and at the begining of the second chapter (J 79) further equates purified *tathāgatagarbha* and stainless suchness with "the fundamental change" (*āśrayaparivṛtti*). Thus, the first point in the explanation of the fundamental change in DDV corresponds to the first one in the explanation of *bodhi* in the *Uttaratantra* (both points also being called "nature"). The following four points of the explanation of the fundamental change in DDV describe this fundamental change in the sense of being a fundamental change in terms of suchness (*tathatāparivṛtti*).

137 Note that, in terms of their contents, the following two points, (g) and (h), of the presentation of the fundamental change pertain to nonconceptual wisdom too. This is also reflected in DDVV saying that (g) belongs to the defining characteristics of nonconceptual wisdom, while (h) elucidates the training in order to attain this wisdom. Thus, in terms of contents (rather than outline), the discussion of nonconceptual wisdom covers 40% of DDV.

138 See Appendix 1 and Weller 1965, p. 97.

139 Compare this point with the second point of the *Uttaratantra*'s explanation of *bodhi*, which speaks about twofold wisdom (nonconceptual wisdom and the wisdom of subsequent attainment) as the "cause" of enlightenment. Here RGVV (J 79.13–14) explains this twofold wisdom as the cause of the fundamental change, which (as mentioned before) is stainless suchness. The remaining six points of explaining enlightenment as listed in *Uttaratantra* II.2 are its result, function, endowment with qualities, manifestation as the three kāyas, permanence, and

inconceivability. Directly or indirectly, all these points are also discussed in DDV's explanations on the nature of phenomena.

140 Though Takasaki 1966 (pp. 41–44 and 187) claims a significant difference in the uses of *parivṛtti* and *parāvṛtti*, Schmithausen 1969a and others showed that this is generally not the case.

141 For overviews and further details, see Davidson 1985 and 1989, Makransky 1997 (pp. 62–83), Robertson 2008 (pp. 20–26, 36–77, and 448–52), Sakuma 1990, Schmithausen 1969a (pp. 90–104), and Takasaki 1966 (pp. 41–44 and 187).

142 This sūtra is not the very short and still available Pāli *Revatasutta* (*Udāna* 5.7), which mentions nothing about *āśrayaparivṛtti* or *āśrayapariśuddhi.*

143 D106, fol. 49a.2–6. Like the rest of the *Saṃdhinirmocanasūtra*'s tenth chapter, this passage is quoted in the *Viniścayasaṃgrahaṇī* (D4038, vol. zi, fol. 191a.1–5). *Saṃdhinirmocanasūtra* VIII.13 (ibid., fol. 29b.3–5) also mentions the term "fundamental change," but provides no explanation, just saying that all the dharmas with which bodhisattvas familiarize through calm abiding and superior insight flow and merge into suchness, enlightenment, nirvāṇa, and the fundamental change.

144 *Saṃdhinirmocanasūtra* X.10 (D106, fols. 54b.5–55a.1) elaborates on the distinction between the dharmakāya and the vimuktikāya as follows. Through the blessings of powerful beings and the force of the karma of sentient beings, intense light shines forth from the fire crystals and water crystals that exist in the sun and the moon (according to ancient Indian cosmology, these crystals are the sources of the light of the sun and moon). However, such light does not radiate from other fire crystals and water crystals (such as on earth). Or precious gems only radiate once they have been polished. Likewise, the great light of wisdom and innumerable images of emanations for sentient beings arise only from the dharmakāya and not from the vimuktikāya of śrāvakas and pratyekabuddhas. For the dharmakāya is accomplished by virtue of having thoroughly trained through cultivating the means and prajñā of focusing on the immeasurable dharmadhātu (see also Ratnākaraśānti's *Prajñāpāramitopadeśa* below in the Introduction's section on the "fundamental change," which similarly explains this difference by using the example of fire crystals and moon crystals). Sthiramati's *Triṃśikābhāṣya* (Lévi ed. p. 44.11–14; D4064, fol. 171a.5–7) distinguishes the vimuktikāya and the dharmakāya by defining them as the fundamental changes that are attained through the relinquishment of the impregnations of the negative tendencies that exist in śrāvakas and bodhisattvas, respectively, with the former fundamental change being surpassable and the latter, unsurpassable. Asvabhāva's *Mahāyānasaṃgrahopanibandhana* (D4051, fol. 214.1–4) on I.48 explains the difference between vimuktikāya and dharmakāya as follows. The former refers to being free from merely the afflictive obscurations, while the latter consists of being free from all afflictive and cognitive obscurations including their latent tendencies, being adorned by all wonderful buddha qualities (such as the ten powers, the four fearlessnesses, and so on), being the matrix of all richness, and being able to act as one pleases. Therefore, it is the attainment of supreme sovereignty. This difference is comparable to an ordinary town person, upon being freed from iron shackles, attaining merely the result of the suffering of bondage having ceased, but beyond that not being endowed with any special features of overlordship, whereas a prince, immediately upon being freed from bondage, receives coronation and is endowed with the most consummate form of overlordship. The *Uttaratantra* describes these two kāyas as the two aspects of the complete relinquishment of the two obscurations in perfect buddhahood, without relating these kāyas to the distinction between bodhisattvas and arhats. Thus, when talking about the dharmakāya as the actual state of buddhahood in general, it is understood that both types of obscurations have been relinquished in it. In this sense, it then includes the vimuktikāya.

145 D107, fol. 164b.5.

146 Compare the ninth and tenth chapters of the *Mahāyānasaṃgraha* speaking about the impure aspect of the dependent nature changing into its pure aspect (see the section on *āśrayaparivṛtti* in the *Mahāyānasaṃgraha* below).

147 D107, fol. 143b.1–2.

148 In general, the term "impregnations of negative tendencies" (*dauṣṭhulya*) refers to body and/or mind being blocked, contaminated, and unworkable. Thus, Sthiramati's commentary on the *Mahāyānasūtrālaṃkāra* (D4034, vol. mi, fol. 193a.7–193b.1) explains the impregnations of negative tendencies as twofold—those of the body consist of negative actions such as killing and stealing, while those of the mind consist of negative states of mind such as attachment, malice, and wrong views. Another twofold division of the impregnations of negative tendencies consists of the latent tendencies of the afflictive obscurations and the cognitive obscurations. The *Abhidharmasamuccaya* (D4049, fols. 99b.7–100a.3) lists twenty-four kinds of impregnations of negative tendencies in terms of (1) expressions (which are omnipresent); (2) feelings; (3) afflictions; (4) karma; (5) maturation; (6) afflictive obscurations; (7) karmic obscurations; (8) maturational obscurations; (9) obscurations; (10) examination; (11) food; (12) sexual union; (13) dreams; (14) illnesses; (15) aging; (16) death; (17) fatigue; (18) being solid; (19) being great; (20) being medium; (21) being small; (22) afflictive obscurations; (23) obscurations of meditative absorption; and (24) cognitive obscurations. Sthiramati's *Abhidharmasamuccayavyākhyā* (D4054, fol. 230a.4–230b.7) explains that all of these refer to certain latent tendencies in the ālaya-consciousness. (1) refers to the latent tendencies of the omnipresent clinging to the names of all phenomena, which have followed one since beginningless time. They are also called "the latent tendencies of proliferating reference points" because the aspects of such clinging to names arise again and again. (2)–(4) refer to the latent tendencies of contaminated feelings, afflictions, and karma, respectively. (5) are the latencies of dysfunctional karmic maturations; (6) the nonexhaustion and the long continuum of the afflictions; (7) obstacles to the path, such as the five actions without interval; (8) the antagonistic factors of the clear realization of reality—obtaining the bodies of hell beings and so on; (9) the obstacles to engaging in virtue—being overpowered by striving for sense pleasures and so on; (10) the obstacles to being ordained—being overwhelmed by examining sense pleasures and so on; (11) not eating moderately (either very little or too much); (12) the physical and mental harm due to intercourse; (13) the seemingly physical body that is experienced by virtue of being asleep; (14) the experiences of unease due to the elements in the body being unbalanced; (15) being powerless in terms of the change of these elements; (16) all faculties being disturbed when dying; (17) physical exhaustion due to long walks and so on; (18) being joined to all the preceding latent tendencies in their respectively concordant ways and thus not passing into nirvāṇa; (19)–(21) being engaged in the realms of desire, form, and formlessness, respectively; (22) the antagonistic factors of the enlightenments of śrāvakas and pratyekabuddhas; (23) the antagonistic factors of accomplishing the nine meditative absorptions of progressive abiding; and (24) the antagonistic factors of omniscience. All of these are fully relinquished on the path of nonlearning when the liberations of mind and prajñā are accomplished. Sthiramati's *Sūtrālaṃkāravṛttibhāṣya* (D4034, vol. mi, fols. 120b.6–121a.1) explains that those two liberations refer to the freedom from the afflictions (nirvāṇa) and the freedom from ignorance (omniscient wisdom), respectively. The first one means to be liberated from the afflictions to be relinquished through the paths of seeing and familiarization, which arises from the lack of attachment. The liberation of prajñā means realizing, just as it is, that the liberation of mind actually *is* liberation, which arises from the lack of ignorance.

149 D107, fol. 143a.2–5 (Nanjio 1923, p. 221).

150 Ibid., fols. 167b.3–4 and 169b.6–7. Compare *The Chapter Called The Essence of the Words of All Buddhas from the Laṅkāvatārasūtra* (D108, fol. 200b.6–7) saying that, by

virtue of becoming free from mind, mentation, and consciousness, bodhisattvas will attain the tathāgatakāya through the progression of the fundamental change. In sūtras such as the *Laṅkāvatārasūtra* and in the Yogācāra system, mind (*citta*), mentation (*manas*), and consciousness (*vijñāna*) refer to the ālaya-consciousness, the afflicted mind, and the remaining six consciousnesses, respectively. Note that the *Laṅkāvatārasūtra* (D107, fol. 109b.4–5) and D108 (fol. 240a.7) say elsewhere that the fundamental change happens on the eighth bhūmi.

151 D107, fol. 92a.4–5. An almost identical passage is found in D108 (fol. 222b.5–6).

152 D107, fol. 189b.6.

153 D107, fol. 148b.3–4 (Nanjio 1923, p. 233). Almost literally the same statement is found in D108 (fol. 278b.5–6), with the variation that liberation is the fundamental change of external referents and the body of conceptions.

154 D107, fol. 58b.4–5. X.879 (D108, fol. 191b.4) states that the result of the fundamental change is a buddha's accomplishment of the welfare of all beings:

> By virtue of the fundamental change,
> Just as with all kinds of gems,
> The welfare of sentient beings is promoted
> Like a reflection on water.

155 According to Suzuki 1998 (p. 296), these two refer to the imaginary and dependent natures.

156 D107, fols. 135b.7–136a.1 (Nanjio 1923, p. 202).

157 This is "the sphere of the personally experienced wisdom of the noble ones."

158 *Svacittadṛśyagocara* ("the sphere of what appears being one's own mind").

159 Suzuki 1998, pp. 184–85.

160 Taishō 1545, pp. 688c26–689a3.

161 Taishō 1552, p. 906a18–20. It seems however that this is a later insertion into the text, since another probably earlier list just above (p. 906a15) lacks *āśrayaparivṛtti*. This is further confirmed by the fact that, among the three Chinese translations of the **Abhidharmasārabhāṣya* (Taishō 28, 1550, and 1551), the term in a similar list of factors that lead to the elimination of afflictions appears only in the first one, thus most likely being inserted later by the editor Dharmatrāta (fourth century) or even the translator Saṅghavarman.

162 Shastri 1970, p. 215.

163 Ibid., p. 663.

164 Ibid., p. 1096.

165 D4038, vol. zhi, fols. 241b.6–242a.2 (the Tibetan reads *lus gyur pa*, while the Chinese suggests *āśrayaparivṛtti*).

166 For example, *Suttavibhaṅga* I.10.6. For further sources on such sex changes, see Davidson 1985, p. 193.

167 Though the *Yogācārabhūmi* is traditionally attributed to Asaṅga, it is clearly a compilation of several layers of historically and doxographically quite different materials, including older abhidharma materials, general early mahāyāna explanations, as well as early and more evolved Yogācāra-specific materials. Therefore, this text is discussed here before the five texts attributed to Maitreya and the other works attributed to Asaṅga.

168 For examples, see the *Śrāvakabhūmi* edition by Shukla 1973, pp. 196.12–197.6 and 200.2–8; D4036, fols. 76a.7–76b.4 and 78a.6–7. The text explains *praśrabdhi* as "joyful ease" (*prāmodya, prīti*) and also as the "easing off" or "subsiding" (*pratipraśrabdhi*) of the impregnations of negative tendencies. This joyful ease is further described as being both the outcome of the process of purifying those tendencies and the very remedy (*pratipakṣa*) in this process. In the latter sense, the progressive increase of joyful ease is directly proportional to the gradual purification or subsiding of those tendencies.

169 D4039, fol. 272a.7–272b.1

170 Ibid., fol. 192b.2–4.

171 *Bodhisattvabhūmi* edition by Dutt 1966, pp. 253.14ff.; D4037, fol. 190a.2–4.

172 *Śrāvakabhūmi* edition by Shukla 1973, pp. 283.6–284.3; D4036, fols. 104b.7–105a.5. The same four factors are also found in a list of eight things to do in the *Śrutamayībhūmi* of the *Yogācārabhūmi* (D4035, fol. 165a.3), which elsewhere (ibid., fol. 168a.3–4) defines the purity of the foundation as being free from the impregnations of negative tendencies that consist of the afflictions related to the three realms of saṃsāra.

173 D4038, vol. zhi, fol. 127a.3–127b.4.

174 *Śrāvakabhūmi* edition by Shukla 1973, p. 200.2–15; D4036, fol. 78a.5–78b.1.

175 *Bodhisattvabhūmi* edition by Dutt 1966, p. 265.2–12; D4037, fol. 197a.4–197b.1.

176 D4038, vol. zhi, fols. 8a.7 and 225a.2–3 as well as vol. zi, fol. 15b.1.

177 D4047, fols. 317a.5–318a.7.

178 Compare the similar use of these examples in DDV, *Mahāyānasūtrālaṃkāra* XI.13, *Madhyāntavibhāga* I.16, and *Uttaratantra* I.30 (see OED's explanation of these examples).

179 Ibid., fol. 8a.2–7.

180 The Chinese says here that the fundamental change and the ālaya-consciousness are contrary to each other, that is, they are incompatible. As Sakuma 1990 (vol. 1, p. 129) points out, in light of a phrase in the preceding quote from the *Viniścayasaṃgrahaṇī* ("The ālaya-consciousness . . . entails appropriating, whereas the fundamental change . . . lacks appropriating"), *anālaya* is to be understood here as *anupādāna*—"not adhering or appropriating" (following the primary meaning of the Sanskrit verb root *ālī*, from which the word *ālaya* derives,that is, "to adhere" or "to stick"). Thus, the fundamental change is the opposite of the ālaya-consciousness, which appropriates, adheres to, and sustains the continuum of one's entire psychophysical existence, including all the latent tendencies for future such existences.

181 Ibid., fol. 28a.2–3.

182 D4035, fols. 282b.4–283a.4.

183 "Disposition," "seed," and "being accomplished" all indicate that suchness itself is the cause or foundation of the fundamental change that consists of pure suchness (or the purity of suchness).

184 Here "what is to be understood" and "what is to be relinquished" can be understood as referring to the reality of suffering and the reality of its origin, respectively (as opposed to "what is to be perceived/manifested" and "what is to be relied on"—the realities of cessation and the path, respectively). Also, in Yogācāra texts, "what is to be understood" and "what is to be relinquished" typically refer to the imaginary nature and the dependent nature, respectively, while the perfect nature is "what is to be perceived." On this, see also the commentaries on DDV below.

185 D4038, vol. zi, fols. 122a.5–124a.3.

186 D4038, vol. zhi, fol. 145a.3–4.

187 D4035, fols. 13b.7–14a.1.

188 D4038, vol. zi, fol. 124a.3–124b.3.

189 The text (ibid., fol. 91a.3–4) also says that the fundamental changes of śrāvakas and pratyekabuddhas are called "vimuktikāya" and are not equal to the fundamental change of buddhas, which is the dharmakāya.

190 Ibid., fols. 27b.7–28a.6.

191 *Bodhisattvabhūmi* edition by Dutt 1966, pp. 279.25–280.4; D4037, fols. 208b.6–209a.1.

192 D4047, fol. 334a.6–334b.4.

193 D4038, vol. zi, fol. 14b.5–15b1.

194 Ibid., vol. zhi, fol. 224b.5–6.

195 D4034, fol. 113b.1–5.

196 The term used here is *āśrayasānyathā.*

197 D4034, vol. mi, fols. 113b.6–114b.3.

198 Ibid., fols. 114b.6–115a.3.

199 Ibid., fol. 115a.4–115b.7.

200 Ibid., fols. 116a.2–117b.6.

201 Note that *Uttaratantra* I.27a gives the fact that "buddha wisdom enters into the hosts of beings" as one of the three reasons why all sentient beings are said to have *tathāgatagarbha.*

202 The following comments on IX.41–47 as well as the concluding verse IX.48 are based on D4034, vol. mi, fols. 126a.1–129a.6.

203 Note that verses IX.41–45 correspond to XI.44–46 below.

204 It is not clear why the fundamental change of the fourth skandha of formations is not discussed here (see, however, *Mahāyānasaṃgraha* X.5 below in the section on *āśrayaparivṛtti* in the *Mahāyānasaṃgraha*).

205 D4034, vol. mi, fol. 134a.1–7.

206 Note that this description corresponds to the threefold fundamental change as found in the *Abhidharmasamuccaya* (see the corresponding section below).

207 Sthiramati's comments are literally confirmed by Ngülchu Togmé's commentary on this verse (Dngul chu thogs med 1979, pp. 174–75), which concludes, "Thus, the nature of phenomena is realized through meditative equipoise, and meditative equipoise is realized through subsequent attainment. Since this is uninterrupted, it is the characteristic of inexhaustible mastery." Note that the translators Jamspal et al. of Asaṅga 2004 (pp. 93–94) present a greatly abbreviated, but partly mistaken, form of Sthiramati's above explanation (misidentifying "the real" as the ālaya-consciousness). Against Sthiramati and Asvabhāva, Jamspal et al. also prefer to follow the Gelugpa scholar dBal Mang, who takes "the wisdom of the real" as referring to the wisdom of meditative equipoise, thus, as Jamspal et al. put it, "tacitly correcting Sthiramati's (or the translator's) equation of *vastujñāna* with mundane, aftermath intuition."

208 D4029, fols. 72b.5–73a.1.

209 D275, fol. 37a.5–6.

210 Ibid., fol. 44a.5–7.

211 D3997, fols. 270b.2–271b.5.

212 Taishō 1530, p. 324a9–10 (attributed to Bandhuprabha and others).

213 D4034, vol. mi, fols. 135b.6–136a.2.

214 Ibid., fol. 176a.2–176b.1.

215 Ibid., fols. 196a.1–197b.7.

216 (1) The discriminating awareness of dharmas means to fully know the individual characteristics of all phenomena, or to teach the eighty-four thousand doors of dharma as various remedial means in accordance with sentient beings's different ways of thinking. (2) The discriminating awareness of meanings refers to fully knowing the divisions and classifications of all phenomena, that is, knowing the meanings that are expressed by the words and statements about the general characteristics of phenomena (impermanence, suffering, emptiness, and identitylessness) and their ultimate characteristic (the lack of arising and ceasing). (3) The discriminating awareness of semantics means to know the languages, symbols, and terms of all the various kinds of sentient beings and to be able to please them through this, to be able to teach many meanings through a single word, and to be free from words that are mistaken, rushed, or repetitive. (4) The discriminating awareness of self-confidence refers to being able to hear the dharma from others and eliminate one's own doubts, explain the dharma to others and thus eliminate their doubts, and speak meaningfully, swiftly, without interruptions, and unimpededly.

217 D4034, vol. mi, fol. 272a.7–272b.3.

218 Ibid., fol. 280a.6–280b.5.

219 Asvabhāva (D4029, fol. 115b.5) adds that this fundamental change right upon the vajra-like samādhi represents the fundamental change of the path.

220 D4034, vol. tsi, fols. 213a.5–214a.4.

221 DDV (K) lines 121–25 (see also lines 24, 27, and 252–53).

222 D4028, fols. 32a.5–33a.7.

223 Ibid., fol. 37b.1–7.

224 Ibid., fol. 38a.3–38b.5.

225 J 21; D4025, fol. 85b.1–3.

226 J 38–39; D4025, fol. 95a.5–95b.2.

227 J 79; D4025, fol. 115a.7–115b.6.

228 J 82; D4025, fol. 119b.1.

229 J 80; D4025, fol. 116a.5–7.

230 J 82, fol. 116b.6–7.

231 As mentioned above, this differs from *Mahāyānasūtrālaṃkāra* IX.42 and its commentaries describing wisdom as the result of the fundamental change.

232 The Sanskrit in Pradhan's restoration of the *Abhidharmasamuccaya* (p. 76.9–11) is *nirantarāśrayaparivṛtti*. *Nirantara* can mean "having no interval," "compact," "perpetual," and "immediately." The Tibetan in D4049 has "fundamental change without exception" (*gnas ma lus par gyur pa*).

233 These consist of the fruitional aspects of the eightfold path of the noble ones at the level of the path of nonlearning (correct view, thought, speech, aims of action, livelihood, vigor, mindfulness, and samādhi), mind being utterly and completely liberated, and the vision of the wisdom of that liberation.

234 D4049, fols. 99b.5–100b.1.

235 D4054, fol. 231a.6–231b.2. Jinaputra's *Abhidharmasamuccayabhāṣya* (D4053, fol. 67b.4–7) says almost literally the same (the *Tengyur* attributes both commentaries to Jinaputra, but modern scholars tend to take Sthiramati as the author of D4054). See also Sthiramati's comments on *Mahāyānasūtrālaṃkāra* IX.56 above.

236 Skt. vipākavijñāna, Tib. rnam smin gyi rnam shes (another name for the ālaya-consciousness).

237 Asvabhāva's *Mahāyānasaṃgrahopanibandhana* (D4051, fols. 195b.3 and 214a.1–2) gives the further examples of the ālaya-consciousness being like a disease or a poison and the latent tendencies for listening, like a medicine or an antidote. When having taken the medicine or the antidote, they may coexist with the disease or the poison for a certain time, but the medicine and the antidote are not identical with the disease or the poison, nor are the disease or the poison the seeds of the medicine or the antidote. Also, though medicinal drops may be stored in a vase with poison, it is impossible for them to arise from the poison as their cause. The same applies for the latent tendencies for listening.

238 Asvabhāva (ibid., fol. 214b.1) glosses "being included in the dharmakāya and vimuktikāya, respectively" as being the cause of the dharmakāya and the vimuktikāya, respectively.

239 Asvabhāva (ibid., fol. 214b.4) glosses "fundamental change" as being similar to the manner in which one's health improves after having taken a powerful medicine.

240 In India, wild geese (*haṃsa*) are said to be able to filter out the milk from a mixture of milk and water.

241 I.45–49 (D4048, fols. 10b.2–11a.6). As for the Sanskrit term *śrutavāsanā*, in itself it can be understood as "latent tendencies *of* listening," "latent tendencies *through* listening," or "latent tendencies *for* listening" (the Tibetan *thos pa'i bag chags* seems rather to suggest the former). Accordingly, one finds a range of explanations of this term. In the above quote from the *Mahāyānasaṃgraha*, the latent tendencies for listening are described in both of the above senses. On the one hand, they are said to be a "remedy," "mundane," and increasing " by virtue of being associated with listening, reflection, and meditation that are performed many times." On the other hand, the term refers to "the seeds of supramundane mind," "the natural outflow of the pure dharmadhātu," "the seeds of the dharmakāya," and is "included in the dharmakāya." Thus, on the one hand, the latent tendencies for listening spring from studying the teachings and make one study them again, thus serving as the causes for eventually attaining the dharmakāya. However, since those tendencies are primordially present in the mind stream through the nature of phenomena, they are the natural outflow of the dharmadhātu and merely revived through listening, but not newly created. The Buddhist teachings are seen as the natural outflow or activity of the dharmadhātu upon its being fully realized by a buddha. When these teachings meet with the latent tendencies of listening in the minds of other beings, those tendencies are activated and thus are also called the natural outflow of the dharmadhātu—the nature of the mind—of those beings. The comments on all the above expressions in the Eighth Karmapa's commentary on the *Abhisamayālaṃkāra* (Mi bskyod rdo rje 2003, vol. 1, pp. 212–14) account for the latent tendencies for listening being thus said to be both mundane and supramundane, but clearly treat them primarily from an ultimate perspective. The Karmapa says that they are "not something that must be input newly under the influence of conditions"; "what allows one to listen to all

the twelve branches of a buddha's speech"; "the capacity of uncontaminated cognition that is active through the power of the nature of phenomena"; and "allowing the enlightened activity of the dharmakāya to engage the mind streams of sentient beings." Also, they do not really increase, but "it is only the power of the decline of the factors to be relinquished that appears as if the latent tendencies for listening, which are the natural outflow of the completely pure dharmadhātu, increase from small to medium and so on." The meaning of their being "mundane" is explained as referring only to their being the remedy for what is mundane, but, in being the natural outflow of the supramundane dharmadhātu, they are not contained in mundane mind streams. The gist of their being a "natural outflow of the dharmadhātu" is said to lie in this term addressing the need for some factor that is other than the completely pure dharmadhātu itself and at the same time outside of all impure phenomena. Thus, from the perspective of this factor of the natural outflow being associated with a mind stream on the path, it is presented as a bodhisattva and yet also as being included in the dharmakāya. In this way, "in the single body of a yogin that appears as the dependent nature, there are two modes of engagement—the mode of engagement of the continuum of consciousness, and the mode of engagement of the power of wisdom." Thus, depending on whether the latent tendencies for listening are regarded from the perspective of seeming reality, the path, and ordinary consciousness or from the perspective of ultimate reality, the ground/fruition, and nonconceptual supramundane wisdom (both perspectives are found in the *Mahāyānasaṃgraha* and the Karmapa's commentary), these tendencies can be described as either mundane, conditioned, and acquired (being a remedy, increasing, associated with listening, reflection, and meditation) or as supramundane, unconditioned, and innate (being the capacity of uncontaminated cognition that is active through the power of the nature of phenomena, being an outflow of the dharmadhātu, and belonging to the dharmakāya). According to the Eighth Karmapa, these tendencies are the spontaneous impulses and habits of listening to and engaging in the dharma that are the natural expression of one's own buddha nature as the causal condition. Thus, the facts of the dharma, teachers, and texts appearing for oneself as well as being attracted to and engaging them come about through the main cause that consists of the revival of these internal tendencies appearing as if external, with the compassion and the enlightened activities of buddhas and bodhisattvas aiding as the dominant or contributing conditions. Fundamentally speaking, all of this happens nowhere else and as nothing else other than appearances in the minds of the disciples, which in these cases are not stained by obscurations.

242 I.57 (D4048, fol. 11b.6–7).

243 Here, the *Mahāyānasaṃgrahabhāṣya* (D4050, fol. 162b.7) glosses "fundamental change" as "the fundamental change of a particular form of the wisdom of focusing on all mahāyāna dharmas without combining them." The *Mahāyānasaṃgrahopanibandhana* (D4051, fol. 247b.4) explains the fundamental change in terms of minds and mental factors arising in a manner of being without stains by virtue of having realized suchness. Or through suchness having become pure, all buddhadharmas such as the powers and fearlessnesses are accomplished.

244 III.12 (D4048, fol. 25b.5–7); the phrases in [ ] are from the commentaries by Vasubandhu and Asvabhāva.

245 Here, the *Mahāyānasaṃgrahopanibandhana* (D4051, fols. 274b.4–275a.1) explains the nonabiding nirvāṇa as the fundamental change in which bodhisattvas abide in a manner that is without form. In it, through prajñā, the power of the afflictions is eliminated and no chance for their arising is provided. At the same time, through compassion, saṃsāra is not abandoned either. "The foundation" in terms of this fundamental change is the dependent nature—saṃsāra (mistaken minds and mental factors). "Its aspect that belongs to what is afflicted" refers to the phenomena that have manifest as the imaginary nature as already stated in Chapter Two. Nirvāṇa belongs to the aspect of the dependent nature that lacks any entities of the imaginary nature.

Thus, the dependent nature is the foundation or matrix that changes because it is connected to both saṃsāra and nirvāṇa. "Its change" refers to liberation through enjoying that change (from its afflicted aspect into its purified aspect). Chapter Two of the *Mahāyānasaṃgraha* highlights the fluid character of all three natures, with the dependent nature as the controvertible medium that can manifest as either dualistic delusion (the imaginary nature) or nondual liberation (the perfect nature). For example, the text says, "[The three natures] are not to be described as either being different or not different. In one sense, the dependent nature is dependent; in another sense, it is imaginary; and in yet another sense, it is perfect. In what sense is the dependent nature called 'dependent'? It is dependent in that it originates from the seeds of dependent latent tendencies. In what sense is it called 'imaginary'? Because it is both the cause of [false] imagination and what is imagined by it. In what sense is it called 'perfect'? Because it does not at all exist in the way it is imagined" (II.17; D4048, fols. 16b.6–17a.2). "Thus, in terms of its imaginary aspect, this very dependent nature is saṃsāra. In terms of its perfect aspect, it is nirvāṇa. You may wonder, 'In the *Abhidharmasūtra* the Bhagavān spoke of three dharmas—those that are included in the set of what is afflicted, what is purified, and both. What did the Buddha have in mind when he said that?' The existence of the imaginary nature in the dependent nature is that which is included in the set of what is afflicted. The existence of the perfect nature in the dependent nature is that which is included in the set of what is purified. The dependent nature is that which is included in both. This is what the Buddha had in mind when he taught [the above]. 'What example is there for that meaning?' The example is a gold-bearing lump of soil. In the case of a gold-bearing lump of soil, three [aspects] can be observed—the earth element, the lump of soil, and gold. [First, only] the lump of soil, which [actually] does not exist [as such] in the earth element, is seen, while the gold, which does exist, is not seen. Once [the lump of soil] is touched by fire, it does not appear like that, but the gold appears. The earth element appearing as a lump of soil is a false appearance. When appearing as gold, it appears just as it is. Therefore, the earth element is included in both parts. Likewise, through cognizance being untouched by the fire of nonconceptual wisdom, this cognizance appears as what is false (the imaginary nature), but not as true reality (the perfect nature). Once cognizance has been touched by the fire of nonconceptual wisdom, this cognizance appears as true reality (the perfect nature), but does not appear as what is false (the imaginary nature). Thus, the cognizance that is false imagination—the dependent nature—is included in both aspects, just as the earth element is in a gold-bearing lump of soil" (II.28–29; D4048, fols. 19b.5–20b.4). Here Asvabhāva's commentary (D4051, fol. 232a.4–6) explains that the earth element refers to the elemental principle of earth (which is not earth in a literal sense, but defined as what accounts for the general qualities of being hard and solid). The actual lump of soil with its color and shape is what derives from this elemental principle, while the gold is the seed or the refined essence of it. In other words, gold also partakes of the elemental principle of being hard and solid. Thus, the earth element is connected with both the lump of soil and the gold. In brief, the *Mahāyānasaṃgraha* presents the dependent nature as the process or the experiential structure in which the world presents itself as a seemingly delusive reality for beings whose minds have a dualistic perceptual structure (which is the imaginary nature). The perfect nature is the underlying fundamental process or structure of mind's true nature and its own expressions as they are unwarped by this dualistic perceptual structure. In more technical terms, the dependent nature is the basic "stuff" or stratum of which all saṃsāric experiences and appearances consist. It creates the basic split of bare experience into seemingly real perceivers that apprehend seemingly real objects. The duality of subject and object—the imaginary nature—does not even exist on the level of seeming reality, but the mind that creates this split does exist and functions on this level. However, what appears as the dependent nature in no way exists ultimately since the Yogācāra texts repeatedly describe it as illusionlike and so on and as what is to be relinquished, while the perfect nature is what is to be revealed—emptiness in the sense that what appears as dependent false imagination is primordially never established as the imaginary nature. It may be argued that the *Mahāyānasaṃgraha*'s notion of the fundamental change consisting of the change of the afflicted aspect of the dependent nature into its purified aspect (in the sense of an actual transformation of one phenomenon into another) differs radically from explanations of "the fundamental change" as the ālaya-consciousness ceasing altogether or unchanging suchness being freed from adventitious stains. However, it should be noted that the *Mahāyānasaṃgraha* also repeatedly explains the dependent nature as being as unreal as an illusion and so on and that it needs to be relinquished. Thus, the "impure aspect" of the dependent nature is simply its manifestation as the unreal and mistaken duality of the imaginary nature, while its "pure aspect" is the manifestation of its true nature—the perfect nature. In this way, the dependent nature is in a sense like H_2O, which can manifest as ice or water.

246 To see saṃsāra as peaceful is definitely a mahāyāna novelty that is not found in the abhidharma literature or even older Yogācāra materials, which agree on solely nirvāṇa being peaceful, while saṃsāra is dreadful and to be relinquished. Compare also the fourth of "the four seals" that qualify a teaching as being Buddhist—"nirvāṇa alone is peace."

247 These two verses correspond to *Mahāyānasūtrālaṃkāra* XIX.53–54 (see above).

248 IX.1–3 (D4048, fols. 35b.7–37a.3).

249 Here, the *Mahāyānasaṃgrahopanibandhana* (D4051, fol. 275b.3–4) comments that when the aspect of the dependent nature that belongs to what is afflicted—the entities of apprehender and apprehended—has come to an end, the dependent nature is liberated from all obscurations. Therefore, it has changed into the aspect of the dependent nature that belongs to what is purified and abides as the mastery over all dharmas. It has changed away from the entities of apprehender and apprehended.

250 In more detail, the ten masteries are mastery over (1) lifespan (being able to live for infinite eons), (2) mind (engaging in firmly dwelling in samādhi through infinite wisdom), (3) necessities (displaying all worldly realms by blessing them with many embellishments), (4) karma (displaying karmic maturations just at the time when they can be blessed), (5) birth (displaying births everywhere in the worldly realms), (6) creative willpower (displaying all worldly realms as being completely filled with buddhas), (7) aspiration prayers (displaying enlightenment in any buddha realm and at any time they please), (8) miraculous powers (displaying all kinds of miraculous feats, such as going to all buddha realms), (9) dharma (displaying the light of the dharma doors without center and periphery), (10) wisdom (displaying a buddha's powers, fearlessnesses, unique qualities, major and minor marks, and becoming completely perfectly enlightened).

251 X.3 (D4048, fols. 37b.1–38a.2).

252 These five are taught in Chapter Five and are also provided in the *Mahāyānasaṃgrahopanibandhana* (D4051, fol. 277a.7–277b.1)—in each moment, bodhisattvas (1) destroy all impregnations of negative tendencies, (2) through being free from discriminating notions about variety, attain delight in the dharma, (3) correctly understand the light of dharma as being immeasurable and unfragmented everywhere, (4) characteristics that are not conceived and are in accordance with what is pure arise for them, and (5) they more and more seize the causes in order to completely perfect and accomplish the dharmakāya.

253 X.4 (D4048, fol. 38a.2–4). Here the *Mahāyānasaṃgrahopanibandhana* (D4051, fol. 277b.3–4) glosses "fundamental change" by saying that the fundamental change—the dharmakāya—is attained through the twofold wisdom of nonconceptuality and its subsequent attainment.

254 X.5 (D4048, fol. 38a.4–7). The *Mahāyānasaṃgrahopanibandhana* (D4051, fol. 277b.4–5) says that śrāvakas, out of fear of suffering, sever the continuum of their skandhas. Since bodhisattvas embrace their skandhas with skill in means, they change them into being without flaws

and nonvirtue. Note also that this presentation of the fundamental changes of the five skandhas here differs greatly from the one in *Mahāyānasūtrālaṃkāra* IX.41–47 and XI.44–46.

255 According to the *Mahāyānasaṃgrahopanibandhana* (D4051, fol. 279a.6–279b.1), this refers to the nature of the dharmakāya because the dharmakāya is utterly pure, and it becomes pure through the change of the ālaya-consciousness. Once the ālaya-consciousness in the form of the seeds of everything that is afflicted has been eliminated through its remedies, it will be compatible with all the many qualities without negativity (Paramārtha's Chinese translation of the *Mahāyānasaṃgrahabhāṣya* explicitly says here that, through the remedies, one becomes dissociated from the impure aspects of the ālaya-consciousness, while becoming associated with its pure aspects). This change is to be understood as in the case of a poison becoming a medicine if its toxicity is removed by another medicine.

256 X.7 (D4048, fol. 38b.2–6).

257 X.35 (D4048, fol. 42b.2).

258 Lévi ed. pp. 43.20–44.14; D4064, fols. 170b.6–171a.7. Vinītadeva's *Triṃśikāṭīkā* (D4070, fol. 61a.7–61b.3) agrees with this, glossing the impregnations of negative tendencies as "the seeds of the afflictions, which are referred to as what is unworkable."

259 Pandeya 1999, pp. 96.10 and 102.5–6; D4032, fols. 250b.2 and 254a.7.

260 Pandeya 1999, pp. 79.8 and 93.14–15; D4032, fols. 239b.6, 249a.1–2, and 282b.5 (not in Pandeya).

261 Pandeya 1999, pp. 40.5–41.15; D4032, fols. 214a.6–215a.2.

262 Note the similarity of this explanation to the final section of Vasubandhu's DDVV on the same three examples.

263 Śrāvaka and pratyekabuddha arhats and buddhas.

264 D4079, fol. 141a.7–141b.7.

265 Though the Sanskrit *śarīra* usually means "body," according to Monier-Williams, its original meaning is "support" or "supporter," which—as can be seen from what follows—is obviously what is meant here. Therefore, in this quote, I render *āśraya* as support.

266 D1424, fols. 153a.5–154a.4. Note that the Sanskrit manuscripts of this text (in Tucci 1971) have *āśrayaparāvṛtti* throughout, while the Tibetan reads *rten yongs su gyur pa* (instead of the usual rendering *gnas gzhan du gyur pa*).

267 D3808, fol. 216a.3–5.

268 Ibid., fol. 68b.2–3: "The imaginary lacks both arising and ceasing, it is nothing but appearing and not appearing. The dependent lacks both increase and decrease, it is nothing but the imaginary. The perfect lacks both being afflicted and being purified, it is nothing but pure by nature."

269 D3811, fol. 200a.7–200b.2.

270 D3808, fol. 63a.5–7.

271 Ibid., fol. 187b.4–5.

272 This most probably refers to the four types of fundamental change of the eight consciousnesses into the four wisdoms as explained above—the ālaya-consciousness changing into into mirrorlike wisdom (*ādarśajñāna*); the afflicted mind (*kliṣṭamanas*), into the wisdom of equality (*samatājñāna*); the mental consciousness (*manovijñāna*), into discriminating wisdom (*pratyavekṣājñāna*); and the five sense consciousnesses, into all-accomplishing wisdom (*krityānuṣṭhānajñāna*).

273 D3808, fol. 212a.3–4.

274 Ibid., fol. 289a.3–5.

275 D3811, fols. 212b.5–213a.1.

276 Interestingly, despite the decidedly Yogācāra terminologies and explanations in both this text and its commentary, both are included in the Madhyamaka section of the *Tengyur.*

277 D3891, fol. 23a.6–23b.6.

278 This is not an etymological, but a common Sanskrit hermeneutical, explanation of the meaning of *citta.*

279 D3891, fol. 26a.1–26b.7.

280 Rang byung rdo rje 2006c, p. 102. This explanation is followed by quoting *Mahāyānasaṃgraha* X.4–7 (see above). Elsewhere in his commentary, the Karmapa says that the dharmadātu is virtuous in the end since the wisdom with its enlightened activity that is called "fundamental change" operates until saṃsāra is emptied. This represents valid cognition due to being undeceiving. It is steady since it is changeless. It is the lack of self since it is not suitable for superimpositions through thoughts and thus cannot be superimposed as "mine" either. Thus, in this sense of being changeless and unmistaken, it is the perfect nature (ibid., p. 49). The nirvāṇa of buddhahood means that mind free from any stains first seems to be ensnared by the innumerable cocoons of the afflictions and then undergoes a fundamental change as taught above. Its nature dwells in all sentient beings, but as it is inconceivable for their thinking and evaluation, it is like a reflection of the moon in water. The time of reaching final consummation by directly and fully seeing this supreme nature of the mind means to attain the completely stainless dharmakāya. Once its adventitious stains have become nonexistent, primordially stainless mind is called "buddhahood." This fundamental change in terms of the stainless dharmakāya does not mean having become nothing whatsoever. Rather, the waves of thoughts have changed into the sea of wisdom, which is the final consummation of the emptiness that is endowed with the supreme of all aspects—the six pāramitās and so on (ibid., pp. 118–19). For more explanations on the notion of fundamental change in this and other Tibetan commentaries on the *Dharmadhātustava* as well as in the Third Karmapa's *Profound Inner Reality, Distinction between Consciousness and Wisdom, Pointing Out the Tathāgata Heart,* and their commentaries, see Brunnhölzl 2007b and 2009.

281 To take the dharmadhātu as a fifth wisdom (dharmadhātu wisdom) has its origin in the Buddhist tantras (the sūtras and Yogācāra texts only explain four wisdoms and the pure dharmadhātu). However, as in Abhayākaragupta's text here, this presentation was also employed in some late Indian Buddhist nontantric works and eventually became the predominant general template in Tibet. The Third Karmapa's autocommentary on his *Profound Inner Reality* (Rang byung rdo rje n.d., pp. 201 and 205) explains that the dharmadhātu wisdom is the utterly pure essence of the other four wisdoms which is both the disposition for buddhahood and its result. In it, saṃsāra and nirvāṇa are complete, it has neither beginning nor end, is neither single nor multiple, and thus is free from all reference points. For more details on the eight consciousnesses and their fundamental change into the four (five) wisdoms, see Brunnhölzl 2009.

282 D3903, fols. 273a.1–274b.2.

283 D3859, vol. zha, 88b.1–2.

284 Ibid., vol. za, fol. 83b.5.

285 Ibid., vol. za, fol. 340a.2.

286 D3870, fol. 32a.1 (also fol. 82b.4).

287 Ibid., fols. 325b.7.–327b.3.

288 P. 501.

289 P. 528.

290 P. 552.

291 Pp. 553–54.

292 XIII.18–19.

293 Verses 36–37.

294 Part 2, IV.69.

295 Pp. 555–56.

296 Pp. 556–57.

297 Kaṇāda was the founder of the Vaiśeṣikas and the reference to his view here seems to allude to the Vaiśeṣika position that the self, when attaining liberation, not only transcends the world, but even ceases to be the subject of any experience, even of itself.

298 Pp. 605–8.

299 I.154–55.

300 Pp. 610–13.

301 Pp. 141–42.

302 J 79 (D4025, fol. 115a.7–115b.1).

303 Tib. yongs su log pa. The most likely Sanskrit correlate is *(vi)nivṛtti*, which can mean "return," "disappearance," "cessation," or "destruction." Obviously, the latter two meanings correspond to *parivṛtti*'s meanings "ending" and "termination." As can be seen from some of the excerpts from Indian commentaries above, this is not an uncommon way of explaining *parivṛtti*.

304 Line 80a (*gnas po gzhan du gyur pa ni*; here translated in accordance with GC; however, as seen above, this seems to be just a variant rendering of *āśrayaparāvṛtti*).

305 Pp. 453–54.

306 Pp. 471–72.

307 Verse 6.

308 P. 458.

309 P. 459.

310 P. 469.

311 D4028, fol. 38b.4–5.

312 *Uttaratantra* I.155.

313 P. 339.

314 P. 339.

315 P. 456.

316 For more details on this, see the endnotes to the translation of this section of GC.

317 Pp. 153–54.

318 Fols. 12b.2–4 and 13b.5–6.

319 Fols. 22b.6–24b.3.

320 Fol. 25a.4–25b.3.

321 Pp. 36–39.

322 For more details on how the Tibetan commentaries explain the fundamental change in DDV, see the translation section with its endnotes.

323 D4034, vol. mi, fols. 118b.7–119a.3.

324 Ibid., fols. 256a.7–257b.1.

325 That is, not just nominal but actual causes and results, with the cause producing the result as something different from the cause.

326 Mi bskyod rdo rje 2003, vol. 1, p. 210.

327 II.210cd–211ab.

328 D4026, fols. 146b.6–7 and 171a.3–4.

329 The following is an elaboration, based on DDVV and the Tibetan commentaries, on the brief outline of DDV's presentation of nonconceptual wisdom given above. For more details, see the translation section below.

330 This is a more advanced meditative state than any of the eight meditative absorptions of the form realm and the formless realm. It represents the temporary cessation of the first seven consciousnesses (i.e., except the ālaya-consciousness) and their mental factors.

331 The following is just a brief summary of what these three texts say. For a translation of the entire eighth chapter with the relevant excerpts from these commentaries, see Brunnhölzl 2007a.

332 Note that these five verses are also quoted in the *Mahāyānasaṃgraha* (III.18; D4048, fol. 26a.6–26b.3), which calls them "verses about clear realization."

333 "Mental discourse" (Skt. manojalpa, Tib. yid kyi brjod pa) is a term for all appearances in terms of apprehender and apprehended being nothing but expressions of mind's continuous constructive play (or, put less politely, being just ongoing mental chatter).

334 Compare the similar explanations of this progression through the four levels of the path of preparation to the path of seeing in the *Dharmadharmatāvibhāga* (lines 173–78 and 259–63 in DDV (K)), *Madhyāntavibhāga* I.6–7ab (quoted below in GC, p. 465), *Mahāyānasūtrālaṃkāra* XIV.23–28, *Mahāyānasaṃgraha* III.13 and III.17–18, *Triṃśikākārikā* 26–30, *Trisvabhāvanirdeśa* 36–37ab, and *Laṅkāvatārasūtra* X.256–257 (except for the *Trisvabhāvanirdeśa* and *Mahāyānasaṃgraha* III.17, all are quoted below in OED, pp. 585–87, 535, 567–68, and 569–70, respectively). Though most of these passages (except for *Mahāyānasūtrālaṃkāra* XIV.23–28 and *Mahāyānasaṃgraha* III.13) do not explicitly relate their contents to the path of preparation, their Indian and Tibetan commentaries usually do so.

335 According to the *Mahāyānasaṃgrahopanibandhana* (D4029, fol. 60b.5–6), "that foundation" refers to nonconceptual wisdom, that is, the collection of flaws is eliminated based on nonconceptual wisdom.

336 Both the *Mahāyānasaṃgrahabhāṣya* (D4026, fol. 146b.5–6) and the *Mahāyānasaṃgrahopanibandhana* (D4029, fol. 61a.4–5) say that these bodhisattvas place their insight in the dharmadhātu of the root mind that focuses on all combined dharmas. The *Bhāṣya* (D4050, fol. 164b.2) on III.18 (which is a quote of *Mahāyānasūtrālaṃkāra* VI.6–10) explains this "root mind" as above and explicitly equates it with nonconceptual wisdom. According to Asvabhāva (D4051, fol. 250b.1), "root" refers to the tenth bhūmi because it is the grandmother of all sūtras.

337 According to the *Mahāyānasaṃgrahopanibandhana* (ibid., fol. 250b.4–6), the dhātu of all the dharmas on which the root mind focuses is emptiness, and it is the wisdom of subsequent attainment that places its mindfulness on this emptiness. As for "the wise realizing that the flow of mindfulness is mere conception," the continuum of mindfulness is the engagement in the dharmadhātu as perceived by the root mind. Since it is "mere conception," all this engagement does not really exist as it seems to appear. "Wise" means that those bodhisattvas apprehend the dharmadhātu through both nonconceptual wisdom and the wisdom of subsequent attainment.

338 D4034, fols. 78b.3–82a.6. According to Asvabhāva's *Mahāyānasūtrālaṃkāraṭīkā* (D4029, fol. 61a.6–7), VI.6 teaches the path of accumulation; VI.7ab, the path of preparation; VI.7cd, the path of seeing; VI.9, the path of familiarization; and VI.10, the final path of familiarization—the entrance into the buddhabhūmi. Vasubandhu's *Mahāyānasaṃgrahabhāṣya* (D4050, fol. 164b.4) agrees except for saying that the path of seeing is taught by VI.7cd and VI.8. Asvabhāva's *Mahāyānasaṃgrahopanibandhana* (D4051, fols. 249b.4–251a.1) says that, in due order, VI.6–10 refer to the paths of accumulation, preparation, seeing, familiarization, and the tenth bhūmi.

339 D4026, fol. 197b.1.

340 D4034, fol. 212b.7.

341 D3891, fol. 10a.4–6.

342 Ibid., fol. 24a.2–24b.5.

343 In other words, the only way in which nonconceptual wisdom as the perceiving subject can realize the dharmadhātu free from duality is by virtue of this wisdom's being free from seeing any duality.

344 Ibid., fol. 25b.1–2.

345 Ibid., fol. 30a.2–30b.2.

346 Ibid., fol. 31a.4–31b.3.

347 Ibid., fol. 38b.4–5.

348 My translation of DDVV below relies on the Sanskrit where available, while noting variants in the Tibetan in C, D, G, N, and P.

349 For a summary of DDVV, see Anacker 1992 and 1999b. For detailed outlines of the text, see Robertson 2008 (pp. 245–60).

350 Tib. stag tshang lo tsā ba shes rab rin chen.

351 As mentioned above, Kong sprul blo gros mtha' yas 2005 (p. 24) says the same.

352 The last part of the text's name can also be understood as "The Discrimination of the Light of Wisdom," thus referring to DDV's main topic of nonconceptual wisdom.

353 Tib. brag dkar sprul sku blo bzang dpal ldan bstan 'dzin snyan grags.

354 For a translation of this commentary in its entirety, see Volume Four of Robertson's *A Study of the Dharmadharmatāvibhaṅga* (forthcoming).

355 Comparing the time when the author of LBC flourished with the date of the composition of LDC, the former was in all likelihood composed before the latter. Nevertheless, Lobsang Dayang obviously had no access to it when he composed his LDC, which is not too surprising given that many Tibetan texts were not widely distributed at that time.

356 A khu shes rab rgya mtsho's *Dpe rgyun dkon pa 'ga' zhig gi tho yig* (Lokesh Chandra 1963, vol. 3, nos. 11472 and 11474) says that both Ngog and Chaba also wrote commentaries on the last four amomng the five works of Maitreya.

357 *Dkar chag mthong bas yid 'phrog chos mdzod dbye ba'i lde mig*. A bibliography of Sa-skya-pa literature prepared at the order of H. H. the Sakya Tridzin, based on a compilation of the Venerable Khenpo Appey and contributions by other Sakyapa scholars (New Delhi: Ngawang Topgyal, 1987).

358 Tib. bsod nams rgyal mtshan; the third head of the Sakya School.

359 *Bianfa faxing lun — Shiqin shi lun* [Dharmadharmatāvibhāga — the Commentary of Vasubandhu]. Hong Kong: Vajrayāna Buddhism Association Limited.

360 For all the variants in DDV (P), DDV (K), and DDVV in the Peking, Derge, Cone, Narthang, and Ganden editions of the *Tengyur*, see Mathes 1996 (my translations of these three texts follow Mathes's critical editions).

361 According to the Tibetan tradition, to present the title of a text both in the original Sanskrit and the language into which it is translated serves three purposes—creating trust in the genuine origin of the teachings at hand, planting the habitual tendencies of Sanskrit as a sacred language, and blessing one's mind stream.

362 The Sanskrit fragment in Sāṃkṛtyāyana 1935 has *dvayam idaṃ sarvaṃ/ dharma[tā] dharmatāsaṃgrahāt/*, which is better reflected in the Tibetan in DDVV.

363 Unlike DDV (K) and the version in DDVV, DDV (P) obviously treats "their matrix" as point four and "what is in common and not in common," as point five.

364 Tib. tho gling (an ancient kingdom in western Tibet).

365 DDV (P) has only "care, defeat," while the version in DDVV reads "benefit, harm." DDV (K) lists all four terms, thus arriving at an eightfold versus a sixfold matrix of the phenomena that are in common in terms of sentient beings.

366 DDV (K) *rgyu*, but all other versions and commentaries (except for MC) have *rgyud*.

367 Numbers in { } refer to the folio numbers of D.

368 "The invincible one"—an epithet of Maitreya.

369 VV (fol. 1a.2) identifies Vasubandhu's primary guru as Asaṅga (*gurubhya āryāsaṅgaḥ*).

370 C *de nyid kyis snang pas* D *de nyid kyis snang bas* GNP *de nyid kyis snang ba'i*. Most likely, *de nyid kyis* refers to Maitreya as the author of this text, which makes *snang ba'i* the preferable reading. With the reading *gnang bas*, Mathes 1996 understands this as "with their permission," thus referring it back to "gurus." However, "gurus" has a plural ending, while *de nyid* is singular.

371 These two sentences explain possible understandings of the Sanskrit compound *triyānanirvāṇa*, which is a typical exegetical approach in Indian commentaries. Similar explanations of other composita are found throughout DDVV.

372 *thams cad du don med*. This could also mean "it does not exist ultimately." Most commentaries do not clarify this one way or the other, but MC (fol. 5a.6) has "in absolutely all respects without being established as referents to be expressed (*rnam pa thams cad nas thams cad du brjod bya'i don du grub pa med*)," while SGC (fol. 2b.2) says "all of them do not exist ultimately (*de yang thams cad don la med*)."

373 These three are divisions of the twelve links of dependent origination—(a) the afflictiveness of afflictions consists of ignorance, craving, and grasping; (b) the afflictiveness of karma, of karmic formations, and becoming; and (c) the afflictiveness of birth, of the remaining seven links. For more details, see OED on this section of DDV.

374 CDGNP all read *ming 'dogs pa*, but VV (fol. 1a.4) confirms that this must be *mi 'dogs pa*—"it is not commonly referred to as mistakenness, because nonexistence is absent" (*na bhrāntyupacāraḥ abhāvābhāvāt*).

375 CDGNP only have *chos* instead of the obvious *chos nyid.*

376 DDGNP omit this phrase, which is inserted in accordance with DDV (P) and what follows in DDVV.

377 Tib. *re zhig*. This usually renders Skt. *tāvat*, which typically introduces a first argument (as in this case) or a counterposition.

378 This refers back to the following passages in DDV above: "What appears as duality and according designations is false imagination, which is the defining characteristic of phenomena . . . If any one of these two—nonexistence and appearance—did not exist, mistakenness, unmistakenness, afflicted phenomena, and purified phenomena would not be tenable. These two are neither one nor are they distinct because there is [a difference as well as] no difference in terms of existence and nonexistence."

379 CDGNP all read 'khod pa instead of 'khor ba.

380 CDGNP *lus can ma yin pa*, VV (fol. 1a.5) *amūrt[t]atvād iti.*

381 *'di* [CD *'dir*] *dge ba dang mi dge ba nyid gang gis de las nyid du rtogs par 'gyur bar de'i dbang du byas pa ste bstan pa yin no.* VV (fol. 1a.5–6) glosses *yena iti yena kuśalatvenā[nā] kuśalatvena vā tatkarmatvaṃ kāyavāgvijñaptyoḥ karmatvaṃ.*

382 VV (fol. 1a.6) glosses this phrase as *grāhyapratibhāsā cāsau grāhakavijñaptiś ceti*, probably unraveling the karmadhāraya compound **grāhyapratibhāsagrāhakavijñapti.*

383 VV (fol. 1a.6–7) glosses the reason here (*sādhāraṇatvād*—"because such is common/universal/equally applicable to all") as "because a cognizance that is the apprehender and appears as the apprehended is what arises for all [beings]" (*sādhāraṇatvād iti sarv[v]eṣam eva grāhyapratibhāsagrāhakavijñapter utpatteḥ*).

384 GNP omit "minds and."

385 VV (fol. 1a.7) glosses this as "ordinary beings" (*pṛthagjana*).

386 VV (fol. 1a.7) glosses "their very own cognizance" (*svavijñaptir eva*) as "their very own [cognitive] aspect" (*svākāra eva*).

387 VV (fol. 1a.7) glosses this as "yogins."

388 The phrase in [ ] corresponds to VV's (fol. 1a7–1b.1) gloss *paracittapratibimbaḥ.*

389 VV (fol. 1b.1) glosses this as "the two of apprehender and apprehended" (*grāhyagrāhakau*).

390 *gnyis yongs su ma grub par rab tu grub pa'i phyir ro.* The most straighforward reading of just the Tibetan would be something like "For it is established that the two are not established at all" (followed by RC and MC). However, given that this is not much more than a tautology and given DDVV's and VV's comments on this phrase (which are followed by SCG and LZC), the most probable Sanskrit equivalent for *yongs su grub pa* is *pariniṣpanna* in its sense of "existing" or being "real," while *rab tu grub pa* seems to render *prasiddha* in its sense of being "well known" or even "notorious."

391 VV (fol. 1b.1) glosses *viruddhavijñānam* as "perceiving a single female body as a corpse and so on, which is not possible in a form that is a [real] entity" (*ekasyaṃ pramadātanau ku(?) ṇapādijñānanam/ na ca vasturupe (!) etad yujyate*). This refers to monks who, due to their cultivation of the meditation on the repulsiveness of the body, perceive women as being like corpses, skeletons, and so on, while other men may perceive them as sexually attractive or neutral. From a Yogācāra point of view, such contrary perceptions would not be possible if there were really existent external entities, which—by virtue of their existing independently of the perceiver—would have to be perceived as exactly the same by everybody. Since such is not the case, it is

said that there are no such external independent objects. Thus, the Yogācāras do not say that an actual object is simply perceived differently by everybody, but that the mental appearances that are triggered by the respective latent tendencies of different beings and look like external objects *are* the objects of these respective beings, without there being any common external referent that triggered these different mental appearances.

392 This is the beginning of the Sanskrit fragment DDVV (S). The translation follows the Sanskrit and refers to variations in CDGNP.

393 Given that suchness is the only true existent and is that which becomes free from adventitious stains, one could also read the last two sentences as "through being free from all stains, [suchness] has become nothing but suchness. That [suchness] is an object in being nothing but that [suchness without stains] is called "the arrival at its nature."

394 DDVV (S) *vastu* CDGNP *dngos po.*

395 VV (fol. 1b.1–2) unravels the compound *sādhāraṇabhajanavijñaptitathatāparivṛttiḥ* as *sādhāraṇabhajanavijñaptes tathatārupena parivṛttiḥ/ parāvarttanam/* ("the change of the cognizance that is the container into/as the nature of suchness").

396 DDVV (S) *trividhatathatāparivṛtti* CDGNP *de bzhin nyid rnam pa gsum yongs su gyur pa* ("the change of three kinds of suchness").

397 DDVV (S) *tadanvaya* CD *de'i rjes su song ba* GNP *de la rjes su song ba.*

398 CDGNP omit this word.

399 In due order, VV (fol. 1b.4–5) glosses these three as "the realization of the real dharmas (qualities) (*bhūtadharmāvagamaḥ*)," "the instructions on the profound and vast dharma (*gambhīrodāradharmadeśanā*)," and "what is to be known being perceived directly (*jñeyapratyakṣībhāvo*)." As for "seeing," CDGNP have *kun tu ston pa*, which usually renders Skt. ādarsanam or *saṃdarśanam* (which can also mean "gazing steadfastly," "appearance," and "manifestation"). VV just says *darśana*, while the compound °*deśanādarśana*° in DDVV (S) could contain either *darśana* or *ādarśana.*

400 DDVV (S) *tadutkūlanikūlaprakhyānāt* CDGNP *de la ni mtho dman can du snang ba'i phyir ro.*

401 DDVV (S) and VV *darśana* CDGNP *ston pa* DDV (P) *mthong ba* DDV (K) *gzigs pa.*

402 DDVV (S) *pratilambhaś ca* CDGNP *thob pas.*

403 DDVV (S) *vicitra* ("wondrous" or "manifold") CDGNP *ngo mtshar.*

404 DDVV (S) *aprameya* CDGNP *bsam gyis mi khyab pa.*

405 DDVV (S) *sattavkṛtyānuṣṭhānāśrayāprameyāvyāhatābhijñādiguṇapratilambhataḥ* CDNG *sems can gyi bya ba sgrub pa'i rten thogs pa med pa'i mngon par shes pa la sogs pa bsam gyis mi khyab pa'i yon tan thob pa'i phyir.*

406 DDVV (S) *pratilambho* CDGNP *thob pa las.*

407 CDGNP omit "great."

408 DDVV (S) *sarvadharmasaṃbhinnālambanatas tattathatālambanaś ca* CDGNP *'dres pa dang ma 'dres pa'i chos thams cad la dmigs pa dang/ de'i de bzhin nyid la dmigs pa las so* (the latter is followed and explained by OED).

409 CDGNP omit "distinctive."

410 CDGNP omit "the four."

411 CDGNP omit “for the arising.”

412 DDVV (S) *paridīpito bhavet* CDGNP *bstan pa yin no.*

413 Here and in the comment below, CDGNP omit “the dharmas of.”

414 CDGNP omit “characteristics.”

415 DDVV (S) *pratilabdhabhāvanādhigama* CDGNP *bsgoms pas rtogs par bya ba thob pa.*

416 CDGNP omit “the relinquishment of the characteristics.”

417 DDVV (S) *sulakṣyatvāt* CDGNP *rtogs par sla ba'i phyir.*

418 DDVV (S) *vijñaptyartha* CDGNP *rnam par rig par bya ba'i don.*

419 CDGNP all mistakenly read *dmigs pa mi dmigs pa'i sbyor ba.*

420 DDVV (S) *lakṣaṇa* CDGNP *mtshan nyid* DDV (P) and DDV (K) *chos nyid.*

421 DDVV (S) *tad anenārūpy anidarśanam apratiṣṭham anābhāsam avijñaptikam aniketam. Avikalpapraveśadhāraṇī* (Matsuda 1996, p. 96.5–6; D142, fol. 3b.4) *avikalpo 'rūpo 'nidarśano 'pratiṣṭhito 'nābhāso 'vijñaptir aniketana.* CDGNP *de ltar 'dis ni brtag tu med pa/ bstan du med pa/ mi gnas pa/ snang ba med pa/ rnam par rig pa med pa/ gnas pa med pa.* Here *arūpi/arūpo* correspond well to *gzugs med pa* in DDV (P). However, probably in order to avoid *gzugs med pa* being understood as its more common meaning “without form,” CDGNP as well as DDV (K) have *brtag tu med pa.* This usually translates *atarka* (“bad reasoning or logic”), but here either means “inconceivable” or “unexaminable” (see GC). As also MC (fol. 17a.5) and GC (p. 465.23–24), respectively, point out, this list of six terms is found in the *Kāśyapaparivarta* (Weller 1965, vol. 2, p. 97) and the *Avikalpapraveśadhāraṇī*. However, in the latter, this quote is found in the context of explicitly discussing the characteristics of nonconceptuality, while the context in the *Kāśyapaparivarta* is a different one. Therefore, since the context of this quote in the *Avikalpapraveśadhāraṇī* fits better with the context of DDV here explaining the defining characteristics of nonconceptual wisdom, it is more likely that DDV here quotes from that dhāraṇī.

422 DDVV (S) *tatra dvayena grāhyagrāhakabhavena nirūpayitum aśakyatvāt* CDGNP *de la gzung ba dang 'dzin pa'i dngos po la gnyis su brtag tu med pa'i phyir.* Here ends the Sanskrit fragment.

423 Thus, in due order, “ungraspable” and so on correspond to the six points of the nonappearance of duality and so on in the immediately preceding paragraph of DDV.

424 DGNP *de'i yul can gyi mtshan ma.* This could also be read as “its characteristics of having an object.”

425 CDGNP *ston pa*, DDV (P) *mthong ba*, DDV (K) *gzigs pa* (see above).

426 GP *don med par 'dzin pa* CDN *don dam par 'dzin pa* (“clinging [to them] as being ultimate”).

427 Here and in the next three instances below, CDGNP have *shes pa* instead of *ye shes* (both, however, translate the same Sanskrit word, *jñāna*).

428 See, for example, *Majjhima Nikāya* 22.13–14 (*Alagaddūpamasutta*; translated in *The Middle Length Sayings of the Buddha* by Bhikku Ñāṇamoli and Bhikku Bodhi (Boston: Wisdom Publications, 1995), pp. 228–29) and the *Vajracchedikāprajñāpāramitāsūtra* §6 (D16, fol. 123a.3; translated in *Perfect Wisdom* by E. Conze (Totnes (UK): Buddhist Publishing Group 2002), p. 151).

429 Though the phrase “since beginningless time” (unlike “due to being ignorant about suchness,”) is not explicitly indicated as a part of DDV in DDVV (and thus missing in DDV (K)),

DDVV obviously contains other instances of phrases from DDV that lack explicit quotation marks and are simply embedded in the text of DDVV. Thus, in conformity with DDV (P), "since beginningless time" is considered to be a part of DDV.

430 CDGNP *rgyu dang bas pa'i 'bras bu*. However, VV (fol. 1b.7) has *sahetuphalaḥ* (which corresponds to both versions of DDV reading *rgyu dang 'bras bur bcas pa*) and glosses it as "false imagination" (which corresponds to the comment in CDGNP). The translation follows the latter.

431 The translation of this sentence is tentative (CDGNP *dmigs pa med kyang yul dang bcas pa yod pas so*). No other commentary refers to this sentence in DDVV, but, in line with DDV, all agree that nonconceptual wisdom does not have any object. Nevertheless, Khenpo Tsultrim Gyamtso Rinpoche (oral conversation) glossed this phrase as meaning that (unlike the eyes and so on) nonconceptual wisdom, despite its lack of observing, *does* have an object, which is the dharmadhātu beyond duality.

432 GNP *gzhi'i dngos po byed pa* CD *gzhi'i dngos po med pa*.

433 This could also be read as "It has already been explained that, no matter how false imagination appears, it does not exist."

434 This refers to a mirage toward which thirsty antelopes run.

435 CDGNP all read *gtogs*. This would mean something like, "Other than just being associated with adventitious fog and so on, is not a part of such [adventitious stains] . . ." However, in analogy with the phrasing of the following two examples, it seems more appropriate to emend *gtogs* to *rtogs*, which is also what is found in this sentence in LZC (p. 38).

436 The Tibetan tradition regards these five texts as representing Maitreya's own words, which were later written down by Asaṅga upon his return from Tuṣita, where Maitreya had taught them to him.

437 Tib. gsal ba'i tshul khrims. This accords with Bu ston rin chen grub 1931–32 (vol. 2, p. 137; Obermiller retrotranslates as *Prasannaśīlā) and Tāranātha 1980 (p. 155), who add that Asaṅga's father was a Kṣatriya, while Vasubandhu's was a Brahman. Their mother is said to have made aspiration prayers to give birth to sons who would uphold the Buddhist teachings. However, contrary to common oral Tibetan tradition, Tāranātha explicitly says that she was not a nun who had relinquished her vows to give birth to these sons. Paramārtha's (499–569) biography of Vasubandhu (in Chinese) says that the mother's name was Viriñcī and that both Asaṅga's and Vasubandhu's father was a Brahman, with whom she also had a third son, called Viriñcivatsa.

438 This seems to be a reference to Yogācāra materials in general rather than to the specific text called *Yogācārabhūmi*, which is usually considered to be authored by Asaṅga. Otherwise, this phrase here would suggest that this text was actually spoken by Maitreya and thus has a status equal to the five above that are regarded as Maitreya's own words.

439 According to Tāranātha 1980 (pp. 158–59), there are different accounts on how much time Asaṅga spent in Tuṣita—six months, fifteen years, twenty-five years, or fifty years.

440 The five works on the bhūmis are the *Bahubhūmivastu*, *Viniścayasaṃgrahaṇī*, *Vastusaṃgrahaṇī*, *Paryāyasaṃgrahaṇī*, and *Vivaraṇasaṃgrahaṇī*. These five form the five sections of the *Yogācārabhūmi*. The two sūtra collections (or two summaries) are the *Abhidharmasamuccaya* and the *Mahāyānasaṃgraha*.

441 As mentioned in note 72, Vasubandhu's "eightfold *prakaraṇa* collection" already includes his *Mahāyānasūtrālaṃkārabhāṣya*, *Madhyāntavibhāgabhāṣya*, and *Dharmadharmatāvibhāgavṛtti*.

442 OED *a ta*.

443 In Indo-Tibetan treatises in general and as a typical feature of the five Maitreya texts, "the body" of a text refers to its initial synopsis, while the remainder of the text represents its "limbs" or "branches."

444 Skt. sākṣātkaraṇīyam, Tib. mngon sum bya ba (the Sanskrit literally means "to be put before one's eyes/senses").

445 OED usually comments on the version of the prose text as it is found in DDVV, which also corresponds the best to the Sanskrit fragments presented in Sāṃkṛtyāyana 1935 (see Mathes 1996).

446 These are the five chapter headings of the *Madhyāntavibhāga*.

447 These are the five chapter headings of the *Uttaratantra*.

448 Traditionally, every Indo-Tibetan Buddhist treatise has to fulfill four criteria—proper subject matter, purpose, essential purpose, and connection (usually abbreviated by just the phrase "purpose and connection"). (1) Proper subject matters from a Buddhist point of view are contained in the three kinds of proper treatises (meaningful in a Buddhist sense; leading to relinquishing suffering; and mainly focusing on practice) versus the six types of specious ones as described in Asaṅga's *Viniścayasaṃgrahaṇī* (D4038, fol. 205a.3–7). The latter include meaningless treatises (on topics such as whether crows have teeth), those with wrong meanings (from a Buddhist perspective, such as discussing an eternal soul), treatises on cheating others, heartless ones (such as on warfare or killing animals), and those that mainly focus on study or debate. (2) The proper purpose of a text means that it must serve as a convenient avenue for penetrating the intended meaning of the teachings. (3) The essential purpose is to engage in this meaning with enthusiasm and eventually attain a buddha's omniscience. (4) The proper connection refers to the one between the purpose and the essential purpose. Also, in terms of the subject matter, the earlier parts of the contents of the text must be properly connected with the following.

449 Note that the terminology here suggests the underlying principles of the four realities of the noble ones. Usually the reality of suffering is what is to be understood; the reality of the origin of suffering, what is to be relinquished; the reality of the cessation of suffering, what is to be made fully perceptible; and the reality of the path, what is to be relied on in order to attain that cessation. In terms of the path, the four elements in the phrase "one comprehends this [nature], ascertains it, [makes it] appear, and completes it through familiarizing with it" correspond to the paths of accumulation, preparation, seeing, and familiarization, respectively.

450 D4028, fol. 27b.5–6.

451 As for the excerpts from other Tibetan commentaries in the endnotes, I generally only render passages that differ from DDVV and OED and/or add to what these two commentaries say. Here, according to LZC (pp. 2–3), after having understood the points to be adopted and to be rejected, the obscurations (phenomena) are to be relinquished, while their remedy—the purified nature of phenomena that has undergone the fundamental change—is to be made fully perceptible. These two are distinguished through their defining characteristics in terms of being different aspects, but not in terms of being different objects. LDC (fol. 3b.4–5) says that the distinction of the characteristics of phenomena and the nature of phenomena refers to the characteristics of the nature of a single entity appearing differently for a mistaken and an unmistaken state of mind, just like a mottled rope appearing as a snake and like its being empty of a snake, respectively. This distinction does not refer to the characteristics of objects with different natures, such as a pillar and a vase, appearing distinctly to the mind.

452 Together with the above explanation that saṃsāra (phenomena) consists of afflicted phenomena and nirvāṇa (the nature of phenomena), of purified phenomena, this corresponds exactly to verse 17 in Vasubandhu's *Trisvabhāvanirdeśa*:

> The imaginary and the dependent
> Are to be known as the defining characteristic of afflictiveness,
> While the perfect [nature] is asserted
> As the defining characteristic of being purified.

In *Mahāyānasaṃgraha* II.2–4 (D4048, fol. 13a.3–13b.3), the dependent nature is defined as "the cognizances that entail the seeds of the ālaya-consciousness and consist of false imagination." The imaginary nature is explained as "mere cognizance appearing as referents, though there are no referents." The perfect nature is "the total absence of the characteristic of referents [the imaginary nature] in the dependent characteristic."

453 OED uses both *mi bden pa* (lit. "not being real") and *bden pa med pa* ("lacking real existence"). However, in terms of meaning, the former comes down to the latter and is thus translated accordingly throughout.

454 Here (a) and (b) obviously allude to the two kinds of the perfect nature—the unchanging and the unmistaken perfect nature. Compare *Mahāyānasaṃgraha* III.8–9 (D4048, fols. 24b.2–25a.2) on the example of misperceiving a rope for a snake and its relationship to the three natures: "How should [bodhisattvas] comprehend [mere cognizance]? . . . They comprehend it just as in the case of a rope appearing as a snake in a dark house. [To see] a rope [as] a snake is mistaken because there is no [snake]. Those who realize this point turn away from the perception of a snake where there is none and dwell in the perception of a rope. [However,] when taken in a subtle way, such is also mistaken since [a rope] consists of [nothing but] the characteristics of color, smell, taste, and what can be touched. [Thus,] based on the perception of color and so on, the perception of a rope has to be discarded too. Likewise, [any notion of] real referents with regard to the mental discourse that appears as the six kinds of letters and referents is eliminated in those six kinds, just as the perception of a snake [is eliminated through the perception of a rope]. Then, based on the perception of the perfect nature, the perception of mere cognizance (*vijñaptimātra*) is also to be dissolved. Thus, through comprehending the characteristics of referents, which are [nothing but] appearances of mental discourse, bodhisattvas comprehend the imaginary nature. Through comprehending mere cognizance, they comprehend the dependent nature. You may wonder, 'How do they comprehend the perfect nature?' They comprehend it by putting an end to the notion of mere cognizance too. At that point, for bodhisattvas who have dissolved the notion of referents, there is no chance for the mental discourse that arises from the causes which are the latent tendencies for listening to arise as any appearance of referents. Therefore, not even an appearance as mere cognizance arises. When such bodhisattvas rest in nonconceptual names with regard to all referents and dwell in the dharmadhātu in a direct manner, there arises their nonconceptual wisdom, in which what is observed and what observes are equal. In this way, such bodhisattvas comprehend the perfect nature."

455 *Mūlamadhyamakakārikā* XXV.19 (OED condenses this into *'khor ba dang ni mya ngan 'das/ 'di gnyis khyad par cung zad ni/ shin tu phra ba'ang yod ma yin).*

456 V.19.

457 D4028, fol. 27b.6–7.

458 According to RC (p. 117) and MC (fol. 4a.6–4b.1), "what is to be relinquished after being understood" is saṃsāra, while "what is to be made fully perceptible" is nirvāṇa. SC (p. 149) glosses "what is to be understood" as the imaginary; "what is to be relinquished," as the

dependent; and "what is to be made fully perceptible," as the perfect nature. What is thus divided into three by way of defining characteristics or isolates is respectively summarized into two (phenomena and their nature) and this text was composed out of the wish to distinguish the manner in which this summarizing applies to these three in detail. LZC (p. 2–3) explains "what is to be understood" as "what is to be adopted and to be rejected"; "what is to be relinquished," as "obscuring phenomena"; and "what is to be made fully perceptible," as the remedy—the nature of phenomena, which is characterized by the fundamental change that has the defining characteristic of being purified. The distinction between phenomena and their nature is not made in terms of their being different objects, but in terms of their defining characteristics of being different aspects.

459 Both RC (pp. 117–18) and MC (fol. 4b.3–5) gloss "all this" as all topics of the Buddha's teachings because phenomena and their nature include all knowable objects. MC continues that if one determines these two well, one will not be ignorant about any topic in the teachings. SC (p. 150) explains "all this" as all knowable objects, which are twofold—saṃsāric afflicted phenomena and purified phenomena (the nature of phenomena). According to LZC (p. 3), all the Buddha's presentations of skandhas, dhātus, āyatanas, the four realities, the two realities, the three natures, and so on are included in seeming phenomena (nonexistents that appear) and the nature of phenomena (the dhātu that is the ultimate basic nature) because all of saṃsāra and nirvāṇa is included in these two.

460 I.8ab.

461 According to RC (p. 118), phenomena are saṃsāra because they bear their own specific characteristics (the definition of "phenomenon") and are the phenomena that are founded upon the dharmadhātu, or because they are constituted by the duality of apprehender and apprehended. The nature of phenomena is the nirvāṇa of the three yānas because the latter is attained through realizing the nature of phenomena. DLC (p. 183) says that the reason for distinguishing between phenomena and their nature is that these two are what is to be relinquished and what is to be adopted, respectively. SC (p. 150) explains that this nirvāṇa does not only refer to the nature of phenomena that has become pure of adventitious stains, but to the natural nirvāṇa that applies to both ground and fruition. The nirvāṇas of the three yānas consist of the wisdoms that are respectively free from apprehender and apprehended or the two extremes of superimposition and denial in terms of a personal identity, that and any phenomenal identity with regard to the apprehended, and the former two plus any phenomenal identity with regard to the apprehender. According to MC (fols. 4b.5–5a.2), what constitutes phenomena is saṃsāra (what appears as the duality of apprehender and apprehended) because the nature of the mode of appearance of mistakenness (the phenomena that represent the bases to be understood and to be relinquished by those who wish for liberation and omniscience) is contained in just this. The nature of phenomena is the nirvāṇa of the three yānas. Through the power of seeing that this saṃsāra as it appears lacks any personal identity and any natures that are established as phenomena, the nirvāṇa that is the fundamental change is attained—through having engaged correctly in the actual mode of being there is finally no discord between the actual mode of being and the mode of appearance. Therefore, what is to be known and made fully perceptible in a correct manner is contained in just this. LZC (p. 4) says that the nature of phenomena is the nirvāṇa of the three yānas because nirvāṇa is what is to be attained through the three yānas. Ultimately, the nature of phenomena is the nonabiding nirvāṇa of the mahāyāna, which bears the defining characteristic of being the fundamental change. LDC (fol. 4b.2–3) explains that the three realms of saṃsāra constitute phenomena because they have the characteristic of circling in saṃsāra in the form of the threefold afflictiveness in terms of afflictions, karma, and birth under the sway of mistaking the phenomena of apprehender and apprehended for the two kinds of identity (personal and phenomenal). The nirvāṇa of the three yānas constitutes the nature of phenomena because nirvāṇa is attained

through realizing the suchness in which the two kinds of identity with regard to the phenomena of apprehender and apprehended have been put to an end.

462 Later OED speaks of two dharmakāyas—the first one is the stainless dharmadhātu and the second one, the very profound dharmakāya, which is a name for the two rūpakāyas.

463 I.10–11ab.

464 I.145.

465 I.86.

466 I.2 (D4048, fol. 2b.6–7).

467 D107, fol. 182a.3–4. OED line c *bden pa gnyis kyi rang bzhin du* ("and the nature of the two realities").

468 D107, fols. 81b.7–82a.1. OED line b *dngos po* ("entity") instead of *rang bzhin* ("nature").

469 As mentioned above, the five dharmas are (1) names (labels such as "a book"), (2) causal features (the bases for such labels—dualistically appearing entities that perform functions and have certain characteristics), (3) imagination (the eight kinds of consciousness and their mental factors), (4) perfect wisdom (the nonconceptual cognizing subject of suchness), and (5) suchness (the ultimate object to be focused on through the path—the dharmadhātu). Thus, perfect wisdom (the unmistaken perfect nature) and suchness (the unchanging perfect nature) make up the perfect nature in terms of subject and object, respectively. Needless to say, this explanation of the perfect nature as two is a pedagogical device to describe what is realized and what realizes it from the dualistic perspective of ordinary beings, but in no way implies any notion of a separate subject and object at the level of a buddha's mind realizing, or rather constituting, ultimate reality.

470 OED *'di gsum gyi spyi la*, which does not make sense and is emended to *'di gsum gyi phyi ma*.

471 As Rang byung rdo rje n.d. (p. 35) explicitly says, the unfolding disposition is nothing but the four wisdoms, which are the stainless essence of the eight consciousnesses.

472 I.2 (D4048, fol. 3b.1–2). The Sanskrit verb root *ālī*, from which the word *ālaya* derives, means "to adhere, stick, come close to, settle down upon, stoop."

473 I.17 (ibid., fol. 6b.2).

474 These two kinds of dependent origination are described in *Mahāyānasaṃgraha* I.19. Without elaboration, *Mahāyānasaṃgraha* I.28 mentions a third kind of dependent origination, "the dependent origination of experience." According to TOK (vol. 2, pp. 427–28), this describes the way in which the six consciousnesses (the primary minds) arise and cease based on the four conditions. Here the experiencer is the mental factor of feeling, and what is experienced is the mental factor of contact between object and consciousness. Feeling further produces the mental factor of impulse in the following way. In the case of a pleasant object, a pleasant feeling arises, which in turn leads to desire and the impulse of not wishing for the mind to become separated from that object. In the case of unpleasant or neutral objects, respectively, aversion and the wish to be separated from such objects or indifference and no such wish arise. Together, the three mental factors of feeling, contact, and impulse are said to blemish the primary minds.

475 I.45 (ibid., fol. 10b.2–4).

476 I.46 (ibid., fol. 10b.5–6).

477 OED *mi rtog*, which is emended to *mi rtogs*.

478 According to RC (p. 118), the definition of phenomena pertains to conceptual and nonconceptual cognitions that appear as the duality of apprehender and apprehended. The nonconceptual cognitions that represent mere dualistic appearances are the five sense consciousnesses. What appears as the according designations—term generalities and object generalities—is the conceptual mind. SC (p. 150) says that phenomena—saṃsāra, seeming reality—consist of both what appears as duality for nonconceptual consciousnesses and the cognizances that appear as the designations of apprehender and apprehended through terms that designate these according to what appears for the conceptions that apprehend terms and referents. For all of these are false imagination because MC (fol. 5a.3–5) explains that "according designations" refers to clinging to appearances as they appear and then designating them with all kinds of names. Just as a picture lacks highs and lows, but appears as if it had highs and lows, dualistic appearances are not ultimately established in the way they appear. Just like what appears for blurred vision, they are merely one's own false imagination. For while there are no (actual) objects, they appear for the mind. Śākya mchog ldan 1988b (p. 36) says that "phenomena" consist of the duality of apprehender and apprehended as well as the conceptions that appear as this duality, that is, the imaginary and the dependent natures, respectively.

479 As it stands, this passage is not found in any of Maitreya's texts. However, the first line is an abbreviation of a passage in the prose version of the *Dharmadharmatāvibhāga* below ("If what appears as the apprehended does not exist, it is established that what appears as the apprehender does not exist either.") and it also resembles *Abhisamayālaṃkāra* V.7ab. In general, the meaning of these two lines is not only found throughout the texts of Maitreya, Asaṅga, Vasubandhu, and other Yogācāras, but also in some Madhyamaka works, such as Nāgārjuna's *Bodhicittavivaraṇa* (verses 39–40) and Candrakīrti's *Madhyamakāvatāra* VI.96.

480 D4206 (fol. 87a.1–2) on verse 6.

481 From the perspective of the six consciousnesses being results, even in the Yogācāra system of no external referents it is fine to say that these consciousnesses arise from their respective causal condition (the ālaya-consciousness), dominant conditions (the six sense faculties), object conditions (the six objects), and immediate conditions (the ceasing of the immediately preceding moment of mind). In general, however, the four conditions in Yogācāra texts simply stand for the entirety of causes and conditions that are produced by the latent tendencies within the ālaya-consciousness. Though these conditions can be understood as sheer dependent origination, they in fact refer to nothing but particular cases of mind's imaginative play. Being just nominal pedagogic devices, these conditions do not refer to any really existing entities, let alone external material ones. Dependent origination is understood as the infinite web of all the different facets (be they labeled as the four conditions, false imagination, or something else) of the incessant constructive activity of the mind interacting with each other, just as waves keep crisscrossing and interfering with each other, constantly forming new ones. Through the power of mutual dependence, the emerging latent tendencies from the ālaya-consciousness, which then look like objects, sense faculties, immediate conditions, and resultant consciousnesses, appear as if they were causes and conditions. However, ultimately, there is no real arising or ceasing in this dynamic process. For example, it may appear that a magician causes many illusory beings to be born, some to die, some to come, and some to leave, but nothing of this really happens because these very "beings" do not exist in the first place. Just as these illusory "beings" depend on the necessary conditions to produce their appearance, what appear as those four conditions are nothing but the products of sheer false imagination, whose actual nature is not realized.

482 XI.40. The three natures are also often called "the three characteristics."

483 The former (Tib. rnam grangs pa'i kun brtags) refers to mental images of conventionally existent phenomena (such as when thinking of a book or a person), any dualistic appearances for nonconceptual consciousnesses, and nonexistents that still seem to appear clearly (such as

purple mice when drunk). The latter (Tib. mtshan nyid chad pa'i kun brtags) refers to sheer mental imputations of what does not exist at all in any way, such as a truly existent self or external material objects.

484 Here, obviously due to a copying mistake, OED repeats the above passage "are not at all established as having the natures of such [referents] . . . In brief, it consists of names and causal features."

485 XI.38. The causal features of appearances and their latent tendencies are presented here as the imaginary nature because they are the bases for imputing names and the causes for these features to appear, respectively. However, the actual essence of the imaginary nature is only what is stated in line c of this verse—mere appearances being made into names and reference points.

486 OED *'di lta bu'o*, which must be a corruption of *'di bum pa'o* (given the preceding phrase "a round belly and so on," which represents the classical Tibetan way of defining the characteristics of a vase).

487 XI.39. The characteristic of false imagination is to misconceive referents as if they existed just as they are labeled and to misconceive names as existing in the same way as the referents they label.

488 DDV's passage "Since what does not exist appears, it is false. In all [respects], it is without referents and is mere conception. Therefore, it is imagination" is explained as a unit by most other commentaries. RC (pp. 118–19) says that the dualistic appearances of the five sense consciousnesses are false because, contrary to the way they appear as duality, they do not exist as duality. The mental consciousness that appears as according designations is false because none of it exists as referents/ultimately (*thams cad don du med pa*). Both what appears as duality and what appear as designations are called "imagination," which is without referents/not existing ultimately (*don med*), meaning that it is actually suchness. As mentioned before, one can read *don med* in DDV as "without referents" or "not existing ultimately." Most commentaries are not explicit one way or the other, but SGC supports the latter, saying "all of them do not exist ultimately" (*de yang thams cad don la med*; fol. 2b.2) and RC could also suggest this meaning here and above when it says *thams cad don du med pa* (however, see MC below in this note). RC continues that suchness is the natural nirvāṇa because it is the mere conception that cannot be distinguished through apprehender, apprehended, objects of designations, what designates them, and so on. This section teaches that all minds and mental factors of the three realms constitute saṃsāra. DLC (pp. 183–84) explains that it is reasonable to call the mind that looks toward the outside "false" because it is the mind that is mistaken about appearances and because it consists of the clear appearance of what does not exist. It is equally reasonable to call it "imagination." For at all times it lacks any ultimate object and is mere mental conception. SC (p. 150) says that all phenomena are false because dualistic appearances and designations appear without existing. The element that is the apprehended aspect which appears as such under the sway of mistakenness, while not existing, is imagination. MC (fol. 5a.5–5b.1) explains that, while there are no (actual) objects, they appear for the mind. Therefore, though dualistic appearances exist from the perspective of appearance, ultimately they are false. Therefore, the designations and labels like "this and this" by the inner mind, which are based on dualistic appearances, are, in absolutely all respects, not established as referents to be expressed (*rnam pa thams cad nas thams cad du brjod bya'i don du grub pa med*) and are mere imputations by one's own conception. Therefore, all the many expressions for phenomena are established as mere imagination. In brief, this teaches that all phenomena of dualistic appearance and the clinging to such duality, apart from merely being imaginary, lack any nature of their own and yet appear. According to LDC (fols. 4b.5–5a.5), the defining characteristic of phenomena is the dependent nature, which is the sphere of false imagination. It consists of the five sense consciousnesses, for which apprehender and apprehended appear to be established as being separate, and the mental consciousness, for

which all phenomena appear as being established through their own specific characteristics as the bases for accordingly labeling and designating them as certain natures and their distinct features through terms and conceptions. Therefore, the nonconceptual sense consciousnesses of the dualistic appearances of apprehender and apprehended are false because their lack of any substantial difference between apprehender and apprehended appears to be established as such a difference. The mental consciousness—the conceptions that represent the awakening of the latent tendencies of expression (on these, see the corresponding comments in OED below)—is false because all phenomena that are imagined as certain natures and their distinct features through terms and conceptions do not exist as actual referents established by virtue of their own specific characteristics. All these six consciousnesses are called "false imagination" because they are mere conceptions in terms of what is actually nonexistent being existent (all of this is based on and elaborates on LBC [fol. 3a.1–4]). This teaches that the imaginary appearances of the mistaken cognition that is false imagination do not exist ultimately, while the mistaken cognition that is false imagination exists ultimately. For DDVV says, "It is without referents because a nature of appearances is not established. It is mere conception because appearances exist merely as mistakenness." Also, *Madhyāntavibhāga* I.1ab says:

> False imagination exists.
> Duality is not present in it.

It appears, LDC says, that Rongtön was unable to elucidate this meaning because his mind apparently tended toward the position that the dependent nature is ultimately nonexistent. Finally, compare Ratnākaraśānti's explanation of "false imagination" in his *Prajñāpāramitopadeśa* (D4079, fol. 142a.7–142b.7). He says that since all phenomena are mere mind, mere consciousness, and mere lucidity, there is no external referent that is apprehended by cognizance. Therefore, cognizance does not exist as having the nature of an apprehender either. Since both apprehender and apprehended are mental discourse, they are the imaginary nature of all phenomena. They are imagined based on the false imagination that, despite there being no referents, appears as the referents that arise from the latent tendencies of clinging to the imaginary nature. False imagination is the dependent nature of phenomena, mistakenness, error, and wrong cognition. Since its aspects of apprehender and apprehended appear solely under the sway of being mistaken and being impaired, it is delusive. Therefore, it is called "false imagination"—its nature is false or unreal. What is correct or real is mere lucidity. Thus, these aspects of apprehender and apprehended are referred to as "the characteristics of mistakenness" and the "characteristics of entertaining reference points" because they are the focal objects of mistakenness. They are also called "the characteristics of duality" because they appear as if they were two. All these characteristics of entertaining reference points cease within supramundane wisdom. Therefore, it is described as "nonmistakenness" and "perfect (or correct) wisdom." Consequently, this wisdom is also the unmistaken perfect nature because it is perfect by virtue of being unmistaken. Suchness is the unchanging perfect nature because it is perfect by virtue of being unchanging. Thus, the dependent nature is nothing but this false imagination, but it is not perfect wisdom.

489 See *Vimalakīrtinirdeśasūtra*, Chapter 9 ("The Dharma-Door of Nonduality"; Thurman 1997, p. 77).

490 XI.41. According to Vasubandhu's *Bhāṣya* (D4026, fol. 172a.6–172b.2), the defining characteristics of the perfect nature—suchness—are threefold. (1) Its own specific characteristic is as follows. It is the nonexistence of all imaginary phenomena and, since it exists as the very nonexistence of these phenomena, it is existent. Thus, it is also the equality of existence and nonexistence because this existence and nonexistence are not different. (2) Its defining characteristic of being afflicted and purified consists of its (seeming) lack of peace by virtue of adventitious afflictions and its (fundamental) being at peace by virtue of its being natural purity. (3) It has the defining characteristic of nonconceptuality because it is without any reference points and

therefore is not the sphere of conceptions. Sthiramati's *Sūtrālaṃkāravṛttibhāṣya* (D4034, vol. mi, fols. 187b.7–188a.5) comments that what is called "the perfect nature" is the defining characteristic of the dharmadhātu, emptiness, and suchness. (1) Since the entities of apprehender and apprehended do not exist in this perfect nature, it is called "nonexistence." Since the emptiness free from apprehender and apprehended is not nonexistent, it is called "existence." Therefore, *Madhyāntavibhāga* I.1bc explains:

> Duality is not present in it.
> But emptiness is present in it . . .

As for "the equality of existence and nonexistence," in the existence of emptiness, the nonexistence of apprehender and apprehended abides, and in the nonexistence of apprehender and apprehended, the existence of emptiness abides. Therefore, *Madhyāntavibhāga* I.cd explains:

> But emptiness is present in it,
> And it is also present in this [emptiness].

This corresponds to *Mahāyānasūtrālaṃkāra* IX.78ab ("Just that which is nonexistence is the supreme existence")—just that which is the nonexistence of the duality of apprehender and apprehended is the highest existence because it exists as the perfect nature. In his direct comments on IX.78ab, Sthiramati (fol. 144a.4) says that, on the first bhūmi, bodhisattvas realize that the imaginary nature does not exist. Thus, what is designated as "the highest existence" is the very fact that the imaginary nature—the nature of apprehender and apprehended—has actually become nonexistent (in a bodhisattva's mind stream) for the first time. Asvabhāva's *Mahāyānasūtrālaṃkāraṭīkā* (D4029, fol. 91a.1–3) also refers here to IX.78ab, saying that suchness is buddhahood. Thus, just that which is the nonexistence of duality (the imaginary nature) is the existence of suchness, and just that which is the existence of suchness is the nonexistence of the imaginary nature. Vasubandhu (D4026, fol. 161a.7) comments on these two lines by saying that just that which is the nonexistence as the imaginary nature is the supreme existence as the perfect nature. (2) Since emptiness is associated with adventitious stains, it is the lack of peace. Since it has the nature of natural luminosity and purity, it is peace. (3) Since the perfect nature is free from all reference points of apprehender and apprehended, it is not an object of dialecticians. Therefore, it is nonconceptuality.

491 There are two basic models for the relationship between the three natures. Model (1), which is found in most Indian Yogācāra texts, explains that the perfect nature consists of the dependent nature being empty of the imaginary nature. Model (2) is usually presented in Tibetan *Shentong* works and says that the perfect nature is empty of both the imaginary and dependent natures. However, there are indeed Indian precursors of model (2), such as Vasubandhu's *Śatasāhasrikāpañcaviṃśatisāhasrikāṣṭādaśasāhasrikāprajñāpāramitābṛhaṭṭīkā* (D3808) and Jagaddalanivāsin's *Bhagavatyāmnāyānusāriṇī* (D3811). For details and the compatibility of the two models in terms of their basic purport, see Brunnhölzl 2004 (pp. 485–86) and 2011a.

492 I.14–15.

493 V.13cd–14ab. The detailed explanation of these ten areas to be investigated and resolved through the prajñā cultivated during the meditation of superior insight follows in verses 14cd–22. According to Mipham Rinpoche's commentary on the *Madhyāntavibhāga* ('Ju mi pham rgya mtsho c. 1990c, pp. 756–57), the ten kinds of unmistakenness are about (1) letters as the means of expression (being comprehensible only by virtue of their being properly connected and the listener/reader being familiar with such connections), (2) the meaning to be expressed (the imaginary being without a nature of its own), (3) mental engagement in the fact that the cause of dualistic appearances is mere dependent cognizance, (4) not straying into the two extremes by virtue of realizing that, just like illusions, phenomena appear in a dualistic manner but are not real, (5) the specific characteristic—the perfect nature free from apprehender and apprehended,

(6) the general characteristic of phenomena—the realization that all phenomena do not go beyond the true reality of being empty of duality, (7) purity and impurity deriving from realizing and not realizing true reality, respectively, (8) the realization that purity and impurity appear, but are adventitious, because the true nature is pure in character, (9) no aversion toward accomplishing the decrease of afflicted phenomena because they are primordially pure, and (10) lacking arrogance resulting from excellent qualities because there is no increase of purified phenomena.

494 RC (p. 119) explains that the defining characteristic of nirvāṇa, which is constituted by the nature of phenomena, is its being of one taste as the emptiness that cannot be distinguished through apprehender, apprehended, objects of designations, what designates them, and so on. DLC (p. 184) explains that the defining characteristic of the nature of phenomena is the suchness in which, from the perspective of analysis, the forms and so on that appear for nonconceptual kinds of consciousness and the objects of designation and what designates them that appear for the conceptual consciousness lack any distinction in terms of their lack of real existence. According to SC (p. 150), as implied by the above explanation of phenomena consisting of false imagination, it is correct imagination that must be understood as the nature of phenomena because it is the wisdom that represents the direct opposite of false imagination. Śākya mchog ldan 1988b (p. 36) says that the nature of phenomena is the wisdom without the duality of apprehender and apprehended, that is, the perfect nature. MC (fol. 5b.1–3) explains that the defining characteristic of the nature of phenomena is the opposite of the defining characteristic of phenomena—the suchness that is the object to be personally experienced and cannot be distinguished through dualistic appearances (apprehender and apprehended) and the clinging to them (the conventions of objects of designations and what designates them). LBC (fol. 3a.6–3b.1) says that suchness is the natural nirvāṇa because it is of one taste as the emptiness that cannot be distinguished as apprehender, apprehended, objects of designations, what designates them, and so on. According to LDC (fol. 5a.6—5b.2), the defining characteristic of the nature of phenomena is the suchness in which, from the perspective of the seeing in the meditative equipoise of the noble ones, all reference points in terms of an internal apprehender and an external apprehended appearing to be established as different substances and all reference points that appear as being established through their own specific characteristics as the bases that are imagined as certain natures and their distinct features by what is to be designated (objects), what designates them (the subject), and so on have vanished. Through these two elements of the defining characteristic of the nature of phenomena, it is taught to be the emptiness of having negated any substantially different apprehender and apprehended in terms of the nonconceptual sense consciousnesses and the conceptual mental consciousness.

495 As mentioned before, among the twelve links of dependent origination, (a) the afflictiveness of afflictions consists of ignorance, craving, and grasping; (b) the afflictiveness of karma, of karmic formations and becoming; and (c) the afflictiveness of birth, of the remaining seven links. According to Mipham Rinpoche's commentary on the *Madhyāntavibhāga* V.24c ('Ju mi pham rgya mtsho c. 1990c, pp. 769–70), (a) has three further aspects: view, the three main afflictions (ignorance, hatred, and desire), and striving for rebirth. Their respective remedies are emptiness, signlessness, and wishlessnes. (b) means committing virtuous and nonvirtuous deeds. The remedy for this is not committing any such deeds. (c) also has three aspects. The first one is rebirth in a further saṃsāric existence. The second one means that, after having been reborn until death, primary minds and mental factors arise in each moment. The third one is the continuum of being reborn, that is, the processes of dying, being alive, and being in the intermediate state. Their respective remedies are to realize the nonexistence of birth, arising, and any nature.

496 These are also known as "the impregnations of the negative tendencies of expression" (*abhilāpadauṣṭhulya*), which are said to exist in the ālaya-consciousness in an omnipresent manner since beginningless time. Obviously, these terms are related to the typical Yogācāra term

"mental discourse" (*manojalpa*), which refers to the entirety of mind's imaginary constructions in terms of subjects and their objects.

497 This paragraph is a summary of *Mahāyānasaṃgraha* II.2–3 (D4048, fol. 13a.3–13b.2). The dependent nature—false imagination or mere cognizance—expresses itself in eleven forms: (1) refers to the five sense faculties (the first five inner dhātus), (2) refers to the afflicted mind, (3) is mentation (the sixth inner dhātu), (4) are the six external objects (the six outer dhātus), (5) are the six consciousnesses (the dhātus of consciousness), (6) refers to the stream of saṃsāra being uninterrupted, (7) is the perception of numbers, (8) is the perception of the outer world, (9) refers to speech that uses conventional terms which refer to what is seen, heard, perceived (by the remaining three sense consciousnesses), and known (by the conceptual consciousness), (10) means views about a self, what is "mine," and others, and (11) consists of the different ways in which all six kinds of beings manifest. As outlined above, the three types of latent tendencies are the respective causes of certain ones among these eleven sets, which are all just various modulations (Skt. *pariṇāma*) of mind, without any of them existing as something other than mind.

498 RC (p. 119) says that the defining characteristic of phenomena is established as follows. What appears as the duality of apprehender and apprehended is mistakenness because it appears as the duality of apprehender and apprehended that does not exist ultimately, just like the appearance of two moons. This very appearance as duality is the cause of afflictiveness. For, based on the appearance of duality, the clinging to duality arises and, based on the latter, attachment and so on arise. MC (fol. 5b.3–4) explains that since referents that are entities thus do not exist and yet appear, they are appearances of mistakenness, just as in the case of blurred vision. MC echoes the last two sentences of RC above, but replaces "attachment and so on" by "all kinds of latent tendencies."

499 These two lines are found in both his *Pramāṇavārttika* (III. 283ab) and *Pramāṇaviniścaya* (I.32ab). However, it should be noted that the context in both texts is one of clearly distinguishing between conceptual consciousnesses and nonconceptual perceptions (such as a visual consciousness) on the level of seeming reality rather than saying that all consciousnesses are conceptual (in the wider sense of this term as used here) and therefore have no referents.

500 Verses 37–38.

501 The example of an illusory elephant and its relation to the three natures is explained in verses 27–30 of the *Trisvabhāvanirdeśa*:

> Something magically created through the force of a mantra
> May appear as if it had the character of an elephant,
> But there is merely an appearing aspect there
> And no elephant at all exists.
>
> The elephant is the imaginary nature,
> Its appearance is the dependent,
> And the nonexistence of the elephant there
> Is held to be the perfect.
>
> Likewise, the imagination of what is nonexistent
> Appears from the root-mind as having the character of duality—
> There is absolutely no duality there,
> But a mere appearance does exist.
>
> The root-consciousness is like the mantra,
> Suchness is regarded as similar to the wood,
> Imagination is to be considered like the appearing aspect of the elephant,
> And duality is like the elephant.

In other words, the ālaya-consciousness is the agent that makes the illusory mere appearances of the dependent nature manifest, with their dualistic "content" (here a seemingly external "elephant") being the imaginary nature. The perfect nature, or suchness, is what is actually there, just perceived wrongly (things like a piece of wood were used by Indian magicians as the support that, through the power of mantra and so on, seemed to manifest as an illusory appearance). However, the example of a piece of wood for suchness is not meant to reify the perfect nature as some solid remainder once duality has vanished. Rather, it is a metaphor for the mode of being of things as they actually are. For a modern example for the relationship between the three natures, see the illuminating description of a holographic image in Kaplan 1990. Such an image appears as something external to and distinct from the perceiver, but there is no such image independent of someone's experience of it as a three-dimensional object over there. The image does not exist on the film, and there is also no conglomeration of light waves that makes up this image. How it appears is only imagined. Still, there is an experience of this image. Once the light that triggers this image is turned off, the image disappears. What is left on the subjective level is the experience of seeing that there is no such image.

502 Verse 9.

503 VI.4cd.

504 Verse 35.

505 Verse 4. RC (pp. 119–20) explains that this passage teaches that mistakenness does not arise from either being ultimately nonexistent or from existing as a mere appearance in isolation and that therefore the combination of both is needed for the arising of mistakenness. With regard to what is simply nonexistent, the mistakenness of apprehending it as existent does not arise because apprehending what is nonexistent as being nonexistent is without error. With regard to what is simply existent, a mistaken apprehending it as existent does not arise either because apprehending what is existent as being existent is not mistaken. Therefore, the apprehending of what is ultimately nonexistent as being existent as a mere appearance must arise by virtue of the combination of both being ultimately nonexistent and yet existing as a mere appearance. But if one of these two did not exist, the mistakenness of apprehending what does not exist as being existent would not arise. Likewise, if the mistakenness of the nonduality of apprehender and apprehended appearing as duality did not exist, the arising of afflicted phenomena would not be tenable either since there would be no cause for that. Without mistakenness, there would not be the remedy for mistakenness—unmistakenness—and consequently no purified phenomena, which arise from unmistakenness. According to SC (pp. 151–52), each one among all phenomena from ignorance up through omniscience is twofold in terms of its seeming aspect (phenomena) and its ultimate aspect (the nature of phenomena). For example, what is called "ultimate ignorance" and "great ignorance" is the wisdom that lacks the duality under the sway of ignorance. The seeming aspect of omniscience (the nature of phenomena) is the cognizance that appears as duality and according designations because it consists of false imagination and is not ultimate—it appears as duality to conception as the cognizing subject. However, if the seeming omniscience is identified as false imagination, this does not mean that it must be explained to be empty of the ultimate omniscience as the object of negation. Since it is impossible in this system to explain the perfect nature as the object of negation of emptiness, the conception, together with its apprehended aspect, that appears as omniscience must be identified as the imaginary omniscience. Therefore, omniscience is empty of that. False imagination is presented as saṃsāra from the point of view of the apprehended aspect of all false imaginations. However, one must understand that, from the point of view of its apprehending aspect that looks inwardly, it belongs to the category of purified phenomena. Therefore, the identification of the ultimate omniscience just above is also presented from the point of view of the apprehending aspect of all consciousnesses that looks inwardly. You may wonder whether

it is not sufficient then to explain all identifications of the imaginary nature as instances of seeming or saṃsāric phenomena. It is not for the following two reasons. In this system, saṃsāra is explained to be mere mind, while the imaginary nature is not explained as mere mind. Also, the cognizances that appear as the imaginary nature must be included in the dependent nature. The statement in *Mahāyānasūtrālaṃkāra* XI.34d that "there are no virtuous phenomena" is also made in terms of what appears to consciousness, but not in a general sense. Also, in what are presented as instances of seeming reality, saṃsāra, and phenomena, the defining characteristics of "not being as it appears, yet not being nonexistent primordially" must be complete. MC (fol. 6a.2–5) says that if it were not the case that phenomena are ultimately nonexistent, but if they existed in just the way in which they appear as duality, to apprehend them in this way would not be tenable as mistakenness. But since there would be no means to put an end to mistakenness then, nirvāṇa would be nonexistent in all respects too. On the other hand, if phenomena did not even appear seemingly (just as they are nonexistent ultimately), it would be impossible for anybody to have any mistakenness about apprehender and apprehended. Consequently, afflicted phenomena would be without any foundation. Since afflicted phenomena would not exist, their opposites—purified phenomena—would not exist either, just as nonexistent horns of a rabbit cannot be cut off. Therefore, since nonexistence and appearance are a unity, afflicted phenomena are possible in terms of the mistakenness of apprehending what is nonexistent as existent and the nirvāṇa that is attained through the path of unmistakenness is also possible through realizing that what does not exist is nonexistent. LZC (p. 7) says that this refers to appearance and emptiness not being separate in that phenomena are empty, while appearing, and are appearing, while empty.

506 Compare *Madhyāntavibhāgabhāṣya* (D4027, fol. 4a.7–4b.1) on I.13c saying that emptiness is not different from or the same as false imagination. If emptiness were different from false imagination, it would be impossible for the nature of phenomena to not be other than phenomena, just as being impermanent is not different from impermanent phenomena. If emptiness were the same as false imagination, it would not be the focal object of purification and the general characteristic of all phenomena. Therefore, the defining characteristic of emptiness is to be free from being the same as or something other than false imagination. Compare also the eight reasons in the *Saṃdhinirmocanasūtra* (D106, fols. 6b.4–9b.2) that seeming and ultimate reality are neither one nor different (see Brunnhölzl 2004, pp. 88–94).

507 XI.34.

508 According to RC (p. 120), saṃsāra and nirvāṇa are not one because saṃsāra does not exist ultimately, while nirvāṇa does exist ultimately. Saṃsāra does not exist ultimately because apprehender and apprehended do not exist ultimately and, since they do not exist, there is no phenomenon that could be presented as saṃsāra. Nor are saṃsāra and nirvāṇa different because nirvāṇa is constituted by the mere nonexistence of saṃsāric phenomena. As *Mahāyānasūtrālaṃkāra* VI.2d says: "Therefore, liberation is the termination of this mere error." DLC (p. 184) says that saṃsāra and nirvāṇa are neither one in their defining characteristics nor different in substance. For, from the perspective of reasoning, they differ in that nirvāṇa exists, while saṃsāra does not exist. Still, again from the perspective of reasoning, they do not differ in their existing or not existing as entities because nirvāṇa is the remainder of merely being free from saṃsāra, while saṃsāra is mere mistaken appearance. SC (p. 152) has someone ask, "In this division of the two realities, ultimate reality alone is asserted to be most powerful. Is it therefore held that the ultimate saṃsāra is the fully qualified saṃsāra?" It is by virtue of the ultimate being most powerful that it is not asserted that a seeming saṃsāra exists. If a saṃsāra exists, it is nothing other than the ultimate saṃsāra because one is generally not able to claim the existence of something by virtue of its existing from the perspective of mistakenness. Therefore, in the actual mode of being, there is nothing that can be divided into the two that are saṃsāra and nirvāṇa because it is said that the equality of saṃsāra and nirvāṇa needs

to be realized and because it is explained here in DDV that they are neither one nor different. According to MC (fol. 6a.6–6b.2), the nature of phenomena—naturally pure nirvāṇa—exists primordially as the basic nature, while the dualistically appearing phenomena of saṃsāra (the bearers of this nature) do not exist as this basic nature in the way they appear. Since the nature of phenomena consists of the mere fact that its bearers are not established, these two are merely distinguished in terms of being interdependent as what is to be adopted and rejected, respectively, but they lack any nature of being established as two different referents. LZC (p. 7) says that phenomena and their nature are not one entity because there is a difference in terms of the aspects in which they appear. They are not different entities either because it is the mere nonexistence of the reference points of the characteristics of phenomena that is labeled as "the nature of phenomena." According to LDC (fols. 6b.1–7a.2), phenomena (the dualistic appearances of apprehender and apprehended) and the nature of phenomena that is empty of the duality of apprehender and apprehended are not one in isolate because they differ in terms of respectively not being established and being established as something that withstands analysis through a reasoning consciousness. For the nature of phenomena exists as the fundamental way of being of entities, while phenomena do not exist as such. Nor are phenomena and the nature of phenomena different in nature because both what exists and does not exist as the fundamental nature of entities do not differ in terms of being the nature of a single entity. For what is the nature of phenomena necessarily constitutes the mere nonexistence as the nature of the dualistic appearances of apprehender and apprehended. This point here is to be explained according to the intention of the *Saṃdhinirmocanasūtra*'s discussion of the two realities being neither one nor different. However, the fact that Rongtön's commentary takes it to mean that saṃsāra and nirvāṇa are neither one nor different and then says that saṃsāra and nirvāṇa are not one because they respectively do not and do exist ultimately, clearly shows that he does not know the two ways of this Mere Mentalist system presenting the meaning of existing and not existing in terms of the seeming and the ultimate as they are described by Tsongkhapa in his *Legs bshad snying po*. Also, RC's quotation of the *Mahāyānasūtrālaṃkāra* in the context of saṃsāra and nirvāṇa not being different seems to be unrelated to this context. However, it is not that all statements in the sūtras and the treatises about the two realities being neither one nor different must be explained as meaning not being one in isolate and not being different in nature. Tsongkhapa's lesser *Lam rim* states that some of these statements have oneness and difference in terms of being established by a nature in mind, while some others have neither being one in isolate nor being different in nature in mind.

509 Verse 20. Since verses 20–22 of the *Triṃśikā* are important for an understanding of the three natures, the relevant comments from Sthiramati's *Triṃśikābhāṣya* and Vinītadeva's *Triṃśikāṭīkā* are provided here to supplement OED's very brief presentation. Sthiramati (Lévi ed., p. 39.4–19; D4064, fols. 167b.3–168a.1) explains, "'If these [skandhas] are mere cognizance, how does this not contradict the sūtras? The sūtras say that the three natures are the imaginary, the dependent, and the perfect [natures].' It is not contradictory because the three natures [can] be presented only when mere cognizance does (really) exist. 'How is that?' Therefore, [verse 20] says, . . . 'By whichever imagination' is stated in order to teach the infinite particular conceptions that conceive of [all] inner and outer entities. 'Whichever entity is imagined' refers to [all] inner and outer [entities] up through even the buddhadharmas. [All of them] are said to be the imaginary nature. What is stated as the reason for that is [the phrase] 'which is unfindable.' Since the entities that are the objects of conception thus lack real existence, they are unfindable. Therefore, these entities are nothing but the imaginary nature—they are not the nature that is contingent on causes and conditions. Thus, one sees the operation of many mutually exclusive conceptions about a single entity or its nonexistence, but it is not that many mutually exclusive natures are feasible with regard to a single entity or its nonexistence. Consequently, all these are mere conception because such referents have an imaginary nature. Also the sūtra

collections say, 'Subhūti, phenomena do not exist in the ways that childish ordinary beings cling to them.'" Vinītadeva's *Triṃśikāṭīkā* (D4070, fol. 52a.2–52b.1) says that imagined entities are actually nonentities. One can also see that many different conceptions arise about a single entity. For example, when hearing "A tiger is coming," while there actually is no tiger, brave people wish to fight this tiger and cowards become afraid of it. Since the focal objects of conceptions are nonentities, all beings are nothing but mere conceptions because the objects of conceptions have the nature of being superimpositions.

510 Lines 21ab. Sthiramati (Lévi ed., p. 39.22–27; D4064, fol. 168a.1–4) comments, "Here, 'conception' indicates the dependent nature. The [phrase] 'arises from conditions' refers to the cause for the arising of what is called 'dependent.' In this regard, [false] imagination refers to the different instances of virtuous, nonvirtuous, and neutral minds and mental factors of the three realms. As [*Madhyāntavibhāga* I.8ab] explains:

> False imagination [consists of]
> The minds and mental factors of the three realms.

The meaning of this is that the dependent is produced—it is dependent on other causes and conditions. It is thus taught that it is contingent on, and comes into existence due to, causes and conditions that are other than itself."

511 Lines 21cd–22. Sthiramati (Lévi ed., pp. 40.1–41.2; D4064, fols. 168a.4–169a.2) comments: "It is 'the perfect [nature]' because it is the perfection of being unchanging. 'Its' refers to the dependent. 'From the former' [means] 'from the imaginary.' In conception, the entities of apprehender and apprehended are imagined. Thus, while apprehender and apprehended do definitely not exist in that conception, they are imagined. [This] is called 'the imaginary.' The perfect nature is the dependent's being always and at all times absolutely free from that apprehender and apprehended . . .Therefore, as for 'it,' the perfect [nature] is the dependent's being always free from the imaginary nature. This very being free is the nature of phenomena, which is not suitable to be other or not other than phenomena. The perfect [nature] is the true nature of the dependent. Therefore, it should be understood that the perfect [nature] is neither other nor not other than the dependent. If the perfect [nature] were other than the dependent, in that case the dependent would not be empty of the imaginary. 'So why is it not other?' In that case the perfect [nature] would not be the pure focal object because, just like the dependent, it would have the character of being afflicted. Likewise, the dependent would not have the character of being afflicted because it is not other than the perfect [nature], but is just like the perfect [nature] . . . This is similar to impermanence, suffering, and identitylessness being neither other nor not other than what is conditioned and so on. If impermanence were other than what is conditioned, in that case what is conditioned would be permanent. 'So why is it not other?' In that case what is conditioned would have the nature of vanishing, just like impermanence. The same is to be said for suffering and so on. 'If the dependent lacks apprehender and apprehended, how is it apprehended? If it is not apprehended, how does one know that it exists?' Therefore, [line 22b] says, 'When the one is not seen, the [other] one is not seen [either].' 'The one is not seen' refers to the perfect nature. 'The [other] one is not seen [either]' refers to the dependent nature. When what is to be seen by supramundane nonconceptual wisdom [during meditative equipoise]—the perfect nature—'is not seen,' [that is,] not realized and not directly perceived, the dependent is what is to be perceived by the pure mundane wisdom attained subsequent to that [nonconceptual wisdom]. Therefore, it is not apprehended by other cognitions. Consequently, without having seen the perfect [nature], the dependent is not apprehended [either]. However, it is not that it is not apprehended by the wisdom that is attained subsequent to supramundane wisdom. As the *Nirvikalpapraveśadhāraṇī* says, 'Through [the wisdom] that is attained subsequent to that, they see all phenomena as being like illusions, mirages, dreams, echoes, [reflections of] the moon in water, and magical creations.' Here phenomena are held

to be contained in the dependent. The perfect [nature] is like space—the wisdom of one taste. As [the same text] says, 'Through nonconceptual wisdom [bodhisattvas] see all phenomena as being equal to the center of space.' For they see the sheer suchness of dependent phenomena." Vinītadeva (D4070, fols. 53a.6–55b.3) says that mere cognizance thus has three natures. Mere cognizance by itself is the dependent nature. What is superimposed onto it as apprehender and apprehended is the imaginary nature. That very [dependent nature]'s being absolutely free from these two is the perfect nature. As for the pure mundane wisdom of subsequent attainment, it is pure because it is attained through the power of supramundane wisdom during meditative equipoise. It is mundane because it arises as the aspects of apprehender and apprehended. Therefore, the dependent nature is apprehended by the pure mundane wisdom that is attained through the power of supramundane wisdom. Those who assert that the dependent nature is the sphere of supramundane wisdom do not realize the dependent nature—since the dependent is taught to have the nature of conception, how could it be the sphere of supramundane wisdom? As for this pure mundane wisdom during subsequent attainment realizing all phenomena to be illusionlike and so on, just as those who see a mirage or a magical appearance realize that it does not really exist as the aspect of water or a person as which it appears, pure mundane wisdom realizes that all minds and mental factors, which mistakenly appear as apprehender and apprehended, are free from these aspects of apprehender and apprehended. Or just as illusions and so on arise from other conditions, the dependent too arises in dependence on other conditions. Therefore, it is said to be illusionlike and so on. All explanations in the mahāyāna about illusions and such are given with regard to the dependent nature and thus it is taught that the dependent is apprehended by pure mundane wisdom. The perfect nature is of one taste, just like space (that is, without any variety and of singular appearance), and thus is the sphere of the wisdom of one taste or singular appearance. Or the perfect nature is of one taste like space and wisdom is also of one taste as that. Nonconceptual supramundane wisdom sees the sheer suchness of all phenomena that are called "dependent." This sheer suchness has the nature of being singular just like space—that suchness is said to lack any variety is because all minds and mental factors are equal in lacking the entities of apprehender and apprehended.

512 Obviously this, does not accord with *Triṃśikā* 21cd and its commentaries, but represents the above-mentioned model (2) of the relationship between the three natures (the perfect nature being empty of both the imaginary and dependent natures).

513 Verse 28.

514 The *Mahāyānasaṃgraha* discusses the three natures primarily in its second and third chapters. For example, *Mahāyānasaṃgraha* II.15 (D4048, fol. 16a.5–16b.1) says, "You may wonder, 'Why is it called dependent?' Because it is what has arisen from its own seeds of latent tendencies and therefore is dependent in terms of [these other] conditions. After it has arisen, its own being is unable to last for more than a moment. Therefore, it is called 'dependent.' You may wonder, 'If the imaginary nature is the appearance of nonexistent referents that is based on the [dependent nature], how is it imaginary and why is it called "imaginary"?' It is imaginary because it is the cause for the arising of the mistakenness of the mental consciousness that entails innumerable aspects of imagination. It is called 'imaginary' because [its] lack of specific characteristics is observed as mere imagination. You may wonder, 'If the perfect nature is the characteristic of the total nonexistence of this [imaginary nature in the dependent nature], why is it perfect and why is it called "perfect"?' It is perfect because it does not change into anything else. It is called 'perfect' in the sense of 'supreme' because it is the pure focal object and the supreme of all virtuous phenomena." *Mahāyānasaṃgraha* II.17 (ibid., fols. 16b.6–17a.2) explains, "In one sense, the dependent nature is dependent; in another sense, it is imaginary; and in yet another sense, it is perfect. In what sense is the dependent nature called 'dependent'? It is dependent in that it originates from the seeds of dependent latent tendencies. In what sense is it called 'imaginary'? Because it is both the cause of [false] imagination and what is imagined by it.

In what sense is it called 'perfect'? Because it does not at all exist in the way in which the imaginary [appears]." *Mahāyānasaṃgraha* II.28–29 (ibid., fols. 19b.4–20a.4) adds, "'With what in mind did the Bhagavān teach in the *Brahmāparipṛccha[sūtra]* that the Tathāgata neither observes saṃsāra nor observes nirvāṇa?' He taught this by having in mind that there is no difference between saṃsāra and nirvāṇa because the dependent nature is [both] the imaginary and perfect natures. Thus, [in terms of] this very dependent nature being the phenomena of the imaginary, it is saṃsāra. [In terms of its] being the phenomena of the perfect [nature], it is nirvāṇa . . . The existence of the imaginary nature in the dependent nature is that which is included in the set of what is afflicted. The existence of the perfect nature in the dependent nature is that which is included in the set of what is purified. The dependent nature is that which is included in both . . . In the case of a gold-bearing lump of soil, three [aspects] can be observed—the earth element, the lump of soil, and gold. [First, only] the lump of soil, which [actually] does not exist [as such] in the earth element, is seen, while the gold, which does exist, is not seen. Once [the lump of soil] is touched by fire, it does not appear like that, but the gold appears. The earth element appearing as a lump of soil is a false appearance. When appearing as gold, it appears just as it is. Therefore, the earth element is included in both parts. Likewise, through cognizance being untouched by the fire of nonconceptual wisdom, this cognizance appears as what is false (the imaginary nature), but not as true reality (the perfect nature). Once cognizance has been touched by the fire of nonconceptual wisdom, this cognizance appears as true reality (the perfect nature), but does not appear as what is false (the imaginary nature). Thus, the cognizance that is false imagination—the dependent nature—is included in both aspects, just as the earth element is in a gold-bearing lump of soil." According to Asvabhāva's commentary on this (P5552, fol. 284a.2–4), the earth element refers to the elemental principle of earth (defined as the general qualities of being hard and solid), with both the lump of soil and gold containing this elemental principle of being hard and solid. *Mahāyānasaṃgraha* II.25–27 (D4048, fols. 18b.5–19b.4) explains the conventional existence as well as the illusionlike nature of the dependent nature and how the three natures should be understood properly: "'If it does not exist as it appears, why is the dependent nature not totally nonexistent? And if it does not exist, the perfect nature does not exist [either], so how is it not the case that everything is nonexistent?' [This is not the case] because if the dependent and perfect natures were nonexistent, there would be the flaw of afflicted and purified phenomena not existing. [However,] afflicted and purified phenomena are observable. Therefore, it is not that everything is nonexistent . . . 'In this teaching that is the very extensive teaching of the mahāyāna of the buddha bhagavāns, how should the imaginary nature be understood?' It should be understood through the teachings on the synonyms of nonexistents. 'How should the dependent nature be understood?' It should be understood to be like an illusion, a mirage, a dream, an optical illusion, a reflection, an echo, [the reflection of] the moon in water, and a magical creation. 'How should the perfect nature be understood?' It should be understood through the teachings on the four kinds of purified phenomena. As for these four kinds of purified phenomena, (1) what is naturally pure is suchness, emptiness, the true end, signlessness, and the ultimate. Also the dharmadhātu is just this. (2) What is pure without stains is just that [which is naturally pure] not possessing any obscurations. (3) The pure path to attain that [which is pure without stains] consists of all the dharmas concordant with enlightenment, the pāramitās, and so on. (4) The pure object in order to generate this [path] is the teaching of the genuine dharma of the mahāyāna. In this way, since this [dharma] is the cause of what is pure, it is not the imaginary [nature]. Since it is the natural outflow of the pure dharmadhātu, it is not the dependent [nature either]. All purified phenomena are included in these four kinds . . . You may wonder, 'Why is the dependent nature taught in such a way as being like an illusion and so on?' It is in order to eliminate the mistaken doubts of others about the dependent nature. Thus, in order to eliminate the doubts of those others who think, 'How can the absence of referents become an object of experience?' it is [taught] to be like an illusion. In order to eliminate the doubts of those who think, 'How can minds and mental factors arise without referents?' it is [taught] to be like a mirage. In order to eliminate the doubts of those who think, 'How can there be experiences of what is desired and undesired if there are no referents?' it is [taught] to be like a dream. In order to eliminate the doubts of those who think, 'If there are no referents, how can the desired and undesired results of virtuous and nonvirtuous actions be accomplished?' it is [taught] to be like a reflection. In order to eliminate the doubts of those who think, 'How can various consciousnesses arise if there are no referents?' it is [taught to be] like an optical illusion. In order to eliminate the doubts of those who think, 'How can various conventional expressions come about if there are no referents?' it is [taught] to be like an echo. In order to eliminate the doubts of those who think, 'If there are no referents, how can the experiential object of the samādhi of apprehending true actuality come about?' it is [taught] to be like [a reflection of] the moon in water. In order to eliminate the doubts of those who think, 'If there are no referents, how can unerring bodhisattvas be reborn as they wish in order to accomplish their activity for sentient beings?' it is [taught] to be like a magical creation." In line with both the first chapter of the *Madhyāntavibhāga* and DDV, *Mahāyānasaṃgraha* II. 32 (ibid., fol. 21a.6–21b.2) says, "'How are their defining characteristics to be explained?' In the dependent characteristic, the imaginary characteristic does not exist, but the perfect characteristic exists in it. Thus, through not seeing or seeing true reality, respectively, these two [—the perfect and the imaginary natures—] are simultaneously not observed or observed as being existent and nonexistent, respectively. It is by virtue of the imaginary not existing and the perfect existing in the dependent nature that such occurs. For when the [imaginary nature] is observed, the [perfect nature] is not observed and when the [imaginary nature] is not observed, the [perfect nature] is observed." See also the other quotations from these two chapters above and below.

515 RC (p. 121) says that, by way of these six points, all saṃsāric phenomena are determined through study and reflection and thus understood in an unmistaken manner. Therefore, this is their unsurpassable comprehension. SC (p. 153) comments that the detailed explanation of phenomena frees one from being ignorant about the basic nature of saṃsāra. Acording to MC (fol. 6b.3–5), this manner of comprehending the natures of phenomena as the factors to be relinquished is unsurpassable because one is able to easily determine all of them without exception.

516 As mentioned before, this refers back to the following passages in DDV above: "What appears as duality and according designations is false imagination, which is the defining characteristic of phenomena . . . If any one of these two—nonexistence and appearance—did not exist, mistakenness, unmistakenness, afflicted phenomena, and purified phenomena would not be tenable. These two are neither one nor are they distinct because there is a difference as well as no difference in terms of existence and nonexistence."

517 OED omits *snang ba*.

518 The last two sentences are literally taken from DDVV (fol. 30a.2–3). Thus, OED *khas blang pa* is emended to *khas blang pas*.

519 According to RC (p. 122), what cycles and the place where it cycles constitute the matrix that pervades all saṃsāric phenomena, with "matrix" meaning the realms of sentient beings and the container.

520 Literally, "the connection of having arisen from something."

521 These two types of connection are the only ones that are accepted as existing between phenomena in Buddhism. Thus, if something is not connected in either way to consciousness, it is totally unrelated to it and thus cannot appear to it. Depending on the point of view, dream appearances can be said to be connected to cognition in terms of having the same nature as cognition and/or arising from it, while something that is never seen has neither connection to cognition. Both RC (p. 122) and MC (fol. 7a.6–7b.1) comment that the world is in common because it appears in common to the cognizances that seem to be in common in those sentient

beings in whom concordant latent tendencies awake. RC continues that the term "seem" indicates that the awakening of concordant latent tendencies is referred to by the conventional expression "in common," but does not exist in the actual mode of being.

522 "Being born from dominant conditions" seems to refer to the other three types of being born besides being born from a womb that Buddhism describes—being born from an egg, being born from heat and moisture (certain animals, such as microbes), and miraculous birth (such as gods and beings in hell).

523 OED *zhes bya ba* is emended to *zhes bya bas* since the entire sentence is literally taken from DDVV (fol. 30a.7–30b.1).

524 Thus, the distinction here is between phenomena in the mind streams of sentient beings being dominating conditions versus being object conditions (among the four conditions described in the Buddhist theory of causation). This distinction accords with Dharmakīrti's *Saṃtānāntarasiddhi* (D4219, fol. 358a.2) saying that the mind stream of another being represents a dominant condition (and not an object condition). Vinītadeva's commentary on this (D4238, fol. 42b.4ff.) explains that this includes the looks, the movements, and the conducts triggered by that mind stream. Compare also Vasubandhu's *Viṃśatikā* 18ab (*anyonādhipatitvena vijñaptiniyamo mithaḥ/*):

> By virtue of mutual domination
> The certainty of cognizance is reciprocal.

According to the autocommentary, "it is by virtue of a specific cognizance in a given mind stream that a specific cognizance in [another] mind stream arises, but not by virtue of a specific [external] referent." Thus, in Yogācāra, the seeming commonality of the perceptions of different beings is not explained through an external material world that is literally common to (and independent of) all who perceive it, but through the mental processes of different beings influencing each other directly. RC (p. 122) and MC (fols. 7b.3–8b.4) say that the manner of birth being in common refers to something like the result of a body being born from a womb through the common causes that consist of one's own karma functioning as the cause and the semen and ovum of one's parents functioning as the cooperative conditions. As for behavior being in common, triggered by the perceptible physical and verbal actions of others, one engages in looking and speaking to them and so on. Somebody taking care of someone else can happen through the dharma or material things, while defeat occurs through verbal quarrels, waging battles, and so on. Benefit refers to protecting others from fear and so on, while harm comes through beating and so on. In all these cases, others function as the dominant conditions, while the phenomena of one's mind stream function as the primary cause for a result that is perceived in common. It is from this point of view that they are called "in common." MC continues that, conventionally, these results are produced through the coming together of those causes and conditions. However, ultimately, through speaking of "dominant conditions" here, Maitreya teaches that there are no external referents that are other than cognizance and serve as object conditions. Also, since the appearances that seem to be in common (such as the outer container) are nothing other than the mere apprehended aspect of internal cognizance, external referents that are in common are not established.

525 Differing from the above "birth" in the set of what is in common in terms of sentient beings (which refers to the actual process of birth that is perceptible by others), in this sequence after "death" and "transition," "birth" refers to conception (which cannot be perceived by others)—the consciousness of a being entering into its next life at the end of the intermediate state after having died in its last life.

526 RC (pp. 123–24) and MC (fol. 8a.5) gloss "cognizance" as the seven consciousnesses other than the ālaya-consciousness, while LZC (p. 10) speaks of six. RC also quotes the *Laṅkāvatārasūtra* (D107, fols. 202b.2 and 202b.4–5):

> Through the ever-abiding ocean of the ālaya
> Being stirred by the wind of objects,
> The waves of various consciousnesses
> Will dance and engage . . .
> Just as ocean and waves
> Are without distinction,
> The consciousnesses and mind are likewise
> Unobservable as being different.

RC concludes this section by saying that the explanations on phenomena being in common and not being in common teach "the matrix" of phenomena because what appear to be in common and not in common arise through latent tendencies being planted in the ālaya.

527 The *Abhidharmasamuccaya* (D4049, fol. 86b.3–4) speaks of the world and sentient beings as "common and uncommon karma," respectively. Both it and the *Viniścayasaṃgrahaṇī* (D4038, vol. zhi, fol. 7a.3–5) also discuss the interactions between beings.

528 OED *'jig rten pa'i* instead of *'dzin pa'i*.

529 Verse 26.

530 OED *phyi rol* instead of *phra rab*.

531 D4206 (fol. 86a.7–86b.3) on verses 1–2.

532 OED *gzung ba med pa'i don du med pa la 'jug pa*. As it stands, this is hard to make sense of—the above is arrived at by omitting the second *med pa*, thus being in accord with the heading of this section. Alternatively, by omitting the first *med pa*, this could also be read as "the comprehension of the nonexistence of [anything] as apprehended referents." RC (p. 124) comments that what appears as something apprehended that is external does not exist as a referent external to consciousness because it is merely one's very own cognition that appears as something in common. It does not exist as another referent apart from the factor that consists of the cognizance that is its apprehender. According to MC (fols. 8b.3–9a.6), what appears as something apprehended that is in common and external is not established as an external referent that is different from internal cognition and whose nature is matter. For it is just the internal cognizances which are the apprehenders in those in whom certain latent tendencies awaken in a concordant manner that appear as the aspects of certain external referents, just like reflections in a dream. Therefore, there is no external referent that is other than consciousness. Thus, what is called "an external referent that is something to be viewed in common" refers simply to the aspects that appear in common in many beings whose mind streams are not the same. Therefore, these aspects are established as not being different from the apprehenders in those individual mind streams. As for the reason for this, if what is called "an external referent that is something to be viewed in common" (which is adduced as a proof for the existence of external referents) is only presented as "an external referent that is in common" by virtue of the manner of certain appearances in individual mind streams being similar, these appearances are simply appearances of those individual mind streams, but it is never possible for them to be in common. A common "external referent" that is other than those mere appearances in individual mind streams can never be pinpointed as being "this" through reasoning. For one would have to present such an object as existing apart from what appears in the mind. However, since there is no valid cognition that could evaluate it without having appeared in the mind, it is not reasonable to present such an external object. Therefore, if one examines well this "external referent

that is something to be viewed in common" and if one ascertains that the reason for presenting it as "being in common" consists of certain appearances in individual mind streams being similar, though these appearances are similar, there is no need to establish a common external referent that is the common cause of those individual appearances, just as similar appearances arise for people whose eyes are affected by a mantra used in producing illusions (a more modern example would be a hologram). Thus, in beings in whom concordant latent tendencies awaken, places and so on will appear in a similar manner for as long as the power of these latent tendencies has not been exhausted. However, there is no externally existent referent that is the single cause for these similar appearances. Just as there are, with regard to what humans perceive as water, different visible appearances for the six kinds of beings with different karmic appearances, what appear to be external and in common should be understood as being merely one's own internal mind's own appearances.

533 The last sentence is not part of DDV, but only appears in DDVV (fol. 31a.4–5).

534 With a few additions, this paragraph corresponds to DDVV (fol. 31a.4–6). RC (pp. 124–25) comments that it is the apprehending cognizances of those in meditative equipoise and of those not in meditative equipoise that are not mutual objects. For those who are not in meditative equipoise, it is their own conceptions that appear as objects and, for those who are in meditative equipoise, the experiential object of samādhi does not appear as the nature of the mind of someone other, but as a reflection of this mind. SC (p. 152) has someone object, "If what is to be apprehended by the cognitions of knowing the minds of others that exist in noble ones and nonnoble ones does not exist, this contradicts the position of this system that there exist other mind streams. But if it does exist, doesn't it follow that apprehender and apprehended are different in substance?" In this context of explaining the Madhyamaka of ground and fruition being inseparable, it is indeed not explained that other mind streams are established, but the direct answer to the above dispute accords with the meaning of the passage in DDV that speaks about the minds of others not mutually serving as objects for either those in meditative equipoise or those not in meditative equipoise. MC (fols. 9a.6–10b.1) presents the following objection: "Indeed, no one is able to refute that all appearances are appearances in the mind. However, this does not prove that all appearances are one in substance with mind, nor does it prove that there are no external referents that cast appearances into the mind. For this is just as in the case of someone being clairvoyant about the minds of others—though such clairvoyance exists, it does not prove that, just like external referents, the minds of others do not exist, nor does it prove that the appearance of someone else's mind is one in substance with one's own mind." Though it is possible to know the minds of others through the power of an awareness-mantra (used to propitiate mundane and supramundane deities in order to partake of their activity), samādhi, and so on, the mind streams of others are not direct objects for either the minds of those in meditative equipoise or the minds of those not in meditative equipoise. For those who are not in meditative equipoise, it is their own conceptions that appear as aspects that resemble the minds of others. For those who are in meditative equipoise, similarly to the aspects of knowing the past and the future, a reflection of the minds of others—a mere aspect that resembles these minds—appears. Therefore, the two ways of cognizing an object that arises in the form of its aspect through the mind focusing on that object and cognizing an object that arises as the nature of an experience that is one in substance with the mind itself are dissimilar—though the minds of yogins may know the suffering, happiness, and so on in the minds of ordinary beings in the manner of focusing on them, it is not that, by virtue of this, the minds of these yogins have the same experiences as these others do. You may wonder, "If, just like the minds of others, external referents too are not experienced directly, but are experienced by virtue of the appearance of an aspect, how is that contradictory?" If it weren't the case that it is cognition itself that, under the influence of the awakening of internal latent tendencies, appears as if being referents, even if there existed external referents, they would not appear, just as water

does not appear for hungry ghosts and forms do not appear for the gods in the formless realm of Infinite Space. On the other hand, if internal latent tendencies have awakened as their clearly manifest forms, there is no need for separate external referents, just as pus appears for hungry ghosts and an all-pervasive appearance of space appears for those in Infinite Space. Therefore, all that ever happens is that appearances arise under the influence of mind, but it is not that mind arises under the influence of appearances. Likewise, it is not that a mind stream arises under the influence of other minds because one is not able to hold that, if only one mind stream passes into nirvāṇa, all others do so too. "Since buddhas fully perceive all phenomena, whatever appears to them is one in substance with their wisdom. However, in that case, the mind stream of a buddha and the mind streams of sentient beings would be one." It is said that buddhas lack any notions of their own mind stream and the mind streams of different sentient beings—their mind stream consists of the wisdom that is the fundamental change in accord with the nature of phenomena. Therefore, it cannot be measured in terms of it and all phenomena being one or different, just as *Mūlamadhyamakakārikā* XVIII.7cd says:

> The unarisen and unceasing
> Nature of phenomena is like nirvāṇa.

535 "These two" refers to the two types of conceptions about the apprehender being regarded as either a substantially existent or an imputedly existent person.

536 V.7.

537 III.353bd.

538 DDVV (fol. 31a.7–31b.1) explains that "What is arising without beginning is the ignorance about suchness, which is the appearing of a duality that does not exist—the cause of mistakenness." MC (fol. 11a.4–6) glosses this as "the arising or awakening or ripening of the latent tendencies of dualistic appearances that have continued as such since beginnless time, possess the [operational] mode of obscuring true reality, and abide together with natural luminosity."

539 Compare the Third Karmapa's autocommentary on his *Profound Inner Reality* (Rang byung rdo rje n.d., p. 21): "The [inconceivable] point of enlightenment is that [the basic element] is associated with these stains since beginningless time, but because these stains are adventitious, they are not established as any real substance."

540 XVIII.104.

541 I.21–22ab.

542 Lines 14cd–15.

543 Compare also the sequence of the four yogic practices as explained below (OED, pp. 585–87). RC (p. 125) comments that, as for cognition apprehending objects, what appears as the apprehender is established as not existing as anything that is another referent because it is just one's own mind that appears as objects, while what appears as the apprehended is established as not existing as anything that is another referent. By virtue of the teaching that the duality of apprehender and apprehended does not exist ultimately, the comprehension of the nonexistence of the appearance of apprehender and apprehended is established because the nonexistence of the duality of apprehender and apprehended is determined through study and reflection and the actuality of the nonduality of apprehender and apprehended becomes fully perceptible through meditation. Though the duality of apprehender and apprehended does not exist ultimately, the causes for the appearance of that duality are the latent tendencies of clinging to apprehender and apprehended since beginningless time because the arising of the clinging to apprehender and apprehended is established by virtue of those tendencies. Nevertheless, it can be relinquished because, though the clinging to duality does not engage in the actual mode of

being, the realization of the lack of that duality does so. For while the duality of apprehender and apprehended is not really established, the lack of duality is established well. DLC (p. 187) says that what appear as apprehender and apprehended are established as being nonexistent ultimately because all appearances are the beginningless arising of the latent tendencies of being ignorant about suchness and imagining it to be unreal, which represents the mere energy of the seeds in the ālaya-consciousness. For one sees the arising of mutually exclusive consciousnesses (such as seeing water, pus, and so on) with regard to a single object. Therefore, to proclaim the assertion that what appear as water, pus, and so on are actually different objects as representing the system of Great Madhyamaka is a philosophical system that is even more inferior than Mere Mentalism. MC (fols. 10b.2–11b.1) says that if it is established that what appears as the apprehended does not exist by its own nature as anything other than the apprehender, it is established that what appears as the apprehender is not established either. For an apprehender is established in dependence on something apprehended, but it is not established on its own. Thus, being free from all aspects of the duality of apprehender and apprehended, the mere inexpressible awareness that is naturally luminous and lacks subject and object is not different from suchness—the perfect nature empty of the two types of identity. Let alone by the Mādhyamikas, this must even be realized by the Mere Mentalists. According to the Mere Mentalists, with the actuality of the sixteen emptinesses being complete in the nature of this luminous awareness, it cannot be conceived or expressed as any phenomena in terms of apprehender and apprehended (such as internal, external, and so on). Therefore, it is asserted to be free from reference points. However, there remains the subtle philosophical position of presenting the nature of this inexpressible cognition as being really established. On the other hand, it is the correct Madhyamaka if this position is refuted through reasoning and thus the very cognition that lacks apprehender and apprehended is asserted as one's own mind that is primordially pure luminosity, lacks real existence, and is in union with being empty. Therefore, the difference between these two mahāyāna systems of Mere Mentalism and Madhyamaka lies only in having or not having cut through that subtle essential point of clinging, while their practices in meditative equipoise and subsequent attainment are pretty much the same. Therefore, it is due to this point that the great scholars and siddhas of India treated these two systems as being virtually without difference in terms of the practice of the mahāyāna. By virtue of understanding the manner of there being no apprehender and apprehended as explained above and through resting one-pointedly in meditative equipoise in this actuality, the direct comprehension of the nonexistence of the appearance of apprehender and apprehended is established, that is, the nature of phenomena without duality will be seen. You may consider it unreasonable that, while this nondual nature of phenomena exists primordially, it does not appear, whereas the mistakenness of dualistic appearances arises. However, the latent tendencies of the dualistic appearances of apprehender and apprehended, which have continued since beginningless time, obscure true reality and abide together with mind's natural luminosity. Since it is established that they arise or awaken or mature, mistakenness and saṃsāra arise from this cause. It is also not the case that one is not able to relinquish these latent tendencies due to their abiding together with mind's luminosity since beginningless time because it is well established that the two of apprehender and apprehended are not established at all. When one familiarizes with this after having understood it, one will see it directly. SGC (fol. 4b.3–4), following DDVV, says that, though the two of apprehender and apprehended are not established at all, by virtue of the reason that one sees the arising of consciousnesses that are in contradiction to this and so on, they are established/commonly known. LZC (p. 13) follows DDVV virtually verbatim. LBC (fols. 6b.6–7a.2) and LDC (fol. 10a.5–10b.2) both gloss "while the two are not established at all, they are commonly known" according to the Tibetan as "while apprehender and apprehended are not established through reasoning as being substantially different, it is established through reasoning that apprehender and apprehended do not exist as being substantially different." Therefore, since this conforms with the actual way of being of phenomena, one is able to eventually relinquish dualistic appearances despite their arising by virtue of clinging to duality since beginningless time.

544 RC (p. 126) says that the comprehension of the nature of phenomena through these six points is unsurpassable because one will understand all phenomena of nirvāṇa without exception. The six points are the defining characteristic of what is to be known, the matrix that is the basis of what is to be known, penetrating the nature of phenomena, directly making contact with the nature of phenomena, recollecting it, and arriving at the nature of that recollection. MC (fol. 11b.3–5) says that the defining characteristic of the nature of phenomena is what is to be known, the matrix is the basis for its arising (or the basis on which the observation of the nature of phenomena is founded), and the arrival at the nature of the nature of phenomena is its perfection or completion. SC (p. 153) comments that the detailed explanations on comprehending the nature of phenomena and nonconceptual wisdom make one understand the manner of cultivating the path to liberation, just as it is. However, these explanations do not solely refer to the uncommon mahāyāna because the divisions of the nature of phenomena as they are discussed here explain the nirvāṇas of all three yānas. The introduction of Jamgön Kongtrul's commentary on the *Uttaratantra* (Kong sprul blo gros mtha' yas 2005, p. 24) says that, among these six points, the first one is what one should understand; the middling four, what one should familiarize with; and the last one, the fruition.

545 Sthiramati's *Triṃśikābhāṣya* (Lévi ed., pp. 41.2–42.9; D4064, fol. 169a.2–169b.7) on verses 23–25 comments on the three natures as the three kinds of lack of nature as follows: "'If the dependent is substantial, why is it that the sūtras teach that "all phenomena are without nature, unarisen, and unceasing"?' There is no contradiction. Therefore, [verse 23 says]:

> It is with regard to the three kinds of lack of nature
> Of the three kinds of nature
> That the lack of nature
> Of all phenomena is taught.

This teaches [their] number in order to state that there are only three natures and not four. By virtue of their respective own characteristics, they seem to exist. [Therefore, they are said to be natures.] The threefold lack of nature consists of the lack of nature in terms of characteristics, the lack of nature in terms of arising, and the ultimate lack of nature. All phenomena have the character of the imaginary, the dependent, and the perfect [natures]. Now, in order to teach what the lack of nature of which one among the three natures is, [lines 24–25ab] say:

> The first one lacks a nature
> In terms of characteristics, the next one
> Lacks existence on its own,
> And the following is the lack of nature as such.
> It is the ultimate of phenomena
> And therefore it is suchness too.

'The first one' is the imaginary nature—it is the lack of nature in terms of characteristics because its characteristics are [only] ascribed. It is said that what has the characteristic of form is form, what has the characteristic of experience is feeling, and so on. Therefore, since these do not have any nature of their own, they represent the lack of nature in terms of a nature of their own, just like a flower in the sky. 'The next one' is the dependent nature. Just like an illusion, it does not exist [on its own] since it arises from other conditions. Therefore, it lacks [any real] arising in the way it appears. Consequently, it is called 'the lack of nature in terms of arising.' [As for the perfect nature, lines 25ab] say:

> It is the ultimate of phenomena
> And therefore it is suchness too.

'Highest' *(parama)* refers to supramundane wisdom because it is unsurpassable. Its referent (artha) is the highest referent. Or, in the sense of being of one taste everywhere, just like space, and in the sense of being stainless and unchanging, the perfect nature is called 'the ultimate' (paramārtha). Thus, the perfect nature is the ultimate [reality] of all phenomena that have the character of being dependent. Since it is referred to as their true nature, this perfect nature is the ultimate lack of nature because the perfect nature is the nature of the lack of entity *(abhāvasvabhāva)*. 'Is it to be referred as the perfect [nature] just because of being referred to as the ultimate?' It is not. 'What is it then?' 'It is suchness too.' As for the word 'too,' it is not that only the term suchness is to be referred [here]. 'What then?' All the many [terms] that are included in the [set of] synonyms of the dharmadhātu are to be referred. [According to line 25c,] 'Since it is such at all times' it is suchness. Thus, at all times, in ordinary beings, learners, and nonlearners, it is such but never otherwise. Therefore, it is called 'suchness.' 'Is suchness—the perfect [nature]—the very being of mere cognizance or is the very being of mere cognizance something else?' Therefore, [line 25d] says, 'It is the very being of mere cognizance.' This is said because of the realization of the characteristic of utter purity. It is said:

> The mind abides in [mere] names
> Since merely that is seen at that time.
> By virtue of abiding in [mere] names
> [Any] observing of cognizance is relinquished.
> At that point, through the succession of [such] familiarization,
> One makes contact with the dhātu of nonobservation,
> Is liberated from all obscurations,
> And attains mastery then.

The words 'It is the very being of mere cognizance' teach clear realization." Vinītadeva's *Triṃśikāṭīkā* (D4070, fols. 56a.5–58a.7) elaborates on the lack of nature in terms of the imaginary nature that the characteristics of form, feeling, and so on are just characteristics or means in order to know entities but are not the ultimate nature of entities. Thus, they function as general characteristics, but generalities are not existing entities. For example, a victory banner may be used in order to point out a house, but the victory banner is not the nature of the house. Likewise, statements such as "what exists as form" function as characteristics in order to know entities. Therefore, since form and so on lack a nature of their own, they are imaginary. On the lack of nature in terms of the dependent nature, Vinītadeva says that the dependent arises through the power of other factors, but lacks any existence of its own. Therefore, it is a lack of nature. Here, the term "existence" refers to arising. Or the dependent lacks arising in the way in which the aspects of apprehender and apprehended appear. Therefore, it is called "the lack of nature in terms of arising." Since it has the nature of being free from that appearing of apprehender and apprehended, it is taught as this lack of nature. Here the term "nature" refers to arising. On the lack of nature in terms of the perfect nature, Vinītadeva comments that since the perfect nature is the ultimate reality of all dependent phenomena, it is the very lack of nature. For it has the nature of the nonexistence of apprehender and apprehended. The perfect nature is the ultimate (*paramārtha*) by virtue of being the focal object or referent (*artha*) of highest (*parama*) supramundane wisdom. In particular, Sthiramati's above passage "Since it is referred to as their true nature . . ." teaches the reason for the perfect nature being connected to the dependent. Thus, it is the true nature of dependent phenomena. Therefore, it is their ultimate reality. "If the perfect nature is the ultimate reality of these dependent phenomena, why is it the lack of entity?" Therefore, Sthiramati said, "the perfect [nature] . . ." The perfect nature is the nature of the lack of entity; therefore, it is called "lack of nature." Or the term "lack of entity" refers to the emptiness that is free from what is other (**pararahitaśūnyatā*), which refers to the nature of entities (*bhāvasvabhāva*). The synonyms for the dharmadhātu include emptiness, the true limit, signlessness, nonduality, the dhātu of nonconceptuality, what is inexpressible, what is unarisen and unceasing, what is unconditioned, and nirvāṇa. As for suchness being such at all times, minds and mental factors are always free from apprehender and apprehended. Since minds and mental factors never abandon this nature, the freedom from apprehender and apprehended exists in them just like that and never changes into anything else. Therefore, one speaks of "suchness" just as water remains in its own nature even when polluted. The perfect nature is what is called "the very being of mere cognizance"—it is nothing other. Through realizing the perfect nature, the characteristic of utter purity is realized. Therefore, it is the very being of mere cognizance. The reason for realizing the characteristic of utter purity is as follows. When yogins have dismantled the apprehended at the time of heat and peak, at the time of poised readiness the mind abides in mere names. When having become free from the aspect of the apprehended in this way, it is seen as mere names. As it is taught, "When having dismantled the apprehended, the mind abides in mere cognizance. For one knows that it is this mere cognizance that arises as the appearances of form and so on, whereas referents such as form do not exist." The term "name" refers to mere cognizance because it is said that "'name' means the skandhas without form." Through the mind abiding in names in this way, at the time of the supreme dharma any focusing on cognizance is relinquished. For if the apprehended is not observed, the apprehender is not observed either. The term "cognizance" refers to the aspect of the apprehender. After apprehender and apprehended have been dismantled in this way, at the point of the arising of the path of seeing, through the power of familiarization, one makes contact with, that is, directly realizes or perceives, the dhātu of nonconceptuality. The term "dhātu of nonconceptuality" refers to the dharmadhātu. When the dharmadhātu is realized, through proceeding higher and higher one is liberated from all obscurations and masters all qualities such as samādhi. The [line] "It is the very being of mere cognizance" teaches clear realization. Or since the path also represents the perfect nature, it is taught to be mere cognizance. Therefore, it is supramundane wisdom that is taught as the term "mere cognizance" here. It is in this way that one realizes the characteristic of utter purity, which means to realize the dharmadhātu.

546 II.32 (D4048, fol. 24b.1).

547 Note that the *Mahāyānasaṃgraha* above only says that, in the dependent nature, the imaginary nature is not observed, while the perfect nature is observed. However, as OED explained several times before (in perfect harmony with many Indian Yogācāra texts), the dependent nature is unreal and a part of the obscurations. Also, mere cognizance (*vijñaptimâtra*) is not always understood as an equivalent of the dependent nature. By definition, the latter entails apprehender and apprehended, while the former is sometimes explained as a term for nondual pure awareness without apprehender and apprehended, that is, nonconceptual wisdom as one of the two aspects of the perfect nature. To highlight this point, Yogācāra texts often distinguish between *vijñaptimātra* (or *cittamātra*) and *vijñaptimātratā* (or *cittamātratā*)—the latter being the very nature of the former. Thus, from this perspective, there is no problem in saying that both the imaginary and the dependent are not seen in such nonconceptual wisdom, while the nature of phenomena (or suchness), as the other aspect of the perfect nature, is seen. On the other hand, mere cognizance is also sometimes understood in the sense of being just the apprehender.

548 According to the *Abhidharmasamuccaya*, (1)–(3), (8), and (9) represent the sūtrapiṭaka of the śrāvakas; (4)–(6) and (10), the vinayapiṭaka; (7) and (12), the sūtrapiṭaka of bodhisattvas; and (11), the abhidharmapiṭaka of both the hīnayāna and the mahāyāna.

549 RC (p. 127) comments that the matrix consists of all afflicted and purified phenomena as well as all sūtras because what is purified must be attained through cutting through superimpositions by way of studying and reflecting on those phenomena and the path must be practiced by way of focusing on the sūtras. MC (fols. 11b.6–12a.2) also glosses phenomena as all afflicted and purified phenomena and gives the following reasons for phenomena and sūtras being the

matrix. Nirvāṇa is attained through determining the ways of what is to be adopted and what is to be rejected among all phenomena on the conventional level and determining that all phenomena are not observable ultimately. Through engaging in the sūtras by way of study and reflection, one will not be ignorant about the manner of practicing the path.

550 This indicates a universe that includes three sets of world systems. The first set (a chiliocosm) consists of one thousand worlds as presented in ancient Indian cosmology, with each one containing Mount Meru, the four continents, and so on. The second set (a dichiliocosm) consists of the first set plus one thousand worlds that each have the size of the first set, and the third set consists of the first two sets plus one thousand worlds that each have the size of the second set.

551 II.14–16.

552 D4027, fol. 9b.1–7. According to Mipham Rinpoche's commentary on the *Madhyāntavibhāga* ('Ju mi pham rgya mtsho c. 1990c, pp. 693–97), in the nature of the dharmadhātu (the object to be realized) there are no different types. Still, in the subject that realizes this dharmadhātu (the meditative equipoises of the ten bhūmis) there are differences in terms of its increasingly pure seeing of the dharmadhātu, though there is no difference in these meditative equipoises in terms of the manner in which dualistic appearances vanish within the dharmadhātu free from reference points. Therefore, just as one is not able to distinguish the traces of a bird in space, one cannot distinguish the bhūmis from the perspective of meditative equipoise. When bodhisattvas progress from bhūmi to bhūmi, the respectively corresponding factors to be relinquished are relinquished through the particular wisdoms of the meditative equipoises of the respective bhūmis. Through the power of that, particular kinds of certainty about the dharmadhātu arise during subsequent attainment. Thus, the manner in which the factors to be relinquished are relinquished is explained here from the point of view of the aspects of those certainties. (1) When the dharmadhātu has been seen directly in the meditative equipoise of the first bhūmi, during its subsequent attainment there arises the realization that the dharmadhātu has the nature of being all-pervading and omnipresent. In this way, the meditative equipoise of the first bhūmi is that which induces this subsequent certainty because the latter is attained based on the former. Or one could say that bodhisattvas realize that the dharmadhātu entails the actuality of omnipresence. Consequently, the obstacle for not realizing this actuality of the omnipresence of the dharmadhātu is the obscuration of this bhūmi. Since this obscuration is relinquished through the arising of the wisdom of the first bhūmi, that certainty during subsequent attainment arises automatically. This is also the case because all phenomena have become of the nature of the dharmadhātu when the dharmadhātu is seen directly, and therefore the nature of phenomena that is the equality of oneself and others is attained. The same goes for the remaining bhūmis. (2) The wisdom of the second bhūmi consists of the actuality of the further eminence, or the supreme increase, of the realization of the dharmadhātu. This means that bodhisattvas who have attained this wisdom practice purification through even greater efforts than before. (3) On the third bhūmi bodhisattvas realize that studying the words of the Buddha—the natural outflow of the dharmadhātu—is the supreme purpose to be strived for. Thus, for the sake of a single verse of dharma, they even cross a pit that is filled by a fire the size of a trichiliocosm. They do so because they see that the dharmadhātu is the most significant and supreme undeceiving one among all objects to be realized, and that there is no superior cause for its realization than to study the words of buddha. (4) On the fourth bhūmi bodhisattvas realize the actuality of nonclinging (such as clinging to any phenomena as being what is "mine")—they even put an end to craving for the dharma, let alone any clinging to what is not the dharma. (5) On the fifth bhūmi they realize the actuality that the phenomena included in the mind streams of themselves and others are not different. They also see that their own mind streams are not different from the buddhas and bodhisattvas of the three times. Furthermore, the sūtras describe this as the ten equalities of completely pure mind and intention—(a)–(c)

the equality of past, present, and future buddhas in their intentions with respect to the completely pure dharma, (d) the equality of intention with respect to completely pure ethics, (e) completely pure sentient beings, (f) completely pure elimination of views, doubts, and regrets, (g) completely pure knowledge of what is the path and what is not the path, (h) completely pure knowledge of the path, (i) completely pure increasing application of the dharmas concordant with enlightenment, and (j) completely pure maturation of sentient beings. Through these equalities bodhisattvas realize that the dharmakāya of all buddhas is not different from their own mind stream (according to the *Daśabhūmikasūtra*, the ten equalities are the equality of all phenomena in (1) their lack of defining characteristics, (2) their lack of characteristics, (3) their nonarising from the four extremes, (4) their nonarising, (5) their being void, (6) their primordial purity, (7) their lack of reference points, (8) their lack of being adopted or rejected, (9) phenomena being like dreams, optical illusions, water moons, reflections, and magical creations, and (10) their being entities or nonentities). (6) On the sixth bhūmi bodhisattvas see the actuality of profound dependent origination. Therefore, this is the realization that there is no phenomenon that is first afflicted and later becomes pure. (7) On the seventh bhūmi, through realizing signlessness, they realize the actuality of all phenomena having the single taste of not being different. (8) On the eighth bhūmi, through attaining the poised readiness for nonarising, they realize the actuality of all phenomena existing as equality, in which there is neither decrease nor increase. In general, through the wisdoms of the three pure bhūmis, bodhisattvas realize the dharmadhātu as the matrix of the fourfold mastery over the nonconceptual dharmadhātu, pure realms, wisdom, and enlightened activity. On the eighth bhūmi they attain mastery over nonconceptuality because they lack any reference points and characteristics by virtue of resting in meditative equipoise in the dharmadhātu in the manner of one taste. They also attain mastery over pure realms because there appear, and they display, limitless appearances of buddha realms and maṇḍalas of retinues. (9) On the ninth bhūmi they attain mastery over the wisdom of teaching the dharma through the four types of discriminating awareness. (10) During the subsequent attainment of the tenth bhūmi bodhisattvas attain mastery over enlightened activity happening in exactly the way they wish. In this manner, the wisdoms of the meditative equipoises of the last three bhūmis are the cause or matrix of those masteries. Since this is the case through the power of bodhisattvas focusing on the dharmadhātu, the dharmadhātu should be understood as the actual matrix in which those qualities arise. Bodhisattvas are able to ascertain this through seeing it directly, whereas ordinary beings should understand it through inference. It is true that there is some degree of simply inducing certainty about the dharmadhātu being omnipresent, without decrease and increase, and so on even on the level of engagement through aspiration. However, during the subsequent attainments of having directly encountered the pure dharmadhātu through the wisdoms of the respective bhūmis, bodhisattvas attain the effortless certainty that cuts through superimpositions through the power of their experience. This is to be understood as the increasingly pure special seeing of the nature of the dharmadhātu that consists of the phases of progressing from bhūmi to bhūmi. Thus, the ignorance that obscures seeing the nature of the dharmadhātu as it is bears the names "great dullness" or "cognitive obscurations." For its nature consists of the ten obscurations that are not afflictions, while the ten bhūmis represent the remedies for the antagonistic factors of the wisdoms of these ten bhūmis. That is, through attaining the respective bhūmis, these obscurations are relinquished for good. See also Brunnhölzl 2010, Appendix I1H1db ("The distinctive features of realization").

553 IV.32–34ab. "Focusing on the Buddha and so on" refers to the skill in the means to abide in signlessness through eliminating signs and characteristics by way of confidence in the three jewels. The sphere of vigor consists of all six pāramitās, and "the consummate intention" is bodhicitta.

554 Ibid., IV.34cd.

555 Usually called "the branches conducive to penetration" (Skt. nirvedhabhāgīya, Tib. nges 'byed cha mthun), which refer to the four levels of the path of preparation—heat, peak, poised readiness, and supreme dharma.

556 MC (fol. 12a.3–4) explains "penetration" (for "discernment") in DDV (K)/(P) as penetrating or identifying the nature of phenomena through mentally engaging in it by way of the threefold prajñā of study, reflection, and meditation according to the meaning of the sūtras on the paths of accumulation and preparation. LDC (fol. 11a.3–4) adds that the path of accumulation consists primarily of studying and reflecting on the nature of phenomena, while the path of preparation consists primarily of meditating on it.

557 OED *shes bya mtshan nyid dag pa nyid*, which is repeated at the end of this section. The pertinent section of the *Mahāyānasaṃgraha* says *shes bya'i mtshan nyid la 'jug pa*.

558 III.1 (D4048, fol. 23a.7–23b.1).

559 D4037, fol. 2b.4.

560 I.39.

561 I.149–50.

562 IV.11ab.

563 IV.11cd.

564 I.34d.

565 III.2 (D4048, fol. 23b.1–2).

566 III.3 (ibid., fol. 23b.2–4).

567 III.4 (ibid., fol. 23b.4–5). OED has slight variations.

568 According to *Mahāyānasaṃgraha* III.5 (ibid., fols. 23b.5–24b.2), the third training means to consider that even beings who have accumulated comparatively limited virtues will obtain excellent conditions in their next life according to their present striving, so why should oneself as a bodhisattva who accumulates limitless virtues not obtain complete perfection?

569 III.6 (ibid., fol. 24a.2–4).

570 This is a very brief summary of *Mahāyānasaṃgraha* III.7 (ibid., fol. 24a.4–24b.2). On the path of preparation, bodhisattvas engage in four investigations, based on their mental discourse that arises from the causes which are the latent tendencies for listening, consists of proper mental engagement, appears as the dharma and its meanings, and is endowed with the view. These four investigations refer to the process of understanding names, referents, their natures, and their distinctive features as being nothing but internal mental discourse and imputations, while not existing as actual referents separate from the mind. The result of this process is the fourfold understanding of how things really are (*yathābhūtaparijñāna*). Through these four investigations and their resulting understanding, bodhisattvas realize that their conceptions that appear as letters and referents are nothing but mere cognizance (for the dissolution of mere cognizance too, see *Mahāyānasaṃgraha* III.8 quoted above). In the above passage in OED, it is not exactly clear what "both" means—the *Mahāyānasaṃgraha* says that the imputations of both a nature and distinctive features are not observable as actual referents (but also that names and referents too are not observable as such). Asvabhāva's *Mahāyānasaṃgrahopanibandhana* (D4051, fols. 244b.6–245a.2) explains that both the four objects of investigation (names and so on) and the results of these investigations are not observable, and that the four investigations serve to ascertain that the imaginary nature is unobservable. The four investigations and understandings are also found in the *Bodhisattvabhūmi* (D4037, fols. 29b.5–30b.7) and *Mahāyānasūtrālaṃkāra*

XIX.47 (see the comments on the two related verses in *Mahāyānasaṃgraha* I.16 below; OED, pp. 584–85).

571 OED omits "for the nonexistence of referents."

572 III.13 (D4048, fol. 25b.2–4). Thus, according to this presentation, on the first three levels of the path of preparation bodhisattvas conceptually realize that something apprehended does not really exist, which is one part of true reality (the other one being the nonexistence of the apprehender). On the last level, they also realize that, due to the nonexistence of the apprehended, the apprehender does not exist either. It is in this sense of mind being an independent apprehender that the notion of mere cognizance is abandoned too. On the immediately following path of seeing they then realize, in a direct and nonconceptual manner, the suchness that is free from any duality of apprehender and apprehended.

573 See 2.2.2.2.2.7.3.7.2.3. The progression of realization below (OED, pp. 584–87).

574 The set of four that consists of cognition, subsequent cognition, and so on refers to the distinct moments of wisdom of directly realizing the sixteen aspects (such as impermanence) of the four realities (this set of four applies to each one of these realities). "The six levels of dhyāna" consist of (1) the preparatory stage of the first dhyāna of the form realm, (2) the ordinary first dhyāna, (3) the special first dhyāna, and (4)–(6) the remaining three dhyānas.

575 According to *Mahāyānasaṃgraha* III.10, its *Bhāṣya* (D4050, fols. 158b.7–159a.3) and the *Mahāyānasaṃgrahopanibandhana* (D4051, fols. 245b.6–246a.7), "names" are to be understood as one's own cognizance appearing as names. Here bodhisattvas are aware that everything is just names in this sense. There are ten spheres of such names on which bodhisattvas focus—(1) phenomena, (2) persons, (3) dharmas (the twelve types of the Buddha's speech), (4) their meanings, (5) brief statements (such as "all phenomena are without identity"), (6) detailed statements (such as "form is without identity, feelings are without identity . . ."), (7) dispositions (*gotra*; the letters of the Sanskrit alphabet, since they are the causes of words and speech), (8) what is impure (ordinary beings who possess the stains of the afflictions), (9) what is pure (the noble ones who see reality and have relinquished those stains), and (10) what is final (the focal objects of the supramundane wisdom that focuses on all dharmas without combination and the wisdom attained subsequent to it, that is, what consists of prajñāpāramitā, the ten bhūmis, and so on). Among these ten, the first nine are associated with conceptions, while the last one is without conceptions.

576 III.9 and III.11 (D4048, fols. 24b.6–25a.5; OED's version is slightly abbreviated).

577 VI.8.

578 XVIII.58ab.

579 XVIII.58cd.

580 XVIII.59ab.

581 XVIII.59cd.

582 XVIII.60ab.

583 OED *mdo* instead of *dga' ba.*

584 XVIII.60cd.

585 XVIII.61ab.

586 XVIII.61cd.

587 XVIII.62ab.

588 XVIII.62cd.

589 As the quote from the *Madhyāntavibhāga* just below shows, joy is usually counted as the branch of benefit, while the branch of the lack of afflictions consists of suppleness, samādhi, and equanimity.

590 IV.8cd–9ab.

591 XIV.28–29ab.

592 Both RC (p. 127) and MC (fol. 12a.4–6) gloss "the correct view" as supramundane and "suchness" as being pure of the stains to be relinquished through seeing. MC also says that the view is attained through the eye of prajñā and that "in a direct manner" refers to its not just being an object generality (a concept about an object). Furthermore, "the attainment of suchness" refers to the meditative equipoise of the path of seeing, while "the experience of suchness" occurs during its subsequent attainment by virtue of the correct view.

593 Obviously, here "recollection" (*anusmṛti*) does not refer to a memory of something or to some other conceptual state, but has the sense of repeatedly and clearly bringing to mind, or cultivating, the direct and nonconceptual realization of the nature of phenomena as experienced on the path of seeing. In other words, the mind immerses itself in that realization again and again, until it is never separated from it.

594 The thirty-seven dharmas consist of consist of seven sets of practices—(1) the four applications of mindfulness, (2) the four correct exertions, (3) the four limbs of miraculous powers, (4) the five faculties, (5) the five powers, (6) the seven branches of enlightenment, and (7) the eightfold path of the noble ones. Sets (1)–(3) make up the lesser, medium, and greater levels of the path of accumulation, (4)–(5) respectively correspond to the first two (heat and peak) and the second two (poised readiness and supreme dharma) of the four levels of the path of preparation, (6) is equivalent to the path of seeing, and (7) represents the path of familiarization. Together with the the thirty-four aspects of bodhisattvas and the thirty-nine aspects of buddhas, these thirty-seven make up the 110 aspects of the knowledge of all aspects that are decribed in the fourth chapter of the *Abhisamayālaṃkāra*. In addition, there are the twenty-seven aspects in terms of the knowledge of entities and the thirty-six aspects in terms of the knowledge of the path, thus altogether 173 aspects in terms of these three knowledges that a bodhisattva has to cultivate. For details, see Brunnhölzl 2011b, pp. 28–41 and 144–63.

595 The *Bhāṣya* (D4050, fols. 162b.5–6 and 180b.1) glosses "focuses in combination" as "focuses on the topics on which the learned focus" and "focuses on all dharmas combined and taken together." The *Mahāyānasaṃgrahopanibandhana* (D4051, fol. 258b.3) glosses this expression as "knowing all dharmas." According to *Saṃdhinirmocanasūtra* VIII.13 (Powers 1994, pp. 160–63), bodhisattvas focus on all dharma teachings either without combining them or in combination. The first one means that they, in their calm abiding and superior insight, focus on individual teachings in the sūtras as they have apprehended, and reflected upon, them. The second one means that they group all these teachings together and take them as a single unit, thinking that all of them flow and merge into suchness, enlightenment, nirvāṇa, and the fundamental change. See also OED below (p. 560).

596 III.14 (D4048, fol. 25b.4–6).

597 XIV.42.

598 XIV.43ab.

599 XIV.43cd.

600 OED mistakenly repeats the passage "therefore masters the perfection . . . nonconceptual wisdom," the first time ending in *ye shes nyid yin pa'i phyir* and the second time, in *ye shes kyi las yin no* (the translation combines both endings).

601 XIV.44ab.

602 XX.17ac.

603 XX.17d–18.

604 XX.19ab.

605 XX.19cd.

606 As outlined in *Mahāyānasūtrālaṃkāra* XI.45–46, this refers to the fundamental change of the sixth and seventh consciousnesses on the eighth bhūmi and the ensuing fourfold mastery over nonconceptuality and pure realms (on the eighth bhūmi), wisdom (on the ninth one), and enlightened activity (on the tenth one). For more details, see the Third Karmapa's *Profound Inner Reality* and *Distinction between Consciousness and Wisdom* (Brunnhölzl 2009, pp. 157–59 and 294–301).

607 XX.20ac.

608 XX.20d.

609 I.127–129 (OED only quotes I.129). I.127–128 list the nine examples for buddha nature being obscured by adventitious stains, such as a buddha statue in a decaying lotus.

610 XIII.16. This verse also appears in the second chapter of the *Mahāyānasaṃgraha*. Vasubandhu's *Bhāṣya* (D4026, fol. 188b.4–6) comments that the following two facts scare childish beings—that phenomena do not exist, yet are observable, and that the dharmadhātu is naturally without afflictiveness and yet becomes pure later. Through showing that these two facts are like illusions and space, respectively, these fears are removed.

611 For Vasubandhu's *Bhāṣya* on verses XIII.16–19 together, see note 643.

612 In general, "roots of virtue" are divided into three sets. Those that are conducive to merit refer to the virtues of those who have not entered the Buddhist path. Those that are conducive to liberation are those on the path of accumulation proper and represent the virtues that eventually liberate from suffering. Those that are conducive to penetration are those on the path of preparation, with "penetration" referring to the path of seeing.

613 XIV.1.

614 Tib. lam sran.

615 This refers to the ālaya-consciousness and the three natures, respectively.

616 The last two sentences list the seven vajra points of the *Uttaratantra*.

617 IV.47. These are the signs of irreversibility of bodhisattvas on the path of seeing in terms of focusing on the reality of suffering (verses IV.48–51 present the signs with regard to the other three realities).

618 XX.21. In due order, the four results in *Mahāyānasūtrālaṃkāra* XX.19–21 as discussed above are thus occurring on the seventh, eighth, ninth, and tenth bhūmis.

619 In the *Mahāyānasaṃgraha*, the fourth chapter on the causes and results of engaging in the characteristics of knowable objects discusses the pāramitās, while its fifth chapter on the familiarization with these causes and results deals with the ten bhūmis. In the *Mahāyānasūtrālaṃkāra*, it is Chapter XVI that explains the pāramitās.

620 I.48–70.

621 I.67.

622 I.68.

623 According to *Mahāyānasūtrālaṃkāra* XI.45–46 and other sources, the first two kinds of mastery are those over nonconceptuality and pure realms.

624 These four lines correspond almost literally to *Abhisamayālaṃkāra* IV.52.

625 The last two lines correspond to *Madhyāntavibhāga* II.1ab.

626 These three lines resemble *Mahāyānasūtrālaṃkāra* VI.9.

627 Tib. thod rgal. This is a specific training on the bodhisattva path of familiarization in which one begins by ascending and descending through the four dhyānas and the four formless meditative absorptions in due order. Next, one ascends through these eight by way of alternating each one of them with the meditative absorption of cessation and finally enters a state of mind within the desire realm of not being in meditation. Then, one descends in the same manner. Lastly, one ascends and descends by alternating each of the dhyānas, formless absorptions, and the meditative absorption of cessation with that state of mind of not being in meditation. Obviously, this is not to be confused with the Dzogchen meditation of the same name.

628 This corresponds to the nirvāṇas of śrāvakas and pratyekabuddhas.

629 The Sanskrit *upagata* (Tib. *nye bar son pa*) can also mean "gone to," "met," "attained," "undergone," and "experienced."

630 Compare the first and second chapters of the *Uttaratantra*, which first explain the suchness with stains (*samalā tathatā*) and then equate the purified buddha nature with the suchness without stains (*nirmalā tathatā*).

631 RC (p. 128) says that the arrival at the place of complete familiarity—the nature of the path of familiarization on which one familiarizes with the dharmadhātu—is the path of nonlearning, that is, the attainment of the fundamental change of suchness being stainless. When that fundamental change is attained, after the appearances of the duality of apprehender and apprehended have vanished all appears as nothing but suchness. Therefore, this is the perfection of the fundamental change. Verse 6 of the *Kāyatrayāvatāra* says:

> Apart from stainless suchness
> And nonconceptual wisdom,
> There are no other dharmas
> Of the buddhas whatsoever.

According to MC (fol. 12b.2–4), once suchness has become without adventitious stains, all phenomena appear as nothing but suchness since their mode of appearance and their actual mode of being are the same in all respects. Though the sheer fundamental change exists already on the first bhūmi, its full completion occurs only on this final bhūmi.

632 In terms of isolates, but not in nature, the instantaneous training in the seventh chapter of the *Abhisamayālaṃkāra* is said to consist of four instants in terms of nonmaturation (being in the process of overcoming the most subtle stains of the infinite uncontaminated phenomena of wisdom), maturation (wisdom overcoming even the most subtle stains in a single instant), the lack of characteristics (realizing all phenomena as dreamlike), and nonduality (no longer seeing phenomena as the duality of apprehender and apprehended).

633 These five are taught in Chapter Five and also provided in Asvabhāva's *Mahāyānasaṃgrahopanibandhana* (D4051, fol. 277a.7–277b.1)—in each moment, bodhisattvas (1) destroy all impregnations of negative tendencies, (2) through being free from discriminating notions about variety, attain delight in the dharma, (3) correctly understand the light of dharma as being immeasurable and unfragmented everywhere, (4) characteristics that are not conceived and are in accordance with what is pure arise for them, and (5) they more and more seize the causes in order to completely perfect and accomplish the dharmakāya.

634 X.4 (D4048, fol. 38a.2–4).

635 "Progression" seems to refer to the second and main subpoint into which OED below divides the seventh (mental engagement) among the ten points that describe the fundamental change.

636 XIV.44cd–46.

637 MC (fol. 12b.5–6) says that this comprehension of the fundamental change is unsurpassable because the final fruition is attained through understanding and practicing the actuality of the fundamental change, just as it is, by way of these ten points.

638 DLC (p. 188) says that, among the ten points of the fundamental change, (1)–(3) respectively refer to its definition, its instances, and the persons in whom the fundamental change happens. (4)–(5) represent its qualities. (6)–(8) are the means to attain it (the collection of its causes, the manner of apprehending it, and the phases of that). (9)–(10) are as in OED. According to SC (pp. 153–54), the detailed explanation of the manner of comprehending the fundamental change dispels any ignorance about the fundamental state and the final fruition of all three yānas. Here "foundation" refers to the true nature of the mind in all three yānas and "change" means that, through the power of becoming familiar with it, afflicted phenomena do not manifest by virtue of purified phenomena. The ultimate state of both kinds of phenomena indeed exists as nothing other than dharmadhātu wisdom. However, through the explanation by way of dividing the sheer fundamental change in terms of isolates into the ālaya-consciousness and ālaya-wisdom, it is easy to identify, respectively, what the roots of what is to be relinquished and what is to be made a living experience are. It may be said, "If the identification of the fruition is explained to be the fundamental change, ground and fruition are presented as being inseparable. Therefore, isn't this rather narrow?" It is not because it is explained that, at the time of meditative equipoise, there is nothing to be removed or added, and therefore there is no need to depend on any efforts in terms of the fundamental change.

639 XIII.18–19. As mentioned above, Vasubandhu's *Bhāṣya* (D4026, fols. 188b.4–189a.1) comments on XIII.16–19 that the following two facts scare childish beings—that phenomena do not exist, yet are observable, and that the dharmadhātu is naturally without afflictiveness and yet becomes pure later. Through showing that these two facts are like illusions and space, respectively, those fears are removed. In due order, the examples in XIII.17–18 serve the same purpose—just as a picture lacks highs and lows, false imagination lacks the duality of apprehender and apprehended. Just as naturally clear water becomes visibly clear when its turbidities are allowed to settle, naturally luminous mind is only blemished by adventitious stains. Except for the mind of dharmatā, no other mind—that is, the dependent nature—is proclaimed to be naturally luminous. Therefore, here "mind" is nothing but the mind that is the nature of phenomena.

640 Verses 36–37.

641 Part 2, IV.69.

642 DLC (p. 189) says that, through having cultivated the path for the sake of the adventitious stains (what is to be relinquished) not appearing and suchness (what is to be attained) appearing, suchness has become stainless. This is the nature of the fundamental change, and the comprehension of this nature means to understand it merely through study and reflection. According to MC (fol. 13a.2–3), suchness being without adventitious stains means that stainless suchness' own nature appears just as it is.

643 As for the term "entity" (Skt. vastu, Tib. dngos po) here, both DDV and DDVV use it in the singular and the latter glosses it as "the threefold fundamental change of suchness." Following DDV (K), RC (p. 129), MC (fol. 13a.3), SC (fol. 5b.3), and LZC (p. 17) gloss it as

"substance" (Tib. rdzas), but provide no further explanations on either term. "Substance" is one of the several meanings of *vastu*, which can also mean "thing," "the real," "essential property," and "pith." In this sense, one would understand this threefold fundamental change of suchness as the entity or substance of the fundamental change, that is, that which is its makeup. According to GC (p. 458), however, "entity" is used here in the sense of distinctive feature, just as when calling an ox "substance" and the whiteness of that ox, "entity." To use the term "substance" here seems to be somewhat of a translation flaw. OED seems to understand "entity" as referring to the three sets of entities that undergo a fundamental change.

644 IV.61 (OED omits line a).

645 IX.43.

646 As explained above, the teachings of the buddhas are the natural outflow of their stainless dharmadhātu, or dharmakāya.

647 This refers to the part of the mental consciousness that directly perceives objects in a manner similar to the sense consciousnesses and the part that is the conceptual mind.

648 IX.44.

649 IX.42.

650 IX.45.

651 As mentioned above, VV (fol. 1b.4–5) respectively glosses these three aspects of the fundamental change as "the realization of the real dharmas (*bhūtadharmāvagamaḥ*)," "the instructions on the profound and vast dharma (*gambhīrodāradharmadeśanā*)," and "what is to be known being perceived directly (*jñeyapratyakṣībhāvo*)." RC (pp. 129–30) speaks of (1) the fundamental change of the suchness of the cognizance that is the common container and the body, (2) the fundamental change of the suchness of the dharmadhātu of the sūtra collection, which consists of speech, and (3) the fundamental change of the suchness of minds and mental factors—the cognizance that is the dhātu of sentient beings which is not in common. MC (fol. 13a.3–13b.6) agrees with this and further glosses (2) as the means of expression that appears as the aspects of words, phrases, and letters. In general, there is no phenomenon whatsoever except for the dharmadhātu. Therefore, though it is the case that, at the time of the fundamental change, there exist as many inconceivable qualities of this fundamental change in the uncontaminated dhātu as there are bearers of the nature of phenomena, here (1) the suchness of the fundamental change of everything that appears as the container and, implicitly, as the body, which is without center or fringe, is all-pervasive. This is the attainment of the dharmakāya. (2) The attainment of the sāmbhogikakāya is the mastery over the qualities of the uninterrupted and inexhaustible melody of the dharma that is the fundamental change of everything which is included in the formations of speech (illustrated by the sūtra collection). (3) The attainment of the nairmāṇikakāya consists of being endowed with the knowledge of the five wisdoms—the fundamental change of what consists of mind (the ālaya-consciousness and the seven other consciousnesses that are based on it). Or, in due order, these three fundamental changes refer to the distinctive features of (1) pure realms and bodies appearing, (2) teaching the genuine dharma, and (3) knowing all aspects of knowable objects through the wisdoms of suchness and variety. When not having undergone the fundamental change yet, what consists of forms and the sounds of speech is suitable to appear as being in common, while the mind is not in common. At the time of the fundamental change, all phenomena just appear as suchness, but there are no differences or impurities. Therefore, everything appears in the special manner of being nothing but pure self-appearance. Nevertheless, from the perspective of the appearances of those who have not undergone this fundamental change, this very suchness appears in different ways as the teacher (the Buddha), the teachings, and so on.

652 D106, fol. 22b.1. As it stands, the second line is not contained in the sūtra, but the entire verse reads:

> The uncontaminated dhātu of those who are liberated
> Is subtle, inconceivable, equal, without difference,
> Accomplishing all aims, devoid of suffering and afflictions,
> Inexpressible as two, blissful, and firm.

According to RC (p. 130), by virtue of the three kinds of fundamental change, in due order, the dharmakāya, the sāmbhogikakāya, and the nairmāṇikakāya are attained. The first two represent the experiential spheres of buddhas and bodhisattvas, respectively, while the third one is also the experiential sphere of śrāvakas and pratyekabuddhas. MC (fols. 13b.6–14a.5) agrees with this and gives the following reasons. The two masteries over the appearances of (1) pure realms and bodies and (2) limitless genuine dharmas exist in buddhas and bodhisattvas, but not in śrāvakas and pratyekabuddhas. Śrāvakas and pratyekabuddhas are also able to see the nairmāṇikakāya which possesses omniscient wisdom. Or, from the point of view of the fundamental change of their afflicted mind which is based on the ālaya-consciousness, they are endowed with a mere fraction of the third fundamental change. Therefore, though the third fundamental change is indeed taught as if in common for all four types of noble ones, śrāvakas and pratyekabuddhas lack the fully complete fundamental change of mind as a whole.

653 DLC (p. 189) explains that the distinctive feature of pure appearances is by virtue of pure buddha realms; the one of pure seeing, by virtue of the pure dharmakāya; the one of pure instruction, by virtue of the pure sāmbhogikakāya; and the one of attaining pure mastery, by virtue of attaining the nairmāṇikakāya. MC (fol. 14a.6) says that the distinctive features of the fundamental change refer to the one of buddhas and bodhisattvas because they attain the ultimate fundamental change through the power of the nonconceptual wisdom in which the two kinds of identitylessness are fully complete.

654 Bodhisattvas on the first bhūmi make ten great aspirations—(1) to provide for the worship of all buddhas without exception, (2) to maintain the religious discipline that has been taught by all the buddhas and to preserve the teaching of the buddhas, (3) to see all the incidents in the earthly career of a buddha, (4) to realize bodhicitta, to practice all the duties of bodhisattvas, to acquire all the pāramitās, and to purify all the stages of their career, (5) to mature all beings and establish them in the knowledge of a buddha, (6) to perceive the whole universe, (7) to purify and cleanse all the buddha realms, (8) to enter the mahāyāna and to produce a common intention and purpose in all bodhisattvas, (9) to make all actions of body, speech, and mind fruitful and successful, and (10) to attain supreme and perfect enlightenment and to teach the dharma.

655 In general, "superior intention" is a term for the superior altruistic attitude of bodhisattvas, which means that they have solely the welfare of others in mind. They do so with the same spontaneous intensity with which ordinary beings usually strive for their own well-being. This attitude is said to be the immediate prerequisite or cause for the arising of uncontrived genuine bodhicitta even in ordinary beings. Here, however, "pure superior intention" indicates the generation of bodhicitta on the first seven bodhisattvabhūmis.

656 RC (p. 131) speaks of aspiration prayers as the motivation of wishing to attain buddhahood, and of the training on the bhūmis as being for the sake of realizing all knowable objects (such as the five fields of knowledge) and relinquishing what is to be relinquished. Similarly, DLC (p. 189) glosses aspiration prayers as "the prior generation of bodhicitta." MC (fol. 14b.3–14b.6) glosses the prerequisite of the focal object as cutting through superimpositions onto the two realities through focusing on all vast and profound words of the Buddha that teach the path and fruition of the mahāyāna.

657 IV.12–14.

658 OED omits this phrase.

659 DLC (pp. 189–90) says that nonconceptual wisdom is indispensable for attaining the fundamental change and, in due order, glosses the six points of comprehending it as its object condition and so on, its function, its cause, the manner in which objects appear to it, its qualities, and its distinctive features. According to MC (fol. 15a.2–6), nonconceptual wisdom is the foundation of the ultimate fundamental change because the full perception, and the turning into the nature, of the actuality of suchness—the primordially pure basic nature—must be attained through the nonconceptual wisdom that realizes this suchness just as it is. For it is never attained otherwise because nonconceptual wisdom is the foundation for that attainment. This wisdom is comprehended through comprehending (1) the focal objects through which it is generated, when focusing on them, (2) the relinquishment of the characteristics that are its antagonistic factors (RC: adverse conditions), (3) the correct yogic practices as the manner in which it is generated in the mind stream, (4) the defining characteristics in terms of its function or experiential sphere, (5) the benefit that is based on it, and (6) the thorough knowledge about what its own nature is like.

660 VIII.21 (D4048, fol. 35b.4).

661 I.26.

662 This is an abbreviated paraphrase of this text's comments on I.26 (J 26; D4025, fols. 87b.6–88a.4).

663 This refers to the functions of the thirty-two qualities of the dharmakāya (the ten powers, the four fearlessnesses, and the eighteen unique qualities of a buddha), as described in the *Dhāraṇīśvararājasūtra* (D147, fols. 185a.6–215a.3).

664 V.9–11. RC (p. 132) explains the four focal objects as first relying on spiritual friends who teach the mahāyāna, then aspiring for the dharma taught by them, gaining certainty through reasonings inspired by one's aspiration, and completing the accumulations by way of mentally engaging in a proper manner in the meaning about which one has gained certainty. DLC (p. 190) says that the collection of causes for the nonconceptual wisdom that primarily consists of the meditative equipoise of the path of seeing is fourfold. Its object condition consists of the Buddha's words that teach the mahāyāna. Its causal condition is the aspiration on the mahāyāna path of accumulation. Its immediate condition is the certainty and familiarity that arises from the reflection on the path of preparation. Its dominant condition is the completion of the accumulations during one incalculable eon. According to MC (fol. 15b.1–2), one must focus on the vast and profound scriptures that teach the mahāyāna, which means one should rely on mahāyāna spiritual friends and listen to their unmistaken instructions. Then, one should give rise to supreme aspiration for these teachings, generate doubt-free certainty about their meanings through the four expedients, and thus complete the accumulations as in RC. The four expedients are those of (1) the nature of phenomena, (2) dependence, (3) entities performing functions, and (4) justification or demonstration of evidence (perceptual, inferential, and scriptural valid cognitions). To note, though the four expedients (Skt. yukti; Tib. rigs pa) are usually rendered as "the four reason(ing)s" in translations from Tibetan, the *Śrāvakabhūmi*'s discussion of these four clarifies that *yukti* here is equivalent to *yoga* and *upāya*, any of which can mean "application," "means," and "expedient." Also RGVV (J 73) gives the same two synonyms for *yukti* in its discussion of the nature of phenomena being such an expedient.

665 The phrase "is to be understood" is added here from DDVV.

666 OED *dag pa* emended to *bdag*.

667 In *Uttaratantra* I.35–38 buddha nature is described through being endowed with these four pāramitās. "Supreme purity" consists of buddha nature's timeless natural purity and its purity due to being without stains at the end of the path. "Supreme self" refers to its being free from conceptions about a self as well as the lack of a self. "Supreme bliss" means its mastery over the nonarising of suffering and its origin. "Supreme permanence" refers to its lack of arising and ceasing in all situations and its uninterrupted and natural enlightened activity. These four notions of purity, self, bliss, and permanence are not to be confused with the four mistaken notions of ordinary beings, who cling to the five skandhas as being pure, a self, blissful, and permanent. From a mahāyāna perspective, the temporary remedies for the latter four are the realizations that, on the level of seeming reality, the skandhas are actually impure, without a self, suffering, and impermanent. However, since all eight of those notions are merely conceptually imputed and ultimately untrue, buddha nature is free from them.

668 DLC (p. 190) glosses the antagonistic factors as "attachment and so on"; their remedies, as the meditation on "repulsiveness and so on"; suchness, as "being empty of duality"; and "fruition," as "enlightenment." RC (p. 132) glosses the antagonistic factors as "attachment and so on"; their remedies, as "the means of relinquishment"; suchness, as "the focal object"; and the dharmas of realization, as "the (cognizing) subject." MC (fols. 15b.3–16a.5) adds that these four refer to characteristics of mind being conceited. Both gloss "suchness" as the focal object and "realization" as the cognizing subject. According to MC, the characteristic of suchness is subtle because it is the unsurpassable remedy for all factors to be relinquished and is the supreme object to be realized. The fourth characteristic—the realizations or fruitions of the path (such as the correct view and the ten powers)—is relinquished after all the others. It is associated with the mind streams of bodhisattvas for a long time because the subtle striving of wishing to attain higher realizations is not given up on the paths and bhūmis. Thus, bodhisattvas are associated with it in the form of subtle conceptions about it until nonconceptual wisdom has completely matured (according to RC, this fourth characteristic is only present up through the seventh bhūmi). LZC (p. 21) speaks of the characteristics of the factors to be relinquished (the antagonistic factors), purified phenomena (the remedies), what is to be realized (suchness), and the dharmas of realization. These refer to the four kinds of conceptions about something apprehended in terms of factors to be relinquished, remedies, and so on because it is taught that bodhisattvas need to be free from all reference points of apprehending.

669 OED *rnam par mi rtog pa la 'jug pa'i mdo.*

670 OED *de bzhin nyid kyi mnyam par 'dzin* emended to *de bzhin nyid ni gnyen por 'dzin.*

671 In the *Avikalpapraveśadhāraṇī* the first characteristic is called "nature" (Skt. prakṛti; indicating the five skandhas as what is to be relinquished), while the fourth one is called "attainment" (Skt. prāpti). In the example (D142, fol. 4a.1–4b.4), the gradual removal of rock, silver, gold, and various gems corresponds to the progressive elimination of the four characteristics, while the wish-fulfilling gem that emerges at the end of this process stands for finally entering the dhātu of nonconceptuality. As discussed in Brunnhölzl 2007b and 2009, the Third Karmapa's commentaries on his *Profound Inner Reality* and the *Dharmadhātustava* also mention these four characteristics and the example of a beryl, referring to the *Avikalpapraveśadhāraṇī* (however, the *dhāraṇī* only speaks of a wish-fulfilling gem, not a beryl). For more details on the four kinds of characteristics and their relinquishment as explained in the *Avikalpapraveśadhāraṇī* and KCA, see Appendix 1.

672 Verse 26. Sthiramati's *Triṃśikābhāṣya* (Lévi ed., p. 42.18–23; D4064, fol. 170a.3–5) comments, "'Twofold grasping' refers to the grasping at something apprehended and the grasping at an apprehender. As for 'the aftereffects of this [twofold grasping],' it plants seeds in the ālaya-consciousness, which [then] gives rises to future twofold grasping. For as long as the mind of a yogin does not dwell in mere cognizance, which has the characteristic of nonduality,

the aftereffects of apprehender and apprehended do not come to an end, which means that they are not relinquished. Here it is taught that, without having relinquished the perception of outer [objects], the perception of inner [apprehenders] is not relinquished either. Therefore, [ordinary beings] think, 'I apprehend form and so on with [my] eyes and so on.'" Vinītadeva's *Triṃśikāṭīkā* (D4070, fol. 58b.1–6) has someone ask, "If mere cognizance is free from apprehender and apprehended, why are all beings so overly attached to thinking that their eyes and so on see form and so on?" For as long as the consciousnesses of sentient beings do not dwell in mere cognizance, the aftereffects of their twofold grasping will not come to a halt. If these have not come to a halt, those beings are overly attached to thinking that a certain apprehender apprehends a certain apprehended object. The true nature of the mind is the very being of mere cognizance. For as long as the consciousness of a yogin does not dwell in mere cognizance, which is free from the two characteristics of apprehender and apprehended, and clings to apprehender and apprehended, the aftereffects or latent tendencies of twofold grasping (clinging to something apprehended and clinging to an apprehender) are not relinquished.

673 Verse 27. Sthiramati (Lévi ed., pp. 42.23–43.8; D4064, fol. 170a.5–170b.2) explains, "'Is it the case then that by virtue of observing mere cognizance free from referents, one dwells in the true nature of the mind?' This is not the case. What then? [Verse 27 says]: . . . Therefore, [lines 27ab] . . . are also stated in order to dispel the grasping of those with pride who, merely through having studied this, [think,] 'I dwell in pure mere cognizance.' 'All this is mere cognizance' refers to being free from referents, that is, observing that 'outer referents do not exist,' which [still] means to grasp at and picture [something]. 'Before' [means] 'being present.' 'Propped up' refers to [something being propped up] by the mind as one has studied it. Due to the variety of focal objects of yogic training, [Vasubandhu] speaks of 'anything,' such as a skeleton or a livid, rotten, maggot-ridden, or decomposed [corpse]. 'Not dwelling in "merely that [cognizance]"' [is said] because of not having relinquished the observing of consciousness [itself]." Vinītadeva (D4070, fol. 59a.3–59b.7) says that to observe mere cognizance does not mean to dwell in the true nature of the mind because when there is still clinging due to the arising of such an aspect of thinking, "All this is mere cognizance," a certain focal object is propped up before one's mind. If anything is propped up before one's mind, one does not really dwell in mere cognizance. For, after having stopped all other focusing, one still focuses on that mere cognizance itself. As long as one conceives of any inner or outer focal objects, how could one dwell in the true nature of the mind? Another explanation here is that those with pride, who have trained in yoga in a flawed way and are puffed up by virtue of merely having studied the presentations about mere cognizance, think, "I dwell in pure mere cognizance and do not imagine any apprehender or apprehended." This verse is given in order to counteract their mistaken pride. Also, through making anything—even a tiny fraction of mere cognizance itself—into a focal object and focusing on it by way of setting it before one's mind in accordance with what one has studied about it, one does not dwell in it, but engages in some contrived clear focusing on apprehender and apprehended. One simply focuses by way of this aspect, "All this is mere cognizance." The synonyms of "focusing" or "observing" here are "grasping," "entertaining characteristics," and "clinging." Though this is the context of focusing on mere cognizance, Sthiramati mentions the focal objects of skeletons and so on because these appear as focal objects as if they were external.

674 Verse 28. Sthiramati (Lévi ed., p. 43.8–20; D4064, fol. 170b.2–6) explains, "'So when does one relinquish the grasping at consciousness or dwell in the very being of mere mind (*cittamātratā*)?' Therefore, [verse 28] says: . . . When consciousness does not observe, see, grasp, or cling to anything outside of the mind (be it the focal object that is the teachings, the focal object that is the instructions, or the focal objects that are ordinary forms, sounds, and so on), at that time, through seeing what is in accordance with true reality, which is unlike being blind, one relinquishes the grasping at consciousness and also dwells in mind's own true nature (*svacittadharmatā*). The reason for this is said to be that 'there is no apprehender without

something apprehended.' If there is something to be apprehended, there is an apprehender, but such is not the case without something to be apprehended. If there is nothing to be apprehended, one realizes that there is no apprehender either—it is not just that there is nothing to be apprehended. Thus, the supramundane nonconceptual wisdom, which is equal in terms of lacking anything to be observed and anything that observes, arises. The aftereffects of clinging to apprehender and apprehended are relinquished and mind itself dwells in mind's own true nature." Vinītadeva (D4070, fol. 60a.3–60b.4) says that once all focusing has been eliminated and consciousness does not focus on anything outside of the mind, the mind truly dwells in mere cognizance. Here, the term "consciousness" refers to grasping, and the term "apprehender" means clinging. Therefore, it is taught that, at this point, the clinging to an apprehender is relinquished too. At this point, one dwells in the true nature of the mind because one realizes that without anything apprehended there is no apprehender either—it is not that one realizes just the lack of something to be apprehended. "Which qualities are attained through having eliminated apprehender and apprehended?" The supramundane wisdom of equality arises, the latencies of clinging to apprehender and apprehended are relinquished, and one's mind dwells in its true nature, which is called "mere cognizance." "The equality by virtue of what is observed and what observes being equal" is supramundane wisdom. This means that, just as there is no conceiving of and clinging to anything to be observed, there is no conceiving of and clinging to anything that observes either.

675 OED *rnam rig dmigs pa*, but according to what was just explained, this must be *rnam rig mi dmigs pa*.

676 Verse 29. Sthiramati (Lévi ed., pp. 43.20–45.2; D4064, fols. 170b.6–171b.6) comments, "'When one dwells in the very being of mere cognizance, how should that be referred to?' Therefore, [verses 29–30] say:

> . . .
> It is the undefiled dhātu
> That is inconceivable, virtuous, and stable.
> It is the blissful vimuktikāya
> And what is called "the dharma[kāya] of the great sage."

These two verses teach that, based on the path of seeing, yogins who engage in mere cognizance give rise to the consummate fruition through progressively going higher and higher. Since there is no mind there that is an apprehender and no perception of apprehended referents, [line 29a says] 'no-mind and nonperception.' Since it is not familiar and does not arise in the world and is nonconceptual, it is said to be beyond the world, which is said to be supramundane wisdom. After wisdom, in order to teach that there is a fundamental change, [line 29b] says, 'This is the fundamental change.' 'Foundation' here refers to the ālaya-consciousness with all the seeds. As for its change, once the entity that consists of the impregnations of negative tendencies, [karmic] maturation, and the latent tendencies of duality has come to an end, it changes into the entity that consists of what is truly workable, the dharmakāya, and nondual wisdom. 'Through relinquishing what is this fundamental change attained?' Therefore, [line 29b] says 'by virtue of having relinquished the twofold impregnations of negative tendencies.' 'Twofold' refers to the impregnations of the negative tendencies of the afflictive obscurations and the impregnations of the negative tendencies of the cognitive obscurations. 'Impregnations of negative tendencies' are the unworkable ālaya, that is, the seeds of the afflictive and cognitive obscurations. As for the fundamental change, the one that is attained through having relinquished the impregnations of the negative tendencies that exist in śrāvakas is said to be 'the vimuktikāya.' The one that is attained through having relinquished the impregnations of the negative tendencies that exist in bodhisattvas is said to be 'what is called the dharma[kāya] of the great sage.' It is taught that by virtue of the difference between the two kinds [of obscurations], [there is] a surpassable and an unsurpassable fundamental change. Here is a stanza:

> The appropriating consciousness should be understood
> To have the characteristics of the two obscurations—
> The seeds of all and the seeds of the afflictions.
> The two are bound there in those two.

['The two'] refers to śrāvakas and bodhisattvas. The seeds of the afflictions [exist] in the former and the seeds of the two obscurations, in the others. Through overcoming those [two], omniscience is attained. As for [line 30a,] 'It is the undefiled dhātu,' it is the very nature of the fundamental change that is called 'the undefiled dhātu' because it lacks any impregnations of negative tendencies. It is undefiled because it is free from all defilements. It is the dhātu because it is the cause of the dharmas of the noble ones. The term 'dhātu' here has the meaning of 'cause.' It is 'inconceivable' because it is not the sphere of dialectics, is personally experienced [by the noble ones], and is without example. It is 'virtuous' because it is the focal object of purification, means being at ease, and consists of the uncontaminated dharmas. It is 'stable' because it is permanent and inexhaustible. It is bliss because it is permanent—what is impermanent is suffering. This [dhātu] is permanent and therefore blissful. Through having relinquished the afflictive obscurations, it is the vimuktikāya of the śrāvakas. The defining characteristic of this fundamental change is also said to be 'what is called "the dharma[kāya]."' It is said to be 'the dharmakāya of the great sage' because it is the perfect accomplishment of the fundamental change due to the great sage's relinquishment of afflictive and cognitive obscurations through having cultivated the bhūmis and pāramitās. It is said to be the dharmakāya because it represents not giving up saṃsāra, while not being afflicted by it, and the attainment of mastery over all dharmas." Vinītadeva (D4070, fols. 61a.2–63a.4) adds that "no-mind," "nonperception," and "supramundane wisdom" refer to the time of the path of seeing. "The fundamental change" and so on refer to progressively going higher and higher. The two kāyas represent the consummate fruition. You may wonder why the realization of mind as such is called "no-mind and nonperception." Since the supramundane mind lacks any other mind that apprehends it, it is no-mind. Since the supramundane mind does not perceive anything to be apprehended whatsoever, it is nonperception. As for the nature of the two obscurations, it is the appropriating ālaya-consciousness, which is to be understood as bondage. "The seeds of the afflictions and the seeds of all" indicates this ālaya-consciousness, in which the seeds of the two obscurations exist. It is described in this way since it contains "the seeds of all" (the two obscurations of bodhisattvas) and "the seeds of the afflictions" (the obscurations of śrāvakas). Since the supreme fundamental change is the collection of the dharmas of the bhūmis and pāramitās, it is called "dharmakāya." Or the dharmakāya is the matrix of all the dharmas that are mastered by bodhisattvas. Another explanation of why the Buddha is called "great sage" is because he is free from any speech that is motivated by any primary or secondary afflictions.

677 VI.8.

678 VI.9. For comments on these two verses, see the introduction. As described there, in due order, verses VI.6–9 of the *Mahāyānasūtrālaṃkāra* are matched with the paths of accumulation, preparation, seeing, and familiarization in all Indian commentaries. Thus, they do not exactly correspond to the particular order of the four yogic practices as outlined by OED here.

679 The training in the equality of saṃsāra and nirvāṇa is described in *Abhisamayālaṃkāra* IV.60. According to the commentaries, the simple training in this equality happens from the path of accumulation onward, but the fully qualified training in this equality occurs only on the eighth bhūmi.

680 Despite OED saying "buddhahood" above, the context here is the training of bodhisattvas on the eighth to tenth bhūmis.

681 This refers to the vajra seat in Bodhgayā (*bodhimaṇḍa*), the place where all buddhas become enlightened.

682 According to RC (p. 133), the four practices consist of focusing on mere mind, not observing external referents, not observing the apprehender that focuses on referents, and focusing on the suchness in which both apprehender and apprehended are not observed. DLC (p. 190) says that the training in observing everything as mere cognizance is the attainment of the illumination about the nonexistence of the apprehended. Based on that, the training in not observing the apprehended is the increase of that illumination. Based on that, the training in not even observing observation as mere cognizance is the engagement in one side of suchness. Finally, the training in observing sheer suchness through not observing the duality of apprehender and apprehended is the immediate or uninterrupted samādhi (right before the path of seeing). In due order, these four trainings are the causes of nonconceptual wisdom, corresponding to the levels of heat, peak, poised readiness, and the supreme dharma of the path of preparation. According to MC (fol. 16a.5–16b.2), one begins with observing all phenomena as being mere mind. Based on that, one trains in the apprehended being unobservable. Based on that, one engages in the apprehender (or that which focuses on the apprehended) being unobservable too. Finally, based on that, one trains in not observing apprehender and apprehended in any way whatsoever, that is, in focusing on suchness. This is the progression of the manner in which nonconceptual wisdom is generated in the mind stream because it is easy to realize that external referents lack a nature of their own, while it is more difficult to realize that the apprehender is unobservable too. The manner of this progression corresponds to what is taught about the four levels of heat (the samādhi of attaining the illumination of prajñā) and so on. LZC (p. 22) says that one observes all appearing phenomena as mere cognizance. Then, one does not observe a basis for these appearances that consists of external referents. Next, if there is no basis to be apprehended that consists of referents, there is no cognizance that is an apprehender. Therefore, what appears or what is observed—mere cognizance—is not observable either. Finally, the nonobservation of both referents and mind and their being nondual is the observation of nonobservation.

683 Compare *Laṅkāvatārasūtra* X.256–257 (D107, fol. 168b.5–6; translation according to the Sanskrit and the *Kangyur* version):

> By relying on mere mind
> One does not imagine outer objects.
> By resting in the focal object of suchness
> One should go beyond mere mind too.
> Having gone beyond mere mind,
> One must even go beyond nonappearance.
> The yogin who rests in nonappearance
> Sees the mahāyāna.

Note that the first two lines in OED's quote almost literally correspond to *Bodhicittavivaraṇa* 25cd. Also, either OED's "old translation" or OED itself obviously omits lines 256b–257a and have a negative in line 257d, which changes the overall meaning significantly. The negative in line 257d is also found in the *Kangyur* versions of the sūtra, while it is lacking in the identical verses 54–55 in Nāgārjuna's *Bhāvanākrama* and the citations of these two verses in Śāntarakṣita's *Madhyamakālaṃkāravṛtti* (D3885, fol. 79b.3–4), Kamalaśīla's *Madhyamakālaṃkārapañjikā* (D3886, fols. 128b.2–129a.3) and first *Bhāvanākrama* (D3915, fol. 33a.3–33b.6), and Ratnākaraśānti's texts. In his translation of the sūtra, Suzuki 1979 (p. 247) says that most Sanskrit manuscripts have *na* ("not"), but that one has *sa* ("he"). Nanjio's

Sanskrit edition also has *sa*. Naturally, the main difference hinges on how one understands the two occurrences of "nonappearance." The Third Karmapa obviously takes the "old translation" as highlighting his own explicit statement above that there are appearances of wisdom on the bhūmis, though they are not conceptualized on the three pure bhūmis. Kamalaśīla's detailed explanation of these verses in his *Bhāvanākrama* (translation in Brunnhölzl 2004, pp. 300–302) takes the first "nonappearance" as referring to the cognition that lacks the duality of apprehender and apprehended, and this cognition is to be transcended. The second one signifies the wisdom in which not even nondual wisdom appears, which is the path of seeing—the true seeing of the mahāyāna. This means that there is nothing to be seen when the light of perfect wisdom dawns through the examination of all phenomena with the eye of prajñā. However, such nonseeing of any phenomenon is not like being blind, closing one's eyes, or not mentally engaging in seeing. The *Madhyamakālaṃkārapañjikā* adds that it is through self-awareness in meditative equipoise that the yogin's mind is experienced as being nondual and without appearance and is described accordingly during subsequent attainment. Thus, though wisdom does not appear as something that can be referred to as nondual wisdom (or anything else, for that matter), since all phenomena lack a nature of their own, given Kamalaśīla's mentioning of the light of wisdom and self-awareness, at least in terms of experiential events on the subject side, he does not seem to refer to a total lack of appearance of anything whatsoever in meditative equipoise. Ratnākaraśānti's *Prajñāpāramitopadeśā* (D4079, fols. 161a.5–162a.4) explains these verses according to the four yogas of focusing on (1) entities, (2) mere mind, (3) suchness, and (4) nonappearance. (1) The first yoga is taught implicitly—as long as one does not identify phenomena as such and such, one is not able to apprehend their emptiness either. (2) The second yoga refers to seeing these phenomena as being mere mind empty of apprehender and apprehended, which still entails appearance. (3) The third yoga means to apprehend the nonappearance of the characteristics of phenomena, viewing them as sheer lucidity. (4) The fourth yoga is the seeing by virtue of the nonappearance of any characteristics of both phenomena and the nature of phenomena. In more detail, "mere mind" in the first line of these two verses refers to the cognition of focusing on mere mind, which represents yoga (2). "Not imagine" means to go beyond yoga (1) of still imagining or examining external referents. "The focal object of suchness" refers to yoga (3)—wisdom focusing on suchness, with "having gone beyond mere mind" meaning to continue to train in this, while not yet having accomplished something previously nonexistent. Such an accomplishment is marked by "One must even go beyond nonappearance." Here "nonappearance" means that the characteristics of phenomena do not appear, which means that one focuses on suchness alone. To go beyond even that is indicated by "the yogin who rests in nonappearance," which refers to seeing that the characteristics of phenomena and the nature of phenomena do not appear at all. This means resting in yoga (4). "Mahāyāna" refers to the uncontaminated path of bodhisattvas superior to śrāvakas and pratyekabuddhas. "Sees" means perceive directly because the wisdom at this stage *is* the mahāyāna. As for how one proceeds through this mahāyāna, who proceeds, and where to, the next verse in the *Laṅkāvatārasūtra* (X.258) says:

> Peace is entered effortlessly,
> Purified through aspiration prayers.
> The highest identityless wisdom
> Sees the mahāyāna.

As for how one proceeds, "effortlessly" means that one transits through the supramundane bhūmis without exertion. These bhūmis are "peace" because they lack afflictions and conceptions. "Purified through aspiration prayers" means that inferior forms of enlightenment are ruled out. As for who proceeds and to where, "identityless wisdom" is so because it is utterly without appearance. It is "the highest" because all obscurations, including their latent tendencies, are relinquished. This means the bodhicitta of a buddha, which will be seen by yogins of the mahāyāna. The late Nyingma master Düjom Rinpoche (Bdud 'joms 'jigs bral ye shes rdo rje 1991, p. 183) comments on these two verses as follows: "Accordingly, after Mind Only has been provisionally taught and then genuinely transcended, the apparitionless Madhyamaka is taught; and when that too has been transcended, the apparitional Madhyamaka is revealed. If that is not reached, it is said that the profound meaning of the greater vehicle is not perceived. It is, in general, erroneous to describe everything expressed by the word *mind* as the Mind Only doctrine, for there are occasions when the abiding nature free from all extremes, [known] inclusively as the nature of just what is, the genuine goal, the natural nirvāṇa, the expanse of reality, the mind of inner radiance, and the intellect of Samantabhadra, is indicated by the word *mind* . . . One should not therefore mistake that which is spoken of as mind-as-such, the inner radiance transcending the mind of saṃsāra and its mental events, for the Mind Only system, which does not transcend consciousness."

684 This passage is, for example, found in the *Pañcaviṃśatisāhasrikāprajñāpāramitāsūtra* (D9, vol. kha, fol. 215b.2–3), the *Daśabhūmikasūtra* (Rahder ed., p. 65), and the *Tathāgatagarbhasūtra* (D258, fol. 248b.5–6). According to DLC (pp. 190–91), as for the manner in which objects appear to nonconceptual wisdom, to abide in the nature of phenomena that lacks the duality of apprehender and apprehended and is inexpressible through terms or conceptions means to comprehend the abiding in it because this is the manner in which this object (the nature of phenomena) abides. MC (fol. 16b.3–6) says that the three defining characteristics consist of nonconceptual wisdom abiding in the very own nature of the nature of phenomena, resting in it without appearances, and resting in it with appearances. As for the first one, nonconceptual wisdom rests in suchness (the true nature of all phenomena) because it abides in the nature of phenomena that cannot be split by mind into the duality of apprehender and apprehended or into the two realities and is inexpressible through speech as any extreme or aspect whatsoever. Ultimately, through realizing that the two realities are inseparable and of one taste, buddha wisdom sees them just as they are. On the paths of learning, nonconceptual wisdom exists in a form that is approximately concordant with this. LZC (p. 23) glosses "the nature of phenomena" as being indestructible and without the duality of apprehender and apprehended, saṃsāra and nirvāṇa, and what is to be adopted and to be rejected.

685 OED here and above *brtag tu med pa* (see the note in the corresponding section of DDVV).

686 OED *phyi nang stong pa*, but the emptiness of the internal and the external means that both the inner sense faculties and their outer objects are without nature. Also, the next point is related to the emptiness of the external.

687 This emptiness refers to the lack of nature of the entire universe (usually understood as also including all sentient beings in it).

688 OED *'di ltar mi snang na don snang bar 'gyur ba'i phyir*, which is translated in light of what is said above and below about suchness appearing once dualistic phenomena do not appear.

689 RC (pp. 133–34) glosses "duality" as the duality of apprehender and apprehended in terms of the nonconceptual (sense) consciousnesses, and "according designations" as what appears as the duality of apprehender and apprehended in terms of the sixth consciousness. Through DDV saying that these two kinds of duality do not appear, it teaches that the imaginary nature does not appear, while the nonappearance of sense faculties and so on teaches that the dependent nature does not appear. Thus, no objects whatsoever appear for nonconceptual wisdom. According to DLC (p. 191), one comprehends the defining characteristics of nonconceptual wisdom not only in terms of the manner in which its object (suchness) abides, but also by way of the manner in which other objects appear to this mental state of nonconceptual wisdom, that is, by virtue of their nonappearance. MC (fols. 16b.6–18a.2) glosses "duality" as RC does and then says that the conceptual mind clings to the dualistic appearances of the sense

consciousness and designates them in accordance with how they appear, which refers to mental discourse or the sixth consciousness conceiving of apprehender and apprehended. Since all six appearances mentioned do not appear, they appear as the suchness that is of one taste and cannot be differentiated by anything, which is referred to as "dualistic appearances vanishing in emptiness." Therefore, nonconceptual wisdom is ungraspable by the sense consciousnesses and so on, indemonstrable by speech, without a foundation or support for the arising of cognition, without appearing as an object, without cognizance as a cognizing subject, and without a base that is a container as a common support. The *Kāśyapaparivarta* says, "Kāśyapa, 'permanence' is an extreme. 'Impermanence' is a second extreme. That which is the middle of these two extremes is ungraspable, indemonstrable, ungrounded, without appearance, without cognizance, and without base. Kāśyapa, this is called 'the middle way, the correct discrimination of phenomena.'" In this text, the same format is applied to identity and identitylessness, saṃsāra and nirvāṇa, existence and nonexistence, and so on. Therefore, what is called "nonconceptual wisdom without appearances" is the wisdom without appearances that is self-luminous, equal to space, and beyond the nature of those six kinds of appearances. As for its own nature, it is the wisdom that is beyond consciousness and not included in any of the eighteen conditioned or unconditioned dhātus. Therefore, its nature is not fragmented through those appearances, but self-luminous in that it is nondual with the nature of phenomena. If this is taught in terms of the isolate of the wisdom of suchness, while never moving away from this natural state, the seeing of all appearances in an equal and unmixed manner takes place through the wisdom of variety. Thus, it is feasible for these two aspects of nonconceptual wisdom to operate unified as a pair without contradiction. For while not moving away from the actuality of all phenomena being of equal taste within the natural state of the nature of phenomena (suchness), all bearers of this nature just appear, but these two [aspects] are not contradictory. Likewise, within the self-appearances of the wisdom that sees the nature of phenomena, appearances dawn in an unimpeded manner. However, it is from the point of view of their being unobservable as such and such appearances that this fully complies with the meaning of the above teaching on nonconceptual wisdom being without appearances because those appearances are beyond the nature of the dualistic appearances of ordinary beings. This is a very crucial and profound point. LZC (p. 24) says that nonconceptual wisdom is "without cognizance" because a nature of cognizance is not established. Thus, since it is defined by being ungraspable and so on, it is free from all reference points. Referring to the *Avikalpapraveśadhāraṇī*, Ratnākaraśānti's *Madhyamakālaṃkāravṛtti* (D4072, fol. 118a.3–7) explains "ungraspable" and so on as follows. Being graspable is by virtue of analysis, but since nonconceptual wisdom is beyond the analysis of all conceptions, it is ungraspable. Being demonstrable refers to clarifying something for others through means such as teaching, but since nonconceptual wisdom is beyond that, it is indemonstrable. All sense faculties are conception because they appear as what makes one apprehend. Thus, the perceptual supports that are the sense faculties are grounded, whereas nonconceptual wisdom is beyond them and thus is ungrounded. All objects are conception because they appear as what is apprehended, but nonconceptual wisdom is beyond that and thus is without appearance. Cognizance refers to the six consciousnesses, which are also conception, because they appear as apprehenders, but nonconceptual wisdom is beyond that and thus without cognizance. Likewise, afflictions and secondary afflictions are conception because they appropriate what is without any foundation. Since nonconceptual wisdom does not do so, it is without base. The same author's *Prajñāpāramitopadeśa* (4079, fol. 160a.2–6) agrees with the first four points, but explains "without base" as referring to nonconceptual wisdom being without the base of the conceptions that consist of the afflictive and cognitive obscurations and being the remedy that overcomes these two obscurations. See also Kamalaśīla's explanation of these five in Appendix 1.

690 This paragraph of DDV and its commentary are also based on the *Avikalpapraveśadhāraṇī* (Matsuda 1996, p. 96.6–9; D142, fol. 3b.4–6). See also KCA in Appendix 1. Ratnākaraśānti's

Prajñāpāramitopadeśā (D4079, fol. 160b.4–7) also quotes this passage from the *Avikalpapraveśadhāraṇī* and explains the ways in which subsequently attained wisdom sees all phenomena like illusions and so on as follows. "Illusions" refer to the world that consists of sentient beings because they appear as unreal men, women, and so on. "Mirages" stand for the outer world as the container because it appears as delusive water and so on. "Dreams" refer to experiencing objects because there are no (real) entities. "Optical illusions" represent physical actions, which are like a shadow, because they are without any movement (of their own). "Echoes" represent verbal actions because there are no (real) sounds. "Reflections" refer to forms appearing on the surface of a mirror. "Magical creations" illustrate the mental actions of bodhisattvas during meditative equipoise because images of referents appear in it without there being any referents. "The moon in water" represents the mental actions of bodhisattvas when not in meditative equipoise because these actions are moistened by the water of mental suppleness (the effect of meditative equipoise). In addition, "magical creations" also illustrate the mental actions of bodhisattvas that happen under the influence of others because these actions are dependent on others.

691 XI.29. "Dispassionate" renders Skt. *nirmārāh* (which can also mean "without obstacle"), while the Tibetan says "without pride" (corresponding to Skt. *nirmānāḥ*).

692 The following comments on these verses VIII.6–14 (D4048, fol. 34b.2–7) are mainly based on the commentaries by Vasubandhu and Asvabhāva (for details, see Brunnhölzl 2007a, endnotes 158–65). "Aspect" refers to that which subjectively appears for nonconceptual wisdom—its cognitive "content"—when it observes its specific object of suchness. "Signlessness" means to refrain from mentally engaging in any characteristics. Thus, the very lack of cognitive aspects is nonconceptual wisdom's unique cognitive aspect.

693 Meaning only derives from correctly and uninterruptedly pronouncing (verbally or mentally) a row of letters or syllables and thus connecting them in a conceptual manner. As for all phenomena being inexpressible, the object of expression and what expresses it are mutually dependent, neither being able to arise without the other. However, their nature is entirely different—the object one wishes to express is a specifically characterized phenomenon of direct perception, while the means to express that object is a conceptual term or image in the conceptual mind. Since a conceptual image can never really capture the uniqueness of a concrete object, nothing can be really expressed.

694 The two paths here are the path of accumulation and the path of support, the former consisting of the practice of the first four pāramitās and the latter being the pāramitā of dhyāna. Through those combined, prajñāpāramitā—nonconceptual wisdom—eventually arises.

695 Through making efforts in cultivating nonconceptual wisdom, one is born into the maṇḍala of a nairmāṇikakāya. Through attaining the actuality of nonconceptual wisdom, one is born into the maṇḍala of a sāmbhogikakāya. Such "maturation" does not have the usual meaning of the result of ordinary karmic actions manifesting, but is the very remedy for karmic maturation.

696 Through being continuously reborn into those maṇḍalas in one's lives to come, nonconceptual wisdom keeps flourishing, manifesting in specific and progressively superior ways.

697 The outcome is nirvāṇa, which is simply attained on the first bodhisattvabhūmi and is greatly perfected on the remaining bhūmis. Or on the first bhūmi (the path of seeing), the essence of all bhūmis is attained. Therefore, this is the primary outcome of nonconceptual wisdom. On the path of familiarization, nonconceptual wisdom is then perfected in the form of the remaining nine bhūmis.

698 On the first bhūmi, the three kāyas are already attained, but it is only on the tenth bhūmi that they become completely pure. In addition, culmination includes attainment of the ten masteries: over (1) lifespan, (2) mind, (3) necessities, (4) karma, (5) birth, (6) creative willpower, (7) aspiration prayers, (8) miraculous powers, (9) wisdom, and (10) dharma.

699 The nonconceptual wisdom due to preparatory application means that bodhisattvas first hear about nonconceptuality from others and then analyze it through reasoning, thus giving rise to devoted interest for it. Since this initial kind of wisdom approaches, and eventually turns into, the actual nonconceptual wisdom, it is given that same name too. The benefit of this wisdom is to be untainted by coarse evil actions. The cause for that is to have confidence and devoted interest in actual nonconceptual wisdom, which serves as the remedy for falling into the lower realms.

700 As explained below under 2.2.2.2.2.7.3.7.2.2. The manner of mental engagement (OED, pp. 584–85), dualistic phenomena do not appear for nonconceptual wisdom, but the nature of phenomena does appear. According to RC (p. 134), during meditative equipoise all that appears is suchness because all phenomena appear equal to the center of space. During subsequent attainment appearances appear without having any real existence because all conditioned phenomena appear like illusions and so on. DLC (p. 191) explains that during meditative equipoise all phenomena appear as the lucid awareness that is without dualistic appearances, just like the center of space. During subsequent attainment all conditioned phenomena appear as the union of appearance and emptiness, just like illusions, dreams, and so on. MC (fol. 18a.2–6) says that during meditative equipoise all phenomena are of equal taste and are unobservable by virtue of the nature of suchness—they appear as equality just as in the example of the center of space. By virtue of the wisdom of subsequent attainment, all conditioned phenomena without exception (no matter how and as what they appear) do appear, but they appear like illusions, mirages, dreams, and so on, whose natures are not established. The final state of lacking any distinction between meditative equipoise and subsequent attainment, in which they are a unity, occurs on the buddhabhūmi. On the bhūmis, this happens in an approximately concordant manner. It also happens in a partially similar manner, when the symbolic wisdom of the path of mantra arises in the mind stream because its means are profound. In this way, one must understand the essential point of both the manner in which buddhas see through their twofold wisdom of suchness and variety and the fact that it is not contradictory for the meditative equipoises on the paths of learning to be with and without appearances. Therefore, this explanation is very important. LDC (fols. 14a.7–15a.3) explains that what appears during meditative equipoise appears as nothing but the freedom from reference points because all phenomena equally appear as being utterly empty, just like the center of space. What appears during subsequent attainment appears as nothing but delusion because all conditioned phenomena appear like illusions. Though this applies in general, a single moment of nonconceptual wisdom on the buddhabhūmi, from the perspective of its seeing the nature of phenomena, lacks dualistic appearances. However, from the perspective of its seeing the bearers of this nature, it has dualistic appearances. That these two are not contradictory is the intention of DDV here. According to LZC (p. 25), as for the basic nature of phenomena—the great appearance of nonappearance—demonstrating the defining characteristic of the wisdom of realizing emptiness, all phenomena lack any distinction in terms of what is made to appear and what makes it appear, thus appearing equal to the center of space because they are free from all reference points of the characteristics of subject and object. All appearances of the conditioned bearers of the nature of phenomena are false because they are understood to be unreal appearances, just like illusions and so on. SC (p. 153) says that the explanation here of the nonconceptual wisdom of meditative equipoise being solely without appearances bears the intention that objects do not exist as other referents, but this does not contradict the fact that one's samādhi's own reflections emerge as entailing appearance. When one needs to understand the ways of seeing of the four wisdoms in a distinct manner, what they are actually aware of must be presented as the dharmadhātu—there is nothing other than that.

701 VIII.2–6 (for details, see Brunnhölzl 2011b, pp. 111–15). Note that these verses describe the qualities of the dharmakāya—its twenty-sevenfold enlightened activity is described separately in VIII.34cd–40.

702 XII.9cd–13.

703 This refers to what are known as "the sixty aspects of Brahmā's melodious voice." For details, see the *Mahāvyutpatti* (section 20, nos. 445–504, which are explained in detail in the *Munimatālaṃkāra*) and TOK, vol. 3, pp. 625–26 (see Appendix VI in Brunnhölzl 2011b).

704 DLC (p. 191) says that the first two benefits represent one's own welfare, while the latter two are the welfare of others. According to MC (fol. 18a.6–18b.4), the attainment of the dharmakāya is the ultimate fundamental change free from the two obscurations. The attainment of the great bliss that is uncontaminated and absolutely unchanging is supreme through its being beyond all kinds of contaminated bliss, including its latent tendencies, which is changing and not lasting. One also attains the two masteries over the pure, spontaneous, and unmistaken seeing of all knowable objects that consist of suchness and variety and over effortlessly teaching to limitless beings to be guided the profound and vast principles of the dharma—the various kinds of dharma doors that accord with their respective individual inclinations. These four benefits of nonconceptual wisdom are taught because it is the cause of giving rise to ultimate relinquishment and realization. LZC (pp. 25–26) says that the dharmakāya is the fundamental change that is the knowledge of suchness—the nature of phenomena, emptiness. The mastery over seeing is the knowledge of the variety of all knowable objects. Buddhas engage in the manifold ways of teaching as it is appropriate through their mastery over displaying the deeds of a buddha, such as dwelling in Tuṣita.

705 V.23–26. According to RC (p. 135), the first four clingings are superimpositions because of clinging to what is ultimately nonexistent as being existent, while the fifth one represents the denial of the conventional existence of mere appearances. DLC (p. 192) says that nonconceptual wisdom has the specific characteristic of relinquishing these five bases for mistakenness. MC (fol. 19a.1–6) explains that nonconceptual wisdom is the remedy that eliminates all bad views of clinging to extremes because it engages in the basic nature of the inseparability of the two realities—the suchness that is free from superimposition and denial. The five types of clinging are called "clinging to nonexistents" because they all engage in what is unreal. For ignorant mind clings to what does not exist ultimately in these five ways as being the aspects of the two kinds of identity, arising and ceasing, difference, and denial. In those who are endowed with nonconceptual wisdom, all bad mistaken views as illustrated by these four kinds of superimposition and the one kind of denial are absent. LZC (p. 27) says that nonconceptual wisdom is the remedy for clinging to a nature of what is unreal.

706 The preparatory stage of the first dhyāna and the ordinary first dhyāna entail both these mental factors of coarse examination and fine analysis, while the special first dhyāna entails only analysis without examination. From the second dhyāna onward there is no more conceptual examination and analysis. However, these dhyānas have other features, such as inner serenity (resulting from mindfulness, alertness, and equanimity), bliss, and being in one-pointed samādhi.

707 According to both RC (p. 135) and MC (fols. 19a.1–20a.5), simply not engaging mentally in the reference points of worldly conventions (that is, blending names and referents) does not qualify as nonconceptual wisdom, just as in the cases of babies and young animals. MC adds that, though the potential for blending terms and referents exists in the mind streams of small babies, since they do not know yet how to engage in coneptual examination and analysis, they do not apprehend referents through blending them with their names. RC's example for the complete subsiding of conceptions is the meditative absorption of cessation, which MC also adds to the three in DDVV and OED. MC further explains that the defining characteristics of nonconceptual wisdom are taught by way of excluding five cases of missing the point of what nonconceptual wisdom is. Nonconceptual wisdom means indeed not seeing any aspects to be observed whatsoever, nor apprehending anything as anything whatsoever. However, this perceptual mode, which is actually the seeing of the suchness of all phenomena, is like people born blind seeing forms. From the perspective of those who just see this life, nonconceptual

wisdom cannot be demonstrated at once in an affirmative manner. Therefore, though its nature is to not conceive of anything, through unerringly realizing that the actuality of the nature of phenomena is unobservable as any extreme whatsoever, in precise accordance with the nature of phenomena, nonconceptual wisdom does not apprehend it as anything whatsoever. However, it is not taught to be nonconceptual by virtue of not cognizing anything at all or by virtue of a total cessation of cognition. Therefore, though nonconceptual wisdom does not conceive of any aspects of extremes or reference points whatsoever, within the actuality of the basic nature being unobservable, the appearances of personally experienced wisdom free from the blurs of doubt dawn from within. This is what one should understand to be nonconceptual wisdom. Note that *Mahāyānasaṃgraha* VIII.2 also lists the same five misconceptions about nonconceptual wisdom. In the chapter on true reality in the *Bodhisattvabhūmi* section of the *Viniścayasaṃgrahaṇī* (D4038, vol. zi, fol. 27a.1–7), the five factors to be excluded from the nonconceptual prajñā of apprehending true reality are referred to as lacking mental engagement in anything whatsoever (*ci yid la mi byed pa*), transcendence, nonentity (*dngos po med pa*), nature (*rang bzhin*), and entertaining mental formations about focal objects (*dmigs pa la mngon par 'du byed pa*). The text explains, "If [this prajñā] were [nonconceptual] by virtue of lacking mental engagement, it would therefore not be suitable to apply [the phrase] 'being endowed with proper mental engagement to it because it would follow that this [phrase can] also [be applied] to being asleep, drunk, or crazy. If it were [nonconceptual] by virtue of transcending [conception in the dhyānas and so on], how would this consequently not contradict the passage '[All] phenomena that are the minds and mental factors of the three realms are conceptions'? If it were [nonconceptual] by virtue of being a nonentity, prajñā would consequently not be a phenomenon that is a mental factor. If it were [nonconceptual] by virtue of its nature, how would prajñā consequently not [always] have the characteristics of [having an intrinsic] nature and being completely unsullied? If it were [nonconceptual] by virtue of entertaining mental formations about a focal object, how would this consequently not be a denigration of nonconceptual prajñā being the very lack of mental formations about a focal object? You may wonder, 'If these aspects are not reasonable, how should one regard this prajñā as being nonconceptual?' To answer, [it is nonconceptual] because it lacks mental formations about focal objects. Its focal object is suchness (the dharma that is not in accord with [being] an entity or a nonentity), and this [suchness] is nonconceptual. Though [this prajñā] lacks mental formations about that [suchness], when the prajñā of suchness that is endowed with samādhi arises through the force of previous [engagement], it apprehends the characteristics of that focal object in a directly perceiving manner. Thus, it is called 'nonconceptual.'"

708 As before, the following comments on these verses (VIII.18, D4048, fol. 35a.5–6) are mainly based on the commentaries by Vasubandhu and Asvabhāva (for details, see Brunnhölzl 2007a, endnotes 173–74). Someone may argue, "If nonconceptual wisdom focused on conception (the imaginary and the dependent), it would not be nonconceptual. It does not focus on anything other either because there is nothing else that exists as a knowable object. Also, if nonconceptual wisdom is a knowledge, it would need an object to be known. And if it is not a knowledge, how could it be called wisdom? Thus, neither possibility is feasible." This is answered by these two stanzas. Nonconceptual wisdom does not engage in conception (false imagination or the dependent) because it is impossible for any focusing on conception to be nonconceptual. Nor does it focus on something else since it focuses on the nature of phenomena, which cannot be said to be either the same as or different from phenomena. Nonconceptual wisdom cannot be said to focus on either conception or nonconception. Unlike the wisdoms of preparatory application and subsequent attainment, actual nonconceptual wisdom is not a knowledge since it is nonconceptual (that is, it does not operate in the conceptual manner of those two wisdoms) and does not engage in conception. Nor can it be said to be nonknowledge since it is preceded by the wisdom due to preparatory application as its cause and engages in the nature of phenomena.

Since there is no split into apprehender and apprehended in this wisdom, one cannot pinpoint anything that knows or anything that is known. This lack of difference is precisely the nonconceptuality of that wisdom—its being not different from what is known is like space and the appearances therein. Nonconceptual wisdom is not nonconceptual like the wisdom due to preparatory application, which still operates in terms of apprehender and apprehended. Rather, since it operates in such a way that it is not different from whatever it apprehends and knows, it engages in equality, which is nonconceptuality per se. The sūtras say that all phenomena are naturally nonconceptual since what is conceived—the imaginary—does not exist. However, this does not mean that there is no need to make any efforts for the sake of realizing this and that all sentient beings are thus naturally liberated already. For though all phenomena are naturally nonconceptual, the wisdom of directly realizing that phenomena are that way has not dawned in sentient beings. In bodhisattvas, however, that wisdom has arisen since there is nothing to conceive for them. Therefore, they are liberated, while others are not.

709 OED follows DDVV in reading *shes pa*.

710 RC (p. 136) and MC (fol. 20a.6–20b.2) say that the nonconceptual wisdom of buddhas and bodhisattvas does not conceive of saṃsāra and nirvāṇa as being what is to be rejected and to be adopted, respectively. It is not limited in terms of relinquishment and realization, but completely perfect. It is lasting because, by virtue of the dharmakāya's nature being permanent, it always engages in the welfare of others for as long as saṃsāra exists.

711 See DDVV (fol. 31a.7–31b.1): "What arises without beginning is the ignorance about suchness, which is the cause of mistakenness—the appearance of duality that does not exist."

712 Skt. anuśaya, Tib. phra rgyas. The Sanskrit literally means being closely attached to something and refers to the afflictions adhering to their objects. The Tibetan rendering ("subtle-expanding") highlights the fact that these afflictions usually begin in a rather subtle or inconspicuous way and then develop and grow in strength.

713 The cognitive obscurations were already discussed at length under 2.2.2.2.2.2. The matrix of the nature of phenomena (OED, pp. 529–32).

714 OED *sbyong ngo*, which is emended to *byung ngo*.

715 I.73.

716 DLC (p. 192) says that functions (4) and (5) are due to the realization of suchness and variety and the completion of the two welfares, respectively. According to MC (fols. 20b.2–21a.2), the distancing of the flux of conceptions is a result produced by a person because nonconceptual wisdom overcomes the arising of these conceptions (that is, their latent tendencies). The accomplishment of unsurpassable bliss is a dominated result because nonconceptual wisdom accomplishes the bliss of realizing all phenomena in an unmistaken manner, which is the absolutely permanent bliss. That nonconceptual wisdom frees from the afflictive and cognitive obscurations is a result of freedom because it overcomes the contaminations, including their latent tendencies. Its unimpeded engagement in seeing all aspects of knowable objects through the wisdom of subsequent attainment is a result that concords with its cause. Its functions of purifying buddha realms, maturing sentient beings, and granting and completely perfecting the phenomenon of the knowledge of all aspects to one's own mind stream as well as bestowing it upon others are counted as one and make up the result of maturation in this context. RC (p. 136) says that unsurpassable uncontaminated bliss is more eminent than those of śrāvakas and pratyekabuddhas. The five functions are what accomplish the fruition that consists of the three kāyas. Like MC, RC also matches the five functions of nonconceptual wisdom with the five kinds of results, but differs in identifying only the granting of the knowledge of all aspects as a result of maturation, while purifying buddha realms and maturing sentient beings are results

produced by a person. Unlike MC, RC does not provide any reasons for matching the five functions with the five results. LZC (pp. 30–31) explains "maturing sentient beings" as maturing the causes that make all sentient beings to be guided attain the fruition.

717 Among the fourteen summarizing points of the *Avikalpapraveśadhāraṇī* in Kamalaśīla's commentary, these points represent (8)–(10) and (12)–(14); see Appendix 1.

718 The words "enlightenment" (*byang chub*), "courageous" (*dpa' ba*), and "(have in) mind" (*sems (pa)*) make up the Tibetan *byang chub sems dpa'* for "bodhisattva." In Sanskrit, *bodhi* means "realization," "awakening," or "enlightenment," and *sattva* has many meanings, the most important ones in this context being "a being," "(disposition of) mind," "spiritual essence," "(strength of) character," "courage," "resolution," and "magnanimity." Thus, bodhisattvas are those who have given rise to bodhicitta, the mental disposition of having enough courage and magnanimity for the resolve of setting their mind solely on the goal of buddhahood for the sake of all sentient beings. The courage in this lies in being afraid neither of the infinite number of sentient beings to be liberated nor the infinite time it takes to liberate them nor the great hardships one has to go through in order to accomplish this.

719 Compare *Mahāyānasaṃgraha* II.2 (D4048, fol. 13a.3–4), which explains the dependent nature as "the cognizances that entail the seeds of the ālaya-consciousness and consist of false imagination." These cognizances are elevenfold as explained above in OED (pp. 510–11).

720 According to the *Mahāyānasaṃgraha* (I.6; D4048, fol. 3b.6–7) these four are the views about a real personality, self-conceit, attachment to the self, and ignorance. For details on "mentation," "the immediate mind" and the afflicted mind in general and according to the Third Karmapa, see Brunnhölzl 2009, pp. 30–34 and 109–113.

721 Note that, just as DDV (K), but unlike DDV (P), OED does not consider "since beginningless time" as a part of DDV.

722 Since OED follows DDV's confusing wording *rgyu dang bcas pa'i 'bras bu*, a more literal reading of OED here would be "results including their causes appear mutually, but they do not really exist."

723 The two texts by Rāhulabhadra in the *Tengyur* do not contain this verse.

724 RC (pp. 137–38) calls these sections of DDV "the manner of mentally engaging in the saṃsāra of dualistic appearances," which consists of the twofold actual manner of mental engagement and, based on that, the dawn of a bodhisattva's engagement in nonconceptual wisdom. As for the twofold mental engagement, first, bodhisattvas mentally engage in reflecting on the dualistic appearances of saṃsāra as follows: "The ālaya that contains all seeds, into which beginningless false imagination with its dualistic appearances of apprehender and apprehended plants latent tendencies, is the cause for the appearance of the nonexistent duality of apprehender and apprehended. This ālaya and the operating consciousnesses that represent a continuum that is different from, and based on, it arise from being ignorant about suchness. The ālaya (the cause) and the appearance of the duality of apprehender and apprehended (its result) appear from the perspective of mistakenness, but do not exist as they appear." Second, bodhisattvas mentally engage in the manner in which dualistic appearances obscure the nature of phenomena: "By virtue of apprehender and apprehended, including their cause, appearing, the nondual nature of phenomena does not appear. By virtue of the duality of apprehender and apprehended not appearing, the nature of phenomena appears." Based on these two kinds of mental engagement, bodhisattvas engage in nonconceptual wisdom. DLC (p. 193) says that the point of mental engagement is presented by way of (1) the collection of its causes and (2) its defining characteristics. The first one consists of (1a) the manner of proper mental engagement through study and reflection on the path of accumulation and (1b) the manner of bringing forth

the clear illumination that arises from meditation on the path of preparation. The above sections of DDV correspond to (1a). That is, if one needs to see suchness directly during the meditative equipoise of the path of seeing, one needs to identify the primary obstacle for this, which consists of our present dualistic appearances because these are just nonexistents that clearly appear. For the cause for this appearance of what does not exist is as follows. Through the condition of being ignorant about suchness and by virtue of the seeds of the ālaya-consciousness that imagine suchness to be unreal, from the perspective of mistakenness, apprehender, apprehended, objects of designation, and what designates them appear in a dualistic manner despite not existing ultimately. Based on this ālaya-consciousness, different continua of persons and so on need to be presented. Therefore, this invalidates the position of those who say that there are buddhas with different continua after the ālaya-consciousness has undergone the fundamental change. MC (fol. 21a.2–21b.5) says that through ignorance about suchness (the basic nature of all phenomena), the ālaya-consciousness contains all seeds of the phenomena which appear as apprehender and apprehended and are imagined from the perspective of mistaken mind, though they are unreal. This ālaya is the cause for the appearance of the duality of apprehender and apprehended, while these two do not exist. The appearance of all kinds of phenomena from the continuum of consciousness that is tainted by the latent tendencies of reference points since beginningless time is like a dream. The operating consciousnesses that are based on the ālaya and yet have different causes appear as the types of mind that definitely apprehend their specific objects (MC mentions the variant reading "continuum" for "cause" here in DDV (K)). Under the sway of false imagination, dualistic phenomena appear, while not existing. Therefore, what entails cause (the ālaya) and result (the seven consciousnesses with their objects—the phenomena that consist of the dualistic appearances of apprehender and apprehended) appears in this way from the perspective of mistakenness, but it does not exist ultimately. Just like mirages and so on, it is only false imagination. In other words, by virtue of the duality of apprehender and apprehended appearing, the nature of phenomena does not appear. By virtue of apprehender and apprehended not appearing, the nature of phenomena does appear. Thus, it is under the sway of false imagination that sentient beings circle in saṃsāra and do not see the nature of phenomena. If bodhisattvas understand and mentally engage in this point in a proper manner, it represents the manner of their first engaging in nonconceptual wisdom for the following reasons. It is under the sway of conceptions that saṃsāra appears—there is no other cause whatsoever. Therefore, there is no essential point for determining afflicted phenomena that is more profound than this. Also, through understanding that dualistic appearances are not established as they appear and therefore are mere false imagination, bodhisattvas engage in nonconceptual wisdom through relinquishing their clinging to these dualistic appearances existing as such. Consequently, this point is also very profound in terms of the essential point of the path of accomplishing purified phenomena. According to LZC (p. 32), for as long as one is obscured by the reference points of the mistaken appearances of apprehender and apprehended, the nature of phenomena—emptiness or suchness free from all reference points—does not appear because it is its very makeup to lack any reference points. By virtue of any characteristics of reference points (such as apprehender and apprehended) not appearing, the nature of phenomena does appear. The proper mental engagement of bodhisattvas in what is explained here to be nonexistent represents their engagement in nonconceptual wisdom during the phase of the path of preparation.

725 The first verse is *Mahāyānasūtrālaṃkāra* XIX.47. According to the *Mahāyānasūtrālaṃkārabhāṣya* (D4050, fol. 245a.7–245b.2), the first two investigations refer to names and referents being adventitious in relation to each other. The second two investigations refer to the imputations of a nature and the distinctive features of something being mere imputations upon having made a connection between a name and its referent. Both verses appear in *Mahāyānasaṃgraha* III.16 (D4048, fol. 26a.4–5). The *Mahāyānasaṃgrahopanibandhana*

(D4051, fol. 249a.4–6) says that "threefold conception" in the second verse refers to the remaining three conceptions about names, natures, and distinctive features (since those about referents have been relinquished), which are finally seen to not exist as real entities either. Thus, the first two lines of the first verse represent engaging in the imaginary nature; the next two lines, engaging in the dependent nature; and the second verse, engaging in the perfect nature. See also the discussion of the four investigations above (OED, pp. 535–36).

726 (1) The mind is made to *settle* on a focal object. (2) By prolonging that, it is made to *settle continuously*. (3) If it strays away from that object, it is *resettled repeatedly*. (4) In order that it does not stray away, it is *settled closely* on the object with mindfulness. (5) Not considering sense pleasures, the mind is *tamed*. (6) Through considering distractions as shortcomings, the mind is *pacified*. (7) Even if obvious thoughts occur, through not readily pursuing them, the mind is *pacified completely*. (8) Through putting an end to dullness and agitation, the mind is *made one-pointed*. (9) Once it is familiar [with that], it is *settled evenly* without any effort.

727 These are (1) investigation, (2) examination, (3) fine analysis, (4) calm abiding, (5) superior insight, (6) their union, (7) lucidity, (8) nonconceptuality, (9) equanimity, (10) uninterrupted continuity, and (11) nondistraction.

728 This is found in the *Saṃdhinirmocanasūtra* and consists of the kinds of superior insight that arise from characteristics, investigation, and discrimination. The first one means to identify what identitylessness means and thus mentally engage in its characteristics, but not by using a lot of reasoning. Investigation refers to relying on reasoning to gain certainty. Discrimination means to further analyze points about which one has already gained certainty.

729 This means to analyze all afflicted and purified phenomena in terms of the meanings of words, entities, characteristics, classes, time, and reasoning.

730 XIV.23.

731 XIV.24.

732 XIV.25.

733 XIV.26–27ab (OED omits lines 26cd).

734 XIV.27cd. According to RC (pp. 138–39), the above fourfold progression represents "the manner of cultivating the yoga of relinquishing dualistic appearances." By virtue of not observing the duality of apprehender and apprehended, bodhisattvas observe them as mere cognizance. By virtue of observing them as mere cognizance, they do not observe any external referents. By virtue of not observing any referents to be apprehended, they do not observe mere cognizance—the apprehender as the cognizing subject—either. By virtue of not observing that duality of apprehender and apprehended during the phase of the path of preparation, they engage in observing nothing but suchness, which cannot be differentiated by the two of apprehender and apprehended. DLC (p. 193) explains this section as (1b) the manner of bringing forth the clear illumination that arises from meditation on the path of preparation (see DLC's comments in note 728). That is, the level of heat of the path of preparation means that what is observed or appears by virtue of having studied and reflected on the above proper mental engagement is observed as mere cognizance. The level of peak is that, based on that, external referents are not observed. Poised readiness refers to not observing the apprehender of mere referents either. The supreme dharma is the observation of nothing but suchness in which apprehender and apprehended lack any difference. These four correspond to the four levels of attaining illumination, its increase, and so on that were explained above. MC (fols. 21b.5–22a.1) says that, by virtue of having become familiar with observing and mentally engaging as explained above, bodhisattvas observe all phenomena as mere cognizance or mere mind. By virtue of that, they do not observe external referents as anything to be clung to. By virtue of not observing referents in this way,

they do not observe them as the mere cognizance that apprehends them as such and such either. By virtue of not observing that apprehender, they engage in observing nondual suchness, which cannot be differentiated as apprehender and apprehended—the actuality that is beyond thought and speech. According to LZC (p. 33), by virtue of focusing on imagination (the appearance of nonexistents), bodhisattvas observe all appearances as mind—mere cognizance. Therefore, they lack the observation of external referents—such referents do not exist because it is mere cognizance itself that appears as referents. By virtue of referents not being established or observable, bodhisattvas do not observe mere cognizance either—if there are no referents to be cognized, cognizance is not reasonable. By virtue of not observing that cognizance, they engage in observing the lack of difference between those two (the subjects and objects in terms of apprehender and apprehended) by virtue of their not existing as two. For if a difference between these two existed, that is, if these two actually existed, they would be realized as such.

735 RC (p. 139) says that the appearance of nothing but suchness, in which the two of apprehender and apprehended are unobservable, is nonconceptual wisdom because it is characterized by not observing any characteristics of reference points of the duality of apprehender and apprehended. This wisdom has two distinctive features—it lacks the object that is the duality of apprehender and apprehended and it lacks being observable by mind. SGC (fol. 9a.5) agrees with the last sentence. DLC (pp. 193–94) explains this section of mental engagement as (2) the defining characteristics of the actual mental engagement in nonconceptual wisdom (see DLC's comments in note 718). The meditative equipoise of the path of seeing of directly realizing the nonobservability of any difference between apprehender and apprehended is nonconceptual wisdom because it is the wisdom that is characterized by lacking objects (unlike something like an eye consciousness apprehending form), lacking the observation of object generalities (unlike something like a thought about a vase), and not observing any characteristics of reference points (such as existence and nonexistence). According to MC (fol. 22a.1–3), the nonobservation of any phenomena that belong to the distinction that consists of the duality of apprehender and apprehended is called "nonconceptual wisdom." It lacks even the slightest object to be observed and it lacks observation as anything by a subject. Therefore, since it is characterized by not observing even the slightest of all characteristics (such as apprehender, apprehended, existence, and nonexistence), one cannot come up with even the most subtle reason for presenting it as belonging to the sphere of conception. LZC (p. 33) explains that the nonobservation of the two of apprehender and apprehended being different is the nonconceptual wisdom of emptiness. It lacks an object and lacks cognizance because it is characterized by emptiness in that is does not observe any reference points of characteristics.

736 The content of this verse corresponds to *Mahāyānasaṃgraha* II.21 (D4048, fol. 17b.5–7) and also resembles *Mahāyānasūtrālaṃkāra* XI.77, but I could not identify it as it stands (it is not contained in any prajñāpāramitā sūtra). Though Dignāga's *Prajñāpāramitārthasaṃgraha* (verses 19–54) explains these ten characteristics or "conceptual distractions" in more detail and links them to passages in the *Prajñāpāramitā Sūtra in Eight Thousand Lines*, these ten are not mentioned by name in any known prajñāpāramitā sūtra.

737 II.22; D4048, fols. 17b.7–18b.1. With some variations, the quoted passages in this section are found in the *Pañcaviṃśatisāhasrikāprajñāpāramitāsūtra* (D9, vol. ka, fols. 42b.2–43b.4). Besides the *Mahāyānasaṃgraha*, they also occur in *Mahāyānasūtrālaṃkāra* XI.77 and its *Bhāṣya* as well as in Dignāga's *Prajñāpāramitārthasaṃgraha* (verses 19–54). The latter two texts use the same passages from the sūtras as the *Mahāyānasaṃgraha* to illustrate the remedies for the ten distractions.

738 II.26; D4048, fol. 19a.2–5.

739 OED adds "taught above" at the end. However, this is not contained in DDV, but is an addition by DDVV.

740 As mentioned above, these five are abiding in signlessness through eliminating characteristics by way of confidence in the three jewels, vigor in the six pāramitās, the mindfulness of bodhicitta, nonconceptual samādhi, and the prajñā of knowing all aspects of phenomena.

741 *Abhisamayālaṃkāra* I.19–20 and its commentaries describe twenty-two kinds of generating bodhicitta (the following comments on them are based on the commentaries by the Fifth Shamarpa and the Eighth Karmapa). Among these twenty-two, the first three correspond to the lesser, medium, and great path of accumulation, respectively, while the fourth one refers to the path of preparation. (1) The one that is associated with the resolve to attain enlightenment for the sake of all beings resembles the earth since it is the basis for all pure dharmas (the buddha qualities and the collection of their causes). (2) The one that is associated with the intention that, when focusing on bringing together all six pāramitās, is oriented toward the benefit and happiness in this and all future lifetimes resembles gold since it does not change until enlightenment. (3) The one that is associated with the superior intention to familiarize with and accomplish all virtuous dharmas (such as the four foundations of mindfulness) is like the waxing moon since all these virtuous dharmas will increase. (4) The one that is associated with the training in familiarizing, in an approximately concordant manner, with all three knowledges (the knowledge of all aspects, the knowledge of the path, and the knowledge of all entities) being without nature is like fire since it is the supreme remedial training that burns the firewood of the obscurations of the three knowledges.

742 These two practices are described in the seventh and eighth points of the knowledge of all aspects—the first topic of the *Abhisamayālaṃkāra.* In general, armorlike practice refers to donning the great armor of the mental vigor to strive for the welfare of others through the basic motivation of bodhicitta. In particular, this practice consists of engaging in the six pāramitās in such a way that the practice of each one of them includes the practice of all. The ninefold practice of engagement, generally speaking, refers to the application of this mental vigor that is its cause. In particular, it includes the trainings in the dhyānas and formless absorptions, the four immeasurables, the pāramitās, the ten bhūmis, nonreferential prajñā, the three greatnesses (great mind, relinquishment, and realization), the supernatural knowledges, and the knowledge of all aspects.

743 IV.4.

744 The five faculties are the same as the five dharmas of confidence and so on above.

745 XIV.8–10ab.

746 MC (fol. 22a.4–5) says that, on the level of engagement through aspiration, bodhisattvas do not directly realize the actuality of the nature of phenomena, but train in this actuality by way of aspiring for it through relying on the prajñās of study, reflection, and meditation.

747 The fifth generation of bodhicitta that corresponds to the path of seeing and is associated with the pāramitā of generosity is like a treasure since it satisfies all sentient beings without ever becoming depleted.

748 MC (fol. 22a.5–6) says that, on the first bhūmi, the actuality of the nature of phenomena is directly realized, that is, not just as an object generality.

749 Again, OED adds "taught above" at the end.

750 RC (p. 139) explains that the first seven bhūmis are called "impure" because characteristics of reference points still arise despite one's not wishing so. The last three bhūmis are "pure" because one does not engage in any characteristics of reference points.

751 IX.2 (D4048, fol. 36b.3–5).

752 The sixth generation of bodhicitta that is associated with the pāramitā of ethics is like a jewel mine since it functions as the source of all infinite and precious mundane and supramundane qualities. The one that is associated with patience is like an ocean since its ground is unperturbed—one's mind is unruffled by any physical and mental sufferings. The one that is associated with vigor is like a vajra since, by virtue of one's firm trust in the causes and the result of unsurpassable enlightenment, it cannot be split through the activities of māras or one's own antagonistic factors. The one that is associated with dhyāna is like Mount Meru since it is not agitated by distractions. The one that is associated with prajñā is like medicine since it pacifies the two obscurations, including their latent tendencies, which are like diseases that produce suffering. The one that is associated with the skillful means of dedication is like a friend since it does not abandon the welfare of sentient beings in any situation. The one that is associated with the ten great aspiration prayers and so forth is like a wish-fulfilling gem since the fruitions of these aspirations are accomplished as aspired. The one that is associated with power is like the sun since it ripens the harvest of those to be guided through teaching the dharma by way of the four discriminating awarenesses in ways that are individually appropriate. The one that is associated with the wisdoms of suchness and variety is like a song of the gandharvas or a pleasant dharma melody since it teaches the dharma for which those to be guided aspire. The one that is associated with the six supernatural knowledges is like a king since it accomplishes the welfare of others through these supernatural knowledges with unimpeded power. The one that is associated with the two accumulations is like a treasure-vault since it is the foundation or treasure of many collections of merit and wisdom. The one that is associated with the thirty-seven dharmas concordant with enlightenment is like a highway since the noble ones travel on it. The one that is associated with compassion as the essence of superior insight is like a vehicle since it moves by not abiding in either saṃsāra or nirvāṇa. The one that is associated with the power of total recall of not forgetting the words and the meanings of the dharma (which is associated with mindfulness) and the self-confidence of explaining them to others in an unimpeded manner (which is associated with prajñā) is like a fountain or a well that is an inexhaustible source of bringing forth fresh water and yet retaining its essence. The one that is associated with the feast of dharma of embracing the ultimate way of being of the three jewels through explaining the four seals of the dharma is like a pleasant melody that satisfies all, just as the sweetly resounding sound of the drum of the gods or their nectar do, since the four seals and so on resound sweetly for those who wish to attain liberation and omniscience. The one that is associated with the single path that all buddhas travel is like a river since the welfare of others is an incessant stream. The one that is associated with the dharmakāya is like a big cloud (the cause for abundance) since it is the source for the activities of the nairmāṇikakāya for the welfare of all beings being displayed in all worldly realms. According to most commentaries on the *Abhisamayālaṃkāra*, the first nine among these correspond to the second through tenth bhūmis; the next five, to the special paths of the three pure bhūmis; and the last three, to the buddhabhūmi in terms of preparation, main part, and conclusion (for details, see Brunnhölzl 2010, pp. 239–41 and 389–92).

753 The Sanskrit *śuddhamatī* is the female form of "being endowed with excellence." Through mistaking *matī* ("endowed") for *mati* ("mind," "intelligence," "insight"), the term became mistranslated as *legs pa'i blo gros* ("Excellent Insight") in Tibetan. Thus, explanations of the name of the ninth bhūmi in Tibetan commentaries usually gloss the latter rendering.

754 OED just says *nges pa*, which the context suggests to emend to *nges tshig*.

755 MC (fol. 22b.2–3) says that the deeds of a buddha are uninterrupted for as long as space and sentient beings exist. The training in completion is the phase of the arrival at the very nature of the nature of phenomena, in which the two obscurations have been relinquished—it is the changeless wisdom that is nondual with the dharmadhātu. According to LZC (p. 35), this means to have become of the nature of nonconceptual wisdom, which is the phase of the wisdom of the fundamental change being of a single taste.

756 II.2.

757 The dharmakāya is permanent by nature because it is without any change. The sāmbhogikakāya is permanent in terms of continuity because it is endowed with the five certainties. The nairmāṇikakāya is permanent in the sense of an uninterrupted series because the enlightened activity of all the different forms of nairmāṇikakāyas is uninterrupted until saṃsāra is empty.

758 II.62.

759 According to II.63–68, in due order, the seven reasons for the rūpakāyas being permanent are that (1) their causes, such as the two accumulations, are infinite, (2) the number of beings to be guided is infinite, (3) buddhas always strive for the benefit of these beings through great love and compassion, (4) due to their miraculous powers, buddhas are able to remain for the sake of beings' benefit for as long as saṃsāra lasts, (5) seeing the oneness of saṃsāra and nirvāṇa, there is no need for rejecting the one or adopting the other, (6) they are unassailable by saṃsāra's suffering due to constantly dwelling in blissful samādhi, and (7) having mastered all buddha qualities, they are not sullied by any saṃsāric phenomena, such as karma and afflictions. The three reasons for the dharmakāya being permanent are that (1) the lord of death has been vanquished, (2) the nature of the dharmakāya is not the one of conditioned phenomena, and (3) it is the ultimate protector and refuge for all beings.

760 Nonconceptual wisdom or buddhahood is permanent because it has the characteristic of being pure suchness, is the result of previous boundless aspiration prayers, and its activity never comes to a halt.

761 Here "supports" refers to the sāmbhogikakāya's and nairmāṇikakāya's retinues, speech, sizes of the body, major and minor marks, enjoyments of the taste of dharma, and so on being distinct in each realm in which they appear.

762 These consist of two kinds of food with regard to living in this life—(1) coarse food (*kavalīkārāhāra*) in order to sustain the sense faculties and (2) the food of touch (*sparśāhāra*) in order to sustain consciousness as what is supported by the faculties, and two kinds of food with regard to future lives—(3) the food of mental volition (*manaḥsaṃcetanāhāra*) in order to propel one into other existences and (4) the food of consciousness (*vijñānāhāra*) in order to complete those other existences.

763 This is an abbreviated and sometimes paraphrased version of *Mahāyānasaṃgraha* X.1-9 and X.28–29 (D4048, fols. 37a.3–39a.5 and 40a.2–41a.3). Obviously, OED omits point (10)—enlightened activity—in the summarizing verse at the beginning of this section. *Mahāyānasaṃgraha* X.31 (ibid., fols. 41b.5–42a.2) says on this that the dharmadhātu in all buddhas always performs the five activities of protecting beings against (1) harm such as blindness, deafness, and madness (merely through seeing a buddha), (2) falling into the lower realms (through preventing them from committing nonvirtue and introducing them to virtue), (3) what are not the means for liberation (through turning tīrthikas away from their efforts for liberation through the wrong means and establishing them in the teachings of the buddhas), (4) the views about a real personality (through providing the path that transcends the three realms), and (5) inferior yānas (through establishing śrāvakas as well as bodhisattvas of uncertain disposition who have entered other yānas in the practice of the mahāyāna).

764 The *Tengyur* does not contain a text by this name.

765 RC (p. 140) says that if there were no fundamental change of having relinquished the obscurations, there would be no support for the afflictions not operating. For that support is the wisdom of having relinquished the obscurations, but without the fundamental change, the relinquishment of the obscurations is not feasible. According to MC (fols. 22b.6–23b.1), if there

were no fundamental change of the factors to be relinquished having been relinquished and the realizations having been attained through the path, there would be no support for already relinquished afflictions not operating again in the mind stream. For example, in the case of the factors to be relinquished through seeing not arising again in the mind stream of a bodhisattva in which they have been relinquished, it is by virtue of that bodhisattva having attained a fundamental change in which the mind stream has changed that there is no chance for those factors to be relinquished to operate again in that mind stream. Otherwise, if the mind stream had not undergone the fundamental change, even if the obscurations have already been relinquished one time, they would arise again just as before. The same applies up through the buddhabhūmi—when a mind stream has not undergone the fundamental change, it serves as a support for the operating of the respective factors to be relinquished, but when it has undergone the fundamental change, it serves as the support for those factors to be relinquished not operating. You may wonder, "Once the seeds to be relinquished are destroyed just like seeds burned by fire, they simply do not arise again. So, even if there is no 'fundamental change,' how is that contradictory to their not re-arising?" Though the seeds to be relinquished are destroyed, this relinquishment needs to be presented by indicating the distinctive features of the mind stream in which it happened, but it is not feasible in terms of a mind stream that shows no such distinctive features. For without demonstrating this relinquishment through specifying that certain distinctive features of a mind stream in which remedial wisdom has been generated represent "the termination of contaminations," one does not know the manner in which those seeds have been destroyed either. Thus, it is by virtue of these distinctive features of a fundamental change when compared to before that the seeds to be relinquished do not re-arise in a mind stream in which they have been terminated, but this is unlike the case of the support having become nonexistent after the continuum of the mind stream has become extinct. Therefore, that contaminations arise in mind streams with certain distinctive features and do not arise in mind streams with certain others is by virtue of not having or having attained a fundamental change, respectively, just as there is no chance for appearances of falling hairs in an eye without blurred vision. LZC (p. 36) glosses "the support for afflictions not operating" as the wisdom that engages in the nature of phenomena.

766 Among the two kinds of the perfect nature, nonconceptual wisdom is usually identified with the unmistaken perfect nature.

767 RC (p. 140) says that there would be no support for the operating of the path that eliminates the obscurations. For without the fundamental change, being pure of the obscurations is not feasible and therefore the path that eliminates the stains is not feasible either. According to MC (fol. 23b.1–4), there would be no support for the operating of the path that is the remedy for the factors to be relinquished. For the supports for respectively higher paths operating in the distinctive mind streams that are referred to as "a person on the path of seeing," "a person on the second bhūmi," and so on are the respectively preceding fundamental changes, and without the respectively preceding ones, the arising of the respectively following ones is not possible. This is comparable to there being no chance for the stem and so on of a plant to grow if there is no fundamental change of its seed into its sprout. For the respective fundamental changes along the path, both the conventional terms for these fundamental changes and their actualities apply, just as the actuality of the buddhabhūmi is called "the path of nonlearning." LZC (p. 36) glosses "the path" as the means to engage in the nature of phenomena.

768 Lit. "Husk-Eater." Kaṇāda was the founder of the Vaiśeṣikas and received his name because he was able to meditate for a long time while sustaining himself by eating only grain husks. He was also called "Owl" (Skt. Ulūka, Tib. 'ug pa) because, upon his accomplishment of Īśvara, the deity alighted on a stone liṅgam in his meditation cave in the form of an owl, who was then asked by Kaṇāda for confirmation of his attainment. The reference to his view here seems to allude to the Vaiśeṣika position that the self, when attaining liberation, not only transcends the world, but even ceases to be the subject of any experience, even of itself.

769 RC (p. 140) says that the flaw of there being no basis for designating the persons who have passed into nirvāṇa is by virtue of these persons being designated as such based on their attainment of the fundamental change of being without stains. According to MC (fols. 23b.4–24a.6), what is taken as the basis for being designated as "a saṃsāric person" is a continuum of the contaminated skandhas. Likewise, what is taken as the basis for being designated as "a nirvāṇic person" is the fundamental change of this continuum into being uncontaminated. Without that fundamental change, there would be no basis for designating the sheer continuum of the skandhas (such as the mind) as a nirvāṇic person, just as there is no such basis during the phase of the skandhas not having undergone the fundamental change before. Furthermore, there would be no basis for designating the persons who have passed into nirvāṇa within the dhātu without any remainder of the skandhas (as asserted by the śrāvakas and pratyekabuddhas) as "those who have passed into nirvāṇa." For if there were no fundamental change, such a designation would be a name without any basis, just like the name "horns of a rabbit." You may think, "Even if there is no fundamental change here, what is wrong with that? To designate the mere cessation of the previous skandhas as 'nirvāṇa' is just like referring to the termination of an illness as 'being without illness.'" If there is the certainty that the continuum of the previous skandhas has become extinct and does not arise again, it is exactly this that represents the existence of the fundamental change of that continuum. For this fundamental change consists of both the support for the certainty that "this person has passed into nirvāṇa and does not fall into saṃsāra again" and the basis for such a designation. Therefore, one cannot claim that such a fundamental change does not exist. However, if one claims its nonexistence, the extinction and the lack of re-arising of the continuum of the previous skandhas do not exist either because both the support and the basis of designation of that extinction and lack of re-arising do not exist. Though bodhisattvas, through the path of the mahāyāna, also pass into nirvāṇa within the dhātu without any remainder of the contaminated skandhas, they pass into the particular nirvāṇa in which the stream of uncontaminated kāyas and wisdoms is uninterrupted. In that case, there is obviously no need to mention that this represents the nature of their fundamental change. LZC (p. 36) glosses the fundamental change as "the fundamental change of emptiness and dependent origination."

770 OED *nyes pa ni bzhi pa'o*, but *bzhi pa* is an addition by DDVV.

771 IX.2 (D4048, fol. 36b.5–6). RC (p. 140) says that the flaw of there being no basis for designating the differences between the three types of enlightenment is by virtue of those types of enlightenment actually being classified due to the differences of their respective fundamental changes. MC (fol. 24a.6–24b.3) agrees with this and elaborates that the three types of enlightenment must be presented by virtue of the differences in terms of their being pure of certain parts of the obscurations or all of them. However, without the fundamental change there would be no basis for designating such differences. At the time of passing into nirvāṇa within the dhātu without any remainders of the skandhas, there would be no basis with regard to which one could designate these differences between the three types of enlightenment. Therefore, all explanations on their qualities of relinquishment and realization being greater or lesser and so on would be pointless, just like explanations on whether the son of a barren woman is handsome or not. Since these four shortcomings have not been discussed in detail in previous Indian and Tibetan commentaries, may those with insight delight in their detailed explanation here.

772 DLC (pp. 194–95) says that the first two flaws would accrue if the natural purity of suchness did not exist, while the latter two would follow if suchness' being free from adventitious stains did not exist. For just as the operation of afflictions and the mere factors to be relinquished needs a support, their nonoperation needs one too. Likewise, the operation of the remedies needs a support. Both of these are not reasonable in anything other than the basis that is the unchanging perfect nature. The statements "This is the nirvāṇa without remainder of the persons who are śrāvakas" and "This is the enlightenment of śrāvakas" are only tenable

with regard to cessation in terms of being free from adventitious stains, but not with regard to anything else. For the (ordinary) mind of mere awareness entails arising and ceasing, the factors to be relinquished and their remedies are not tenable in a single support, and the continuum (of dualistic mind) has become extinct in the nirvāṇa without remainder.

773 OED *de las bzlog pas phan yon rnams pa nyid* emended to *de las bzlog pa phan yon rnam pa bzhi nyid* according to DDVV.

774 According to MC (fols. 24b.6–25b.2), the wisdom of the fundamental change is the basis for designating the various kinds of liberation—enlightenment and nirvāṇa, the source of inexhaustible qualities, and the supreme support for accomplishing, as one wishes, all temporary and ultimate welfares of all sentient beings without exception for as long as space exists. Having understood this, fortunate persons should engage in accomplishing this wisdom. LZC (pp. 36–37) says that if the wisdom of the fundamental change—the nature being empty and appearances being dependent origination—exists, on a mere conventional level there is a support for the afflictions not operating, a support for engaging in the path, a basis for the conventional term "nirvāṇa," and a basis for designating the generating of the mindsets of the three kinds of enlightenment.

775 OED *gnas pa*, which, according to the context, is emended to *gnas gyur*.

776 *Mahāyānasūtrālaṃkāra* XIX.53–54 and *Mahāyānasaṃgraha* IX.2 (D4048, fol. 37a.1–2).

777 IX.2 (D4048, fol. 37a.2–3).

778 XI.15.

779 RC (p. 141) says that illusions and so on are examples for the appearance of the duality of apprehender and apprehended, which does not exist in the actual mode of being because it appears from the perspective of mistakenness, though not existing in actuality. According to MC (fol. 25a.2–4), the phenomena of saṃsāra (what appears under the sway of mere false imagination) are called "nonexistent phenomena"—they appear while lacking any nature of their own. LZC (p. 37) explains that this section refers to the dispute about the appearance of unreal conditioned phenomena and presents the following objection: "If something does not exist, it does not appear, but if it appears, it must be real." The answer is that though nonexistent phenomena appear, they do so only for false imagination, but they are not real, just like illusions and so on.

780 OED *bzhin no* instead of *yin no*.

781 RC (pp. 141–42) says that space and so on are examples for the foundation of the fundamental change—the natural nirvāṇa. For though space may be associated with clouds, space does not have the nature of clouds nor vice versa, and therefore they coexist in a manner of being separable. Since space is pure of the nature of clouds and clouds are pure of the nature of space, one also speaks of "purity by nature." The same applies for gold being covered by a film and water being murky. Or these examples for the fundamental change can be understood as follows. Though the natural nirvāṇa is naturally pure before, it is associated with adventitious stains and therefore is impure. Later, this very natural purity has become pure of adventitious stains and therefore one speaks of "the attainment of the fundamental change." This corresponds to the manner in which space is naturally pure before and later has become pure of clouds as well as the ways in which gold and water become free from a film and silt, respectively. According to MC (fol. 25a.4–25b.3), in terms of their actual mode of being, all phenomena are primordially without any stains (such as apprehender and apprehended), but this actual mode of being is obscured under the sway of mistakenness and thus, in terms of their mode of appearance, phenomena appear as if being impure. During that time one says that they "did not undergo the fundamental change." Once the actual mode of being and the mode of appearance

concord in all respects through the power of those stains having been eliminated by the path, the final fundamental change is attained. You may wonder, "Isn't it the case that the nature of phenomena is not feasible as having the nature of primordial purity, but actually entails a change because it entails two different phases—not having and having undergone the fundamental change?" This is not the case. Primordially pure space is associated with adventitious fog and so on; gold, with dirt; water, with silt; and the sun, with obscurations such as clouds, but their respective natures are not impaired by these obscurations. Also, when their natures free from these obscurations have become manifest, it is not that these natures arise newly. Likewise, it is through the power of having become free from adventitious stains that the fundamental change is attained. This fundamental change is to be understood as merely the fact that the actuality of natural luminosity, which did not appear before by virtue of having been obscured by adventitious stains, appears later by virtue of the power of the path. LZC (pp. 37–39) says that this section refers to a dispute about what is unconditioned. In itself, the fundamental change is not something that entails change. For though the phenomena that appear as the conditioned bearers of the nature of phenomena undergo a fundamental change, in the nature of phenomena—emptiness free from reference points—any nature is not established, and therefore change is not established either. LZC follows DDVV in saying that the fundamental change is taught through the examples of gold and water as being congruent with their properties only in terms of their qualities, without considering their respective (material) substances. However, contrary to DDVV ("Through the example of space, however, it is taught in its entirety"), LZC explains that though the example of space is one in terms of its (immaterial) substance being concordant with the fundamental change, it is only an example that concords with a fraction of the qualities of the fundamental change, but not in its entirety. For Maitreya says in *Uttaratantra* IV.96cd:

> It is similar to space and yet dissimilar
> In that [the latter] is not the basis of virtue.

Note that the examples of space, gold, and water also appear with the same meaning in *Mahāyānasūtrālaṃkāra* XI.13 and *Madhyāntavibhāga* I.16. Similar to DDVV, Vasubandhu's *Mahāyānasūtrālaṃkārabhāṣya* (D4026, fol. 168a.3–6) says that the perfect nature is to be purified from adventitious stains, though it is naturally pure of the afflictions, just like space, gold, and water. Space and so on are not impure by nature, nor is it not held that their purity is by virtue of becoming free from adventitious stains. Sthiramati's *Sūtrālaṃkāravṛttibhāṣya* (D4034, vol. mi, fol. 174a.1–174b.1) elaborates that from the states of ordinary beings up through those of nobles ones, emptiness is always free from the duality of apprehender and apprehended. However, that it nevertheless appears as apprehender and apprehended for ordinary beings is the imaginary nature. The dependent nature is the foundation of mistakenness because it functions as the cause of imagining what looks like apprehender and apprehended, just as when wrongly imagining a rope to be a snake. The perfect nature has the character of being inexpressible because it is not feasible to be pinpointed by any words, names, or letters. It is also free from reference points because it lacks any phenomena in terms of apprehender and apprehended. The imaginary nature (apprehender and apprehended) is what is to be understood as being nonexistent, just like the horns of a rabbit. The dependent nature is what is to be relinquished because the stains of apprehender and apprehended that exist in the dependent must be eliminated. The perfect nature is what is to be purified. For though its nature is completely pure and stainless, it still must be purified from adventitious stains, which resembles the natural purity of space, gold, and water needing to be purified from their respective adventitious stains of clouds, earth, and silt. Compare also Sthiramati's comments (ibid., fol. 75a.3–5) on the last characteristic of the ultimate—"not purified and yet purified again"—in *Mahāyānasūtrālaṃkāra* VI.1, which discusses the ultimate as the emptiness in which there is actually nothing to be purified and which is only obscured by adventitious stains. Just as space, gold, water, and a crystal are naturally pure, the ultimate is pure in that it is of the nature of emptiness. Just as the natural purity of space cannot be purified by washing it with water or the like, in the nature of emptiness there are no stains to be purified. Therefore, it is said to be "not purified." Though there are no stains to be removed in this nature, it is not that the afflictive and cognitive obscurations that exist in emptiness in an adventitious manner are not to be removed—indeed they must be removed and purified, a process like removing adventitious clouds from space, or adventitious earth and stones from gold. This is called "the ultimate becoming pure." Sthiramati's *Madhyāntavibhāgaṭīkā* (Pandeya 1999, pp. 40.5–41.15; D4032, fols. 214a.6–215a.2) elaborates on Vasubandhu's *Madhyāntavibhāgabhāṣya* on I.16 (D4027, fol. 4b.4–6) as follows. The divisions of emptiness are being afflicted and pure as well as being with and without stains. Being afflicted refers to false imagination, while its relinquishment means being pure. However, at the times of being afflicted and pure, respectively, there is nothing but emptiness that is afflicted or pure. That emptiness is presented as afflicted and pure, respectively, is based on its not having or having undergone the fundamental change. By virtue of the flaws of noncognition and wrong cognition, those who are not learned cling to apprehender and apprehended and their mind streams become stained by afflictions such as desire. Thus, it is due to emptiness not appearing for them that they are considered as "being with stains." By virtue of their realization of true reality, the noble ones lack mistaken states of mind. Thus, in them, emptiness is spotless like space and appears in an uninterrupted manner, due to which they are referred to as "having relinquished the stains." It is in this way that emptiness is to be regarded as depending on being afflicted and being pure, but one should not think that its nature is stained because it is luminous by nature. You may wonder, "In what is unchanging, different phases are not seen, whereas change is connected to arising and ceasing. Therefore, since emptiness is a phenomenon that entails change in that it is with and without stains, respectively, why is it not impermanent?" There is no change of emptiness from the phase of being afflicted to its phase of being pure, but it always remains as true reality and thus does not change into anything else. Here "change" refers to emptiness becoming free from adventitious stains, but not to its nature changing into anything else. Therefore, its nature is completely pure, similar to space, gold, and water. Since these do not have the nature of their stains, they never change into being of the nature of these stains. Therefore, both when they are stained by adventitious stains and when they have become pure of them, their natures do not change into anything else. On the other hand, those who claim that the very same entity first has the defining characteristic of being afflicted and later has the nature of being pure will never be able to deny that such an entity is a phenomenon that is altered due to its having changed into being of another nature. Nor will those who think that both being afflicted and being pure are adventitious be able to explain the fundamental change as the irreversible attainment of nirvāṇa. Therefore, emptiness is not impermanent. *Uttaratantra* I.30 gives the examples of a wish-fulfilling jewel, space, and water for buddha nature always being without afflictions naturally. According to the commentaries, these three examples match buddha nature because of their general characteristic (being naturally pure of adventitious stains) and their specific characteristics—the wish-fulfilling jewel stands for the power of the dharmakāya to accomplish all wishes and so on, space resembles suchness never changing into anything else, and water illustrates the moistening nature of the buddha disposition, whose compassion pervades all beings and thus makes the sprouts of their roots of virtue grow. In particular, GC (pp. 271–72) explains that suchness is not a nonimplicative negation, but a phenomenon of awareness. Therefore, it is endowed with both power and compassion. Also, the dharmakāya and the disposition are merely divisions of nothing but suchness in terms of its being pure and impure, respectively. Consequently, power, changelessness, and compassion are not substantial characteristics. Furthermore, the dharmakāya realizes unconditioned suchness and is also endowed with compassion. If suchness is directly realized, consummate power (such as the supernatural knowledges) and compassion arise naturally. Likewise, the disposition is endowed with the dharmakāya, since it primordially possesses the qualities such as the ten powers, and it never changes or deteriorates, even when wandering through all kinds of higher and lower realms. On the path, it is through the power of aspiring for the profound buddhadharmas that suchness will be realized, and by virtue of that, compassion for all beings who do not realize it arises. This also shows the progression of the four yogas of Mahāmudrā. Through the yoga of one-pointedness, bodhisattvas rest the mind unmoved by thoughts like clear water. Through this, they realize spacelike suchness free from reference points. By virtue of that, through the yoga of one taste, they realize the suchness of the aspects of what is outwardly oriented (the eyes and so on) as being pure. Finally, when the jewellike yoga of nonmeditation free from effort arises in them, through their meditation being directing toward taking care of beings, their compassion arises effortlessly and thus the welfare of others is accomplished naturally. This, GC says, is what Padampa Sangyé holds.

782 See *Uttaratantra* I.95cd–152. In these examples, the lotus and so on stand for increasingly subtler obscurations, while the buddha statue and so on represent the respective natural qualities of buddha nature that are revealed (for details, see Arya Maitreya, Jamgön Kongtrül Lodrö Thayé, Khenpo Tsultrim Gyamtso Rinpoche 2000, pp. 148–73).

783 I.154–55.

784 The last sentence corresponds to an almost identical passage in Asaṅga's RGVV on these two verses (J 76; D4025, fol. 114ba.4). As for the emptiness endowed with the supreme of all aspects, "aspects" indicates all its excellent remedial qualities, such as the six pāramitās. Thus, it is both emptiness and that which makes one attain unsurpassable buddhahood. Another way to understand this expression is that it refers to the inseparability of appearance and emptiness, or luminosity and emptiness. Karma Trinlépa's commentary on the *Profound Inner Reality* (Karma 'phrin las pa phyogs las rnam rgyal 1975, p. 329) says, "Here my guru, the mighty victor [Chötra Gyatso] holds the following. Since the emptiness endowed with the supreme of all aspects and the sugata heart are equivalent, being endowed with the supreme of all aspects refers to the sugata heart being actually endowed with the sixty-four qualities of freedom and maturation, and the meaning of emptiness is that this is not established as anything identifiable or as any characteristics. Therefore, he asserts that making it a living experience—cultivating this lucid yet nonconceptual [state]—is Mahāmudrā meditation."

785 It is interesting and typical for the Third Karmapa's approach of treating Yogācāra and Madhyamaka as being of equal importance and complementary that, in the context of a commentary on a Yogācāra text on the fundamental change of nondual nonconceptual wisdom, this fundamental change that is to be attained through studying this text and making it a living experience is identified as the hallmark of the Madhyamaka teachings— "the freedom from extremes." The last line in OED's colophon is not only remarkable because of this, but because the term "freedom from extremes" also stands for the view of "the earlier Mādhyamikas" in Tibet (referring to what was understood as the correct Madhyamaka view before Tsongkhapa). This view was proclaimed by masters such as Patsab Lotsāwa and his four main disciples; the Sakya masters Rendawa, Gorampa Sönam Sengé, and Dagtsang Lotsāwa; the Eighth Karmapa, Mikyö Dorjé; Pawo Rinpoche, and others. This approach uses Madhyamaka analysis that results in an unqualified negation of all four positions of the typical Madhyamaka tetralemma without asserting anything instead in order to completely overcome all conceptualizations and reference points. In this way, it is certainly an accurate characterization of the Indian Madhyamaka approach. However, "the later Mādhyamikas"—the Gelugpa School—criticized this view by saying that "lack of real existence" is the correct Madhyamaka view and thus not to be negated. At the same time, there were attempts to discredit "the Madhyamaka of freedom from extremes" through associating it with the notorious stereotype of the Chinese Hvashang Mahāyāna.

786 Tib. kun dga' byams pa, a student of the Third Karmapa.

787 OED *ma ha jña na*. The location of this colophon on the translators of DDV seems somewhat out of place in OED here. One would rather expect it to be mentioned right before OED's concluding verses above.

788 1308 and 1332 were other Monkey Years during the Third Karmapa's lifetime, but the first one seems too early (his other works of similar content were all written between 1322 and 1327; see Brunnhölzl 2009, p. 86). In 1332, Rangjung Dorje was on his long journey to, and stay at, the Chinese court and not in Upper Dechen.

789 Tib. bde chen steng. The Third Karmapa's retreat place in the mountains above the main seat of the Karmapas, Tsurpu (Tib. mtshur phu) Monastery north of Lhasa.

790 Numbers in { } indicate the page numbers of 'Gos lo tsā ba gzhon nu dpal 2003b.

791 Except for the phrase "which is labeled with the name 'enlightenment,'" this sentence is from RGVV (J 79; D4025, fol. 115a.7).

792 J 79 (D4025, fol. 115a.7–115b.1). As mentioned above, the eight points of explaining enlightenment as listed in *Uttaratantra* II.2 are its nature, cause, result, function, endowment with qualities, manifestation as the three kāyas, permanence, and inconceivability. All of them are discussed directly or indirectly in DDV's section on the nature of phenomena, on which GC comments below.

793 Tib. yongs su log pa (Skt. most probably *(vi)nivṛtti*, which can mean "return," "cessation," "disappearance," or "destruction"). Though the Tibetan *log pa* (an intransitive verb) also means "return" or "reverse," GC obviously does not understand it in this way here, such as the pure dharmadhātu returning or reverting to its natural uncontaminated state. Given GC's gloss below, the term is clearly taken to mean "cease" or "come to an end" (which is one of the meanings of *parivṛtti*).

794 D3890, line 80a (*gnas po gzhan du gyur pa ni*; according to Jñānacandra's commentary, this seems to be just a variant rendering of *āśrayaparāvṛtti*).

795 See also GC's commentary on RGVV on II.1 (pp. 471.24–472.2): "As for there being these eight points, what is expressed by the name 'tathāgata heart' is the basic element or cause which is not liberated from the cocoon of the afflictions, that is, which serves as the foundation (*gnas*) for the production of afflictions. It is a foundation because it functions as the support for afflictiveness. Once it has become pure of its stains, including their latent tendencies, and this has become irreversible, it does not function as the foundation for afflictions [anymore] and has therefore reversed from [what it was] before. Since it [now] functions as the support for purified phenomena alone, it should be understood as the nature of the fundamental change. The two that [are called] 'basic element' and 'fundamental change' are only differentiated by virtue of there being or not being stains—their nature is this very suchness." Different from DDVV, OED, and other commentaries, GC obviously takes suchness as being the single foundation of both afflicted and purified phenomena, which is also repeated several times below.

796 Here GC quotes DDV (K)'s entire section on the detailed explanation of the nature of phenomena (*rnam pa drug gis chos nyid la . . . nam mkha' chu dang gser sogs bzhin*) according to GNP.

797 As mentioned above, the introduction of Jamgön Kongtrul's commentary on the *Uttaratantra* (Kong sprul blo gros mtha' yas 2005, p. 24) also states that the *Dharmadharmatāvibhāga* is like a commentary on the second chapter of the *Uttaratantra* and that the former's term "nature of phenomena" and the latter's term "stainless suchness" have the same meaning.

798 Phrases in **bold** indicate the words of DDV (K).

799 The last sentence is also found in the introduction to Jamgön Kongtrul's commentary on the *Uttaratantra* (Kong sprul blo gros mtha' yas 2005, p. 24).

800 For details on GC's understanding of the nature of phenomena as being "the continuum of stainless mind," see the concluding section on the three examples of space, gold, and water for the nature of phenomena.

801 XIII.19.

802 D4028, fol. 38b.2.

803 Verses 43–45.

804 *tshul chos nyid bzhin du yid la byed pa* glosses DDV (K) *tshul bzhin yid la byed pa* ("the proper mental engagement").

805 IV.53.

806 Verse 6.

807 Tib. don. As this gloss and the following comments show, GC obviously understands *dgos pa* in its more common sense of "purpose" and not as "prerequisites."

808 The other three wheels are living in a favorable place, relying on great beings, and making one's own excellent aspirations.

809 Matsuda 1996, pp. 94–95 (D142, fols. 2b.1–3a.6). The translation follows the Sanskrit.

810 The eleventh bhūmi is the buddhabhūmi.

811 This refers to a passage in KCA (D4000, fol. 128b.2): "As for 'nonconceptual,' it is nonconceptual by virtue of not being conceptual in mistaken ways because wrong conceptions are relinquished. It is nonconceptual with regard to this because it does not conceptualize [it]—it is suchness and perfect wisdom."

812 Kamalaśīla (ibid., fol. 131a.6) says that "without correct discrimination (*yang dag par so sor rtog pa*), one is not able to not become mentally engaged in characteristics such as forms that have become an appearance."

813 The latter reasoning is also known as "the vajra sliver reasoning," which refutes that phenomena arise from themselves, others, both, or without any cause.

814 This example and its meaning are found in the *Kāśyapaparivarta* and other sūtras. Though wooden sticks do not have the characteristics of fire, a fire comes forth from rubbing them and then burns these very two wooden sticks, upon which also the fire disappears on its own. Likewise, when the conceptions of remedies interact with those about factors to be relinquished, discriminating prajñā arises. Eventually, on the path of seeing, this turns into nonconceptual prajñā, which then simultaneously consumes both the factors to be relinquished and their remedies, since these depend on each other. Once both have vanished, nonconceptual prajñā subsides on its own since it has fulfilled its function of freeing the mind from the imaginations of what is to be relinquished and its remedies.

815 D4000, fols. 135b.7–136a.2.

816 Ibid., fol. 136a.2.

817 The translation follows DNP, pointing to significant variations in GC. In the latter, this paragraph starts with *'di dag tu 'gyur te/* and ends with *zhes bcom ldan 'das kyis rnam par mi rtog par 'jug pa las gsungs na de dag dang 'dir gsungs pa ji ltar mi 'gal zhe na/*.

818 GC *snying po*, but later comments correctly as *gnyen po*.

819 GC *'thob pa.*

820 GC "With regard to the entities of seeming [reality], . . ." (*dngos po kun rdzob pa rnams la*).

821 Lines 7cd.

822 GC links the last sentence to this one, reading, "In order that those who do not fully penetrate true reality realize true reality, . . ." (*de kho na nyid yongs su mi shes pa dag gis de kho na nyid rtogs pa'i don du*).

823 This is another way of referring to conceptualizing the above three characteristics of remedial factors, true reality, and fruition (or attainment).

824 Verse 36.

825 Lines 5cd.

826 DNP omit this word.

827 With some variations, the same quote is found in Jñānakīrti's *Tattvāvatāra* (P4532, fol. 72a.1–2) after his gloss of the ultimate seeing in the mahāyāna in *Laṅkāvatārasūtra* X.257 as being Mahāmudrā (see note 854).

828 Instead of this sentence, GC has ". . . since it is said, 'However, conceptions that analyze characteristics are discriminations of names, and discrimination has the character of apprehending characteristics'" (*'on kyang mtshan ma ni dpyod pa'i rnam par rtog pa ming gi 'du shes te/ 'du shes ni mtshan mar 'dzin pa'i bdag nyid can no/ zhes gsungs pa'i phyir ro*).

829 II.92–97ab (*Tattvadaśakaṭīkā* omits lines 93ab). Since this quote differs considerably in the *Tattvadaśakaṭīkā* in DNP, GC, the Tibetan version of the sūtra in the *Kangyur*, and the available Sanskrit version (ed. Vaidya), the translation follows the latter (the same also goes for the next quote from that sūtra following just below).

830 Tib. *zung 'jug pa'i dbu ma.*

831 GC omits this line.

832 GC "It is *not* unarisen by nature."

833 GC *rtog med sems kyi rnal 'byor la'ang/ bsam med par yang de mi rtog rnam pa kun mchog rnam pa med/ blo yi dbang po thams cad pa/ dngos dang dngos med bdag nyid can/ dngos dang dngos med rnam par spangs/ mtha' bzhi las ni rnam par grol/ mtha' bzhi po yang yang dag ldan/ sna tshogs sgro 'dogs sgro ma btags/ mi mthun phyogs kyi de nyid ni/ 'bras bu'o dpyod pas dpyad du med/ de dang de brten yang dag skyes/ rang gi ngo bos ma skyes min/ bems po min phyir rang nyid rig shes byed min la blta bya min/ rang bzhin med phyir ther zug min/ de nyid rnam 'gyur med phyir rtag/.* For the most part, this corresponds to the section in Sahajavajra's own *Sthitisamuccaya* (D2227, fols. 98b.6–99a1) that speaks about the Mahāmudrā practice of those of the most supreme faculties (note that parts of these verses are also reminiscent of certain lines in Maitrīpa's *Mahāyānavimśikā* and *Tattvavimśikā*). The translation here follows GC, which differs, sometimes significantly, from both *Sthitisamuccaya* DNP and the version of this quote as found in *Tattvadaśakaṭīkā* DNP (both the latter also differ from each other). The *Sthitisamuccaya* varies as follows:

> Through the yoga of nonconceptual mind,
> That very mind is not to be conceptualized/examined.
> It is the entirely supreme among all aspects,
> Without aspect, beyond being an object of the sense faculties,
> . . .

And yet equally based on the four extremes,
Not abiding as various superimpositions,
And great bliss without attachment.
This very fruition is the antagonistic factors
And this very examination is nonexamination.
It arises by virtue of the attainment of conditions,
But has the nature of nonarising.
It is not matter, nor is it known
Or seen through self-awareness.
Through examination, space is a nonentity—
It is unchanging and stable.

(D *sems ni rtog med sbyor bas kyang/ sems de nyid ni brtag mi bya/ kun nas thams cad mchog yin te/ rnam med dbang po'i yul las 'das/ dngos dang dngos med rang bzhin nyid/ dngos dang dngos med rnam par spangs/ mtha' bzhi las ni rnam grol zhing/ mtha' bzhi dag ni mnyam par brten/ sna tshogs sgro btags gnas pa med/ chags med bde ba chen po nyid/ 'bras bu de nyid mi mthun phyogs/ brtags pa de nyid ma brtags pa'o/ de rkyen thob pas skye ba ste/ skye ba med pa'i rang bzhin te/ bems po med de rang rig pas/ mi shes pa dang ma mthong ba/ brtags pas nam mkha' dngos med de/ de ni mi 'gyur brtan pa'o/*). *Tattvadaśakaṭīkā* D *sems pa'i rnam rtog sbyor ba dang/ de ni bsam med rtog pa med/ rnam pa kun mchog thams cad kyi/ dbang po las 'das rnam pa med/ dngos dang dngos med bdag nyid de/ dngos dang dngos med rnam par spangs/ mtha' bzhi dang ni mnyam ldan pas/ mtha' bzhi las ni rnam par grol/ sna tshogs bzhag pa'i sna tshogs med/ dogs pa med pas bde ba che/ 'bras bu de nyid rnam rtog rnams/ dpyod pa nyid ni dpyad pa med/ de dang de skyes thob pa rnams/ ma skyes pa yi rang bzhin no/ de phyir rang rig ma skyes phyir/ rang gi[s] ma skyes 'dod pa yin/ dpyod pa'i mtha' la mi gnas so/ rtog pa'i mtha' las 'gyur ba med/* (for a translation, see Brunnhölzl 2007a, pp. 179–80).

834 Verse 35.

835 GC *gnas* (as in the identical quote above) DNP *rgyu*.

836 II.98, 101, 102, 106, 105.

837 Verse 30.

838 GC continually refers to this text as *mdo* instead of *gzungs*. For the sake of consistency, I use *dhāraṇī*.

839 Verse 3 in its entirety says:

This entity is indeed enlightenment,
Which is due to having the nature of nonattachment.
Attachment is born from mistakenness,
And mistakenness is held to be without basis.

(*bodhir asau bhaved bhāvaḥ saṅgaṃ tyaktvā svabhāvataḥ / āsaṅgo bhrāntito jāto bhrāntir asthānikā matā //*). For Sahajavajra's commentary, see Brunnhölzl 2007a, pp. 165–67.

840 Thus, the inference here would read: "Seeming [phenomena] as the subject lack specific characteristics because they are dependent origination." The same subject and predicate apply to other Madhyamaka reasonings, such as the vajra sliver reasoning.

841 D4000, fol. 7a.5–6.

842 Ibid., fol. 4a.3 (see the first quote from this text above).

843 In the context of the reality of the path, GC (pp. 113.6–114.8) identifies a bodhisattva's nonconceptual wisdom on the paths of seeing and familiarization as the nature of the

path. After outlining the *Dharmadharmatāvibhāga*'s five distinctive features that are excluded from being nonconceptual wisdom, its nature is identified as being the direct perception that is free from conceptions which entail terms and referents. The reason for calling it "nonconceptual" is that it serves as the remedy for the conceptions of clinging to the four characteristics of antagonistic factors, the remedy, suchness, and the dharmas of realization (for details, see GC below). Then (p. 114.8–12), the text summarizes the above discussion on the relinquishment of these characteristics: "What is discussed in the *Dharmadharmatāvibhāga* in this way is the presentation of the meaning of the *Avikalpapraveśa[dhāraṇī]*. When engaging in the meaning of this sūtra, there appear to be two approaches. Master Kamalaśīla holds that the conceptions to be relinquished are relinquished through discriminating prajñā alone. The commentary on Maitrīpa's *Tattvadaśaka* maintains that [those conceptions] are not relinquished through discriminating [prajñā], but through the samādhi of reality as it is, which is to know that the nature of the [conceptions] to be relinquished is luminosity. Here it is reasonable to follow Maitrīpa who has found this text." On Maitrīpa's particular approach, GC (pp. 137.23–138.2) elaborates: "Thus, when those who practice according to the pith instructions of Mahāmudrā that originated from Maitrīpa rest in nothing whatsoever, free from any mental engagement in the three times, thoughts that distract from that may arise. Then, they look at just what arises, whatever it may be, without wavering. Such looking is called 'examining thoughts as they are.' Through such an [approach], even if all other thoughts have subsided, there is some subtle thought, 'The mind meditates on and rests in something to be meditated.' When they look nakedly at that subtle thought, it will also cease and a mind will arise that is, just like space, free from center and boundary." Thus, contrary to Kamalaśīla's—at least initially—inferential approach to superior insight, in Maitrīpa's approach direct cognitions of the true nature of one's mind can be experienced, and are used, right from the beginning and may happen simultaneously with calm abiding. In this way, Maitrīpa's approach of revealing the luminous emptiness of whatever appears in the mind covers all apprehended characteristics or mental factors to be relinquished as well, through which they simply vanish, or rather, are exposed as what they really are, which is the very heart of Mahāmudrā.

844 Here GC's actual comments on the words of DDV (K) resume.

845 Note that in the fourth yogic practice GC does not acknowledge the *observation* of the nonobservation of duality.

846 X.256–257 (D107, fol. 168b.5–6; see OED's comments on this passage of DDV).

847 VI.8.

848 I.6–7ab.

849 These are "one-pointedness (*rtse gcig*)," "freedom from reference points (*spros bral*)," "one taste (*ro gcig*)," and "nonmeditation (*sgom med*)." Note that GC (pp. 61.22–67.3) also reads these four yogas into a passage of the *Laṅkāvatārasūtra*, referring to the relevant passage in the *Phyag rgya chen po lam zab mthar thug zhang gi man ngag* (translated in Martin 1992, pp. 278–79) by the early Kagyü master Lama Shang (Tib. bla ma zhang g.yu brag pa brston 'grus grags pa; 1122–1193).

850 Note that Jñānakīrti's *Tattvāvatāra* (P4532, fols. 70b.1–72a.6) explains the first verse of *Laṅkāvatārasūtra* X.256–257 in a standard way by identifying the first three yogic practices. On the second verse he comments as follows. Since suchness is unborn, it neither exists as an entity nor as a lack of entities. This means that suchness is the complete lack of reference points since entities and the lack of entities include all possible reference points. Through realizing that, all beings are understood as having the nature of the dharmakāya, thus going beyond the understanding of mere mind. The yogin must even transcend the state of true reality not appearing in the manner of being a unity or a multiplicity and the like. To fully rest in the nonappearance

of any reference points whatsoever is to realize true reality, here called "the mahāyāna," with another form of that name being "Mahāmudrā." Thus, Jñānakīrti indicates that the final realization of the freedom from reference points even in the sūtra tradition of the mahāyāna is nothing but Mahāmudrā, which he further equates with the famous "nonseeing is the supreme seeing" in the prajñāpāramitā sūtras (elsewhere, he repeatedly equates prajñāpāramitā and emptiness with Mahāmudrā). He also clarifies that such nonseeing is of course not just the same sheer absence of any mental engagement as when being asleep or closing one's eyes. For more details, see Brunnhölzl 2007a, pp. 135–36.

851 D142, fol. 3b.4.

852 GC comments here on both *brtag tu med pa* ("unexaminable") in DDV (K) and *gzugs med pa* ("ungraspable") in DDV (P), with the latter corresponding to *arūpi* in DDV (S).

853 D142, fol. 6a.4–6.

854 In the context of explaining the reality of the path as part of the jewel of the dharma (*Uttaratantra* I.9–12), GC (pp. 113. 2–114. 8) further elaborates on the nature of nonconceptual wisdom: "The nature [of the path] consists of the paths of seeing and familiarization of bodhisattvas. As for the reason to refer to them as 'path,' both the paths of seeing and familiarization are the causes for attaining this dharmakāya of a tathāgata, which bears the name of the cessation of suffering, through realizing it. Therefore, they are the path because they search for [this dharmakāya] {note that some of the meanings of Skt. *mārga* are "seeking," "search," "tracing out"}. The nature of the path refers to nonconceptual wisdom, which consists of the bodhisattvabhūmis. This [wisdom] is twofold through being divided in terms of the paths of seeing and familiarization." Next, GC quotes DDVV on the five features that are excluded from being nonconceptual wisdom, which is then summarized as follows: "This word 'nonconceptual' [in 'nonconceptual wisdom'], which is a negative, [can be understood as referring to] three [meanings]—nonexistence [of conceptions], being other [than conceptions], or being the remedy [for conceptions]. From among these, when it refers to the [sheer] nonexistence [of conceptions], since such a nonexistence is not a cognition, it is not suitable as what comprehends suchness. Therefore, it is not tenable [that 'nonconceptual' refers to such a nonexistence]. As for being other [than conceptions], from among those five factors [to be excluded], if this referred to the result that is conceptual cognition not being produced, it would follow that also the five sense consciousnesses of small children are that [nonconceptual wisdom]. If it referred to cognitions that are not produced through conception, also a consciousness that is in deep sleep would be that [nonconceptual wisdom]. If it referred to cognitions that transcend, and are free from, conception by virtue of temporary remedies, also the meditative absorption of the second dhyāna that exists in the mind streams of tīrthikas would be that [nonconceptual wisdom]. If it referred to entities that are other than conceptions, it would follow that also form and so on are that [nonconceptual wisdom]. If it referred to just something that is similar, also the thought, 'I shall not entertain conceptions about suchness' would be that [nonconceptual wisdom]. Since the first four are not cognitions that comprehend suchness, they are not nonconceptual wisdom. As for the last one, though it represents some directing of cognition toward suchness, in itself it is a conception. Therefore, it is not nonconceptual wisdom [either]. Here, all five kinds of such analysis refer to analyses of the conceptions that entail terms and referents, but not to [analyses of the kind of conceptions that make up all] the minds and mental factors of the three realms because the sense consciousnesses of small children [belong to those conceptions that] are [the minds and mental factors of] the three realms. This means that, here, nonconceptual wisdom must be taken as a direct perception that is free from the conceptions that entail terms and referents. Therefore, it refers to what has analyzed these conceptions that entail terms and referents. The negative 'nonconceptual' in this [term 'nonconceptual wisdom'] refers to [this wisdom being a] remedy—the remedy for the fourfold clinging to characteristics. [In the

Dharmadharmatāvibhāga] the fourfold clinging to characteristics refers to the characteristics of antagonistic factors, the remedy, suchness, and the dharmas of realization. It is the clinging to these four characteristics that is called 'conception,' while [nonconceptual wisdom] is their remedy. Thus, this is the intention behind calling it 'nonconceptual.'" Elsewhere, GC (p. 472.8–20) also elaborates on wisdom as the cause of enlightenment being twofold: "Supramundane [wisdom] excellently penetrates [all] knowable objects and lacks conceptions and obscurations since these are mundane—it is [the wisdom of] meditative equipoise. [The wisdom after] having risen from this meditative equipoise that is attained subsequent [to it] through the power of that meditative equipoise, through the appearing of all kinds of seeming phenomena, venerates buddhas, purifies [buddha] realms, and matures sentient beings. Since it does not directly see ultimate reality [during this], it does not penetrate knowable objects in an excellent manner and represents the [cognizing] subject of the seeming. Consequently, since it is a phenomenon that [still] represents an obscuration and its own nature is conceptual, it is [considered to be] mundane. Though [this [wisdom] lacks the conceptions that entail terms and referents, it is by virtue of its being a phenomenon with dualistic appearances that it is referred to as conceptual. Also, up through the seventh bhūmi, even subtle conceptions that entail terms and referents arise. These supramundane and mundane wisdoms are the two causes of the fundamental change . . . The result of these two wisdoms is of two kinds—one speaks of 'freedom,' which consists of being free from the afflictive obscurations by virtue of supramundane [wisdom] and being free from the cognitive obscurations by virtue of mundane [wisdom]. The suchness of these very two obscurations—the self-awareness that is liberated from the two obscurations—is the reality of cessation. The two obscurations represent [the reality of] the origin [of suffering], and their result is [the reality of] suffering, which consists of saṃsāra and the inconceivable death and transition of the mental body that is included under nirvāṇa. The two wisdoms are [the reality of] the path and that twofold freedom, [the reality of] cessation. In due order, by virtue of being free from the afflictive obscurations, one's own welfare is accomplished and by virtue of being free from the cognitive obscurations, the welfare of others is accomplished. This is the function [of enlightenment]."

855 Lit. "there is no one else whosoever to be searched for who surpasses buddhas" (*sangs rgyas kyi ni gong na gzhan btsal bar bya ba su yang med pa*).

856 GC *yang dag pa'i kun tu rtog pa* ("correct imagination").

857 GC's *shes pa gzhan las rab tu phye ba* obviously takes *rab tu phye ba* itself (which usually renders the Sanskrit *prabhāvita* for "characterized") in the sense of "being distinct" or "more distinguished."

858 This numbering refers back to GC's above division of the ten points of the fundamental change into the presentation of the fundamental change and the reasonings to establish it (p. 305). Within the first division, the first five points make up (1) its nature; the sixth and seventh, (2) its causes; and the eighth one (the training), (3) the fruition. The reasonings consist of points nine and ten.

859 What the *Abhidharmasamuccaya* (D4049, fol. 96a.2–3) actually says on this in the context of the four remedies is as follows: "What is the invalidating remedy? It means to regard contaminated formations as shortcomings. What is the relinquishing remedy? It refers to the paths of preparation and the uninterrupted paths. What is the sustaining remedy? It is the paths of liberation. What is the distancing remedy? It refers to the higher paths of these." According to most Indian and Tibetan commentaries on the *Abhisamayālaṃkāra*, in dependence on the phases of (a) still being in the process of eradicating the respective factors to be relinquished on a given path or (b) having already eradicated them, these four are as follows. (1) The invalidating remedy is the path of preparation (focusing on the four realities of the noble ones and invalidating the obscurations in terms of their sixteen aspects). (2) The relinquishing remedy refers to the

uninterrupted paths (the actual process of eradicating even the seeds of the respective factors to be relinquished). (3) The sustaining remedy refers to the paths of liberation (experiencing and sustaining the attained freedom from the factors that have been relinquished through the preceding uninterrupted paths). (4) The distancing remedy refers to the special paths (enhancing the realizations that were attained through the preceding paths of liberation). In this way, the first two remedies belong to phase (a) and the last two to phase (b).

860 D4028, fol. 38b.4–5.

861 *Uttaratantra* I.155. The way in which GC interprets the three examples of space and so on is quite uncommon in that he takes all three to illustrate the natural luminosity of mind as being a "substance that operates by way of being an uninterrupted series [of moments] (*rgyun gyis 'jug pa'i rdzas*)." In the context of the *Uttaratantra*'s discussion of buddha nature being all-pervading in all three of its states (being impure, partly pure and completely pure), GC (p. 339.6–7) explicitly confirms this: "When the fundamental change is taught in [Vasubandhu's] commentary on the *Dharmadharmatāvibhāga* through the examples of water, gold, and space, it is explained in all three examples that there is a continuum" (note that DDVV explicitly applies the qualifier "operating by way of being an uninterrupted series" only to water and clearly distinguishes the examples of water and gold from the one of space). The immediately preceding sentence in Vasubandhu's commentary (D4028, fol. 38b.4) to which this remark refers says, "Since there is no such [alteration], the nature of phenomena and the fundamental change that is constituted by it are permanent." Thus, it seems that GC understands this permanence of the nature of phenomena as an endless and uninterrupted continuation of moments, of which only the continuum of space is a fully congruent example, whereas gold and water also represent continua, but are not everlasting. Note that this notion of permanence is also found in *Mahāyānasūtrālaṃkāra* IX.66cd, in which the dharmakāya, the sāmbhogikakāya, and the nairmāṇikakāya are respectively said to be permanent in three ways—by nature, in terms of continuity, and in terms of an uninterrupted series (Skt. prabandhena, Tib. rgyun gyis). That Gö Lotsāwa indeed takes the nature of phenomena, the fundamental change, and nonconceptual wisdom to be continua of moments is confirmed by GC (p. 339.8–13) continuing: "Therefore, it is not the case that space—which is the mere existence of providing room, has a momentary nature, and possesses a continuum—is nonexistent. Here, in terms of time, the space at the beginning of an eon is not the space at the time of [its] destruction [and thus also momentary in a sense]. In terms of location, the very substance that is the mere existence of providing room within a golden container is not the mere existence of providing room in an earthen container. Likewise, the moments of the basic element of sentient beings, which has the property of awareness and operates by way of being an uninterrupted series, do not turn into the moments of buddha wisdom. However, the two mere existences of providing room in a golden and an earthen container, respectively, are not different in type. Likewise, the nonconceptuality of buddhas and the nonconceptuality of sentient beings are very much similar in kind, and there also are conventional expressions for their being one, such as saying, 'I and the buddhas say the same.'" Thus, for Gö Lotsāwa, the nature of phenomena, the fundamental change, and nonconceptual wisdom all have the nature of momentariness, and can thus be taken as the continuity of the stainless true nature of one's mind. This is explicitly made clear in GC's above comments on the defining characteristic of the nature of phenomena (p. 456.18–20): ". . . the commentary [by Vasubandhu] explains [the nature of phenomena] to be nothing but the continuum of stainless mind," which is supported by referring to *Mahāyānasūtrālaṃkāra* XIII.19 and DDVV, both saying that the nature of phenomena is the pure luminous mind. Now, interestingly, it is both this momentary nature of the nature of phenomena as the continuum of luminosity and the fact that this luminosity is observed after not having been observed before that show for Gö Lotsāwa that Vasubandhu's commentary belongs to the Madhyamaka tradition because, he says, the great Yogācāra treatises do not explain that there is a naturally pure continuum of luminosity within the continuum of

the afflictions. It is not really clear what Gö Lotsāwa means by "great Yogācāra treatises" here, and a thorough analysis of this point is beyond the scope of this book. However, in brief, Gö Lotsāwa can hardly refer to Vasubandhu's texts since he considers him to be a Mādhyamika (otherwise, he would have to explain why only DDVV is Madhyamaka, while Vasubandhu's other texts are not). As for the other works of Maitreya, the explanation of emptiness in the first chapter of the *Madhyāntavibhāga* is strikingly similar to the nature of phenomena in DDV and the suchness of the *Uttaratantra*. Also, the *Mahāyānasūtrālaṃkāra* speaks about suchness existing and not being different in all sentient beings, which is also the meaning of beings possessing *tathāgatagarbha* (see IX.37). The text also uses the example of turbid water becoming clear merely due to the removal of its turbidities, which is the same in the case of mind being purified of its adventitious stains (XIII.18–19; see OED, p. 555; for the consistent comments of Vasubandhu, Sthiramati, and Asvabhāva on *tathāgatagarbha* as referring to suchness or identitylessness being the same in all phenomena/beings, see Brunnhölzl 2009, p. 62 and endnote 135). What Gö Lotsāwa might have had in mind could be passages such as *Mahāyānasaṃgraha* I.45–49, in which a clear line is drawn between an impure ālaya-consciousness and a pure supramundane mind, which does not exist in the mind streams of ordinary beings, but arises from the latent tendencies for listening that are the natural outflow of the pure dharmadhātu. However, it is also stated there that these latent tendencies abide together with the ālaya-consciousness as a continuum until the latter dissolves.

862 KCA is organized according to the five principles of how to properly comment on the sūtras that are found in Vasubandhu's *Vyākhyāyukti* (D4061, fol. 30b.3):

> Those who relate the meaning of the sūtras
> Should state their purpose, their topical summary,
> The meaning of the words, their coherence,
> And the rebuttal of objections.

According to KCA (fols. 123a.6–124a.1), the purpose of this dhāraṇī is to enter the dhātu of nonconceptuality and to relinquish the entire web of conceptions through the special characteristics of mindfulness and prajñā. Its ultimate purpose is to then attain the state of a buddha's omniscience through the progressive purifications of the bhūmis. Thus, it teaches the means to enter the dhātu of nonconceptuality. Through studying and meditating on this dhāraṇī, all obscurations will be terminated and unobscured wisdom will dawn. In this way, omniscience will be attained. This dhāraṇī is explicitly said to be the remedy for conceptions, but since all flaws arise from wrong conceptions, it is also the remedy for all flaws. As for the topical summary of this dhāraṇī (the second one among the above five principles), KCA says that it consist of fourteen points. These are (1) the setting of the dhāraṇī, (2) the opening of the discourse, (3) the encouragement to retain it, (4) the request to teach it, (5) making the retinue into a proper vessel, (6) taking one's stand, (7) the correct practice in order to relinquish characteristics, (8) entering the dhātu of nonconceptuality, (9) the characteristics of that dhātu, (10) the signs of having entered it, (11) the benefit of that, (12) its activity, (13) an example, and (14) the means to enter that dhātu. The headings inserted by me in the translation correspond to these fourteen points.

863 In the following, numbers preceded by M in { } refer to the folio numbers in the Sanskrit edition in Matsuda 1996 (based on two untitled manuscripts from Gilgit and Nepal). Numbers preceded by D in { } indicate the folio numbers of the Derge edition of the text (D142). Unless noted otherwise, the translation follows the Sanskrit. As is usual with the translations in the Tibetan canon, the first page of D142 lists the title of the text in both Sanskrit and Tibetan.

864 KCA (fol. 126a.2–4) explicitly says that the phrases "Thus have I heard" (*evaṃ mayā śrutam*) and "the Bhagavān was residing in Rājagṛha . . ." (*bhagavān rājagṛhe . . .*) are linked through the phrase "at one time" (*ekasmin samaye*). This indicates that the one who has heard the dhāraṇī (Ānanda) was actually present when the Buddha taught this text. "At one time" means

that teachings like this dhāraṇī are rare and also that there were many other times of Ānanda hearing numerous other teachings by the Buddha when he stayed in various other places.

865 KCA (fols. 126b.2–127a.1) explains that the manner in which the Buddha resides is threefold—through his physical conduct, through his speech explaining the dharma (both representing the welfare of others), and through his mind being settled in perfect inner equipoise (his own welfare). As for the third one, "palace" means that the Buddha's mind is serene because he is free from all obscuring stains, which is the Buddha's inconceivable samādhi. "The heart of the nonconceptual dharmadhātu" resembles the inner sanctuary in a palace or house—the Buddha resides right in the heart of the dharmadhātu through having realized it. This "palace" is superior to all three realms of saṃsāra because it transcends them by virtue of being uncontaminated. Or since this "palace" is the special abode that arises from supramundane virtue and thus is not owned by any craving within the three realms, there is nothing like it in the three realms. It is the sphere of bodhisattvas with the eye of the wisdom that is purified through the immeasurable, profound, and vast accumulations of merit and wisdom. It is not the sphere of the wisdom eyes of śrāvakas and so on, which resemble eyes struck by jaundice since śrāvakas and so on only have the wisdom that aspires for what is inferior.

866 M only has "Maheśvara."

867 KCA (fol. 128a.4–128b.7) explains that, according to the prajñāpāramitā sūtras, bodhisattvas are "mahāsattvas" because they don the mental armor in order to liberate a great assembly of sentient beings, have a great mind, and have great abandonment. Or it is due to seven features—their great dharma (the vast dharma such as the prajñāpāramitā sūtra in one hundred thousand lines), great mindset (the mindset of bodhicitta—striving for unsurpassable completely perfect enlightenment), great motivation (wishing to benefit all beings and make them happy), great aspiration (for the vast and profound dharma), great accumulation (immeasurable accumulations of merit and wisdom), and great time (attaining buddhahood through making efforts for three incalculable eons). All these refer to the causes of buddhahood, while great accomplishment (attaining unsurpassable enlightenment by virtue of these causes) is the result. In due order, the translations of the names of the bodhisattvas listed here as well as the meanings of some of them (KCA does not comment on all) are as follows. Avikalpa ("Nonconceptuality") refers to not conceptualizing in any improper manner. It means suchness and perfect wisdom, which are attained due to having relinquished wrong conceptions. Avikalpaprabhāsa ("Shine of Nonconceptuality") refers to the lucidity and brilliance due to having attained this nonconceptuality. Avikalpacandra ("Moon of Nonconceptuality") means that this nonconceptuality illuminates like the moon. Nirvikalpavīra ("Hero of Nonconceptuality") means being brave due to having gained mastery over nonconceptual wisdom. Nirvikalpadharmanirdeśakuśala ("Skilled in Teaching the Dharma of Nonconceptuality") means being skilled in explaining the dharma of nonconceptuality (the mahāyāna) directly and indirectly after having gained mastery over nonconceptuality. Nirvikalpasvabhāva ("Nature of Nonconceptuality") refers to having the very character of nonconceptual wisdom. Nirvikalpamati means "Mind of Nonconceptuality"; Nirvikalpanāda, "Roar of Nonconceptuality"; and Nirvikalpaspharaṇa, "Pervasive Nonconceptuality." Nirvikalpasvara ("Mighty Nonconceptuality") and Nirvikalpamaheśvara ("Great Mighty Nonconceptuality") refer to having gained (great) mastery over nonconceptual wisdom. Nirvikalpamahāmaitrīsvara ("Mighty Great Love of Nonconceptuality") means to have gained mastery over great nonconceptual and nonreferential love. Avalokiteśvara ("The Mighty Beholder") means having gained mastery over considering with a loving mind all sentient beings who are and who are not proper receptacles. That only those bodhisattvas are mentioned by name in the dhāraṇī is because they are the main bodhisattvas. For at that time the dharma was taught beginning with nonconceptuality. That is, only those who have cast away the conceptions of improper mental engagement are able to listen to and aspire for this dharma, whereas others are not.

868 KCA (fol. 129a.2) glosses "the nonconceptuality of all phenomena" as their being beyond existence, nonexistence, and so on. Thus, nonconceptuality is inexpressible.

869 KCA (fol. 130b.1–5) explains that "taking one's stand" refers to the two prajñās arising from hearing (studying) and reflecting. Bodhisattvas need to take their stand in them in order to realize nonconceptuality, which is twofold—suchness and nonconceptual wisdom. "The dharma related to nonconceptuality" is the dharma that is explained for the sake of that realization. This dharma consists of the entire mahāyāna because, according to the *Saṃdhinirmocanasūtra*, all of it flows into and merges with suchness and enlightenment. "To hear" indicates the prajñā of hearing (or studying) this dharma. That bodhisattvas "place their intention on nonconceptuality" means that they develop and increase the prajñā of reflection through their confidence in, and striving for, the two kinds of nonconceptuality (suchness and nonconceptual wisdom) as they are explained. In particular, "to place their intention" means that the confident prajñā of reflection of bodhisattvas cannot be shaken by others.

870 M only has "those characteristics of conceptions" (*tāni vikalpanimittāni*).

871 According to KCA (fols. 130b.6–132b.2), the phrase "relinquish all characteristics of conceptuality" introduces the seventh summary point (the correct practice to relinquish characteristics,) which means to engage in the prajñā of meditation based on the two preceding prajñās of study and reflection. The characteristics here are fourfold—(1) the characteristics of antagonistic factors (nature), (2) the characteristics of their remedial factors, (3) the characteristics of true reality, and (4) the characteristics of the result of having familiarized with the remedies. Since they are increasingly subtle, their order of relinquishment in terms of being more or less coarse is taught in a way that resembles the order of washing stains out of a garment. Thus, the characteristics of a nature are to be relinquished first. The characteristics of a nature consist of the mind, under the sway of ignorance since time without beginning, effortlessly entertaining the notion that everything has a nature of its own. In brief, this means to engage in the two entities of apprehender and apprehended. Among the five skandhas, the skandha of form is engaged as the entities that make up the apprehended, while the other four skandhas are engaged as the entities that make up the apprehender. All skandhas are contaminated in that they are appropriated by the afflictions. So if these characteristics of a nature are beginningless, how can they be relinquished? Obviously, they cannot be eliminated from the mind in the same way as pulling out a thorn from the body. Rather, "What becomes perceptible, that is, what appears, is to be relinquished through not mentally engaging in it." Here "mental nonengagement" does not refer to the mere absence of any mental engagement because an absence is not tenable as an entity that is the cause of anything. For without discriminating true reality one is not able to mentally engage in the characteristics of form and so on that appear. (Note that this explanation of "mental nonengagement" as "discriminating true reality"—*bhūtapratyavekṣā*—is also found in Kamalaśīla's *Bhāvanākrama*, in which he uses *Laṅkāvatārasūtra* X.256–258 to explain the gradual process of such discrimination as a combination of the approaches of Yogācāra and Madhyamaka, which culminates in "not seeing" any phenomena—the supreme seeing of perfect nonconceptual wisdom; for a translation, see Brunnhölzl 2004, pp. 300–302.) Anything other than such mental engagement of discriminating true reality is not mental nonengagement. For otherwise it would follow that other things, such as form, are mental nonengagement too, while none of them functions as the remedy for these characteristics (see the section in the *Dharmadharmatāvibhāga* about the five features that are to be eliminated as representing nonconceptual wisdom). Therefore, the intention behind "mental nonengagement" is that it refers to the mental nonengagement that is characterized by being the discrimination of true reality which does not accord with mentally engaging (in characteristics). Or it is due to mental nonengagement being the result of the discrimination of true reality that the latter is called "mental nonengagement." Through teaching mental nonengagement as merely the result, it is obvious that, implicitly, it must also refer to its cause. It is through such mental nonengagement

that one is able to relinquish the four kinds of characteristics. For when yogins discriminate what appear as the characteristics of form and so on by virtue of mistaken aspects under the sway of ignorance, at the point when they do not observe these characteristics anymore, they have relinquished the clinging to them. Once they have relinquished that clinging, they also realize the lack of characteristics (or signlessness). Upon the obscurations having been relinquished, stainless wisdom dawns and the relinquishment of all latencies of desire and so on without exception is attained too. According to the *Ratnameghasūtra*, once one has become an expert in knowing the flaws of clinging to characteristics, one engages in the yoga of emptiness in order to become free from all reference points. Through having familiarized with emptiness a lot, no matter which states one's mind may enter, if one searches for the nature of those states, in which the mind delights, one realizes that they are empty. If one searches for the mind itself, it is also realized to be empty. And when searching for the mind that conducts this examination, one realizes that it is empty too. Through realizing emptiness in this way, one engages in the yoga of signlessness. Though the mental nonengagement that is characterized by being the discrimination of true reality is the nature of nonconceptuality, it is consumed by the fire of perfect wisdom that arises from it, just as two sticks are burnt by the fire that arises from having rubbed them together. Therefore, those who wish for the arising of nonconceptual wisdom should first cultivate the superior insight that is characterized by discriminating true reality—it will relinquish all characteristics. Yogins should analyze all phenomena in terms of dependent origination, their being without coming and going, their lack of arising from themselves, others, and both, their parts, and so on. In short, however they may analyze, they should discriminate in line with the arising of the conviction that real entities do not exist.

872 M only has "those characteristics of conceptions."

873 KCA (fols. 132b.4–133b.2) comments that the remedies consists of the pāramitās because these are the remedies for the obscurations of all afflictions, such as avarice. All samādhis, prajñā, the pāramitās, and the bhūmis are the remedies for characteristics because omniscience will not be attained without its causes. "By way of analyzing a nature" refers to conceiving of the existence of specific characteristics of generosity and so on. In the case of generosity, its nature is threefold—giving riches, protection from fear, and the dharma. The nature of ethics is to turn away from all flawed conduct and engage in all virtue. The nature of patience is to be enduring, not to retaliate, and to be open and ready for true reality. The nature of all vigor is to truly delight in virtues. The nature of dhyāna is a one-pointed mind. The nature of prajñā is to discriminate entities in a correct, thorough, and exhaustive manner. "By way of analyzing qualities" refers to conceiving of the results of the six pāramitās—in due order, great wealth; an excellent body as the cause of the higher realms; good looks and many retinues; indivisible retinues and uninterrupted wealth; being free from physical harm; and all faculties being sharp, abundant physical and mental pleasures, and mastery over most assemblies of people. The general result of all pāramitās is that oneself and all others are taken care of. "By way of analyzing an essence" refers to conceiving of all that was dedicated for great enlightenment as having become inexhaustible and being the cause for attaining enlightenment.

874 KCA (fols. 133b.2–134a.7) says that true reality is the freedom from the entire web of reference points, such as existence and nonexistence. Bodhisattvas may think, "Though generosity and so on lack a nature of their own, the entities that make up the ultimate, such as emptiness, exist by virtue of their own specific characteristics. Otherwise, if the ultimate did not exist either, pure conduct would be pointless." However, such conceptions are to be relinquished too. Since emptiness and so on are nothing but the characteristic of sheer personal and phenomenal identitylessness, there are no entities such as emptiness that exist by virtue of their own specific characteristics. Otherwise, if emptiness and so on had the nature of entities and such, how could one put an end to conceptions about their being entities? The *Ratnameghasūtra* says that if the characteristic that is the lack of the personal and phenomenal identities that are

superimposed onto all illusionlike phenomena were not the ultimate, the persons and phenomena as they are imagined by childish beings would be real. Therefore, childish beings would see true reality by virtue of their clinging to persons and phenomena and thus effortlessley attain liberation. Consequently, any attempt at cultivating the path of the noble ones in order to attain nirvāṇa would be pointless. "By way of analyzing specific characteristics" refers to conceiving of entities that exist by virtue of their own specific characteristics. Or it refers to conceiving of the nature of "emptiness"—the freedom from the personal and phenomenal identities that are superimposed onto all illusionlike phenomena. This is "suchness" because it is the actuality that is never anything other. It is "the true end" because it is the unmistaken actuality. It is "signlessness" because it is free from all characteristics. It is "the ultimate" because it is the sphere of the highest nonconceptual wisdom. It is "the dharmadhātu" because it is the cause of all buddhadharmas. Thus, to think of the specific characteristics of each one of these words, such as emptiness, in light of their being existent entities means to entertain characteristics. "By way of analyzing qualities" refers to thinking that all buddha qualities without exception will be attained through having familiarized with emptiness and so on. "By way of analyzing an essence" refers to thinking of emptiness and so on as being true reality because they are undeceiving, perfect in being unchanging, the perfect nature, irrefutable in all respects through valid cognition, correctly established through valid cognition, and constitute the dharmakāyas of all buddhas. "Relinquishing these characteristics through not mentally engaging in them" refers to not conceiving of them as having the nature of existents, nonexistents, and so on. Since emptiness and so on are nothing but the sheer characteristic of personal and phenomenal identitylessness, they do not exist as having the nature of entities. However, they are not totally nonexistent like the horns of a rabbit either because they are labeled as the nature of phenomena by virtue of all illusionlike phenomena being free from any identities that are superimposed as persons and phenomena. Once that is realized, conceptions about their having a nature and so on are to be relinquished.

875 KCA (fols. 134b.1–135b.6) says that bodhisattvas may think, "Though the pāramitās as well as the ultimate (emptiness) as the focal object of the pāramitās lack a nature of their own, the entities that have the nature of being what is attained by virtue of having familiarized with the remedies and the ultimate do exist because they are the results. Otherwise, how could bodhisattvas actually enter the bhūmis?" These thoughts are to be relinquished too because also the bhūmis and so on are without arising ultimately. "The attainment of the poised readiness for the dharma of nonarising, the attainment of the prophecy, and the attainment of the purity of buddha realms" refer to bodhisattvas on the eighth bhūmi. "The attainment of maturing sentient beings and the attainment of the empowerment" refer to bodhisattvas on the ninth and tenth bhūmis, respectively. Since these three bhūmis are endowed with special qualities, such as operating in an effortless manner, they are superior to other bhūmis. Therefore, the dhāraṇī speaks of distinct characteristics of conceptions about them. However, these characteristics of conceptions about the bhūmis and so on only occur in beginner yogins and not in bodhisattvas on the bhūmis because they are impossible to have on the bhūmis. "By way of analyzing specific characteristics" refers to conceiving of the bhūmis and so on as entities that exist by virtue of their respective own specific characteristics. That is, through bodhisattvas having entered what is flawless on the first bhūmi, this bhūmi is presented as the remedy for being ignorant about persons and phenomena. Through ethics being completely pure, the second bhūmi is the remedy for being ignorant about the mistakenness of subtle infractions of ethics. Through having gained mastery over mundane meditative absorptions, the third bhūmi is the remedy for being ignorant about the desire of the desire realm. Through firmly dwelling in the factors concordant with enlightenment as they were attained, the fourth bhūmi is the remedy for the ignorance of craving for the dharmas of meditative absorptions. Through familiarizing with the realities by way of dwelling in the factors concordant with enlightenment embraced by means, on the fifth

bhūmi bodhisattvas fully turn their back on both saṃsāra and nirvāṇa, and that bhūmi is the remedy for the ignorance of mentally engaging in facing those two. Through dwelling in signlessness, the sixth bhūmi is the remedy for being ignorant about greatly engaging in signlessness and for being ignorant about engaging in saṃsāra. Through dwelling in signlessness even in unfavorable situations, the seventh bhūmi is the remedy for the ignorance of entertaining subtle characteristics. Through dwelling in signlessness without effort, the eighth bhūmi is the remedy for the ignorance of making efforts with regard to, and engaging in, signlessness. Through having attained the four discriminating awarenesses, the ninth bhūmi is the remedy for being ignorant about the mastery over explaining the dharma in all aspects. Through having gained mastery over a buddha's realm, retinue, emanations, and so on, the tenth bhūmi is the remedy for being ignorant about the great supernatural knowledge. In brief, through having attained the knowledge that is without attachment and obstruction with regard to all phenomena in all respects, this bhūmi is the remedy for the ignorance that obstructs the subtle wisdom about all knowable objects. As for "by way of analyzing qualities," in one single moment of time bodhisattvas on the first bhūmi (1) attain one hundred samādhis, (2) see one hundred buddhas, (3) are blessed by them, (4) shake one hundred worldly realms, (5) go to one hundred realms, (6) illuminate one hundred realms, (7) mature one hundred sentient beings, (8) remain for one hundred eons, (9) operate from the beginning to the end of one hundred eons, (10) open one hundred doors of dharma, (11) display one hundred of their own bodies, and (12) display one hundred excellent retinues that surround each one of those bodies. These twelve qualities are multiplied one thousand times on the second bhūmi; one hundred thousand times on the third; ten billion times on the fourth; one hundred billion times on the fifth; ten trillion times on the sixth; and one hundred sextillion times on the seventh. On the eighth they are equal to the number of the minutest particles in one million trichiliocosms. On the ninth they are as many as the particles in one million countless buddha realms. On the tenth they are as many as the particles in a septillion inexpressible buddha realms. On the buddhabhūmi one knows all the minutest particles contained in all worldly realms to the end of space, thus knowing all aspects of all entities contained in all directions and times without exception. "By way of analyzing an essence" refers to conceptions about the bhūmis and so on due to their being the supreme of all mundane and supramundane phenomena and being the causes for the consummate welfares of oneself and others. "Relinquishing these characteristics through not mentally engaging in them" refers to relinquishing the clinging to the bhūmis and so on as being entities because all phenomena are of one taste in that they are without arising ultimately.

876 Here the translation follows D and KCA (*rnam par mi rtog pa'i dbyings la shin tu brtson pa yin*). M has "strive hard through being nonconceptual" (*suprayukto bhavaty avikalpena /*).

877 KCA (fols. 135b.7–137a.2) says that "striving hard for the dhātu of nonconceptuality" refers to having actually entered the path of entering the dhātu of nonconceptuality. In this way, through aspiration and prajñā, yogins relinquish the entire web of the characteristics of conceptions about existence and so on. Through aspiring for true reality with a state of mind that is free from examination, analysis, and expression, and is of one taste, they effortlessly familiarize with, and abide in, true reality in a very lucid manner. The continuum of mind resting within that should be undistracted. When it becomes distracted occasionally, the mind should be calmed and then redirected toward true reality. When the mind is seen to dwell in meditative equipoise free from agitation and dullness, one should let go of all effort and rest in equanimity, for at that point any effort will be a distraction. Thus, yogins effortlessly familiarize with, and rest in, true reality for as long as they wish through the power of aspiration. When wishing to rise from this samādhi, they think, "Though all phenomena do not arise ultimately, they do arise in the manner of illusions and so on in dependence on distinct particular causes and conditions. Therefore, since I wish to attain the state of buddhahood in order to benefit all sentient beings, I should make efforts in gathering the vast and immeasurable accumulations of merit and wisdom." Just

like an illusionist, they should make efforts in accomplishing all the illusionlike accumulations of merit and wisdom that are endowed with emptiness and compassion and are dedicated for unsurpassable enlightenment. Having done so, the dhyāna of emptiness endowed with the supreme of all aspects will be accomplished. According to the *Ratnacūḍasūtra*, the emptiness endowed with the supreme of all aspects is the one that does not lack the six pāramitās, means, and so on. The *Vimalakīrtinirdeśasūtra* says that to teach prajñā alone without any means is a fetter of bodhisattvas. For as long as yogins have not entered the bhūmis, their familiarization with true reality on the level of engagement through aspiration as described here is presented as "the correct practice" and "the proper samādhi," which is in conformity with eventually making contact with the dhātu of nonconceptuality.

878 M omits this phrase and starts with "By virtue of pursuing that correct practice through familiarization . . ."

879 KCA (fol. 137a.3–137b.4) explains that, through having cultivated for a long time the progression of study, reflection, and meditation in terms of the correct practice to relinquish characteristics, the familiarization with true reality reaches its culmination and the dharmadhātu free from all conceptions and reference points is realized. This is the arising of the supreme supramundane wisdom that is the valid cognition which is very lucid, stainless, immovable, and steady, like the continuum of a candle flame without wind. It effortlessly engages the nature of ultimate bodhicitta and consists of the path of seeing that directly perceives the true reality of all phenomena being identityless. At that point, yogins have entered nonconceptuality, which is also the attainment of the first bhūmi. "Pursuing that correct practice through reliance" indicates the causal entities of the prajñā of study, that is, relying on the scriptures. "Pursuing it through familiarization" refers to the prajñā of reflection. "Pursuing it through enhancement" refers to the prajñā of meditation because it is the enhancement of undistracted continuous familiarization. "Pursuing it through correct mental engagement" means to pursue it through practicing these three prajñās in an unmistaken manner. This is done "in a spontaneous and effortless manner." For by virtue of having gathered the immeasurable accumulations of merit and wisdom due to uninterrupted devoted familiarization for a long time, through the power of the supreme pliable samādhi calm abiding and superior insight operate in union, while being free from all flaws such as faintheartedness and agitation. Once the path of effortless engagement has arisen, this means that bodhisattvas "make contact with the dhātu of nonconceptuality in a spontaneous manner" because they perceive it directly. Having entered the first bhūmi, the higher bhūmis will be purified subsequently. In due order, the four phrases "By virtue of pursuing that correct practice through reliance . . . correct mental engagement" can also be understood as corresponding to the four factors conducive to penetration during the path of preparation.

880 M inserts here the phrase "due to being beyond all characteristics of conceptions," which is not found in D and KCA. It appears to be redundant, when matching the six initial phrases of this passage with the six terms at its end, as KCA does (see next note).

881 KCA (fols. 137b.4–138a.6) explains that the dhātu of nonconceptuality is called "nonconceptual" because it is "beyond all conceptions that analyze," that is, it cannot be examined by any of one's conceptions. Therefore, it is "ungraspable." It is "beyond all conceptions in terms of demonstrating and illustrating" because it cannot be demonstrated to others as being such and such. Therefore, it is indemonstrable. It is "beyond all conceptions in terms of sense faculties" because it is utterly beyond the nature of everything that is conceived as the characteristics of the inner āyatanas. Therefore, it is unfounded because it is not based on any of the inner āyatanas. It is "beyond all conceptions in terms of objects" because it is utterly beyond the nature of everything that is conceived as the characteristics of the outer āyatanas. Therefore, it is without appearance because it does not appear as something like an object such as form. It is "beyond

all conceptions in terms of cognizance" because it is utterly beyond the nature of everything that is conceived as the characteristics of cognizance (such as the eye consciousness). Therefore, it is not cognizance because it does not have the nature of the six types of consciousness. It is "not the locus of all afflictive, secondary afflictive, and cognitive obscurations" because in the naturally luminous dharmadhātu there is no support for any adventitious obscurations that consist of the afflictions and secondary afflictions. Therefore, it is without base because it lacks a base for any obscurations. Consequently, it is called "nonconceptual" because it is utterly beyond the conceptions about all those phenomena. This is its defining characteristic, which is sixfold—being ungraspable and so on. To express it in that way is not in terms of the kind of existence that is called "seeming reality" because true reality is utterly beyond all that. If it were the sphere of conventions, it would be the seeming and not the ultimate.

882 KAC (fols. 138b.2–140a.6) says that the reason for bodhisattvas abiding in the dhātu of nonconceptuality through the nonconceptual wisdom that is not different from what is to be known is that, by virtue of engaging in the nonobservability of all phenomena, they do not observe any distinction between what knows and what is known. Therefore, they "see all phenomena as being like the center of space" because none of the characteristics explained above arise anymore in any way whatsoever. So who sees at that time? Ultimately, a yogin's own continuum, which has the nature of a person and so on, does not exist at all. Therefore, there is no seeing either. However, though there is no nature ultimately, on the level of seeming reality the cognition of the mere aspect of an object (such as form) that arises for it is labeled in the world with conventional expressions such as "Devadatta sees." Likewise, here, though wisdom lacks any nature ultimately, through the power of having familiarized with true actuality, when self-awareness realizes the lack of nature through the aspect of all phenomena lacking a nature, it is said that "a yogin's wisdom sees." Though all phenomena are without nature ultimately, isn't it asserted on the level of seeming reality that the wisdom of yogins is different from the cognitions of ordinary beings? Otherwise, how could distinct persons, such as śrāvakas, pratyekabuddhas, and bodhisattvas, be presented? What does not have a cause even on the level of seeming reality does not arise at all, just as there is no arising of horns of a rabbit in seeming reality. What has a cause arises in a manner that is delusive ultimately, just like illusions and reflections. However, this dependent origination is not tenable ultimately because then illusions and so on would be ultimate too. What originates dependently cannot withstand scrutiny as being different from how illusions and so on are. It is empty of former and later ends, and its middle cannot be apprehended as an entity that is singular or multiple either. It is not tenable that it arises from itself, something other, or both. If it were labeled as "ultimately existent" in accordance with its own continuum being described as being identityless, since it depends on and arises from others, it can be labeled in this way as one wishes. However, one must still declare that the defining characteristics of the ultimate are different from illusions and so on. Otherwise, illusions and so on would not be mistakenness because they also originate dependently. Since cognition now arises as aspects such as an illusory elephant, if this illusion were real as the nature of cognition, it would be untenable for cognition to arise as any other aspect because being the same and other are mutually exclusive. Nondual wisdom does not arise as the aspect of duality because it is contradictory for false duality to exist in what is singular. It would arise from being unarisen and would not cease after it has arisen because a progression of existence and nonexistence in a singularity is contradictory. As Nāgārjuna says:

> In a nature, existence
> And nonexistence are not tenable.
> As they are mutually exclusive,
> How could existence and nonexistence be suitable in a singularity?
>
> If something existed through a nature of its own,
> It would not become nonexistent.

It would never be tenable for
A nature of its own to change into anything else.

(The first verse is unidentified; the second one is *Mūlamadhyamakakārikā* XV.8).

Therefore, though illusions are delusive, they arise under the sway of conditions such as an elixir and a mantra having come together. Likewise, the illusions of ordinary beings arise under the sway of karma and afflictions. Similarly, the illusion of the yogic wisdom of yogins arises through the power of the accumulations of merit and wisdom. Just like illusions, causes and conditions are satisfying when not examined. Since they have the nature of being connected by virtue of a series of causes without beginning, all of this is not contradictory. As for "the wisdom that is attained subsequent" to supramundane nonconceptual wisdom, it sees everything that makes up the world of sentient beings as being illusionlike because what appear as the forms of sentient beings are like the elephants in an illusion. Everything that makes up the world of the container is like a mirage because, just like a mirage, outer objects appear in a delusive manner. The nature of places and possessions resembles a dream because, just as in a dream, desire for those delusive appearances arises. The nature of physical actions resembles an optical illusion because, just like an optical illusion, they appear, though all phenomena are without acting. The nature of verbal actions is like an echo because, just like an echo, they are delusive, but are heard. The behavior in the desire realm is like a reflection because the maturational results of former actions appear in accordance with how these actions were committed before. The maturational results of the actions that consist of the samādhis that engage in the form realm and the formless realm resemble a reflection of the moon in water because those samādhis are like water. What consists of pure buddha realms and so on is like a magical creation because it is created by one's own completely pure mind. Or the inner āyatanas are like an illusion because they appear as the nature of sentient beings and so on, though sentient beings do not exist. The six āyatanas of consciousness and all mental factors resemble a mirage because they, just like a mirage, appear as delusive aspects. The outer āyatanas are like a dream because, just as in a dream, forms are delusive and yet appear as objects. The rūpakāyas of buddhas that are adorned by the marks of a great being and so on resemble an optical illusion because they appear in that way under the influence of the completely pure dharmakāya. The dharma that is taught is like an echo because, just like an echo, it is obtained through the influence of the buddhas. The results of former actions are like a reflection because all phenomena arise in accordance with karma. What consists of the pure realms of buddhas is like a reflection of the moon in water because it appears like the moon in the water of the mind that is free from all obscurations. All conditioned phenomena are like a magical creation because, despite being delusive, they appear as magical creations in accordance with the coming together of their specific causes and conditions. Thus, the sign of having entered the dhātu of nonconceptuality is the arising of the wisdom that resembles an illusion and so on after having risen from the spacelike wisdom when resting in meditative equipoise in the true reality of all phenomena.

883 M has "vast mastery over dwelling in the great teaching" (*mahādeśanāvihāravibhutva vaipulyatān*). KCA (fol. 140a.6–140b.3) explains that the two types of wisdom just discussed have four benefits. The first two are the consummate welfare of oneself and the latter two, the consummate welfare of others. To dwell in vast great bliss is attained through attaining the mastery over manifesting dwelling in the supreme inexhaustible bliss that is without evil. Vast great excellence of mind, which here refers to samādhi, is attained through attaining the mastery over manifesting special qualities, such as the supreme of all supernatural knowledges. Vast great prajñā is attained through being skilled in the discrimination of all aspects of sentient beings' antagonistic factors, their remedies, what they should adopt, and what they should reject. Vast great wisdom is attained through attaining the knowledge of whether sentient beings are or are not proper receptacles. Vast mastery over great teaching is attained through gaining mastery over teaching the dharma in all its aspects in accordance with those sentient beings.

884 KCA (fol. 140b.4–5) says that, at the time of buddhahood, the effortless activity of buddhas arises in an uninterrupted manner. Therefore, it always accomplishes every aspect of the welfare of all sentient beings in accordance with their respective karmic fortunes.

885 The phrase "various great radiant precious substances that are wish-fulfilling jewels" (M *bhāsurāṇāṃ vicitrāṇāṃ mahācintāmaṇiratnānāṃ*) in its plural form and in its connection with silver, gold, and various gems seems a little bit confusing when compared to the "great treasure of a wish-fulfilling jewel" below, which is clearly differentiated from the silver, gold, and various gems that lie above it. Possibly, as KCA indicates below, silver and so on are considered here as wish-fulfilling in terms of the mundane desires of gods and humans, while the actual wish-fulfilling jewel stands for fulfilling the supreme supramundane desire of attaining buddhahood.

886 KCA (fols. 140b.6–142a.6) explains that this section has two parts—the example and its meaning. "Formations" are of various kinds, with "afflictiveness" consisting of the afflictiveness of afflictions, karma, and birth that operate since beginningless time and "duality" consisting of clinging to the extremes of permanence and extinction and so on. Under the sway of ignorance, worldly people cling to these extremes all the time and therefore "are engrossed in duality." Since these distinct types of formations are produced by the distinct conceptions about a nature, they lack a core and thus resemble a "rock mountain." Since the threefold afflictiveness of afflictions, karma, and birth operates since beginningless time in an uninterrupted manner, it is like "very hard" rock. Since it is difficult to be free from clinging to all pairs of extremes until buddhahood is attained, "being engrossed in duality" is like "solid" rock. "Without [any further] exertion of digging" is the example for the path of entering the dhātu of nonconceptuality through engaging in the union of calm abiding and superior insight. "Being rich" refers to the teachings and "great wealth," to gold and so on. The realization of the dhātu of nonconceptuality is like finding a wish-fulfilling jewel that is the cause of accomplishing all desired goals without exception, thus being the example for attaining the kāya of a tathāgata. Therefore, it is taught to be the single thing to be adopted. Whoever aspires for and has trust in the dhātu of nonconceptuality (which is like the treasure of a wish-fulfilling jewel) and thus gives rise to great enthusiasm for digging through the mountain of formations that is made of the rock of the conceptions about a nature, which are to be relinquished, will accomplish buddhahood (which is like a precious wish-fulfilling jewel), but others will not. "The person who knows about that great treasure through supernatural knowledge" refers to the Buddha. He is the only one to teach this meaningful and profound dharma that is not held in common with the tīrthikas, thus being worthy of being an object of refuge and so on. He is the "tathāgata" because he has gone to suchness (*tathatā*) or because he has gone to the unsurpassable state just like (*tatha*) the buddhas before him. He is an "arhat" because he has overcome the enemies such as desire and because he is worthy of being venerated by the entire world. He is "the completely perfect buddha" because he has perfectly realized true reality, which is like knowing the great treasure. Just as it is correct that hoes and so on are proper means to dig, while others are not, one is able to relinquish characteristics without mentally engaging in them only through the discrimination of true reality, but not through anything else. Therefore, as the example for mental nonengagement, the text speaks of "digging." For it is through this discrimination of true reality while not mentally engaging that the relinquishment of conceptions about characteristics is accomplished. Since generosity and so on that are embraced by conceptions resemble silver and so on and thus are not great, they may serve as the causes for the richness of gods or humans, but they are not the causes for attaining buddhahood, which is like a great wish-fulfilling jewel. The causes for buddhahood are generosity and so on that are embraced by nonconceptual wisdom. In order to teach that, the text presents the examples of silver and so on for the conceptions about remedies and so on. Though the conceptions about remedies and so on are taken to be real within the nature of conceptions, they are particular object entities by virtue of being conceived and therefore exist as the causes for progressively attaining particular results. This is why the text gives the examples

of "rocks that appear to be silver, gold, and various gems." The precious substances of gold and so on are the examples for conceptions about the bhūmis, but not for the bhūmis themselves. In order to teach that the bhūmis always are like a treasure of a wish-fulfilling jewel, "obtaining the great treasure of the precious wish-fulfilling jewel" is the example for making contact with the dhātu of nonconceptuality, which is the attainment of the first bhūmi. In this way, the progressive stages of entering the dhātu of nonconceptuality should be understood.

887 The translation follows D (*rnam pa thams cad mkhyen pa nyid shin tu rnam par byang ba'o*) and KCA's according comments. M has "The three realms are nothing other than the knowledge of all aspects because of being purified (*sarvākārajñatāyā nānyat traidhātukaṃ vyavadānād*)."

888 D omits this sentence.

889 D has "all conceptions about the knowledge of all aspects" (*rnam pa thams cad mkhyen pa'i rnam par rtog pa thams cad*).

890 KCA (fols. 142a.6–145a.1) says that the question, "How then do bodhisattva mahāsattvas examine the characteristics of conceptions as taught [above] and enter the dhātu of nonconceptuality?" derives from the following thought: "Without examination, one is not able to relinquish characteristics, and without relinquishing characteristics, one will not enter the dhātu of nonconceptuality. Therefore, one doubtlessly needs to examine." When it was taught above that characteristics are relinquished through the discrimination of true reality, which is called "mental nonengagement," it was not explained how one should discriminate true reality. Therefore, this section here, starting with "bodhisattva mahāsattvas who dwell in the dhātu of nonconceptuality," teaches the means to do so. The intention behind the term "dhātu of nonconceptuality" here is that it refers to the path of preparation because in the actual dwelling in this dhātu, characteristics about form and so on are not perceptible. In order to teach that one should discriminate true reality in such a way that one relinquishes the two extremes and thus enters the middle path by any means, the text teaches the nature of the extreme of superimposition, the nature of the extreme of denial, and how to enter the middle path. The extreme of superimposition is twofold—superimposing persons and phenomena. "My form" and "the form of others" represent superimpositions of persons because the clinging to form and so on as what is mine arises through the clinging to a self. The extreme of superimposing phenomena is twofold—superimposing phenomena as a nature and its particulars. "This is form" represents the former, and the next four phrases represent the latter. For since form and so on are primordially unarisen, ultimately, any arising, ceasing, and so on of form and so on are impossible. Form is conceived as "arising and ceasing" because it is something that has the quality of arising and ceasing in every moment. "Form is afflicted" because it entails dependent origination in its progressive order. "Form is purified" because it entails dependent origination in its reverse order. The remaining phrases, starting with "Form does not exist," represent the extreme of denial. In order to teach that a person does not exist in the same way in which phenomena such as form exist on the level of seeming reality, the text says, "Form does not exist." This teaches the extreme of denying a person, which only exists by way of being imputed onto form and so on because such a person does not even exist on the level of seeming reality. "Form does not exist by a nature of its own" is the denial of a nature, while the next five phrases represent denials of its particulars. All refer to the extreme of denial in terms of denying what is imputedly existent. Since all are cases of clinging to something as nonexistent that were preceded by clinging to it as existent, when conceived in that way, they become the clinging to something as existent. Therefore, one should not conceive of form as being nonexistent either. That "form does not exist as a cause" means that it does not exist as having the nature of a cause. That it "does not exist as a result" means that there is nothing that has become a result. "Karma" refers to the ability of form to impel its own specific result. "Linkage" refers to being connected with its own specific result and so on. "Process" refers to difference. "The cognizance that appears as form" is ultimately unarisen too and therefore is as delusive as form. In order to teach that the

clinging to form as being mere cognizance also represents an extreme of superimposition, the text speaks of "form being mere cognizance." However, since the cognizance that appears as form exists on the level of seeming reality in the same way that dreams and so on do, the text says, "Just as form does not exist, so does the cognizance that appears as form not exist." This teaches the extreme of denial in terms of denying cognizance on the level of seeming reality. Having taught the two extermes in this way, the text proceeds to teach how to enter the middle path. Yogins who analyze the ultimate "do not observe form nor do they observe the cognizance that appears as form." Therefore, they neither superimpose anything onto it nor do they cling to the extreme of denial. "However, it is not that the cognizance that appears as form and so on is utterly and completely nonexistent." The intention here is that, otherwise, this would contradict what is seen and so on. The intention behind the term "cognizance" in "Any other phenomenon apart from cognizance is not observable" is that cognizance refers to mistakenness in all respects because it displays what is wrong. Therefore, all phenomena simply have the nature of being what is conceived by mere mistakenness. The intention behind this is that, apart from being just such mistakenness, they lack any independent nature of their own. As the *Laṅkāvatārasūtra* says:

> In terms of the seeming, entities arise.
> In terms of the ultimate, they lack a nature of their own.
> To err about the lack of nature
> Is held to be the correct seeming.

(*Laṅkāvatārasūtra* X.120 reads:

> In terms of the seeming, everything exists.
> In terms of the ultimate, it does not exist.
> Ultimately, the lack of nature of phenomena is seen.
> To perceive the lack of nature [as something] is said to be the seeming.)

Therefore, all entities are taught in terms of seeming reality, which establishes that cognizance is not utterly nonexistent. The phrase "This cognizance is not perceived as the lack of existence" refutes that the dharmadhātu and cognizance, which is of the nature of the seeming, are the same (KCA wrongly has *mi 'dra ba*). The dharmadhātu, whose nature is to be free from all entities that are persons and phenomena, is expressed here by the term "lack of existence." It is reasonable that the very nature of cognizance, onto which the entities of persons and phenomena are superimposed, is not the same as persons and phenomena because what is real and what is not real are mutually exclusive. However, the text also teaches that the dharmadhātu and cognizance are not utterly different either, saying that "the lack of existence is not perceived apart from cognizance." The dharmadhātu is the characteristic of the lack of persons and phenomena in that very cognizance. Since that is designated as the nature of phenomena, ultimately, this nature and what bears this nature are not different. As for the dharmadhātu and cognizance not being perceived as being one, if the dharmadhātu and cognizance were alike in all respects, the dharmadhātu would be perceptible by everybody. Consequently, everybody would perceive true reality. There would also be the flaw that, just like the dharmadhātu, cognizance would be real and unafflicted. On the reverse, just like cognizance, the dharmadhātu would be conditioned and afflicted. As for the dharmadhātu and cognizance not being perceived as being different, if the dharmadhātu is the freedom from what is superimposed as persons and phenomena (the nature of the seeming) onto this very cognizance, that is, if it is the characteristic of the nonexistence of these superimpositions, how could it be different from that cognizance? If it were different, the sheer identitylessness of conditional phenomena would not be the characteristic of the ultimate. Also, those who are bound by the characteristics of conditional phenomena would not be surpassed by yogins because yogins would realize the dharmadhātu as something entirely different from cognizance. Therefore, the dhātu of nonconceptuality is what cannot be expressed as being one or different, just like a conch and its being white. This lack of characteristics of the dharmadhātu "is not perceived as an existent" because anything that has the nature of being existent is not observed in it. "Nor is it perceived as a nonexistent" since an existent is unobservable and therefore something that has the nature of being nonexistent—what is attained through excluding what is existent—does not exist either. As *Mūlamadhyamakakārikā* XV.5 says, what is other than existent has the characteristic of nonexistence. Therefore, if what is existent is not established, what is nonexistent is not established either. Even if one regards "what is not conceived by any aspects of all those conceptions (such as those about arising and ceasing)" as "the dhātu of nonconceptuality," one still entertains conceptions. Therefore, one should not regard it in that way either. "The way of entering the dhātu of nonconceptuality" thus refers to the means to enter it, which has the characteristic of relinquishing the two extremes. How to examine the two extremes was taught above, and it is based on discriminating the manner of entering the middle path in this way that bodhisattvas accordingly dwell in the dhātu of nonconceptuality. The same manner of discriminating the two extremes of superimposition and denial and entering the middle path, as it was explained here for form, is to be applied to everything else from feelings up through the knowledge of all aspects. In particular, as for the knowledge of all aspects, ultimately, all obscurations are not to be relinquished because they have the nature of being superimposed by mistakenness and thus are primordially unarisen, just as a head cannot be cut off twice. Therefore, since there is nothing to be relinquished, being omniscient is not due to relinquishment. Consequently, to think that "the knowledge of all aspects relinquishes the obscurations" also represents an extreme of superimposition and thus is to be relinquished by yogins. To think that "the knowledge of all aspects is the very phenomenon that is purified" also is a conception because it means clinging to the two extremes of purity and impurity. Thus, through the force of clinging to the knowledge of all aspects as being pure, one superimposes impurity onto everything else because the one depends on the other. Therefore, one conceives in a dualistic manner. However, in all phenomena being unarisen and being of one taste, there are no divisions such as pure and impure. Therefore, after having relinquished all pairs of extremes, the learned do not even dwell in the middle. The remaining statements about the knowledge of all aspects are to be explained in the same way as the above ones about form.

891 Here the translation follows D (*'dzin pa dang / yi ger 'bri ba dang / 'chang ba dang / klog pa'i bsod nams*). M is reconstructed as "through retaining, reading, and reciting" (*udgrahaṇalekhanavācanād*).

892 D has "full of generosity/gifts" (*yongs su gang ba'i sbyin pa*).

893 KCA (fol. 145a.1–145b.2) explains that the first verse teaches the progression of the causes for entering the dhātu that is the cause of nonconceptuality, while the second one teaches the benefit of that. "The children of the Victor who reflected on nonconceptuality in this dharma" refers to having studied the dharma that pertains to nonconceptuality and then having settled into reflecting about that nonconceptuality. "By transcending conceptions difficult to traverse" means to relinquish the four kinds of characteristics of conceptions about a nature and so on. "Gradually attain nonconceptuality" means that yogins, through progressively engaging in all that, attain supramundane nonconceptual wisdom. Or "gradually" can also be linked to the phrase "transcending conceptions difficult to traverse," which thus teaches the gradual entrance into the dhātu of nonconceptuality. "By virtue of that" means by virtue of the causes for attaining nonconceptual wisdom. "To discover the bliss of nonconceptuality" means to realize it. The text speaks of "the bliss of nonconceptuality" because nonconceptuality itself is bliss or because bliss is the fruition of nonconceptuality, with "peaceful" and the following terms all representing particular qualities of this bliss. It is "peaceful" because it is free from all reference points. It is "immovable" because it is stable due to not deteriorating. It is "supreme" because it is more eminent than any other kinds of mundane and supramundane bliss. It is "powerful" because it is perceived as one wishes and for as long as one wishes. As for this bliss being "equal yet unequal," it is equal because it is common to all buddhas and bodhisattvas, and it is unequal because it is

not in common with śrāvakas and so on. Or it is equal due to having attained the realization that all phenomena are equality, and it is unequal because there is no other bliss that is equally supreme. Or it is equal because of its being utterly peaceful, and it is unequal because of possessing qualities such as being immovable.

894 I list here important works relevant to the current study, but for reasons of space I do not include Buddhist sūtras and some of the other canonical works cited in the text or notes.

Bibliography

Indic Works[894]

Abhayākaragupta. *Munimatālaṃkāra*. (Thub pa'i dgongs pa'i rgyan). D3903.

Asaṅga. *Abhidharmasamuccaya*. (Chos mngon pa kun las btus pa). Sanskrit edition/retrotranslation from Tibetan by P. Pradhan. Santiniketan, India: Visva-Bharati, 1950. D4049.

——. *Bodhisattvabhūmi*. (Byang chub sems dpa'i sa). Sanskrit edition by N. Dutt. Patna, India: K.P. Jayaswal Research Institute, 1966. D4037.

——. *Mahāyānasaṃgraha*. (Theg chen bsdus pa). D4048.

——. *Ratnagotravibhāgavyākhyā* or *Mahāyānottaratantraśāstravyākhyā*. (Theg pa chen po'i rgyud bla ma'i bstan bcos rnam par bshad pa). Sanskrit edition by E. H. Johnston. Patna, India: Bihar Research Society, 1950. D4025.

——. *Śrāvakabhūmi*. (Nyan thos kyi sa). Sanskrit edition by K. Shukla. Patna, India: K.P. Jayaswal Research Institute, 1973. D4036.

——. *Viniścayasaṃgrahaṇī*. (Rnam par gtan la dbab pa bsdu ba). D4038.

——. *Yogācārabhūmi*. (Rnal 'byor spyod pa'i sa). D4035.

Asvabhāva. *Mahāyānasaṃgrahopanibandhana*. (Theg pa chen po bsdus pa'i bshad sbyar). D4051.

——. *Mahāyānasūtrālaṃkāraṭīkā*. (Theg pa chen po mdo sde'i rgyan gyi rgya cher bshad pa). D4029.

Dharmakīrti. *Pramāṇavārttika*. (Tshad ma rnam 'grel). D4210.

Dignāga. *Ālambanaparīkṣā*. (Dmigs pa brtag pa). D4205.

——. *Ālambanaparīkṣāvṛtti*. (Dmigs pa brtag pa'i 'grel pa). D4206.

Jagaddalanivāsin. *Bhagavatyāmnāyānusāriṇīnāmavyākhyā*. (Bcom ldan 'das ma'i man ngag gi rjes su 'brang ba zhes bya ba'i rnam par bshad pa). D3811.

Jñānacandra. *Kāyavṛtti*. (Sku gsum 'grel pa). D3891.

Jñānaśrīmitra. *Jñānaśrīmitranibandhāvali*. Ed. Anantalal Thakur. Tibetan Sanskrit Series 5. Patna, India: K.P. Jayaswal Research Institute, 1987.

Kamalaśīla. *Avikalpapraveśadhāraṇīṭīkā*. (Rnam par mi rtog par 'jug pa'i gzungs kyi rgya cher 'grel pa). D4000.

Maitreya. *Abhisamayālaṃkāra*. (Mngon rtogs rgyan). Sanskrit edition by T. Stcherbatsky and E. Obermiller. Bibliotheca Buddhica 23. Leningrad, 1929; G. Tucci, Baroda, 1932; U. Wogihara, Tokyo, 1932–35; K. Kajiyoshi in *Hannya-kyō no kenkyu*, 1944, pp. 275–320. D3786.

——. *Dharmadharmatāvibhāga*. (Chos dang chos nyid rnam par byed pa). D4022/4023.

——. *Madhyāntavibhāga*. (Dbus dang mtha' rnam par 'byed pa). D4021.

——. *Mahāyānasūtrālaṃkāra*. (Theg pa chen po'i mdo sde rgyan). Sanskrit edition in S. Lévi 1907. D4020.

——. *Ratnagotravibhāgamahāyānottaratantraśāstra*. (Theg pa chen po'i rgyud bla ma). Sanskrit edition by E. H. Johnston. Patna, India: The Bihar Research Society, 1950 (includes the *Ratnagotravibhāgavyākhyā*). D4024.

Nāgamitra. *Kāyatrayāvatāramukha*. (Sku gsum la 'jug pa'i sgo). D3890.

Nāgārjuna. *Bodhicittavivaraṇa*. (Byang chub sems kyi 'grel pa). D4556.

——. *Dharmadhātustava*. (Chos dbyings bstod pa). D1118.

——. *Prajñānāmamūlamadhyamakakārikā*. (Dbu ma rtsa ba'i tshig le'ur byas pa shes rab ces bya ba). D3824.

——. *Yuktiṣaṣṭikā*. (Rigs pa drug cu pa). D3825

Ratnākaraśānti. *Bhramahāranāmasādhana*. ('Khrul pa spong ba zhes bya ba'i sgrub pa'i thabs). D1245.

——. *Khasamanāmaṭīkā*. (Nam mkha' dang mnyam pa zhes bya ba'i rgya cher 'grel pa). D1424.

——. *Kusumāñjaliguhyasamājanibandha*. (Gsang ba 'dus pa'i bshad sbyar snyim pa'i me tog). D1851.

——. *Madhyamakālaṃkāravṛttimadhyamapratipadāsiddhināma*. (Dbu ma rgyan gyi 'grel pa dbu ma'i lam grub pa zhes bya ba). D4072.

——. *Prajñāpāramitābhāvanopadeśa*. (Shes rab kyi pha rol tu phyin pa bsgom pa'i man ngag). D4076/4545.

——. *Prajñāpāramitopadeśa*. (Shes rab kyi pha rol tu phyin pa'i man ngag). D4079.

——. *Sūtrasamuccayabhāṣyaratnālokālaṃkāranāma*. (Mdo kun las btus pa'i bshad pa rin po che snang ba'i rgyan ces bya ba). D3935.

Sthiramati. *Madhyāntavibhāgaṭīkā*. (Dbus dang mtha' rnam par 'byed pa'i 'grel bshad). Sanskrit editions: S. Lévi, ed. Paris: Bibliothèque de l'École des Hautes Études, 1932; S. Yamaguchi, ed. Tokyo: Suzuki Research Foundation, 1966. R. Pandeya, ed. Delhi: Motilal Banarsidass 1999. D4032.

——. *Sūtrālaṃkāravṛttibhāṣya*. (Mdo sde rgyan gyi 'grel bshad). D4034.

——. *Triṃśikābhāṣya*. (Sum cu pa'i bshad pa). Sanskrit edition in S. Lévi 1925. D4064.

Vairocanarakṣita. *Dharmadharmatāvibhāgakatipayapadavivṛtti*. Photocopies of a Sanskrit manuscript at Seminar für Indologie und Buddhismuskunde der Universität Göttingen.

Vasubandhu. *Abhidharmakośa*. (Chos mngon pa'i mdzod). Sanskrit edition in Shastri 1970. D4089.

——. *Abhidharmakośabhāṣya*. (Chos mngon pa'i mdzod kyi bshad pa). Sanskrit edition in Shastri 1970. D4090.

——. *Dharmadharmatāvibhāgavṛtti*. (Chos dang chos nyid rnam par 'byed pa'i 'grel pa). D4028.

——. *Madhyāntavibhāgabhāṣya*. (Dbus mtha' rnam 'byed kyi 'grel pa). D4027.

——. *Mahāyānasūtrālaṃkārabhāṣya*. (Theg pa chen po'i mdo sde rgyan gyi 'grel pa). D4026.

——. *Śatasāhasrikāpañcaviṃśatisāhasrikāṣṭādaśasāhasrikāprajñāpāramitābṛhaṭṭīkā*. (Sher phyin 'bum pa dang nyi khri lnga stong pa dang khri brgyad stong pa'i rgya cher 'grel pa; abbr. Yum gsum gnod 'joms). D3808.

——. *Triṃśikākārikā*. (Sum cu pa'i tshig le'ur byas pa). Sanskrit edition in S. Lévi 1925. D4055.

Vinītadeva. *Triṃśikāṭīkā*. (Sum cu pa'i 'grel bshad). D4070.

Tibetan Works

Bcom ldan 'das rig pa'i ral gri. 1981. *Byams chos lnga'i lta khrid*. In Kong sprul blo gros mtha' yas 1979–81, vol. 18: 167–70.

——. 2006. *Chos dang chos nyid rnam 'byed kyi bsdus don*. In *Bcom ldan rig pa'i ral gri'i gsung 'bum*, vol. 5: 647–50. Lhasa: Published by Khams sprul bsod nams don grub.

Bdud 'joms 'jigs bral ye shes rdo rje. 1991. *The Nyingma School of Tibetan Buddhism*. 2 vols. Translated by Gyurme Dorje and M. Kapstein. Boston: Wisdom Publications.

Blo bzang dpal ldan bstan 'dzin snyan grags. n.d. *Chos dang chos nyid rnam 'byed kyi 'grel pa lam gyi snying po*. n.p. Also in *Blo bzang dpal ldan bstan 'dzin snyan grags gyi gsung 'bum*, vol. 13: 837–70. Chengdu: Dmangs khrod dpe dkon sdud sgrig khang, 2001.

Blo bzang rta dbyangs. 1975–1976. *Chos dang chos nyid rnam par 'byed pa'i 'grel pa legs bshad rin chen sgrom phye*. In *The Collected Works of rJe btsun Blo bzang rta dbyangs*, vol. ca: 339–79. New Delhi: Published by Gurudeva.

Bu ston rin chen grub. 1931–32. *History of Buddhism*. 2 vols. Translated by E. Obermiller. Heidelberg: Otto Harrassowitz.

Chos grags bstan 'phel. 1990. *Dbu ma gzhan stong pa'i byung ba cung zad brjod pa nges don ngag gi rol mo*. In *Dbu ma gzhan stong skor bstan bcos phyogs bsdus deb dang po*, 1–11. Rumtek (Sikkim, India): Karma Shri Nalanda Institute.

Chos grags rgya mtsho (Karmapa VII). 1985. *The Ocean of Texts on Reasoning* (*Tshad ma legs par bshad pa thams cad kyi chu bo yongs su 'du ba rigs pa'i gzhung lugs kyi rgya mtsho*). 4 vols. Rumtek (Sikkim, India): Karma Thupten Chosphel and Phuntsok.

Chos kyi 'byung gnas (Situpa VIII) and 'Be lo tshe dbang kun khyab. 1972. *Sgrub brgyud karma kaṃ tshang brgyud pa rin po che'i rnam par thar pa rab 'byams nor bu zla ba chu shel gyi phreng ba*. 2 vols. New Delhi: Gyaltsan and Kesang Legshay.

Dngul chu thogs med bzang po dpal. 1979. *Theg pa chen po mdo sde rgyan gyi 'grel pa rin po che'i phreng ba*. Bir, India: Dzongsar Institute Library.

Dol po pa shes rab rgyal mtshan. 1998. *Ri chos nges don rgya mtsho*. Beijing: Mi rigs dpe skrun khang.

Dpa' bo gtsug lag phreng ba. 2003. *History of the Dharma, A Feast for the Learned* (*Dam pa'i chos kyi 'khor lo bsgyur ba rnams kyi byung ba gsal bar byed pa mkhas pa'i dga' ston*). 2 vols. Sarnath: Vajra Vidya Library.

Go bo rab 'byams pa bsod nams seng ge. 1979. *Shes rab kyi pha rol tu phyin pa'i man ngag gi bstan bcos mngon rtogs rgyan gyi gzhung snga phyi'i 'brel dang dka' gnas la dpyad pa sbas don zab mo'i gter gyi kha 'byed*. In *Go bo rab 'byams pa bsod nams seng ge'i bka' 'bum*, vol. 7: 1–453. Dehradun: Sakya College.

'Gos lo tsā ba gzhon nu dpal. 1996. *The Blue Annals*. Translated by G. N. Roerich. Delhi: Motilal Banarsidass.

——. 2003a. *Deb ther sngon po*. 2 vols. Sarnath: Vajra Vidya Library.

——. 2003b. *Theg pa chen po'i rgyud bla ma'i bstan bcos kyi 'grel bshad de kho na nyid rab tu gsal ba'i me long*. Nepal Research Centre Publications 24. Edited by Klaus-Dieter Mathes. Stuttgart: Franz Steiner Verlag.

'Ju mi pham rgya mtsho. 1984. *Mngon rtogs rgyan gyi mchan 'grel pun da ri ka'i do shel*. In *Collected Writings of 'Jam-mgon 'Ju Mi-pham-rgya-mtsho*, vol. 4: 1–347. Paro, Bhutan: Lama Ngodrup and Sherab Drimay.

——. c. 1990a. *Collected Works* (*gsungs 'bum*). Sde dge dgon chen edition. Edited by Dilgo Khyentse Rinpoche. Kathmandu.

——. c. 1990b. *Chos dang chos nyid rnam par 'byed pa'i tshig le'ur byas pa'i 'grel pa ye shes snang ba rnam 'byed*. In 'Ju mi pham rgya mtsho c. 1990a, vol. pa: 1–51.

——. c. 1990c. *Dbus dang mtha' rnam par 'byed pa'i 'grel pa od zer phreng ba*. In 'Ju mi pham rgya mtsho c. 1990a, vol. pa: 660–784.

Gzhan phan chos kyi snang ba (a.k.a. Mkhan po gzhan dga'). 1983a. *Chos dang chos nyid rnam par 'byed pa'i tshig le'ur byas pa'i mchan 'grel*. In *Gzhung chen bcu gsum rdzong gsar yig cha*, vol. 3: 1–22. New Delhi: Publ. by Konchhog Lhadrepa.

——. 1983b. *Sher phyin mchan 'grel yan lag*. In *Gzhung chen bcu gsum rdzong gsar yig cha*, vol. 3: 71–75. New Delhi: Publ. by Konchhog Lhadrepa.

Karma 'phrin las pa phyogs las rnam rgyal. 1975. *Dri lan yid kyi mun sel zhes bya ba lcags mo'i dris lan*. In *The Songs of Esoteric Practice (Mgur) and Replies to Doctrinal Questions (Dri lan) of Karma-'phrin-las-pa*. Containing a reproduction of volume GA, *Chos kyi rje karma phrin las pa'i gsung 'bum las rdo rje mgur kyi phreng ba rnams* (Songs of esoteric practice given on various occasions), and volume CHA, *Chos kyi rje Karma phrin las pa'i gsung 'bum las thun mong ba'i dri lan gyi phreng ba rnams* (Replies to various doctrinal questions and polemics). New Delhi: Publ. by Ngawang Tobgay.

Kong sprul blo gros mtha' yas. 1979–81. *Gdams ngag mdzod*. 18 vols. Paro, Bhutan: Published by Lama Ngodrup and Sherab Drimey.

——. 1982. *Theg pa'i sgo kun las btus pa gsung rab rin po che'i mdzod bslab pa gsum legs par ston pa'i bstan bcos shes bya kun khyab*; includes its autocommentary, *Shes bya kun la khyab pa'i gzhung lugs nyung ngu'i tshig gis rnam par 'grol ba legs bshad yongs 'du shes bya mtha' yas pa'i rgya mtsho* (abbreviated as *Shes bya kun kyab mdzod*). 3 vols. Beijing: Mi rigs dpe skrun khang.

——. 2005. *Theg pa chen po rgyud bla ma'i bstan bcos snying po'i don mngon sum lam gyi bshad srol dang sbyar ba'i rnam par 'grel ba phyir mi ldog pa seng ge nga ro*. Seattle: Nitartha *international*. Also as Rumtek blockprint, n.d.

Krang dbyi sun et al. 1985. *Bod rgya tshig mdzod chen mo*. 2 vols. Beijing: Mi rigs dpe skrun khang.

Kun dga' grol mchog. 1981. *Jo nang khrid bgrya*. In Kong sprul blo gros mtha' yas 1979–81, vol. 18: 1–374.

Lodho Zangpo, Khenpo. (Mkhan po blo gros bzang po). 1982. "A Commentary on the Dharmadharmatavibhaga." *Bulletin of Tibetology* 18 (2): 24–63.

Mi bskyod rdo rje (Karmapa VIII). 1990. *Dbu ma gzhan stong smra ba'i srol legs par phye ba'i sgron me*. In *Dbu ma gzhan stong skor bstan bcos phyogs bsdus deb dang po*, 13–48. Rumtek (Sikkim, India): Karma Shri Nalanda Institute.

——. 1996. *The Chariot of the Tagbo Siddhas* (*Dbu ma la 'jug pa'i rnam bshad dpal ldan dus gsum mkhyen pa'i zhal lung dvags brgyud grub pa'i shing rta*). Seattle: Nitartha *international*.

——. 2003. *The Noble One Resting at Ease* (*Shes rab kyi pha rol tu phyin pa'i lung chos mtha' dag gi bdud rtsi'i snying por gyur pa gang la ldan pa'i gzhi rje btsun mchog tu dgyes par ngal gso'i yongs 'dus brtol gyi ljon pa rgyas pa*). 2 vols. Seattle: Nitartha *international*.

Rang byung rdo rje (Karmapa III). 2006a. *Dpal rgyal dbang ka rma pa sku phreng gsum pa rang byung rdo rje'i gsung 'bum*. 11 vols. Lhasa: Dpal brtsegs bod yig dpe rnying zhib 'jug khang.

——. 2006b. *Chos dang chos nyid rnam par 'byed pa'i bstan bcos kyi rnam par bshad pa'i rgyan*. In Rang byung rdo rje 2006a, vol. cha: 488–613.

——. 2006c. *Dbu ma chos dbyings bstod pa'i rnam par bshad pa*. In Rang byung rdo rje 2006a, vol. ja: 1–125.

——. n.d. *Zab mo nang gi don gsal bar byed pa'i 'grel pa*. Rumtek (Sikkim, India).

Rngog lo tsā ba blo ldan shes rab. 1993. *Theg chen rgyud bla ma'i don bsdus pa*. Dharamsala, India: Library of Tibetan Works and Archives.

Rong ston shes bya kun gzigs. 1998. *Chos dang chos nyid rnam par 'byed pa'i rnam bshad legs par 'doms pa lha'i rnga bo che*. In *Dbu mtha' rnam 'byed dang chos dang chos nyid rnam 'byed rtsa 'grel*, 113–44. Chengdu: Si khron mi rigs dpe skrun khang.

——. 1999. *Rgyud bla ma'i sgom rim mi pham dgongs don*. In *Rong ston shākya rgyal mtshan gyi gsung skor*, vol. kha: 527–29. Kathmandu: Sakya College.

Sa bzang ma ti paṇ chen 'jam dbyangs blo gros rgyal mtshan. 1999. *Theg pa chen po'i rgyud bla ma'i bstan bcos kyi rnam par bshad pa nges don rab gsal snang ba*. In *Sa skya pa'i mkhas pa rnams kyi gsung skor*: vol. 4: 1–520. Kathmandu: Sa skya rgyal yongs gsung rab slob gnyer khang.

Śākya mchog ldan. 1975. *Dbu ma'i 'byung tshul rnam par bshad pa'i gtam yid bzhin lhun po*. In *The Complete Works (gsuṅ 'bum) of gSer-mdog Paṇ-chen Śākya-mchog-ldan*, vol. 4: 209–48. Thimpu, Bhutan: Edited by Kunzang Tobgey.

——. 1988a. *'Dzam gling sangs rgyas bstan pa'i rgyan mchog yongs rdzogs gnas lngar mkhyen pa'i paṇḍita chen po gser mdog paṇ chen shākya mchog ldan gyi gsung 'bum legs bshad gser gyi bdud rtsi* (Collected Works). 24 vols. Delhi: Publ. by Nagwang Topgyel.

——. 1988b. *Byams chos lnga'i nges don rab tu gsal ba zhes bya ba'i bstan bcos*. In Śākya mchog ldan 1998a, vol. da: 1–38.

——. 1988c. *Byams chos lnga'i lam gyi rim pa gsal bar byed pa'i bstan bcos rin chen sgrom gyi sgo 'byed*. In Śākya mchog ldan 1988a, vol. da: 39–155.

Shes rab phun tshogs. 2007. *Dbu ma gzhan stong la 'jug pa'i sgo gong ma'i gsung gi bdud rtsi*. Sarnath: Vajra Vidya Institute Library.

Stag tshang lo tsā ba shes rab rin chen. 2007. *Chos dang chos nyid rnam 'byed kyi rnam bshad*. In *Stag tshang lo tsā ba shes rab rin chen gyi gsung 'bum*, vol. 2: 182–96. Beijing: Krung go'i bod rig pa dpe skrun khang.

Tāranātha. 1980. *History of Buddhism in India*. Translated by Lama Chimpa and Alaka Chattopadhyaya. Calcutta: Bagchi.

——. 1982–1987. *The Collected Works of Jo-nang rje-btsun Tāranātha*. 17 vols. Leh, Ladakh: Published by C. Namgyal and Tsewang Taru, Smanrtsis Shesrig Dpemdzod.

——. n.d. *Collected Works*. 'Dzam thang edition. TBRC no. W22276.

Tsultrim, Phuntsok. 1990. *Dharmadharmatāvibhaṅgakārikā of Maitreyanath (With a commentary by Vasubandhu)*. Biblioteca Indo-Tibetica 19. Sarnath, India: The Central Institute for Higher Tibetan Studies.

Yu mo ba mi bskyod rdo rje. 1983. *Set of Four Bright Lamps* (*Gsal sgron skor bzhi*). Gangtok: Sherab Gyaltsen and Lama Dawa.

Modern Works

Anacker, Stefan. 1978. "The Meditational Therapy of the *Madhyāntavibhāgabhāṣya*." In *Mahāyāna Buddhist Meditation: Theory and Practice*, edited by Minoru Kiyota, 83–113. Honolulu: University of Hawai'i Press.

——. 1986. *Seven Works of Vasubandhu*. Delhi: Motilal Banarsidass.

——. 1992. "An Unravelling of the *Dharma-Dharmatā-Vibhāga-Vṛtti* of Vasubandhu." *AS* 46 (1): 26–36.

——. 1999a. "Summary of the *Dharmadharmatāvibhāga*." In *Encyclopedia of Indian Philosophies*, vol. 8: 477–78.

——. 1999b. "Summary of the *Dharmadharmatāvibhāgavṛtti*." In *Encyclopedia of Indian Philosophies*, vol. 8: 588–96.

Aramaki, Noritoshi. 1967–1968. "Paratantrasvabhāva—A Diagrammatic Account." *JIBS* 15 (2): 40–54 and 16 (2): 29–41.

——. 2005. "The *Dharmadharmatāvibhāga* or the Ontological Differentiation Between Beings and Being-as-such." *The Society of Buddhist Studies Otani University*, No. 81: 102–80.

Arnold, Dan. 2003. "Verses on Nonconceptual Awareness: A Close Reading of *Mahāyānasaṃgraha* 8.2–13." *Indian International Journal of Buddhist Studies* 4: 19–49.

——. 2005. "Is Svasaṃvitti Transcendental?" *Asian Philosophy* 15 (1): 77–111.

Arya Maitreya, Jamgön Kongtrül Lodrö Thayé, Khenpo Tsultrim Gyamtso Rinpoche. 2000. Translated by R. Fuchs. *Buddha Nature*. Ithaca: Snow Lion Publications.

Asaṅga. 2004. *The Universal Vehicle Discourse Literature* (*Mahāyānasūtrālaṁkāra*). Translated by L. Jamspal et al. Treasury of the Buddhist Sciences, editor-in-chief Robert A. F. Thurman. New York: American Institute of Buddhist Studies, Columbia University.

Bailey, H. W., and E. H. Johnston. 1935. "A Fragment of the Uttaratantra in Sanskrit." *Bulletin of the School of Oriental Studies* 8 (1): 77–89.

Boquist, Åke. 1993. *Trisvabhāva: A Study of the Development of the Three-Nature-Theory in Yogācāra Buddhism*. Lund Studies in African and Asian Religions 8. Lund: Dept. of History of Religions, University of Lund.

Brunnhölzl, Karl. 2004. *The Center of the Sunlit Sky*. Ithaca: Snow Lion Publications.

——, trans. and introd. 2007a. *Straight from the Heart: Buddhist Pith Instructions*. Ithaca: Snow Lion Publications.

——, trans. and introd. 2007b. *In Praise of Dharmadhātu*. Ithaca: Snow Lion Publications.

——, trans. and introd. 2009. *Luminous Heart*. Ithaca: Snow Lion Publications.

——. 2010. *Gone Beyond: The Prajñāpāramitā Sūtras,* The Ornament of Clear Realization, *and Its Commentaries in the Tibetan Kagyü Tradition*. Vol. 1. Ithaca: Snow Lion Publications.

——. 2011a. *Prajñāpāramitā, Indian* "gzhan stong pas," *and the Beginning of Tibetan* gzhan stong. Wiener Studien zur Tibetologie und Buddhismuskunde, Heft 74. Vienna: Arbeitskreis für tibetische und buddhistische Studien, Universität Wien.

——. 2011b. *Gone Beyond: The Prajñāpāramitā Sūtras,* The Ornament of Clear Realization, *and Its Commentaries in the Tibetan Kagyü Tradition*. Vol. 2. Ithaca: Snow Lion Publications.

Buescher, Hartmut. 2008. *The Inception of Yogācāra-Vijñānavāda*. Beiträge zur Kultur- und Geistesgeschichte Asiens, Nr. 62. Österreichische Akademie der Wissenschaften Philosophisch-Historische Klasse, Sitzungsberichte, 776. Band. Wien: Verlag der Österreichische Akademie der Wissenschaften.

Burchardi, Anne. 2006. "A Provisional List of Tibetan Commentaries on the *Ratnagotravibhāga*." *Tibet Journal* 31 (4): 3–46.

Cha, John Younghan. 1996. "A Study of the *Dharmadharmatāvibhāga*: An Analysis of the Religious Philosophy of the Yogācāra, together with an Annotated Translation of Vasubandhu's Commentary." Ph.D. diss., Northwestern University.

D'Amato, Mario. 2007. "Trisvabhāva in the *Mahāyānasūtrālaṃkāra*." www.empty-universe.com/yogacara/trisvabhava_in_msa.pdf.

Dargyay, Lobsang. 1990. "What is Non-Existent and What is Remanent in Śūnyatā." *JIP* 18: 81–91.

Davidson, Ronald M. 1985. "Buddhist Systems of Transformation: Asraya-parivrtti/-paravrtti among the Yogacara." Ph.D. diss., University of California.

——. 1989. "*Āśrayaparāvṛtti* and *Mahāyānābhidharma*: Some Problems and Perspectives." In *Amalā Prajñā: Aspects of Buddhist Studies*, edited by N. H. Samtani, 253–62. Delhi: Sri Satguru Publications.

Dragonetti, Carmen. 2000. "Marginal Note on the Idealistic Conception of *citta-mātra*." *JIABS* 23 (2): 165–75.

Dreyfus, Georges, and Christian Lindtner. 1989. "The Yogācāra Philosophy of Dignāga and Dharmakīrti." *Studies in Central and East Asian Religions* 2: 27–52.

Galloway, Brian. 1980. "A Yogācāra Analysis of the Mind, Based on the Vijñāna Section of Vasubandhu's *Pañcaskandhaprakaraṇa* with Guṇaprabha's Commentary." *JIABS* 3 (2): 7–20.

Gokhale, V. V. 1977–78. "Yogācāra Works Annotated by Vairocanarakṣita (discovered in the Tibetan photographic materials at the K.P. Jayaswal Research Institute at Patna)." *Annuals of the Bhandarkar Oriental Research Institute* 58–59: 635–44.

Griffiths, Paul J. 1986. *On Being Mindless*. La Salle, Ill.: Open Court.

——. 1994. "What Else Remains in Śūnyatā? An Investigation of Terms for Mental Imagery in the *Madhyāntavibhāga*-Corpus."*JIABS* 17 (1): 1–25.

Griffiths, Paul J., et al. 1989. *The Realm of Awakening*. Oxford: Oxford University Press.

Hakamaya, Noriaki. 1980. "The Realm of Enlightenment in *Vijñaptimātratā*: The Formulation of the 'Four Kinds of Pure Dharmas.'" *JIABS* 3 (1): 22–41.

Hall, Bruce C. 1986. "The Meaning of Vijñapti in Vasubandhu's Concept of Mind." *JIABS* 9 (1): 7–23.

Hanson, Elena F. 1998. "Early Yogācāra and Its Relation to Nāgārjuna's Madhyamaka: Change and Continuity in the History of Mahāyāna Buddhist Thought." Ph.D. diss., Harvard University.

Harris, Ian Charles. 1991. *The Continuity of Madhyamaka and Yogācāra in Indian Mahāyāna Buddhism*. Leiden, Netherlands: E. J. Brill.

Hattori, Masaaki. 1982. "The Dream Example in Vijñānavāda Treatises." In *Indological and Buddhist Studies: Volume in Honour of Professor J. W. de Jong on His Sixtieth Birthday*, edited by L. A. Hercus et al., 235–41. Canberra: Australian National University, Faculty of Asian Studies.

——. 1985. "The Transformation of the Basis (*āśraya-parāvṛtti*) in the Yogācāra System of Philosophy." In Dieter Henrich, ed., *All-Einheit: Wege eines Gedankens in Ost und West*. Stuttgart: Klett-Cotta, 100–108.

Inui, H. 1998. "Shoe kongōchōkyō no haikei ni aru daijyōbukkyō: Nyoraizōshisō tono kankei wo chūshin ni." *Kōyasandaigaku mikkyōbunka kenkyūjokiyō* 10: 39–57.

——. 2000. "Shoe kongōchōkyō no kihon ni aru nyoraizōshisō." *Mikkyō no keisei to ruden: Kōyasandaigaku mikkyōbunka kenkyūjokiyō bessatsu* 2: 53—88.

Jaini, Padmanabh. 1985. "The Sanskrit Fragments of Vinītadeva's *Triṃśikā-Ṭīkā*." *Bulletin of the School of Oriental and African Studies* 48: 470–92.

Kano, Kazuo. 2006. "rNgog Blo-ldan Shes-rab's Summary of the *Ratnagotravibhāga*." Ph.D. diss., University of Hamburg.

Kaplan, Stephen. 1990. "A Holographic Alternative to a Traditional Yogācāra Simile: An Analysis of Vasubandhu's Trisvabhāva Doctrine." *Eastern Buddhist* 23: 56–78.

Kawamura, Leslie S. 1975. "Vinītadeva's Contribution to the Buddhist Mentalistic Trend." Ph.D. diss., University of Saskatchewan.

——. 1984. "The *Dharmadharmatāvibhāga*." *JIBS* 32 (2): 1107–14.

——. 1989. "Two Indigenous Tibetan Commentaries on the *Dharmadharmatāvibhāga*." *Acta Orientalia Academiae Scientiarum Hungaricae* 43 (2–3): 467–74.

——. 1993. "*Āśrayaparivṛtti* in the *Dharma-dharmatā-vibhāga*." In *Studies in Original Buddhism and Mahayana Buddhism in Commemoration of Late Professsor Dr. Fumimaro Watanabe*, Edited by E. Mayeda, vol. 1: 73–90. Kyoto: Nagata Bunshōdō.

Keenan, John P. 1980. "A Study of the *Buddhabhūmyupadeśa*: The Doctrinal Development of the Notion of Wisdom in Yogācāra Thought." Ph.D. diss., University of Wisconsin.

——. 1982. "Original Purity and the Focus of Early Yogacara." *JIABS* 5 (1): 7–18.

——. 2002. *The Interpretation of the Buddha Land*. Berkeley: Numata Center for Buddhist Translation and Research.

King, Richard. 1994. "Early Yogācāra and Its Relationship with the Madhyamaka School." *Philosophy East and West* 44 (4): 659–83.

——. 1998. "Vijñaptimātratā and the Abhidharma Context of Early Yogācāra." *Asian Philosophy* 8 (1): 5–18.

Lévi, Sylvain. 1907. *Mahāyāna-Sūtrālaṃkāra*: Exposé de la doctrine du Grand Véhicule selon le système Yogācāra. Ed. et trad. d'après un manuscrit rapporté du Népal par Sylvain Lévi. Tome 1. Texte. Paris: Bibliothèque de l'École des Hautes Études, Sciences historiques et philologiques, fascicule 159.

——. 1925. *Vijñaptimātratāsiddhi: Deux traités de Vasubandhu: Viṁśatikā et Triṁśikā*. Paris: Bibliothèque des Hautes Études, Sciences historiques et philologiques, fasc. 245.

Lindtner, Christian. 1992. "The *Laṅkāvatārasūtra* in Early Indian Madhyamaka Literature." *AS* 46 (1): 244–79.

——. 1997. "*Cittamātra* in Indian Mahāyāna until Kamalaśīla." *Wiener Zeitschrift für die Kunde Südasiens* 41: 159–206.

Lokesh Chandra. 1963. *Materials for a History of Tibetan Literature*. 3 vols. Śata-Piṭaka Series 28–30. New Delhi: International Academy of Indian Culture.

Makransky, John J. 1997. *Buddhahood Embodied*. Albany: State University of New York Press.

Martin, Dan. 1992. "A Twelfth-century Tibetan Classic of Mahāmudrā, *The Path of Ultimate Profundity: The Great Seal Instructions of Zhang*." *JIABS* 15 (2): 243–319.

Mathes, Klaus-Dieter. 1990. "Untersuchung der Phänomene und ihrer Natur (Chos daṅ chos-ñid rnam-par 'byed-pa tshig le'ur byas-pa). Eine Lehrschrift der buddhistischen Yogācāra-Schule in tibetischer Überlieferung." Magister Artium Thesis, Rheinische Friedrich-Wilhelms-Universität zu Bonn.

——. 1996. *Unterscheidung der Gegebenheiten von ihrem wahren Wesen (Dharmadharmatāvibhāga)*. Swisttal-Odendorf, Germany: Indica et Tibetica Verlag.

——. 2002. "'Gos Lo tsâ ba gZhon nu dpal's Extensive Commentary on and Study of the *Ratnagotravibhāgavyākhyā*." In *Religion and Secular Culture in Tibet*, edited by H. Blezer with the assistance of A. Zadoks. Proceedings of the International Association of Tibetan Studies 2000, Brill's Tibetan Studies Library, vol. 2/2: 79–96. Leiden, Netherlands: E. J. Brill.

——. 2005. "'Gos Lo tsā ba gZhon nu dpal's Commentary on the *Dharmatā* Chapter of the *Dharmadharmatāvibhāgakārikās*." *Studies in Indian Philosophy and Buddhism, University of Tokyo*, 12: 3–39.

——. 2007a. "The Ontological Status of the Dependent (*paratantra*) in the *Saṃdhinirmocanasūtra* and the *Vyākhyāyukti*." In *Indica and Tibetica: Festschrift für Michael Hahn. Zum 65. Geburtstag Űberreicht von Freunden und Schülern*, edited by Konrad Klaus and Jens-Uwe Hartmann. Wiener Studien zur Tibetologie und Buddhismuskunde 66: 323–40. Vienna: Arbeitskreis für tibetische und buddhistische Studien, Universität Wien.

——. 2007b. "The 'Principle of True Nature' (*dharmatâ-yukti*) as a Justification for Positive Descriptions of Reality in Mahâyâna Buddhism." *Logic and Belief in Indian Philosophy*. Warsaw Indological Studies, vol. 3: 127–139.

——. 2008. *A Direct Path to the Buddha Within*. Boston: Wisdom Publications.

——. Forthcoming. "The *Gzhan stong* Model of Reality—Some More Material on Its Origin, Transmission, and Interpretation." In Proceedings of the XVth Congress of the International Association of Buddhist Studies, Atlanta 2008. *JIABS* 34.

Matsuda, Kazunobu. 1996. "*Nirvikalpapraveśadhāraṇī*, Sanskrit Text and Japanese Translation." *Bulletin of Research Institute of Bukkyo University* 3: 89–113.

Matsunaga, Y. 1980. *Mikkyōkyōten seiritsu shiron*. Tokyo: Hōzōkan.

Meinert, Carmen. 2003. "Structural Analysis of the *Bsam gtan mig sgron*: A Comparison of the Fourfold Correct Practice in the Āryāvikalpapraveśanāmadhāraṇī and the Contents of the Four Main Chapters of the *Bsam gtan mig sgron*." *JIABS* 26 (1): 175–95.

Nagao, Gadjin M. 1964. *Madhyāntavibhāga-bhāṣya*. Tokyo: Suzuki Research Foundation.

——. 1991. *Mādhyamika and Yogācāra: A Study of Mahāyāna Philosophy.* Trans. L. Kawamura. Albany: State University of New York Press.

——. 1994. *An Index to Asaṅga's* Mahāyānasaṃgraha. 2 vols. Tokyo: International Institute for Buddhist Studies.

Nanjio, Bunyiu, ed. 1923. *The Laṅkāvatāra Sūtra.* Bibliotheca Otaniensis 1. Kyoto: Otani University Press.

Nozawa, Josho. 1955. "The *Dharmadharmatāvibhaṅga* and the *Dharmadharmatāvibhaṅgavṛtti.* Tibetan Texts (together with a Sanskrit–fragment of the DhDhVV), edited and collated, based upon the Peking and Derge editions." In *Studies in Indology and Buddhology Presented in Honour of Prof. Susumu Yamaguchi on the Occasion of His Sixtieth Birthday*, ed. Gadjin Nagao and Josho Nozawa, 9–49. Kyoto: Hosaka.

Pandeya, Ramchandra. 1999. *Madhyānta-vibhāga-śāstra: Containing the Kārikā-s of Maitreya, Bhāṣya of Vasubandhu and Ṭīkā by Sthiramati.* Delhi: Motilal Banarsidass.

Potter, Karl H., ed. 1999. *Encyclopedia of Indian Philosophies.* Vol. 8, Buddhist Philosophy from 100 to 350 A.D. Delhi: Motilal Banarsidass.

——, ed. 2003a. *Encyclopedia of Indian Philosophies.* Vol. 9, Buddhist Philosophy from 350 to 600 A.D. Delhi: Motilal Banarsidass.

——. 2003b. "Mapping the Three Natures onto the Two Levels." In *Encyclopedia of Indian Philosophies*, vol. 9: 58–69.

Powell, James K. 1998. "The Great Debate in Mahāyāna Buddhism: The Nature of Consciousness." Ph.D. diss., University of Wisconsin.

Powers, John, trans. 1994. *Wisdom of Buddha: The Saṁdhinirmocana Mahāyāna Sūtra.* Berkeley: Dharma Publishing.

Robertson, Raymond E. 2006–2008. *A Study of the Dharmadharmatāvibhaṅga.* 2 vols. (vols. 3 and 4 forthcoming). Beijing: China Tibetology Publishing House.

Ruegg Seyfort, David. 1963. "The Jo naṅ pas: A School of Buddhist Ontologists according to the *Grub mtha' žel gyi me loṅ.*" *Journal of the American Oriental Society* 83: 73–91.

——. 1969. *La théorie du tathāgatagarbha et du gotra.* Publications de l'École Française d'Extrême-Orient 70. Paris: École Française d'Extrême-Orient

Sakuma, Hidenori. 1990. *Die Āśrayaparivṛtti–Theorie in der Yogācārabhūmi*, Teil 1 und 2. Alt- und Neu-Indische Studien 40. Stuttgart: F. Steiner Verlag.

Sāṃkṛtyāyana, Rāhula. 1935. "Search for Sanskrit Manuscripts in Tibet." *The Journal of the Bihar and Orissa Research Society* 24 (4): 163 (introduction and conclusion of the *Dharmadharmatāpravibhāgasūtra*).

Schmithausen, Lambert. 1969a. *Der Nirvāṇa-Abschnitt in der* Viniścayasaṃgrahaṇī *der* Yogācārabhūmiḥ. Veröffentlichungen der Kommission für Sprachen und Kulturen Süd- und Ostasiens 8. Österreichische Akademie der Wissenschaften, philosophisch-historische Klasse, Sitzungsberichte, 264. Band, 2. Abhandlung. Wien: Hermann Böhlaus.

——. 1969b. "Zur Literaturgeschichte der älteren Yogācāra-Schule." *Zeitschrift der Deutschen Morgenländischen Gesellschaft*, Supplementa I: 811–23.

——. 1987. *Ālayavijñāna: On the Origin and the Early Development of a Central Concept of Yogācāra Philosophy.* 2 vols. Tokyo: International Buddhist Institute for Buddhist Studies.

——. 2000. "On Three *Yogācārabhūmi* Passages Mentioning the Three *Svabhāvas* or *Lakṣaṇas*." In *Wisdom, Compassion, and the Search for Understanding*, ed. J. Silk, 245-63. Honolulu: University of Hawai'i Press.

——. 2001. "Zwei charakteristische Lehren der Yogācāras." In *Buddhismus in Geschichte und Gegenwart* 5: 5–14. Universität Hamburg.

Scott, Jim. 2004. *Maitreya's Distinguishing Phenomena and Pure Being*. Ithaca: Snow Lion Publications.

Shastri, Swami Dwarikada. 1970. *Abhidharmakośa & Bhāṣya of Acharya Vasubandhu with Sphuṭārthā Commentary of Ācārya Yaśomitra*. Part I (I and II *Kośasthāna*), critically edited. Vārāṇasī: Bauddha Bharati.

Shastri, Yajneshwar S. 1989. Mahāyānasūtrālaṃkāra *of Asaṅga: A Study in Vijñānavāda Buddhism*. Delhi: Sri Satguru Publications.

Sparham, Gareth. 2001. "Demons on the Mother: *Objections to the Perfect Wisdom Sūtras in Tibet*." In *Changing Minds*, ed. Guy Newland, 193–214. Ithaca: Snow Lion Publications.

Sponberg, Alan. 1979. "Dynamic Liberation in Yogacara Buddhism." *JIABS* 2 (1): 44–64.

——. 1981. "The Trisvabhāva Doctrine in India and China." *Bukkyō Bunka Kenkyujo Kiyo* 21: 97–119.

Stearns, Cyrus. 2010. *The Buddha from Dölpo*. Ithaca: Snow Lion Publications.

Sutton, Florin Giripescu. 1991. *Existence and Enlightenment in the* Laṅkāvatāra-sūtra*: A Study in the Ontology and Epistemology of the Yogācāra-School of Mahāyāna-Buddhism*. Albany: State University of New York Press.

Suzuki, Daisetz Teitaro. 1979. *The Laṅkāvatārasūtra*. Boulder: Prajñā Press.

——. 1998. *Studies in the Lankavatara Sutra*. (Reprint; originally published in 1930). Delhi: Munshiram Manoharlal Publishers.

Takasaki, Jikido. 1959. "*Tenne*—Āśrayaparivṛtti *to* Āśrayaparāvṛtti." *Nihon Bukkyō-gaku Sōnenpō* (25): 89–110.

——. 1966. *A Study on the* Ratnagotravibhāga (Uttaratantra). Serie Orientale Roma 33. Rome: Istituto Italiano per il Medio ed Estremo Oriente.

——. 1989. *Hōshōron. Indo Koten Sōsho. Tokyo: Kōdansha.*

——. 1999. *Hōshōron, Hokkaimusabetsuron. Shin kokuyaku daizōkyō ronshobu 1. Tokyo: Daizōshuppan.*

Takeuchi, Shoko. 1977. "Phenomena and Reality in Vijñaptimātra Thought: On the Usages of the Suffix 'tā' in Maitreya's Treatises." In *Buddhist Thought and Asian Civilization: Essays in Honor of Herbert V. Guenther on His Sixtieth Birthday*, edited by Leslie Kawamura and Keith Scott, 254–67. Emeryville: Dharma Publishing.

Thrangu Rinpoche. 2004. *Distinguishing Dharma and Dharmata by Maitreya*. Boulder and Auckland (New Zealand): Namo Buddha Publications and Zhyisil Chokyi Ghatsal Publications.

Thurman, Robert A. F., trans. 1997. *The Holy Teaching of Vimalakīrti*. University Park: Pennsylvania State University Press.

Tola, Fernando, and Carmen Dragonetti. 1982. "Dignāga's *Ālambanaparīkṣāvṛtti*." *JIP* 10: 105–34.

——. 1983. "The *Trisvabhāvakārikā* of Vasubandhu." *JIP* 11: 225–66.

——. 2004. *Being as Consciousness: Yogācāra Philosophy of Buddhism.* Delhi: Motilal Banarsidass.

Tucci, Giuseppe. 1971. "Ratnākaraśānti on *Āśraya-Parāvṛtti.*" In *Opera Minora*, vol. 2: 529–32. Rome: Rome University.

——. 1986. *Minor Buddhist Texts.* (Reprint; originally published as Serie Orientale Roma 9 in 1956/58). Delhi: Motilal Banarsidass.

Waldron, William. 1994–95. "How Innovative Is the Ālayavijñāna?" *JIP* 22 (3): 199–258 and 23 (1): 9–51.

——. 2003. *The Buddhist Unconscious: The Ālaya-vijñāna in the Context of Indian Buddhist Thought.* London: RoutledgeCurzon.

Weller, Friedrich. 1965. *Zum Kāśyapaparivarta.* Heft 2. Verdeutschung des sanskrit-tibetischen Textes. Abhandlungen der sächsischen Akademie der Wissenschaften zu Leipzig. Philologisch-historische Klasse, Bd. 57, Heft 3. Berlin: Akademie-Verlag.

Williams, Paul. 1983. "On Rang Rig." In *Contributions on Tibetan Buddhist Religion and Philosophy.* Proceedings of the Csoma de Körös Symposium held at Velm-Vienna, Austria, 13–19 September 1981, edited by E. Steinkellner and H. Tauscher, vol. 2: 321–32. Wiener Studien zur Tibetologie und Buddhismuskunde 11. Vienna: Arbeitskreis für tibetische und buddhistische Studien, Universität Wien.

——. 1998. *The Reflexive Nature of Awareness.* Surrey: Curzon Press.

Wilson, Joe B. 2001. "Gung thang and Sa bzang Ma ti Paṇ chen on the Meaning of 'Foundational Consciousness' (ālaya, kun gzhi)." In *Changing Minds*, edited by Guy Newland, 215-30. Ithaca: Snow Lion Publications.

Yao, Zhihua. 2003. "Knowing That One Knows: The Buddhist Doctrine of Self-Cognition." Ph.D. diss., Boston University.

Index

Six-armed Mahākāla